California Probate Code

2023 Edition

(Volume 2 of 2)

Aurum Codex Print™

Division 6 - WILLS AND INTESTATE SUCCESSION

Part 1 - WILLS

Chapter 1 - GENERAL PROVISIONS

Section 6100 - Individuals that may make will

(a) An individual 18 or more years of age who is of sound mind may make a will.
(b) A conservator may make a will for the conservatee if the conservator has been so authorized by a court order pursuant to Section 2580. Nothing in this section shall impair the right of a conservatee who is mentally competent to make a will from revoking or amending a will made by the conservator or making a new and inconsistent will.

Ca. Prob. Code § 6100
Amended by Stats. 1995, Ch. 730, Sec. 7. Effective January 1, 1996.

Section 6100.5 - Not mentally competent to make will

(a) An individual is not mentally competent to make a will if, at the time of making the will, either of the following is true:

(1) The individual does not have sufficient mental capacity to be able to do any of the following:

(A) Understand the nature of the testamentary act.

(B) Understand and recollect the nature and situation of the individual's property.

(C) Remember and understand the individual's relations to living descendants, spouse, and parents, and those whose interests are affected by the will.

(2) The individual suffers from a mental health disorder with symptoms including delusions or hallucinations, which delusions or hallucinations result in the individual's devising property in a way that, except for the existence of the delusions or hallucinations, the individual would not have done.

(b) This section does not supersede existing law relating to the admissibility of evidence to prove the existence of mental incompetence or mental health disorders.

(c) Notwithstanding subdivision (a), a conservator may make a will on behalf of a conservatee if the conservator has been authorized to do so by a court order pursuant to Section 2580.

Ca. Prob. Code § 6100.5
Amended by Stats 2019 ch 9 (AB 46),s 18, eff. 1/1/2020.

Section 6101 - Property disposed of by will

A will may dispose of the following property:

(a) The testator's separate property.

(b) The one-half of the community property that belongs to the testator under Section 100.

(c) The one-half of the testator's quasi-community property that belongs to the testator under Section 101.

Ca. Prob. Code § 6101
Enacted by Stats. 1990, Ch. 79.

Section 6102 - Persons to whom disposition of property may be made

A will may make a disposition of property to any person, including but not limited to any of the following:

(a) An individual.

(b) A corporation.

(c) An unincorporated association, society, lodge, or any branch thereof.

(d) A county, city, city and county, or any municipal corporation.

(e) Any state, including this state.

(f) The United States or any instrumentality thereof.

(g) A foreign country or a governmental entity therein.

Ca. Prob. Code § 6102
Enacted by Stats. 1990, Ch. 79.

Section 6103 - Applicability of law prior to January 1, 1985

Except as otherwise specifically provided, Chapter 1 (commencing with Section 6100), Chapter 2 (commencing with Section 6110), Chapter 3 (commencing with Section 6120), Chapter 4 (commencing with Section 6130), Chapter 6 (commencing with Section 6200), and Chapter 7 (commencing with Section 6300) of this division, and Part 1 (commencing with Section 21101) of Division 11, do not apply where the testator died before January 1, 1985, and the law applicable prior to January 1, 1985, continues to apply where the testator died before January 1, 1985.

Ca. Prob. Code § 6103
Amended by Stats 2002 ch 138 (AB 1784), s 6, eff. 1/1/2003.

Section 6104 - Execution or revocation procured by duress, menace, fraud, undue influence

The execution or revocation of a will or a part of a will is ineffective to the extent the execution or revocation was procured by duress, menace, fraud, or undue influence.

Ca. Prob. Code § 6104
Enacted by Stats. 1990, Ch. 79.

Section 6105 - Validity of will made conditional by its own terms

A will, the validity of which is made conditional by its own terms, shall be admitted to probate or rejected, or denied effect after admission to probate, in conformity with the condition.

Ca. Prob. Code § 6105
Enacted by Stats. 1990, Ch. 79.

Chapter 2 - EXECUTION OF WILLS

Section 6110 - Requirements

(a) Except as provided in this part, a will shall be in writing and satisfy the requirements of this section.
(b) The will shall be signed by one of the following:

    (1) By the testator.

    (2) In the testator's name by some other person in the testator's presence and by the testator's direction.

    (3) By a conservator pursuant to a court order to make a will under Section 2580.
(c)

    (1) Except as provided in paragraph (2), the will shall be witnessed by being signed, during the testator's lifetime, by at least two persons each of whom (A) being present at the same time, witnessed either the signing of the will or the testator's acknowledgment of the signature or of the will and (B) understand that the instrument they sign is the testator's will.

    (2) If a will was not executed in compliance with paragraph (1), the will shall be treated as if it was executed in compliance with that paragraph if the proponent of the will establishes by clear and convincing evidence that, at the time the testator signed the will, the testator intended the will to constitute the testator's will.
    Ca. Prob. Code § 6110
Amended by Stats 2008 ch 53 (AB 2248),s 1, eff. 1/1/2009.

Section 6111 - Holographic will

(a) A will that does not comply with Section 6110 is valid as a holographic will, whether or not witnessed, if the signature and the material provisions are in the handwriting of the testator.
(b) If a holographic will does not contain a statement as to the date

of its execution and:

(1) If the omission results in doubt as to whether its provisions or the inconsistent provisions of another will are controlling, the holographic will is invalid to the extent of the inconsistency unless the time of its execution is established to be after the date of execution of the other will.

(2) If it is established that the testator lacked testamentary capacity at any time during which the will might have been executed, the will is invalid unless it is established that it was executed at a time when the testator had testamentary capacity. **(c)** Any statement of testamentary intent contained in a holographic will may be set forth either in the testator's own handwriting or as part of a commercially printed form will.

Ca. Prob. Code § 6111
Amended by Stats. 1990, Ch. 710, Sec. 13. Operative July 1, 1991, by Sec. 48 of Ch. 710.

Section 6111.5 - Admissibility of extrinsic evidence

Extrinsic evidence is admissible to determine whether a document constitutes a will pursuant to Section 6110 or 6111, or to determine the meaning of a will or a portion of a will if the meaning is unclear.

Ca. Prob. Code § 6111.5
Added by Stats. 1990, Ch. 710, Sec. 14. Operative July 1, 1991, by Sec. 48 of Ch. 710.

Section 6112 - Witnesses

(a) Any person generally competent to be a witness may act as a witness to a will.

(b) A will or any provision thereof is not invalid because the will is signed by an interested witness.

(c) Unless there are at least two other subscribing witnesses to the will who are disinterested witnesses, the fact that the will makes a devise to a subscribing witness creates a presumption that the witness procured the devise by duress, menace, fraud, or undue influence. This presumption is a presumption affecting the burden of proof. This presumption does not apply where the witness is a person to whom the devise is made solely in a fiduciary capacity.

(d) If a devise made by the will to an interested witness fails because the presumption established by subdivision (c) applies to the devise and the witness fails to rebut the presumption, the interested witness shall take such proportion of the devise made to the witness in the will as does not exceed the share of the estate which would be distributed to the witness if the will were not established. Nothing in this subdivision affects the law that applies where it is established that the witness procured a devise by duress, menace, fraud, or undue influence.

Ca. Prob. Code § 6112
Enacted by Stats. 1990, Ch. 79.

Section 6113 - Validly executed

A written will is validly executed if its execution complies with any of the following:

(a) The will is executed in compliance with Section 6110 or 6111 or Chapter 6 (commencing with Section 6200) (California statutory will) or Chapter 11 (commencing with Section 6380) (Uniform International Wills Act).

(b) The execution of the will complies with the law at the time of execution of the place where the will is executed.

(c) The execution of the will complies with the law of the place where at the time of execution or at the time of death the testator is domiciled, has a place of abode, or is a national.

Ca. Prob. Code § 6113
Enacted by Stats. 1990, Ch. 79.

Chapter 3 - REVOCATION AND REVIVAL

Section 6120 - Methods of revoking

A will or any part thereof is revoked by any of the following:

(a) A subsequent will which revokes the prior will or part expressly or by inconsistency.

(b) Being burned, torn, canceled, obliterated, or destroyed, with the intent and for the purpose of revoking it, by either (1) the testator or (2) another person in the testator's presence and by the testator's direction.

Ca. Prob. Code § 6120
Enacted by Stats. 1990, Ch. 79.

Section 6121 - Duplicate burned, torn, canceled, obliterated or destroyed

A will executed in duplicate or any part thereof is revoked if one of the duplicates is burned, torn, canceled, obliterated, or destroyed, with the intent and for the purpose of revoking it, by either (1) the testator or (2) another person in the testator's presence and by the testator's direction.

Ca. Prob. Code § 6121
Enacted by Stats. 1990, Ch. 79.

Section 6122 - Dissolution or annulment of marriage after will executed

(a) Unless the will expressly provides otherwise, if after executing a will the testator's marriage is dissolved or annulled, the dissolution or annulment revokes all of the following:

(1) Any disposition or appointment of property made by the will to the former spouse.

(2) Any provision of the will conferring a general or special power of appointment on the former spouse.

(3) Any provision of the will nominating the former spouse as executor, trustee, conservator, or guardian.
(b) If any disposition or other provision of a will is revoked solely by this section, it is revived by the testator's remarriage to the former spouse.
(c) In case of revocation by dissolution or annulment:

(1) Property prevented from passing to a former spouse because of the revocation passes as if the former spouse failed to survive the testator.

(2) Other provisions of the will conferring some power or office on the former spouse shall be interpreted as if the former spouse failed to survive the testator.

(d) For purposes of this section, dissolution or annulment means any dissolution or annulment which would exclude the spouse as a surviving spouse within the meaning of Section 78. A decree of legal separation which does not terminate the status of spouses is not a dissolution for purposes of this section.

(e) Except as provided in Section 6122.1, no change of circumstances other than as described in this section revokes a will.

(f) Subdivisions (a) to (d), inclusive, do not apply to any case where the final judgment of dissolution or annulment of marriage occurs before January 1, 1985. That case is governed by the law in effect prior to January 1, 1985.

Ca. Prob. Code § 6122

Amended by Stats 2016 ch 50 (SB 1005),s 86, eff. 1/1/2017.

Amended by Stats 2002 ch 664 (AB 3034), s 179, eff. 1/1/2003.

Amended by Stats 2001 ch 893 (AB 25), s 50, eff. 1/1/2002.

Section 6122.1 - Domestic partnership terminated after will executed

(a) Unless the will expressly provides otherwise, if after executing a will the testator's domestic partnership is terminated, the termination revokes all of the following:

(1) Any disposition or appointment of property made by the will to the former domestic partner.

(2) Any provision of the will conferring a general or special power of appointment on the former domestic partner.

(3) Any provision of the will nominating the former domestic partner as executor, trustee, conservator, or guardian.

(b) If any disposition or other provision of a will is revoked solely by this section, it is revived by the testator establishing another domestic partnership with the former domestic partner.

(c) In case of revocation by termination of a domestic partnership:

(1) Property prevented from passing to a former domestic partner because of the revocation passes as if the former domestic partner failed to survive the testator.

(2) Other provisions of the will conferring some power or office on the former domestic partner shall be interpreted as if the former domestic partner failed to survive the testator.

(d) This section shall apply only to wills executed on or after January 1, 2002.

Ca. Prob. Code § 6122.1

Added by Stats 2001 ch 893 (AB 25), s 51, eff. 1/1/2002.

Section 6123 - Second will revoking first will revoked

(a) If a second will which, had it remained effective at death, would have revoked the first will in whole or in part, is thereafter revoked by acts under Section 6120 or 6121, the first will is revoked in whole or in part unless it is evident from the circumstances of the revocation of the second will or from the testator's contemporary or subsequent declarations that the testator intended the first will to take effect as executed.

(b) If a second will which, had it remained effective at death, would have revoked the first will in whole or in part, is thereafter revoked by a third will, the first will is revoked in whole or in part, except to the extent it appears from the terms of the third will that the testator intended the first will to take effect.

Ca. Prob. Code § 6123

Enacted by Stats. 1990, Ch. 79.

Section 6124 - Presumption will destroyed with intent to revoke

If the testator's will was last in the testator's possession, the testator was competent until death, and neither the will nor a duplicate original of the will can be found after the testator's death, it is presumed that the testator destroyed the will with intent to revoke it. This presumption is a presumption affecting the burden of producing evidence.

Ca. Prob. Code § 6124
Enacted by Stats. 1990, Ch. 79.

Chapter 4 - REFERENCE TO MATTERS OUTSIDE THE WILL

Section 6130 - Incorporation by reference

A writing in existence when a will is executed may be incorporated by reference if the language of the will manifests this intent and describes the writing sufficiently to permit its identification.

Ca. Prob. Code § 6130
Enacted by Stats. 1990, Ch. 79.

Section 6131 - Disposition of property by reference to acts and events

A will may dispose of property by reference to acts and events that have significance apart from their effect upon the dispositions made by the will, whether the acts and events occur before or after the execution of the will or before or after the testator's death. The execution or revocation of a will of another person is such an event.

Ca. Prob. Code § 6131
Enacted by Stats. 1990, Ch. 79.

Section 6132 - Reference to writing directing disposition of tangible personal property not otherwise specifically disposed of by will

(a) Notwithstanding any other provision, a will may refer to a writing that directs disposition of tangible personal property not otherwise specifically disposed of by the will, except for money that is common coin or currency and property used primarily in a trade or business. A writing directing disposition of a testator's tangible personal property is effective if all of the following conditions are satisfied:

(1) An unrevoked will refers to the writing.

(2) The writing is dated and is either in the handwriting of, or signed by, the testator.

(3) The writing describes the items and the recipients of the property with reasonable certainty.

(b) The failure of a writing to conform to the conditions described in paragraph (2) of subdivision (a) does not preclude the introduction of evidence of the existence of the testator's intent regarding the disposition of tangible personal property as authorized by this section.

(c) The writing may be written or signed before or after the execution of the will and need not have significance apart from its effect upon the dispositions of property made by the will. A writing that meets the requirements of this section shall be given effect as if it were actually contained in the will itself, except that if any person designated to receive property in the writing dies before the testator, the property shall pass as further directed in the writing and, in the absence of any further directions, the disposition shall lapse.

(d) The testator may make subsequent handwritten or signed changes to any writing. If there is an inconsistent disposition of tangible personal property as between writings, the most recent writing controls.

(e)

(1) If the writing directing disposition of tangible personal property omits a statement as to the date of its execution, and if the omission results in doubt whether its provisions or the provisions of another writing inconsistent with it are controlling, then the writing omitting the statement is invalid to the extent of its inconsistency unless the time of its execution is established to be after the date of execution of the other writing.

(2) If the writing directing disposition of tangible personal property omits a statement as to the date of its execution, and it is established that the testator lacked testamentary capacity at any time during which the writing may have been executed, the writing is invalid unless it is established that it was executed at a time when the testator had testamentary capacity.

(f)

(1) Concurrent with the filing of the inventory and appraisal required by Section 8800, the personal representative shall also file the writing that directs disposition of the testator's tangible personal property.

(2) Notwithstanding paragraph (1), if the writing has not been found or is not available at the time of the filing of the inventory and appraisal, the personal representative shall file the writing no later than 60 days prior to filing the petition for final distribution pursuant to Section 11640.

(g) The total value of tangible personal property identified and disposed of in the writing shall not exceed twenty-five thousand dollars ($25,000). If the value of an item of tangible personal property described in the writing exceeds five thousand dollars ($5,000), that item shall not be subject to this section and that item shall be disposed of pursuant to the remainder clause of the will. The value of an item of tangible personal property that is disposed of pursuant to the remainder clause of the will shall not be counted towards the twenty-five thousand dollar ($25,000) limit described in this subdivision.

(h) As used in this section, the following definitions shall apply:

(1) "Tangible personal property" means articles of personal or household use or ornament, including, but not limited to, furniture, furnishings, automobiles, boats, and jewelry, as well as precious metals in any tangible form, such as bullion or coins and articles held for investment purposes. The term "tangible personal property" does not mean real property, a mobilehome as defined in Section 798.3 of the Civil Code, intangible property, such as evidences of indebtedness, bank accounts and other monetary deposits, documents of title, or securities.

(2) "Common coin or currency" means the coins and currency of the United States that are legal tender for the payment of public and private debts, but does not include coins or currency kept or acquired for their historical, artistic, collectable, or investment value apart from their normal use as legal tender for payment.

Ca. Prob. Code § 6132

Added by Stats 2006 ch 280 (AB 2568),s 1, eff. 1/1/2007.

Chapter 6 - CALIFORNIA STATUTORY WILL

Article 1 - DEFINITIONS AND RULES OF CONSTRUCTION

Section 6200 - Definitions and rules of construction govern construction

Unless the provision or context clearly requires otherwise, these definitions and rules of construction govern the construction of this chapter.

Ca. Prob. Code § 6200

Repealed and added by Stats. 1991, Ch. 1055, Sec. 20.

Section 6201 - Testator

"Testator" means a person choosing to adopt a California statutory will.

Ca. Prob. Code § 6201

Repealed and added by Stats. 1991, Ch. 1055, Sec. 20.

Section 6202 - [Repealed]

Ca. Prob. Code § 6202

Repealed by Stats 2001 ch 417 (AB 873), s 10, eff. 1/1/2002.

Section 6203 - Executor

"Executor" means both the person so designated in a California statutory will and any other person acting at any time as the executor or administrator under a California statutory will.

Ca. Prob. Code § 6203
Repealed and added by Stats. 1991, Ch. 1055, Sec. 20.

Section 6204 - Trustee

"Trustee" means both the person so designated in a California statutory will and any other person acting at any time as the trustee under a California statutory will.
   Ca. Prob. Code § 6204
Repealed and added by Stats. 1991, Ch. 1055, Sec. 20.

Section 6205 - Descendants

"Descendants" mean children, grandchildren, and their lineal descendants of all generations, with the relationship of parent and child at each generation being determined as provided in Section 21115. A reference to "descendants" in the plural includes a single descendant where the context so requires.
   Ca. Prob. Code § 6205
Amended by Stats 2002 ch 138 (AB 1784), s 7, eff. 1/1/2003.

Section 6206 - Reference to Uniform gifts to Minors Act or Uniform Transfers to Minors Act

A reference in a California statutory will to the "Uniform Gifts to Minors Act of any state" or the "Uniform Transfers to Minors Act of any state" includes both the Uniform Gifts to Minors Act of any state and the Uniform Transfers to Minors Act of any state. A reference to a "custodian" means the person so designated in a California statutory will or any other person acting at any time as a custodian under a Uniform Gifts to Minors Act or Uniform Transfers to Minors Act.
   Ca. Prob. Code § 6206
Repealed and added by Stats. 1991, Ch. 1055, Sec. 20.

Section 6207 - Masculine includes feminine, singular includes plural

Masculine pronouns include the feminine, and plural and singular words include each other, where appropriate.

Ca. Prob. Code § 6207

Repealed and added by Stats. 1991, Ch. 1055, Sec. 20.

Section 6208 - Performance of act

(a) If a California statutory will states that a person shall perform an act, the person is required to perform that act.

(b) If a California statutory will states that a person may do an act, the person's decision to do or not to do the act shall be made in the exercise of the person's fiduciary powers.

Ca. Prob. Code § 6208

Repealed and added by Stats. 1991, Ch. 1055, Sec. 20.

Section 6209 - Distribution made to person's descendants

Whenever a distribution under a California statutory will is to be made to a person's descendants, the property shall be divided into as many equal shares as there are then living descendants of the nearest degree of living descendants and deceased descendants of that same degree who leave descendants then living; and each living descendant of the nearest degree shall receive one share and the share of each deceased descendant of that same degree shall be divided among his or her descendants in the same manner.

Ca. Prob. Code § 6209

Repealed and added by Stats. 1991, Ch. 1055, Sec. 20.

Section 6210 - Person

"Person" includes individuals and institutions.

Ca. Prob. Code § 6210

Repealed and added by Stats. 1991, Ch. 1055, Sec. 20.

Section 6211 - Reference to person "if living" or who "survives me"

Reference to a person "if living" or who "survives me" means a person who survives the decedent by 120 hours. A person who fails to survive the decedent by 120 hours is deemed to have predeceased the decedent for the purpose of a California statutory will, and the beneficiaries are determined accordingly. If it cannot be established by clear and convincing evidence that a person who would otherwise be a beneficiary has survived the decedent by 120 hours, it is deemed that the person failed to survive for the required period. The requirement of this section that a person who survives the decedent must survive the decedent by 120 hours does not apply if the application of the 120-hour survival requirement would result in the escheat of property to the state.

Ca. Prob. Code § 6211
Repealed and added by Stats. 1991, Ch. 1055, Sec. 20.

Article 2 - GENERAL PROVISIONS

Section 6220 - Individuals who may execute will

Any individual of sound mind and over the age of 18 may execute a California statutory will under the provisions of this chapter.

Ca. Prob. Code § 6220
Repealed and added by Stats. 1991, Ch. 1055, Sec. 20.

Section 6221 - Execution of will

A California statutory will shall be executed only as follows:
(a) The testator shall complete the appropriate blanks and shall sign the will.
(b) Each witness shall observe the testator's signing and each witness shall sign his or her name in the presence of the testator.

Ca. Prob. Code § 6221
Repealed and added by Stats. 1991, Ch. 1055, Sec. 20.

Section 6222 - Execution of attestation clause

The execution of the attestation clause provided in the California statutory will by two or more witnesses satisfies Section 8220.
   Ca. Prob. Code § 6222
Repealed and added by Stats. 1991, Ch. 1055, Sec. 20.

Section 6223 - One statutory will; included in will

(a) There is only one California statutory will.
(b) The California statutory will includes all of the following:

   (1) The contents of the California statutory will form set out in Section 6240, excluding the questions and answers at the beginning of the California statutory will.

   (2) By reference, the full texts of each of the following:

      (A) The definitions and rules of construction set forth in Article 1 (commencing with Section 6200).

      (B) The property disposition clauses adopted by the testator. If no property disposition clause is adopted, Section 6224 shall apply.

      (C) The mandatory clauses set forth in Section 6241.
(c) Notwithstanding this section, any California statutory will or California statutory will with trust executed on a form allowed under prior law shall be governed by the law that applied prior to January 1, 1992.
   Ca. Prob. Code § 6223
Repealed and added by Stats. 1991, Ch. 1055, Sec. 20.

Section 6224 - More than one property disposition clause selected

If more than one property disposition clause appearing in paragraphs 2 or 3 of a California statutory will is selected, no gift is made. If more than one property disposition clause in paragraph 5 of a California statutory will form is selected, or if none is selected, the residuary estate of a testator who signs a California statutory will shall be distributed to the testator's heirs as if the testator did not make a will.

Ca. Prob. Code § 6224
Repealed and added by Stats. 1991, Ch. 1055, Sec. 20.

Section 6225 - Clauses considered in determining meaning

Only the texts of property disposition clauses and the mandatory clauses shall be considered in determining their meaning. Their titles shall be disregarded.

Ca. Prob. Code § 6225
Repealed and added by Stats. 1991, Ch. 1055, Sec. 20.

Section 6226 - Revocation and amendment; additions and deletions; validity of document executed on form

(a) A California statutory will may be revoked and may be amended by codicil in the same manner as other wills.
(b) Any additions to or deletions from the California statutory will on the face of the California statutory will form, other than in accordance with the instructions, shall be given effect only where clear and convincing evidence shows that they would effectuate the clear intent of the testator. In the absence of such a showing, the court either may determine that the addition or deletion is ineffective and shall be disregarded, or may determine that all or a portion of the California statutory will is invalid, whichever is more likely to be consistent with the intent of the testator.
(c) Notwithstanding Section 6110, a document executed on a California statutory will form is valid as a will if all of the following requirements are shown to be satisfied by clear and convincing evidence:

(1) The form is signed by the testator.

18

(2) The court is satisfied that the testator knew and approved of the contents of the will and intended it to have testamentary effect.

(3) The testamentary intent of the maker as reflected in the document is clear.

Ca. Prob. Code § 6226

Repealed and added by Stats. 1991, Ch. 1055, Sec. 20.

Section 6227 - Dissolution or annulment of marriage after executing will

(a) If after executing a California statutory will the testator's marriage is dissolved or annulled, or the testator's registered domestic partnership is terminated, the dissolution, annulment, or termination revokes any disposition of property made by the will to the former spouse and any nomination of the former spouse as executor, trustee, guardian, or custodian made by the will. If any disposition or nomination is revoked solely by this section, it is revived by the testator's remarriage to, or entry into a subsequent registered domestic partnership with, the former spouse.

(b) In case of revocation by dissolution or annulment:

(1) Property prevented from passing to a former spouse because of the revocation passes as if the former spouse failed to survive the testator.

(2) Provisions nominating the former spouse as executor, trustee, guardian, or custodian shall be interpreted as if the former spouse failed to survive the testator.

(c) For purposes of this section, dissolution or annulment means any dissolution or annulment that would exclude the spouse as a surviving spouse within the meaning of Section 78. A decree of legal separation which does not terminate the status of spouses is not a dissolution or annulment for purposes of this section.

(d) This section applies to any California statutory will, without regard to the time when the will was executed, but this section does not apply to any case where the final judgment of dissolution or annulment of marriage occurs before January 1, 1985; and, if the final judgment of dissolution or annulment of marriage occurs before January 1, 1985, the case is governed by the law that applied prior to January 1, 1985.

   Ca. Prob. Code § 6227

Amended by Stats 2016 ch 50 (SB 1005),s 87, eff. 1/1/2017.

Article 3 - FORM AND FULL TEXT OF CLAUSES

Section 6240 - Statutory will form

The following is the California Statutory Will form:
QUESTIONS AND ANSWERS ABOUT THIS CALIFORNIA STATUTORY WILL
The following information, in question and answer form, is not a part of the California Statutory Will. It is designed to help you understand about Wills and to decide if this Will meets your needs. This Will is in a simple form. The complete text of each paragraph of this Will is printed at the end of the Will.
1. What happens if I die without a Will? If you die without a Will, what you own (your "assets") in your name alone will be divided among your spouse, domestic partner, children, or other relatives according to state law. The court will appoint a relative to collect and distribute your assets.
2. What can a Will do for me? In a Will you may designate who will receive your assets at your death. You may designate someone (called an "executor") to appear before the court, collect your assets, pay your debts and taxes, and distribute your assets as you specify. You may nominate someone (called a "guardian") to raise your children who are under age 18. You may designate someone (called a "custodian") to manage assets for your children until they reach any age from 18 to 25.
3. Does a Will avoid probate? No. With or without a Will, assets in your name alone usually go through the court probate process. The court's first job is to determine if your Will is valid.
4. What is community property? Can I give away my share in my Will? If you are married or in a domestic partnership and you or your spouse earned money during your marriage or domestic partnership from work and wages, that money (and the assets bought with it) is community property. Your Will can only give

away your one-half of community property. Your Will cannot give away your spouse's one-half of community property.

5. Does my Will give away all of my assets? Do all assets go through probate? No. Money in a joint tenancy bank account automatically belongs to the other named owner without probate. If your spouse, domestic partner, or child is on the deed to your house as a joint tenant, the house automatically passes to him or her. Life insurance and retirement plan benefits may pass directly to the named beneficiary. A Will does not necessarily control how these types of "nonprobate" assets pass at your death.

6. Are there different kinds of Wills? Yes. There are handwritten Wills, typewritten Wills, attorney-prepared Wills, and statutory Wills. All are valid if done precisely as the law requires. You should see a lawyer if you do not want to use this Statutory Will or if you do not understand this form.

7. Who may use this Will? This Will is based on California law. It is designed only for California residents. You may use this form if you are single, married, a member of a domestic partnership, or divorced. You must be age 18 or older and of sound mind.

8. Are there any reasons why I should NOT use this Statutory Will? Yes. This is a simple Will. It is not designed to reduce death taxes or other taxes. Talk to a lawyer to do tax planning, especially if (i) your assets will be worth more than $600,000 or the current amount excluded from estate tax under federal law at your death, (ii) you own business-related assets, (iii) you want to create a trust fund for your children's education or other purposes, (iv) you own assets in some other state, (v) you want to disinherit your spouse, domestic partner, or descendants, or (vi) you have valuable interests in pension or profit-sharing plans. You should talk to a lawyer who knows about estate planning if this Will does not meet your needs. This Will treats most adopted children like natural children. You should talk to a lawyer if you have stepchildren or foster children whom you have not adopted.

9. May I add or cross out any words on this Will? No. If you do, the Will may be invalid or the court may ignore the crossed out or added words. You may only fill in the blanks. You may amend this Will by a separate document (called a codicil). Talk to a lawyer if you want to do something with your assets which is not allowed in this form.

10. May I change my Will? Yes. A Will is not effective until you die. You may make and sign a new Will. You may change your Will at any time, but only by an amendment (called a codicil). You can give away or sell your assets before your death. Your Will only acts on what you own at death.

11. Where should I keep my Will? After you and the witnesses sign the Will, keep your Will in your safe deposit box or other safe place. You should tell trusted family members where your Will is kept.

12. When should I change my Will? You should make and sign a new Will if you marry, divorce, or terminate your domestic partnership after you sign this Will. Divorce, annulment, or termination of a domestic partnership automatically cancels all property stated to pass to a former spouse or domestic partner under this Will, and revokes the designation of a former spouse or domestic partner as executor, custodian, or guardian. You should sign a new Will when you have more children, or if your spouse or a child dies, or a domestic partner dies or marries. You may want to change your Will if there is a large change in the value of your assets. You may also want to change your Will if you enter a domestic partnership or your domestic partnership has been terminated after you sign this Will.

13. What can I do if I do not understand something in this Will? If there is anything in this Will you do not understand, ask a lawyer to explain it to you.

14. What is an executor? An "executor" is the person you name to collect your assets, pay your debts and taxes, and distribute your assets as the court directs. It may be a person or it may be a qualified bank or trust company.

15. Should I require a bond? You may require that an executor post a "bond." A bond is a form of insurance to replace assets that may be mismanaged or stolen by the executor. The cost of the bond is paid from the estate's assets.

16. What is a guardian? Do I need to designate one? If you have children under age 18, you should designate a guardian of their "persons" to raise them.

17. What is a custodian? Do I need to designate one? A "custodian" is a person you may designate to manage assets for someone (including a child) who is under the age of 25 and who receives assets under your Will. The custodian manages the assets and pays as much as the custodian determines is proper for health, support, maintenance, and education. The custodian delivers what is left to the person when the person reaches the age you choose (from 18 to 25). No bond is required of a custodian.

18. Should I ask people if they are willing to serve before I designate them as executor, guardian, or custodian? Probably yes. Some people and banks and trust companies may not consent to serve or may not be qualified to act.

19. What happens if I make a gift in this Will to someone and that person dies before I do? A person must survive you by 120 hours to take a gift under this Will. If that person does not, then the gift fails and goes with the rest of your assets. If the person who does not survive you is a relative of yours or your spouse, then certain assets may go to the relative's descendants.

20. What is a trust? There are many kinds of trusts, including trusts created by Wills (called "testamentary trusts") and trusts created during your lifetime (called "revocable living trusts"). Both kinds of trusts are long-term arrangements in which a manager (called a "trustee") invests and manages assets for someone (called a "beneficiary") on the terms you specify. Trusts are too complicated to be used in this Statutory Will. You should see a lawyer if you want to create a trust.

21. What is a domestic partner? You have a domestic partner if you have met certain legal requirements and filed a form entitled "Declaration of Domestic Partnership" with the Secretary of State. Notwithstanding Section 299.6 of the Family Code, if you have not filed a Declaration of Domestic Partnership with the Secretary of State, you do not meet the required definition and should not use the section of the Statutory Will form that refers to domestic partners even if you have registered your domestic partnership with another governmental entity. If you are unsure if you have a domestic partner or if your domestic partnership meets the required definition, please contact the Secretary of State's office.

INSTRUCTIONS

1. READ THE WILL. Read the whole Will first. If you do not understand something, ask a lawyer to explain it to you.

2. FILL IN THE BLANKS. Fill in the blanks. Follow the instructions in the form carefully. Do not add any words to the Will (except for filling in blanks) or cross out any words.

3. DATE AND SIGN THE WILL AND HAVE TWO WITNESSES SIGN IT. Date and sign the Will and have two witnesses sign it. You and the witnesses should read and follow the Notice to Witnesses found at the end of this Will. *You do not need to have this document notarized. Notarization will not fulfill the witness requirement.

* *

NOTICE OF INCOMPLETE TEXT: The California Statutory Will appears in the hard-copy publication of the chaptered bill. See Sec. 88, Chapter 50 (pp. 77-82), Statutes of 2016.

* *

   Ca. Prob. Code § 6240
Amended by Stats 2016 ch 50 (SB 1005),s 88, eff. 1/1/2017.
Amended by Stats 2010 ch 88 (AB 1986),s 1, eff. 1/1/2011.
Amended by Stats 2003 ch 32 (AB 167), s 5, eff. 1/1/2004.
Amended by Stats 2001 ch 893 (AB 25), s 52, eff. 1/1/2002.

Section 6241 - Mandatory clauses

The mandatory clauses of the California statutory will form are as follows:

(a) Intestate Disposition. If the testator has not made an effective disposition of the residuary estate, the executor shall distribute it to the testator's heirs at law, their identities and respective shares to be determined according to the laws of the State of California in effect on the date of the testator's death relating to intestate succession of property not acquired from a predeceased spouse.

(b) Powers of Executor.

   (1) In addition to any powers now or hereafter conferred upon executors by law, including all powers granted under the Independent Administration of Estates Act, the executor shall have the power to:

   (A) Sell estate assets at public or private sale, for cash or on credit terms.

(B) Lease estate assets without restriction as to duration.

(C) Invest any surplus moneys of the estate in real or personal property, as the executor deems advisable.

(2) The executor may distribute estate assets otherwise distributable to a minor beneficiary to one of the following:

(A) The guardian of the minor's person or estate.

(B) Any adult person with whom the minor resides and who has the care, custody, or control of the minor.

(C) A custodian of the minor under the Uniform Transfers to Minors Act as designated in the California statutory will form. The executor is free of liability and is discharged from any further accountability for distributing assets in compliance with the provisions of this paragraph.

(3) On any distribution of assets from the estate, the executor shall have the discretion to partition, allot, and distribute the assets in the following manner:

(A) In kind, including undivided interest in an asset or in any part of it.

(B) Partly in cash and partly in kind.

(C) Entirely in cash. If a distribution is being made to more than one beneficiary, the executor shall have the discretion to distribute assets among them on a pro rata or non pro rata basis, with the assets valued as of the date of distribution.

(c) Powers of Guardian. A guardian of the person nominated in the California statutory will shall have the same authority with respect to the person of the ward as a parent having legal custody of a child would have. All powers granted to guardians in this paragraph may be exercised without court authorization.

Ca. Prob. Code § 6241

Repealed and added by Stats. 1991, Ch. 1055, Sec. 20.

Section 6242 - Rules applicable to statutory will form

(a) Except as specifically provided in this chapter, a California statutory will shall include only the texts of the property disposition clauses and the mandatory clauses as they exist on the day the California statutory will is executed.

(b) Sections 6205, 6206, and 6227 apply to every California statutory will, including those executed before January 1, 1985. Section 6211 applies only to California statutory wills executed after July 1, 1991.

(c) Notwithstanding Section 6222, and except as provided in subdivision (b), a California statutory will is governed by the law that applied prior to January 1, 1992, if the California statutory will is executed on a form that (1) was prepared for use under former Sections 56 to 56.14, inclusive, or former Sections 6200 to 6248, inclusive, of the Probate Code, and (2) satisfied the requirements of law that applied prior to January 1, 1992.

(d) A California statutory will does not fail to satisfy the requirements of subdivision (a) merely because the will is executed on a form that incorporates the mandatory clauses of Section 6241 that refer to former Section 1120.2. If the will incorporates the mandatory clauses with a reference to former Section 1120.2, the trustee has the powers listed in Article 2 (commencing with Section 16220) of Chapter 2 of Part 4 of Division 9.

Ca. Prob. Code § 6242

Amended by Stats 2004 ch 183 (AB 3082), s 279, eff. 1/1/2005.

Section 6243 - Applicability of general law of California

Except as specifically provided in this chapter, the general law of California applies to a California statutory will.

Ca. Prob. Code § 6243

Repealed and added by Stats. 1991, Ch. 1055, Sec. 20.

Chapter 7 - UNIFORM TESTAMENTARY ADDITIONS TO TRUSTS ACT

Section 6300 - Devise made by will to trustee of trust

(a) A devise, the validity of which is determinable by the law of this state, may be made by a will to the trustee of a trust established or to be established by the testator, by the testator and some other person, or by some other person (including a funded or unfunded life insurance trust, although the settlor has reserved any or all rights of ownership of the insurance contracts) if the trust is identified in the testator's will and its terms are set forth in a written instrument (other than a will) executed before, concurrently with, or within 60 days after the execution of the testator's will or in the valid last will of a person who has predeceased the testator (regardless of the existence, size, or character of the trust property). The devise is not invalid because the trust is amendable or revocable, or both, or because the trust was amended after the execution of the will or after the death of the testator.
(b) Unless the testator's will provides otherwise, the property so devised (1) is not deemed to be held under a testamentary trust of the testator but becomes a part of the trust to which it is given and (2) shall be administered and disposed of in accordance with the provisions of the instrument or will setting forth the terms of the trust, including any amendments thereto made before or after the death of the testator (regardless of whether made before or after the execution of the testator's will).
(c) Unless otherwise provided in the will, a revocation or termination of the trust before the death of the testator causes the devise to lapse.

Ca. Prob. Code § 6300
Amended by Stats 2017 ch 33 (AB 309),s 1, eff. 1/1/2018.

Section 6301 - Will executed prior to September 17, 1965

This chapter does not invalidate any devise made by a will executed prior to September 17, 1965.

Ca. Prob. Code § 6301
Enacted by Stats. 1990, Ch. 79.

Section 6303 - Title of chapter

This chapter may be cited as the Uniform Testamentary Additions to Trusts Act.
Ca. Prob. Code § 6303
Enacted by Stats. 1990, Ch. 79.

Chapter 8 - NONPROBATE TRANSFER TO TRUSTEE NAMED IN DECEDENT'S WILL

Section 6320 - Definitions

As used in this chapter, unless the context otherwise requires:
(a) "Designation" means a designation made pursuant to Section 6321.
(b) "Instrument" includes all of the following:

(1) An insurance, annuity, or endowment contract (including any agreement issued or entered into by the insurer in connection therewith, supplemental thereto, or in settlement thereof).

(2) A pension, retirement benefit, death benefit, stock bonus, profit-sharing or employees' saving plan, employee benefit plan, or contract created or entered into by an employer for the benefit of some or all of his or her employees.

(3) A self-employed retirement plan, or an individual retirement annuity or account, established or held pursuant to the Internal Revenue Code.

(4) A multiple-party account, as defined in Section 5132.

(5) Any other written instrument of a type described in Section 5000.
Ca. Prob. Code § 6320

Amended by Stats. 1992, Ch. 178, Sec. 31.4. Effective January 1, 1993.

Section 6321 - Designation of trustee entitled to designate beneficiary, payee or owner

An instrument may designate as a primary or contingent beneficiary, payee, or owner a trustee named or to be named in the will of the person entitled to designate the beneficiary, payee, or owner. The designation shall be made in accordance with the provisions of the contract or plan or, in the absence of such provisions, in a manner approved by the insurer if an insurance, annuity, or endowment contract is involved, and by the trustee, custodian, or person or entity administering the contract or plan, if any. The designation may be made before or after the execution of the designator's will and is not required to comply with the formalities for execution of a will.

Ca. Prob. Code § 6321
Amended by Stats. 1992, Ch. 178, Sec. 31.6. Effective January 1, 1993.

Section 6322 - Requirements for designation to be effective

The designation is ineffective unless the designator's will contains provisions creating the trust or makes a disposition valid under Section 6300.

Ca. Prob. Code § 6322
Enacted by Stats. 1990, Ch. 79.

Section 6323 - Benefits or rights resulting from designation payable directly to trustee

Subject to the provisions of Section 6325, the benefits or rights resulting from the designation are payable or transferable directly to the trustee, without becoming subject to administration, upon or at any time after admission of the designator's will to probate. A designation pursuant to this chapter does not have the effect of naming a trustee of a separate inter vivos trust but the rights and benefits or the proceeds thereof when paid to the trustee are, or become a part of, the testamentary trust or trusts established pursuant to the designator's will or shall be added to an inter vivos trust or trusts if the disposition is governed by Section 6300.

Ca. Prob. Code § 6323
Enacted by Stats. 1990, Ch. 79.

Section 6324 - Designator's debts

Except as otherwise provided in the designator's will, the rights and benefits and their proceeds paid or transferred to the trustee are not subject to the debts of the designator to any greater extent than if they were paid or transferred to a named beneficiary, payee, or owner other than the estate of the designator.

Ca. Prob. Code § 6324
Enacted by Stats. 1990, Ch. 79.

Section 6325 - Jurisdiction of court

(a) The court in which the proceedings are pending for administration of the estate of the decedent has jurisdiction, before or after payment or transfer of benefits and rights or their proceeds to the trustee, to:

  (1) Determine the validity of the trust.

  (2) Determine the terms of the trust.

  (3) Fill vacancies in the office of trustee.

  (4) Require a bond of a trustee in its discretion and in such amount as the court may determine for the faithful performance of duties as trustee, subject to the provisions of Article 3 (commencing with Section 1570) of Chapter 16 of Division 1.1 of the Financial Code and Section 15602 of this code.

  (5) Grant additional powers to the trustee, as provided in

Section 16201.

(6) Instruct the trustee.

(7) Fix or allow payment of compensation of a trustee as provided in Sections 15680 to 15683, inclusive.

(8) Hear and determine adverse claims to the trust property by the personal representative, surviving spouse, or other third person.

(9) Determine the identity of the trustee and the trustee's acceptance or rejection of the office and, upon request, furnish evidence of trusteeship to a trustee.

(10) Order postponement of the payment or transfer of the benefits and rights or their proceeds.

(11) Authorize or direct removal of the trust or trust property to another jurisdiction pursuant to the procedure provided in Chapter 5 (commencing with Section 17400) of Part 5 of Division 9.

(12) Make any order incident to the foregoing or to the accomplishment of the purposes of this chapter.
(b) The personal representative of the designator's estate, any trustee named in the will or designation or successor to such trustee, or any person interested in the estate or trust may petition the court for an order under this section. Notice of hearing of the petition shall be given in the manner provided in Section 17203, except as the court may otherwise order.
    Ca. Prob. Code § 6325
Amended by Stats 2014 ch 71 (SB 1304),s 138, eff. 1/1/2015.

Section 6326 - Applicability of Division 9

As to matters not specifically provided in Section 6325, the provisions of Division 9 (commencing with Section 15000) apply to the trust.

Ca. Prob. Code § 6326
Enacted by Stats. 1990, Ch. 79.

Section 6327 - Appeal

An appeal may be taken from any of the following:
(a) Any order described in Part 3 (commencing with Section 1300) of Division 3 made pursuant to this chapter.
(b) An order making or refusing to make a determination specified in paragraph (1), (2), or (8) of subdivision (a) of Section 6325.
(c) As provided in Section 1304 for an order made pursuant to Section 6326.
   Ca. Prob. Code § 6327
Amended by Stats 2003 ch 32 (AB 167), s 6, eff. 1/1/2004.

Section 6328 - Payment by obligor to personal representative of designator

If no qualified trustee makes claim to the benefits or rights or proceeds within one year after the death of the designator, or if satisfactory evidence is furnished within such one-year period showing that no trustee can qualify to receive them, payment or transfer may be made, unless the designator has otherwise provided, by the obligor to the personal representative of the designator or to those thereafter entitled, and the obligor is discharged from liability.
   Ca. Prob. Code § 6328
Enacted by Stats. 1990, Ch. 79.

Section 6329 - Trusts not invalidated

Enactment of this chapter does not invalidate trusts, otherwise valid, not made pursuant to the provisions of this chapter.
   Ca. Prob. Code § 6329
Enacted by Stats. 1990, Ch. 79.

Section 6330 - Chapter construed as restatement and continuation of prior act

This chapter, insofar as it is substantially the same as former Chapter 10 (commencing with Section 175) of former Division 1, repealed by Section 18 of Chapter 842 of the Statutes of 1983, shall be construed as a restatement and continuation thereof and not as a new enactment. After December 31, 1984, a reference in a written instrument to the previously existing provisions relating to the subject matter of this chapter shall be deemed to be a reference to the corresponding provisions of this chapter.

Ca. Prob. Code § 6330
Enacted by Stats. 1990, Ch. 79.

Chapter 9 - DEVISE SUBJECT TO CALIFORNIA UNIFORM TRANSFERS TO MINORS ACT

Section 6341 - Will provides that devised property subject to Act

If a testator's will provides that devised property shall be paid or delivered or transferred to a custodian subject to the California Uniform Gifts to Minors Act or the California Uniform Transfers to Minors Act:

(a) All of the provisions of the California Uniform Transfers to Minors Act, Part 9 (commencing with Section 3900) of Division 4, including, but not limited to, the definitions and the provisions concerning powers, rights, and immunities contained in that act, are applicable to the devise during the period prior to distribution of the property.

(b) Unless the will clearly requires otherwise, if the person named as the beneficiary for whose benefit the custodial property is to be held attains the age at which the custodianship was to terminate prior to the order of distribution, the devise shall be deemed to be a direct devise to the person named as the beneficiary for whose benefit the custodial property was to be held.

(c) The personal representative of the testator's estate, upon entry of an order for distribution, shall make distribution pursuant to the order for distribution by transferring the devised property in the form and manner provided by the California Uniform Transfers to Minors Act.

(d) If a vacancy in the custodianship exists prior to full distribution of the devised property by the personal representative, a successor custodian shall be appointed for any undistributed property in the manner provided by the California Uniform Transfers to Minors Act.

Ca. Prob. Code § 6341
Enacted by Stats. 1990, Ch. 79.

Section 6345 - Successor or substitute custodians

The will may provide for successor or substitute custodians and may specify the standard of compensation of the custodian.

Ca. Prob. Code § 6345
Enacted by Stats. 1990, Ch. 79.

Section 6347 - Designated custodian deemed devisee; duty to participate in proceedings in estate on behalf of minor

(a) Except as otherwise provided in the will or ordered by a court, each custodian designated in the will and the person for whom the property is to be held shall be deemed a devisee for the purpose of receiving notices which may be required or permitted to be sent to a devisee in the estate of the testator.

(b) Unless required by the will or ordered by the court, a custodian does not have a duty to participate in the proceedings in the estate on behalf of the minor, and in no event does the custodian have a duty to so participate until the custodian has filed a written notice of acceptance of the office of custodian with the clerk of the court in which administration of the estate of the testator is pending.

Ca. Prob. Code § 6347
Enacted by Stats. 1990, Ch. 79.

Section 6348 - Jurisdiction over proceedings and matters concerning undistributed property

Until distribution of the property pursuant to an order for

distribution is completed, the court in which administration of the estate of the testator is pending has exclusive jurisdiction over all proceedings and matters concerning undistributed property, including, but not limited to, the appointment, declination, resignation, removal, bonding, and compensation of, and the delivery or transfer of the undistributed property to, a custodian. After distribution of any property is completed, the court has no further jurisdiction over the distributed property and the property shall be held subject to the California Uniform Transfers to Minors Act.

Ca. Prob. Code § 6348
Enacted by Stats. 1990, Ch. 79.

Section 6349 - Not exclusive method for making devises; provisions of Act not limited

(a) This chapter shall not be construed as providing an exclusive method for making devises to or for the benefit of minors.
(b) Nothing in this chapter limits any provision of the California Uniform Transfers to Minors Act, Part 9 (commencing with Section 3900) of Division 4.

Ca. Prob. Code § 6349
Enacted by Stats. 1990, Ch. 79.

Chapter 11 - UNIFORM INTERNATIONAL WILLS ACT

Section 6380 - Definitions

In this chapter:
(a) "International will" means a will executed in conformity with Sections 6381 to 6384, inclusive.
(b) "Authorized person" and "person authorized to act in connection with international wills" means a person who by Section 6388, or by the laws of the United States including members of the diplomatic and consular service of the United States designated by Foreign Service Regulations, is empowered to supervise the execution of international wills.

Ca. Prob. Code § 6380
Enacted by Stats. 1990, Ch. 79.

Section 6381 - Validity of will

(a) A will is valid as regards form, irrespective particularly of the place where it is made, of the location of the assets and of the nationality, domicile, or residence of the testator, if it is made in the form of an international will complying with the requirements of this chapter.

(b) The invalidity of the will as an international will does not affect its formal validity as a will of another kind.

(c) This chapter does not apply to the form of testamentary dispositions made by two or more persons in one instrument.

    Ca. Prob. Code § 6381

Enacted by Stats. 1990, Ch. 79.

Section 6382 - Requirements of will

(a) The will shall be made in writing. It need not be written by the testator himself or herself. It may be written in any language, by hand or by any other means.

(b) The testator shall declare in the presence of two witnesses and of a person authorized to act in connection with international wills that the document is the testator's will and that the testator knows the contents thereof. The testator need not inform the witnesses, or the authorized person, of the contents of the will.

(c) In the presence of the witnesses, and of the authorized person, the testator shall sign the will or, if the testator has previously signed it, shall acknowledge his or her signature.

(d) If the testator is unable to sign, the absence of the testator's signature does not affect the validity of the international will if the testator indicates the reason for his or her inability to sign and the authorized person makes note thereof on the will. In that case, it is permissible for any other person present, including the authorized person or one of the witnesses, at the direction of the testator, to sign the testator's name for the testator if the authorized person makes note of this also on the will, but it is not required that any person sign the testator's name for the testator.

(e) The witnesses and the authorized person shall there and then attest the will by signing in the presence of the testator.

Ca. Prob. Code § 6382

Enacted by Stats. 1990, Ch. 79.

Section 6383 - Signatures

(a) The signatures shall be placed at the end of the will. If the will consists of several sheets, each sheet shall be signed by the testator or, if the testator is unable to sign, by the person signing on his or her behalf or, if there is no such person, by the authorized person. In addition, each sheet shall be numbered.

(b) The date of the will shall be the date of its signature by the authorized person. That date shall be noted at the end of the will by the authorized person.

(c) The authorized person shall ask the testator whether the testator wishes to make a declaration concerning the safekeeping of the will. If so and at the express request of the testator, the place where the testator intends to have the will kept shall be mentioned in the certificate provided for in Section 6384.

(d) A will executed in compliance with Section 6382 is not invalid merely because it does not comply with this section.

Ca. Prob. Code § 6383

Enacted by Stats. 1990, Ch. 79.

Section 6384 - Certificate establishing requirements of chapter fulfilled

The authorized person shall attach to the will a certificate to be signed by the authorized person establishing that the requirements of this chapter for valid execution of an international will have been fulfilled. The authorized person shall keep a copy of the certificate and deliver another to the testator. The certificate shall be substantially in the following form:

CERTIFICATE(Convention of October 26, 1973)

1.I, _____ (name, address, and capacity) _____ , a person authorized to act in connection with international wills,

2.certify that on _____ (date) _____ at _____ (place) _____

3._____ (testator) (name, address, date and place of birth)
_____ in my presence and that of the witnesses

4.(a)_____ (name, address, date and place of birth)_____

(b)_____ (name, address, date and place of birth)_____ has declared that the attached document is his will and that he knows the contents thereof.

5.I furthermore certify that:

6.(a)in my presence and in that of the witnesses

(1) the testator has signed the will or has acknowledged his signature previously affixed.

(2)following a declaration of the testator stating that he was unable to sign his will for the following reason

_____, I have mentioned this declaration on the will,* and the signature has been affixed by _____ (name and address)* _____

7.(b)the witnesses and I have signed the will;

8.(c)each page of the will has been signed by_____ and numbered;*

9.(d)I have satisfied myself as to the identity of the testator and of the witnesses as designated above;

10.(e)the witnesses met the conditions requisite to act as such according to the law under which I am acting;

11. (f) the testator has requested me to include the following statement concerning the safekeeping of his will:*

12.   PLACE OF EXECUTION
13.   DATE
14.   SIGNATURE and, ifnecessary, SEAL
_____*to be completed if appropriate

Ca. Prob. Code § 6384
Enacted by Stats. 1990, Ch. 79.

Section 6385 - Certificate conclusive of formal validity

In the absence of evidence to the contrary, the certificate of the authorized person is conclusive of the formal validity of the instrument as a will under this chapter. The absence or irregularity of a certificate does not affect the formal validity of a will under this chapter.

Ca. Prob. Code § 6385
Enacted by Stats. 1990, Ch. 79.

Section 6386 - Revocation

The international will is subject to the ordinary rules of revocation of wills.

Ca. Prob. Code § 6386
Enacted by Stats. 1990, Ch. 79.

Section 6387 - Interpreting and applying chapter

Sections 6380 to 6386, inclusive, derive from Annex to Convention of October 26, 1973, Providing a Uniform Law on the Form of an International Will. In interpreting and applying this chapter, regard shall be had to its international origin and to the need for uniformity in its interpretation.

Ca. Prob. Code § 6387
Enacted by Stats. 1990, Ch. 79.

Section 6388 - Individuals admitted to practice law in state authorized persons

Individuals who have been admitted to practice law before the courts of this state and who are in good standing as active law practitioners of this state are authorized persons in relation to international wills.

Ca. Prob. Code § 6388
Enacted by Stats. 1990, Ch. 79.

Section 6389 - Registry

The Secretary of State shall establish a registry system by which authorized persons may register in a central information center information regarding the execution of international wills, keeping that information in strictest confidence until the death of the maker and then making it available to any person desiring information about any will who presents a death certificate or other satisfactory evidence of the testator's death to the center. Information that may be received, preserved in confidence until death, and reported as indicated is limited to the name, social security or other individual identifying number established by law, if any, address, date and place of birth of the testator, and the intended place of deposit or safekeeping of the instrument pending the death of the maker. The Secretary of State, at the request of the authorized person, may cause the information it receives about execution of any international will to be transmitted to the registry system of another jurisdiction as identified by the testator, if that other system adheres to rules protecting the confidentiality of the information similar to those established in this state.

Ca. Prob. Code § 6389
Enacted by Stats. 1990, Ch. 79.

Section 6390 - Reference to former law deemed reference to chapter

After December 31, 1984, a reference in a written instrument, including a will, to the former law (repealed by Chapter 892 of the Statutes of 1984) shall be deemed to be a reference to the corresponding provision of this chapter.

Ca. Prob. Code § 6390
Enacted by Stats. 1990, Ch. 79.

Part 2 - INTESTATE SUCCESSION

Chapter 1 - INTESTATE SUCCESSION GENERALLY

Section 6400 - Generally

Any part of the estate of a decedent not effectively disposed of by will passes to the decedent's heirs as prescribed in this part.

Ca. Prob. Code § 6400
Enacted by Stats. 1990, Ch. 79.

Section 6401 - Intestate share of surviving spouse

(a) As to community property, the intestate share of the surviving spouse is the one-half of the community property that belongs to the decedent under Section 100.

(b) As to quasi-community property, the intestate share of the surviving spouse is the one-half of the quasi-community property that belongs to the decedent under Section 101.

(c) As to separate property, the intestate share of the surviving spouse is as follows:

(1) The entire intestate estate if the decedent did not leave any surviving issue, parent, brother, sister, or issue of a deceased brother or sister.

(2) One-half of the intestate estate in the following cases:

(A) Where the decedent leaves only one child or the issue of one deceased child.

(B) Where the decedent leaves no issue, but leaves a parent or parents or their issue or the issue of either of them.

(3) One-third of the intestate estate in the following cases:

(A) Where the decedent leaves more than one child.

(B) Where the decedent leaves one child and the issue of one or more deceased children.

(C) Where the decedent leaves issue of two or more deceased children.

Ca. Prob. Code § 6401

Amended by Stats 2014 ch 913 (AB 2747),s 32, eff. 1/1/2015.
Amended by Stats 2002 ch 447 (AB 2216), s 1, eff. 7/1/2003.

Section 6402 - Intestate estate not passing to surviving spouse or if no surviving spouse

Except as provided in Section 6402.5, the part of the intestate estate not passing to the surviving spouse, under Section 6401, or the entire intestate estate if there is no surviving spouse, passes as follows:

(a) To the issue of the decedent, the issue taking equally if they are all of the same degree of kinship to the decedent, but if of unequal degree those of more remote degree take in the manner provided in Section 240.

(b) If there is no surviving issue, to the decedent's parent or parents equally.

(c) If there is no surviving issue or parent, to the issue of the parents or either of them, the issue taking equally if they are all of the same degree of kinship to the decedent, but if of unequal degree those of more remote degree take in the manner provided in Section 240.

(d) If there is no surviving issue, parent or issue of a parent, but the decedent is survived by one or more grandparents or issue of grandparents, to the grandparent or grandparents equally, or to the issue of those grandparents if there is no surviving grandparent, the issue taking equally if they are all of the same degree of kinship to the decedent, but if of unequal degree those of more remote degree take in the manner provided in Section 240.

(e) If there is no surviving issue, parent or issue of a parent, grandparent or issue of a grandparent, but the decedent is survived by the issue of a predeceased spouse, to that issue, the issue taking equally if they are all of the same degree of kinship to the predeceased spouse, but if of unequal degree those of more remote degree take in the manner provided in Section 240.

(f) If there is no surviving issue, parent or issue of a parent, grandparent or issue of a grandparent, or issue of a predeceased spouse, but the decedent is survived by next of kin, to the next of kin in equal degree, but where there are two or more collateral kindred in equal degree who claim through different ancestors, those who claim through the nearest ancestor are preferred to those claiming through an ancestor more remote.

(g) If there is no surviving next of kin of the decedent and no surviving issue of a predeceased spouse of the decedent, but the decedent is survived by the parents of a predeceased spouse or the issue of those parents, to the parent or parents equally, or to the issue of those parents if both are deceased, the issue taking equally if they are all of the same degree of kinship to the predeceased spouse, but if of unequal degree those of more remote degree take in the manner provided in Section 240.

Ca. Prob. Code § 6402

Amended by Stats 2014 ch 913 (AB 2747),s 32.5, eff. 1/1/2015.
Amended by Stats 2002 ch 447 (AB 2216), s 2, eff. 7/1/2003.

Section 6402.5 - Portion of decedent's estate attributable to decedent's predeceased spouse

(a) For purposes of distributing real property under this section if the decedent had a predeceased spouse who died not more than 15 years before the decedent and there is no surviving spouse or issue of the decedent, the portion of the decedent's estate attributable to the decedent's predeceased spouse passes as follows:

(1) If the decedent is survived by issue of the predeceased spouse, to the surviving issue of the predeceased spouse; if they are all of the same degree of kinship to the predeceased spouse they take equally, but if of unequal degree those of more remote degree take in the manner provided in Section 240.

(2) If there is no surviving issue of the predeceased spouse but the decedent is survived by a parent or parents of the predeceased spouse, to the predeceased spouse's surviving parent or parents equally.

(3) If there is no surviving issue or parent of the predeceased spouse but the decedent is survived by issue of a parent of the predeceased spouse, to the surviving issue of the parents of the predeceased spouse or either of them, the issue taking equally if they are all of the same degree of kinship to the predeceased spouse, but if of unequal degree those of more remote degree take in the manner provided in Section 240.

(4) If the decedent is not survived by issue, parent, or issue of a parent of the predeceased spouse, to the next of kin of the decedent in the manner provided in Section 6402.

(5) If the portion of the decedent's estate attributable to the decedent's predeceased spouse would otherwise escheat to the state because there is no kin of the decedent to take under Section 6402, the portion of the decedent's estate attributable to the predeceased spouse passes to the next of kin of the predeceased spouse who shall take in the same manner as the next of kin of the decedent take under Section 6402.

(b) For purposes of distributing personal property under this section if the decedent had a predeceased spouse who died not more than five years before the decedent, and there is no surviving spouse or issue of the decedent, the portion of the decedent's estate attributable to the decedent's predeceased spouse passes as follows:

(1) If the decedent is survived by issue of the predeceased spouse, to the surviving issue of the predeceased spouse; if they are all of the same degree of kinship to the predeceased spouse they take equally, but if of unequal degree those of more remote degree take in the manner provided in Section 240.

(2) If there is no surviving issue of the predeceased spouse but the decedent is survived by a parent or parents of the predeceased spouse, to the predeceased spouse's surviving parent or parents equally.

(3) If there is no surviving issue or parent of the predeceased spouse but the decedent is survived by issue of a parent of the predeceased spouse, to the surviving issue of the parents of the predeceased spouse or either of them, the issue taking equally if they are all of the same degree of kinship to the predeceased spouse, but if of unequal degree those of more remote degree take in the manner provided in Section 240.

(4) If the decedent is not survived by issue, parent, or issue of a parent of the predeceased spouse, to the next of kin of the decedent in the manner provided in Section 6402.

(5) If the portion of the decedent's estate attributable to the decedent's predeceased spouse would otherwise escheat to the state because there is no kin of the decedent to take under Section 6402, the portion of the decedent's estate attributable to the predeceased spouse passes to the next of kin of the predeceased spouse who shall take in the same manner as the next of kin of the decedent take under Section 6402.

(c) For purposes of disposing of personal property under subdivision (b), the claimant heir bears the burden of proof to show the exact personal property to be disposed of to the heir.

(d) For purposes of providing notice under any provision of this code with respect to an estate that may include personal property subject to distribution under subdivision (b), if the aggregate fair market value of tangible and intangible personal property with a written record of title or ownership in the estate is believed in good faith by the petitioning party to be less than ten thousand dollars ($10,000), the petitioning party need not give notice to the issue or next of kin of the predeceased spouse. If the personal property is subsequently determined to have an aggregate fair market value in excess of ten thousand dollars ($10,000), notice shall be given to the issue or next of kin of the predeceased spouse as provided by law.

(e) For the purposes of disposing of property pursuant to subdivision (b), "personal property" means that personal property in which there is a written record of title or ownership and the value of which in the aggregate is ten thousand dollars ($10,000) or more.

(f) For the purposes of this section, the "portion of the decedent's estate attributable to the decedent's predeceased spouse" means all of the following property in the decedent's estate:

(1) One-half of the community property in existence at the time of the death of the predeceased spouse.

(2) One-half of any community property, in existence at the time of death of the predeceased spouse, which was given to the decedent by the predeceased spouse by way of gift, descent, or devise.

(3) That portion of any community property in which the predeceased spouse had any incident of ownership and which vested in the decedent upon the death of the predeceased spouse by right of survivorship.

(4) Any separate property of the predeceased spouse which came to the decedent by gift, descent, or devise of the predeceased spouse or which vested in the decedent upon the death of the predeceased spouse by right of survivorship.
(g) For the purposes of this section, quasi-community property shall be treated the same as community property.
(h) For the purposes of this section:

(1) Relatives of the predeceased spouse conceived before the decedent's death but born thereafter inherit as if they had been born in the lifetime of the decedent.

(2) A person who is related to the predeceased spouse through two lines of relationship is entitled to only a single share based on the relationship which would entitle the person to the larger share.
Ca. Prob. Code § 6402.5
Enacted by Stats. 1990, Ch. 79.

Section 6403 - Failure to survive decedent by 120 hours

(a) A person who fails to survive the decedent by 120 hours is deemed to have predeceased the decedent for the purpose of intestate succession, and the heirs are determined accordingly. If it cannot be established by clear and convincing evidence that a person who would otherwise be an heir has survived the decedent by 120 hours, it is deemed that the person failed to survive for the required period. The requirement of this section that a person who survives the decedent must survive the decedent by 120 hours does not apply if the application of the 120-hour survival requirement would result in the escheat of property to the state.

(b) This section does not apply to the case where any of the persons upon whose time of death the disposition of property depends died before January 1, 1990, and such case continues to be governed by the law applicable before January 1, 1990.

Ca. Prob. Code § 6403
Enacted by Stats. 1990, Ch. 79.

Section 6404 - Applicable provisions if no taker of intestate estate

Part 4 (commencing with Section 6800) (escheat) applies if there is no taker of the intestate estate under the provisions of this part.

Ca. Prob. Code § 6404
Enacted by Stats. 1990, Ch. 79.

Section 6406 - Relatives of halfblood

Except as provided in Section 6451, relatives of the halfblood inherit the same share they would inherit if they were of the whole blood.

Ca. Prob. Code § 6406
Amended by Stats. 1993, Ch. 529, Sec. 3. Effective January 1, 1994.

Section 6407 - Relatives conceived before decedent's death but born thereafter

Relatives of the decedent conceived before the decedent's death but born thereafter inherit as if they had been born in the lifetime of the decedent.

Ca. Prob. Code § 6407
Enacted by Stats. 1990, Ch. 79.

Section 6409 - Property treated as advancement

(a) If a person dies intestate as to all or part of his or her estate, property the decedent gave during lifetime to an heir is treated as an advancement against that heir's share of the intestate estate only if one of the following conditions is satisfied:

(1) The decedent declares in a contemporaneous writing that the gift is an advancement against the heir's share of the estate or that its value is to be deducted from the value of the heir's share of the estate.

(2) The heir acknowledges in writing that the gift is to be so deducted or is an advancement or that its value is to be deducted from the value of the heir's share of the estate.

(b) Subject to subdivision (c), the property advanced is to be valued as of the time the heir came into possession or enjoyment of the property or as of the time of death of the decedent, whichever occurs first.

(c) If the value of the property advanced is expressed in the contemporaneous writing of the decedent, or in an acknowledgment of the heir made contemporaneously with the advancement, that value is conclusive in the division and distribution of the intestate estate.

(d) If the recipient of the property advanced fails to survive the decedent, the property is not taken into account in computing the intestate share to be received by the recipient's issue unless the declaration or acknowledgment provides otherwise.

Ca. Prob. Code § 6409
Amended by Stats 2002 ch 138 (AB 1784), s 8, eff. 1/1/2003.

Section 6410 - Debt owed decedent; failure of debtor to survive decedent

(a) A debt owed to the decedent is not charged against the intestate share of any person except the debtor.

(b) If the debtor fails to survive the decedent, the debt is not taken into account in computing the intestate share of the debtor's issue.

Ca. Prob. Code § 6410
Enacted by Stats. 1990, Ch. 79.

Section 6411 - Person who is or has been not a citizen or national of the United States

No person is disqualified to take as an heir because that person or a person through whom the person claims is or has been a person who is not a citizen or national of the United States.
Ca. Prob. Code § 6411
Amended by Stats 2021 ch 296 (AB 1096),s 54, eff. 1/1/2022.
Enacted by Stats. 1990, Ch. 79.

Section 6412 - Estates of dower and curtesy

Except to the extent provided in Section 120, the estates of dower and curtesy are not recognized.
Ca. Prob. Code § 6412
Enacted by Stats. 1990, Ch. 79.

Section 6413 - Related to decedent through two lines of relationship

A person who is related to the decedent through two lines of relationship is entitled to only a single share based on the relationship which would entitle the person to the larger share.
Ca. Prob. Code § 6413
Enacted by Stats. 1990, Ch. 79.

Section 6414 - Death of decedent before January 1, 1985

(a) Except as provided in subdivision (b), this part does not apply where the decedent died before January 1, 1985, and the law applicable prior to January 1, 1985, continues to apply where the decedent died before January 1, 1985.
(b) Section 6412 applies whether the decedent died before, on, or after January 1, 1985.
(c) Where any of the following provisions is applied in a case where the decedent died before January 1, 1985, any reference in that provision to this part shall be deemed to be a reference to former Division 2 (commencing with Section 200) which was repealed by

Section 19 of Chapter 842 of the Statutes of 1983:

(1) Section 377 of the Code of Civil Procedure.

(2) Section 3524 of the Penal Code.
Ca. Prob. Code § 6414
Enacted by Stats. 1990, Ch. 79.

Chapter 2 - PARENT AND CHILD RELATIONSHIP

Section 6450 - Existence of relationship for purposes of determining intestate succession

Subject to the provisions of this chapter, a relationship of parent and child exists for the purpose of determining intestate succession by, through, or from a person in the following circumstances:
(a) The relationship of parent and child exists between a person and the person's natural parents, regardless of the marital status of the natural parents.
(b) The relationship of parent and child exists between an adopted person and the person's adopting parent or parents.
Ca. Prob. Code § 6450
Added by Stats. 1993, Ch. 529, Sec. 5. Effective January 1, 1994.

Section 6451 - Adoption

(a) An adoption severs the relationship of parent and child between an adopted person and a natural parent of the adopted person unless both of the following requirements are satisfied:

(1) The natural parent and the adopted person lived together at any time as parent and child, or the natural parent was married to or cohabiting with the other natural parent at the time the person was conceived and died before the person's birth.

(2) The adoption was by the spouse of either of the natural parents or after the death of either of the natural parents.
(b) Neither a natural parent nor a relative of a natural parent, except for a wholeblood brother or sister of the adopted person or

the issue of that brother or sister, inherits from or through the adopted person on the basis of a parent and child relationship between the adopted person and the natural parent that satisfies the requirements of paragraphs (1) and (2) of subdivision (a), unless the adoption is by the spouse or surviving spouse of that parent.

(c) For the purpose of this section, a prior adoptive parent and child relationship is treated as a natural parent and child relationship.

Ca. Prob. Code § 6451

Added by Stats. 1993, Ch. 529, Sec. 5. Effective January 1, 1994.

Section 6452 - Parent not inheriting from or through child

(a) A parent does not inherit from or through a child on the basis of the parent and child relationship if any of the following apply:

(1) The parent's parental rights were terminated and the parent-child relationship was not judicially reestablished.

(2) The parent did not acknowledge the child.

(3) The parent left the child during the child's minority without an effort to provide for the child's support or without communication from the parent, for at least seven consecutive years that continued until the end of the child's minority, with the intent on the part of the parent to abandon the child. The failure to provide support or to communicate for the prescribed period is presumptive evidence of an intent to abandon.

(b) A parent who does not inherit from or through the child as provided in subdivision (a) shall be deemed to have predeceased the child, and the intestate estate shall pass as otherwise required under Section 6402.

Ca. Prob. Code § 6452

Added by Stats 2013 ch 39 (AB 490),s 2, eff. 1/1/2014.

Section 6453 - Determining whether parent is "natural parent"

For the purpose of determining whether a person is a "natural parent" as that term is used in this chapter:

(a) A natural parent and child relationship is established where that relationship is presumed and not rebutted pursuant to the Uniform Parentage Act (Part 3 (commencing with Section 7600) of Division 12 of the Family Code).

(b) A natural parent and child relationship may be established pursuant to any other provisions of the Uniform Parentage Act, except that the relationship may not be established by an action under subdivision (c) of Section 7630 of the Family Code unless any of the following conditions exist:

(1) A court order was entered during the parent's lifetime declaring parentage.

(2) Parentage is established by clear and convincing evidence that the parent has openly held out the child as that parent's own.

(3) It was impossible for the parent to hold out the child as that parent's own and parentage is established by clear and convincing evidence, which may include genetic DNA evidence acquired during the parent's lifetime.

(c) A natural parent and child relationship may be established pursuant to Section 249.5.

Ca. Prob. Code § 6453

Amended by Stats 2018 ch 116 (SB 1436),s 1, eff. 1/1/2019.
Amended by Stats 2004 ch 775 (AB 1910), s 9, eff. 1/1/2005.

Section 6454 - Existence of relationship between person and foster parent or stepparent

For the purpose of determining intestate succession by a person or the person's issue from or through a foster parent or stepparent, the relationship of parent and child exists between that person and the person's foster parent or stepparent if both of the following requirements are satisfied:

(a) The relationship began during the person's minority and continued throughout the joint lifetimes of the person and the person's foster parent or stepparent.

(b) It is established by clear and convincing evidence that the foster parent or stepparent would have adopted the person but for a legal barrier.

Ca. Prob. Code § 6454
Added by Stats. 1993, Ch. 529, Sec. 5. Effective January 1, 1994.

Section 6455 - Doctrine of equitable adoption

Nothing in this chapter affects or limits application of the judicial doctrine of equitable adoption for the benefit of the child or the child's issue.

Ca. Prob. Code § 6455
Added by Stats. 1993, Ch. 529, Sec. 5. Effective January 1, 1994.

Part 3 - FAMILY PROTECTION

Chapter 1 - TEMPORARY POSSESSION OF FAMILY DWELLING AND EXEMPT PROPERTY

Section 6500 - Entitled to possession of family dwelling, wearing apparel, household furniture, etc.

Until the inventory is filed and for a period of 60 days thereafter, or for such other period as may be ordered by the court for good cause on petition therefor, the decedent's surviving spouse and minor children are entitled to remain in possession of the family dwelling, the wearing apparel of the family, the household furniture, and the other property of the decedent exempt from enforcement of a money judgment.

Ca. Prob. Code § 6500
Enacted by Stats. 1990, Ch. 79.

Section 6501 - Filing petition for order; notice of hearing

A petition for an order under Section 6500 may be filed by any interested person. Notice of the hearing on the petition shall be given as provided in Section 1220.

Ca. Prob. Code § 6501
Enacted by Stats. 1990, Ch. 79.

Chapter 2 - SETTING ASIDE EXEMPT PROPERTY OTHER THAN FAMILY DWELLING

Section 6510 - Persons to whom property may be set apart

Upon the filing of the inventory or at any subsequent time during the administration of the estate, the court in its discretion may on petition therefor set apart all or any part of the property of the decedent exempt from enforcement of a money judgment, other than the family dwelling, to any one or more of the following:

(a) The surviving spouse.

(b) The minor children of the decedent.

Ca. Prob. Code § 6510
Enacted by Stats. 1990, Ch. 79.

Section 6511 - Filing petition for order; notice of hearing

A petition for an order under Section 6510 may be filed by any interested person. Notice of the hearing on the petition shall be given as provided in Section 1220.

Ca. Prob. Code § 6511
Enacted by Stats. 1990, Ch. 79.

Chapter 3 - SETTING ASIDE PROBATE HOMESTEAD

Section 6520 - Setting apart probate homestead

Upon the filing of the inventory or at any subsequent time during the administration of the estate, the court in its discretion may on petition therefor select and set apart one probate homestead in the manner provided in this chapter.

Ca. Prob. Code § 6520
Enacted by Stats. 1990, Ch. 79.

Section 6521 - Persons homestead set apart for

The probate homestead shall be set apart for the use of one or more of the following persons:
(a) The surviving spouse.
(b) The minor children of the decedent.
   Ca. Prob. Code § 6521
Enacted by Stats. 1990, Ch. 79.

Section 6522 - Property from which homestead selected

(a) The probate homestead shall be selected out of the following property, giving first preference to the community and quasi-community property of, or property owned in common by, the decedent and the person entitled to have the homestead set apart:

   (1) If the homestead is set apart for the use of the surviving spouse or for the use of the surviving spouse and minor children, out of community property or quasi-community property.

   (2) If the homestead is set apart for the use of the surviving spouse or for the use of the minor children or for the use of the surviving spouse and minor children, out of property owned in common by the decedent and the persons entitled to have the homestead set apart, or out of the separate property of the decedent or, if the decedent was not married at the time of death, out of property owned by the decedent.
(b) The probate homestead shall not be selected out of property the right to possession of which is vested in a third person unless the third person consents thereto. As used in this subdivision, "third person" means a person whose right to possession of the property (1) existed at the time of the death of the decedent or came into existence upon the death of the decedent and (2) was not created by testate or intestate succession from the decedent.
   Ca. Prob. Code § 6522
Amended by Stats. 1990, Ch. 710, Sec. 17. Operative July 1, 1991, by Sec. 48 of Ch. 710.

Section 6523 - Considerations in selecting and setting apart homestead

(a) In selecting and setting apart the probate homestead, the court shall consider the needs of the surviving spouse and minor children, the liens and encumbrances on the property, the claims of creditors, the needs of the heirs or devisees of the decedent, and the intent of the decedent with respect to the property in the estate and the estate plan of the decedent as expressed in inter vivos and testamentary transfers or by other means.
(b) The court, in light of subdivision (a) and other relevant considerations as determined by the court in its discretion, shall:

    (1) Select as a probate homestead the most appropriate property available that is suitable for that use, including in addition to the dwelling itself such adjoining property as appears reasonable.

    (2) Set the probate homestead so selected apart for such a term and upon such conditions (including, but not limited to, assignment by the homestead recipient of other property to the heirs or devisees of the property set apart as a homestead) as appear proper.
    Ca. Prob. Code § 6523
Enacted by Stats. 1990, Ch. 79.

Section 6524 - Set apart for limited period designated in order

The property set apart as a probate homestead shall be set apart only for a limited period, to be designated in the order, and in no case beyond the lifetime of the surviving spouse, or, as to a child, beyond its minority. Subject to the probate homestead right, the property of the decedent remains subject to administration including testate and intestate succession. The rights of the parties during the period for which the probate homestead is set apart are governed, to the extent applicable, by the Legal Estates Principal and Income Law, Chapter 2.6 (commencing with Section 731) of Title 2 of Part 1 of Division 2 of the Civil Code.

Ca. Prob. Code § 6524
Enacted by Stats. 1990, Ch. 79.

Section 6525 - Person who may file petition; notice of hearing

(a) A petition to select and set apart a probate homestead may be filed by any interested person.
(b) Notice of the hearing on the petition shall be given as provided in Section 1220 to all of the following persons:

(1) Each person listed in Section 1220.

(2) Each known heir whose interest in the estate would be affected by the petition.

(3) Each known devisee whose interest in the estate would be affected by the petition.

Ca. Prob. Code § 6525
Enacted by Stats. 1990, Ch. 79.

Section 6526 - Liability for claims

(a) Property of the decedent set apart as a probate homestead is liable for claims against the estate of the decedent, subject to the probate homestead right. The probate homestead right in property of the decedent is liable for claims that are secured by liens and encumbrances on the property at the time of the decedent's death but is exempt to the extent of the homestead exemption as to any claim that would have been subject to a homestead exemption at the time of the decedent's death under Article 4 (commencing with Section 704.710) of Chapter 4 of Division 2 of Title 9 of Part 2 of the Code of Civil Procedure.
(b) The probate homestead right in the property of the decedent is not liable for claims against the person for whose use the probate homestead is set apart.
(c) Property of the decedent set apart as a probate homestead is liable for claims against the testate or intestate successors of the

decedent or other successors to the property after administration, subject to the probate homestead right.

Ca. Prob. Code § 6526

Enacted by Stats. 1990, Ch. 79.

Section 6527 - Order modifying term or conditions of right or terminating right

(a) The court may by order modify the term or conditions of the probate homestead right or terminate the probate homestead right at any time prior to entry of an order for final distribution of the decedent's estate if in the court's discretion to do so appears appropriate under the circumstances of the case.

(b) A petition for an order under this section may be filed by any of the following:

(1) The person for whose use the probate homestead is set apart.

(2) The testate or intestate successors of the decedent or other successors to the property set apart as a probate homestead.

(3) Persons having claims secured by liens or encumbrances on the property set apart as a probate homestead.

(c) Notice of the hearing on the petition shall be given to all the persons listed in subdivision (b) as provided in Section 1220.

Ca. Prob. Code § 6527

Enacted by Stats. 1990, Ch. 79.

Section 6528 - Declaration of homestead for benefit of surviving spouse or minor not affected

Nothing in this chapter terminates or otherwise affects a declaration of homestead by, or for the benefit of, a surviving spouse or minor child of the decedent with respect to the community, quasi-community, or common interest of the surviving spouse or minor child in property in the decedent's estate. This section is declaratory of, and does not constitute a change in, existing law.

Ca. Prob. Code § 6528
Enacted by Stats. 1990, Ch. 79.

Chapter 4 - FAMILY ALLOWANCE

Section 6540 - Persons entitled to allowance; persons who may be given allowance

(a) The following are entitled to such reasonable family allowance out of the estate as is necessary for their maintenance according to their circumstances during administration of the estate:

(1) The surviving spouse of the decedent.

(2) Minor children of the decedent.

(3) Adult children of the decedent who are physically or mentally incapacitated from earning a living and were actually dependent in whole or in part upon the decedent for support.
(b) The following may be given such reasonable family allowance out of the estate as the court in its discretion determines is necessary for their maintenance according to their circumstances during administration of the estate:

(1) Other adult children of the decedent who were actually dependent in whole or in part upon the decedent for support.

(2) A parent of the decedent who was actually dependent in whole or in part upon the decedent for support.
(c) If a person otherwise eligible for family allowance has a reasonable maintenance from other sources and there are one or more other persons entitled to a family allowance, the family allowance shall be granted only to those who do not have a reasonable maintenance from other sources.
Ca. Prob. Code § 6540
Enacted by Stats. 1990, Ch. 79.

Section 6541 - Authority of court to grant or modify allowance; order for allowance

(a) The court may grant or modify a family allowance on petition of any interested person.

(b) With respect to an order for the family allowance provided for in subdivision (a) of Section 6540:

(1) Before the inventory is filed, the order may be made or modified either (A) ex parte or (B) after notice of the hearing on the petition has been given as provided in Section 1220.

(2) After the inventory is filed, the order may be made or modified only after notice of the hearing on the petition has been given as provided in Section 1220.

(c) An order for the family allowance provided in subdivision (b) of Section 6540 may be made only after notice of the hearing on the petition has been given as provided in Section 1220 to all of the following persons:

(1) Each person listed in Section 1220.

(2) Each known heir whose interest in the estate would be affected by the petition.

(3) Each known devisee whose interest in the estate would be affected by the petition.

Ca. Prob. Code § 6541
Enacted by Stats. 1990, Ch. 79.

Section 6542 - Commencement of allowance

A family allowance commences on the date of the court's order or such other time as may be provided in the court's order, whether before or after the date of the order, as the court in its discretion determines, but the allowance may not be made retroactive to a date earlier than the date of the decedent's death.

Ca. Prob. Code § 6542
Enacted by Stats. 1990, Ch. 79.

Section 6543 - Termination

(a) A family allowance shall terminate no later than the entry of the order for final distribution of the estate or, if the estate is insolvent, no later than one year after the granting of letters.
(b) Subject to subdivision (a), a family allowance shall continue until modified or terminated by the court or until such time as the court may provide in its order.
Ca. Prob. Code § 6543
Enacted by Stats. 1990, Ch. 79.

Section 6544 - Costs of proceedings

The costs of proceedings under this chapter shall be paid by the estate as expenses of administration.
Ca. Prob. Code § 6544
Enacted by Stats. 1990, Ch. 79.

Section 6545 - Undertaking given upon appeal preventing stay

Notwithstanding Chapter 2 (commencing with Section 916) of Title 13 of Part 2 of the Code of Civil Procedure, the perfecting of an appeal from an order made under this chapter does not stay proceedings under this chapter or the enforcement of the order appealed from if the person in whose favor the order is made gives an undertaking in double the amount of the payment or payments to be made to that person. The undertaking shall be conditioned that if the order appealed from is modified or reversed so that the payment or any part thereof to the person proves to have been unwarranted, the payment or part thereof shall, unless deducted from any preliminary or final distribution ordered in favor of the person, be repaid and refunded into the estate within 30 days after the court so orders following the modification or reversal, together with interest and costs.

Ca. Prob. Code § 6545
Enacted by Stats. 1990, Ch. 79.

Chapter 6 - SMALL ESTATE SET-ASIDE

Section 6600 - Decedent's estate defined; property excluded in determining estate of decedent or value

(a) Subject to subdivision (b), for the purposes of this chapter, "decedent's estate" means all the decedent's personal property, wherever located, and all the decedent's real property located in this state.

(b) For the purposes of this chapter:

(1) Any property or interest or lien thereon which, at the time of the decedent's death, was held by the decedent as a joint tenant, or in which the decedent had a life or other interest terminable upon the decedent's death, shall be excluded in determining the estate of the decedent or its value.

(2) A multiple-party account to which the decedent was a party at the time of the decedent's death shall be excluded in determining the estate of the decedent or its value, whether or not all or a portion of the sums on deposit are community property, to the extent that the sums on deposit belong after the death of the decedent to a surviving party, P.O.D. payee, or beneficiary. As used in this paragraph, the terms "multiple-party account," "party," "P.O.D. payee," and "beneficiary" have the meanings given those terms in Article 2 (commencing with Section 5120) of Chapter 1 of Part 2 of Division 5.

Ca. Prob. Code § 6600
Enacted by Stats. 1990, Ch. 79.

Section 6601 - Minor child defined

As used in this chapter, "minor child" means a child of the decedent who was under the age of 18 at the time of the decedent's death and who survived the decedent.

Ca. Prob. Code § 6601
Enacted by Stats. 1990, Ch. 79.

Section 6602 - Petition may be filed requesting order if net value of estate not in excess of $85,000

A petition may be filed under this chapter requesting an order setting aside the decedent's estate to the decedent's surviving spouse and minor children, or one or more of them, as provided in this chapter, if the net value of the decedent's estate, over and above all liens and encumbrances at the date of death and over and above the value of any probate homestead interest set apart out of the decedent's estate under Section 6520, does not exceed eighty-five thousand nine hundred dollars ($85,900), as adjusted periodically in accordance with Section 890.

Ca. Prob. Code § 6602
Amended by Stats 2019 ch 122 (AB 473),s 2, eff. 1/1/2020.

Section 6603 - Venue for filing petition

The petition shall be filed in the superior court of a county in which the estate of the decedent may be administered.

Ca. Prob. Code § 6603
Enacted by Stats. 1990, Ch. 79.

Section 6604 - Allegations and information required in petition

(a) The petition shall allege that this chapter applies and request that an order be made setting aside the estate of the decedent as provided in this chapter.
(b) The petition shall include the following:

(1) If proceedings for administration of the estate are not pending, the facts necessary to determine the county in which the estate of the decedent may be administered.

(2) The name, age, address, and relation to the decedent of each heir and devisee of the decedent, so far as known to the petitioner.

(3) A specific description and estimate of the value of the decedent's estate and a list of all liens and encumbrances at the date of death.

(4) A specific description and estimate of the value of any of the decedent's real property located outside this state that passed to the surviving spouse and minor children of the decedent, or any one or more of them, under the will of the decedent or by intestate succession.

(5) A specific description and estimate of the value of any of the decedent's property described in subdivision (b) of Section 6600 that passed to the surviving spouse and minor children of the decedent, or any one or more of them, upon the death of the decedent.

(6) A designation of any property as to which a probate homestead is set apart out of the decedent's estate under Section 6520.

(7) A statement of any unpaid liabilities for expenses of the last illness, funeral charges, and expenses of administration.

(8) The requested disposition of the estate of the decedent under this chapter and the considerations that justify the requested disposition.

Ca. Prob. Code § 6604
Enacted by Stats. 1990, Ch. 79.

Section 6605 - Petition filed when proceedings for administration pending; petition filed concurrently with petition for probate

(a) If proceedings for the administration of the estate of the decedent are pending, a petition under this chapter shall be filed in those proceedings without the payment of an additional fee.

(b) If proceedings for the administration of the estate of the decedent have not yet been commenced, a petition under this chapter may be filed concurrently with a petition for the probate of the decedent's will or for administration of the estate of the decedent, or, if no petition for probate or for administration is being filed, a petition under this chapter may be filed independently.

(c) A petition may be filed under this chapter at any time prior to the entry of the order for final distribution of the estate.

Ca. Prob. Code § 6605

Enacted by Stats. 1990, Ch. 79.

Section 6606 - Persons who may file petition

(a) A petition may be filed under this chapter by any of the following:

(1) The person named in the will of the decedent as executor.

(2) The surviving spouse of the decedent.

(3) The guardian of a minor child of the decedent.

(4) A child of the decedent who was a minor at the time the decedent died.

(5) The personal representative if a personal representative has been appointed for the decedent's estate.

(b) The guardian of a minor child of the decedent may file the petition without authorization or approval of the court in which the guardianship proceeding is pending.

Ca. Prob. Code § 6606

Enacted by Stats. 1990, Ch. 79.

Section 6607 - Notice of hearing on petition

(a) Where proceedings for the administration of the estate of the decedent are not pending when the petition is filed under this chapter and the petition under this chapter is not joined with a petition for the probate of the decedent's will or for administration of the estate of the decedent, the petitioner shall give notice of the hearing on the petition as provided in Section 1220 to (1) each person named as executor in the decedent's will and to (2) each heir or devisee of the decedent, if known to the petitioner. A copy of the petition shall be sent with the notice of hearing to the surviving spouse, each child, and each devisee who is not petitioning.

(b) If the petition under this chapter is filed with a petition for the probate of the decedent's will or with a petition for administration of the estate of the deceased spouse, notice of the hearing on the petition shall be given to the persons and in the manner prescribed by Section 8003 and shall be included in the notice required by that section.

(c) If proceedings for the administration of the estate of the decedent are pending when the petition is filed under this chapter and the hearing of the petition for probate of the will or administration of the estate of the decedent is set for a day more than 15 days after the filing of the petition filed under this chapter, the petition under this chapter shall be set for hearing at the same time as the petition for probate of the will or for administration of the estate, and notice of hearing on the petition filed under this chapter shall be given by the petitioner as provided in Section 1220. If the hearing of the petition for probate of the will or for administration of the estate is not set for hearing for a day more than 15 days after the filing of the petition under this chapter, (1) the petition filed under this chapter shall be set for hearing at least 15 days after the date on which it is filed, (2) notice of the hearing on the petition filed under this chapter shall be given by the petitioner as provided in Section 1220, and (3) if the petition for probate of the will or for administration of the estate has not already been heard, that petition shall be continued until that date and heard at the same time unless the court otherwise orders.

Ca. Prob. Code § 6607
Enacted by Stats. 1990, Ch. 79.

Section 6608 - Inventory and appraisal filed with court

If a petition is filed under this chapter, the personal representative, or the petitioner if no personal representative has been appointed, shall file with the clerk of the court, prior to the hearing of the petition, an inventory and appraisal made as provided in Part 3 (commencing with Section 8800) of Division 7. The personal representative or the petitioner, as the case may be, may appraise the assets which a personal representative could appraise under Section 8901.

Ca. Prob. Code § 6608
Enacted by Stats. 1990, Ch. 79.

Section 6609 - Making order

(a) If the court determines that the net value of the decedent's estate, over and above all liens and encumbrances at the date of death of the decedent and over and above the value of any probate homestead interest set apart out of the decedent's estate under Section 6520, does not exceed eighty-five thousand nine hundred dollars ($85,900), as adjusted periodically in accordance with Section 890, as of the date of the decedent's death, the court shall make an order under this section unless the court determines that making an order under this section would be inequitable under the circumstances of the particular case.

(b) In determining whether to make an order under this section, the court shall consider the needs of the surviving spouse and minor children, the liens and encumbrances on the property of the decedent's estate, the claims of creditors, the needs of the heirs or devisees of the decedent, the intent of the decedent with respect to the property in the estate and the estate plan of the decedent as expressed in inter vivos and testamentary transfers or by other means, and any other relevant considerations. If the surviving spouse has remarried at the time the petition is heard, it shall be presumed that the needs of the surviving spouse do not justify the setting aside of the small estate, or any portion thereof, to the surviving spouse. This presumption is a presumption affecting the burden of proof.

(c) Subject to subdivision (d), if the court makes an order under this section, the court shall assign the whole of the decedent's estate, subject to all liens and encumbrances on property in the estate at the date of the decedent's death, to the surviving spouse and the minor children of the decedent, or any one or more of them.
(d) If there are any liabilities for expenses of the last illness, funeral charges, or expenses of administration that are unpaid at the time the court makes an order under this section, the court shall make the necessary orders for payment of those unpaid liabilities.
(e) Title to property in the decedent's estate vests absolutely in the surviving spouse, minor children, or any or all of them, as provided in the order, subject to all liens and encumbrances on property in the estate at the date of the decedent's death, and there shall be no further proceedings in the administration of the decedent's estate unless additional property in the decedent's estate is discovered.

Ca. Prob. Code § 6609
Amended by Stats 2019 ch 122 (AB 473),s 3, eff. 1/1/2020.

Section 6610 - Final order conclusive on all persons

Upon becoming final, an order under Section 6609 shall be conclusive on all persons, whether or not they are then in being.

Ca. Prob. Code § 6610
Enacted by Stats. 1990, Ch. 79.

Section 6611 - Liability for unsecured debts of decedent

(a) Subject to the limitations and conditions specified in this section, the person or persons in whom title vested pursuant to Section 6609 are personally liable for the unsecured debts of the decedent.
(b) The personal liability of a person under this section does not exceed the fair market value at the date of the decedent's death of the property title to which vested in that person pursuant to Section 6609, less the total of all of the following:

(1) The amount of any liens and encumbrances on that property.

(2) The value of any probate homestead interest set apart under Section 6520 out of that property.

(3) The value of any other property set aside under Section 6510 out of that property.

(c) In any action or proceeding based upon an unsecured debt of the decedent, the surviving spouse of the decedent, the child or children of the decedent, or the guardian of the minor child or children of the decedent, may assert any defense, cross-complaint, or setoff which would have been available to the decedent if the decedent had not died.

(d) If proceedings are commenced in this state for the administration of the estate of the decedent and the time for filing claims has commenced, any action upon the personal liability of a person under this section is barred to the same extent as provided for claims under Part 4 (commencing with Section 9000) of Division 7, except as to the following:

(1) Creditors who commence judicial proceedings for the enforcement of the debt and serve the person liable under this section with the complaint therein prior to the expiration of the time for filing claims.

(2) Creditors who have or who secure an acknowledgment in writing of the person liable under this section that that person is liable for the debts.

(3) Creditors who file a timely claim in the proceedings for the administration of the estate of the decedent.

(e) Section 366.2 of the Code of Civil Procedure applies in an action under this section.

Ca. Prob. Code § 6611

Amended by Stats. 1992, Ch. 178, Sec. 32. Effective January 1, 1993.

Section 6612 - Estate administered as if no petition filed

If a petition filed under this chapter is filed with a petition for the probate of the decedent's will or for administration of the estate of the decedent and the court determines not to make an order under Section 6609, the court shall act on the petition for probate of the decedent's will or for administration of the estate of the decedent in the same manner as if no petition had been filed under this chapter, and the estate shall then be administered in the same manner as if no petition had been filed under this chapter.

Ca. Prob. Code § 6612
Enacted by Stats. 1990, Ch. 79.

Section 6613 - Attorney's fees

The attorney's fees for services performed in connection with the filing of a petition and the obtaining of a court order under this chapter shall be determined by private agreement between the attorney and the client and are not subject to approval by the court. If there is no agreement between the attorney and the client concerning the attorney's fees for services performed in connection with the filing of a petition and obtaining of a court order under this chapter and there is a dispute concerning the reasonableness of the attorney's fees for those services, a petition may be filed with the court in the same proceeding requesting that the court determine the reasonableness of the attorney's fees for those services. If there is an agreement between the attorney and the client concerning the attorney's fees for services performed in connection with the filing of a petition and obtaining a court order under this chapter and there is a dispute concerning the meaning of the agreement, a petition may be filed with the court in the same proceeding requesting that the court determine the dispute.

Ca. Prob. Code § 6613
Enacted by Stats. 1990, Ch. 79.

Section 6614 - Law applicable if death before July 1, 1987

Sections 6600 to 6613, inclusive, do not apply if the decedent died before July 1, 1987. If the decedent died before July 1, 1987, the case continues to be governed by the law applicable to the case prior to July 1, 1987.

Ca. Prob. Code § 6614
Enacted by Stats. 1990, Ch. 79.

Section 6615 - Reference to repealed provisions

A reference in any statute of this state or in a written instrument, including a will or trust, to a provision of former Sections 640 to 647.5, inclusive, repealed by Chapter 783 of the Statutes of 1986, shall be deemed to be a reference to the comparable provisions of this chapter.

Ca. Prob. Code § 6615
Enacted by Stats. 1990, Ch. 79.

Part 4 - ESCHEAT OF DECEDENT'S PROPERTY

Section 6800 - Generally

(a) If a decedent, whether or not the decedent was domiciled in this state, leaves no one to take the decedent's estate or any portion thereof by testate succession, and no one other than a government or governmental subdivision or agency to take the estate or a portion thereof by intestate succession, under the laws of this state or of any other jurisdiction, the same escheats at the time of the decedent's death in accordance with this part.

(b) Property that escheats to the state under this part, whether held by the state or its officers, is subject to the same charges and trusts to which it would have been subject if it had passed by succession and is also subject to the provisions of Title 10 (commencing with Section 1300) of Part 3 of the Code of Civil Procedure relating to escheated estates.

Ca. Prob. Code § 6800
Enacted by Stats. 1990, Ch. 79.

Section 6801 - Real property

Real property in this state escheats to this state in accordance with Section 6800.

Ca. Prob. Code § 6801
Enacted by Stats. 1990, Ch. 79.

Section 6802 - Tangible personal property

All tangible personal property owned by the decedent, wherever located at the decedent's death, that was customarily kept in this state prior to the decedent's death, escheats to this state in accordance with Section 6800.

Ca. Prob. Code § 6802
Enacted by Stats. 1990, Ch. 79.

Section 6803 - Tangible personal property subject to superior court control

(a) Subject to subdivision (b), all tangible personal property owned by the decedent that is subject to the control of a superior court of this state for purposes of administration under this code escheats to this state in accordance with Section 6800.

(b) The property described in subdivision (a) does not escheat to this state but goes to another jurisdiction if the other jurisdiction claims the property and establishes all of the following:

(1) The other jurisdiction is entitled to the property under its law.

(2) The decedent customarily kept the property in that jurisdiction prior to the decedent's death.

(3) This state has the right to escheat and take tangible personal property being administered as part of a decedent's estate in that jurisdiction if the decedent customarily kept the property in this state prior to the decedent's death.

Ca. Prob. Code § 6803
Enacted by Stats. 1990, Ch. 79.

Section 6804 - Intangible personal property

All intangible property owned by the decedent escheats to this state in accordance with Section 6800 if the decedent was domiciled in this state at the time of the decedent's death.

Ca. Prob. Code § 6804

Enacted by Stats. 1990, Ch. 79.

Section 6805 - Intangible personal property subject to superior court control

(a) Subject to subdivision (b), all intangible property owned by the decedent that is subject to the control of a superior court of this state for purposes of administration under this code escheats to this state in accordance with Section 6800 whether or not the decedent was domiciled in this state at the time of the decedent's death.

(b) The property described in subdivision (a) does not escheat to this state but goes to another jurisdiction if the other jurisdiction claims the property and establishes all of the following:

(1) The other jurisdiction is entitled to the property under its laws.

(2) The decedent was domiciled in that jurisdiction at the time of the decedent's death.

(3) This state has the right to escheat and take intangible property being administered as part of a decedent's estate in that jurisdiction if the decedent was domiciled in this state at the time of the decedent's death.

Ca. Prob. Code § 6805

Enacted by Stats. 1990, Ch. 79.

Section 6806 - Benefit from trust established under plan providing health and welfare, pension, vacation, severance, etc.

Notwithstanding any other provision of law, a benefit consisting of money or other property distributable from a trust established under a plan providing health and welfare, pension, vacation, severance, retirement benefit, death benefit, unemployment insurance or similar benefits does not pass to or escheat to the state under this part but goes to the trust or fund from which it is distributable, subject to the provisions of Section 1521 of the Code of Civil Procedure. However, if such plan has terminated and the trust or fund has been distributed to the beneficiaries thereof prior to distribution of such benefit from the estate, such benefit passes to the state and escheats to the state under this part.

Ca. Prob. Code § 6806
Enacted by Stats. 1990, Ch. 79.

Division 7 - ADMINISTRATION OF ESTATES OF DECEDENTS

Part 1 - GENERAL PROVISIONS

Chapter 1 - PASSAGE OF DECEDENT'S PROPERTY

Section 7000 - Generally

Subject to Section 7001, title to a decedent's property passes on the decedent's death to the person to whom it is devised in the decedent's last will or, in the absence of such a devise, to the decedent's heirs as prescribed in the laws governing intestate succession.

Ca. Prob. Code § 7000
Enacted by Stats. 1990, Ch. 79.

Section 7001 - Rights of beneficiaries, creditors, other persons

The decedent's property is subject to administration under this code, except as otherwise provided by law, and is subject to the rights of beneficiaries, creditors, and other persons as provided by law.

Ca. Prob. Code § 7001
Enacted by Stats. 1990, Ch. 79.

Chapter 2 - JURISDICTION AND COURTS

Article 1 - JURISDICTION AND VENUE

Section 7050 - Superior court jurisdiction

The superior court has jurisdiction of proceedings under this code concerning the administration of the decedent's estate.
Ca. Prob. Code § 7050
Amended by Stats. 1994, Ch. 806, Sec. 22. Effective January 1, 1995.

Section 7051 - Venue of proceedings if decedent domicile in state at time of death

If the decedent was domiciled in this state at the time of death, the proper county for proceedings concerning administration of the decedent's estate is the county in which the decedent was domiciled, regardless of where the decedent died.
Ca. Prob. Code § 7051
Enacted by Stats. 1990, Ch. 79.

Section 7052 - Venue of proceedings if decedent not domicile in state at time of death

If the decedent was not domiciled in this state at the time of death, the proper county for proceedings under this code concerning the administration of the decedent's estate is one of the following:
(a) If property of the nondomiciliary decedent is located in the county in which the nondomiciliary decedent died, the county in which the nondomiciliary decedent died.
(b) If no property of the nondomiciliary decedent is located in the county in which the nondomiciliary decedent died or if the nondomiciliary decedent did not die in this state, any county in which property of the nondomiciliary decedent is located, regardless of where the nondomiciliary decedent died. If property of the nondomiciliary decedent is located in more than one county, the proper county is the county in which a petition for ancillary administration is first filed, and the court in that county has

jurisdiction of the administration of the estate.

Ca. Prob. Code § 7052

Enacted by Stats. 1990, Ch. 79.

Article 2 - DISQUALIFICATION OF JUDGE

Section 7060 - Grounds

(a) In addition to any other ground provided by law for disqualification of a judge, a judge is disqualified from acting in proceedings under this code concerning the administration of the decedent's estate, except to order the transfer of a proceeding as provided in Article 3 (commencing with Section 7070), if any of the following circumstances exist:

(1) The judge is interested as a beneficiary or creditor.

(2) The judge is named as executor or trustee in the will.

(3) The judge is otherwise interested.

(b) A judge who participates in any manner in the drafting or execution of a will, including acting as a witness to the will, is disqualified from acting in any proceeding prior to and including the admission of the will to probate or in any proceeding involving its validity or interpretation.

(c) The amendments made to former Section 303 by Section 27 of Chapter 923 of the Statutes of 1987 do not apply in any proceeding commenced prior to July 1, 1988.

Ca. Prob. Code § 7060

Enacted by Stats. 1990, Ch. 79.

Article 3 - TRANSFER OF PROCEEDINGS

Section 7070 - No judge of court qualified to act

The court or judge shall order a proceeding under this code concerning the administration of the decedent's estate transferred to another county if there is no judge of the court in which the proceeding is pending who is qualified to act. This section does not apply if a judge qualified to act is assigned by the chairman of the Judicial Council to sit in the county and hear the proceeding.

Ca. Prob. Code § 7070
Enacted by Stats. 1990, Ch. 79.

Section 7071 - County to which proceeding transferred

Transfer of a proceeding under this article shall be to another county in which property of the decedent is located or, if there is no other county in which property of the decedent is located, to an adjoining county.

Ca. Prob. Code § 7071
Enacted by Stats. 1990, Ch. 79.

Section 7072 - Retransfer to court in which proceeding originally commenced

Upon petition of the personal representative or other interested person before entry of the order for final distribution of the estate, a proceeding transferred under this article may be retransferred to the court in which the proceeding was originally commenced if the court determines that both of the following conditions are satisfied:
(a) Another person has become judge of the court where the proceeding was originally commenced who is not disqualified to act in the administration of the estate.
(b) The convenience of the parties interested would be promoted by the retransfer.

Ca. Prob. Code § 7072
Enacted by Stats. 1990, Ch. 79.

Chapter 3 - RULES OF PROCEDURE

Article 2 - NEW TRIALS

Section 7220 - Cases in which motion may be made

In proceedings under this code concerning the administration of the decedent's estate, a motion for a new trial may be made only in the following cases:

(a) Contest of a will or revocation of probate of a will.

(b) Cases in which a right to jury trial is expressly granted, whether or not the case was tried by a jury.

Ca. Prob. Code § 7220

Amended by Stats 2015 ch 303 (AB 731),s 418, eff. 1/1/2016.
Enacted by Stats. 1990, Ch. 79.

Article 3.5 - JUDGMENTS AND ORDERS

Section 7250 - Personal representatives and sureties released when judgment becomes final

(a) When a judgment or order made pursuant to the provisions of this code concerning the administration of the decedent's estate becomes final, it releases the personal representative and the sureties from all claims of the heirs or devisees and of any persons affected thereby based upon any act or omission directly authorized, approved, or confirmed in the judgment or order. For the purposes of this section, "order" includes an order settling an account of the personal representative, whether an interim or final account.

(b) Nothing in this section affects any order, judgment, or decree made, or any action taken, before July 1, 1988. The validity of any action taken before July 1, 1988, is determined by the applicable law in effect before July 1, 1988, and not by this section.

(c) This section shall not apply where the judgment or order is obtained by fraud or conspiracy or by misrepresentation contained in the petition or account or in the judgment as to any material fact. For purposes of this subdivision, misrepresentation includes, but shall not be limited to, the omission of a material fact.

Ca. Prob. Code § 7250

Amended by Stats. 1993, Ch. 794, Sec. 2. Effective January 1, 1994.

Article 4 - ORDERS AND TRANSACTIONS AFFECTING PROPERTY

Section 7260 - Transaction defined

As used in this article, "transaction" means a transaction affecting title to property in the estate, including, but not limited to, the following:

(a) In the case of real property, a conveyance (including a sale, option, or order confirming a sale or option), a lease, the creation of a mortgage, deed of trust, or other lien or encumbrance, the setting apart of a probate homestead, or the distribution of property.

(b) In the case of personal property, a transfer of the property or the creation of a security interest or other lien on the property.

Ca. Prob. Code § 7260

Enacted by Stats. 1990, Ch. 79.

Section 7261 - Statement of authority in instrument

If a transaction affecting real property in the estate is executed by the personal representative in accordance with the terms of a court order, the instrument shall include a statement that the transaction is made by authority of the order authorizing or directing the transaction and shall give the date of the order.

Ca. Prob. Code § 7261

Enacted by Stats. 1990, Ch. 79.

Section 7262 - Effect of transaction in accordance with order authorizing transaction

A transaction executed by the personal representative in accordance with an order authorizing or directing the transaction has the same effect as if the decedent were living at the time of the transaction and had carried it out in person while having legal capacity to do so.

Ca. Prob. Code § 7262

Enacted by Stats. 1990, Ch. 79.

Section 7263 - Certified copy of order recorded

If an order is made setting apart a probate homestead, confirming a sale or making a distribution of real property, or determining any other matter affecting title to real property in the estate, the personal representative shall record a certified copy of the order in the office of the county recorder in each county in which any portion of the real property is located.

Ca. Prob. Code § 7263
Enacted by Stats. 1990, Ch. 79.

Article 5 - UNITED STATES AS INTERESTED PERSON

Section 7280 - Generally

Where compensation, pension, insurance, or other allowance is made or awarded by a department or bureau of the United States government to a decedent's estate, the department or bureau has the same right as an interested person to do any of the following:

(a) Request special notice.

(b) Commence and prosecute an action on the bond of a personal representative.

(c) Contest an account of a personal representative.

Ca. Prob. Code § 7280
Enacted by Stats. 1990, Ch. 79.

Chapter 4 - PUBLIC ADMINISTRATORS

Article 1 - TAKING TEMPORARY POSSESSION OR CONTROL OF PROPERTY

Section 7600 - Notice of property that ought to be in public administrator's possession

If a public officer or employee knows of property of a decedent that is subject to loss, injury, waste, or misappropriation and that ought to be in the possession or control of the public administrator, the officer or employee shall inform the public administrator.

Ca. Prob. Code § 7600
Enacted by Stats. 1990, Ch. 79.

Section 7600.5 - Notice public administrator of death of person in hospital without known next of kin

If a person dies in a hospital, convalescent hospital, or board and care facility without known next of kin, the person in charge of the hospital or facility shall give immediate notice of that fact to the public administrator of the county in which the hospital or facility is located. If the notice required by this section is not given, the hospital or facility is liable for (1) any cost of interment incurred by the estate or the county as a result of the failure and (2) any loss to the estate or beneficiaries caused by loss, injury, waste, or misappropriation of property of the decedent as a result of the failure.

Ca. Prob. Code § 7600.5
Enacted by Stats. 1990, Ch. 79.

Section 7600.6 - Notice to public administrator by funeral director

A funeral director in control of the decedent's remains pursuant to subdivision (c) of Section 7100 of the Health and Safety Code shall notify the public administrator if none of the persons described in paragraphs (2) to (6), inclusive, of subdivision (a) of Section 7100 of the Health and Safety Code exist, can be found after reasonable inquiry, or can be contacted by reasonable means.

Ca. Prob. Code § 7600.6
Amended by Stats. 1998, Ch. 253, Sec. 3. Effective January 1, 1999.

Section 7601 - Public administrator to take possession of decedent's property if no personal representative appointed

(a) If no personal representative has been appointed, the public administrator of a county shall take prompt possession or control of property of a decedent in the county that is deemed by the public administrator to be subject to loss, injury, waste, or misappropriation, or that the court orders into the possession or control of the public administrator after notice to the public administrator as provided in Section 1220.
(b) If property described in subdivision (a) is beyond the ability of the public administrator to take possession or control, the public administrator is not liable for failing to take possession or control of the property.

Ca. Prob. Code § 7601
Amended by Stats 2004 ch 888 (AB 2687), s 2, eff. 1/1/2005.

Section 7602 - Duties of public administrator authorized to take possession

(a) A public administrator who is authorized to take possession or control of property of a decedent under this article shall make a prompt search for other property, a will, and instructions for disposition of the decedent's remains.
(b) If a will is found, the public administrator or custodian of the will shall deliver the will as provided in Section 8200.
(c) If instructions for disposition of the decedent's remains are found, the public administrator shall promptly deliver the instructions to the person upon whom the right to control disposition of the decedent's remains devolves as provided in Section 7100 of the Health and Safety Code.
(d) If other property is located, the public administrator shall take possession or control of any property that, in the sole discretion of the public administrator, is deemed to be subject to loss, injury, waste, or misappropriation and that is located anywhere in this state or that is subject to the laws of this state. The public administrator does not have any liability for loss, injury, waste, or misappropriation of property of which he or she is unable to take possession or control.
Ca. Prob. Code § 7602
Amended by Stats 2004 ch 888 (AB 2687), s 3, eff. 1/1/2005.

Section 7603 - Certification of fact of authorization to take possession

(a) A public administrator who is authorized to take possession or control of property of a decedent pursuant to this article may issue a written certification of that fact. The written certification is effective for 30 days after the date of issuance.
(b) The public administrator may record a copy of the written certification in any county in which is located real property of which the public administrator is authorized to take possession or control

under this article.

(c) A financial institution, government or private agency, retirement fund administrator, insurance company, licensed securities dealer, or other person shall, without the necessity of inquiring into the truth of the written certification, without requiring a death certificate, without charge, and without court order or letters being issued:

(1) Provide the public administrator complete information concerning property held in the sole name of the decedent, including the names and addresses of any beneficiaries.

(2) Grant the public administrator access to a safe-deposit box rented in the sole name of the decedent for the purpose of inspection and removal of any will or instructions for disposition of the decedent's remains. Costs and expenses incurred in drilling or forcing a safe-deposit box shall be borne by the estate of the decedent.

(3) Surrender to the public administrator any property of the decedent that, in the sole discretion of the public administrator, is deemed to be subject to loss, injury, waste, or misappropriation.

(d) Receipt of the written certification provided by this section:

(1) Constitutes sufficient acquittance for providing information or granting access to the safe-deposit box, for removal of the decedent's will and instructions for disposition of the decedent's remains, and for surrendering property of the decedent.

(2) Fully discharges the financial institution, government or private agency, retirement fund administrator, insurance company, licensed securities dealer, or other person from any liability for any act or omission of the public administrator with respect to the property or the safe-deposit box.

Ca. Prob. Code § 7603

Amended by Stats 2004 ch 888 (AB 2687), s 4, eff. 1/1/2005.

Section 7604 - Costs incurred in preservation of estate and reasonable compensation

If the public administrator takes possession or control of property of a decedent under this article, but another person is subsequently appointed personal representative or subsequently takes control or possession, the public administrator is entitled to reasonable costs incurred for the preservation of the estate, together with reasonable compensation for services. The costs and compensation are a proper expense of administration.

Ca. Prob. Code § 7604
Amended by Stats. 1994, Ch. 806, Sec. 24. Effective January 1, 1995.

Section 7605 - Continuing education requirements

On or before January 1, 2010, the public administrator shall comply with the continuing education requirements that are established by the California State Association of Public Administrators, Public Guardians, and Public Conservators.

Ca. Prob. Code § 7605
Added by Stats 2008 ch 237 (AB 2343),s 3, eff. 1/1/2009.

Article 2 - APPOINTMENT AS PERSONAL REPRESENTATIVE

Section 7620 - Petition for appointment; acceptance of appointment when ordered; summary disposition of estate

The public administrator of the county in which the estate of a decedent may be administered shall promptly:
(a) Petition for appointment as personal representative of the estate if no person having higher priority has petitioned for appointment and the total value of the property in the decedent's estate exceeds one hundred fifty thousand dollars ($150,000).
(b) Petition for appointment as personal representative of any other estate the public administrator determines is proper.
(c) Accept appointment as personal representative of an estate

when so ordered by the court, whether or not on petition of the public administrator, after notice to the public administrator as provided in Section 7621.

(d) Proceed with summary disposition of the estate as authorized by Article 4 (commencing with Section 7660), if the total value of the property in the decedent's estate does not exceed the amount prescribed in Section 13100 and a person having higher priority has not assumed responsibility for administration of the estate.

   Ca. Prob. Code § 7620

Amended by Stats 2011 ch 117 (AB 1305),s 1, eff. 1/1/2012.

Amended by Stats 2004 ch 888 (AB 2687), s 5, eff. 1/1/2005.

Section 7621 - Appointment and issuance of letters

(a) Except as otherwise provided in this section, appointment of the public administrator as personal representative shall be made, and letters issued, in the same manner and pursuant to the same procedure as for appointment of and issuance of letters to personal representatives generally.

(b) Appointment of the public administrator may be made on the court's own motion, after notice to the public administrator as provided in Section 1220.

(c) Letters may be issued to "the public administrator" of the county without naming the public administrator.

(d) The public administrator's oath and official bond are in lieu of the personal representative's oath and bond. Every estate administered under this chapter shall be charged an annual bond fee in the amount of twenty-five dollars ($25) plus one-fourth of one percent of the amount of an estate greater than ten thousand dollars ($10,000). The amount charged is an expense of administration and that amount shall be deposited in the county treasury. If a successor personal representative is appointed, the amount of the bond fee shall be prorated over the period of months during which the public administrator acted as personal representative. Upon final distribution by the public administrator, any amount of bond charges in excess of one year shall be a prorated charge to the estate.

Ca. Prob. Code § 7621
Amended by Stats. 1995, Ch. 160, Sec. 1. Effective January 1, 1996.

Section 7622 - Administration of estate; compensation

Except as otherwise provided in this chapter:

(a) The public administrator shall administer the estate in the same manner as a personal representative generally, and the provisions of this code concerning the administration of the decedent's estate apply to administration by the public administrator.

(b) The public administrator is entitled to receive the same compensation as is granted by this division to a personal representative generally. The attorney for the public administrator is entitled to receive the same compensation as is granted by this division to an attorney for a personal representative generally. However, the compensation of the public administrator and the public administrator's attorney may not be less than the compensation in effect at the time of appointment of the public administrator or the minimum amount provided in subdivision (b) of Section 7666, whichever is greater.

Ca. Prob. Code § 7622
Amended by Stats 2004 ch 888 (AB 2687), s 6, eff. 1/1/2005.

Section 7623 - Additional compensation

(a) As used in this section, "additional compensation" means the difference between the reasonable compensation of the public administrator in administering the estate and the compensation awarded the public administrator under Chapter 1 (commencing with Section 10800) of Part 7.

(b) The public administrator may be awarded additional compensation if any of the following conditions are satisfied:

(1) A person having priority for appointment as personal representative has been given notice under Section 8110 of the public administrator's petition for appointment, and the person has not petitioned for appointment in preference to the public administrator.

(2) The public administrator has been appointed after the resignation or removal of a personal representative.

Ca. Prob. Code § 7623
Enacted by Stats. 1990, Ch. 79.

Section 7624 - Payment of money remaining after final distribution

(a) If after final distribution of an estate any money remains in the possession of the public administrator that should be paid over to the county treasurer pursuant to Chapter 5 (commencing with Section 11850) of Part 10, the court shall order payment to be made within 60 days.

(b) Upon failure of the public administrator to comply with an order made pursuant to subdivision (a), the district attorney of the county shall promptly institute proceedings against the public administrator and the sureties on the official bond for the amount ordered to be paid, plus costs.

Ca. Prob. Code § 7624
Enacted by Stats. 1990, Ch. 79.

Article 3 - DEPOSIT OF MONEY OF ESTATE

Section 7640 - Generally

(a) The public administrator shall, upon receipt, deposit all money of the estate in an insured account in a financial institution or with the county treasurer of the county in which the proceedings are pending.

(b) Upon deposit under this section the public administrator is discharged from further responsibility for the money deposited until the public administrator withdraws the money.

Ca. Prob. Code § 7640
Enacted by Stats. 1990, Ch. 79.

Section 7641 - Withdrawal of money deposited

Money deposited in a financial institution or with the county treasurer under this article may be withdrawn upon the order of the public administrator when required for the purposes of administration.

Ca. Prob. Code § 7641

Enacted by Stats. 1990, Ch. 79.

Section 7642 - Interest or dividends credited

(a) The public administrator shall credit each estate with the highest rate of interest or dividends that the estate would have received if the funds available for deposit had been individually and separately deposited.

(b) Interest or dividends credited to the account of the public administrator in excess of the amount credited to the estates pursuant to subdivision (a) shall be deposited in the county general fund.

Ca. Prob. Code § 7642

Enacted by Stats. 1990, Ch. 79.

Section 7643 - Duties of court treasurer

(a) The county treasurer shall receive and safely keep all money deposited with the county treasurer under this chapter and pay the money out on the order of the public administrator when required for the purposes of administration. The county treasurer and sureties on the official bond of the county treasurer are responsible for the safekeeping and payment of the money.

(b) The county treasurer shall deliver to the State Treasurer or the Controller all money in the possession of the county treasurer belonging to the estate, if there are no beneficiaries or other persons entitled to the money, or the beneficiaries or other persons entitled to the money do not appear and claim it. Delivery shall be made under the provisions of Article 1 (commencing with Section 1440) of Chapter 6 of Title 10 of Part 3 of the Code of Civil Procedure.

Ca. Prob. Code § 7643

Enacted by Stats. 1990, Ch. 79.

Section 7644 - Money presumptively abandoned

(a) If a deposit in a financial institution is made under this article, money remaining unclaimed at the expiration of five years after the date of the deposit, together with the increase and proceeds of the deposit, shall be presumed abandoned in any of the following circumstances:

(1) The deposit belongs to the estate of a known decedent for which a personal representative has never been appointed.

(2) The deposit belongs to the estate of a known decedent for which a personal representative has been appointed but no order of distribution has been made due to the absence of interested persons or the failure of interested persons diligently to protect their interests by taking reasonable steps for the purpose of securing a distribution of the estate.

(b) The Controller may, at any time after the expiration of the five-year period, file a petition with the court setting forth the fact that the money has remained on deposit in a financial institution under the circumstances described in subdivision (a) for the five-year period, and requesting an order declaring that the money is presumptively abandoned and directing the holder of the money to pay the money to the State Treasurer.

(c) Upon presentation of a certified copy of a court order made under subdivision (b), the financial institution shall forthwith transmit the money to the State Treasurer for deposit in the State Treasury. The deposit shall be made as provided in Section 1310 of the Code of Civil Procedure. All money deposited in the State Treasury under the provisions of this section shall be deemed to be deposited in the State Treasury under the provisions of Article 1 (commencing with Section 1440) of Chapter 6 of Title 10 of Part 3 of the Code of Civil Procedure. The deposit shall be transmitted, received, accounted for, and disposed of as provided by Title 10 (commencing with Section 1300) of Part 3 of the Code of Civil Procedure.

Ca. Prob. Code § 7644
Enacted by Stats. 1990, Ch. 79.

Article 4 - SUMMARY DISPOSITION OF SMALL ESTATES

Section 7660 - Generally

(a) If a public administrator takes possession or control of an estate pursuant to this chapter, the public administrator may, acting as personal representative of the estate, summarily dispose of the estate in the manner provided in this article in either of the following circumstances:

(1) The total value of the property in the decedent's estate does not exceed the amount prescribed in Section 13100. The authority provided by this paragraph may be exercised only upon order of the court. The order may be made upon ex parte application. The fee to be allowed to the clerk for the filing of the application is two hundred five dollars ($205). The authority for this summary administration of the estate shall be evidenced by a court order for summary disposition.

(2) The total value of the property in the decedent's estate does not exceed fifty thousand dollars ($50,000). The authority provided by this paragraph may be exercised without court authorization.

(A) A public administrator who is authorized to summarily dispose of property of a decedent pursuant to this paragraph may issue a written certification of Authority for Summary Administration. The written certification is effective for 30 days after the date of issuance.

(B) A financial institution, government or private agency, retirement fund administrator, insurance company, licensed securities dealer, or other person shall, without the necessity of inquiring into the truth of the written certification of Authority for Summary Administration and without court order or letters being issued, do all of the following:

(i) Provide the public administrator complete information concerning any property held in the name of the decedent, including the names and addresses of any beneficiaries or joint owners.

(ii) Grant the public administrator access to a safe-deposit box or storage facility rented in the name of the decedent for the purpose of inspection and removal of property of the decedent. Costs and expenses incurred in accessing a safe-deposit box or storage facility shall be borne by the estate of the decedent.

(iii) Surrender to the public administrator any property of the decedent that is held or controlled by the financial institution, agency, retirement fund administrator, insurance company, licensed securities dealer, or other person.

(C) Receipt by a financial institution, government or private agency, retirement fund administrator, insurance company, licensed securities dealer, or other person of the written certification provided by this article shall do both of the following:

(i) Constitute sufficient acquittance for providing information or granting access to a safe-deposit box or a storage facility and for surrendering any property of the decedent.

(ii) Fully discharge the financial institution, government or private agency, retirement fund administrator, insurance company, licensed securities dealer, or other person from liability for any act or omission of the public administrator with respect to the property, a safe-deposit box, or a storage facility.
(b) Summary disposition may be made notwithstanding the existence of the decedent's will, if the will does not name an executor or if the named executor refuses to act.
(c) Nothing in this article precludes the public administrator from filing a petition with the court under any other provision of this code concerning the administration of the decedent's estate.
(d) Petitions filed pursuant to this article shall contain the information required by Section 8002.
(e) If a public administrator takes possession or control of an estate pursuant to this chapter, this article conveys the authority of a

personal representative as described in Section 9650 to the public administrator to summarily dispose of the estates pursuant to the procedures described in paragraphs (1) and (2) of subdivision (a).

(f) The fee charged under paragraph (1) of subdivision (a) shall be distributed as provided in Section 68085.4 of the Government Code. When an application is filed under that paragraph, no other fees shall be charged in addition to the uniform filing fee provided for in Section 68085.4 of the Government Code.

Ca. Prob. Code § 7660

Amended by Stats 2012 ch 162 (SB 1171),s 139, eff. 1/1/2013.

Amended by Stats 2011 ch 117 (AB 1305),s 2, eff. 1/1/2012.

Amended by Stats 2009 ch 22 (SB X4-13),s 32, eff. 7/28/2009.

Amended by Stats 2008 ch 311 (SB 1407),s 29, eff. 1/1/2009.

Amended by Stats 2005 ch 75 (AB 145),s 149, eff. 7/19/2005, op. 1/1/2006

Amended by Stats 2004 ch 888 (AB 2687), s 7, eff. 1/1/2005.

Section 7661 - Power of administrator acting under authority of article

A public administrator acting under authority of this article may:

(a) Withdraw money or take possession of any other property of the decedent that is in the possession or control of a financial institution, government or private agency, retirement fund administrator, insurance company, licensed securities dealer, or other person.

(b) Collect any debts owed to the decedent, including, but not limited to, any rents, issues, or profits from the real and personal property in the estate until the estate is distributed.

(c) Sell any personal property of the decedent, including, but not limited to, stocks, bonds, mutual funds and other types of securities. Sales may be made with or without notice, as the public administrator elects. Title to the property sold passes without the need for confirmation by the court.

(d) Sell any real property of the decedent. The sale shall be accomplished through one of the following procedures:

(1) The sale may be conducted subject to Article 6 (commencing with Section 10300) of Chapter 18 of Part 5.

(2) With approval specified in the original court order for summary disposition of the estate, the sale of real property may be accomplished using a Notice of Proposed Action according to the following requirements:

(A) The publication of the sale shall be accomplished according to Sections 10300 to 10307, inclusive.

(B) The appraisal of the property and determination of the minimum sale price of 90 percent of the appraised value shall be accomplished according to Section 10309.

(C) If an offer meets the approval of the public administrator and the offered price is at least 90 percent of the appraised value, a notice of proposed action shall be made according to Sections 10581 to 10588, inclusive. If objection is not made to the notice of proposed action, the sale may be completed without a court confirmation of the sale. The sale may be consummated by recording a public administrator's deed and a copy of the court order for summary disposition that authorized the use of the notice of proposed action.

(D) If an objection to the notice of proposed action is made pursuant to Section 10587, the sale shall be confirmed in court according to Sections 10308 to 10316, inclusive. The sale may be consummated by recording an administrator's deed and a copy of the court order confirming the sale.

(E) If objection to the notice of proposed action is not made under Section 10587, the public administrator may still elect to have the sale confirmed in court according to Sections 10308 to 10316, inclusive, if the public administrator deems that is in the best interest of the estate. Title to the property sold passes with the public administrator's deed.

Ca. Prob. Code § 7661
Amended by Stats 2004 ch 888 (AB 2687), s 8, eff. 1/1/2005.

Section 7662 - Order of paying out money of estate

The public administrator acting under authority of this article shall pay out the money of the estate in the order prescribed in Section 11420, for expenses of administration, charges against the estate, and claims presented to the public administrator before distribution of the decedent's property pursuant to Section 7663. A creditor whose claim is paid under this section is not liable for contribution to a creditor whose claim is presented after the payment.

Ca. Prob. Code § 7662

Amended (as amended by Stats. 1990, Ch. 710) by Stats. 1991, Ch. 82, Sec. 23. Effective June 30, 1991. Operative July 1, 1991, by Sec. 31 of Ch. 82.

Section 7663 - Distribution to decedent's beneficiaries; deposit with county treasurer if no beneficiaries

(a) After payment of debts pursuant to Section 7662, but in no case before four months after court authorization of the public administrator to act under this article or after the public administrator takes possession or control of the estate, the public administrator shall distribute to the decedent's beneficiaries any money or other property of the decedent remaining in the possession of the public administrator.

(b) If there are no beneficiaries, the public administrator shall deposit the balance with the county treasurer for use in the general fund of the county, subject to Article 3 (commencing with Section 50050) of Chapter 1 of Part 1 of Division 1 of Title 5 of the Government Code. If the amount deposited exceeds five thousand dollars ($5,000), the public administrator shall at the time of the deposit give the Controller written notice of the information specified in Section 1311 of the Code of Civil Procedure.

Ca. Prob. Code § 7663

Amended by Stats. 1996, Ch. 401, Sec. 2. Effective January 1, 1997.

Section 7664 - Liability for unsecured debts of decedent

A person to whom property is distributed under this article is personally liable for the unsecured debts of the decedent. Such a debt may be enforced against the person in the same manner as it could have been enforced against the decedent if the decedent had not died. In an action based on the debt, the person may assert any defenses available to the decedent if the decedent had not died. The aggregate personal liability of a person under this section shall not exceed the fair market value of the property distributed to the person, valued as of the date of the distribution, less the amount of any liens and encumbrances on the property on that date. Section 366.2 of the Code of Civil Procedure applies in an action under this section.

Ca. Prob. Code § 7664
Amended by Stats. 1992, Ch. 178, Sec. 33. Effective January 1, 1993.

Section 7665 - Statement by public administrator; file of receipts and records

(a) The public administrator shall file with the clerk a statement showing the property of the decedent that came into possession of the public administrator and the disposition made of the property, together with receipts for all distributions. This subdivision does not apply to proceedings under paragraph (2) of subdivision (a) of Section 7660.
(b) The public administrator shall maintain a file of all receipts and records of expenditures for a period of three years after disposition of the property pursuant to Section 7663.

Ca. Prob. Code § 7665
Enacted by Stats. 1990, Ch. 79.

Section 7666 - Compensation

(a) Except as provided in Section 7623 and in subdivision (b), the compensation payable to the public administrator and the attorney, if any, for the public administrator for the filing of an application pursuant to this chapter and for performance of any duty or service connected with that filing is as set forth in Part 7 (commencing with Section 10800).

(b) The public administrator is entitled to a minimum compensation of three thousand dollars ($3,000).

Ca. Prob. Code § 7666

Amended by Stats 2022 ch 151 (SB 928),s 1, eff. 1/1/2023.
Amended by Stats 2004 ch 888 (AB 2687), s 9, eff. 1/1/2005.

Part 2 - OPENING ESTATE ADMINISTRATION

Chapter 1 - COMMENCEMENT OF PROCEEDINGS

Section 8000 - Proceedings commenced by petition

(a) At any time after a decedent's death, any interested person may commence proceedings for administration of the estate of the decedent by a petition to the court for an order determining the date and place of the decedent's death and for either or both of the following:

(1) Appointment of a personal representative.

(2) Probate of the decedent's will.

(b) A petition for probate of the decedent's will may be made regardless of whether the will is in the petitioner's possession or is lost, destroyed, or beyond the jurisdiction of the state.

Ca. Prob. Code § 8000

Enacted by Stats. 1990, Ch. 79.

Section 8001 - Waiver of right to appointment as personal representative

Unless good cause for delay is shown, if a person named in a will as executor fails to petition the court for administration of the estate within 30 days after the person has knowledge of the death of the decedent and that the person is named as executor, the person may be held to have waived the right to appointment as personal representative.

Ca. Prob. Code § 8001
Enacted by Stats. 1990, Ch. 79.

Section 8002 - Information contained in petition

(a) The petition shall contain all of the following information:

(1) The date and place of the decedent's death.

(2) The street number, street, and city, or other address, and the county, of the decedent's residence at the time of death.

(3) The name, age, address, and relation to the decedent of each heir and devisee of the decedent, so far as known to or reasonably ascertainable by the petitioner.

(4) The character and estimated value of the property in the estate.

(5) The name of the person for whom appointment as personal representative is petitioned.
(b) If the decedent left a will:

(1) The petitioner shall attach to the petition a photographic copy of the will. In the case of a holographic will or other will of which material provisions are handwritten, the petitioner shall also attach a typed copy of the will.

(2) If the will is in a foreign language, the petitioner shall attach an English language translation. On admission of the will to probate, the court shall certify to a correct translation into English, and the certified translation shall be filed with the will.

(3) The petition shall state whether the person named as executor in the will consents to act or waives the right to appointment.
Ca. Prob. Code § 8002
Enacted by Stats. 1990, Ch. 79.

Section 8003 - Setting hearing on petition; notice of hearing

(a) The hearing on the petition shall be set for a day not less than 15 nor more than 30 days after the petition is filed. At the request of the petitioner made at the time the petition is filed, the hearing on the petition shall be set for a day not less than 30 nor more than 45 days after the petition is filed. The court may not shorten the time for giving the notice of hearing under this section.

(b) The petitioner shall serve and publish notice of the hearing in the manner prescribed in Chapter 2 (commencing with Section 8100).

Ca. Prob. Code § 8003
Enacted by Stats. 1990, Ch. 79.

Section 8004 - Appointment of personal representative contested

(a) If appointment of the personal representative is contested, the grounds of opposition may include a challenge to the competency of the personal representative or the right to appointment. If the contest asserts the right of another person to appointment as personal representative, the contestant shall also file a petition and serve notice in the manner provided in Article 2 (commencing with Section 8110) of Chapter 2, and the court shall hear the two petitions together.

(b) If a will is contested, the applicable procedure is that provided in Article 3 (commencing with Section 8250) of Chapter 3.

Ca. Prob. Code § 8004
Enacted by Stats. 1990, Ch. 79.

Section 8005 - Matters upon which witnesses examined at hearing; matters to be established at hearing

(a) At the hearing on the petition, the court may examine and compel any person to attend as a witness concerning any of the following matters:

(1) The time, place, and manner of the decedent's death.

(2) The place of the decedent's domicile and residence at the time of death.

(3) The character and value of the decedent's property.

(4) Whether or not the decedent left a will.
(b) The following matters shall be established:

(1) The jurisdictional facts, including:

(A) The date and place of the decedent's death.

(B) That the decedent was domiciled in this state or left property in this state at the time of death.

(C) The publication of notice under Article 3 (commencing with Section 8120) of Chapter 2.

(2) The existence or nonexistence of the decedent's will.

(3) That notice of the hearing was served as provided in Article 2 (commencing with Section 8110) of Chapter 2.
Ca. Prob. Code § 8005
Enacted by Stats. 1990, Ch. 79.

Section 8006 - Order determining time and place of decedent's death and jurisdiction of court; matters incorrectly stated in petition but actually established

(a) If the court finds that the matters referred to in paragraph (1) of subdivision (b) of Section 8005 are established, the court shall make an order determining the time and place of the decedent's death and the jurisdiction of the court. Where appropriate and on satisfactory proof, the order shall admit the decedent's will to probate and appoint a personal representative. The date the will is admitted to probate shall be included in the order.

(b) If through defect of form or error the matters referred to in paragraph (1) of subdivision (b) of Section 8005 are incorrectly stated in the petition but actually are established, the court has and retains jurisdiction to correct the defect or error at any time. No such defect or error makes void an order admitting the will to probate or appointing a personal representative or an order made in any subsequent proceeding.

Ca. Prob. Code § 8006
Enacted by Stats. 1990, Ch. 79.

Section 8007 - Oder admitting will to probate or appointing personal representative conclusive determination of court jurisdiction

(a) Except as provided in subdivision (b), an order admitting a will to probate or appointing a personal representative, when it becomes final, is a conclusive determination of the jurisdiction of the court and cannot be collaterally attacked.

(b) Subdivision (a) does not apply in either of the following cases:

(1) The presence of extrinsic fraud in the procurement of the court order.

(2) The court order is based on the erroneous determination of the decedent's death.

Ca. Prob. Code § 8007
Enacted by Stats. 1990, Ch. 79.

Chapter 2 - NOTICE OF HEARING

Article 1 - CONTENTS

Section 8100 - Form

The notice of hearing of a petition for administration of a decedent's estate, whether delivered under Article 2 (commencing with Section 8110) or published under Article 3 (commencing with Section

8120), shall state substantially as follows:

NOTICE OF PETITION TO ADMINISTER
ESTATE OF _____, ESTATE NO. _____

To all heirs, beneficiaries, creditors, and contingent creditors of
_____ and persons who may be otherwise interested in
the will or estate, or both:A petition has been filed by
_____ in the Superior Court of California, County of
_____, requesting that _____ be appointed as
personal representative to administer the estate of _____
[and for probate of the decedent's will, which is available for
examination in the court file].[The petition requests authority to
administer the estate under the Independent Administration of
Estates Act. This will avoid the need to obtain court approval for
many actions taken in connection with the estate. However,
before taking certain actions, the personal representative will be
required to give notice to interested persons unless they have
waived notice or have consented to the proposed action. The
petition will be granted unless good cause is shown why it should
not be.]
The petition is set for hearing in Dept. No.
at _____ (Address) _____ on _____ (Date of hearing) _____
at _____ (Time of hearing) _____ .

IF YOU OBJECT to the granting of the petition, you should appear
at the hearing and state your objections or file written objections
with the court before the hearing. Your appearance may be in
person or by your attorney.
IF YOU ARE A CREDITOR or a contingent creditor of the deceased,
you must file your claim with the court and mail a copy to the
personal representative appointed by the court within the later of
either (1) four months from the date of first issuance of letters to a
general personal representative, as defined in subdivision (b) of
Section 58 of the California Probate Code, or (2) 60 days from the
date of delivery of the notice to you under Section 9052 of the
California Probate Code.
YOU MAY EXAMINE the file kept by the court. If you are interested

in the estate, you may request special notice of the filing of an inventory and appraisal of estate assets or of any petition or account as provided in Section 1250 of the California Probate Code.

_____ (Name and address of petitioner or petitioner's attorney)
_____

Ca. Prob. Code § 8100
Amended by Stats 2017 ch 319 (AB 976),s 63, eff. 1/1/2018.
Amended by Stats 2012 ch 207 (AB 2683),s 2, eff. 1/1/2013.

Article 2 - SERVICE OF NOTICE OF HEARING

Section 8110 - Persons served

At least 15 days before the hearing of a petition for administration of a decedent's estate, the petitioner shall deliver notice of the hearing pursuant to Section 1215 on all of the following persons:
(a) Each heir of the decedent, so far as known to or reasonably ascertainable by the petitioner.
(b) Each devisee, executor, and alternative executor named in any will being offered for probate, regardless of whether the devise or appointment is purportedly revoked in a subsequent instrument.
Ca. Prob. Code § 8110
Amended by Stats 2017 ch 319 (AB 976),s 64, eff. 1/1/2018.

Section 8111 - Testamentary trust of property for charitable purposes or devise for charitable purposes

If the decedent's will involves or may involve a testamentary trust of property for charitable purposes other than a charitable trust with a designated trustee resident in this state, or involves or may involve a devise for charitable purposes without an identified devisee, notice of hearing accompanied by a copy of the petition and of the will shall be delivered pursuant to Section 1215 to the Attorney General as provided in Section 1209.
Ca. Prob. Code § 8111
Amended by Stats 2017 ch 319 (AB 976),s 65, eff. 1/1/2018.

Section 8112 - Notice of administration to decedent's creditors

A general personal representative shall give notice of administration of the estate of the decedent to creditors under Chapter 2 (commencing with Section 9050), and to public entities under Chapter 5 (commencing with Section 9200), of Part 4.

Ca. Prob. Code § 8112

Enacted by Stats. 1990, Ch. 79.

Section 8113 - Notice to diplomatic or consular official of foreign country

If a citizen of a foreign country dies without leaving a will or leaves a will without naming an executor, or if it appears that property will pass to a citizen of a foreign country, notice shall be given to a recognized diplomatic or consular official of the foreign country maintaining an office in the United States.

Ca. Prob. Code § 8113

Enacted by Stats. 1990, Ch. 79.

Article 3 - PUBLICATION

Section 8120 - Required

In addition to service of the notice of hearing as provided in Article 2 (commencing with Section 8110), notice of hearing of a petition for administration of a decedent's estate shall also be published before the hearing in the manner provided in this article.

Ca. Prob. Code § 8120

Enacted by Stats. 1990, Ch. 79.

Section 8121 - First publication date; procedure for publication

(a) The first publication date of the notice shall be at least 15 days before the hearing. Three publications in a newspaper published once a week or more often, with at least five days intervening between the first and last publication dates, not counting the publication dates, are sufficient.

(b) Notice shall be published in a newspaper of general circulation in the city where the decedent resided at the time of death, or where the decedent's property is located if the court has jurisdiction under Section 7052. If there is no such newspaper, or if the decedent did not reside in a city, or if the property is not located in a city, then notice shall be published in a newspaper of general circulation in the county which is circulated within the area of the county in which the decedent resided or the property is located. If there is no such newspaper, notice shall be published in a newspaper of general circulation published in this state nearest to the county seat of the county in which the decedent resided or the property is located, and which is circulated within the area of the county in which the decedent resided or the property is located.

(c) For purposes of this section, "city" means a charter city as defined in Section 34101 of the Government Code or a general law city as defined in Section 34102 of the Government Code.

Ca. Prob. Code § 8121

Enacted by Stats. 1990, Ch. 79.

Section 8122 - Notice published in good faith compliance with section 8121 sufficient

The Legislature finds and declares that, to be most effective, notice of hearing should be published in compliance with Section 8121. However, the Legislature recognizes the possibility that in unusual cases due to confusion over jurisdictional boundaries or oversight such notice may inadvertently be published in a newspaper that does not satisfy Section 8121. Therefore, to prevent a minor error in publication from invalidating what would otherwise be a proper proceeding, the Legislature further finds and declares that notice published in a good faith attempt to comply with Section 8121 is sufficient to provide notice of hearing and to establish jurisdiction if the court expressly finds that the notice was published in a newspaper of general circulation published within the county and widely circulated within a true cross-section of the area of the county in which the decedent resided or the property was located in substantial compliance with Section 8121.

Ca. Prob. Code § 8122
Enacted by Stats. 1990, Ch. 79.

Section 8123 - Caption of notice

The caption of a notice under this article shall be in 8-point type or larger and the text shall be in 7-point type or larger.

Ca. Prob. Code § 8123
Enacted by Stats. 1990, Ch. 79.

Section 8124 - Affidavit showing due publication

A petition for administration of a decedent's estate shall not be heard by the court unless an affidavit showing due publication of the notice of hearing has been filed with the court. The affidavit shall contain a copy of the notice and state the date of its publication.

Ca. Prob. Code § 8124
Enacted by Stats. 1990, Ch. 79.

Section 8125 - Information for creditors omitted in subsequent notice

Notwithstanding Section 8100, after the notice of hearing is published and an affidavit filed, any subsequent publication of the notice ordered by the court may omit the information for creditors and contingent creditors.

Ca. Prob. Code § 8125
Enacted by Stats. 1990, Ch. 79.

Chapter 3 - PROBATE OF WILL

Article 1 - PRODUCTION OF WILL

Section 8200 - Custodian's duty to deliver will to clerk of court and mail copy to executor; release of will copy attachment to petition for probate

(a) Unless a petition for probate of the will is earlier filed, the custodian of a will shall, within 30 days after having knowledge of the death of the testator, do both of the following:

(1) Deliver the will, personally or by registered or certified mail, to the clerk of the superior court of the county in which the estate of the decedent may be administered.

(2) Deliver a copy of the will pursuant to Section 1215 to the person named in the will as executor, if the person's whereabouts is known to the custodian, or if not, to a person named in the will as a beneficiary, if the person's whereabouts is known to the custodian.
(b) A custodian of a will who fails to comply with the requirements of this section shall be liable for all damages sustained by any person injured by the failure.
(c) The clerk shall release a copy of a will delivered under this section for attachment to a petition for probate of the will or otherwise on receipt of payment of the required fee and either a court order for production of the will or a certified copy of a death certificate of the decedent.
(d) The fee for delivering a will to the clerk of the superior court pursuant to paragraph (1) of subdivision (a) shall be as provided in Section 70626 of the Government Code. If an estate is commenced for the decedent named in the will, the fee for any will delivered pursuant to paragraph (1) of subdivision (a) shall be reimbursable from the estate as an expense of administration.
Ca. Prob. Code § 8200
Amended by Stats 2017 ch 319 (AB 976),s 66, eff. 1/1/2018.
Amended by Stats 2013 ch 61 (SB 826),s 2, eff. 1/1/2014.
Amended by Stats 2012 ch 41 (SB 1021),s 86, eff. 6/27/2012.

Section 8201 - Order to person to produce will

If, on petition to the superior court of the county in which the estate of the decedent is being or may be administered alleging that a person has possession of a decedent's will, the court is satisfied that the allegation is true, the court shall order the person to produce the will.

Ca. Prob. Code § 8201
Enacted by Stats. 1990, Ch. 79.

Section 8202 - Copy of will admitted to probate

If the will of a person who was domiciled in this state at the time of death is detained in a court of any other state or country and cannot be produced for probate in this state, a certified photographic copy of the will may be admitted to probate in this state with the same force and effect as the original will. The same proof shall be required as if the original will were produced.

Ca. Prob. Code § 8202
Enacted by Stats. 1990, Ch. 79.

Section 8203 - Transfer of will to clerk of court in county in which proceeding pending

 If a will has been delivered to the clerk of the superior court in a county in which no proceeding is pending to administer the testator's estate, that court may order the will transferred to the clerk of the superior court in a county in which such a proceeding is pending. A petition for the transfer may be presented and heard without notice, but shall not be granted without proof that a copy of the petition has been delivered pursuant to Section 1215 to the petitioner and any persons who have requested special notice in the proceeding in the court to which the will is to be transferred. The petition and order shall include the case number of the proceeding in the court to which transfer is prayed. Certified copies of the petition, any supporting documents, and the order shall be transmitted by the clerk along with the original will, and these copies shall be filed in the proceeding by the clerk of the recipient court.

Ca. Prob. Code § 8203

Amended by Stats 2017 ch 319 (AB 976),s 67, eff. 1/1/2018.

Article 2 - PROOF OF WILL

Section 8220 - Proved on evidence of subscribing witness

Unless there is a contest of a will:

(a) The will may be proved on the evidence of one of the subscribing witnesses only, if the evidence shows that the will was executed in all particulars as prescribed by law.

(b) Evidence of execution of a will may be received by an affidavit of a subscribing witness to which there is attached a photographic copy of the will, or by an affidavit in the original will that includes or incorporates the attestation clause.

(c) If no subscribing witness resides in the county, but the deposition of a witness can be taken elsewhere, the court may direct the deposition to be taken. On the examination, the court may authorize a photographic copy of the will to be made and presented to the witness, and the witness may be asked the same questions with respect to the photographic copy as if the original will were present.

Ca. Prob. Code § 8220

Enacted by Stats. 1990, Ch. 79.

Section 8221 - Proof of handwriting

If no subscribing witness is available as a witness within the meaning of Section 240 of the Evidence Code, the court may, if the will on its face conforms to all requirements of law, permit proof of the will by proof of the handwriting of the testator and one of the following:

(a) Proof of the handwriting of any one subscribing witness.

(b) Receipt in evidence of one of the following documents reciting facts showing due execution of the will:

    (1) A writing in the will bearing the signatures of all subscribing witnesses.

(2) An affidavit of a person with personal knowledge of the circumstances of the execution.

Ca. Prob. Code § 8221
Enacted by Stats. 1990, Ch. 79.

Section 8222 - Holographic will

A holographic will may be proved in the same manner as other writings.

Ca. Prob. Code § 8222
Enacted by Stats. 1990, Ch. 79.

Section 8223 - Lost or destroyed will

The petition for probate of a lost or destroyed will shall include a written statement of the testamentary words or their substance. If the will is proved, the provisions of the will shall be set forth in the order admitting the will to probate.

Ca. Prob. Code § 8223
Enacted by Stats. 1990, Ch. 79.

Section 8224 - Testimony of witness preserved or official reporter's transcript of testimony

The testimony of each witness in a proceeding concerning the execution or provisions of a will, the testamentary capacity of the decedent, and other issues of fact, may be reduced to writing, signed by the witness, and filed, whether or not the will is contested. The testimony so preserved, or an official reporter's transcript of the testimony, is admissible in evidence in any subsequent proceeding concerning the will if the witness has become unavailable as a witness within the meaning of Section 240 of the Evidence Code.

Ca. Prob. Code § 8224
Enacted by Stats. 1990, Ch. 79.

Section 8225 - Recording fact that will admitted to probate

When the court admits a will to probate, that fact shall be recorded in the minutes by the clerk and the will shall be filed.

Ca. Prob. Code § 8225

Enacted by Stats. 1990, Ch. 79.

Section 8226 - Admission to probate conclusive; prior admission of another will; petition by proponent of will

(a) If no person contests the validity of a will or petitions for revocation of probate of the will within the time provided in this chapter, admission of the will to probate is conclusive, subject to Section 8007.

(b) Subject to subdivision (c), a will may be admitted to probate notwithstanding prior admission to probate of another will or prior distribution of property in the proceeding. The will may not affect property previously distributed, but the court may determine how any provision of the will affects property not yet distributed and how any provision of the will affects provisions of another will.

(c) If the proponent of a will has received notice of a petition for probate or a petition for letters of administration for a general personal representative, the proponent of the will may petition for probate of the will only within the later of either of the following time periods:

(1) One hundred twenty days after issuance of the order admitting the first will to probate or determining the decedent to be intestate.

(2) Sixty days after the proponent of the will first obtains knowledge of the will.

Ca. Prob. Code § 8226

Amended by Stats. 1997, Ch. 724, Sec. 19. Effective January 1, 1998.

Article 3 - CONTEST OF WILL

Section 8250 - Objection to probate filed by contestant

(a) When a will is contested under Section 8004, the contestant shall file with the court an objection to probate of the will. Thereafter, a summons shall be issued and served, with a copy of the objection, on the persons required by Section 8110 to be served with notice of hearing of a petition for administration of the decedent's estate. The summons shall be issued and served as provided in Chapter 3 (commencing with Section 412.10) and Chapter 4 (commencing with Section 413.10) of Title 5 of Part 2 of the Code of Civil Procedure. The summons shall contain a direction that the persons summoned file with the court a written pleading in response to the contest within 30 days after service of the summons.

(b) A person named as executor in the will is under no duty to defend a contest until the person is appointed personal representative.

Ca. Prob. Code § 8250

Amended by Stats 2011 ch 308 (SB 647),s 11, eff. 1/1/2012.

Section 8251 - Answer or demur to objection; failure to timely respond to summons

(a) The petitioner and any other interested person may jointly or separately answer the objection or demur to the objection within the time prescribed in the summons.

(b) Demurrer may be made on any of the grounds of demurrer available in a civil action. If the demurrer is sustained, the court may allow the contestant a reasonable time, not exceeding 15 days, within which to amend the objection. If the demurrer is overruled, the petitioner and other interested persons may, within 15 days thereafter, answer the objection.

(c) If a person fails timely to respond to the summons:

(1) The case is at issue notwithstanding the failure and the case may proceed on the petition and other documents filed by the time of the hearing, and no further pleadings by other persons are necessary.

(2) The person may not participate further in the contest, but the person's interest in the estate is not otherwise affected. Nothing in this paragraph precludes further participation by the petitioner.

(3) The person is bound by the decision in the proceeding.
Ca. Prob. Code § 8251
Enacted by Stats. 1990, Ch. 79.

Section 8252 - Burden of proofs at trial

(a) At the trial, the proponents of the will have the burden of proof of due execution. The contestants of the will have the burden of proof of lack of testamentary intent or capacity, undue influence, fraud, duress, mistake, or revocation. If the will is opposed by the petition for probate of a later will revoking the former, it shall be determined first whether the later will is entitled to probate.
(b) The court shall try and determine any contested issue of fact that affects the validity of the will.
Ca. Prob. Code § 8252
Enacted by Stats. 1990, Ch. 79.

Section 8253 - Examination of subscribing witnesses

At the trial, each subscribing witness shall be produced and examined. If no subscribing witness is available as a witness within the meaning of Section 240 of the Evidence Code, the court may admit the evidence of other witnesses to prove the due execution of the will.
Ca. Prob. Code § 8253
Enacted by Stats. 1990, Ch. 79.

Section 8254 - Orders and judgment rendered by court

The court may make appropriate orders, including orders sustaining or denying objections, and shall render judgment either admitting the will to probate or rejecting it, in whole or in part, and appointing a personal representative.

Ca. Prob. Code § 8254
Enacted by Stats. 1990, Ch. 79.

Article 4 - REVOCATION OF PROBATE

Section 8270 - Petition to revoke probate

(a) Within 120 days after a will is admitted to probate, any interested person, other than a party to a will contest and other than a person who had actual notice of a will contest in time to have joined in the contest, may petition the court to revoke the probate of the will. The petition shall include objections setting forth written grounds of opposition.

(b) Notwithstanding subdivision (a), a person who was a minor or who was incompetent and had no guardian or conservator at the time a will was admitted to probate may petition the court to revoke the probate of the will at any time before entry of an order for final distribution.

Ca. Prob. Code § 8270
Enacted by Stats. 1990, Ch. 79.

Section 8271 - Summons on filing petition

(a) On the filing of the petition, a summons shall be directed to the personal representative and to the heirs and devisees of the decedent, so far as known to the petitioner. The summons shall contain a direction that the persons summoned file with the court a written pleading in response to the petition within 30 days after service of the summons. Failure of a person timely to respond to the summons precludes the person from further participation in the revocation proceeding, but does not otherwise affect the person's interest in the estate.

(b) The summons shall be issued and served with a copy of the petition and proceedings had as in the case of a contest of the will.

(c) If a person fails timely to respond to the summons:

(1) The case is at issue notwithstanding the failure and the case may proceed on the petition and other documents filed by the time of the hearing, and no further pleadings by other persons are necessary.

(2) The person may not participate further in the contest, but the person's interest in the estate is not otherwise affected.

(3) The person is bound by the decision in the proceeding.
Ca. Prob. Code § 8271
Amended by Stats. 1998, Ch. 581, Sec. 25. Effective January 1, 1999.

Section 8272 - Effect of revocation

(a) If it appears on satisfactory proof that the will should be denied probate, the court shall revoke the probate of the will.
(b) Revocation of probate of a will terminates the powers of the personal representative. The personal representative is not liable for any otherwise proper act done in good faith before the revocation, nor is any transaction void by reason of the revocation if entered into with a third person dealing in good faith and for value.
Ca. Prob. Code § 8272
Enacted by Stats. 1990, Ch. 79.

Chapter 4 - APPOINTMENT OF PERSONAL REPRESENTATIVE

Article 1 - GENERAL PROVISIONS

Section 8400 - Appointment required to administer estate; appointment effective when letters issued; warning on order appointing

(a) A person has no power to administer the estate until the person is appointed personal representative and the appointment becomes effective. Appointment of a personal representative becomes effective when the person appointed is issued letters.
(b) Subdivision (a) applies whether or not the person is named executor in the decedent's will, except that a person named executor in the decedent's will may, before the appointment is made or

becomes effective, pay funeral expenses and take necessary measures for the maintenance and preservation of the estate.

(c) The order appointing a personal representative shall state in capital letters on the first page of the order, in at least 12-point type, the following: "WARNING: THIS APPOINTMENT IS NOT EFFECTIVE UNTIL LETTERS HAVE ISSUED."

Ca. Prob. Code § 8400
Amended by Stats. 1996, Ch. 862, Sec. 16. Effective January 1, 1997.

Section 8401 - Deposit of property by petitioner with trust company or financial institution

(a) Notwithstanding Section 8400, a petitioner for appointment as personal representative may deliver property in the petitioner's possession to a trust company or financial institution for deposit, or allow a trust company or financial institution to retain on deposit property already in its possession, as provided in Chapter 3 (commencing with Section 9700) of Part 5.

(b) The petitioner shall obtain and file with the court a written receipt including the agreement of the trust company or financial institution that the property on deposit, including any earnings thereon, shall not be allowed to be withdrawn except on order of the court.

(c) In receiving and retaining property under this section, the trust company or financial institution is protected to the same extent as though it had received the property from a person who had been appointed personal representative.

Ca. Prob. Code § 8401
Enacted by Stats. 1990, Ch. 79.

Section 8402 - Persons not competent to act as personal representative

(a) Notwithstanding any other provision of this chapter, a person is not competent to act as personal representative in any of the following circumstances:

(1) The person is under the age of majority.

(2) The person is subject to a conservatorship of the estate or is otherwise incapable of executing, or is otherwise unfit to execute, the duties of the office.

(3) There are grounds for removal of the person from office under Section 8502.

(4) The person is not a resident of the United States.

(5) The person is a surviving business partner of the decedent and an interested person objects to the appointment.
(b) Paragraphs (4) and (5) of subdivision (a) do not apply to a person named as executor or successor executor in the decedent's will.

Ca. Prob. Code § 8402
Amended by Stats 2016 ch 703 (AB 2881),s 19, eff. 1/1/2017.

Section 8403 - Oath taken before letters issued

(a) Before letters are issued, the personal representative shall take and subscribe an oath to perform, according to law, the duties of the office. The oath may be taken and dated on or after the time the petition for appointment as personal representative is signed, and may be filed with the clerk at any time after the petition is granted.
(b) The oath constitutes an acceptance of the office and shall be attached to or endorsed on the letters.

Ca. Prob. Code § 8403
Enacted by Stats. 1990, Ch. 79.

Section 8404 - Acknowledgment of receipt of statement of duties filed before letters issued

(a) Before letters are issued, the personal representative (other than a trust company or a public administrator) shall file an acknowledgment of receipt of a statement of duties and liabilities of the office of personal representative. The statement shall be in the form prescribed by the Judicial Council.

(b) The court may by local rule require the acknowledgment of receipt to include the personal representative's birth date and driver's license number, if any, provided that the court ensures their confidentiality.

(c) The statement of duties and liabilities prescribed by the Judicial Council does not supersede the law on which the statement is based.

Ca. Prob. Code § 8404

Amended by Stats. 1994, Ch. 806, Sec. 26. Effective January 1, 1995.

Section 8405 - Included in letters

Letters shall be signed by the clerk under the seal of the court and shall include:

(a) The county from which the letters are issued.

(b) The name of the person appointed as personal representative and whether the personal representative is an executor, administrator, administrator with the will annexed, or special administrator.

(c) A notation whether the personal representative is authorized to act under the Independent Administration of Estates Act (Part 6 (commencing with Section 10400) of Division 7), and if so authorized whether the independent administration authority includes or excludes the power to do any of the following:

(1) Sell real property.

(2) Exchange real property.

(3) Grant an option to purchase real property.

(4) Borrow money with the loan secured by an encumbrance upon real property.

Ca. Prob. Code § 8405

Enacted by Stats. 1990, Ch. 79.

Article 2 - EXECUTORS

Section 8420 - Right to appoint personal representative

The person named as executor in the decedent's will has the right to appointment as personal representative.

Ca. Prob. Code § 8420
Enacted by Stats. 1990, Ch. 79.

Section 8421 - Testator intended to commit execution of will and administration of estate to person

If a person is not named as executor in a will but it appears by the terms of the will that the testator intended to commit the execution of the will and the administration of the estate to the person, the person is entitled to appointment as personal representative in the same manner as if named as executor.

Ca. Prob. Code § 8421
Enacted by Stats. 1990, Ch. 79.

Section 8422 - Power to designate executor or coexecutor conferred by will

(a) The testator may by will confer on a person the power to designate an executor or coexecutor, or successor executor or coexecutor. The will may provide that the persons so designated may serve without bond.
(b) A designation shall be in writing and filed with the court. Unless the will provides otherwise, if there are two or more holders of the power to designate, the designation shall be unanimous, unless one of the holders of the power is unable or unwilling to act, in which case the remaining holder or holders may exercise the power.
(c) Except as provided in this section, an executor does not have authority to name a coexecutor, or a successor executor or coexecutor.

Ca. Prob. Code § 8422
Enacted by Stats. 1990, Ch. 79.

Section 8423 - Successor trust company appointed as executor

If the executor named in the will is a trust company that has sold its business and assets to, has consolidated or merged with, or is in any manner provided by law succeeded by, another trust company, the court may, and to the extent required by the Banking Law (Division 1 (commencing with Section 99) of the Financial Code) shall, appoint the successor trust company as executor.

Ca. Prob. Code § 8423
Enacted by Stats. 1990, Ch. 79.

Section 8424 - Person named as executor under age of majority

(a) If a person named as executor is under the age of majority and there is another person named as executor, the other person may be appointed and may administer the estate until the majority of the minor, who may then be appointed as coexecutor.
(b) If a person named as executor is under the age of majority and there is no other person named as executor, another person may be appointed as personal representative, but the court may revoke the appointment on the majority of the minor, who may then be appointed as executor.

Ca. Prob. Code § 8424
Enacted by Stats. 1990, Ch. 79.

Section 8425 - Not all persons named in will appointed as executors

If the court does not appoint all the persons named in the will as executors, those appointed have the same authority to act in every respect as all would have if appointed.

Ca. Prob. Code § 8425
Enacted by Stats. 1990, Ch. 79.

Article 3 - ADMINISTRATORS WITH THE WILL ANNEXED

Section 8440 - Appointment of personal representative by administrator

An administrator with the will annexed shall be appointed as personal representative if no executor is named in the will or if the sole executor or all the executors named in the will have waived the right to appointment or are for any reason unwilling or unable to act.

Ca. Prob. Code § 8440
Enacted by Stats. 1990, Ch. 79.

Section 8441 - Priority for appointment as administrator

(a) Except as provided in subdivision (b), persons and their nominees are entitled to appointment as administrator with the will annexed in the same order of priority as for appointment of an administrator.

(b) A person who takes under the will has priority over a person who does not, but the court in its discretion may give priority to a person who does not take under the will if the person is entitled to a statutory interest that is a substantially greater portion of the estate than the devise to the person who takes under the will and the priority appears appropriate under the circumstances. A person who takes more than 50 percent of the value of the estate under the will or the person's nominee, or the nominee of several persons who together take more than 50 percent of the value of the estate under the will, has priority over other persons who take under the will.

Ca. Prob. Code § 8441
Enacted by Stats. 1990, Ch. 79.

Section 8442 - Authority over decedent's estate

(a) Subject to subdivision (b), an administrator with the will annexed has the same authority over the decedent's estate as an executor named in the will would have.

(b) If the will confers a discretionary power or authority on an executor that is not conferred by law and the will does not extend the power or authority to other personal representatives, the power or authority shall not be deemed to be conferred on an administrator with the will annexed, but the court in its discretion may authorize the exercise of the power or authority.

Ca. Prob. Code § 8442

Enacted by Stats. 1990, Ch. 79.

Article 4 - ADMINISTRATORS

Section 8460 - Appointment if decedent dies intestate

(a) If the decedent dies intestate, the court shall appoint an administrator as personal representative.

(b) The court may appoint one or more persons as administrator.

Ca. Prob. Code § 8460

Enacted by Stats. 1990, Ch. 79.

Section 8461 - Order of priority for appointment

Subject to the provisions of this article, a person in the following relation to the decedent is entitled to appointment as administrator in the following order of priority:

(a) Surviving spouse or domestic partner as defined in Section 37.

(b) Children.

(c) Grandchildren.

(d) Other issue.

(e) Parents.

(f) Brothers and sisters.

(g) Issue of brothers and sisters.

(h) Grandparents.

(i) Issue of grandparents.

(j) Children of a predeceased spouse or domestic partner.

(k) Other issue of a predeceased spouse or domestic partner.

(l) Other next of kin.

(m) Parents of a predeceased spouse or domestic partner.

(n) Issue of parents of a predeceased spouse or domestic partner.

(o) Conservator or guardian of the estate acting in that capacity at the time of death who has filed a first account and is not acting as conservator or guardian for any other person.

(p) Public administrator.

(q) Creditors.

(r) Any other person.

Ca. Prob. Code § 8461

Amended by Stats 2001 ch 893 (AB 25), s 53, eff. 1/1/2002.

Section 8462 - Priority of surviving spouse or domestic partner or relative

The surviving spouse or domestic partner of the decedent, a relative of the decedent, or a relative of a predeceased spouse or domestic partner of the decedent, has priority under Section 8461 only if one of the following conditions is satisfied:

(a) The surviving spouse, domestic partner, or relative is entitled to succeed to all or part of the estate.

(b) The surviving spouse, domestic partner, or relative either takes under the will of, or is entitled to succeed to all or part of the estate of, another deceased person who is entitled to succeed to all or part of the estate of the decedent.

Ca. Prob. Code § 8462

Amended by Stats 2001 ch 893 (AB 25), s 54, eff. 1/1/2002.

Section 8463 - Surviving spouse party to action for separate maintenance, annulment or dissolution of marriage

If the surviving spouse is a party to an action for separate maintenance, annulment, or dissolution of the marriage of the decedent and the surviving spouse, and was living apart from the decedent on the date of the decedent's death, the surviving spouse has priority next after brothers and sisters and not the priority prescribed in Section 8461.

Ca. Prob. Code § 8463

Enacted by Stats. 1990, Ch. 79.

Section 8464 - Person under age of majority or for whom guardian or conservator of estate appointed

If a person otherwise entitled to appointment as administrator is a person under the age of majority or a person for whom a guardian or conservator of the estate has been appointed, the court in its discretion may appoint the guardian or conservator or another person entitled to appointment.

Ca. Prob. Code § 8464
Enacted by Stats. 1990, Ch. 79.

Section 8465 - Nomination of person for appointment

(a) The court may appoint as administrator a person nominated by any of the following persons:

(1) A person otherwise entitled to appointment.

(2) A person who would otherwise be entitled for appointment but who is ineligible for appointment under paragraph (4) of subdivision (a) of Section 8402 because he or she is not a resident of the United States.

(3) The guardian or conservator of the estate of a person otherwise entitled to appointment. The nomination shall be made in writing and filed with the court.

(b) If a person making a nomination for appointment of an administrator is the surviving spouse or domestic partner, child, grandchild, other issue, parent, brother or sister, or grandparent of the decedent, the nominee has priority next after those in the class of the person making the nomination.

(c) If a person making a nomination for appointment of an administrator is other than a person described in subdivision (b), the court in its discretion may appoint either the nominee or a person of a class lower in priority to that of the person making the nomination, but other persons of the class of the person making the nomination have priority over the nominee.

(d) If a person making a nomination for appointment of an administrator is a person described in paragraph (2) of subdivision (a), the court shall not appoint a nominee who is not a California resident to act as administrator. For California residents nominated under paragraph (2) of subdivision (a), the court shall consider whether the nominee is capable of faithfully executing the duties of the office. The court may in its discretion deny the appointment and appoint another person. In determining whether to appoint the nominee, the factors the court may consider include, but are not limited to, the following:

(1) Whether the nominee has a conflict of interest with the heirs or any other interested party.

(2) Whether the nominee had a business or personal relationship with the decedent or decedent's family before the decedent's death.

(3) Whether the nominee is engaged in or acting on behalf of an individual, a business, or other entity that solicits heirs to obtain the person's nomination for appointment as administrator.

(4) Whether the nominee has been appointed as a personal representative in any other estate.
(e) If the court decides to appoint a nominee under the circumstances described in subdivision (d), the court shall require the nominee to obtain bond, unless the court orders otherwise for good cause. Any order for good cause must be supported by specific findings of fact, and shall consider the need for the protection of creditors, heirs, and any other interested parties. Before waiving a bond, the court shall consider all other alternatives, including, but not limited to, the deposit of property in the estate pursuant to Chapter 3 (commencing with Section 9700) of Part 5 on the condition that the property, including any earnings thereon, will not be withdrawn except on authorization of the court. The waiver of all of the heirs of the requirement of a bond shall not constitute good cause.
(f) If the appointed nominee ceases to be a California resident following his or her appointment, he or she shall be deemed to have

resigned as administrator for the purposes of Article 7 (commencing with Section 8520). The court shall not lose jurisdiction of the proceeding by any resignation under this subdivision.

(g) By accepting appointment as personal representative, the nominee shall submit personally to the jurisdiction of the court.

Ca. Prob. Code § 8465

Amended by Stats 2015 ch 54 (AB 548),s 1, eff. 1/1/2016.

Amended by Stats 2012 ch 635 (AB 1670),s 1, eff. 1/1/2013.

Amended by Stats 2001 ch 893 (AB 25), s 55, eff. 1/1/2002.

Section 8466 - Creditor claiming appointment

If a person whose only priority is that of a creditor claims appointment as administrator, the court in its discretion may deny the appointment and appoint another person.

Ca. Prob. Code § 8466

Enacted by Stats. 1990, Ch. 79.

Section 8467 - Several persons having equal priority

If several persons have equal priority for appointment as administrator, the court may appoint one or more of them, or if such persons are unable to agree, the court may appoint the public administrator or a disinterested person in the same or the next lower class of priority as the persons who are unable to agree.

Ca. Prob. Code § 8467

Enacted by Stats. 1990, Ch. 79.

Section 8468 - Failure to claim appointment

If persons having priority fail to claim appointment as administrator, the court may appoint any person who claims appointment.

Ca. Prob. Code § 8468

Enacted by Stats. 1990, Ch. 79.

Section 8469 - Priority given to conservator or guardian of estate

(a) For good cause, the court may allow the priority given by Section 8461 to a conservator or guardian of the estate of the decedent serving in that capacity at the time of death that has not filed a first account, or that is acting as guardian or conservator for another person, or both.

(b) If the petition for appointment as administrator requests the court to allow the priority permitted by subdivision (a), the petitioner shall, in addition to the notice otherwise required by statute, deliver notice of the hearing pursuant to Section 1215 to the public administrator.

Ca. Prob. Code § 8469
Amended by Stats 2017 ch 319 (AB 976),s 68, eff. 1/1/2018.

Article 5 - BOND

Section 8480 - Required; failure to give

(a) Except as otherwise provided by statute, every person appointed as personal representative shall, before letters are issued, give a bond approved by the court. If two or more persons are appointed, the court may require either a separate bond from each or a joint and several bond. If a joint bond is furnished, the liability on the bond is joint and several.

(b) The bond shall be for the benefit of interested persons and shall be conditioned on the personal representative's faithful execution of the duties of the office according to law.

(c) If the person appointed as personal representative fails to give the required bond, letters shall not be issued. If the person appointed as personal representative fails to give a new, additional, or supplemental bond, or to substitute a sufficient surety, under court order, the person may be removed from office.

Ca. Prob. Code § 8480
Amended by Stats. 1998, Ch. 77, Sec. 3. Effective January 1, 1999.

Section 8481 - Waiver of requirement

(a) A bond is not required in either of the following cases:

(1) The will waives the requirement of a bond.

(2) All beneficiaries waive in writing the requirement of a bond and the written waivers are attached to the petition for appointment of a personal representative. This paragraph does not apply if the will requires a bond.
(b) Notwithstanding the waiver of a bond by a will or by all the beneficiaries, on petition of any interested person or on its own motion, the court may for good cause require that a bond be given, either before or after issuance of letters.
Ca. Prob. Code § 8481
Enacted by Stats. 1990, Ch. 79.

Section 8482 - Amount

(a) The court in its discretion may fix the amount of the bond, but the amount of the bond shall be not more than the sum of:

(1) The estimated value of the personal property.

(2) The probable annual gross income of the estate.

(3) If independent administration is granted as to real property, the estimated value of the decedent's interest in the real property.
(b) Notwithstanding subdivision (a), if the bond is given by an admitted surety insurer, the court may establish a fixed minimum amount for the bond, based on the minimum premium required by the admitted surety insurer.
(c) If the bond is given by personal sureties, the amount of the bond shall be twice the amount fixed by the court under subdivision (a).
(d) Before confirming a sale of real property the court shall require such additional bond as may be proper, not exceeding the maximum requirements of this section, treating the expected

proceeds of the sale as personal property.

Ca. Prob. Code § 8482
Enacted by Stats. 1990, Ch. 79.

Section 8483 - Amount when deposited property ordered not withdrawn except upon court authorization

(a) This section applies where property in the estate has been deposited pursuant to Chapter 3 (commencing with Section 9700) of Part 5 on condition that the property, including any earnings thereon, will not be withdrawn except on authorization of the court. **(b)** In a proceeding to determine the amount of the bond of the personal representative (whether at the time of appointment or subsequently), on production of a receipt showing the deposit of property of the estate in the manner described in subdivision (a), the court may order that the property shall not be withdrawn except on authorization of the court and may, in its discretion, do either of the following:

(1) Exclude the property in determining the amount of the required bond or reduce the amount of the bond to an amount the court determines is reasonable.

(2) If a bond has already been given or the amount fixed, reduce the amount to an amount the court determines is reasonable.

Ca. Prob. Code § 8483
Enacted by Stats. 1990, Ch. 79.

Section 8484 - Petition to have amount reduced

If a personal representative petitions to have the amount of the bond reduced, the petition shall include an affidavit setting forth the condition of the estate and notice of hearing shall be given as provided in Section 1220.

Ca. Prob. Code § 8484
Enacted by Stats. 1990, Ch. 79.

Section 8485 - Petition for substitution or release of surety

A personal representative who petitions for substitution or release of a surety shall file with the petition an account in the form provided in Section 10900. The court shall not order a substitution or release unless the account is approved.

    Ca. Prob. Code § 8485

Enacted by Stats. 1990, Ch. 79.

Section 8486 - Reasonable cost of bond allowed

The personal representative shall be allowed the reasonable cost of the bond for every year it remains in force.

    Ca. Prob. Code § 8486

Enacted by Stats. 1990, Ch. 79.

Section 8487 - Applicability of Bond and Undertaking Law

The provisions of the Bond and Undertaking Law (Chapter 2 (commencing with Section 995.010) of Title 14 of Part 2 of the Code of Civil Procedure) apply to a bond given under this division, except to the extent this division is inconsistent.

    Ca. Prob. Code § 8487

Enacted by Stats. 1990, Ch. 79.

Section 8488 - Action against sureties for breach of condition; limitation of action

(a) In case of a breach of a condition of the bond, an action may be brought against the sureties on the bond for the use and benefit of the decedent's estate or of any person interested in the estate.

(b) No action may be maintained against the sureties on the bond of the personal representative unless commenced within four years from the discharge or removal of the personal representative or within four years from the date the order surcharging the personal representative becomes final, whichever is later.

(c) In any case, and notwithstanding subdivision (c) of Section

7250, no action may be maintained against the sureties on the bond unless commenced within six years from the date the judgment under Section 7250 or the later of the orders under subdivision (b) of this section becomes final.

Ca. Prob. Code § 8488

Amended by Stats. 1994, Ch. 806, Sec. 27. Effective January 1, 1995.

Article 6 - REMOVAL FROM OFFICE

Section 8500 - Petition for removal; citation; suspension of representative's powers; hearing

(a) Any interested person may petition for removal of the personal representative from office. A petition for removal may be combined with a petition for appointment of a successor personal representative under Article 7 (commencing with Section 8520). The petition shall state facts showing cause for removal.

(b) On a petition for removal, or if the court otherwise has reason to believe from the court's own knowledge or from other credible information, whether on the settlement of an account or otherwise, that there are grounds for removal, the court shall issue a citation to the personal representative to appear and show cause why the personal representative should not be removed. The court may suspend the powers of the personal representative and may make such orders as are necessary to deal with the property pending the hearing.

(c) Any interested person may appear at the hearing and file a written declaration showing that the personal representative should be removed or retained. The personal representative may demur to or answer the declaration. The court may compel the attendance of the personal representative and may compel the personal representative to answer questions, on oath, concerning the administration of the estate. Failure to attend or answer is cause for removal of the personal representative from office.

(d) The issues shall be heard and determined by the court. If the court is satisfied from the evidence that the citation has been duly served and cause for removal exists, the court shall remove the personal representative from office.

Ca. Prob. Code § 8500
Enacted by Stats. 1990, Ch. 79.

Section 8501 - Letters revoked

On removal of a personal representative from office, the court shall revoke any letters issued to the personal representative, and the authority of the personal representative ceases.

Ca. Prob. Code § 8501
Enacted by Stats. 1990, Ch. 79.

Section 8502 - Grounds

A personal representative may be removed from office for any of the following causes:

(a) The personal representative has wasted, embezzled, mismanaged, or committed a fraud on the estate, or is about to do so.

(b) The personal representative is incapable of properly executing the duties of the office or is otherwise not qualified for appointment as personal representative.

(c) The personal representative has wrongfully neglected the estate, or has long neglected to perform any act as personal representative.

(d) Removal is otherwise necessary for protection of the estate or interested persons.

(e) Any other cause provided by statute.

Ca. Prob. Code § 8502
Enacted by Stats. 1990, Ch. 79.

Section 8503 - Petition of surviving spouse or relative of decedent

(a) Subject to subdivision (b), an administrator may be removed from office on the petition of the surviving spouse or a relative of the decedent entitled to succeed to all or part of the estate, or the nominee of the surviving spouse or relative, if such person is higher in priority than the administrator.

(b) The court in its discretion may refuse to grant the petition:

(1) Where the petition is by a person or the nominee of a person who had actual notice of the proceeding in which the administrator was appointed and an opportunity to contest the appointment.

(2) Where to do so would be contrary to the sound administration of the estate.

Ca. Prob. Code § 8503
Enacted by Stats. 1990, Ch. 79.

Section 8504 - Removal of administrator appointed on ground of intestacy

(a) After appointment of an administrator on the ground of intestacy, the personal representative shall be removed from office on the later admission to probate of a will.

(b) After appointment of an executor or administrator with the will annexed, the personal representative shall be removed from office on admission to probate of a later will.

Ca. Prob. Code § 8504
Enacted by Stats. 1990, Ch. 79.

Section 8505 - Removal for contempt for disobeying court order

(a) A personal representative may be removed from office if the personal representative is found in contempt for disobeying an order of the court.

(b) Notwithstanding any other provision of this article, a personal representative may be removed from office under this section by a court order reciting the facts and without further showing or notice.

Ca. Prob. Code § 8505
Enacted by Stats. 1990, Ch. 79.

Article 7 - CHANGES IN ADMINISTRATION

Section 8520 - Vacancy upon resignation, death or removal of representative

A vacancy occurs in the office of a personal representative who resigns, dies, or is removed from office under Article 6 (commencing with Section 8500), or whose authority is otherwise terminated.

Ca. Prob. Code § 8520
Enacted by Stats. 1990, Ch. 79.

Section 8521 - Vacancy in office of fewer than all representatives

(a) Unless the will provides otherwise or the court in its discretion orders otherwise, if a vacancy occurs in the office of fewer than all personal representatives, the remaining personal representatives shall complete the administration of the estate.

(b) The court, on the filing of a petition alleging that a vacancy has occurred in the office of fewer than all personal representatives, may order the clerk to issue appropriate amended letters to the remaining personal representatives.

Ca. Prob. Code § 8521
Enacted by Stats. 1990, Ch. 79.

Section 8522 - Appointment of successor

(a) If a vacancy occurs in the office of a personal representative and there are no other personal representatives, the court shall appoint a successor personal representative.

(b) Appointment of a successor personal representative shall be made on petition and notice shall be delivered to interested persons in the manner provided in Article 2 (commencing with Section 8110) of Chapter 2, and shall be subject to the same priority as for an original appointment of a personal representative. The personal representative of a deceased personal representative is not, as such, entitled to appointment as successor personal representative.

Ca. Prob. Code § 8522
Amended by Stats 2017 ch 319 (AB 976),s 69, eff. 1/1/2018.

Section 8523 - Orders made between time of vacancy and appointment of successor

The court may make orders that are necessary to deal with the estate of the decedent between the time a vacancy occurs in the office of personal representative and appointment of a successor. Those orders may include appointment of a special administrator.
   Ca. Prob. Code § 8523
Enacted by Stats. 1990, Ch. 79.

Section 8524 - Powers and duties of successor

(a) A successor personal representative is entitled to demand, sue for, recover and collect all the estate of the decedent remaining unadministered, and may prosecute to final judgment any suit commenced by the former personal representative before the vacancy.

(b) No notice, process, or claim given to or served on the former personal representative need be given to or served on the successor in order to preserve any position or right the person giving the notice or filing the claim may thereby have obtained or preserved with reference to the former personal representative.

(c) Except as provided in subdivision (b) of Section 8442 (authority of administrator with will annexed) or as otherwise ordered by the court, the successor personal representative has the powers and duties in respect to the continued administration that the former personal representative would have had.
   Ca. Prob. Code § 8524
Enacted by Stats. 1990, Ch. 79.

Section 8525 - Validity of acts before vacancy; liability of representative whose office vacant

(a) The acts of the personal representative before a vacancy occurs are valid to the same extent as if no vacancy had later occurred.

(b) The liability of a personal representative whose office is vacant, or of the surety on the bond, is not discharged, released, or affected by the vacancy or by appointment of a successor, but continues until settlement of the accounts of the personal representative and delivery of all the estate of the decedent to the successor personal representative or other person appointed by the court to receive it. The personal representative shall render an account of the administration within the time that the court directs.

Ca. Prob. Code § 8525
Enacted by Stats. 1990, Ch. 79.

Article 8 - SPECIAL ADMINISTRATORS

Section 8540 - When appointment by court

(a) If the circumstances of the estate require the immediate appointment of a personal representative, the court may appoint a special administrator to exercise any powers that may be appropriate under the circumstances for the preservation of the estate.

(b) The appointment may be for a specified term, to perform particular acts, or on any other terms specified in the court order.

Ca. Prob. Code § 8540
Enacted by Stats. 1990, Ch. 79.

Section 8541 - Appointment; preference; approval of performance of particular act; correction of errors

(a) Appointment of a special administrator may be made at any time without notice or on such notice to interested persons as the court deems reasonable.

(b) In making the appointment, the court shall ordinarily give preference to the person entitled to appointment as personal representative. The court may appoint the public administrator.

(c) In the case of an appointment to perform a particular act, request for approval of the act may be included in the petition for appointment, and approval may be made on the same notice and at the same time as the appointment.

(d) The court may act, if necessary, to remedy any errors made in the appointment.

Ca. Prob. Code § 8541
Enacted by Stats. 1990, Ch. 79.

Section 8542 - Issuance of letters

(a) The clerk shall issue letters to the special administrator after both of the following conditions are satisfied:

(1) The special administrator gives any bond that may be required by the court under Section 8480.

(2) The special administrator takes the usual oath attached to or endorsed on the letters.
(b) Subdivision (a) does not apply to the public administrator.
(c) The letters of a special administrator appointed to perform a particular act shall include a notation of the particular act the special administrator was appointed to perform.

Ca. Prob. Code § 8542
Enacted by Stats. 1990, Ch. 79.

Section 8543 - Waiver of bond

Subject to subdivision (b) of Section 8481, the court shall direct that no bond be given in either of the following cases:
(a) The will waives the requirement of a bond and the person named as executor in the will is appointed special administrator.
(b) All beneficiaries waive in writing the requirement of a bond and the written waivers are attached to the petition for appointment of the special administrator. This paragraph does not apply if the will requires a bond.

Ca. Prob. Code § 8543
Enacted by Stats. 1990, Ch. 79.

Section 8544 - Powers

(a) Except to the extent the order appointing a special administrator prescribes terms, the special administrator has the power to do all of the following without further order of the court:

(1) Take possession of all of the real and personal property of the estate of the decedent and preserve it from damage, waste, and injury.

(2) Collect all claims, rents, and other income belonging to the estate.

(3) Commence and maintain or defend suits and other legal proceedings.

(4) Sell perishable property.
(b) Except to the extent the order prescribes terms, the special administrator has the power to do all of the following on order of the court:

(1) Borrow money, or lease, mortgage, or execute a deed of trust on real property, in the same manner as an administrator.

(2) Pay the interest due or all or any part of an obligation secured by a mortgage, lien, or deed of trust on property in the estate, where there is danger that the holder of the security may enforce or foreclose on the obligation and the property exceeds in value the amount of the obligation. This power may be ordered only on petition of the special administrator or any interested person, with any notice that the court deems proper, and shall remain in effect until appointment of a successor personal representative. The order may also direct that interest not yet accrued be paid as it becomes due, and the order shall remain in effect and cover the future interest unless and until for good cause set aside or modified by the court in the same manner as for the original order.

(3) Exercise other powers that are conferred by order of the court.
(c) Except where the powers, duties, and obligations of a general personal representative are granted under Section 8545, the special administrator is not a proper party to an action on a claim against

the decedent.

(d) A special administrator appointed to perform a particular act has no duty to take any other action to protect the estate.

Ca. Prob. Code § 8544

Enacted by Stats. 1990, Ch. 79.

Section 8545 - Grant of powers, duties and obligations of general representative

(a) Notwithstanding Section 8544, the court may grant a special administrator the same powers, duties, and obligations as a general personal representative where to do so appears proper. Notwithstanding Section 8541, if letters have not previously been issued to a general personal representative, the grant shall be on the same notice required under Section 8003 for appointment of a personal representative, unless the appointment is made at a hearing on a petition for appointment of a general personal representative and the notice of that petition required under Section 8003 has been given.

(b) Subject to Section 8543, the court may require as a condition of the grant that the special administrator give any additional bond that the court deems proper. From the time of approving and filing any required additional bond, the special administrator shall have the powers, duties, and obligations of a general personal representative.

(c) If a grant is made under this section, the letters shall recite that the special administrator has the powers, duties, and obligations of a general personal representative.

Ca. Prob. Code § 8545

Amended by Stats. 1994, Ch. 806, Sec. 28. Effective January 1, 1995.

Section 8546 - Powers cease on issuance of letters to general administrator

(a) The powers of a special administrator cease on issuance of letters to a general personal representative or as otherwise directed by the court.

(b) The special administrator shall promptly deliver to the general personal representative:

(1) All property of the estate in the possession of the special administrator. The court may authorize the special administrator to complete a sale or other transaction affecting property in the possession of the special administrator.

(2) A list of all creditor claims of which the special administrator has knowledge. The list shall show the name and address of each creditor, the amount of the claim, and what action has been taken with respect to the claim. A copy of the list shall be filed in the court.

(c) The special administrator shall account in the same manner as a general personal representative is required to account. If the same person acts as both special administrator and general personal representative, the account of the special administrator may be combined with the first account of the general personal representative.

Ca. Prob. Code § 8546
Enacted by Stats. 1990, Ch. 79.

Section 8547 - Compensation

(a) Subject to the limitations of this section, the court shall fix the compensation of the special administrator and the compensation of the attorney of the special administrator.

(b) The compensation of the special administrator shall not be allowed until the close of administration, unless the general personal representative joins in the petition for allowance of the special administrator's compensation or the court in its discretion so allows. Compensation for extraordinary services of a special administrator may be allowed on settlement of the final account of the special administrator. The total compensation paid to the special administrator and general personal representative shall not, together, exceed the sums provided in Part 7 (commencing with Section 10800) for compensation for the ordinary and extraordinary services of a personal representative. If the same person does not act as both special administrator and general personal representative, the compensation shall be divided in such proportions as the court determines to be just or as may be agreed to by the special administrator and general personal representative. **(c)** The total compensation paid to the attorneys both of the special administrator and the general personal representative shall not, together, exceed the sums provided in Part 7 (commencing with Section 10800) as compensation for the ordinary and extraordinary services of attorneys for personal representatives. When the same attorney does not act for both the special administrator and general personal representative, the compensation shall be divided between the attorneys in such proportions as the court determines to be just or as agreed to by the attorneys.

(d) Compensation of an attorney for extraordinary services to a special administrator may be awarded in the same manner and subject to the same standards as for extraordinary services to a general personal representative, except that the award of compensation to the attorney may be made on settlement of the final account of the special administrator.

Ca. Prob. Code § 8547
Amended by Stats. 1990, Ch. 710, Sec. 22. Operative July 1, 1991, by Sec. 48 of Ch. 710.

Article 9 - NONRESIDENT PERSONAL REPRESENTATIVE

Section 8570 - Definition

As used in this article, "nonresident personal representative" means a nonresident of this state appointed as personal representative, or a resident of this state appointed as personal representative who later removes from and resides without this state.

Ca. Prob. Code § 8570
Amended by Stats. 1991, Ch. 1055, Sec. 22.

Section 8571 - Bond

Notwithstanding any other provision of this chapter and notwithstanding a waiver of a bond, the court in its discretion may require a nonresident personal representative to give a bond in an amount determined by the court.

Ca. Prob. Code § 8571

Enacted by Stats. 1990, Ch. 79.

Section 8572 - Acceptance of appointment constitutes appointment of Secretary of State as attorney for nonresident; service of process and notice of motion

(a) Acceptance of appointment by a nonresident personal representative is equivalent to and constitutes an irrevocable and binding appointment by the nonresident personal representative of the Secretary of State to be the attorney of the personal representative for the purpose of this article. The appointment of the nonresident personal representative also applies to any personal representative of a deceased nonresident personal representative.

(b) All lawful processes, and notices of motion under Section 377.41 of the Code of Civil Procedure, in an action or proceeding against the nonresident personal representative with respect to the estate or founded on or arising out of the acts or omissions of the nonresident personal representative in that capacity may be served on the Secretary of State as the attorney for service of the nonresident personal representative.

Ca. Prob. Code § 8572

Amended by Stats. 1993, Ch. 589, Sec. 129. Effective January 1, 1994.

Section 8573 - Statement of permanent address signed and filed with court; notice of change of address

A nonresident personal representative shall sign and file with the court a statement of the permanent address of the nonresident personal representative. If the permanent address is changed, the nonresident personal representative shall promptly file in the same manner a statement of the change of address.

Ca. Prob. Code § 8573

Enacted by Stats. 1990, Ch. 79.

Section 8574 - Manner of service of process and notice of motion

(a) Service of process or notice of a motion under Section 377.41 of the Code of Civil Procedure in any action or proceeding against the nonresident personal representative shall be made by delivering to and leaving with the Secretary of State two copies of the summons and complaint or notice of motion and either of the following:

(1) A copy of the statement by the nonresident personal representative under Section 8573.

(2) If the nonresident personal representative has not filed a statement under Section 8573, a copy of the letters issued to the nonresident personal representative together with a written statement signed by the party or attorney of the party seeking service that sets forth an address for use by the Secretary of State.

(b) The Secretary of State shall promptly mail by registered mail one copy of the summons and complaint or notice of motion to the nonresident personal representative at the address shown on the statement delivered to the Secretary of State.

(c) Personal service of process, or notice of motion, on the nonresident personal representative wherever found shall be the equivalent of service as provided in this section.

Ca. Prob. Code § 8574

Amended by Stats. 1993, Ch. 589, Sec. 130. Effective January 1, 1994.

Section 8575 - Proof of compliance with section 8574

Proof of compliance with Section 8574 shall be made in the following manner:

(a) In the event of service by mail, by certificate of the Secretary of State, under official seal, showing the mailing. The certificate shall be filed with the court from which process issued.

(b) In the event of personal service outside this state, by the return of any duly constituted public officer qualified to serve like process, or notice of motion, of and in the jurisdiction where the nonresident personal representative is found, showing the service to have been made. The return shall be attached to the original summons, or notice of motion, and filed with the court from which process issued.

Ca. Prob. Code § 8575
Amended by Stats. 1991, Ch. 1055, Sec. 23.

Section 8576 - Legal effect and validity of service

(a) Except as provided in this section, service made under Section 8574 has the same legal force and validity as if made personally in this state.

(b) A nonresident personal representative served under Section 8574 may appear and answer the complaint within 30 days from the date of service.

(c) Notice of motion shall be served on a nonresident personal representative under Section 8574 not less than 30 days before the date of the hearing on the motion.

Ca. Prob. Code § 8576
Enacted by Stats. 1990, Ch. 79.

Section 8577 - Failure to file statement of permanent address or give notice of address change

(a) Failure of a nonresident personal representative to comply with Section 8573 is cause for removal from office.

(b) Nothing in this section limits the liability of, or the availability of any other remedy against, a nonresident personal representative who is removed from office under this section.

Ca. Prob. Code § 8577
Enacted by Stats. 1990, Ch. 79.

Part 3 - INVENTORY AND APPRAISAL

Chapter 1 - GENERAL PROVISIONS

Section 8800 - Duty to file; time for filing; certification filed

(a) The personal representative shall file with the court clerk an inventory of property to be administered in the decedent's estate together with an appraisal of property in the inventory. An inventory and appraisal shall be combined in a single document.

(b) The inventory and appraisal shall be filed within four months after letters are first issued to a general personal representative. The court may allow such further time for filing an inventory and appraisal as is reasonable under the circumstances of the particular case.

(c) The personal representative may file partial inventories and appraisals where appropriate under the circumstances of the particular case, but all inventories and appraisals shall be filed before expiration of the time allowed under subdivision (b).

(d) Concurrent with the filing of the inventory and appraisal pursuant to this section, the personal representative shall also file a certification that the requirements of Section 480 of the Revenue and Taxation Code either:

(1) Are not applicable because the decedent owned no real property in California at the time of death.

(2) Have been satisfied by the filing of a change in ownership statement with the county recorder or assessor of each county in California in which the decedent owned property at the time of death.

Ca. Prob. Code § 8800

Amended by Stats. 1992, Ch. 1180, Sec. 1. Effective January 1, 1993.

Section 8801 - Supplemental inventory and appraisal

If the personal representative acquires knowledge of property to be administered in the decedent's estate that is not included in a prior inventory and appraisal, the personal representative shall file a supplemental inventory and appraisal of the property in the manner prescribed for an original inventory and appraisal. The supplemental inventory and appraisal shall be filed within four months after the personal representative acquires knowledge of the property. The court may allow such further time for filing a supplemental inventory and appraisal as is reasonable under the circumstances of the particular case.

Ca. Prob. Code § 8801
Enacted by Stats. 1990, Ch. 79.

Section 8802 - Fair market value of item listed

The inventory and appraisal shall separately list each item and shall state the fair market value of the item at the time of the decedent's death in monetary terms opposite the item.

Ca. Prob. Code § 8802
Enacted by Stats. 1990, Ch. 79.

Section 8803 - Copy mailed to persons requesting special notice

On the filing of an inventory and appraisal or a supplemental inventory and appraisal, the personal representative shall, pursuant to Section 1252, deliver a copy to each person who has requested special notice.

Ca. Prob. Code § 8803
Amended by Stats 2017 ch 319 (AB 976),s 70, eff. 1/1/2018.

Section 8804 - Refusal or negligent failure to timely file

If the personal representative refuses or negligently fails to file an inventory and appraisal within the time allowed under this chapter, upon petition of an interested person:
(a) The court may compel the personal representative to file an inventory and appraisal pursuant to the procedure prescribed in Chapter 4 (commencing with Section 11050) of Part 8.
(b) The court may remove the personal representative from office.
(c) The court may impose on the personal representative personal liability for injury to the estate or to an interested person that directly results from the refusal or failure. The liability may include attorney's fees, in the court's discretion. Damages awarded pursuant to this subdivision are a liability on the bond of the

personal representative, if any.

Ca. Prob. Code § 8804
Enacted by Stats. 1990, Ch. 79.

Chapter 2 - INVENTORY

Article 1 - GENERAL PROVISIONS

Section 8850 - Included in inventory; property particularly specified

(a) The inventory, including partial and supplemental inventories, shall include all property to be administered in the decedent's estate.
(b) The inventory shall particularly specify the following property:

(1) Money owed to the decedent, including debts, bonds, and notes, with the name of each debtor, the date, the sum originally payable, and the endorsements, if any, with their dates. The inventory shall also specify security for the payment of money to the decedent, including mortgages and deeds of trust. If security for the payment of money is real property, the inventory shall include the recording reference or, if not recorded, a legal description of the real property.

(2) A statement of the interest of the decedent in a partnership, appraised as a single item.

(3) All money and other cash items, as defined in Section 8901, of the decedent.
(c) The inventory shall show, to the extent ascertainable by the personal representative, the portions of the property that are community, quasi-community, and separate property of the decedent.

Ca. Prob. Code § 8850
Enacted by Stats. 1990, Ch. 79.

Section 8851 - Debt or demand of testator against executor or other person

The discharge or devise in a will of any debt or demand of the testator against the executor or any other person is not valid against creditors of the testator, but is a specific devise of the debt or demand. The debt or demand shall be included in the inventory. If necessary, the debt or demand shall be applied in the payment of the debts of the testator. If not necessary for that purpose, the debt or demand shall be distributed in the same manner and proportion as other specific devises.

Ca. Prob. Code § 8851
Enacted by Stats. 1990, Ch. 79.

Section 8852 - Oath of personal representative

(a) The personal representative shall take and subscribe an oath that the inventory contains a true statement of the property to be administered in the decedent's estate of which the personal representative has knowledge, and particularly of money of the decedent and debts or demands of the decedent against the personal representative. The oath shall be endorsed upon or attached to the inventory.

(b) If there is more than one personal representative, each shall take and subscribe the oath. If the personal representatives are unable to agree as to property to be included in the inventory, any personal representative may petition for a court order determining whether the property is to be administered in the decedent's estate. The determination shall be made pursuant to the procedure provided in Part 19 (commencing with Section 850) of Division 2 or, if there is an issue of property belonging or passing to the surviving spouse, pursuant to Chapter 5 (commencing with Section 13650) of Part 2 of Division 8.

Ca. Prob. Code § 8852
Amended by Stats 2003 ch 32 (AB 167), s 7, eff. 1/1/2004.

Article 2 - DISCOVERY OF PROPERTY OF DECEDENT

Section 8870 - Citation issued for person to answer interrogatories or appear before court to be examined

(a) On petition by the personal representative or an interested person, the court may order that a citation be issued to a person to answer interrogatories, or to appear before the court and be examined under oath, or both, concerning any of the following allegations:

(1) The person has wrongfully taken, concealed, or disposed of property in the estate of the decedent.

(2) The person has knowledge or possession of any of the following:

(A) A deed, conveyance, bond, contract, or other writing that contains evidence of or tends to disclose the right, title, interest, or claim of the decedent to property.

(B) A claim of the decedent.

(C) A lost will of the decedent.

(b) If the person does not reside in the county in which the estate is being administered, the superior court either of the county in which the person resides or of the county in which the estate is being administered may issue a citation under this section.

(c) Disobedience of a citation issued pursuant to this section may be punished as a contempt of the court issuing the citation.

(d) Notice to the personal representative of a proceeding under subdivision (a) shall be given for the period and in the manner provided in Section 1220. Other persons requesting notice of the hearing pursuant to Section 1250 shall be notified by the person filing the petition as set forth in Section 1252.

Ca. Prob. Code § 8870

Amended by Stats. 1996, Ch. 563, Sec. 23. Effective January 1, 1997.

Section 8871 - Interrogatories and answers

Interrogatories may be put to a person cited to answer interrogatories pursuant to Section 8870. The interrogatories and answers shall be in writing. The answers shall be signed under penalty of perjury by the person cited. The interrogatories and answers shall be filed with the court.

Ca. Prob. Code § 8871
Enacted by Stats. 1990, Ch. 79.

Section 8872 - Examination of witnesses

(a) At an examination witnesses may be produced and examined on either side.

(b) If upon the examination it appears that the allegations of the petition are true, the court may order the person to disclose the person's knowledge of the facts to the personal representative.

(c) If upon the examination it appears that the allegations of the petition are not true, the person's necessary expenses, including a reasonable attorney's fee, shall be charged against the petitioner or allowed out of the estate, in the discretion of the court.

Ca. Prob. Code § 8872
Enacted by Stats. 1990, Ch. 79.

Section 8873 - Citation issued to person having possession of property

(a) On petition by the personal representative, the court may issue a citation to a person who has possession or control of property in the decedent's estate to appear before the court and make an account under oath of the property and the person's actions with respect to the property.

(b) Disobedience of a citation issued pursuant to this section may be punished as a contempt of the court issuing the citation.

Ca. Prob. Code § 8873
Enacted by Stats. 1990, Ch. 79.

Chapter 3 - APPRAISAL

Article 1 - PROCEDURE

Section 8900 - Persons making appraisal

The appraisal of property in the inventory shall be made by the personal representative, probate referee, or independent expert as provided in this chapter.

Ca. Prob. Code § 8900

Enacted by Stats. 1990, Ch. 79.

Section 8901 - Property appraised by personal representative

The personal representative shall appraise the following property, excluding items whose fair market value is, in the opinion of the personal representative, an amount different from the face value of the property:

(a) Money and other cash items. As used in this subdivision, a "cash item" is a check, draft, money order, or similar instrument issued on or before the date of the decedent's death that can be immediately converted to cash.

(b) The following checks issued after the date of the decedent's death:

    (1) Checks for wages earned before death.

    (2) Refund checks, including tax and utility refunds, and Medicare, medical insurance, and other health care reimbursements and payments.

(c) Accounts (as defined in Section 21) in financial institutions.

(d) Cash deposits and money market mutual funds, as defined in subdivision (b) of Section 9730, whether in a financial institution or otherwise, including a brokerage cash account. All other mutual funds, stocks, bonds, and other securities shall be appraised pursuant to Sections 8902 to 8909, inclusive.

(e) Proceeds of life and accident insurance policies and retirement plans and annuities payable on death in lump sum amounts.

Ca. Prob. Code § 8901

Amended by Stats. 1994, Ch. 806, Sec. 30. Effective January 1, 1995.

Section 8902 - Appraisal by probate referee

Except as otherwise provided by statute:

(a) The personal representative shall deliver the inventory to the probate referee designated by the court, together with necessary supporting data to enable the probate referee to make an appraisal of the property in the inventory to be appraised by the probate referee.

(b) The probate referee shall appraise all property other than that appraised by the personal representative.

Ca. Prob. Code § 8902

Enacted by Stats. 1990, Ch. 79.

Section 8903 - Waiver of appraisal by probate referee

(a) The court may, for good cause, waive appraisal by a probate referee in the manner provided in this section.

(b) The personal representative may apply for a waiver together with the petition for appointment of the personal representative or together with another petition, or may apply for a waiver in a separate petition filed in the administration proceedings, but the application shall not be made later than the time the personal representative delivers the inventory to the probate referee, if a probate referee has been designated. A copy of the proposed inventory and appraisal and a statement that sets forth the good cause that justifies the waiver shall be attached to the petition.

(c) The hearing on the waiver shall be not sooner than 15 days after the petition is filed. Notice of the hearing on the petition, together with a copy of the petition and a copy of the proposed inventory and appraisal, shall be given as provided in Sections 1215 and 1220 to all of the following persons:

(1) Each person listed in Section 1220.

(2) Each known heir whose interest in the estate would be affected by the waiver.

(3) Each known devisee whose interest in the estate would be affected by the waiver.

(4) The Attorney General, at the office of the Attorney General in Sacramento, if any portion of the estate is to escheat to the state and its interest in the estate would be affected by the waiver.

(5) The probate referee, if a probate referee has been designated.

(d) A probate referee to whom notice is given under this section may oppose the waiver. If the opposition fails and the court determines the opposition was made without substantial justification, the court shall award litigation expenses, including reasonable attorney's fees, against the probate referee. If the opposition succeeds, the court may designate a different probate referee to appraise property in the estate.

(e) If the petition is granted, the inventory and appraisal attached to the petition shall be filed pursuant to Section 8800.

Ca. Prob. Code § 8903

Amended by Stats 2017 ch 319 (AB 976),s 71, eff. 1/1/2018.

Section 8904 - Property appraised by independent expert

(a) A unique, artistic, unusual, or special item of tangible personal property that would otherwise be appraised by the probate referee may, at the election of the personal representative, be appraised by an independent expert qualified to appraise the item.

(b) The personal representative shall make the election provided in subdivision (a) by a notation on the inventory delivered to the probate referee indicating the property to be appraised by an independent expert. The probate referee may, within five days after delivery of the inventory, petition for a court determination whether the property to be appraised by an independent expert is a unique, artistic, unusual, or special item of tangible personal property. If the petition fails and the court determines that the petition was made without substantial justification, the court shall award litigation expenses, including reasonable attorney's fees, against the probate referee.

Ca. Prob. Code § 8904

Enacted by Stats. 1990, Ch. 79.

Section 8905 - Signature on appraisal

A person who appraises property, whether a personal representative, probate referee, or independent expert, shall sign the appraisal as to property appraised by that person, and shall take and subscribe an oath that the person has truly, honestly, and impartially appraised the property to the best of the person's ability.

Ca. Prob. Code § 8905
Enacted by Stats. 1990, Ch. 79.

Section 8906 - Objection to appraisal

(a) At any time before the hearing on the petition for final distribution of the estate, the personal representative or an interested person may file with the court a written objection to the appraisal.

(b) The clerk shall fix a time, not less than 15 days after the filing, for a hearing on the objection.

(c) The person objecting shall give notice of the hearing, together with a copy of the objection, as provided in Section 1220. If the appraisal was made by a probate referee, the person objecting shall also deliver notice of the hearing and a copy of the objection to the probate referee at least 15 days before the date set for the hearing.

(d) The person objecting to the appraisal has the burden of proof.

(e) Upon completion of the hearing, the court may make any orders that appear appropriate. If the court determines the objection was filed without reasonable cause or good faith, the court may order that the fees of the personal representative and attorney and any costs incurred for defending the appraisal be made a charge against the person filing the objection.

Ca. Prob. Code § 8906
Amended by Stats 2017 ch 319 (AB 976),s 72, eff. 1/1/2018.

Section 8907 - Compensation

Neither the personal representative nor the attorney for the personal representative is entitled to receive compensation for extraordinary services by reason of appraising any property in the estate.

Ca. Prob. Code § 8907
Amended by Stats. 1991, Ch. 82, Sec. 24. Effective June 30, 1991. Operative July 1, 1991, by Sec. 31 of Ch. 82.

Section 8908 - Appraisal report or backup data provided by probate referee

A probate referee who appraises property in the estate shall, upon demand by the personal representative or by a beneficiary:
(a) Provide any appraisal report or backup data in the possession of the probate referee used by the referee to appraise an item of property. The probate referee shall not disclose any information that is required by law to be confidential. The probate referee shall provide the appraisal report or backup data without charge. The cost of providing the appraisal report or backup data shall not be allowed as an expense of appraisal but is included in the commission for services of the probate referee.
(b) Justify the appraisal of an item of property if the appraisal is contested, whether by objection pursuant to Section 8906, by tax audit, or otherwise. The probate referee may be entitled to an additional fee for services provided to justify the appraisal, to be agreed upon by the personal representative or beneficiary and referee. If the personal representative or beneficiary and the probate referee are unable to agree, the court shall determine what fee, if any, is appropriate.

Ca. Prob. Code § 8908
Enacted by Stats. 1990, Ch. 79.

Section 8909 - Retention of appraisal report and backup data

A probate referee who appraises property in an estate shall retain possession of all appraisal reports and backup data used by the referee to appraise the property for a period of three years after the appraisal is filed. The probate referee shall, during the three-year period, offer the personal representative the reports and data used by the referee to appraise the property and deliver the reports and data to the personal representative on request. Any reports and data not requested by the personal representative may be destroyed at the end of the three-year period without further notice.

Ca. Prob. Code § 8909
Enacted by Stats. 1990, Ch. 79.

Article 2 - DESIGNATION AND REMOVAL OF PROBATE REFEREE

Section 8920 - Designation of persons appointed by Controller

The probate referee, when designated by the court, shall be among the persons appointed by the Controller to act as a probate referee for the county. If there is no person available who is able to act or if, pursuant to authority of Section 8922 or otherwise, the court does not designate a person appointed for the county, the court may designate a probate referee from another county.

Ca. Prob. Code § 8920
Enacted by Stats. 1990, Ch. 79.

Section 8921 - Designation of person requested by personal representative

The court may designate a person requested by the personal representative as probate referee, on a showing by the personal representative of good cause for the designation. The following circumstances are included within the meaning of good cause, as used in this section:

(a) The probate referee has recently appraised the same property that will be appraised in the administration proceeding.

(b) The probate referee will be making related appraisals in another proceeding.

(c) The probate referee has recently appraised similar property in another proceeding.

Ca. Prob. Code § 8921
Enacted by Stats. 1990, Ch. 79.

Section 8922 - Authority of court not to designate person

The court has authority and discretion not to designate a particular person as probate referee even though appointed by the Controller to act as a probate referee for the county.

Ca. Prob. Code § 8922
Enacted by Stats. 1990, Ch. 79.

Section 8923 - Persons court may designate

The court may not designate as probate referee any of the following persons:
(a) The court clerk.
(b) A partner or employee of the judge or commissioner who orders the designation.
(c) The spouse of the judge or commissioner who orders the designation.
(d) A person, or the spouse of a person, who is related within the third degree either (1) to the judge or commissioner who orders the designation or (2) to the spouse of the judge or commissioner who orders the designation.

Ca. Prob. Code § 8923
Enacted by Stats. 1990, Ch. 79.

Section 8924 - Grounds for removal

(a) The court shall remove the designated probate referee in any of the following circumstances:

(1) The personal representative shows cause, including incompetence or undue delay in making the appraisal, that in the opinion of the court warrants removal of the probate referee. The showing shall be made at a hearing on petition of the personal representative. The personal representative shall deliver pursuant to Section 1215 notice of the hearing on the petition to the probate referee at least 15 days before the date set for the hearing.

(2) The personal representative has the right to remove the first probate referee who is designated by the court. Cause need not be shown for removal under this paragraph. The personal representative may exercise the right at any time before the personal representative delivers the inventory to the probate referee. The personal representative shall exercise the right by filing an affidavit or declaration under penalty of perjury with the court and delivering a copy to the probate referee pursuant to Section 1215. Thereupon, the court shall remove the probate referee without any further act or proof.

(3) Any other cause provided by statute.
(b) Upon removal of the probate referee, the court shall designate another probate referee in the manner prescribed in Section 8920.

Ca. Prob. Code § 8924
Amended by Stats 2017 ch 319 (AB 976),s 73, eff. 1/1/2018.

Article 3 - TIME FOR PROBATE REFEREE APPRAISAL

Section 8940 - Generally

(a) The probate referee shall promptly and with reasonable diligence appraise the property scheduled for appraisal by the probate referee in the inventory that the personal representative delivers to the referee.
(b) The probate referee shall, not later than 60 days after delivery of the inventory, do one of the following:

(1) Return the completed appraisal to the personal representative.

(2) Make a report of the status of the appraisal. The report shall show the reason why the property has not been appraised and an estimate of the time needed to complete the appraisal. The report shall be delivered to the personal representative and filed with the court.

Ca. Prob. Code § 8940
Enacted by Stats. 1990, Ch. 79.

Section 8941 - Hearing on report of status of appraisal

(a) The court shall, on petition of the personal representative or probate referee, or may, on the court's own motion, hear the report of the status of the appraisal. The court may issue a citation to compel the personal representative or the probate referee to attend the hearing.

(b) If the probate referee does not make the report of the status of the appraisal within the time required by this article or prescribed by the court, the court shall, on petition of the personal representative or may, on its own motion, cite the probate referee to appear before the court and show the reason why the property has not been appraised.

(c) Upon the hearing, the court may order any of the following:

(1) That the appraisal be completed within a time that appears reasonable.

(2) That the probate referee be removed. Upon removal of the probate referee the court shall designate another probate referee in the manner prescribed in Section 8920.

(3) That the commission of the probate referee be reduced by an amount the court deems appropriate, regardless of whether the commission otherwise allowable under the provisions of Sections 8960 to 8964 would be reasonable compensation for the services rendered.

(4) That the personal representative deliver to the probate referee all information necessary to allow the probate referee to complete the appraisal. Failure to comply with such an order is grounds for removal of the personal representative.

(5) Such other orders as may be appropriate.
Ca. Prob. Code § 8941
Enacted by Stats. 1990, Ch. 79.

Article 4 - COMMISSION AND EXPENSES OF PROBATE REFEREE

Section 8960 - Generally

(a) The commission and expenses provided by this article as compensation for the services of the probate referee shall be paid from the estate.
(b) The probate referee may not withhold the appraisal until the commission and expenses are paid, but shall deliver the appraisal to the personal representative promptly upon completion.
(c) The commission and expenses of the probate referee are an expense of administration, entitled to the priority for payment provided by Section 11420, and shall be paid in the course of administration.

Ca. Prob. Code § 8960
Enacted by Stats. 1990, Ch. 79.

Section 8961 - Compensation for services

As compensation for services the probate referee shall receive all of the following:
(a) A commission of one-tenth of one percent of the total value of the property for each estate appraised, subject to Section 8963. The commission shall be computed excluding property appraised by the personal representative pursuant to Section 8901 or by an independent expert pursuant to Section 8904.
(b) Actual and necessary expenses for each estate appraised. The referee shall file with, or list on, the inventory and appraisal a verified account of the referee's expenses.

Ca. Prob. Code § 8961
Enacted by Stats. 1990, Ch. 79.

Section 8963 - Amount of commission

(a) Notwithstanding Section 8961 and subject to subdivision (b), the commission of the probate referee shall in no event be less than seventy-five dollars ($75) nor more than ten thousand dollars

($10,000) for any estate appraised.

(b) Upon application of the probate referee, the court may allow a commission in excess of ten thousand dollars ($10,000) if the court determines that the reasonable value of the referee's services exceeds that amount. Notice of the hearing under this subdivision shall be given as provided in Section 1220 to all of the following persons:

(1) Each person listed in Section 1220.

(2) Each known heir whose interest in the estate would be affected by the petition.

(3) Each known devisee whose interest in the estate would be affected by the petition.

(4) The Attorney General, at the office of the Attorney General in Sacramento, if any portion of the estate is to escheat to the state and its interest in the estate would be affected by the petition.

(5) Each person who has requested special notice of petitions filed in the proceeding.

Ca. Prob. Code § 8963
Enacted by Stats. 1990, Ch. 79.

Section 8964 - More than one probate referee making appraisal

If more than one probate referee appraises or participates in the appraisal of property in the estate, each is entitled to the share of the commission agreed upon by the referees or, absent an agreement, that the court allows. In no case shall the total commission for all referees exceed the maximum commission that would be allowable for a single referee.

Ca. Prob. Code § 8964
Enacted by Stats. 1990, Ch. 79.

Article 5 - TRANSITIONAL PROVISION

Section 8980 - Generally

If an inventory is delivered to a probate referee for appraisal before July 1, 1989, all matters relating to the appraisal by the referee, including the property to be included in the appraisal, waiver of the appraisal, and compensation of the referee, are governed by the applicable law in effect before July 1, 1989, and are not governed by this chapter.

Ca. Prob. Code § 8980
Enacted by Stats. 1990, Ch. 79.

Part 4 - CREDITOR CLAIMS

Chapter 1 - GENERAL PROVISIONS

Section 9000 - Definitions

As used in this division:

(a) "Claim" means a demand for payment for any of the following, whether due, not due, accrued or not accrued, or contingent, and whether liquidated or unliquidated:

(1) Liability of the decedent, whether arising in contract, tort, or otherwise.

(2) Liability for taxes incurred before the decedent's death, whether assessed before or after the decedent's death, other than property taxes and assessments secured by real property liens.

(3) Liability of the estate for funeral expenses of the decedent.

(b) "Claim" does not include a dispute regarding title of a decedent to specific property alleged to be included in the decedent's estate.

(c) "Creditor" means a person who may have a claim against estate property.

Ca. Prob. Code § 9000
Amended by Stats 2007 ch 159 (AB 341),s 1, eff. 1/1/2008.

Section 9001 - Notice to creditors

(a) The publication of notice under Section 8120 and the giving of notice of administration of the estate of the decedent under Chapter 2 (commencing with Section 9050) constitute notice to creditors of the requirements of this part.
(b) Nothing in subdivision (a) affects a notice or request to a public entity required by Chapter 5 (commencing with Section 9200).
Ca. Prob. Code § 9001
Enacted by Stats. 1990, Ch. 79.

Section 9002 - Claims filed as provided in part; claims not filed as provided barred

Except as otherwise provided by statute:
(a) All claims shall be filed in the manner and within the time provided in this part.
(b) A claim that is not filed as provided in this part is barred.
Ca. Prob. Code § 9002
Enacted by Stats. 1990, Ch. 79.

Section 9003 - Established claims debts paid in course of administration

A claim that is established under this part shall be included among the debts to be paid in the course of administration.
Ca. Prob. Code § 9003
Enacted by Stats. 1990, Ch. 79.

Section 9004 - Inapplicability to proceedings commenced before July 1, 1988

(a) This part does not apply in any proceeding for administration of a decedent's estate commenced before July 1, 1988.
(b) The applicable law in effect before July 1, 1988, governing the subject matter of this part continues to apply in any proceeding for administration of a decedent's estate commenced before July 1,

1988, notwithstanding its repeal by Chapter 923 of the Statutes of 1987.

Ca. Prob. Code § 9004
Enacted by Stats. 1990, Ch. 79.

Chapter 2 - NOTICE TO CREDITORS

Section 9050 - Generally

(a) Subject to Section 9054, the personal representative shall give notice of administration of the estate to the known or reasonably ascertainable creditors of the decedent. The notice shall be given as provided in Section 1215. For the purpose of this subdivision, a personal representative has knowledge of a creditor of the decedent if the personal representative is aware that the creditor has demanded payment from the decedent or the estate.
(b) The giving of notice under this chapter is in addition to the publication of the notice under Section 8120.

Ca. Prob. Code § 9050
Amended by Stats. 1996, Ch. 862, Sec. 18. Effective January 1, 1997.

Section 9051 - Time for giving

The notice shall be given within the later of:
(a) Four months after the date letters are first issued.
(b) Thirty days after the personal representative first has knowledge of the creditor.

Ca. Prob. Code § 9051
Amended by Stats. 1996, Ch. 862, Sec. 19. Effective January 1, 1997.

Section 9052 - Form

The notice shall be in substantially the following form:

NOTICE OF ADMINISTRATION OFESTATE OF _____,
DECEDENT

Notice to creditors:Administration of the estate of _____
(deceased) has been commenced by _____ (personal

163

representative) in Estate No. _____ in the Superior Court of California, County of _____. You must file your claim with the court and deliver a copy pursuant to Section 1215 of the California Probate Code to the personal representative within the last to occur of four months after _____ (the date letters were first issued to a general personal representative, as defined in subdivision (b) of Section 58 of the California Probate Code), or 60 days after the date this notice was mailed to you or, in the case of personal delivery, 60 days after the date this notice was delivered to you, or you must petition to file a late claim as provided in Section 9103 of the California Probate Code. Failure to file a claim with the court and serve a copy of the claim on the personal representative will, in most instances, invalidate your claim. A claim form may be obtained from the court clerk. For your protection, you are encouraged to file your claim by certified mail, with return receipt requested.

(Date of mailing this notice)   (Name and address of personalrepresentative or attorney)

Ca. Prob. Code § 9052
Amended by Stats 2017 ch 319 (AB 976),s 74, eff. 1/1/2018.
Amended by Stats 2012 ch 207 (AB 2683),s 3, eff. 1/1/2013.

Section 9053 - Liability of personal representative

(a) If the personal representative believes that notice to a particular creditor is or may be required by this chapter and gives notice based on that belief, the personal representative is not liable to any person for giving the notice, whether or not required by this chapter.
(b) If the personal representative fails to give notice required by this chapter, the personal representative is not liable to any person for the failure, unless a creditor establishes all of the following:

(1) The failure was in bad faith.

(2) The creditor had no actual knowledge of the administration of the estate before expiration of the time for filing a claim, and payment would have been made on the creditor's claim in the course of administration if the claim had been properly filed.

(3) Within 16 months after letters were first issued to a general personal representative, the creditor did both of the following:

(A) Filed a petition requesting that the court in which the estate was administered make an order determining the liability of the personal representative under this subdivision.

(B) At least 30 days before the hearing on the petition, caused notice of the hearing and a copy of the petition to be served on the personal representative in the manner provided in Chapter 4 (commencing with Section 413.10) of Title 5 of Part 2 of the Code of Civil Procedure.
(c) Nothing in this section affects the liability of the estate, if any, for the claim of a creditor, and the personal representative is not liable for the claim to the extent it is paid out of the estate or could be paid out of the estate pursuant to Section 9103.
(d) A personal representative has a duty to make reasonably diligent efforts to identify reasonably ascertainable creditors of the decedent.
    Ca. Prob. Code § 9053
EFFECTIVE 1/1/2000. Amended August 30, 1999 (Bill Number: AB 1051) (Chapter 263).

Section 9054 - Conditions not requiring notice

Notwithstanding Section 9050, the personal representative need not give notice to a creditor even though the personal representative has knowledge of the creditor if any of the following conditions is satisfied:
(a) The creditor has filed a claim as provided in this part.
(b) The creditor has demanded payment and the personal representative elects to treat the demand as a claim under Section 9154.

Ca. Prob. Code § 9054
Enacted by Stats. 1990, Ch. 79.

Chapter 3 - TIME FOR FILING CLAIMS

Section 9100 - Generally

(a) A creditor shall file a claim before expiration of the later of the following times:

(1) Four months after the date letters are first issued to a general personal representative.

(2) Sixty days after the date notice of administration is mailed or personally delivered to the creditor. Nothing in this paragraph extends the time provided in Section 366.2 of the Code of Civil Procedure.
(b) A reference in another statute to the time for filing a claim means the time provided in paragraph (1) of subdivision (a).
(c) Nothing in this section shall be interpreted to extend or toll any other statute of limitations or to revive a claim that is barred by any statute of limitations. The reference in this subdivision to a "statute of limitations" includes Section 366.2 of the Code of Civil Procedure.
Ca. Prob. Code § 9100
Amended by Stats 2007 ch 159 (AB 341),s 2, eff. 1/1/2008.
EFFECTIVE 1/1/2000. Amended August 30, 1999 (Bill Number: AB 1051) (Chapter 263).

Section 9101 - Time not extended by vacancy in office of representative

A vacancy in the office of the personal representative that occurs before expiration of the time for filing a claim does not extend the time.
Ca. Prob. Code § 9101
Enacted by Stats. 1990, Ch. 79.

Section 9102 - Claim timely filed

A claim that is filed before expiration of the time for filing the claim is timely even if acted on by the personal representative or by the court after expiration of the time for filing claims.

Ca. Prob. Code § 9102

Amended by Stats 2007 ch 159 (AB 341),s 3, eff. 1/1/2008.

Section 9103 - Claim filed after expiration of time for filing

(a) Upon petition by a creditor or the personal representative, the court may allow a claim to be filed after expiration of the time for filing a claim provided in Section 9100 if either of the following conditions is satisfied:

(1) The personal representative failed to send proper and timely notice of administration of the estate to the creditor, and that petition is filed within 60 days after the creditor has actual knowledge of the administration of the estate.

(2) The creditor had no knowledge of the facts reasonably giving rise to the existence of the claim more than 30 days prior to the time for filing a claim as provided in Section 9100, and the petition is filed within 60 days after the creditor has actual knowledge of both of the following:

(A) The existence of the facts reasonably giving rise to the existence of the claim.

(B) The administration of the estate.

(b) Notwithstanding subdivision (a), the court shall not allow a claim to be filed under this section after the court makes an order for final distribution of the estate.

(c) The court may condition the claim on terms that are just and equitable, and may require the appointment or reappointment of a personal representative if necessary. The court may deny the creditor's petition if a payment to general creditors has been made and it appears that the filing or establishment of the claim would cause or tend to cause unequal treatment among creditors.

(d) Regardless of whether the claim is later established in whole or in part, payments otherwise properly made before a claim is filed under this section are not subject to the claim. Except to the extent provided in Section 9392 and subject to Section 9053, the personal representative or payee is not liable on account of the prior payment. Nothing in this subdivision limits the liability of a person who receives a preliminary distribution of property to restore to the estate an amount sufficient for payment of the distributee's proper share of the claim, not exceeding the amount distributed.

(e) Notice of hearing on the petition shall be given as provided in Section 1220.

(f) Nothing in this section authorizes allowance or approval of a claim barred by, or extends the time provided in, Section 366.2 of the Code of Civil Procedure.

Ca. Prob. Code § 9103

Amended by Stats 2007 ch 159 (AB 341),s 4, eff. 1/1/2008.

Section 9104 - Amendment of revision of claim timely filed

(a) Subject to subdivision (b), if a claim is filed within the time provided in this chapter, the creditor may later amend or revise the claim. The amendment or revision shall be filed in the same manner as the claim.

(b) An amendment or revision may not be made to increase the amount of the claim after the time for filing a claim has expired. An amendment or revision to specify the amount of a claim that, at the time of filing, was not due, was contingent, or was not yet ascertainable, is not an increase in the amount of the claim within the meaning of this subdivision.

(c) An amendment or revision may not be made for any purpose after the earlier of the following times:

(1) The time the court makes an order for final distribution of the estate.

(2) One year after letters are first issued to a general personal representative. This paragraph does not extend the time provided by Section 366.2 of the Code of Civil Procedure or authorize allowance or approval of a claim barred by that section.

Ca. Prob. Code § 9104

Amended by Stats 2007 ch 159 (AB 341),s 5, eff. 1/1/2008.

Chapter 4 - FILING OF CLAIMS

Section 9150 - Generally

(a) A claim may be filed by the creditor or a person acting on behalf of the creditor.

(b) A claim shall be filed with the court and a copy shall be served on the personal representative, or on a person who is later appointed and qualified as personal representative.

(c) Service of the claim on the personal representative shall be made within the later of 30 days of the filing of the claim or four months after letters issue to a personal representative with general powers. Service shall not be required after the claim has been allowed or rejected.

(d) If the creditor does not file the claim with the court and serve the claim on the personal representative as provided in this section, the claim shall be invalid.

Ca. Prob. Code § 9150

Amended by Stats. 1996, Ch. 862, Sec. 24. Effective January 1, 1997.

Section 9151 - Affidavit supporting claim

(a) A claim shall be supported by the affidavit of the creditor or the person acting on behalf of the creditor stating:

(1) The claim is a just claim.

(2) If the claim is due, the facts supporting the claim, the amount of the claim, and that all payments on and offsets to the claim have been credited.

(3) If the claim is not due or contingent, or the amount is not yet ascertainable, the facts supporting the claim.

(4) If the affidavit is made by a person other than the creditor, the reason it is not made by the creditor.

(b) The personal representative may require satisfactory vouchers or proof to be produced to support the claim. An original voucher may be withdrawn after a copy is provided. If a copy is provided, the copy shall be attached to the claim.

Ca. Prob. Code § 9151

Enacted by Stats. 1990, Ch. 79.

Section 9152 - Claim based on written instrument; claim secured by mortgage, deed of trust, etc.

(a) If a claim is based on a written instrument, either the original or a copy of the original with all endorsements shall be attached to the claim. If a copy is attached, the original instrument shall be exhibited to the personal representative or court or judge on demand unless it is lost or destroyed, in which case the fact that it is lost or destroyed shall be stated in the claim.

(b) If the claim or a part of the claim is secured by a mortgage, deed of trust, or other lien that is recorded in the office of the recorder of the county in which the property subject to the lien is located, it is sufficient to describe the mortgage, deed of trust, or lien and the recording reference for the instrument that created the mortgage, deed of trust, or other lien.

Ca. Prob. Code § 9152

Enacted by Stats. 1990, Ch. 79.

Section 9153 - Copy mailed or delivered to personal representative; proof of mailing or delivery

A claim form adopted by the Judicial Council shall inform the creditor that the claim must be filed with the court and a copy delivered pursuant to Section 1215 to the personal representative. The claim form shall include a proof of delivery of a copy of the claim to the personal representative, which may be completed by the creditor.

Ca. Prob. Code § 9153
Amended by Stats 2017 ch 319 (AB 976),s 75, eff. 1/1/2018.

Section 9154 - Election to treat demand for payment as claim filed and established under part

(a) Notwithstanding any other provision of this part, if a creditor makes a written demand for payment within four months after the date letters are first issued to a general personal representative, the personal representative may waive formal defects and elect to treat the demand as a claim that is filed and established under this part by paying the amount demanded before the expiration of 30 days after the four-month period if all of the following conditions are satisfied:

(1) The debt was justly due.

(2) The debt was paid in good faith.

(3) The amount paid was the true amount of the indebtedness over and above all payments and offsets.

(4) The estate is solvent.
(b) Nothing in this section limits application of (1) the doctrines of waiver, estoppel, laches, or detrimental reliance or (2) any other equitable principle.
Ca. Prob. Code § 9154
Enacted by Stats. 1990, Ch. 79.

Chapter 5 - CLAIMS BY PUBLIC ENTITIES

Section 9200 - Time for filing; claim not timely filed barred; public entity defined

(a) Except as provided in this chapter, a claim by a public entity shall be filed within the time otherwise provided in this part. A claim not so filed is barred, including any lien imposed for the claim.
(b) As used in this chapter, "public entity" has the meaning

provided in Section 811.2 of the Government Code, and includes an officer authorized to act on behalf of the public entity.

Ca. Prob. Code § 9200

Enacted by Stats. 1990, Ch. 79.

Section 9201 - Claim arising under listed law, act or code provision

(a) Notwithstanding any other statute, if a claim of a public entity arises under a law, act, or code listed in subdivision (b):

(1) The public entity may provide a form to be used for the written notice or request to the public entity required by this chapter. Where appropriate, the form may require the decedent's social security number, if known.

(2) The claim is barred only after written notice or request to the public entity and expiration of the period provided in the applicable section. If no written notice or request is made, the claim is enforceable by the remedies, and is barred at the time, otherwise provided in the law, act, or code.

(b)

Law, Act, or Code	Applicable Section
Sales and Use Tax Law (commencing with Section 6001 ofthe Revenue and TaxationCode)	Section 6487.1 of the Revenueand Taxation Code
Bradley-Burns Uniform LocalSales and Use Tax Law (com-mencing with Section 7200 ofthe Revenue and TaxationCode)	Section 6487.1 of the Revenueand Taxation Code
Transactions and Use Tax Law(commencing with Section 7251of the Revenue and TaxationCode)	Section 6487.1 of the Revenueand Taxation Code

Motor Vehicle Fuel License Tax Law(commencing with Section 7301 of the Revenue and Taxa-tion Code)	Section 7675.1 of the Revenueand Taxation Code
Use Fuel Tax Law (commencingwith Section 8601 of the Reve-nue and Taxation Code)	Section 8782.1 of the Revenue and Taxation Code
Administration of Franchise andIncome Tax Law (commencingwith Section 18401 of the Reve-nue and Taxation Code)	Section 19517 of the Revenueand Taxation Code
Cigarette Tax Law (commenc-ing with Section 30001 of theRevenue and Taxation Code)	Section 30207.1 of the Reve-nue and Taxation Code
Alcoholic Beverage Tax Law(commencing with Section 32001 of the Revenue and Taxa-tion Code)	Section 32272.1 of the Reve-nue and Taxation Code
Unemployment Insurance Code	Section 1090 of the Unemploy-ment Insurance Code
State Hospitals (commencing withSection 7200 of the Welfare andInstitutions Code)	Section 7277.1 of the Welfareand Institutions Code
Medi-Cal Act (commencingwith Section 14000 of the Wel-fare and Institutions Code)	Section 9202 of the ProbateCode
Waxman-Duffy Prepaid HealthPlan Act (commencing with Sec-tion 14200 of the Welfare andInstitutions Code)	Section 9202 of the ProbateCode

Ca. Prob. Code § 9201
Amended by Stats 2014 ch 144 (AB 1847),s 49, eff. 1/1/2015.

EFFECTIVE 1/1/2000. Amended October 10, 1999 (Bill Number: SB 1229) (Chapter 987).

Section 9202 - Notice to Director of Health Care Services; Director of California Victim Compensation Board; Franchise tax Board

(a) Not later than 90 days after the date letters are first issued to a general personal representative, the general personal representative or estate attorney shall give the Director of Health Care Services notice of the decedent's death in the manner provided in Section 215 if the general personal representative knows or has reason to believe that the decedent received health care under Chapter 7 (commencing with Section 14000) or Chapter 8 (commencing with Section 14200) of Part 3 of Division 9 of the Welfare and Institutions Code, or was the surviving spouse of a person who received that health care. The director has four months after notice is given in which to file a claim.

(b) Not later than 90 days after the date letters are first issued to a general personal representative, the general personal representative or estate attorney shall give the Director of the California Victim Compensation Board notice of the decedent's death in the manner provided in Section 216 if the general personal representative or estate attorney knows that an heir or beneficiary is or has previously been confined in a prison or facility under the jurisdiction of the Department of Corrections and Rehabilitation or confined in any county or city jail, road camp, industrial farm, or other local correctional facility. The director of the board shall have four months after that notice is received in which to pursue collection of any outstanding restitution fines or orders.

(c)

(1) Not later than 90 days after the date letters are first issued to a general personal representative, the general personal representative or estate attorney shall give the Franchise Tax Board notice of the administration of the estate. The notice shall be given as provided in Section 1215.

(2) The provisions of this subdivision shall apply to estates for which letters are first issued on or after July 1, 2008.

(d) Nothing in this section shall be interpreted as requiring the estate attorney, the beneficiary, the personal representative, or the person in possession of property of the decedent to conduct an additional investigation to determine whether a decedent has an heir or beneficiary who has been confined in a prison or facility under the jurisdiction of the Department of Corrections and Rehabilitation, or its Division of Juvenile Facilities, or confined in any county or city jail, road camp, industrial farm, or other local correctional facility.

Ca. Prob. Code § 9202

Amended by Stats 2016 ch 31 (SB 836),s 261, eff. 6/27/2016.
Amended by Stats 2014 ch 508 (AB 2685),s 4, eff. 1/1/2015.
Amended by Stats 2007 ch 105 (AB 361),s 1, eff. 1/1/2008.
Amended by Stats 2005 ch 238 (SB 972),s 4, eff. 1/1/2006

Section 9203 - Validity of proceeding not affected by failure to give notice; distribution made before expiration of time allowed to file claim

(a) Failure of a person to give the written notice or request required by this chapter does not affect the validity of any proceeding under this code concerning the administration of the decedent's estate.

(b) If property in the estate is distributed before expiration of the time allowed a public entity to file a claim, the public entity has a claim against the distributees to the full extent of the public entity's claim, or each distributee's share of the distributed property, whichever is less. The public entity's claim against distributees includes interest at a rate equal to that specified in Section 19521 of the Revenue and Taxation Code, from the date of distribution or the date of filing the claim by the public entity, whichever is later, plus other accruing costs as in the case of enforcement of a money judgment.

Ca. Prob. Code § 9203

EFFECTIVE 1/1/2000. Amended October 10, 1999 (Bill Number: SB 1229) (Chapter 987).

Section 9204 - Order of priority of claims not affected

Nothing in this chapter shall be construed to affect the order of priority of claims provided for under other provisions of law.

Ca. Prob. Code § 9204
Enacted by Stats. 1990, Ch. 79.

Section 9205 - Restitution illegally acquired

This chapter does not apply to liability for the restitution of amounts illegally acquired through the means of a fraudulent, false, or incorrect representation, or a forged or unauthorized endorsement.

Ca. Prob. Code § 9205
Enacted by Stats. 1990, Ch. 79.

Chapter 6 - ALLOWANCE AND REJECTION OF CLAIMS

Section 9250 - Generally

(a) When a claim is filed, the personal representative shall allow or reject the claim in whole or in part.

(b) The allowance or rejection shall be in writing. The personal representative shall file the allowance or rejection with the court clerk and give notice to the creditor as provided in Part 2 (commencing with Section 1200) of Division 3, together with a copy of the allowance or rejection.

(c) The allowance or rejection shall contain the following information:

(1) The name of the creditor.

(2) The total amount of the claim.

(3) The date of issuance of letters.

(4) The date of the decedent's death.

(5) The estimated value of the decedent's estate.

(6) The amount allowed or rejected by the personal representative.

(7) Whether the personal representative is authorized to act under the Independent Administration of Estates Act (Part 6 (commencing with Section 10400)).

(8) A statement that the creditor has 90 days in which to act on a rejected claim.
(d) The Judicial Council may prescribe an allowance or rejection form, which may be part of the claim form. Use of a form prescribed by the Judicial Council is deemed to satisfy the requirements of this section.
(e) This section does not apply to a demand the personal representative elects to treat as a claim under Section 9154.

Ca. Prob. Code § 9250
Amended by Stats 2007 ch 159 (AB 341),s 6, eff. 1/1/2008.
EFFECTIVE 1/1/2000. Amended August 30, 1999 (Bill Number: AB 1051) (Chapter 263).

Section 9251 - Personal representative not authorized to act under Independent Administration of Estates Act

If the personal representative is not authorized to act under the Independent Administration of Estates Act (Part 6 (commencing with Section 10400)):
(a) Immediately on the filing of the allowance of a claim, the clerk shall present the claim and allowance to the court or judge for approval or rejection.
(b) On presentation of a claim and allowance, the court or judge may, in its discretion, examine the creditor and others on oath and receive any evidence relevant to the validity of the claim. The court or judge shall endorse on the claim whether the claim is approved or rejected and the date.

Ca. Prob. Code § 9251
Enacted by Stats. 1990, Ch. 79.

Section 9252 - Personal representative creditor of decedent

(a) If the personal representative or the attorney for the personal representative is a creditor of the decedent, the clerk shall present the claim to the court or judge for approval or rejection. The court or judge may in its discretion require the creditor to file a petition and give notice of hearing.

(b) If the court or judge approves the claim, the claim is established and shall be included with other established claims to be paid in the course of administration.

(c) If the court or judge rejects the claim, the personal representative or attorney may bring an action against the estate. Summons shall be served on the judge, who shall appoint an attorney at the expense of the estate to defend the action.

Ca. Prob. Code § 9252
Enacted by Stats. 1990, Ch. 79.

Section 9253 - Claim barred by statute of limitations

A claim barred by the statute of limitations may not be allowed by the personal representative or approved by the court or judge.

Ca. Prob. Code § 9253
Enacted by Stats. 1990, Ch. 79.

Section 9254 - Contest of validity of claim

(a) The validity of an allowed or approved claim may be contested by any interested person at any time before settlement of the report or account of the personal representative in which it is first reported as an allowed or approved claim. The burden of proof is on the contestant, except where the personal representative has acted under the Independent Administration of Estates Act (Part 6 (commencing Section 10400)), in which case the burden of proof is on the personal representative.

(b) Subdivision (a) does not apply to a claim established by a judgment.

Ca. Prob. Code § 9254
Enacted by Stats. 1990, Ch. 79.

Section 9255 - Allowance or approval in part

(a) The personal representative may allow a claim, or the court or judge may approve a claim, in part. The allowance or approval shall state the amount for which the claim is allowed or approved.
(b) A creditor who refuses to accept the amount allowed or approved in satisfaction of the claim may bring an action on the claim in the manner provided in Chapter 8 (commencing with Section 9350). The creditor may not recover costs in the action unless the creditor recovers an amount greater than that allowed or approved.
Ca. Prob. Code § 9255
Enacted by Stats. 1990, Ch. 79.

Section 9256 - Refusal or neglect to act deemed equivalent of giving notice of rejection

If within 30 days after a claim is filed the personal representative or the court or judge has refused or neglected to act on the claim, the refusal or neglect may, at the option of the creditor, be deemed equivalent to giving a notice of rejection on the 30th day.
Ca. Prob. Code § 9256
Enacted by Stats. 1990, Ch. 79.

Chapter 7 - CLAIMS ESTABLISHED BY JUDGMENT

Section 9300 - Judgments payable in course of administration

(a) Except as provided in Section 9303, after the death of the decedent all money judgments against the decedent or against the personal representative on a claim against the decedent or estate are payable in the course of administration and are not enforceable against property in the estate of the decedent under the Enforcement of Judgments Law (Title 9 (commencing with Section 680.010) of Part 2 of the Code of Civil Procedure).

(b) Subject to Section 9301, a judgment referred to in subdivision (a) shall be filed in the same manner as other claims.

Ca. Prob. Code § 9300

Enacted by Stats. 1990, Ch. 79.

Section 9301 - Final judgment against personal representative in representative capacity

When a money judgment against a personal representative in a representative capacity becomes final, it conclusively establishes the validity of the claim for the amount of the judgment. The judgment shall provide that it is payable out of property in the decedent's estate in the course of administration. An abstract of the judgment shall be filed in the administration proceedings.

Ca. Prob. Code § 9301

Enacted by Stats. 1990, Ch. 79.

Section 9302 - Enforcement of judgment for possession or sale of property

(a) Notwithstanding the death of the decedent, a judgment for possession of property or a judgment for sale of property may be enforced under the Enforcement of Judgments Law (Title 9 (commencing with Section 680.010) of Part 2 of the Code of Civil Procedure). Nothing in this subdivision authorizes enforcement under the Enforcement of Judgments Law against any property in the estate of the decedent other than the property described in the judgment for possession or sale.

(b) After the death of the decedent, a demand for money that is not satisfied from the property described in a judgment for sale of property shall be filed as a claim in the same manner as other claims and is payable in the course of administration.

Ca. Prob. Code § 9302

Enacted by Stats. 1990, Ch. 79.

Section 9303 - Decedent's property subject to execution lien at time of death

If property of the decedent is subject to an execution lien at the time of the decedent's death, enforcement against the property may proceed under the Enforcement of Judgments Law (Title 9 (commencing with Section 680.010) of Part 2 of the Code of Civil Procedure) to satisfy the judgment. The levying officer shall account to the personal representative for any surplus. If the judgment is not satisfied, the balance of the judgment remaining unsatisfied is payable in the course of administration.

Ca. Prob. Code § 9303
Enacted by Stats. 1990, Ch. 79.

Section 9304 - Conversion of attachment lien into judgment lien

(a) An attachment lien may be converted into a judgment lien on property in the estate subject to the attachment lien, with the same priority as the attachment lien, in either of the following cases:

(1) Where the judgment debtor dies after entry of judgment in an action in which the property was attached.

(2) Where a judgment is entered after the death of the defendant in an action in which the property was attached.
(b) To convert the attachment lien into a judgment lien, the levying officer shall, after entry of judgment in the action in which the property was attached and before the expiration of the attachment lien, do one of the following:

(1) Serve an abstract of the judgment, and a notice that the attachment lien has become a judgment lien, on the person holding property subject to the attachment lien.

(2) Record or file, in any office where the writ of attachment and notice of attachment are recorded or filed, an abstract of the judgment and a notice that the attachment lien has become a judgment lien. If the attached property is real property, the plaintiff or the plaintiff's attorney may record the required abstract and notice with the same effect as if recorded by the levying officer.

(c) After the death of the decedent, any members of the decedent's family who were supported in whole or in part by the decedent may claim an exemption provided in Section 487.020 of the Code of Civil Procedure for property levied on under the writ of attachment if the right to the exemption exists at the time the exemption is claimed. The personal representative may claim the exemption on behalf of members of the decedent's family. The claim of exemption may be made at any time before the time the abstract and notice are served, recorded, or filed under subdivision (b) with respect to the property claimed to be exempt. The claim of exemption shall be made in the same manner as an exemption is claimed under Section 482.100 of the Code of Civil Procedure.

Ca. Prob. Code § 9304
Enacted by Stats. 1990, Ch. 79.

Chapter 8 - CLAIMS IN LITIGATION

Article 1 - CLAIM WHERE NO PENDING ACTION OR PROCEEDING

Section 9350 - Applicability of article

This article applies to any claim other than a claim on an action or proceeding pending against the decedent at the time of death.

Ca. Prob. Code § 9350
Enacted by Stats. 1990, Ch. 79.

Section 9351 - Commencing action against personal representative on cause of action against decedent

An action may not be commenced against a decedent's personal representative on a cause of action against the decedent unless a claim is first filed as provided in this part and the claim is rejected in whole or in part.

Ca. Prob. Code § 9351
Enacted by Stats. 1990, Ch. 79.

Section 9352 - Statute of limitations tolled

(a) The filing of a claim or a petition under Section 9103 to file a claim tolls the statute of limitations otherwise applicable to the claim until allowance, approval, or rejection.

(b) The allowance or approval of a claim in whole or in part further tolls the statute of limitations during the administration of the estate as to the part allowed or approved.

Ca. Prob. Code § 9352

Amended by Stats. 1991, Ch. 1055, Sec. 26.

Section 9353 - Claim rejected barred unless

(a) Regardless of whether the statute of limitations otherwise applicable to a claim will expire before or after the following times, a claim rejected in whole or in part is barred as to the part rejected unless, within the following times, the creditor commences an action on the claim or the matter is referred to a referee or to arbitration:

   (1) If the claim is due at the time the notice of rejection is given, 90 days after the notice is given.

   (2) If the claim is not due at the time the notice of rejection is given, 90 days after the claim becomes due.

(b) The time during which there is a vacancy in the office of the personal representative shall be excluded from the period determined under subdivision (a).

Ca. Prob. Code § 9353

Amended by Stats 2007 ch 159 (AB 341),s 7, eff. 1/1/2008.

Section 9354 - Venue for commencing action; notice of pendency of action; court costs

(a) In addition to any other county in which an action may be commenced, an action on the claim may be commenced in the county in which the proceeding for administration of the decedent's estate is pending.

(b) The plaintiff shall file a notice of the pendency of the action with the court clerk in the estate proceeding, together with proof of giving a copy of the notice to the personal representative as provided in Section 1215. Personal service of a copy of the summons and complaint on the personal representative is equivalent to the filing and giving of the notice. Any property distributed under court order, or any payment properly made, before the notice is filed and given is not subject to the claim. The personal representative, distributee, or payee is not liable on account of the prior distribution or payment.

(c) The prevailing party in the action shall be awarded court costs and, if the court determines that the prosecution or defense of the action against the prevailing party was unreasonable, the prevailing party shall be awarded reasonable litigation expenses, including attorney's fees.

Ca. Prob. Code § 9354
Enacted by Stats. 1990, Ch. 79.

Article 2 - CLAIM WHERE ACTION OR PROCEEDING PENDING

Section 9370 - Generally

(a) An action or proceeding pending against the decedent at the time of death may not be continued against the decedent's personal representative unless all of the following conditions are satisfied:

(1) A claim is first filed as provided in this part.

(2) The claim is rejected in whole or in part.

(3) Within three months after the notice of rejection is given, the plaintiff applies to the court in which the action or proceeding is pending for an order to substitute the personal representative in the action or proceeding. This paragraph applies only if the notice of rejection contains a statement that the plaintiff has three months within which to apply for an order for substitution.

(b) No recovery shall be allowed in the action against property in the decedent's estate unless proof is made of compliance with this section.

Ca. Prob. Code § 9370
Enacted by Stats. 1990, Ch. 79.

Article 3 - LITIGATION WHERE NO CLAIM REQUIRED

Section 9390 - Action to establish decedent's liability for which decedent protected by insurance

(a) An action to establish the decedent's liability for which the decedent was protected by insurance may be commenced or continued under Section 550, and a judgment in the action may be enforced against the insurer, without first filing a claim as provided in this part.
(b) Unless a claim is first made as provided in this part, an action to establish the decedent's liability for damages outside the limits or coverage of the insurance may not be commenced or continued under Section 550.
(c) If the insurer seeks reimbursement under the insurance contract for any liability of the decedent, including, but not limited to, deductible amounts in the insurance coverage and costs and attorney's fees for which the decedent is liable under the contract, an insurer defending an action under Section 550 shall file a claim as provided in this part. Failure to file a claim is a waiver of reimbursement under the insurance contract for any liability of the decedent.

Ca. Prob. Code § 9390
Amended by Stats. 1990, Ch. 710, Sec. 23. Operative July 1, 1991, by Sec. 48 of Ch. 710.

Section 9391 - Action to enforce mortgage or other lien on property in decedent's estate

Except as provided in Section 10361, the holder of a mortgage or other lien on property in the decedent's estate, including, but not limited to, a judgment lien, may commence an action to enforce the lien against the property that is subject to the lien, without first filing a claim as provided in this part, if in the complaint the holder of the lien expressly waives all recourse against other property in the estate. Section 366.2 of the Code of Civil Procedure does not apply to an action under this section. The personal representative shall have the authority to seek to enjoin any action of the lienholder to enforce a lien against property that is subject to the lien.

Ca. Prob. Code § 9391

Amended by Stats. 1996, Ch. 862, Sec. 25. Effective January 1, 1997.

Section 9392 - [First of two versions] Liability for claim of creditor by person to whom distribution made

(a) Subject to subdivision (b), a person to whom property is distributed is personally liable for the claim of a creditor, without a claim first having been filed, if all of the following conditions are satisfied:

(1) The identity of the creditor was known to, or reasonably ascertainable by, a general personal representative within four months after the date letters were first issued to the personal representative, and the claim of the creditor was not merely conjectural.

(2) Notice of administration of the estate was not given to the creditor under Chapter 2 (commencing with Section 9050) and neither the creditor nor the attorney representing the creditor in the matter had actual knowledge of the administration of the estate before the time the court made an order for final distribution of the property.

(3) The statute of limitations applicable to the claim under Section 353 of the Code of Civil Procedure has not expired at the time of commencement of an action under this section.

(b) Personal liability under this section is applicable only to the extent the claim of the creditor cannot be satisfied out of the decedent and is limited to the extent of the fair market value of the property on the date of the order for distribution, less the amount of any liens and encumbrances on the property at that time. Personal liability under this section is joint and several, based on the principles stated in Part 4 (commencing with Section 21400) of

Division 11 (abatement).

(c) Nothing in this section affects the rights of a purchaser or encumbrancer of property in good faith and for value from a person who is personally liable under this section.

   Ca. Prob. Code § 9392

Added by Stats. 1990, Ch. 79, Sec. 20. See prevailing Section 9392 (added by Stats. 1990, Ch. 140) as amended by Stats. 1992, Ch. 178.

Section 9392 - [Second of two versions] Liability for claim of creditor by person to whom distribution made

(a) Subject to subdivision (b), a person to whom property is distributed is personally liable for the claim of a creditor, without a claim first having been filed, if all of the following conditions are satisfied:

   (1) The identity of the creditor was known to, or reasonably ascertainable by, a general personal representative within four months after the date letters were first issued to the personal representative, and the claim of the creditor was not merely conjectural.

   (2) Notice of administration of the estate was not given to the creditor under Chapter 2 (commencing with Section 9050) and neither the creditor nor the attorney representing the creditor in the matter has actual knowledge of the administration of the estate before the time the court made an order for final distribution of the property.

   (3) The statute of limitations applicable to the claim under Section 366.2 of the Code of Civil Procedure has not expired at the time of commencement of an action under this section.

(b) Personal liability under this section is applicable only to the extent the claim of the creditor cannot be satisfied out of the estate of the decedent and is limited to a pro rata portion of the claim of the creditor, based on the proportion that the value of the property distributed to the person out of the estate bears to the total value of all property distributed to all persons out of the estate. Personal liability under this section for all claims of all creditors shall not exceed the value of the property distributed to the person out of the estate. As used in this section, the value of property is the fair market value of the property on the date of the order for distribution, less the amount of any liens and encumbrances on the property at that time.

(c) Nothing in this section affects the rights of a purchaser or encumbrancer of property in good faith and for value from a person who is personally liable under this section.

Ca. Prob. Code § 9392

Amended (as added by Stats. 1990, Ch. 140) by Stats. 1992, Ch. 178, Sec. 36. Effective January 1, 1993.

Article 4 - TRANSITIONAL PROVISION

Section 9399 - Applicability

(a) This chapter does not apply to an action commenced before July 1, 1989.

(b) The applicable law in effect before July 1, 1989, continues to apply to an action commenced before July 1, 1989, notwithstanding its repeal by Chapter 1199 of the Statutes of 1988.

Ca. Prob. Code § 9399

Enacted by Stats. 1990, Ch. 79.

Part 5 - ESTATE MANAGEMENT

Chapter 1 - GENERAL PROVISIONS

Article 1 - DUTIES AND LIABILITIES OF PERSONAL REPRESENTATIVE

Section 9600 - Ordinary care and diligence used in management and control of estate

(a) The personal representative has the management and control of the estate and, in managing and controlling the estate, shall use ordinary care and diligence. What constitutes ordinary care and diligence is determined by all the circumstances of the particular estate.

(b) The personal representative:

(1) Shall exercise a power to the extent that ordinary care and diligence require that the power be exercised.

(2) Shall not exercise a power to the extent that ordinary care and diligence require that the power not be exercised.
Ca. Prob. Code § 9600
Enacted by Stats. 1990, Ch. 79.

Section 9601 - Breach of fiduciary duty

(a) If a personal representative breaches a fiduciary duty, the personal representative is chargeable with any of the following that is appropriate under the circumstances:

(1) Any loss or depreciation in value of the decedent's estate resulting from the breach of duty, with interest.

(2) Any profit made by the personal representative through the breach of duty, with interest.

(3) Any profit that would have accrued to the decedent's estate if the loss of profit is the result of the breach of duty.
(b) If the personal representative has acted reasonably and in good faith under the circumstances as known to the personal representative, the court, in its discretion, may excuse the personal representative in whole or in part from liability under subdivision (a) if it would be equitable to do so.
Ca. Prob. Code § 9601
Enacted by Stats. 1990, Ch. 79.

Section 9602 - Personal representative liable for interest pursuant to breach

(a) If the personal representative is liable for interest pursuant to Section 9601, the personal representative is liable for the greater of the following amounts:

(1) The amount of interest that accrues at the legal rate on judgments.

(2) The amount of interest actually received.
(b) If the personal representative has acted reasonably and in good faith under the circumstances as known to the personal representative, the court, in its discretion, may excuse the personal representative in whole or in part from liability under subdivision (a) if it would be equitable to do so.

Ca. Prob. Code § 9602
Amended by Stats. 1998, Ch. 77, Sec. 4. Effective January 1, 1999.

Section 9603 - Other remedies

The provisions of Sections 9601 and 9602 for liability of a personal representative for breach of a fiduciary duty do not prevent resort to any other remedy available against the personal representative under the statutory or common law.

Ca. Prob. Code § 9603
Enacted by Stats. 1990, Ch. 79.

Section 9604 - Chargeable upon special promise to answer for damages out of personal representative's own estate

No personal representative is chargeable upon a special promise to answer in damages for a liability of the decedent or to pay a debt of the decedent out of the personal representative's own estate unless the agreement for that purpose, or some memorandum or note thereof, is in writing and is signed by one of the following:
(a) The personal representative.
(b) Some other person specifically authorized by the personal representative in writing to sign the agreement or the memorandum or note.

Ca. Prob. Code § 9604
Enacted by Stats. 1990, Ch. 79.

Section 9605 - Claim against personal representative not discharged by appointment

Appointment of a person as personal representative does not discharge any claim the decedent has against the person.

Ca. Prob. Code § 9605
Enacted by Stats. 1990, Ch. 79.

Section 9606 - Liability on instrument properly entered into in personal representative's fiduciary capacity

Unless otherwise provided in the instrument or in this division, a personal representative is not personally liable on an instrument, including but not limited to a note, mortgage, deed of trust, or other contract, properly entered into in the personal representative's fiduciary capacity in the course of administration of the estate unless the personal representative fails to reveal the personal representative's representative capacity or identify the estate in the instrument.

Ca. Prob. Code § 9606
Enacted by Stats. 1990, Ch. 79.

Article 2 - COURT SUPERVISION

Section 9610 - Generally

Unless this part specifically provides a proceeding to obtain court authorization or requires court authorization, the powers and duties set forth in this part may be exercised by the personal representative without court authorization, instruction, approval, or confirmation. Nothing in this section precludes the personal representative from seeking court authorization, instructions, approval, or confirmation.

Ca. Prob. Code § 9610
Enacted by Stats. 1990, Ch. 79.

Section 9611 - Authorization and instruction or approval and confirmation

(a) In all cases where no other procedure is provided by statute, upon petition of the personal representative, the court may authorize and instruct the personal representative, or approve and confirm the acts of the personal representative, in the administration, management, investment, disposition, care, protection, operation, or preservation of the estate, or the incurring or payment of costs, fees, or expenses in connection therewith. Section 9613 does not preclude a petition for instructions under this section.

(b) Notice of the hearing on the petition shall be given as provided in Section 1220.

Ca. Prob. Code § 9611
Enacted by Stats. 1990, Ch. 79.

Section 9613 - Direction to act or not to act

(a) On petition of any interested person, and upon a showing that if the petition is not granted the estate will suffer great or irreparable injury, the court may direct the personal representative to act or not to act concerning the estate. The order may include terms and conditions the court determines are appropriate under the circumstances.

(b) Notice of the hearing on the petition shall be given as provided in Section 1220.

Ca. Prob. Code § 9613
Enacted by Stats. 1990, Ch. 79.

Section 9614 - Suspension of powers as to specific property or circumstances or specific duties

(a) On petition of an interested person, the court may suspend the powers of the personal representative in whole or in part, for a time, as to specific property or circumstances or as to specific duties of the office, or may make any other order to secure proper performance of the duties of the personal representative, if it appears to the court that the personal representative otherwise may take some action that would jeopardize unreasonably the interest of the petitioner. Persons with whom the personal representative may transact business may be made parties.

(b) The matter shall be set for hearing within 10 days unless the parties agree otherwise. Notice as the court directs shall be given to the personal representative and attorney of record, if any, and to any other parties named in the petition.

(c) The court may, in its discretion, if it determines that the petition was brought unreasonably and for the purpose of hindering the personal representative in the performance of the duties of the office, assess attorney's fees against the petitioner and make the assessment a charge against the interest of the petitioner.

Ca. Prob. Code § 9614
Enacted by Stats. 1990, Ch. 79.

Article 3 - SUMMARY DETERMINATION OF DISPUTES

Section 9620 - Agreement with third person that judge determine dispute

If there is a dispute relating to the estate between the personal representative and a third person, the personal representative may do either of the following:

(a) Enter into an agreement in writing with the third person to refer the dispute to a temporary judge designated in the agreement. The agreement shall be filed with the clerk, who shall thereupon, with the approval of the court, enter an order referring the matter to the designated person. The temporary judge shall proceed promptly to hear and determine the matter in controversy by summary procedure, without pleadings or discovery. The decision of the designated person is subject to Section 632 of the Code of Civil Procedure. Judgment shall be entered on the decision and shall be as valid and effective as if rendered by a judge of the court in an action against the personal representative or the third person commenced by ordinary process.

(b) Enter into an agreement in writing with the third person that a judge, pursuant to the agreement and with the written consent of the judge, both filed with the clerk within the time specified in Section 9353 for bringing an independent suit on the matter in dispute, may hear and determine the dispute pursuant to the procedure provided in subdivision (a).

Ca. Prob. Code § 9620

Enacted by Stats. 1990, Ch. 79.

Section 9621 - Agreement with third person to submit dispute to arbitration

If there is a dispute relating to the estate between the personal representative and a third person, the personal representative may enter into an agreement in writing with the third person to submit the dispute to arbitration under Title 9 (commencing with Section 1280) of Part 3 of the Code of Civil Procedure. The agreement is not effective unless it is first approved by the court and a copy of the approved agreement is filed with the court. Notice of the hearing on the petition for approval of the agreement shall be given as provided in Section 1220. The order approving the agreement may be made ex parte.

Ca. Prob. Code § 9621

Enacted by Stats. 1990, Ch. 79.

Article 4 - JOINT PERSONAL REPRESENTATIVES

Section 9630 - Generally

(a) Subject to subdivisions (b), (c), and (d):

(1) Where there are two personal representatives, both must concur to exercise a power.

(2) Where there are more than two personal representatives, a majority must concur to exercise a power.

(b) If one of the joint personal representatives dies or is removed or resigns, the powers and duties continue in the remaining joint personal representatives as if they were the only personal representatives until further appointment is made by the court.

(c) Where joint personal representatives have been appointed and one or more are (1) absent from the state and unable to act, or (2) otherwise unable to act, or (3) legally disqualified from serving, the court may, by order made with or without notice, authorize the remaining joint personal representatives to act as to all matters embraced within its order.

(d) Where there are two or more personal representatives, any of them may:

(1) Oppose a petition made by one or more of the other personal representatives or by any other person.

(2) Petition the court for an order requiring the personal representatives to take a specific action for the benefit of the estate or directing the personal representatives not to take a specific action. If a procedure is provided by statute for a petition to authorize the specific action by the personal representatives, the petitioner shall file the petition under the provision relating to that procedure. Otherwise, the petitioner shall file the petition under Section 9611.

Ca. Prob. Code § 9630
Enacted by Stats. 1990, Ch. 79.

Section 9631 - Liability for breach of fiduciary duty

(a) Except as provided in subdivision (b), where there is more than one personal representative, one personal representative is not liable for a breach of fiduciary duty committed by another of the personal representatives.

(b) Where there is more than one personal representative, one personal representative is liable for a breach of fiduciary duty committed by another of the personal representatives under any of the following circumstances:

(1) Where the personal representative participates in a breach of fiduciary duty committed by the other personal representative.

(2) Where the personal representative improperly delegates the administration of the estate to the other personal representative.

(3) Where the personal representative approves, knowingly acquiesces in, or conceals a breach of fiduciary duty committed by the other personal representative.

(4) Where the personal representative's negligence enables the other personal representative to commit a breach of fiduciary duty.

(5) Where the personal representative knows or has information from which the personal representative reasonably should have known of the breach of fiduciary duty by the other personal representative and fails to take reasonable steps to compel the other personal representative to redress the breach.
(c) The liability of a personal representative for a breach of fiduciary duty committed by another of the personal representatives that occurred before July 1, 1988, is governed by prior law and not by this section.
Ca. Prob. Code § 9631
Enacted by Stats. 1990, Ch. 79.

Article 5 - INDEPENDENT ADMINISTRATION

Section 9640 - Generally

Nothing in this part limits or restricts any authority granted to a personal representative under the Independent Administration of Estates Act (Part 6 (commencing with Section 10400)) to administer the estate under that part.
Ca. Prob. Code § 9640
Enacted by Stats. 1990, Ch. 79.

Article 6 - TRANSITIONAL PROVISION

Section 9645 - Action taken before July 1, 1988

(a) Subject to subdivisions (b) and (c), any petition or other matter filed or commenced before July 1, 1988, shall be continued under this part, so far as applicable, except where the court determines that application of a particular provision of this part would substantially interfere with the rights of the parties or other interested persons, in which case the particular provision of this part does not apply and the applicable law in effect before July 1,

1988, applies.

(b) Nothing in this part affects any order, judgment, or decree made, or any action taken, before July 1, 1988.

(c) Notwithstanding the enactment of this part:

(1) An order, judgment, or decree made before July 1, 1988, shall continue in full force and effect in accordance with its terms or until modified or terminated by the court.

(2) The validity of an order, judgment, or decree made before July 1, 1988, is determined by the applicable law in effect before July 1, 1988, and not by this part.

(3) The validity of any action taken before July 1, 1988, is determined by the applicable law in effect before July 1, 1988, and not by this part.

Ca. Prob. Code § 9645
Enacted by Stats. 1990, Ch. 79.

Chapter 2 - ESTATE MANAGEMENT GENERALLY

Section 9650 - Generally

(a) Except as provided by statute and subject to subdivision (c):

(1) The personal representative has the right to, and shall take possession or control of, all the property of the decedent to be administered in the decedent's estate and shall collect all debts due to the decedent or the estate. The personal representative is not accountable for any debts that remain uncollected without his or her fault.

(2) The personal representative is entitled to receive the rents, issues, and profits from the real and personal property in the estate until the estate is distributed.

(b) The personal representative shall pay taxes on, and take all steps reasonably necessary for the management, protection, and preservation of, the estate in his or her possession.

(c) Real property or tangible personal property may be left with or surrendered to the person presumptively entitled to it unless or until, in the judgment of the personal representative, possession of the property by the personal representative will be necessary for purposes of administration. The person holding the property shall surrender it to the personal representative on request by the personal representative.

Ca. Prob. Code § 9650
Enacted by Stats. 1990, Ch. 79.

Section 9651 - Good faith taking of possession of property believing property part of decedent's estate

(a) A personal representative who in good faith takes into possession real or personal property, and reasonably believes that the property is part of the estate of the decedent, is not:

    (1) Criminally liable for so doing.

    (2) Civilly liable to any person for so doing.

(b) The personal representative shall make reasonable efforts to determine the true nature of, and title to, the property so taken into possession.

(c) During his or her possession, the personal representative is entitled to receive all rents, issues, and profits of the property. If the property is later determined not to be part of the estate of the decedent, the personal representative shall deliver the property, or cause it to be delivered, to the person legally entitled to it, together with all rents, issues, and profits of the property received by the personal representative, less any expenses incurred in protecting and maintaining the property and in collecting rents, issues, and profits. The personal representative may request court approval before delivering the property pursuant to this subdivision.

(d) The court may allow the personal representative reasonable compensation for services rendered in connection with the duties specified in this section as to property later determined not to be part of the estate of the decedent, if the court makes one of the following findings:

(1) The services were of benefit to the estate. If the court makes this finding, the compensation and the expenses and costs of litigation, including attorney's fees of the attorney hired by the personal representative to handle the matter, are a proper expense of administration.

(2) The services were essential to preserve, protect, and maintain the property. If the court makes this finding, the court shall award compensation and the expenses and costs of litigation, including attorney's fees of the attorney hired by the personal representative to handle the matter, as an expense deductible from the rents, issues, and profits received by the personal representative, or, if these are insufficient, as a lien against the property.
Ca. Prob. Code § 9651
Enacted by Stats. 1990, Ch. 79.

Section 9652 - Investment of cash

(a) Except as provided in subdivisions (b) and (c), the personal representative shall keep all cash in his or her possession invested in interest-bearing accounts or other investments authorized by law.
(b) The requirement of subdivision (a) does not apply to the amount of cash that is reasonably necessary for orderly administration of the estate.
(c) The requirement of subdivision (a) does not apply to the extent that the testator's will otherwise provides.
Ca. Prob. Code § 9652
Enacted by Stats. 1990, Ch. 79.

Section 9653 - Action for recovery of property of decedent for benefit of creditors

(a) On application of a creditor of the decedent or the estate, the personal representative shall commence and prosecute an action for the recovery of real or personal property of the decedent for the benefit of creditors if the personal representative has insufficient assets to pay creditors and the decedent during lifetime did any of the following with respect to the property:

(1) Made a conveyance of the property, or any right or interest in the property, that is voidable as to creditors under the Uniform Voidable Transactions Act (Chapter 1 (commencing with Section 3439) of Title 2 of Part 2 of Division 4 of the Civil Code).

(2) Made a gift of the property in view of impending death.

(3) Made a direction to transfer a vehicle, undocumented vessel, manufactured home, mobilehome, commercial coach, truck camper, or floating home to a designated beneficiary on the decedent's death pursuant to Section 18102.2 of the Health and Safety Code, or Section 5910.5 or 9916.5 of the Vehicle Code, and the property has been transferred as directed.
(b) A creditor making application under this section shall pay such part of the costs and expenses of the suit and attorney's fees, or give an undertaking to the personal representative for that purpose, as the personal representative and the creditor agree, or, absent an agreement, as the court or judge orders.
(c) The property recovered under this section shall be sold for the payment of debts in the same manner as if the decedent had died seized or possessed of the property. The proceeds of the sale shall be applied first to payment of the costs and expenses of suit, including attorney's fees, and then to payment of the debts of the decedent in the same manner as other property in possession of the personal representative. After all the debts of the decedent have been paid, the remainder of the proceeds shall be paid to the person from whom the property was recovered. The property may be sold in its entirety or in such portion as necessary to pay the debts.
Ca. Prob. Code § 9653
Amended by Stats 2015 ch 44 (SB 161),s 27, eff. 1/1/2016.

Section 9654 - Action for possession or to quiet title to property

The heirs or devisees may themselves, or jointly with the personal representative, maintain an action for possession of property or to quiet title to property against any person except the personal representative.

Ca. Prob. Code § 9654
Enacted by Stats. 1990, Ch. 79.

Section 9655 - Stock or memberships held by estate

With respect to a share of stock of a domestic or foreign corporation held in the estate, a membership in a nonprofit corporation held in the estate, or other property held in the estate, a personal representative may do any one or more of the following:

(a) Vote in person, and give proxies to exercise, any voting rights with respect to the share, membership, or other property.

(b) Waive notice of a meeting or give consent to the holding of a meeting.

(c) Authorize, ratify, approve, or confirm any action which could be taken by shareholders, members, or property owners.

Ca. Prob. Code § 9655
Enacted by Stats. 1990, Ch. 79.

Section 9656 - Insuring property of estate

The personal representative may insure the property of the estate against damage or loss and may insure himself or herself against liability to third persons.

Ca. Prob. Code § 9656
Enacted by Stats. 1990, Ch. 79.

Section 9657 - Profit or losses

The personal representative shall not make profit by the increase, nor suffer loss by the decrease or destruction without his or her fault, of any part of the estate.

Ca. Prob. Code § 9657
Enacted by Stats. 1990, Ch. 79.

Chapter 3 - DEPOSIT OF MONEY AND PERSONAL PROPERTY WITH FINANCIAL INSTITUTIONS

Section 9700 - Authority to deposit money of estate; withdrawal

The personal representative may deposit money of the estate in an insured account in a financial institution in this state. Unless otherwise provided by court order, the money may be withdrawn without order of the court.

Ca. Prob. Code § 9700
Enacted by Stats. 1990, Ch. 79.

Section 9701 - Authority to deposit personal property with trust company; withdrawal

The personal representative may deposit personal property of the estate with a trust company for safekeeping. Unless otherwise provided by court order, the personal property may be withdrawn without order of the court.

Ca. Prob. Code § 9701
Enacted by Stats. 1990, Ch. 79.

Section 9702 - Deposit of securities by trust company serving as personal representative

(a) A trust company serving as personal representative may deposit securities that constitute all or part of the estate in a securities depository, as provided in Section 1612 of the Financial Code.
(b) If securities have been deposited with a trust company by a personal representative pursuant to Section 9701, the trust company may deposit the securities in a securities depository, as provided in Section 1612 of the Financial Code.
(c) The securities depository may hold securities deposited with it in the manner authorized by Section 1612 of the Financial Code.

Ca. Prob. Code § 9702
Amended by Stats 2014 ch 71 (SB 1304),s 139, eff. 1/1/2015.

Section 9703 - Money or property subject to withdrawal only upon court order

(a) Upon application of the personal representative, the court may, with or without notice, order that money or other personal property be deposited pursuant to Section 9700 or 9701 and be subject to withdrawal only upon authorization of the court.

(b) The personal representative shall deliver a copy of the court order to the financial institution or trust company at the time the deposit is made.

(c) No financial institution or trust company accepting a deposit pursuant to Section 9700 or 9701 shall be on notice of the existence of an order that the money or other property is subject to withdrawal only upon authorization of the court unless it has actual notice of the order.

Ca. Prob. Code § 9703
Enacted by Stats. 1990, Ch. 79.

Section 9704 - Order for distribution of money or property deposited

When an order for distribution of money or personal property deposited pursuant to this chapter is made, the financial institution, trust company, or securities depository may deliver the property directly to the distributees and shall file receipts therefor with the clerk.

Ca. Prob. Code § 9704
Enacted by Stats. 1990, Ch. 79.

Section 9705 - Rate of interest on deposit of money by trust company serving as personal representative; deposit in checking account

(a) Subject to subdivision (b), where a trust company is a personal representative and in the exercise of reasonable judgment deposits money of the estate in an account in any department of the corporation or association of which it is a part, it is chargeable with interest thereon at the rate of interest prevailing among banks of the locality on such deposits.

(b) Where it is to the advantage of the estate, the amount of cash that is reasonably necessary for orderly administration of the estate may be deposited in a checking account that does not earn interest which is maintained in a department of the corporation or association of which the trust company is a part.

Ca. Prob. Code § 9705
Enacted by Stats. 1990, Ch. 79.

Chapter 4 - INVESTMENTS AND PURCHASE OF PROPERTY

Section 9730 - Allowed investments pending distribution

Pending distribution of the estate, the personal representative may invest money of the estate in possession of the personal representative in any one or more of the following:

(a) Direct obligations of the United States, or of the State of California, maturing not later than one year from the date of making the investment.

(b) An interest in a money market mutual fund registered under the Investment Company Act of 1940 (15 U.S.C. Sec. 80a-1, et seq.) or an investment vehicle authorized for the collective investment of trust funds pursuant to Section 9.18 of Part 9 of Title 12 of the Code of Federal Regulations, the portfolios of which are limited to United States government obligations maturing not later than five years from the date of investment and to repurchase agreements fully collateralized by United States government obligations.

(c) Units of a common trust fund described in Section 1585 of the Financial Code. The common trust fund shall have as its objective investment primarily in short term fixed income obligations and shall be permitted to value investments at cost pursuant to regulations of the appropriate regulatory authority.

Ca. Prob. Code § 9730
Amended by Stats 2014 ch 71 (SB 1304),s 140, eff. 1/1/2015.

Section 9731 - Investment in securities of United States or state ordered by court

(a) Pending distribution of the estate, upon a showing that it is to the advantage of the estate, the court may order that money of the estate in possession of the personal representative be invested in securities of the United States or of this state.

(b) To obtain an order under this section, the personal representative or any interested person shall file a petition stating the types of securities that are proposed to be purchased and the advantage to the estate of the purchase.

(c) Notice of the hearing on the petition shall be given as provided in Section 1220.

Ca. Prob. Code § 9731
Enacted by Stats. 1990, Ch. 79.

Section 9732 - Investment of money in manner provided by will ordered by court

(a) The court may order that money of the estate in possession of the personal representative be invested in any manner provided by the will if all of the following conditions are satisfied:

(1) The time for filing claims has expired.

(2) All debts, as defined in Section 11401, have been paid or are sufficiently secured by mortgage or otherwise, or there is sufficient cash in the estate aside from the money to be invested to pay all the debts, or the court is otherwise satisfied that all the debts will be paid.

(3) The estate is not in a condition to be finally distributed.

(b) To obtain an order under this section, the personal representative or any interested person shall file a petition showing the general condition of the estate and the types of investments that are proposed to be made.

(c) Notice of the hearing on the petition shall be delivered as provided in Section 1220. In addition, the petitioner shall cause notice of the hearing and a copy of the petition to be delivered pursuant to Section 1215 to all known devisees of property which is proposed to be invested. Where the property proposed to be invested is devised to a trust or trustee, notice of the hearing and a copy of the petition shall be delivered pursuant to Section 1215 to the trustee or, if the trustee has not yet accepted the trust, to the person named in the will as trustee. Delivery pursuant to this subdivision shall be to the person's last known address as provided in Section 1220.

(d) If no objection has been filed by an interested person, the court may make an order authorizing or directing the personal representative to invest such portion of the money of the estate as the court deems advisable in the types of investments proposed in the petition and authorized by the will. If there is no objection by an interested person and no substantial reason why some or all of the investment powers given by the will should not be exercised, the court shall make the order. The order may be for a limited period or until the administration of the estate is completed. Upon petition of the personal representative or any interested person, the order may be renewed, modified, or terminated at any time.

Ca. Prob. Code § 9732
Amended by Stats 2017 ch 319 (AB 976),s 76, eff. 1/1/2018.

Section 9733 - Purchase of annuity ordered by court

(a) Pending distribution of the estate or at the time the court makes an order for final distribution of the estate, on petition of the personal representative or any interested person, the court may, upon good cause shown, order that the personal representative purchase an annuity from an insurer admitted to do business in this state to satisfy a devise of an annuity or other direction in the will for periodic payments to a devisee.

(b) Notice of the hearing on the petition shall be given as provided in Section 1220.

Ca. Prob. Code § 9733
Enacted by Stats. 1990, Ch. 79.

Section 9734 - Exercise of option after court authorization

(a) If an asset of the estate consists of an option right, the personal representative may exercise the option after authorization by order of court upon a showing that the exercise would be to the advantage of the estate and would be in the best interest of the interested persons. The personal representative may use any funds or property in the estate to acquire the property covered by the option.

(b) A petition under this section may be filed by the personal representative or any interested person.

(c) Notice of the hearing on the petition shall be given as provided in Section 1220.

Ca. Prob. Code § 9734
Enacted by Stats. 1990, Ch. 79.

Section 9735 - Purchase of securities or commodities required to perform incomplete contract of sale

(a) After authorization by order of court, the personal representative may purchase securities or commodities required to perform an incomplete contract of sale where the decedent died having sold but not delivered securities or commodities not owned by the decedent. The court's order shall fix the terms and conditions of purchase.

(b) A petition under this section may be filed by the personal representative or by any party to the contract. Notice of the hearing on the petition shall be given as provided in Section 1220.

(c) No notice of hearing need be given where the maximum purchase price is fixed or where the securities or commodities are to be purchased on an established stock, bond, or commodity exchange.

Ca. Prob. Code § 9735
Enacted by Stats. 1990, Ch. 79.

Section 9736 - Holding security in name of nominee

The personal representative may hold a security in the name of a nominee or in any other form without disclosure of the estate so that title to the security may pass by delivery.

Ca. Prob. Code § 9736
Enacted by Stats. 1990, Ch. 79.

Section 9737 - Exercise of subscription rights to purchase additional securities

(a) If an estate by reason of owning securities also owns or receives subscription rights for the purchase of additional securities, the personal representative may exercise the subscription rights after authorization by order of court upon a showing that it is to the advantage of the estate.

(b) To obtain an order under this section, the personal representative or any interested person shall file a petition stating the nature of the subscription rights and the advantage to the estate of exercising them.

(c) Notice of the hearing on the petition shall be given as provided in Section 1220.

Ca. Prob. Code § 9737
Enacted by Stats. 1990, Ch. 79.

Chapter 5 - OPERATION OF DECEDENT'S BUSINESS

Section 9760 - Decedent's business defined; Authority to continue operation; petition requesting order authorizing continued operation

(a) As used in this section, "decedent's business" means an unincorporated business or venture in which the decedent was engaged or which was wholly or partly owned by the decedent at the time of the decedent's death, but does not include a business operated by a partnership in which the decedent was a partner.

(b) If it is to the advantage of the estate and in the best interest of the interested persons, the personal representative, with or without court authorization, may continue the operation of the decedent's business; but the personal representative may not continue the operation of the decedent's business for a period of more than six months from the date letters are first issued to a personal representative unless a court order has been obtained under this section authorizing the personal representative to continue the operation of the business.

(c) The personal representative or any interested person may file a petition requesting an order (1) authorizing the personal representative to continue the operation of the decedent's business or (2) directing the personal representative to discontinue the operation of the decedent's business. The petition shall show the advantage to the estate and the benefit to the interested persons of the order requested. Notice of the hearing on the petition shall be given as provided in Section 1220.

(d) If a petition is filed under this section, the court may make an order that either:

(1) Authorizes the personal representative to continue the operation of the decedent's business to such an extent and subject to such restrictions as the court determines to be to the advantage of the estate and in the best interest of the interested persons.

(2) Directs the personal representative to discontinue the operation of the decedent's business within the time specified in, and in accordance with the provisions of, the order.

Ca. Prob. Code § 9760
Enacted by Stats. 1990, Ch. 79.

Section 9761 - Accounting rendered by surviving partner

If a partnership existed between the decedent and another person at the time of the decedent's death, on application of the personal representative, the court may order any surviving partner to render an account pursuant to Section 15510, 15634, or 16807 of the Corporations Code. An order under this section may be enforced by the court's power to punish for contempt.

Ca. Prob. Code § 9761
Amended by Stats 2003 ch 32 (AB 167), s 8, eff. 1/1/2004.

Section 9762 - Participation in partnership

(a) After authorization by order of court upon a showing that it would be to the advantage of the estate and in the best interest of the interested persons, the personal representative may continue as a general or a limited partner in any partnership in which the decedent was a general partner at the time of death. In its order, the court may specify any terms and conditions of the personal representative's participation as a partner that the court determines are to the advantage of the estate and in the best interest of the interested persons, but any terms and conditions that are inconsistent with the terms of any written partnership agreement are subject to the written consent of all of the surviving partners.

(b) If there is a written partnership agreement permitting the decedent's personal representative to participate as a partner, the personal representative has all the rights, powers, duties, and obligations provided in the written partnership agreement, except as otherwise ordered by the court pursuant to subdivision (a).

(c) If there is not a written partnership agreement, the personal representative has the rights, powers, duties, and obligations that the court specifies in its order pursuant to subdivision (a).

(d) To obtain an order under this section, the personal representative or any interested person shall file a petition showing that the order requested would be to the advantage of the estate and in the best interest of the interested persons. Notice of the hearing on the petition shall be given as provided in Section 1220. In addition, unless the court otherwise orders, the petitioner, not less than 15 days before the hearing, shall cause notice of hearing and a copy of the petition to be delivered pursuant to Section 1215 to each of the surviving general partners at his or her last known address.

Ca. Prob. Code § 9762
Amended by Stats 2017 ch 319 (AB 976),s 77, eff. 1/1/2018.

Section 9763 - Action against surviving partner that decedent could have commenced; rights as limited partner

(a) If the decedent was a general partner, the personal representative may commence and maintain any action against the surviving partner that the decedent could have commenced and maintained.

(b) The personal representative may exercise the decedent's rights as a limited partner as provided in Section 15675 of the Corporations Code.

Ca. Prob. Code § 9763
Enacted by Stats. 1990, Ch. 79.

Section 9764 - Petition for appointment of active member of State Bar to take control of deceased attorney's files and assets

(a) The personal representative of the estate of a deceased attorney who was engaged in a practice of law at the time of his or her death or other person interested in the estate may bring a petition for appointment of an active member of the State Bar of California to take control of the files and assets of the practice of the deceased member.

(b) The petition may be filed and heard on such notice that the court determines is in the best interests of the estate of the deceased member. If the petition alleges that the immediate appointment of a practice administrator is required to safeguard the interests of the estate, the court may dispense with notice only if the personal representative is the petitioner or has joined in the petition or has otherwise waived notice of hearing on the petition.

(c) The petition shall indicate the powers sought for the practice administrator from the list of powers set forth in Section 6185 of the Business and Professions Code. These powers shall be specifically listed in the order appointing the practice administrator.

(d) The petition shall allege the value of the assets that are to come under the control of the practice administrator, including, but not limited by the amount of funds in all accounts used by the deceased member. The court shall require the filing of a surety bond in the amount of the value of the personal property to be filed with the court by the practice administrator. No action may be taken by the practice administrator unless a bond has been fully filed with the court.

(e) The practice administrator shall not be the attorney representing the personal representative.

(f) The court shall appoint the attorney nominated by the deceased member in a writing, including, but not limited to, the deceased member's will, unless the court concludes that the appointment of the nominated person would be contrary to the best interests of the estate or would create a conflict of interest with any of the clients of the deceased member.

(g) The practice administrator shall be compensated only upon order of the court making the appointment for his or her reasonable and necessary services. The law practice shall be the source of the compensation for the practice administrator unless the assets are insufficient in which case, the compensation of the practice administrator shall be charged against the assets of the estate as a cost of administration. The practice administrator shall also be entitled to reimbursement of his or her costs.

(h) Upon conclusion of the services of the practice administrator, the practice administrator shall render an accounting and petition for its approval by the superior court making the appointment. Upon settlement of the accounting, the practice administrator shall be discharged and the surety on his or her bond exonerated.

(i) For the purposes of this section, the person appointed to take control of the practice of the deceased member shall be referred to as the "practice administrator" and the decedent shall be referred to as the "deceased member."

Ca. Prob. Code § 9764

Added by Stats. 1998, Ch. 682, Sec. 5. Effective January 1, 1999.

Section 9765 - Replacement of deceased professional fiduciary

(a) Commencing January 1, 2024, a professional fiduciary is deceased and a vacancy exists, the deceased fiduciary's conservator, agent under power of attorney for asset management, trustee, or interested person may petition for the appointment of one or more individuals, qualified to act as a professional fiduciary under the Professional Fiduciaries Act (Chapter 6 (commencing with Section 6500) of Division 3 of the Business and Professions Code), as a professional fiduciary practice administrator, to take control of the deceased professional fiduciary's files and to be appointed as temporary successor as to those matters for which a vacancy exists as a result of the professional fiduciary's death.

(b) The petition shall request an order appointing a professional fiduciary practice administrator as temporary successor, with all of the powers and duties held by the deceased fiduciary, in each matter in which the deceased fiduciary was acting in a representative capacity, including guardianships of the estate, conservatorships of the person and estate, decedent's estates, court-supervised trusts, and non-court-supervised trusts.

(c) The court shall require the professional fiduciary practice administrator to file a surety bond in each matter in which the professional fiduciary practice administrator is appointed temporary successor, in the amount currently required of the deceased fiduciary or in another amount as the court deems appropriate.

(d) The court may appoint as the professional fiduciary practice administrator the professional fiduciary nominated by the deceased professional fiduciary in a writing, including, but not limited to, the decedent's will or trust, or in the absence thereof, the person nominated by the person having legal standing to act on behalf of the deceased professional fiduciary. The court shall not make the appointment if the court concludes that the appointment of the nominated person would be contrary to the best interests of, or would create a conflict of interest with, any interested party in a matter in which the deceased fiduciary was acting in a fiduciary capacity.

(e) The appointment of the professional fiduciary practice administrator as temporary successor shall terminate, in each of the matters in which the professional fiduciary practice administrator was appointed as temporary successor, 45 days after the entry of the order appointing the professional fiduciary practice administrator, or earlier if another person is appointed.

(f) Notice of the hearing on the petition for appointment of a professional fiduciary practice administrator as temporary successor shall be given to all persons entitled to notice in each of the matters that are the subject of the petition. The court may dispense with notice if the court determines that the immediate appointment of a professional fiduciary practice administrator is required to safeguard the interests of an individual or an asset in a matter in which the deceased fiduciary was acting in a representative capacity.

(g) The professional fiduciary practice administrator shall be compensated for services provided and reimbursement of costs incurred in each matter solely from the assets of that matter subject to the provisions of the applicable document or as determined by the court, and in no event more than the incapacitated fiduciary would have been paid.

(h) The professional fiduciary practice administrator shall do all of the following:

(1) File a copy of the order appointing the professional fiduciary practice administrator as temporary successor in each of the matters in which the court appoints the professional fiduciary practice administrator as temporary successor.

(2) Take control and review all files and writings maintained by the deceased fiduciary for matters in which the deceased fiduciary was acting in a representative capacity.

(3) Within 15 days after the entry of the order appointing the professional fiduciary practice administrator as temporary successor, provide written notice to all interested parties as to each matter in which the deceased fiduciary was acting in a representative capacity who can be reasonably ascertained and located to inform those parties of the appointment of the professional fiduciary practice administrator as temporary successor. The notice shall advise the parties of the need for the appointment for a permanent successor, which shall include the following:

(A) The right of the parties to petition the court for the appointment of a permanent successor.

(B) The right of any interested party to nominate an individual to act as permanent successor, and then the obligation of the professional fiduciary practice administrator to petition for the appointment of the individual nominated, provided an interested party provides the professional fiduciary practice administrator with the name of their nominee within 15 days after the date notice was given.

(C) The ability of the professional fiduciary practice administrator, in the event that none of the interested parties act within the time prescribed above, under subparagraph (A) or (B), to petition the court for appointment of a permanent successor.

(4) Upon the court's appointment of a permanent successor, the professional fiduciary practice administrator shall file an account and report on behalf of the deceased fiduciary for any period of time the deceased fiduciary would have been required to account, as well as for the period of time the professional fiduciary practice administrator served as temporary successor. As part of that account and report, the professional fiduciary practice administrator may request compensation both on behalf of the deceased fiduciary, for services rendered prior to their death, and on their own behalf for services rendered after the deceased fiduciary's death as temporary successor, subject to any limitation on fees and costs that existed for the deceased fiduciary, and may request discharge and exoneration of bond. The account filed for the period during which the matter was administered by the now deceased fiduciary may be verified on information and belief.

(5) Comply with any other obligations imposed by the court.
(i) Each of the time periods prescribed in this section may be extended by the court if the court determines that good cause exists, and if the court determines that the extension is in the best interest of the minor, the conservatee, the decedent's estate, or the current income beneficiaries under a trust, as applicable.
(j) For purposes of this section, the following definitions apply:

(1)"Professional fiduciary practice administrator" means the person appointed pursuant to this section to take over the responsibilities from the deceased fiduciary.

(2)"Vacancy" means that the instrument under which the deceased fiduciary was acting does not name a successor to fill the vacancy, the instrument under which the deceased fiduciary was acting does not provide a nonjudicial method to fill the vacancy, and a cofiduciary, authorized to act solely, was not acting with the deceased fiduciary.

(k) This section does not limit the authority granted to the court under subdivision (j) of Section 2250, Section 8523, and subdivision (e) of Section 15642.

(l) The Judicial Council shall create or revise any forms or rules necessary to implement this section no later than January 1, 2024.

Ca. Prob. Code § 9765
Added by Stats 2022 ch 612 (SB 1024),s 5, eff. 1/1/2023.

Chapter 6 - ABANDONMENT OF TANGIBLE PERSONAL PROPERTY

Section 9780 - Authority to dispose of abandoned tangible personal property

Unless the property is specifically devised, subject to the requirements of this chapter, the personal representative may dispose of or abandon tangible personal property where the cost of collecting, maintaining, and safeguarding the property would exceed its fair market value.

Ca. Prob. Code § 9780
Enacted by Stats. 1990, Ch. 79.

Section 9781 - Exercise of power to dispose without court authorization

Unless otherwise provided in the will, subject to the requirements of this chapter, the personal representative may exercise the power provided in Section 9780 without court authorization or approval.

Ca. Prob. Code § 9781
Enacted by Stats. 1990, Ch. 79.

Section 9782 - Notice of proposed disposition

(a) Except as provided in Section 9785, before disposing of or abandoning property under Section 9780, the personal representative shall give notice of the proposed disposition or abandonment as provided in subdivision (c) to all of the following:

(1) Each known devisee whose interest in the estate would be affected by the proposed action.

(2) Each known heir whose interest in the estate would be affected by the proposed action.

(3) Each person who has filed a request for special notice pursuant to Section 1250.

(4) The Attorney General, at the office of the Attorney General in Sacramento, if any portion of the estate is to escheat to the state and its interest in the estate would be affected by the proposed action.
(b) The notice of the proposed disposition or abandonment shall describe the property to be disposed of or abandoned, indicate the manner in which the property is to be disposed of or abandoned, and specify the date on or after which the property will be disposed of or abandoned.
(c) The notice shall be delivered personally to each person required to be given notice or shall be sent by mail to the person at the person's last known address. If the notice is delivered personally, it shall be delivered to the person not less than five days before the date specified in the notice as the date on or after which the property will be disposed of or abandoned. If the notice is sent by mail, it shall be deposited in the mail not less than 10 days before the date specified in the notice as the date on or after which the property will be disposed of or abandoned.

Ca. Prob. Code § 9782
Enacted by Stats. 1990, Ch. 79.

Section 9783 - Objection to proposed disposition

A person described in Section 9782 may personally deliver or mail a written objection to the disposition or abandonment to the personal representative on or before the date specified in the notice as the date on or after which the property will be disposed of or abandoned. Subject to Section 9788, after receipt of the written objection, the personal representative shall not dispose of or abandon the property without authorization by order of the court obtained under Section 9611.

Ca. Prob. Code § 9783
Amended by Stats 2017 ch 319 (AB 976),s 78, eff. 1/1/2018.

Section 9784 - Application for order restraining proposed disposition

(a) A person described in Section 9782 who objects to the disposition or abandonment of property by the personal representative under Section 9780 may apply to the court in which proceedings for administration of the estate are pending for an order restraining the personal representative from disposing of or abandoning the property without prior court authorization.

(b) The court shall grant the requested order without requiring notice to the personal representative and without cause being shown for the order if the court is satisfied that the estate will not suffer any loss or unreasonable expense if the order is granted. As a condition of granting the order, the court may require the person applying for the order (1) to pay the costs of storing and protecting the property or (2) to provide security by bond or cash deposit that the costs will be paid.

(c) The personal representative is deemed to have notice of the restraining order if it is served upon the personal representative in the manner provided in Section 415.10 or 415.30 of the Code of Civil Procedure, or in the manner authorized by the court, before the date specified in the notice as the date on or after which the property will be disposed of or abandoned.

Ca. Prob. Code § 9784
Enacted by Stats. 1990, Ch. 79.

Section 9785 - Notice not given to persons consenting to disposition or waiving right to notice

Notice of the proposed disposition or abandonment need not be given to any of the following:

(a) A person who consents in writing to the proposed disposition or abandonment.

(b) A person who, in writing, waives the right to notice of the proposed disposition or abandonment.

Ca. Prob. Code § 9785
Enacted by Stats. 1990, Ch. 79.

Section 9786 - Notice of court hearing on petition for court authorization

A person who objects to the disposition or abandonment as provided in Section 9783, or who serves a restraining order issued under Section 9784 in the manner provided in that section, shall be given notice of any court hearing on a petition for court authorization of the disposition or abandonment of the property.

Ca. Prob. Code § 9786
Enacted by Stats. 1990, Ch. 79.

Section 9787 - Court review of disposition

(a) Except as provided in subdivision (b), a person described in Section 9782 who receives notice of the proposed disposition or abandonment as provided in Section 9782, waives the right to have the court later review the disposition or abandonment of the property unless the person does one of the following:

(1) Personally delivers or mails a written objection as provided in Section 9783.

(2) Serves a restraining order obtained under Section 9784 before whichever of the following is the later time:

(A) The date specified in the notice of proposed disposition or abandonment as the date on or after which the property will be disposed of or abandoned.

(B) The date the property has actually been disposed of or abandoned.

(b) Subject to Section 9785, the court may review the disposition or abandonment of the property upon the motion of a person described in subdivision (a) of Section 9782 who establishes that he or she did not actually receive notice of the proposed disposition or abandonment before the time to object expired.

Ca. Prob. Code § 9787

Amended by Stats 2017 ch 319 (AB 976),s 79, eff. 1/1/2018.

Section 9788 - Possession of property by person objecting to disposition at request of personal representative

(a) Notwithstanding Sections 9783 and 9784, the personal representative may abandon or dispose of the property without court authorization if the person who made the objection or obtained the restraining order fails to take possession of the property at his or her expense within 10 days after the personal representative requests that the person do so.

(b) A person who takes possession of estate property pursuant to this section is liable for the safekeeping of the property until a court order is made relieving the person of this obligation.

Ca. Prob. Code § 9788

Enacted by Stats. 1990, Ch. 79.

Chapter 7 - BORROWING, REFINANCING, AND ENCUMBERING PROPERTY

Section 9800 - Court order authorizing

(a) Subject to subdivision (c), after authorization by order of court obtained under this chapter upon a showing that it would be to the advantage of the estate, the personal representative may borrow money on a note, either unsecured or to be secured by a security interest or other lien on the personal property of the estate, or any part thereof, or to be secured by a mortgage or deed of trust on the real property of the estate, or any part thereof, and may give a security interest or other lien on the personal property of the estate, or any part thereof, or a mortgage or deed of trust on the real property of the estate, or any part thereof, in order to do any one or more of the following:

(1) Pay the debts of the decedent or the estate, devises, expenses of administration, and charges against the estate.

(2) Pay, reduce, extend, or renew a security interest or lien or mortgage or deed of trust already existing on property of the estate.

(3) Improve, use, operate, or preserve property in the estate.
(b) The personal representative shall apply the money to the purpose specified in the order.
(c) Where the surviving spouse has elected to have his or her share of the community real property administered in the decedent's estate, the personal representative is authorized to borrow money to be secured by a mortgage or deed of trust on the community real property of the estate, or any part thereof, only with the written consent of the surviving spouse.

Ca. Prob. Code § 9800
Enacted by Stats. 1990, Ch. 79.

Section 9801 - Undivided interest in property less than entire ownership

If property of the estate consists of an undivided interest in real or personal property, or any other interest therein less than the entire ownership, upon a showing that it would be to the advantage of the estate to borrow money to improve, use, operate, or preserve the property jointly with the owners of the other interests therein, or to pay, reduce, extend, or renew a security interest, lien, mortgage, or deed of trust already existing on all of the property, the personal representative, after authorization by order of the court obtained under this chapter, may join with the owners of the other interests in borrowing money and the execution of a joint and several note and such security interest, lien, mortgage, or deed of trust as may be required to secure the payment of the note. The note may be for such sum as is required for the purpose.

Ca. Prob. Code § 9801
Enacted by Stats. 1990, Ch. 79.

Section 9802 - Petition for order

(a) The personal representative or any interested person may file a petition for an order under this chapter.

(b) The petition shall state the purpose for which the order is sought and the necessity for or the advantage to accrue from the order. If applicable, the petition shall also show the amount of money proposed to be borrowed, the rate of interest to be paid, the length of time the note is to run, and a general description of the property proposed to be mortgaged or subjected to the deed of trust, security interest, or other lien.

Ca. Prob. Code § 9802
Enacted by Stats. 1990, Ch. 79.

Section 9803 - Notice of hearing

Notice of the hearing on the petition shall be given as provided in Section 1220.

Ca. Prob. Code § 9803
Enacted by Stats. 1990, Ch. 79.

Section 9804 - Order authorizing or requiring personal representative

(a) Subject to subdivision (c), if the court is satisfied that it will be to the advantage of the estate, the court shall make an order that authorizes or requires that the personal representative do any one or more of the following:

(1) Borrow money and execute a note.

(2) Execute a mortgage or deed of trust or give other security by security interest or other lien.

(3) Pay, reduce, extend, or renew a security interest or lien or mortgage or deed of trust already existing upon property of the estate.

(b) The court in its order may do any one or more of the following:

(1) Order that the amount specified in the petition, or a lesser amount, be borrowed.

(2) Prescribe the maximum rate of interest and the period of the loan.

(3) Require that the interest and the whole or any part of the principal be paid from time to time out of the whole estate or any part thereof.

(4) Require that the personal property used as security, or any buildings on real property to be mortgaged or subjected to the deed of trust, be insured for the further security of the lender and that the premiums be paid out of the estate.

(5) Specify the purpose for which the money to be borrowed is to be applied.

(6) Specify the terms and conditions of any extension or renewal agreement.

(7) Prescribe such other terms and conditions concerning the transaction as the court determines to be to the advantage of the estate.

(c) Where the surviving spouse has elected to have his or her share of the community real property administered in the decedent's estate, an order authorizing or requiring the personal representative to borrow money to be secured by a mortgage or deed of trust upon the community real property of the estate, or any part thereof, may be made only if the written consent of the surviving spouse has been filed with the court.

Ca. Prob. Code § 9804
Enacted by Stats. 1990, Ch. 79.

Section 9805 - Execution and delivery of mortgage or deed of trust

(a) The personal representative shall execute and deliver the mortgage or deed of trust, or execute and deliver the instrument creating the security interest, setting forth therein that it is made by authority of the order, giving the date of the order.

(b) The note and the mortgage or deed of trust or other instrument creating the security interest, if any, shall be signed by the personal representative and shall be acknowledged by the personal representative if the instrument creates a lien on real property.

Ca. Prob. Code § 9805
Enacted by Stats. 1990, Ch. 79.

Section 9806 - Mortgage, deed of trust or security interest made pursuant to court order

(a) Every mortgage, deed of trust, or security interest made pursuant to a court order obtained under this chapter is effectual to mortgage, or to subject to the deed of trust or security interest, all of the following:

(1) All right, title, and interest which the decedent had to the property described therein at the time of the decedent's death.

(2) Any right, title, or interest in the property acquired by the estate of the decedent, by operation of law or otherwise, since the time of the decedent's death.

(3) Any right, title, or interest in the community real property belonging to the decedent's surviving spouse whose written consent has been filed with the court and which is referred to in the court order obtained under this chapter.

(b) Jurisdiction of the court to administer the estate of the decedent vests the court with jurisdiction to make the order for the note and for the security interest, lien, mortgage, or deed of trust. This jurisdiction shall conclusively inure to the benefit of the owner of the security interest or lien, mortgagee named in the mortgage, or the trustee and beneficiary named in the deed of trust, and their heirs and assigns.

(c) No omission, error, or irregularity in the proceedings under this chapter shall impair or invalidate the proceedings or the note, security interest, lien, mortgage, or deed of trust given pursuant to an order under this chapter. Subject to Section 9807, the owner of the security interest or lien, the mortgagee named in the mortgage, or the trustee and beneficiary named in the deed of trust, and their heirs and assigns, have and possess the same rights and remedies on the note and the security interest or lien or mortgage or deed of trust as if it had been made by the decedent prior to his or her death.

Ca. Prob. Code § 9806
Enacted by Stats. 1990, Ch. 79.

Section 9807 - Judgment or claim for deficiency

(a) Except as provided in subdivision (b), no judgment or claim for any deficiency shall be had or allowed against the personal representative or the estate if (1) there is a foreclosure or sale under a security interest, lien, mortgage, or deed of trust and (2) the proceeds of sale of the encumbered property are insufficient to pay the note, the security interest, lien, mortgage, or deed of trust, and the costs or expenses of sale.

(b) If the note, security interest, mortgage, or deed of trust was given to pay, reduce, extend, or renew a lien, security interest, mortgage, or deed of trust existing on property of the estate at the time of death of the decedent and the indebtedness secured thereby was a claim established under Part 4 (commencing with Section 9000), the part of the indebtedness remaining unsatisfied shall be classed with other established claims.

Ca. Prob. Code § 9807
Enacted by Stats. 1990, Ch. 79.

Chapter 8 - ACTIONS AND PROCEEDINGS BY OR AGAINST PERSONAL REPRESENTATIVE

Section 9820 - Authority to commenced or defend actions

The personal representative may:
(a) Commence and maintain actions and proceedings for the benefit of the estate.
(b) Defend actions and proceedings against the decedent, the

personal representative, or the estate.

Ca. Prob. Code § 9820

Enacted by Stats. 1990, Ch. 79.

Section 9822 - Action on bond of former personal representative

The personal representative may bring an action on the bond of any former personal representative of the same estate, for the use and benefit of all interested persons.

Ca. Prob. Code § 9822

Enacted by Stats. 1990, Ch. 79.

Section 9823 - Action for partition

(a) If the decedent leaves an undivided interest in any property, an action for partition of the property may be brought against the personal representative.

(b) The personal representative may bring an action against the other cotenants for partition of any property in which the decedent left an undivided interest.

Ca. Prob. Code § 9823

Enacted by Stats. 1990, Ch. 79.

Chapter 9 - COMPROMISE OF CLAIMS AND ACTIONS; EXTENSION, RENEWAL, OR MODIFICATION OF OBLIGATIONS

Section 9830 - Authority without court authorization, instruction, approval or confirmation

(a) Unless this chapter or some other applicable statute requires court authorization or approval, if it is to the advantage of the estate, the personal representative may do any of the following without court authorization, instruction, approval, or confirmation:

(1) Compromise or settle a claim, action, or proceeding by or for the benefit of, or against, the decedent, the personal representative, or the estate, including the giving of a covenant not to sue.

(2) Extend, renew, or in any manner modify the terms of an obligation owing to or in favor of the decedent or the estate.

(3) Release, in whole or in part, any claim belonging to the estate to the extent that the claim is uncollectible.

(b) Nothing in this section precludes the personal representative from seeking court authorization pursuant to the provisions of this chapter.

(c) Upon petition of an interested person or upon the court's own motion, the court may limit the authority of the personal representative under subdivision (a). Notice of the hearing on the petition shall be given as provided in Section 1220.

Ca. Prob. Code § 9830
Enacted by Stats. 1990, Ch. 79.

Section 9831 - Court authorization required for compromise or settlement of claim, action or proceeding

Unless the time for filing creditor claims has expired, authorization by order of court is required for a compromise or settlement of a claim, action, or proceeding by or for the benefit of, or against, the decedent, the personal representative, or the estate.

Ca. Prob. Code § 9831
Enacted by Stats. 1990, Ch. 79.

Section 9832 - Court authorization required compromise, settlement, extension, renewal or modification

(a) Except as provided in subdivision (b), authorization by order of court is required for a compromise, settlement, extension, renewal, or modification which affects any of the following:

(1) Title to real property.

(2) An interest in real property or a lien or encumbrance on real property.

(3) An option to purchase real property or an interest in real property.

(b) If it is to the advantage of the estate, the personal representative without prior court authorization may extend, renew, or modify a lease of real property in either of the following cases:

(1) Where under the lease as extended, renewed, or modified the rental does not exceed five thousand dollars ($5,000) a month and the term does not exceed one year.

(2) Where the lease is from month to month, regardless of the amount of the rental.

(c) For the purposes of subdivision (b), if the lease as extended, renewed, or modified gives the lessee the right to extend the term of the lease, the length of the term shall be considered as though the right to extend had been exercised.

Ca. Prob. Code § 9832

Amended by Stats. 1990, Ch. 710, Sec. 24. Operative July 1, 1991, by Sec. 48 of Ch. 710.

Section 9833 - Transaction amount or value in excess of $25 000

Authorization by order of court is required for a compromise or settlement of a matter when the transaction requires the transfer or encumbrance of property of the estate, or the creation of an unsecured liability of the estate, or both, in an amount or value in excess of twenty-five thousand dollars ($25,000).

Ca. Prob. Code § 9833

Enacted by Stats. 1990, Ch. 79.

Section 9834 - Claim against or debt of personal representative

Authorization by order of court is required for any of the following:

(a) A compromise or settlement of a claim by the estate against the personal representative or the personal representative's attorney, whether or not the claim arises out of the administration of the estate.

(b) An extension, renewal, or modification of the terms of a debt or similar obligation of the personal representative, or the personal representative's attorney, owing to, or in favor of, the estate.

Ca. Prob. Code § 9834
Enacted by Stats. 1990, Ch. 79.

Section 9835 - Wrongful death or injury of decedent

Authorization by order of court is required for the compromise or settlement of a claim or right of action given to the personal representative by any law for the wrongful death or injury of the decedent, including any action brought by the personal representative in attempting enforcement of the claim or right of action. Authorization to compromise or settle the claim or right of action includes authorization to give a covenant not to sue.

Ca. Prob. Code § 9835
Enacted by Stats. 1990, Ch. 79.

Section 9836 - Venue for obtaining court authorization

The court authorization required by this chapter shall be obtained from the court in which the estate is being administered.

Ca. Prob. Code § 9836
Enacted by Stats. 1990, Ch. 79.

Section 9837 - Petition for order

(a) A petition for an order authorizing a compromise, settlement, extension, renewal, or modification under this chapter may be filed by any of the following:

(1) The personal representative.

(2) Any interested person who has obtained the written approval of the personal representative to file the petition.

(b) The petition shall show the terms of the compromise, settlement, extension, renewal, or modification and its advantage to the estate.

(c) Notice of the hearing on the petition shall be given as provided in Section 1220.

Ca. Prob. Code § 9837

Enacted by Stats. 1990, Ch. 79.

Section 9838 - Conveyance when order requires transfer of real property

(a) If an order made under Section 9837 authorizes a compromise or settlement that requires the transfer of real property of the estate, the personal representative shall execute a conveyance of the real property to the person entitled thereto under the compromise or settlement. The conveyance shall refer to the order authorizing the compromise or settlement and directing that the conveyance be executed. A certified copy of the order shall be recorded in the office of the county recorder in each county in which any portion of the real property is located.

(b) A conveyance made in compliance with the court order authorizing the compromise or settlement and directing the conveyance to be executed vests in the person to whom the property is transferred both of the following:

(1) All the right, title, and interest which the decedent had in the property at the time of the decedent's death.

(2) Any other or additional right, title, or interest in the property acquired by the estate of the decedent, by operation of law or otherwise, prior to the transfer.

Ca. Prob. Code § 9838

Enacted by Stats. 1990, Ch. 79.

Section 9839 - Accounts credited for amount actually paid

If the personal representative pays a claim for less than its full amount, the personal representative's accounts may be credited only for the amount actually paid.

Ca. Prob. Code § 9839
Enacted by Stats. 1990, Ch. 79.

Chapter 10 - ACCEPTANCE OF DEED IN LIEU OF FORECLOSURE OR TRUSTEE'S SALE; GRANT OF PARTIAL SATISFACTION OR PARTIAL RECONVEYANCE

Section 9850 - Court order required

(a) If it is to the advantage of the estate to accept a deed to property which is subject to a mortgage or deed of trust in lieu of foreclosure of the mortgage or sale under the deed of trust, the personal representative may, after authorization by order of the court and upon such terms and conditions as may be imposed by the court, accept a deed conveying the property to the heirs or devisees of the decedent, subject to administration.
(b) To obtain an order under this section, the personal representative or any interested person shall file a petition showing the advantage to the estate of accepting the deed. Notice of the hearing on the petition shall be given as provided in Section 1220.
(c) The court shall make an order under this section only if the advantage to the estate of accepting the deed is shown by clear and convincing evidence.
Ca. Prob. Code § 9850
Enacted by Stats. 1990, Ch. 79.

Section 9851 - Partial satisfaction or partial reconveyance

(a) Except as provided in subdivision (c), if it is to the advantage of the estate for the personal representative to give a partial satisfaction of a mortgage or to cause a partial reconveyance to be executed by a trustee under a trust deed held by the estate, the personal representative may, after authorization by order of the court and upon such terms and conditions as may be imposed by the court, give the partial satisfaction or cause the partial reconveyance to be executed by the trustee.
(b) To obtain an order under this section, the personal representative or any interested person shall file a petition showing the advantage to the estate of giving the partial satisfaction or

causing the partial reconveyance. Notice of the hearing on the petition shall be given as provided in Section 1220.

(c) No authorization by the court is necessary for the personal representative to give a partial satisfaction of a mortgage or to cause a partial reconveyance to be executed by a trustee under a deed of trust held by the estate if the partial satisfaction or partial reconveyance is executed pursuant to the terms of the mortgage or deed of trust held by the estate.

Ca. Prob. Code § 9851
Enacted by Stats. 1990, Ch. 79.

Chapter 11 - CONVEYANCE OR TRANSFER OF PROPERTY CLAIMED TO BELONG TO DECEDENT OR OTHER PERSON

Section 9860 through 9869 - [Repealed]

Ca. Prob. Code § 9860 through 9869
Repealed by Stats 2001 ch 49 (SB 669), s 4, eff. 1/1/2002.

Chapter 12 - PURCHASE OF CLAIMS OR ESTATE PROPERTY BY PERSONAL REPRESENTATIVE OR PERSONAL REPRESENTATIVE'S ATTORNEY

Section 9880 - Direct or indirect purchase or interest in purchase prohibited

Except as provided in this chapter, neither the personal representative nor the personal representative's attorney may do any of the following:

(a) Purchase any property of the estate or any claim against the estate, directly or indirectly.

(b) Be interested in any such purchase.

Ca. Prob. Code § 9880
Enacted by Stats. 1990, Ch. 79.

Section 9881 - Requirements for order authorizing purchase

Upon a petition filed under Section 9883, the court may make an order under this section authorizing the personal representative or the personal representative's attorney to purchase property of the estate if all of the following requirements are satisfied:

(a) Written consent to the purchase is signed by (1) each known heir whose interest in the estate would be affected by the proposed purchase and (2) each known devisee whose interest in the estate would be affected by the proposed purchase.

(b) The written consents are filed with the court.

(c) The purchase is shown to be to the advantage of the estate.

Ca. Prob. Code § 9881

Enacted by Stats. 1990, Ch. 79.

Section 9882 - Will authorizes purchase

Upon a petition filed under Section 9883, the court may make an order under this section authorizing the personal representative or the personal representative's attorney to purchase property of the estate if the will of the decedent authorizes the personal representative or the personal representative's attorney to purchase the property.

Ca. Prob. Code § 9882

Enacted by Stats. 1990, Ch. 79.

Section 9883 - Petition requesting order

(a) The personal representative may file a petition requesting that the court make an order under Section 9881 or 9882. The petition shall set forth the facts upon which the request for the order is based.

(b) If court confirmation of the sale is required, the court may make its order under Section 9881 or 9882 at the time of the confirmation.

(c) Notice of the hearing on the petition shall be given as provided in Section 1220 to all of the following persons:

(1) Each person listed in Section 1220.

(2) Each known heir whose interest in the estate would be affected by the proposed purchase.

(3) Each known devisee whose interest in the estate would be affected by the proposed purchase.

(d) If the court is satisfied that the purchase should be authorized, the court shall make an order authorizing the purchase upon the terms and conditions specified in the order, and the personal representative may execute a conveyance or transfer according to the terms of the order. Unless otherwise provided in the will or in the order of the court, the sale of the property shall be made in the same manner as the sale of other estate property of the same nature.

Ca. Prob. Code § 9883
Enacted by Stats. 1990, Ch. 79.

Section 9884 - Purchase pursuant to contract made during lifetime of decedent

This chapter does not prohibit the purchase of property of the estate by the personal representative or the personal representative's attorney pursuant to a contract in writing made during the lifetime of the decedent if the contract is one that can be specifically enforced and the requirements of Part 19 (commencing with Section 850) of Division 2 are satisfied.

Ca. Prob. Code § 9884
Amended by Stats 2003 ch 32 (AB 167), s 9, eff. 1/1/2004.

Section 9885 - Exercise of option to purchase

This chapter does not prevent the exercise by the personal representative or the personal representative's attorney of an option to purchase property of the estate given in the will of the decedent if the requirements of Chapter 17 (commencing with Section 9980) are satisfied.

Ca. Prob. Code § 9885
Enacted by Stats. 1990, Ch. 79.

Chapter 13 - DEDICATION OR CONVEYANCE TO GOVERNMENTAL ENTITY; EASEMENTS AND ACCESS RIGHTS

Section 9900 - Generally

If it is to the advantage of the estate and in the best interest of the interested persons, the personal representative, after authorization by order of the court obtained under this chapter and upon such terms and conditions as the court may prescribe, may do any of the following either with or without consideration:

(a) Dedicate or convey real property of the estate for any purpose to any of the following:

(1) This state or any public entity in this state.

(2) The United States or any agency or instrumentality of the United States.

(b) Dedicate or convey an easement over real property of the estate to any person for any purpose.

(c) Convey, release, or relinquish to this state or any public entity in this state any access rights to any street, highway, or freeway from any real property of the estate.

(d) Consent as a lienholder to a dedication, conveyance, release, or relinquishment under subdivision (a), (b), or (c) by the owner of property subject to the lien.

Ca. Prob. Code § 9900
Enacted by Stats. 1990, Ch. 79.

Section 9901 - Petition for order; notice of hearing

(a) The personal representative or any interested person may file a petition for an order under this chapter.

(b) Notice of the hearing on the petition shall be given as provided in Section 1220.

Ca. Prob. Code § 9901
Enacted by Stats. 1990, Ch. 79.

Chapter 14 - EXCHANGE OF PROPERTY

Section 9920 - Generally

If it is to the advantage of the estate to exchange property of the estate for other property, the personal representative may, after authorization by order of court obtained under this chapter and upon such terms and conditions as may be prescribed by the court, exchange the property for the other property. The terms and conditions prescribed by the court may include the payment or receipt of part cash by the personal representative.

Ca. Prob. Code § 9920
Enacted by Stats. 1990, Ch. 79.

Section 9921 - Petition

To obtain an order under this chapter, the personal representative or any interested person shall file a petition containing all of the following:

(a) A description of the property.

(b) The terms and conditions of the proposed exchange.

(c) A showing that the proposed exchange is to the advantage of the estate.

Ca. Prob. Code § 9921
Enacted by Stats. 1990, Ch. 79.

Section 9922 - Notice of hearing; exchange of securities

(a) Except as provided in subdivision (b), notice of the hearing on the petition shall be given as provided in Section 1220.

(b) If the petition is for authorization to exchange securities as defined in Section 10200 for different securities, the court, upon a showing of good cause, may order that the notice be given for a shorter period or that the notice be dispensed with. The order provided by this subdivision may be made ex parte.

Ca. Prob. Code § 9922
Enacted by Stats. 1990, Ch. 79.

Section 9923 - Proceedings not invalidated by omission, error or irregularity

No omission, error, or irregularity in the proceedings under this chapter shall impair or invalidate the proceedings or the exchange made pursuant to an order made under this chapter.

Ca. Prob. Code § 9923
Enacted by Stats. 1990, Ch. 79.

Chapter 15 - LEASES

Section 9940 - Lease with option to purchase; right to extend term of lease

For the purpose of this chapter:
(a) "Lease" includes, without limitation, a lease that includes an option to purchase real propery of the estate.
(b) If a lease gives the lessee the right to extend the term of the lease, the length of the term shall be considered as though the right to extend had been exercised.

Ca. Prob. Code § 9940
Enacted by Stats. 1990, Ch. 79.

Section 9941 - Lease without court authorization

If it is to the advantage of the estate, the personal representative may lease, as lessor, real property of the estate without authorization of the court in either of the following cases:
(a) Where the rental does not exceed five thousand dollars ($5,000) a month and the term does not exceed one year.
(b) Where the lease is from month to month, regardless of the amount of the rental.

Ca. Prob. Code § 9941
Amended by Stats. 1990, Ch. 710, Sec. 25. Operative July 1, 1991, by Sec. 48 of Ch. 710.

Section 9942 - Lease after court authorization; option to purchase included in lease

(a) The personal representative may lease, as lessor, real property of the estate after authorization by order of court obtained under this chapter upon a showing that the proposed lease is to the advantage of the estate.

(b) If the proposed lease includes an option to purchase real property of the estate, a petition for an order authorizing the lease shall be filed under this chapter but the applicable provisions for court approval both in this chapter and in Chapter 16 (commencing with Section 9960) apply to the execution of the lease.

Ca. Prob. Code § 9942
Enacted by Stats. 1990, Ch. 79.

Section 9943 - Petition to obtain court order

(a) To obtain an order under this chapter, the personal representative or any interested person shall file a petition containing all of the following:

(1) A general description of the real property proposed to be leased.

(2) The term, rental, and general conditions of the proposed lease.

(3) A showing that the proposed lease is to the advantage of the estate.

(b) If the lease is proposed to be for a term longer than 10 years, the petition shall also state facts showing the need for the longer lease and its advantage to the estate and its benefit to the interested persons.

Ca. Prob. Code § 9943
Enacted by Stats. 1990, Ch. 79.

Section 9944 - Notice of hearing

(a) Notice of the hearing on the petition shall be given as provided in Section 1220 and posted as provided in Section 1230.

(b) Notice of the hearing on the petition also shall be given as provided in Section 10300, but this notice is not required if the will authorizes or directs the personal representative to lease or sell property.

(c) If the lease is proposed to be for a term longer than 10 years, in addition to the notice required by subdivision (a), notice of the hearing shall be given as provided in Section 1220 to all of the following persons:

(1) Each known heir whose interest in the estate would be affected by the proposed lease.

(2) Each known devisee whose interest in the estate would be affected by the proposed lease.

Ca. Prob. Code § 9944
Enacted by Stats. 1990, Ch. 79.

Section 9945 - Consideration of other offer at hearing; order authorizing lease

(a) At the hearing, the court shall entertain and consider any other offer made in good faith at the hearing to lease the same property on more favorable terms.

(b) If the court is satisfied that it will be to the advantage of the estate, and, if the lease is for more than 10 years, that it is to the benefit of interested persons, the court shall make an order authorizing the personal representative to make the lease to the person on the terms and conditions stated in the order. The court shall not make an order authorizing the personal representative to make the lease to any person other than the lessee named in the petition unless the offer made at the hearing is acceptable to the personal representative.

Ca. Prob. Code § 9945
Enacted by Stats. 1990, Ch. 79.

Section 9946 - Terms and conditions of lease authorize in order

(a) Subject to Section 9947, an order authorizing the execution of a lease shall set forth the minimum rental or royalty or both and the period of the lease.

(b) The order may authorize other terms and conditions of the lease, including, with respect to a lease for the purpose of exploration for or production or removal of minerals, oil, gas, or other hydrocarbon substances, or geothermal energy, any one or more of the following provisions:

(1) A provision for the payment of rental and royalty to a depositary.

(2) A provision for the appointment of a common agent to represent the interests of all the lessors.

(3) A provision for the payment of a compensatory royalty in lieu of rental and in lieu of drilling and producing operations on the land covered by the lease.

(4) A provision empowering the lessee to enter into any agreement authorized by Section 3301 of the Public Resources Code with respect to the land covered by the lease.

(5) A provision for a community oil lease or a pooling or unitization by the lessee.

(c) If the lease covers additional property owned by other persons or an undivided or other interest of the decedent less than the entire ownership in the property, the order may authorize the lease to provide for division of rental and royalty in the proportion that the land or interest of each owner bears to the total area of the land or total interests covered by the lease.

Ca. Prob. Code § 9946
Enacted by Stats. 1990, Ch. 79.

Section 9947 - Term of lease

(a) Except as provided in this section, the term of the lease shall be for such period as the court may authorize.

(b) Except as provided in subdivision (c), the court shall not authorize a lease for longer than 10 years if any heir or devisee who has an interest in the property to be leased objects at the hearing.
(c) If the lease is for the purpose of exploration for or production or removal of minerals, oil, gas, or other hydrocarbon substances, or geothermal energy, the court may authorize that the lease be for a fixed period and any of the following:

(1) So long thereafter as minerals, oil, gas, or other hydrocarbon substances or geothermal energy are produced in paying quantities from the property leased or mining or drilling operations are conducted thereon.

(2) If the lease provides for the payment of a compensatory royalty, so long thereafter as such compensatory royalty is paid.

(3) If the land covered by the lease is included in an agreement authorized by Section 3301 of the Public Resources Code, so long thereafter as oil, gas, or other hydrocarbon substances are produced in paying quantities from any of the lands included in any such agreement or drilling operations are conducted thereon.
Ca. Prob. Code § 9947
Enacted by Stats. 1990, Ch. 79.

Section 9948 - Execution, acknowledgment and delivery of lease; jurisdiction of court

(a) The personal representative shall execute, acknowledge, and deliver the lease as directed, setting forth therein that it is made by authority of the order, giving the date of the order.
(b) A lease made pursuant to an order obtained under this chapter is effectual to lease the premises described in the order at the rent, for the term, and upon the terms and conditions prescribed in the order.
(c) Jurisdiction of the court in proceedings under this code concerning the administration of the estate of the decedent vests the court with jurisdiction to make the order for the lease. This jurisdiction shall conclusively inure to the benefit of the lessee and

the lessee's heirs and assigns.

(d) No omission, error, or irregularity in the proceedings under this chapter shall impair or invalidate the proceedings or the lease made pursuant to an order made under this chapter.

Ca. Prob. Code § 9948
Enacted by Stats. 1990, Ch. 79.

Chapter 16 - GRANTING OPTION TO PURCHASE REAL PROPERTY

Section 9960 - Granting option after court order authorizing

After authorization by order of court obtained under this chapter, the personal representative may grant an option to purchase real property of the estate for a period within or beyond the period of administration.

Ca. Prob. Code § 9960
Enacted by Stats. 1990, Ch. 79.

Section 9961 - Petition to obtain order

To obtain an order under this chapter, the personal representative shall file a petition containing all of the following:

(a) A description of the real property.

(b) The terms and conditions of the proposed option.

(c) A showing that granting the option is to the advantage of the estate.

Ca. Prob. Code § 9961
Enacted by Stats. 1990, Ch. 79.

Section 9962 - Purchase price

The purchase price of the real property subject to the option shall be at least 90 percent of the appraised value of the real property. The appraisal shall be made in the manner provided in subdivision (c) of Section 10309 within one year prior to the hearing of the petition.

Ca. Prob. Code § 9962
Enacted by Stats. 1990, Ch. 79.

Section 9963 - Notice of hearing

Notice of the hearing on the petition shall be posted as provided in Section 1230 and given as provided in Section 1220 to all of the following persons:

(a) Each person listed in Section 1220.

(b) Each known heir whose interest in the estate would be affected by the granting of the option.

(c) Each known devisee whose interest in the estate would be affected by the granting of the option.

Ca. Prob. Code § 9963
Enacted by Stats. 1990, Ch. 79.

Section 9964 - Order authorizing

(a) The court shall make an order authorizing the personal representative to grant the option upon the terms and conditions stated in the order if the court is satisfied as to all of the following:

(1) Good reason exists to grant the option and granting the option will be to the advantage of the estate.

(2) It does not appear that a higher offer with respect to the purchase price of the real property subject to the option may be obtained. An offer is a higher offer with respect to purchase price only if the offer satisfies the requirements of Section 10311 governing increased bids in real property sales.

(3) It does not appear that a better offer with respect to the terms of the option may be obtained. An offer is a better offer with respect to the terms of the option only if the offer is materially more advantageous to the estate.

(b) A higher offer made either for cash or on credit, whether on the same or different credit terms, or a better offer, shall be considered only if the personal representative informs the court in person or by counsel, before the court makes its order authorizing the granting of the option, that the offer is acceptable.

Ca. Prob. Code § 9964
Enacted by Stats. 1990, Ch. 79.

Section 9965 - Option subject to Chapter 4, Title 5, Part 2, Civil Code

An option granted pursuant to an order made under this chapter, whether within or beyond the administration of the estate, is subject to Chapter 4 (commencing with Section 884.010) of Title 5 of Part 2 of Division 2 of the Civil Code.

Ca. Prob. Code § 9965
Enacted by Stats. 1990, Ch. 79.

Section 9966 - Validity not impaired by omission error or irregularity

No omission, error, or irregularity in the proceedings under this chapter shall impair or invalidate the proceedings or the granting of an option pursuant to an order made under this chapter.

Ca. Prob. Code § 9966
Enacted by Stats. 1990, Ch. 79.

Chapter 17 - OPTION TO PURCHASE GIVEN IN WILL

Section 9980 - Right to exercise option; time

(a) Where an option to purchase real or personal property is given in a will, the person given the option has the right to exercise the option at any time within the time limits provided by the will. For the purposes of this section, if a time limitation in the will is measured from the death of the testator, that time shall be extended by the period between the testator's death and the issuance of letters testamentary or of administration with the will annexed or by six months, whichever is the shorter period.
(b) If the will does not provide a time limit for exercise of the option, the time limit is one year from the death of the decedent.
(c) Subject to subdivision (b), if the option given in the will is

exercisable under the terms of the will after the time that the estate would otherwise be closed, the property subject to the option shall be distributed subject to the option.

Ca. Prob. Code § 9980
Enacted by Stats. 1990, Ch. 79.

Section 9981 - Order directing transfer or conveyance to person given option

(a) Where an option to purchase real or personal property is given in a will admitted to probate, the court may make an order under this chapter directing the personal representative to transfer or convey the property to the person given the option upon compliance with the terms and conditions stated in the will.
(b) The personal representative or the person given the option to purchase the property may file a petition for an order pursuant to this chapter.
(c) Notice of the hearing on the petition shall be given as provided in Section 1220.

Ca. Prob. Code § 9981
Enacted by Stats. 1990, Ch. 79.

Section 9982 - Requirements to make order

The court shall not make an order under this chapter unless one of the following requirements is satisfied:
(a) The court determines that the rights of creditors will not be impaired by the making of the order.
(b) The court requires a bond in an amount and with such surety as the court shall direct or approve.

Ca. Prob. Code § 9982
Enacted by Stats. 1990, Ch. 79.

Section 9983 - Validity not impaired by omission, error or irregularity

No omission, error, or irregularity in the proceedings under this chapter shall impair or invalidate the proceedings or the transfer or conveyance made pursuant to an order made under this chapter.

Ca. Prob. Code § 9983

Enacted by Stats. 1990, Ch. 79.

Chapter 18 - SALES

Article 1 - GENERAL PROVISIONS

Section 10000 - Cases in which personal representative may sell property of estate

Subject to the limitations, conditions, and requirements of this chapter, the personal representative may sell real or personal property of the estate in any of the following cases:

(a) Where the sale is necessary to pay debts, devises, family allowance, expenses of administration, or taxes.

(b) Where the sale is to the advantage of the estate and in the best interest of the interested persons.

(c) Where the property is directed by the will to be sold.

(d) Where authority is given in the will to sell the property.

Ca. Prob. Code § 10000

Enacted by Stats. 1990, Ch. 79.

Section 10001 - Cases in which interested person may petition for order requiring sale

(a) If the personal representative neglects or refuses to sell the property, any interested person may petition the court for an order requiring the personal representative to sell real or personal property of the estate in any of the following cases:

(1) Where the sale is necessary to pay debts, devises, family allowance, expenses of administration, or taxes.

(2) Where the sale is to the advantage of the estate and in the best interest of the interested persons.

(3) Where the property is directed by the will to be sold.

(b) Notice of the hearing on the petition shall be given as provided in Section 1220.

(c) Notice of the hearing on the petition also shall be given to the personal representative by citation served at least five days before the hearing.

Ca. Prob. Code § 10001
Enacted by Stats. 1990, Ch. 79.

Section 10002 - Compliance with directions in will; order relieving personal representative of duty to comply

(a) Subject to subdivision (b), if directions are given in the will as to the mode of selling or the particular property to be sold, the personal representative shall comply with those directions.

(b) If the court determines that it would be to the advantage of the estate and in the best interest of the interested persons, the court may make an order relieving the personal representative of the duty to comply with the directions in the will. The order shall specify the mode and the terms and conditions of selling or the particular property to be sold, or both. The personal representative or any interested person may file a petition for an order under this subdivision. Notice of the hearing on the petition shall be given as provided in Section 1220.

Ca. Prob. Code § 10002
Enacted by Stats. 1990, Ch. 79.

Section 10003 - Powers of personal representative

Subject to Part 4 (commencing with Section 21400) of Division 11 and to Sections 10001 and 10002, if estate property is required or permitted to be sold, the personal representative may:

(a) Use discretion as to which property to sell first.

(b) Sell the entire interest of the estate in the property or any lesser interest therein.

(c) Sell the property either at public auction or private sale.

Ca. Prob. Code § 10003
Enacted by Stats. 1990, Ch. 79.

Section 10004 - Sale of property as unit

(a) Where the personal representative determines in his or her discretion that, by use or relationship, any assets of the estate, whether real or personal, constitute a unit for purposes of sale, the personal representative may cause the property to be appraised as a unit.

(b) Whether or not the property is appraised as a unit, the personal representative may sell all the assets described in subdivision (a) as a unit and under one bid if the court finds the sale of the assets as a unit to be to the advantage of the estate.

(c) No private sale of the assets as a unit may be made for less than 90 percent of the sum of the appraised values of the personal property and the sum of the appraised values of the real property, appraised separately, or for less than 90 percent of the appraised value if appraised as a unit.

(d) If the assets to be sold as a unit include any real property, the sale shall be made in the manner provided for the sale of real property, and the bid and sale are subject to the limitations and restrictions established for the sale of real property. If the assets to be sold as a unit are entirely personal property, the property shall be sold in the manner provided for the sale of personal property.

Ca. Prob. Code § 10004
Enacted by Stats. 1990, Ch. 79.

Section 10005 - Sale for more than appraised value; sale at loss

(a) If any property in the estate is sold for more than the appraised value, the personal representative shall account for the proceeds of sale, including the excess over the appraised value.

(b) If any property in the estate is sold for less than the appraised value and the sale has been made in accordance with law, the personal representative is not responsible for the loss.

Ca. Prob. Code § 10005
Enacted by Stats. 1990, Ch. 79.

Section 10006 - Consent to cotenants to have interest sold

If property in the estate is to be sold as an undivided interest in a cotenancy, the other cotenants may file in the estate proceeding written consent to have their interests sold pursuant to this chapter. Thereafter, the court's orders made pursuant to this chapter are as binding on the consenting cotenants as on the personal representative.

Ca. Prob. Code § 10006
Enacted by Stats. 1990, Ch. 79.

Article 2 - CONTRACT WITH AGENT, BROKER, OR AUCTIONEER

Section 10150 - Written contract

(a) The personal representative may enter into a written contract with either or both of the following:

(1) A licensed real estate broker to secure a purchaser for any real property of the estate. The broker may associate other licensed real estate brokers for this purpose, including use of a multiple listing service as defined in Section 1087 of the Civil Code.

(2) One or more agents or brokers to secure a purchaser for any personal property of the estate. If the particular property to be sold or the particular manner of sale requires that the agent or broker be licensed, the contract may be made only with an agent or broker that is so licensed.

(b) The contract may provide for payment of a fee, commission, or other compensation out of the proceeds of sale, but the contract is binding and valid as against the estate only for such amount as the court allows pursuant to Article 3 (commencing with Section 10160). No liability of any kind is incurred by the estate under the contract or a sale unless the sale is confirmed by the court, except for the obligations of the estate to the purchaser of personal property as to which title passes pursuant to Section 10259 without court confirmation or approval. The personal representative is not personally liable on the contract by reason of execution of the contract.

(c) The contract may grant an exclusive right to sell property for a period not in excess of 90 days if, prior to execution of the contract granting an exclusive right to sell, the personal representative obtains permission of the court to enter into the contract upon a showing of necessity and advantage to the estate. The court may grant the permission when the personal representative is appointed or at any subsequent time upon ex parte application. The personal representative may execute one or more extensions of the contract granting an exclusive right to sell property, each extension being for a period not to exceed 90 days, if for each extension the personal representative obtains permission of the court upon ex parte application to extend the contract upon a showing of necessity and advantage to the estate of the extension.

Ca. Prob. Code § 10150

Enacted by Stats. 1990, Ch. 79.

Section 10151 - Contract with public auction sale

(a) The personal representative may enter into a written contract with any of the following:

(1) Where the public auction sale will be held in this state, an auctioneer who is qualified to conduct business under Title 2.95 (commencing with Section 1812.600) of Part 4 of Division 3 of the Civil Code.

(2) Where the public auction sale will be held outside this state pursuant to an order made under Section 10254, an auctioneer who is legally permitted in the jurisdiction where the sale will be held to conduct a public auction sale and to secure purchasers by that method for the personal property authorized to be sold by public auction sale in that jurisdiction under the court order.

(b) The contract shall be one that is legally enforceable under the law of the jurisdiction where made.

(c) The contract may provide for payment to the auctioneer of a fee, commission, or other compensation out of the proceeds of sale and for reimbursement of expenses, but the contract is binding and valid as against the estate only for such amounts as the court allows pursuant to Section 10167. No liability of any kind is incurred by the estate under the contract or a sale unless the sale is approved by the court, except for the obligations of the estate to the purchaser of personal property as to which title passes pursuant to Section 10259 without court confirmation or approval. The personal representative is not personally liable on the contract by reason of execution of the contract.

(d) The contract may provide that personal property of two or more estates being administered by the same personal representative may be sold at the same public auction sale. Items of personal property may be sold separately or in a lot with other items from the same estate. A sale pursuant to the contract shall be with reserve. The auctioneer shall comply with the instructions of the personal representative with respect to withdrawal of items, risk of loss, place of delivery, warranties, and other matters.

Ca. Prob. Code § 10151

Amended by Stats 2003 ch 32 (AB 167), s 10, eff. 1/1/2004.

Article 3 - COMPENSATION OF AGENT, BROKER, OR AUCTIONEER

Section 10160 - Requirements for estate to be liable for compensation

The estate is not liable to an agent, broker, or auctioneer under a contract for the sale of property or for any fee, commission, or other compensation or expenses in connection with a sale of property unless the following requirements are satisfied:

(a) An actual sale is made.

(b) If court confirmation or approval is required, the sale is confirmed or approved by the court as required.

(c) The sale is consummated.

Ca. Prob. Code § 10160

Enacted by Stats. 1990, Ch. 79.

Section 10160.5 - Estate not liable to agent or broker

The estate is not liable to an agent or broker under a contract for the sale of property or for any fee, commission, or other compensation or expenses in connection with sale of the property in either of the following cases:

(a) Where the agent or broker, directly or indirectly, is the purchaser of the property.

(b) Where the agent or broker representing the purchaser to whom the sale is confirmed has any interest in the purchaser.

Ca. Prob. Code § 10160.5

Enacted by Stats. 1990, Ch. 79.

Section 10161 - Amount of compensation

(a) Subject to the provisions of this article, whether or not the agent or broker has a contract with the personal representative, the fee, commission, or other compensation of an agent or broker in connection with a sale of property shall be the amount the court, in its discretion, determines to be a reasonable compensation for the services of the agent or broker to the estate.

(b) Unless the agent or broker holds a contract granting an exclusive right to sell the property, an agent or broker is not entitled to any fee, commission, or other compensation for services to the estate in connection with a sale except in the following cases:

(1) Where the agent or broker produces the original bid which is returned to the court for confirmation.

(2) Where the property is sold on an increased bid, made at the time of the hearing on the petition for confirmation, to a purchaser procured by the agent or broker.

(c) If the agent or broker has a contract with the personal representative, the amount of the compensation of the agent or broker in connection with the sale of property shall not exceed the amount provided for in the contract.

Ca. Prob. Code § 10161

Enacted by Stats. 1990, Ch. 79.

Section 10162 - Compensation where bid made by person not represented by agent or broker

(a) Subject to subdivision (b), where the bid returned to the court for confirmation is made by a person who is not represented by an agent or broker and the successful bidder is represented by an agent or broker, the compensation of the agent or broker who procured the purchaser to whom the sale is confirmed shall not exceed one-half of the difference between the amount of the bid in the original return and the amount of the successful bid.

(b) This section does not limit the compensation of the agent or broker who holds a contract under Section 10150 granting him or her the exclusive right to sell the property.

Ca. Prob. Code § 10162
Enacted by Stats. 1990, Ch. 79.

Section 10162.3 - Compensation determined on full amount for which sale confirmed

(a) This section applies if all of the following circumstances exist:

(1) There is no agent or broker holding a contract under Section 10150 granting the exclusive right to sell the property.

(2) The bid returned to court for confirmation is made by a purchaser represented by an agent or broker.

(3) The court confirms the sale to that purchaser either on the bid returned to court for confirmation or on an increased bid made at the time of the hearing on the petition for confirmation.

(b) If all the circumstances described in subdivision (a) exist, the court shall allow the agent or broker who procured the purchaser to whom the sale is confirmed the compensation determined under Section 10161 on the full amount for which the sale is confirmed.

Ca. Prob. Code § 10162.3
Enacted by Stats. 1990, Ch. 79.

Section 10162.5 - Compensation where agent or broker holds contract granting exclusive right to sell

Subject to Section 10162.6, where an agent or broker holds a contract under Section 10150 granting the exclusive right to sell the property, the court shall allow to the agent or broker holding the contract the compensation determined under Section 10161 on:

(a) The full amount for which the sale is confirmed in either of the following circumstances:

(1) The bid returned to the court for confirmation is made by a purchaser who is not represented by an agent or broker and the court confirms the sale to that purchaser on that bid.

(2) The bid returned to the court for confirmation is made by a purchaser who is represented by the agent or broker holding the contract and the court confirms the sale to that purchaser on an increased bid made at the time of the hearing on the petition for confirmation.

(b) The amount of the original bid if both of the following circumstances exist:

(1) The bid returned to court for confirmation is made by a purchaser who is not represented by an agent or broker or who is represented by the agent or broker holding a contract under Section 10150 granting the exclusive right to sell the property.

(2) The court confirms the sale on an increased bid, made at the time of the hearing on the petition for confirmation, to a purchaser who was not procured by a bona fide agent or broker.

Ca. Prob. Code § 10162.5

Enacted by Stats. 1990, Ch. 79.

Section 10162.6 - Compensation payable if sale confirmed to particular purchaser named in contract

(a) This section applies if both of the following circumstances exist:

(1) An agent or broker holds a contract under Section 10150 granting the exclusive right to sell the property.

(2) The contract provides that no compensation is payable to the agent or broker holding the contract if sale is confirmed to a particular purchaser named in the contract.

(b) If the court confirms the sale to the purchaser named in the contract, whether on an original bid returned to the court or on an increased bid made at the time of the hearing on the petition for confirmation, the compensation of any agents or brokers involved in the sale is determined as provided in this article, except that no compensation is payable to the agent or broker holding the contract.

(c) If the court confirms the sale to a purchaser other than the person named in the contract, whether on an original bid returned to the court or on an increased bid made at the time of the hearing on the petition for confirmation, the compensation of the agent or broker holding the contract, and of any other agents or brokers involved in the sale, is determined under this article as if the limitation in the contract did not exist.

Ca. Prob. Code § 10162.6
Enacted by Stats. 1990, Ch. 79.

Section 10162.7 - Confirmation of sale to purchaser procured by another agent or broker

(a) Subject to Section 10162.6, this section applies if all of the following circumstances exist:

(1) There is an agent or broker holding a contract under Section 10150 granting the exclusive right to sell the property.

(2) The bid returned to court for confirmation is made by a purchaser procured by another agent or broker.

(3) The court confirms the sale to that purchaser either on the bid returned to court for confirmation or on an increased bid made at the time of the hearing on the petition for confirmation.

(b) If all the circumstances described in subdivision (a) exist, the court shall allow the compensation determined under Section 10161 on the full amount for which the sale is confirmed. The compensation allowed by the court shall be divided between the agent or broker holding the contract and the other agent or broker as is provided in any agreement between the agent or broker holding the contract and the other agent or broker. If there is no agreement, the compensation on the amount of the original bid returned to the court shall be divided equally between the agent or broker holding the contract and the other agent or broker and, if the sale is confirmed on an increased bid, the other agent or broker shall be paid all of the compensation on the difference between the original bid and the amount for which the sale is confirmed.

Ca. Prob. Code § 10162.7
Enacted by Stats. 1990, Ch. 79.

Section 10163 - Compensation determined on full amount for which sale confirmed

Subject to Sections 10162 and 10162.6, where the original bid returned to the court for confirmation was made by a purchaser who was not procured by an agent or broker, the court shall allow the compensation determined under Section 10161 on the full amount for which the sale is confirmed to the agent or broker who procured the purchaser to whom the sale is confirmed if either of the following conditions is satisfied:

(a) The court confirms a sale on an increased bid, made at the time of the hearing on the petition for confirmation, to a purchaser procured by an agent or broker holding a contract under Section 10150 granting the exclusive right to sell the property.

(b) There is no agent or broker holding a contract under Section 10150 granting the exclusive right to sell the property and the court confirms a sale on an increased bid, made at the time of the hearing on the petition for confirmation, to a purchaser procured by a bona fide agent or broker.

Ca. Prob. Code § 10163
Enacted by Stats. 1990, Ch. 79.

Section 10164 - Sale confirmed on increased bid made at time of hearing by purchaser not procured by agent or broker

(a) This section applies only where the court confirms a sale on an increased bid, made at the time of the hearing on the petition for confirmation, to a purchaser who was not procured by a bona fide agent or broker.

(b) Except as provided in subdivision (c), the court shall allow the compensation determined under Section 10161 on the amount of the original bid to the agent or broker whose original bid was returned to the court.

(c) If an agent or broker holds a contract under Section 10150 granting the exclusive right to sell the property and the original bid returned to the court is made by a purchaser who was procured by another agent or broker, the compensation determined under Section 10161 on the amount of the original bid shall be divided between the agent or broker holding the contract and the other agent or broker as is provided in any agreement between the agent or broker holding the contract and the other agent or broker. If there is no agreement, the compensation shall be divided equally between the agent or broker holding the contract and the other agent or broker.

Ca. Prob. Code § 10164
Enacted by Stats. 1990, Ch. 79.

Section 10165 - Compensation determined on full amount for which sale confirmed on increased bid made at time of hearing

(a) Subject to Section 10162.6, where the court confirms a sale on an increased bid, made at the time of the hearing on the petition for confirmation, to a purchaser procured by a bona fide agent or broker, the court shall allow the compensation determined under Section 10161 on the full amount for which the sale is confirmed, as provided in this section, if either of the following conditions is satisfied:

(1) The original bid returned to the court for confirmation was made by a purchaser who was procured by another agent or broker.

(2) The original bid returned to the court for confirmation was made by a purchaser who was not represented by an agent or broker, and another agent or broker holds a contract under Section 10150 granting the exclusive right to sell the property.

(b) The agent or broker who procured the purchaser to whom the sale is confirmed shall be paid one-half of the compensation on the amount of the original bid and all of the compensation on the difference between the original bid and the amount for which the sale is confirmed.

(c) The other one-half of the compensation on the amount of the original bid shall be paid as follows:

(1) If the original bid returned to the court is made by a purchaser who was procured by the agent or broker holding a contract under Section 10150 granting the exclusive right to sell the property, the entire one-half of the compensation on the original bid shall be paid to that agent or broker.

(2) If the original bid returned to the court is made by a purchaser who was procured by a bona fide agent or broker and there is no agent or broker holding a contract under Section 10150 granting the exclusive right to sell the property, the entire one-half of the compensation on the original bid shall be paid to that agent or broker.

(3) If there is an agent or broker who holds a contract under Section 10150 granting the exclusive right to sell the property and the original bid returned to the court is made by a purchaser who was procured by another agent or broker, the one-half of the compensation on the amount of the original bid shall be divided between the agent or broker holding the contract granting the exclusive right to sell the property and the other agent or broker whose original bid was returned to the court for confirmation as is provided in any agreement between the agent or broker holding the contract and the other agent or broker. If there is no agreement, the one-half of the compensation on the amount of the original bid shall be divided equally between the agent or broker holding the contract and the other agent or broker whose original bid was returned to the court for confirmation.

(4) If there is an agent or broker who holds a contract under Section 10150 granting the exclusive right to sell the property and the original bid returned to the court is made by a purchaser who is not represented by an agent or broker and the court confirms the sale on an increased bid, made at the time of the hearing on the petition for confirmation, to a purchaser procured by another agent or broker, the entire one-half of the compensation on the original bid shall be paid to the agent or broker holding the contract.

(5) If the agent or broker compensated under subdivision (b) holds a contract under Section 10150 granting the exclusive right to sell the property, the entire one-half of the compensation on the original bid shall be paid to the other agent or broker who procured the original bid returned to the court.

Ca. Prob. Code § 10165
Enacted by Stats. 1990, Ch. 79.

Section 10166 - Condition that certain amount of bid paid to agent or broker by personal representative

Notwithstanding that a bid contains a condition that a certain amount of the bid shall be paid to an agent or broker by the personal representative, only such compensation as is proper under this article shall be allowed. Acceptance of the bid by the court binds the bidder even though the compensation allowed by the court is less than that specified by the condition.

Ca. Prob. Code § 10166
Enacted by Stats. 1990, Ch. 79.

Section 10167 - Amount of fees, compensation and expenses of auctioneer

(a) Subject to subdivision (b), whether or not the auctioneer has a contract with the personal representative, the fees, compensation, and expenses of an auctioneer in connection with a sale of property shall be the amount the court, in its discretion, determines to be a reasonable compensation for the services of the auctioneer to the estate.

(b) If the auctioneer has a contract with the personal representative, the amount of the compensation of the auctioneer in connection with the sale of property shall not exceed the amount provided for in the contract.

Ca. Prob. Code § 10167
Enacted by Stats. 1990, Ch. 79.

Section 10168 - Agreement among cooperating agents or brokers

This article does not supersede any agreement cooperating agents or brokers may have among themselves to divide the compensation payable under this article.

Ca. Prob. Code § 10168
Added by Stats. 1990, Ch. 710, Sec. 26. Operative July 1, 1991, by Sec. 48 of Ch. 710.

Article 4 - SPECIAL PROVISIONS APPLICABLE TO PARTICULAR TYPES OF PROPERTY

Section 10200 - Securities

(a) As used in this section, "securities" means "security" as defined in Section 70, land trust certificates, certificates of beneficial interest in trusts, investment trust certificates, mortgage participation certificates, or certificates of deposit for any of the foregoing, but does not include notes secured by a mortgage or deed of trust unless the note or notes have been authorized or permitted to be issued by the Commissioner of Financial Protection and Innovation or have been made by a public utility subject to the Public Utilities Act (Part 1 (commencing with Section 201) of Division 1 of the Public Utilities Code).
(b) After authorization by order of court, securities may be sold or may be surrendered for redemption or conversion. Title to the securities sold or surrendered as authorized by an order obtained under this section passes without the need for subsequent court confirmation.
(c) To obtain an order under this section, the personal representative or any interested person shall file a petition stating

the terms and conditions and the advantage to the estate of the proposed sale or redemption or conversion. If the court authorizes the sale, redemption, or conversion, the court's order shall fix the terms and conditions of sale, redemption, or conversion.

(d) Notice of the hearing on the petition shall be given as provided in Section 1220 and posted as provided in Section 1230, but the court may order that the notice be given for a shorter period or dispensed with.

(e) No notice of sale or of the redemption or conversion need be given if any of the following conditions are satisfied:

(1)The minimum selling price is fixed by the court.

(2)The securities are to be sold on an established stock or bond exchange.

(3)The securities to be sold are securities designated as a national market system security on an interdealer quotation system, or subsystem thereof, by the National Association of Securities Dealers, Inc., sold through a broker-dealer registered under the Securities Exchange Act of 1934 during the regular course of business of the broker-dealer.

(4)The securities are to be surrendered for redemption or conversion.

Ca. Prob. Code § 10200

Amended by Stats 2022 ch 452 (SB 1498),s 207, eff. 1/1/2023.
Amended by Stats 2019 ch 143 (SB 251),s 77, eff. 1/1/2020.

Section 10201 - Savings accounts and mutual capital certificates of savings association or federal association; credit union shared accounts

(a) For purposes of this section:

(1) "Federal association" is defined in Section 5102 of the Financial Code.

(2) "Mutual capital certificate" is defined in Section 5111 of the Financial Code.

(3) "Savings account" is defined in Section 5116 of the Financial Code.

(4) "Savings association" is defined in Section 5102 of the Financial Code.

(5) "Withdrawal value" is defined in Section 5124 of the Financial Code.

(b) Notwithstanding Section 10200, savings accounts and mutual capital certificates of a savings association or federal association may be sold or surrendered for withdrawal by the personal representative, and title thereto passed, without notice of sale, prior order of court, or subsequent confirmation by the court, if an amount of money is obtained upon the sale or withdrawal not less than the withdrawal value of the savings account or the value of the mutual capital certificate.

(c) Notwithstanding Section 10200, credit union share accounts and certificates for funds may be sold or withdrawn by the personal representative, and title thereto passed, without notice of sale, prior order of court, or subsequent confirmation by the court, if an amount of money is obtained upon the sale or withdrawal not less than the withdrawal value of the share account or the value of the certificate for funds.

Ca. Prob. Code § 10201

Enacted by Stats. 1990, Ch. 79.

Section 10202 - Subscription rights for purchase of additional securities

Notwithstanding Section 10200, if an estate by reason of owning securities, also owns or receives subscription rights for the purchase of additional securities, the personal representative may sell all or part of the subscription rights without notice of sale, prior order of court, or subsequent confirmation by the court.

Ca. Prob. Code § 10202
Enacted by Stats. 1990, Ch. 79.

Section 10203 - Leasehold interest

(a) Except as provided in subdivision (b), where property to be sold consists of a leasehold interest, the sale shall be made as in the case of the sale of personal property of the estate.

(b) The sale of a leasehold interest shall be made as in the case of the sale of real property of the estate if the interest to be sold consists of any of the following:

(1) A leasehold interest in real property with an unexpired term of 10 years or longer. For this purpose, the leasehold interest shall be considered to have an unexpired term of 10 years or longer if the lessee has the right to extend the term and the term, if extended, would exceed 10 years.

(2) A leasehold interest in real property together with an option to purchase the leased property or some part thereof.

(3) A lease for the purpose of production of minerals, oil, gas, or other hydrocarbon substances, or geothermal energy.

Ca. Prob. Code § 10203
Enacted by Stats. 1990, Ch. 79.

Section 10204 - Partnership interest

Property of the estate that consists of a partnership interest or an interest belonging to an estate by virtue of a partnership formerly existing may be sold in the same manner as other personal property.

Ca. Prob. Code § 10204
Enacted by Stats. 1990, Ch. 79.

Section 10205 - Chose in action

A chose in action belonging to the estate may be sold in the same manner as other personal property.

Ca. Prob. Code § 10205
Enacted by Stats. 1990, Ch. 79.

Section 10206 - Sale of interest in property under contract for purchase of real property

(a) Except as otherwise provided in this section, if the decedent at the time of death was possessed of a contract for the purchase of real property and the decedent's interest in the property and under the contract is to be sold, the sale shall be made as in the case of the sale of real property of the estate.

(b) If the decedent's interest in the property and under the contract is sold, the sale shall be made subject to all payments which are due at the time of sale or which may thereafter become due on the contract. Except as provided in subdivision (d), if there are any payments due or to become due, the court shall not confirm the sale until the purchaser executes a bond to the personal representative that satisfies the requirements of subdivision (c).

(c) The bond shall be for the benefit and indemnity of the personal representative and the persons entitled to the interest of the decedent in the real property contracted for. The amount of the bond shall be equal to the amount of payments then due and thereafter to become due on the contract, with such sureties as the court may approve. The bond shall be conditioned that the purchaser will (1) make all payments for the property which are then due or which become due after the date of the sale and (2) fully indemnify the personal representative and the person entitled to the interest of the decedent against all demands, costs, charges, and expenses, by reason of any covenant or agreement contained in the contract.

(d) The bond need not be given in either of the following cases:

   (1) Where no claim has been made against the estate on the contract and the time for filing claims has expired.

   (2) Where the person entitled to payment under the contract waives all recourse to the assets of the estate for payment and releases the estate and the personal representative from liability for payment.

Ca. Prob. Code § 10206
Enacted by Stats. 1990, Ch. 79.

Section 10207 - Real property suitable for shift-in-land-use loan to develop grazing or pasture facilities

(a) Real property suitable for a shift-in-land-use loan to develop grazing or pasture facilities may be sold under this section by the personal representative to a grazing or pasture association in conformity with the federal Consolidated Farm and Rural Development Act (7 U.S.C. Sec. 1921, et seq.) after authorization by order of the court.

(b) The personal representative or any interested person may file a petition for an order under this section. Notice of the hearing on the petition shall be given as provided in Section 1220.

(c) An order for sale of property under this section may be made only if the court determines both of the following:

(1) Either the sale is made pursuant to the will of the decedent or all of the following have consented to the sale:

(A) Each known heir whose interest in the estate would be affected by the sale.

(B) Each known devisee who has an interest in the property under the decedent's will.

(2) The sale will not jeopardize the rights of creditors of the estate.

(d) If the court makes an order authorizing sale of the property, the personal representative may make the sale in accord with the terms and conditions set out in the order, subject to the following requirements:

(1) Except as provided in Sections 10002, 10301, 10303, and 10503, notice of the time and place of the sale shall be published pursuant to Section 10300.

(2) The price of the sale made shall be not less than the value of the property as established by an independent and competent appraiser mutually acceptable to the federal government, the grazing or pasture association, and the personal representative.

(3) Except as provided in Sections 10002 and 10503, the sale shall be reported to and confirmed by the court as provided in Article 6 (commencing with Section 10300) before title to the property passes, but the sale may be made irrespective of whether a higher bid is made to the court at the hearing on the petition to confirm the sale.

Ca. Prob. Code § 10207
Enacted by Stats. 1990, Ch. 79.

Article 5 - SALE OF PERSONAL PROPERTY

Section 10250 - Notice of sale

Subject to Sections 10251 and 10252 and except as otherwise provided by statute, personal property of the estate may be sold only after notice of sale is given by one or both of the following methods, as the personal representative may determine:
(a) Posting at the county courthouse of the county in which the proceedings are pending at least 15 days before:

(1) In the case of a private sale, the day specified in the notice of sale as the day on or after which the sale is to be made.

(2) In the case of a public auction sale, the day of the auction.
(b) Publication pursuant to Section 6063a of the Government Code in a newspaper in the county in which the proceedings are pending, such publication to be completed before:

(1) In the case of a private sale, the day specified in the notice of sale as the day on or after which the sale is to be made.

(2) In the case of a public auction sale, the day of the auction.

Ca. Prob. Code § 10250
Enacted by Stats. 1990, Ch. 79.

Section 10251 - Order shortening time of notice of sale

(a) If it is shown that it will be to the advantage of the estate, the court or judge may by order shorten the time of notice of sale to not less than five days.

(b) If the court or judge makes an order under subdivision (a), notice of sale shall be given by one or both of the following methods, as the personal representative may determine:

(1) By posting as provided in Section 10250 except that the posting shall be for at least five days instead of 15 days as required by Section 10250.

(2) By publication as provided in Section 10250 except that the publication shall be pursuant to Section 6061 of the Government Code.

Ca. Prob. Code § 10251
Enacted by Stats. 1990, Ch. 79.

Section 10252 - Cases in which property sold without notice

Personal property may be sold with or without notice, as the personal representative may determine, in any of the following cases:

(a) Where the property is directed by the will to be sold.

(b) Where authority is given in the will to sell the property.

(c) Where the property is perishable, will depreciate in value if not disposed of promptly, or will incur loss or expense by being kept.

(d) Where sale of the property is necessary to provide for the payment of a family allowance pending receipt of other sufficient funds.

Ca. Prob. Code § 10252
Enacted by Stats. 1990, Ch. 79.

Section 10253 - Contents of notice of sale

(a) The notice of sale given pursuant to Section 10250 shall state all of the following:

(1) Whether the sale is to be a private sale or a public auction sale.

(2) In the case of a private sale, the place at which bids or offers will be received and a day on or after which the sale will be made or, in the case of a public auction sale, the time and place of sale.

(3) A brief description of the personal property to be sold.
(b) The notice of sale may state other matters in addition to those required by subdivision (a), including terms and conditions of sale.
Ca. Prob. Code § 10253
Enacted by Stats. 1990, Ch. 79.

Section 10254 - Public auction sale

(a) Unless the court orders otherwise pursuant to subdivision (b):

(1) A sale of personal property at a public auction sale shall be made within this state at the courthouse door, at the auction house, at some other public place, or at the residence of the decedent.

(2) No public auction sale shall be made of any tangible personal property that is not present at the time of sale.
(b) Upon petition of the personal representative or any interested person, the court may order either or both of the following:

(1) That a sale of personal property at public auction be made at any place within or without the United States.

(2) That tangible personal property need not be present at the time of sale.
(c) The personal representative may postpone a public auction sale

of personal property from time to time if all of the following conditions are satisfied:

(1) The personal representative believes that the postponement is to the advantage of the estate.

(2) Notice of the postponement is given by public declaration at the time and place appointed for the sale.

(3) The postponement, together with previous postponements of sale of the property, does not exceed three months.
Ca. Prob. Code § 10254
Enacted by Stats. 1990, Ch. 79.

Section 10255 - Private sale

(a) A private sale of personal property may not be made before the day stated in the notice of sale as the day on or after which the sale will be made, nor later than one year after that day.
(b) In the case of a private sale of personal property, the bids or offers shall be in writing and shall be left at the place designated in the notice of sale, or be delivered to the personal representative personally or to the person specified in the notice of sale, at any time after the first publication or posting of notice of sale and before the making of the sale.
Ca. Prob. Code § 10255
Enacted by Stats. 1990, Ch. 79.

Section 10256 - Bids to comply with terms specified in notice

Whether a sale of personal property is private or at public auction, bids shall substantially comply with any terms specified in the notice of sale.
Ca. Prob. Code § 10256
Enacted by Stats. 1990, Ch. 79.

Section 10257 - Sale on credit

(a) Personal property may be sold for cash or on credit.

(b) Except as may otherwise be ordered by the court pursuant to Section 10258, if a sale is made on credit, not less than 25 percent of the purchase price shall be paid in cash at the time of sale, and the personal representative shall do one of the following:

(**1**) Take the note of the purchaser for the balance of the purchase money, with a security interest in the personal propery sold, to secure the payment of the balance.

(**2**) Enter into a conditional sale contract under which title is retained until the balance is paid.

(c) The terms of the note and security interest or conditional sale contract shall be approved by the court at the time of confirmation of sale.

(d) Where property sold by the personal representative for part cash and part deferred payments consists of an undivided interest in personal property or any other interest therein less than the entire ownership and the owner or owners of the remaining interests therein join in the sale, the note and security interest may be made to the personal representative and such others having an interest in the property. The interest of the personal representative in the note and security interest shall be in the same interest and in the same proportions as the estate's interest in the property prior to the sale.

Ca. Prob. Code § 10257
Enacted by Stats. 1990, Ch. 79.

Section 10258 - Petition for order authorizing sale on credit for less than 25 percent of purchase price paid in cash

(a) On petition of the personal representative, the court may by order authorize a sale of personal property on credit on terms providing for less than 25 percent of the purchase price to be paid in cash at the time of sale, or may waive or modify the requirement that a security interest or other lien shall be retained or taken to secure payment of the balance of the purchase price, where it is shown that the terms are to the advantage of the estate and the property to be sold is of such a nature that it is impracticable to sell the property for a larger cash payment at the time of sale or to retain a security interest or other lien in the property. The order of the court shall fix the terms and conditions of the sale.

(b) Notice of the hearing on the petition shall be posted as provided in Section 1230 and given as provided in Section 1220 to all of the following persons:

(1) Each person listed in Section 1220.

(2) Each known heir whose interest in the estate would be affected by the sale.

(3) Each known devisee whose interest in the estate would be affected by the sale.

Ca. Prob. Code § 10258
Enacted by Stats. 1990, Ch. 79.

Section 10259 - Title passing without need of court confirmation or approval

(a) Title to the following personal property passes upon sale without the need for court confirmation or approval:

(1) Personal property which is perishable, which will depreciate in value if not disposed of promptly, or which will incur loss or expense by being kept.

(2) Personal property the sale of which is necessary to provide for the payment of a family allowance pending receipt of other sufficient funds.

(b) Title to personal property sold at public auction passes without the need for court confirmation or approval upon receipt of the purchase price and:

(1) In the case of tangible personal property, the delivery of the

property to the purchaser.

(2) In the case of intangible personal property, the delivery to the purchaser of the instrument that transfers the title to the property to the purchaser.

(c) The personal representative is responsible for the actual value of the property described in subdivision (a) or (b) unless the sale is reported to and approved by the court.

Ca. Prob. Code § 10259

Enacted by Stats. 1990, Ch. 79.

Section 10260 - Sales reported to and confirmed by court before title passes

(a) Except as provided in Sections 10200, 10201, 10202, 10259, and 10503, all sales of personal property shall be reported to and be confirmed by the court before title to the property passes to the purchaser, notwithstanding that the property is directed by the will to be sold or authority is given in the will to sell the property.

(b) If the personal representative fails to file the report and a petition for confirmation of the sale within 30 days after the sale, the purchaser at the sale may file the report and petition for confirmation of the sale.

(c) Notice of the hearing on the petition for confirmation filed under subdivision (a) or (b) shall be given as provided in Section 1220 and posted as provided in Section 1230.

Ca. Prob. Code § 10260

Enacted by Stats. 1990, Ch. 79.

Section 10261 - Hearing on petition for confirmation

(a) Except as provided in this subdivision, at the hearing on the petition for confirmation of the sale, the court shall examine into the necessity for the sale or the advantage to the estate and the benefit to the interested persons in making the sale. If the decedent's will authorizes or directs the property to be sold, there need be no showing of the necessity of the sale or the advantage to the estate and the benefit to the interested persons in making the sale.

(b) Any interested person may file written objections to the confirmation of the sale at or before the hearing and may testify and produce witnesses in support of the objections.

(c) Before confirming the sale of a partnership interest, whether made to the surviving partner or to any other person, the court shall do both of the following:

(1) Inquire into the condition of the partnership affairs.

(2) Examine any surviving partner if that surviving partner is a resident within the state at the time of the hearing and able to be present in court. The court may issue a citation to compel the surviving partner to attend the hearing.

(d) Upon its own motion or upon the request of the personal representative, the agent or broker, or any other interested person, made at the time of the confirmation hearing or at another time, the court shall fix the compensation of the agent or broker as provided in Article 3 (commencing with Section 10160).

Ca. Prob. Code § 10261

Enacted by Stats. 1990, Ch. 79.

Section 10262 - Acceptance of new bid made to court at hearing on petition for confirmation

(a) Except as provided in subdivision (b), if a written offer to purchase the property is made to the court at the hearing on the petition for confirmation of the sale and the new bid is at least 10 percent more than the amount stated in the report made to the court, the court in its discretion may accept the new bid and confirm the sale to the offeror, or may order a new sale, if all of the following conditions are satisfied:

(1) The original bid as stated in the report to the court is more than one hundred dollars ($100) or, if the original bid is less than one hundred dollars ($100), the new bid is at least one hundred dollars ($100) more than the original bid.

(2) The new bid is made by a responsible person.

(3) The new bid complies with all provisions of law.
(b) If there is more than one offer that satisfies the requirements of subdivision (a), the court shall do one of the following:

(1) Accept the highest such offer and confirm the sale to the offeror.

(2) Order a new sale.
(c) This section does not apply to a sale of property described in Section 10259.
   Ca. Prob. Code § 10262
Enacted by Stats. 1990, Ch. 79.

Section 10263 - Proof that notice given

If notice of the sale was required, before an order is made confirming the sale, it shall be proved to the satisfaction of the court that notice of the sale was given as required by this article, and the order of confirmation shall show that such proof was made.
   Ca. Prob. Code § 10263
Enacted by Stats. 1990, Ch. 79.

Section 10264 - Validity not impaired by omission, error or irregularity

No omission, error, or irregularity in the proceedings under this article shall impair or invalidate the proceedings or the sale pursuant to an order made under this article.
   Ca. Prob. Code § 10264
Enacted by Stats. 1990, Ch. 79.

Article 6 - SALE OF REAL PROPERTY

Section 10300 - Notice of sale

(a) Except as provided in Sections 10301 to 10303, inclusive, and in Section 10503, real property of the estate may be sold only after notice of sale has been published pursuant to Section 6063a of the Government Code (1) in a newspaper published in the county in which the real property or some portion thereof is located or (2) if there is no such newspaper, in such newspaper as the court or judge may direct.

(b) The publication of notice of sale shall be completed before:

(1) In the case of a private sale, the day specified in the notice as the day on or after which the sale is to be made.

(2) In the case of a public auction sale, the day of the auction.
Ca. Prob. Code § 10300
Enacted by Stats. 1990, Ch. 79.

Section 10301 - Posting notice in lieu of publication

(a) If it appears from the inventory and appraisal that the value of the real property to be sold does not exceed five thousand dollars ($5,000), the personal representative may in his or her discretion dispense with publication of notice of sale and, in lieu of publication, post the notice of sale at the courthouse of the county in which the real property or some portion thereof is located.

(b) Except as provided in Section 10302, posting pursuant to this section shall be for at least 15 days before:

(1) In the case of a private sale, the day specified in the notice of sale as the day on or after which the sale is to be made.

(2) In the case of a public auction sale, the day of the auction.
Ca. Prob. Code § 10301
Enacted by Stats. 1990, Ch. 79.

Section 10302 - Order shortening time of notice

(a) If it is shown that it will be to the advantage of the estate, the court or judge may by order shorten the time of notice of sale to not less than five days.

(b) Except as provided in subdivision (c), if the court or judge makes an order under subdivision (a), notice of sale shall be published as provided in Section 10300 except that the publication shall be pursuant to Section 6061 of the Government Code.

(c) In a case described in Section 10301, if the court makes an order under subdivision (a), notice of sale shall be posted as provided in Section 10301 except that the notice of sale shall be posted at least five days before the sale instead of 15 days as required by Section 10301.

Ca. Prob. Code § 10302
Enacted by Stats. 1990, Ch. 79.

Section 10303 - Cases in which property sold without notice

Real property may be sold with or without notice, as the personal representative may determine, in either of the following cases:

(a) Where the property is directed by the will to be sold.

(b) Where authority is given in the will to sell the property.

Ca. Prob. Code § 10303
Enacted by Stats. 1990, Ch. 79.

Section 10304 - Contents of notice

(a) The notice of sale given pursuant to this article shall state all of the following:

(1) Whether the sale is to be a private sale or a public auction sale.

(2) In the case of a private sale, the place at which bids or offers will be received and a day on or after which the sale will be made or, in the case of a public auction sale, the time and place of sale.

(3) The street address or other common designation or, if none, a legal description of the real property to be sold.

(b) The notice of sale may state other matters in addition to those required by subdivision (a), including terms and conditions of sale.

Ca. Prob. Code § 10304
Enacted by Stats. 1990, Ch. 79.

Section 10305 - Sale at public auction

(a) A sale of real property at public auction shall be made in the county in which the property is located. If the property is located in two or more counties, it may be sold in any one of them.
(b) A sale of real property at public auction shall be made between 9 a.m. and 9 p.m., and the sale shall be made on the day specified in the notice of sale unless the sale is postponed.
(c) The personal representative may postpone a public auction sale of real property from time to time if all of the following conditions are satisfied:

(1) The personal representative believes that the postponement is to the advantage of the estate.

(2) Notice of the postponement is given by public declaration at the time and place appointed for the sale.

(3) The postponement, together with previous postponements of sale of the property, does not exceed three months in all.
Ca. Prob. Code § 10305
Enacted by Stats. 1990, Ch. 79.

Section 10306 - Private sale

(a) A private sale of real property may not be made before the day stated in the notice of sale as the day on or after which the sale will be made, nor later than one year after that day.
(b) In the case of a private sale of real property, the bids or offers shall be in writing and shall be left at the place designated in the notice of sale, or be delivered to the personal representative personally or to the person specified in the notice of sale, at any time after the first publication or posting of notice of sale and before the making of the sale.

Ca. Prob. Code § 10306
Enacted by Stats. 1990, Ch. 79.

Section 10307 - Bids to comply with terms of notice

Whether a sale of real property is private or at public auction, bids shall substantially comply with any terms specified in the notice of sale.

Ca. Prob. Code § 10307
Enacted by Stats. 1990, Ch. 79.

Section 10308 - Sales report to and confirmed by court before title passes

(a) Except as provided in Section 10503, all sales of real property shall be reported to and be confirmed by the court before title to the property passes to the purchaser, whether the sale is a private sale or a public auction sale and notwithstanding that the property is directed by the will to be sold or authority is given in the will to sell the property.

(b) If the personal representative fails to file the report and a petition for confirmation of the sale within 30 days after the sale, the purchaser at the sale may file the report and petition for confirmation of the sale.

(c) Notice of the hearing on the petition for confirmation filed under subdivision (a) or (b) shall be given as provided in Section 1220 to the persons designated by that section and to the purchasers named in the petition, and posted as provided in Section 1230.

Ca. Prob. Code § 10308
Amended by Stats. 1992, Ch. 871, Sec. 11. Effective January 1, 1993.

Section 10309 - Appraisal required for confirmation

(a) Except as provided in Section 10207, no sale of real property at private sale shall be confirmed by the court unless all of the following conditions are satisfied:

(1) The real property has been appraised within one year prior to the date of the confirmation hearing.

(2) The valuation date used in the appraisal described in paragraph (1) is within one year prior to the date of the confirmation hearing.

(3) The sum offered for the property is at least 90 percent of the appraised value of the property as determined by the appraisal described in paragraph (1).

(b) An appraisal of the property may be had at any time before the sale or the confirmation of sale in any of the following cases:

(1) Where the property has not been previously appraised.

(2) Where the property has not been appraised within one year before the date of the confirmation hearing.

(3) Where the valuation date used in the latest appraisal is more than one year before the date of the confirmation hearing.

(4) Where the court is satisfied that the latest appraisal is too high or too low.

(c) A new appraisal made pursuant to subdivision (b) need not be made by a probate referee if the original appraisal of the property was made by a person other than a probate referee. If the original appraisal of the property was made by a probate referee, the new appraisal may be made by the probate referee who made the original appraisal without further order of the court or further request for the appointment of a new probate referee. If appraisal by a probate referee is required, a new probate referee shall be appointed, using the same procedure as for the appointment of an original referee, to make the new appraisal if the original probate referee is dead, has been removed, or is otherwise unable to act, or if there is other reason to appoint another probate referee.

Ca. Prob. Code § 10309
Enacted by Stats. 1990, Ch. 79.

Section 10310 - Hearing on petition for confirmation

(a) Except as provided in this subdivision, at the hearing on the petition for confirmation of the sale of the real property, the court shall examine into the necessity for the sale or the advantage to the estate and the benefit to the interested persons in making the sale. If the decedent's will authorizes or directs the property to be sold, there need be no showing of the necessity of the sale or the advantage to the estate and benefit to the interested persons in making the sale.

(b) The court shall examine into the efforts of the personal representative to obtain the highest and best price for the property reasonably attainable.

(c) Any interested person may file written objections to the confirmation of the sale at or before the hearing and may testify and produce witnesses in support of the objections.

Ca. Prob. Code § 10310

Enacted by Stats. 1990, Ch. 79.

Section 10311 - Acceptance of offer made and confirmation of sale

(a) Subject to subdivisions (b), (c), (d), and (e), and except as provided in Section 10207, if a written offer to purchase the real property is made to the court at the hearing on the petition for confirmation of the sale, the court shall accept the offer and confirm the sale to the offeror if all of the following conditions are satisfied:

(1) The offer is for an amount at least 10 percent more on the first ten thousand dollars ($10,000) of the original bid and 5 percent more on the amount of the original bid in excess of ten thousand dollars ($10,000).

(2) The offer is made by a responsible person.

(3) The offer complies with all provisions of law.

(b) Subject to subdivisions (c), (d), and (e), if there is more than one offer that satisfies the requirements of subdivision (a), the court shall accept the highest such offer and confirm the sale to the person making that offer.

(c) The court may, in its discretion, decline to accept the offer that satisfies the requirements of subdivisions (a) and (b); and, in such case, the court shall order a new sale.

(d) If the sale returned for confirmation is on credit and the higher offer is for cash or on credit, whether on the same or different credit terms, or the sale returned for confirmation is for cash and the higher offer is on credit, the court may not consider the higher offer unless the personal representative informs the court in person or by counsel prior to confirmation of sale that the higher offer is acceptable.

(e) For the purpose of this section, the amount of the original bid and any higher offer shall be determined by the court without regard to any of the following:

(1) Any commission on the amount of the bid to which an agent or broker may be entitled under a contract with the personal representative.

(2) Any condition of the bid that a certain amount of the bid be paid to an agent or broker by the personal representative.

Ca. Prob. Code § 10311
Enacted by Stats. 1990, Ch. 79.

Section 10312 - Proof notice given

If notice of the sale was required, before an order is made confirming the sale it shall be proved to the satisfaction of the court that notice of the sale was given as required by this article, and the order of confirmation shall show that the proof was made.

Ca. Prob. Code § 10312
Enacted by Stats. 1990, Ch. 79.

Section 10313 - Order confirming sale and directing conveyances or assignments

(a) The court shall make an order confirming the sale to the person making the highest offer that satisfies the requirements of this article, and directing conveyances or assignments or both to be executed, if it appears to the court that all of the following requirements are satisfied:

(1) Either the sale was authorized or directed to be made by the decedent's will or good reason existed for the sale.

(2) If notice of the sale was required, the proof required by Section 10312 has been made.

(3) The sale was legally made and fairly conducted.

(4) The amount for which the sale is to be confirmed is not disproportionate to the value of the property.

(5) In the case of a private sale, the sale complied with the requirements of Section 10309.

(6) If the sale is confirmed to the original bidder, it does not appear that a sum exceeding the original bid by at least 10 percent more on the first ten thousand dollars ($10,000) of the original bid and 5 percent more on the amount of the original bid in excess of ten thousand dollars ($10,000), exclusive of the expenses of a new sale, may be obtained.

(b) Upon its own motion or upon the request of the personal representative, the agent or broker, or any other interested person, made at the time of the confirmation hearing or at another time, the court shall fix the compensation of the agent or broker as provided in Article 3 (commencing with Section 10160).

(c) If it appears to the court that the requirements of subdivision (a) are not satisfied, the court shall vacate the sale and order a new sale.

(d) If the court orders a new sale under subdivision (c) of this section or under subdivision (c) of Section 10311, notice of the new sale shall be given and the new sale shall in all respects be conducted as if no previous sale had taken place.

Ca. Prob. Code § 10313
Enacted by Stats. 1990, Ch. 79.

Section 10314 - Execution of conveyance or assignment by personal representative

(a) Except as provided in subdivision (b), upon confirmation of the sale, the personal representative shall execute a conveyance to the purchaser which shall refer to the order confirming the sale and directing the conveyance to be executed. A certified copy of the order shall be recorded in the office of the recorder of the county in which the real property or some portion thereof is located.

(b) Upon confirmation of a sale of the decedent's interest under a contract for the purchase of real property by the decedent and after the purchaser has given a bond if one is required under Section 10206, the personal representative shall execute an assignment of the contract to the purchaser.

(c) A conveyance made in compliance with the court order confirming the sale and directing the conveyance to be executed vests in the purchaser both of the following:

 (1) All the right, title, and interest which the decedent had in the property at the time of the decedent's death.

 (2) Any other or additional right, title, or interest in the property acquired by the estate of the decedent, by operation of law or otherwise, prior to the sale.

(d) An assignment made in compliance with the court order confirming the sale of the decedent's interest under a contract for the purchase of real property by the decedent vests in the purchaser all the right, title, and interest of the estate, or of the persons entitled to the interest of the decedent, at the time of sale in the property assigned. The purchaser of the decedent's interest under the contract for the purchase of the real property by the decedent has the same rights and remedies against the vendor of the property as the decedent would have had if living.

Ca. Prob. Code § 10314
Enacted by Stats. 1990, Ch. 79.

Section 10315 - Sale made on credit; property sold for part cash and part deferred payment less than entire ownership

(a) If a sale is made on credit, the personal representative shall take the note of the purchaser for the unpaid portion of the purchase money, with a mortgage or deed of trust on the property to secure payment of the note. The mortgage or deed of trust shall be subject only to encumbrances existing at the date of sale and such other encumbrances as the court may approve.

(b) Where property sold by the personal representative for part cash and part deferred payments consists of an undivided interest in real property or any other interest therein less than the entire ownership and the owner or owners of the remaining interests therein join in the sale, the note and deed of trust or mortgage may be made to the personal representative and such others having an interest in the property. The interest of the personal representative in the note and deed of trust or mortgage shall be in the same interest and in the same proportions as the estate's interest in the property prior to the sale.

Ca. Prob. Code § 10315
Enacted by Stats. 1990, Ch. 79.

Section 10316 - Validity not impaired by omission, error or irregularity

No omission, error, or irregularity in the proceedings under this article shall impair or invalidate the proceedings or the sale pursuant to an order made under this article.

Ca. Prob. Code § 10316
Enacted by Stats. 1990, Ch. 79.

Article 7 - VACATING SALE FOR PURCHASER'S DEFAULT; LIABILITY OF DEFAULTING PURCHASER FOR DAMAGES

Section 10350 - Generally

(a) If after court confirmation of sale of real or personal property the purchaser fails to comply with the terms of sale, the court may, on petition of the personal representative, vacate the order of confirmation, order a resale of the property, and award damages to the estate against the purchaser.

(b) Notice of the hearing on the petition shall be given as provided in Section 1220 to the persons designated by that section and the notice and a copy of the petition shall be given to the buyers and brokers named in the order confirming sale, except that notice need not be given to a defaulting purchaser whose written consent to the petition is filed with the court before the hearing.

(c) Notice of the resale of the property shall be given as provided in this chapter for a sale of the property in the first instance.

(d) Proceedings after notice of the resale shall be as provided in this chapter for a sale of the property in the first instance.

(e) If the property is resold, the defaulting purchaser is liable to the estate for damages equal to the sum of the following:

(1) The difference between the contract price of the first sale and the amount paid by the purchaser at the resale.

(2) Expenses made necessary by the purchaser's breach.

(3) Other consequential damages.

Ca. Prob. Code § 10350

Amended by Stats. 1992, Ch. 871, Sec. 12. Effective January 1, 1993.

Section 10351 - Vacating confirmation and making order confirming sale to new high bidder

(a) The court may vacate the order of confirmation of a sale of real or personal property and make an order confirming the sale to the new high bidder if both of the following requirements are satisfied:

(1) A petition is filed within 60 days after confirmation of the sale showing that (A) the purchaser at the sale has failed to complete the purchase and (B) a bid has been made for the property in the same or a higher amount, on the same or better terms, and in the manner prescribed in the original notice of sale.

(2) The sale has not been vacated pursuant to Section 10350.

(b) Notice of the hearing on the petition shall be given as provided in Section 1220 to the persons designated by that section and the notice and a copy of the petition shall be given to the buyers and brokers named in the order confirming sale, except that notice need not be given to a defaulting purchaser whose written consent to the vacation of the order confirming the sale is filed with the court prior to the hearing.

(c) If the report and petition for confirmation of the second sale are not filed within 60 days of the confirmation of the first sale, the property may be resold only in the manner provided in Section 10350.

Ca. Prob. Code § 10351

Amended by Stats. 1992, Ch. 871, Sec. 13. Effective January 1, 1993.

Article 8 - APPLICATION OF SALE PROCEEDS OF ENCUMBERED PROPERTY; SALE TO LIENHOLDER

Section 10360 - Definitions

As used in this article:

(a) "Amount secured by the lien" includes interest and any costs and charges secured by the lien.

(b) "Encumbered property" means real or personal property that is subject to a lien for a secured debt which is a valid claim against the estate and which has been allowed or approved.

(c) "Lien" means a mortgage, deed of trust, or other lien.

Ca. Prob. Code § 10360

Enacted by Stats. 1990, Ch. 79.

Section 10361 - Order of applying purchase money

(a) If encumbered property is sold, the purchase money shall be applied in the following order:

(1) Expenses of administration which are reasonably related to the administration of the property sold as provided in paragraph (1) of subdivision (a) of Section 11420.

(2) The payment of the expenses of the sale.

(3) The payment and satisfaction of the amount secured by the lien on the property sold if payment and satisfaction of the lien is required under the terms of the sale.

(4) Application in the course of administration.
(b) The application of the purchase money, after the payment of those expenses set forth in paragraphs (1) and (2) of subdivision (a), to the payment and satisfaction of the amount secured by the lien on the property sold shall be made without delay; and, subject to Section 10362, the property sold remains subject to the lien until the purchase money has been actually so applied.

Ca. Prob. Code § 10361
Amended by Stats. 1996, Ch. 862, Sec. 26. Effective January 1, 1997.

Section 10361.5 - Petition to determine amount of expenses related to administration of encumbered property

The personal representative or any interested party may, at any time before payment is made to satisfy all liens on the encumbered property sold, petition for an order determining the amount of expenses of administration that are reasonably related to the administration of that encumbered property as provided in paragraph (1) of subdivision (a) of Section 11420. The petition may be heard as part of a petition for confirmation of sale of personal or real property as provided in Section 10260 or 10308, respectively or may be heard separately. If the petition is presented as part of a petition for confirmation of sale of real or personal property, the notice of hearing otherwise required by this code for a petition for confirmation of sale shall be given in addition to the notice requirements under Section 10361.6.

Ca. Prob. Code § 10361.5
Added by Stats. 1996, Ch. 862, Sec. 27. Effective January 1, 1997.

Section 10361.6 - Service of notice and copy of petition

(a) At least 30 days prior to the day of the hearing, the petitioner shall cause notice of the hearing and a copy of the petition to be served in the manner provided in Chapter 4 (commencing with Section 413.10) of Title 5 of Part 3 of the Code of Civil Procedure on all of the following persons:

(1) The personal representative, if the personal representative is not the petitioner.

(2) The holder of any mortgage or other lien secured by the property that is sold.

(3) All agents or brokers entitled to compensation from the proceeds of the property that is sold.
(b) Except for those persons given notice pursuant to subdivision (a), notice of the hearing, together with a copy of the petition, shall be given as provided in Section 1220 to all of the following persons:

(1) Each person listed in Section 1220.

(2) Each known heir whose interest in the estate would be affected by the petition.

(3) Each known devisee whose interest in the estate would be affected by the petition.

(4) The Attorney General, at the office of the Attorney General in Sacramento, if any portion of the estate is to escheat to the state and its interest in the estate would be affected by the petition.
(c) The court may not shorten the time for giving the notice of hearing under this section.

Ca. Prob. Code § 10361.6
Added by Stats. 1996, Ch. 862, Sec. 28. Effective January 1, 1997.

Section 10362 - Payment of purchase money to pay

amount of lien and expenses of sale

(a) If encumbered property is sold, the purchase money, or so much of the purchase money as is sufficient to pay the amount secured by the lien on the property sold and the expenses of the sale, may be paid to the clerk of the court. Upon the payment being so made, the lien on the property sold ceases.

(b) The clerk of court without delay shall use the money paid to the clerk under this section to pay the expenses of the sale and to pay and satisfy the amount secured by the lien on the property sold. The clerk shall at once return the surplus, if any, to the personal representative unless the court, for good cause shown and after notice to the personal representative, otherwise orders.

Ca. Prob. Code § 10362
Enacted by Stats. 1990, Ch. 79.

Section 10363 - Lienholder purchasing property

(a) At a sale of real or personal property subject to a lien, the lienholder may become the purchaser of the property, even though no claim for the amount secured by the lien on the property sold has been, or could have been, filed, allowed, or approved.

(b) Unless the property is sold subject to the lien:

(1) If the lienholder becomes the purchaser of the property and the amount secured by the lien on the property is a valid claim against the estate and has been allowed or approved, the receipt of the lienholder for the amount due the lienholder from the proceeds of the sale is a payment pro tanto.

(2) If the lienholder becomes the purchaser of the property and no claim for the amount secured by the lien on the property has been filed, allowed, or approved, the court may at the hearing on the petition for confirmation of the sale examine into the validity and enforceability of the lien and the amount secured by the lien, and the court may authorize the personal representative to accept the receipt of the lienholder for the amount secured by the lien as payment pro tanto.

(3) If the lienholder becomes the purchaser of the property and the amount for which the property is purchased is insufficient to pay the expenses of the sale and to discharge the lienholder's lien, whether or not a claim has been filed, allowed, or approved, the lienholder shall pay to the clerk of the court an amount sufficient to cover the expenses of the sale.

(c) Nothing permitted under this section shall be deemed to be an allowance or approval of a claim based upon the lien or the amount secured by the lien.

Ca. Prob. Code § 10363
Enacted by Stats. 1990, Ch. 79.

Article 9 - DAMAGES AND RECOVERY OF PROPERTY

Section 10380 - Neglect or misconduct of personal representative

The personal representative is liable to an interested person for damages suffered by the interested person by reason of the neglect or misconduct of the personal representative in the proceedings in relation to a sale.

Ca. Prob. Code § 10380
Enacted by Stats. 1990, Ch. 79.

Section 10381 - Fraudulent sale

In addition to any other damages for which the personal representative is liable, if the personal representative fraudulently sells real property of the estate contrary to or otherwise than under the provisions of this chapter, the person having an estate of inheritance in the real property may recover from the personal representative, as liquidated damages, an amount equal to double the fair market value of the real property sold on the date of sale.

Ca. Prob. Code § 10381
Enacted by Stats. 1990, Ch. 79.

Section 10382 - Statute of limitations on action to recover property on claim sale void

(a) No action for the recovery of property sold by a personal representative on the claim that the sale is void may be maintained by an heir or other person claiming under the decedent unless the action is commenced within whichever of the following is the later time:

(1) Three years after the settlement of the final account of the personal representative.

(2) Three years after the discovery of any fraud upon which the action is based.
(b) The limitation established by subdivision (a) is not tolled for any reason.

Ca. Prob. Code § 10382
Enacted by Stats. 1990, Ch. 79.

Part 6 - INDEPENDENT ADMINISTRATION OF ESTATES

Chapter 1 - GENERAL PROVISIONS

Section 10400 - Title of part

This part shall be known and may be cited as the Independent Administration of Estates Act.

Ca. Prob. Code § 10400
Enacted by Stats. 1990, Ch. 79.

Section 10401 - Court supervision defined

As used in this part, "court supervision" means the judicial order, authorization, approval, confirmation, or instructions that would be required if authority to administer the estate had not been granted under this part.

Ca. Prob. Code § 10401
Enacted by Stats. 1990, Ch. 79.

Section 10402 - Full authority defined

As used in this part, "full authority" means authority to administer the estate under this part that includes all the powers granted under this part.

    Ca. Prob. Code § 10402

Enacted by Stats. 1990, Ch. 79.

Section 10403 - Limited authority defined

As used in this part, "limited authority" means authority to administer the estate under this part that includes all the powers granted under this part except the power to do any of the following:

(a) Sell real property.

(b) Exchange real property.

(c) Grant an option to purchase real property.

(d) Borrow money with the loan secured by an encumbrance upon real property.

    Ca. Prob. Code § 10403

Enacted by Stats. 1990, Ch. 79.

Section 10404 - Will required to provide estate administered under part

The personal representative may not be granted authority to administer the estate under this part if the decedent's will provides that the estate shall not be administered under this part.

    Ca. Prob. Code § 10404

Enacted by Stats. 1990, Ch. 79.

Section 10405 - Special administrator granted authority to administer estate

A special administrator may be granted authority to administer the estate under this part if the special administrator is appointed with, or has been granted, the powers of a general personal representative.

    Ca. Prob. Code § 10405

Enacted by Stats. 1990, Ch. 79.

Section 10406 - Applicability of part

(a) Subject to subdivision (b), this part applies in any case where authority to administer the estate is granted under this part or where independent administration authority was granted under prior law.

(b) If the personal representative was granted independent administration authority prior to July 1, 1988, the personal representative may use that existing authority on and after July 1, 1988, to borrow money on a loan secured by an encumbrance upon real property, whether or not that existing authority includes the authority to sell real property.

Ca. Prob. Code § 10406

Amended by Stats. 1990, Ch. 710, Sec. 28. Operative July 1, 1991, by Sec. 48 of Ch. 710.

Chapter 2 - GRANTING OR REVOKING INDEPENDENT ADMINISTRATION AUTHORITY

Section 10450 - Petition for authority

(a) To obtain authority to administer the estate under this part, the personal representative shall petition the court for that authority either in the petition for appointment of the personal representative or in a separate petition filed in the estate proceedings.

(b) The petition may request either of the following:

(1) Full authority to administer the estate under this part.

(2) Limited authority to administer the estate under this part.

Ca. Prob. Code § 10450

Enacted by Stats. 1990, Ch. 79.

Section 10451 - Notice of hearing on petition

(a) If the authority to administer the estate under this part is requested in the petition for appointment of the personal representative, notice of the hearing on the petition shall be given for the period and in the manner applicable to the petition for appointment.

(b) Where proceedings for the administration of the estate are pending at the time a petition is filed under Section 10450, notice of the hearing on the petition shall be given as provided in Section 1220 to all of the following persons:

(1) Each person listed in Section 1220.

(2) Each known heir whose interest in the estate would be affected by the petition.

(3) Each known devisee whose interest in the estate would be affected by the petition.

(4) Each person named as executor in the will of the decedent.

(c) The notice of hearing of the petition for authority to administer the estate under this part, whether included in the petition for appointment or in a separate petition, shall include the substance of the following statement: "The petition requests authority to administer the estate under the Independent Administration of Estates Act. This will avoid the need to obtain court approval for many actions taken in connection with the estate. However, before taking certain actions, the personal representative will be required to give notice to interested persons unless they have waived notice or have consented to the proposed action. Independent administration authority will be granted unless good cause is shown why it should not be."

Ca. Prob. Code § 10451
Enacted by Stats. 1990, Ch. 79.

Section 10452 - Granting requested authority

Unless an interested person objects as provided in Section 1043 to the granting of authority to administer the estate under this part and the court determines that the objecting party has shown good cause why the authority to administer the estate under this part should not be granted, the court shall grant the requested authority.

If the objecting party has shown good cause why only limited authority should be granted, the court shall grant only limited authority.

Ca. Prob. Code § 10452
Enacted by Stats. 1990, Ch. 79.

Section 10453 - Bond

(a) If the personal representative is otherwise required to file a bond and has full authority, the court, in its discretion, shall fix the amount of the bond at not more than the estimated value of the personal property, the estimated value of the decedent's interest in the real property authorized to be sold under this part, and the probable annual gross income of the estate, or, if the bond is to be given by personal sureties, at not less than twice that amount.

(b) If the personal representative is otherwise required to file a bond and has limited authority, the court, in its discretion, shall fix the amount of the bond at not more than the estimated value of the personal property and the probable annual gross income of the estate, or, if the bond is to be given by personal sureties, at not less than twice that amount.

Ca. Prob. Code § 10453
Enacted by Stats. 1990, Ch. 79.

Section 10454 - Petition requesting order revoking authority

(a) Any interested person may file a petition requesting that the court make either of the following orders:

(1) An order revoking the authority of the personal representative to continue administration of the estate under this part.

(2) An order revoking the full authority of the personal representative to administer the estate under this part and granting the personal representative limited authority to administer the estate under this part.

(b) The petition shall set forth the basis for the requested order.

(c) Notice of the hearing on the petition shall be given as provided in Section 1220. In addition, the personal representative shall be served with a copy of the petition and a notice of the time and place of the hearing at least 15 days prior to the hearing. Service on the personal representative shall be made in the manner provided in Section 415.10 or 415.30 of the Code of Civil Procedure or in such manner as may be authorized by the court.

(d) If the court determines that good cause has been shown, the court shall make an order revoking the authority of the personal representative to continue administration of the estate under this part. Upon the making of the order, new letters shall be issued without the notation described in subdivision (c) of Section 8405.

(e) If the personal representative was granted full authority and the court determines that good cause has been shown, the court shall make an order revoking the full authority and granting the personal representative limited authority. Upon the making of the order, new letters shall be issued with the notation described in subdivision (c) of Section 8405 that is required where the authority granted is limited authority.

Ca. Prob. Code § 10454
Enacted by Stats. 1990, Ch. 79.

Chapter 3 - ADMINISTRATION UNDER INDEPENDENT ADMINISTRATION AUTHORITY

Article 1 - GENERAL PROVISIONS

Section 10500 - Generally

(a) Subject to the limitations and conditions of this part, a personal representative who has been granted authority to administer the estate under this part may administer the estate as provided in this part without court supervision, but in all other respects the personal representative shall administer the estate in the same manner as a personal representative who has not been granted authority to administer the estate under this part.

(b) Notwithstanding subdivision (a), the personal representative may obtain court supervision as provided in this code of any action to be taken by the personal representative during administration of the estate.

Ca. Prob. Code § 10500

Enacted by Stats. 1990, Ch. 79.

Section 10501 - Actions requiring court supervision

(a) Notwithstanding any other provision of this part, whether the personal representative has been granted full authority or limited authority, a personal representative who has obtained authority to administer the estate under this part is required to obtain court supervision, in the manner provided in this code, for any of the following actions:

(1) Allowance of the personal representative's compensation.

(2) Allowance of compensation of the attorney for the personal representative.

(3) Settlement of accounts.

(4) Subject to Section 10520, preliminary and final distributions and discharge.

(5) Sale of property of the estate to the personal representative or to the attorney for the personal representative.

(6) Exchange of property of the estate for property of the personal representative or for property of the attorney for the personal representative.

(7) Grant of an option to purchase property of the estate to the personal representative or to the attorney for the personal representative.

(8) Allowance, payment, or compromise of a claim of the personal representative, or the attorney for the personal representative, against the estate.

(9) Compromise or settlement of a claim, action, or proceeding by the estate against the personal representative or against the attorney for the personal representative.

(10) Extension, renewal, or modification of the terms of a debt or other obligation of the personal representative, or the attorney for the personal representative, owing to or in favor of the decedent or the estate.

(b) Notwithstanding any other provision of this part, a personal representative who has obtained only limited authority to administer the estate under this part is required to obtain court supervision, in the manner provided in this code, for any of the following actions:

(1) Sale of real property.

(2) Exchange of real property.

(3) Grant of an option to purchase real property.

(4) Borrowing money with the loan secured by an encumbrance upon real property.

(c) Paragraphs (5) to (10), inclusive, of subdivision (a) do not apply to a transaction between the personal representative as such and the personal representative as an individual where all of the following requirements are satisfied:

(1) Either (A) the personal representative is the sole beneficiary of the estate or (B) all the known heirs or devisees have consented to the transaction.

(2) The period for filing creditor claims has expired.

(3) No request for special notice is on file or all persons who filed a request for special notice have consented to the transaction.

(4) The claim of each creditor who filed a claim has been paid, settled, or withdrawn, or the creditor has consented to the transaction.

Ca. Prob. Code § 10501
Amended by Stats. 1992, Ch. 178, Sec. 37. Effective January 1, 1993.

Section 10502 - Powers of personal representative

(a) Subject to the conditions and limitations of this part and to Section 9600, a personal representative who has been granted authority to administer the estate under this part has the powers described in Article 2 (commencing with Section 10510), Article 3 (commencing with Section 10530), and Article 4 (commencing with Section 10550).
(b) The will may restrict the powers that the personal representative may exercise under this part.

Ca. Prob. Code § 10502
Enacted by Stats. 1990, Ch. 79.

Section 10503 - Sale of property

Subject to the limitations and requirements of this part, when the personal representative exercises the authority to sell property of the estate under this part, the personal representative may sell the property either at public auction or private sale, and with or without notice, for such price, for cash or on credit, and upon such terms and conditions as the personal representative may determine, and the requirements applicable to court confirmation of sales of real property (including, but not limited to, publication of notice of sale, court approval of agents' and brokers' commissions, sale at not less than 90 percent of appraised value, and court examination into the necessity for the sale, advantage to the estate and benefit to interested persons, and efforts of the personal representative to obtain the highest and best price for the property reasonably attainable), and the requirements applicable to court confirmation of sales of personal property, do not apply to the sale.

Ca. Prob. Code § 10503
Enacted by Stats. 1990, Ch. 79.

Article 2 - POWERS EXERCISABLE ONLY AFTER GIVING NOTICE OF PROPOSED ACTION

Section 10510 - Generally

The personal representative may exercise the powers described in this article only if the requirements of Chapter 4 (commencing with Section 10580) (notice of proposed action procedure) are satisfied.

Ca. Prob. Code § 10510
Enacted by Stats. 1990, Ch. 79.

Section 10511 - Power to sell or exchange real property

The personal representative who has full authority has the power to sell or exchange real property of the estate.

Ca. Prob. Code § 10511
Enacted by Stats. 1990, Ch. 79.

Section 10512 - Power to sell or incorporate

The personal representative has the power to sell or incorporate any of the following:
(a) An unincorporated business or venture in which the decedent was engaged at the time of the decedent's death.
(b) An unincorporated business or venture which was wholly or partly owned by the decedent at the time of the decedent's death.

Ca. Prob. Code § 10512
Enacted by Stats. 1990, Ch. 79.

Section 10513 - Power to abandon tangible personal property

The personal representative has the power to abandon tangible personal property where the cost of collecting, maintaining, and safeguarding the property would exceed its fair market value.

Ca. Prob. Code § 10513
Enacted by Stats. 1990, Ch. 79.

Section 10514 - Power to borrow and encumber property

(a) Subject to subdivision (b), the personal representative has the following powers:

(1) The power to borrow.

(2) The power to place, replace, renew, or extend any encumbrance upon any property of the estate.
(b) Only a personal representative who has full authority has the power to borrow money with the loan secured by an encumbrance upon real property.
Ca. Prob. Code § 10514
Enacted by Stats. 1990, Ch. 79.

Section 10515 - Power to grant option to purchase real property

The personal representative who has full authority has the power to grant an option to purchase real property of the estate for a period within or beyond the period of administration.
Ca. Prob. Code § 10515
Enacted by Stats. 1990, Ch. 79.

Section 10516 - Power to convey pursuant to option to purchase

If the will gives a person the option to purchase real or personal property and the person has complied with the terms and conditions stated in the will, the personal representative has the power to convey or transfer the property to the person.
Ca. Prob. Code § 10516
Enacted by Stats. 1990, Ch. 79.

Section 10517 - Power to convey to complete contract

The personal representative has the power to convey or transfer real or personal property to complete a contract entered into by the decedent to convey or transfer the property.

Ca. Prob. Code § 10517

Enacted by Stats. 1990, Ch. 79.

Section 10518 - Power to allow, compromise or settle claims

The personal representative has the power to allow, compromise, or settle any of the following:

(a) A third-party claim to real or personal property if the decedent died in possession of, or holding title to, the property.

(b) The decedent's claim to real or personal property title to or possession of which is held by another.

Ca. Prob. Code § 10518

Enacted by Stats. 1990, Ch. 79.

Section 10519 - Power to make disclaimer

The personal representative has the power to make a disclaimer.

Ca. Prob. Code § 10519

Enacted by Stats. 1990, Ch. 79.

Section 10520 - Power to make preliminary distribution

If the time for filing claims has expired and it appears that the distribution may be made without loss to creditors or injury to the estate or any interested person, the personal representative has the power to make preliminary distributions of the following:

(a) Income received during administration to the persons entitled under Chapter 8 (commencing with Section 12000) of Part 10.

(b) Household furniture and furnishings, motor vehicles, clothing, jewelry, and other tangible articles of a personal nature to the persons entitled to the property under the decedent's will, not to exceed an aggregate fair market value to all persons of fifty thousand dollars ($50,000) computed cumulatively through the date of distribution. Fair market value shall be determined on the basis of the inventory and appraisal.

(c) Cash to general pecuniary devisees entitled to it under the decedent's will, not to exceed ten thousand dollars ($10,000) to any one person.

Ca. Prob. Code § 10520

Added by Stats. 1992, Ch. 178, Sec. 38. Effective January 1, 1993.

Article 3 - POWERS THE EXERCISE OF WHICH REQUIRES GIVING OF NOTICE OF PROPOSED ACTION UNDER SOME CIRCUMSTANCES

Section 10530 - Generally

Except to the extent that this article otherwise provides, the personal representative may exercise the powers described in this article without giving notice of proposed action under Chapter 4 (commencing with Section 10580).

Ca. Prob. Code § 10530

Enacted by Stats. 1990, Ch. 79.

Section 10531 - Power to manage and control property

(a) The personal representative has the power to manage and control property of the estate, including making allocations and determinations under the Uniform Principal and Income Act, Chapter 3 (commencing with Section 16320) of Part 4 of Division 9. Except as provided in subdivision (b), the personal representative may exercise this power without giving notice of proposed action under Chapter 4 (commencing with Section 10580).

(b) The personal representative shall comply with the requirements of Chapter 4 (commencing with Section 10580) in any case where a provision of Chapter 3 (commencing with Section 10500) governing the exercise of a specific power so requires.

Ca. Prob. Code § 10531

EFFECTIVE 1/1/2000. Amended July 22, 1999 (Bill Number: AB 846) (Chapter 145).

Section 10532 - Power to contract in order to carry out specific power

(a) The personal representative has the power to enter into a contract in order to carry out the exercise of a specific power granted by this part, including, but not limited to, the powers granted by Sections 10531 and 10551. Except as provided in subdivision (b), the personal representative may exercise this power without giving notice of proposed action under Chapter 4 (commencing with Section 10580).

(b) The personal representative shall comply with the requirements of Chapter 4 (commencing with Section 10580) where the contract is one that by its provisions is not to be fully performed within two years, except that the personal representative is not required to comply with those requirements if the personal representative has the unrestricted right under the contract to terminate the contract within two years.

(c) Nothing in this section excuses compliance with the requirements of Chapter 4 (commencing with Section 10580) when the contract is made to carry out the exercise of a specific power and the provision that grants that power requires compliance with Chapter 4 (commencing with Section 10580) for the exercise of the power.

Ca. Prob. Code § 10532
Enacted by Stats. 1990, Ch. 79.

Section 10533 - Power to deposit and invest money

(a) The personal representative has the power to do all of the following:

(1) Deposit money belonging to the estate in an insured account in a financial institution in this state.

(2) Invest money of the estate in any one or more of the following:

(A) Direct obligations of the United States, or of the State of California, maturing not later than one year from the date of making the investment.

(B) An interest in a money market mutual fund registered under the Investment Company Act of 1940 (15 U.S.C. Sec. 80a-1, et seq.) or an investment vehicle authorized for the collective investment of trust funds pursuant to Section 9.18 of Part 9 of Title 12 of the Code of Federal Regulations, the portfolios of which are limited to United States government obligations maturing not later than five years from the date of investment and to repurchase agreements fully collateralized by United States government obligations.

(C) Units of a common trust fund described in Section 1564 of the Financial Code. The common trust fund shall have as its objective investment primarily in short term fixed income obligations and shall be permitted to value investments at cost pursuant to regulations of the appropriate regulatory authority.

(D) Eligible securities for the investment of surplus state moneys as provided for in Section 16430 of the Government Code.

(3) Invest money of the estate in any manner provided by the will.

(b) Except as provided in subdivision (c), the personal representative may exercise the powers described in subdivision (a) without giving notice of proposed action under Chapter 4 (commencing with Section 10580).

(c) The personal representative shall comply with the requirements of Chapter 4 (commencing with Section 10580) where the personal representative exercises the power to make any investment pursuant to the power granted by subparagraph (D) of paragraph (2) of subdivision (a) or paragraph (3) of subdivision (a), except that the personal representative may invest in direct obligations of the United States, or of the State of California, maturing not later than one year from the date of making the investment without complying with the requirements of Chapter 4 (commencing with Section 10580).

Ca. Prob. Code § 10533
Enacted by Stats. 1990, Ch. 79.

Section 10534 - Power to continue as general partner in partnership

(a) Subject to the partnership agreement and the provisions of the Uniform Partnership Act of 1994 (Chapter 5 (commencing with Section 16100) of Title 2 of the Corporations Code), the personal representative has the power to continue as a general partner in any partnership in which the decedent was a general partner at the time of death.

(b) The personal representative has the power to continue operation of any of the following:

(1) An unincorporated business or venture in which the decedent was engaged at the time of the decedent's death.

(2) An unincorporated business or venture which was wholly or partly owned by the decedent at the time of the decedent's death.

(c) Except as provided in subdivision (d), the personal representative may exercise the powers described in subdivisions (a) and (b) without giving notice of proposed action under Chapter 4 (commencing with Section 10580).

(d) The personal representative shall comply with the requirements of Chapter 4 (commencing with Section 10580) if the personal representative continues as a general partner under subdivision (a), or continues the operation of any unincorporated business or venture under subdivision (b), for a period of more than six months from the date letters are first issued to a personal representative.

Ca. Prob. Code § 10534
Amended by Stats 2003 ch 32 (AB 167), s 11, eff. 1/1/2004.

Section 10535 - Power to pay family allowance

(a) The personal representative has the power to pay a reasonable family allowance. Except as provided in subdivision (b), the personal representative may exercise this power without giving notice of proposed action under Chapter 4 (commencing with Section 10580).

(b) The personal representative shall comply with the requirements of Chapter 4 (commencing with Section 10580) for all of the following:

(1) Making the first payment of a family allowance.

(2) Making the first payment of a family allowance for a period commencing more than 12 months after the death of the decedent.

(3) Making any increase in the amount of the payment of a family allowance.

Ca. Prob. Code § 10535
Enacted by Stats. 1990, Ch. 79.

Section 10536 - Power to lease estate property

(a) The personal representative has the power to enter as lessor into a lease of property of the estate for any purpose (including, but not limited to, exploration for and production or removal of minerals, oil, gas, or other hydrocarbon substances or geothermal energy, including a community oil lease or a pooling or unitization agreement) for such period, within or beyond the period of administration, and for such rental or royalty or both, and upon such other terms and conditions as the personal representative may determine. Except as provided in subdivisions (b) and (c), the personal representative may exercise this power without giving notice of proposed action under Chapter 4 (commencing with Section 10580).

(b) The personal representative shall comply with the requirements of Chapter 4 (commencing with Section 10580) where the personal representative enters into a lease of real property for a term in excess of one year. If the lease gives the lessee the right to extend the term of the lease, the lease shall be considered as if the right to extend has been exercised.

(c) The personal representative shall comply with the requirements of Chapter 4 (commencing with Section 10580) where the personal representative enters into a lease of personal property and the lease is one described in subdivision (b) of Section 10532.

Ca. Prob. Code § 10536
Enacted by Stats. 1990, Ch. 79.

Section 10537 - Power to sell or exchange personal property

(a) The personal representative has the power to sell personal property of the estate or to exchange personal property of the estate for other property upon such terms and conditions as the personal representative may determine. Except as provided in subdivision (b), the personal representative shall comply with the requirements of Chapter 4 (commencing with Section 10580) in exercising this power.
(b) The personal representative may exercise the power granted by subdivision (a) without giving notice of proposed action under Chapter 4 (commencing with Section 10580) in case of the sale or exchange of any of the following:

(1) A security sold on an established stock or bond exchange.

(2) A security designated as a national market system security on an interdealer quotation system, or subsystem thereof, by the National Association of Securities Dealers, Inc., sold through a broker-dealer registered under the Securities Exchange Act of 1934 during the regular course of business of the broker-dealer.

(3) Personal property referred to in Section 10202 or 10259 when sold for cash.

(4) A security described in Section 10200 surrendered for redemption or conversion.
Ca. Prob. Code § 10537
Enacted by Stats. 1990, Ch. 79.

Section 10538 - Power to grant exclusive right to sell property

(a) The personal representative has the following powers:

(1) The power to grant an exclusive right to sell property for a period not to exceed 90 days.

(2) The power to grant to the same broker one or more extensions of an exclusive right to sell property, each extension being for a period not to exceed 90 days.
(b) Except as provided in subdivision (c), the personal representative may exercise the powers described in subdivision (a) without giving notice of proposed action under Chapter 4 (commencing with Section 10580).
(c) The personal representative shall comply with the requirements of Chapter 4 (commencing with Section 10580) where the personal representative grants to the same broker an extension of an exclusive right to sell property and the period of the extension, together with the periods of the original exclusive right to sell the property and any previous extensions of that right, is more than 270 days.

Ca. Prob. Code § 10538
Enacted by Stats. 1990, Ch. 79.

Article 4 - POWERS EXERCISABLE WITHOUT GIVING NOTICE OF PROPOSED ACTION

Section 10550 - Generally

The personal representative may exercise the powers described in this article without giving notice of proposed action under Chapter 4 (commencing with Section 10580).

Ca. Prob. Code § 10550
Enacted by Stats. 1990, Ch. 79.

Section 10551 - Powers exercised without supervision

In addition to the powers granted to the personal representative by other sections of this chapter, the personal representative has all the powers that the personal representative could exercise without court supervision under this code if the personal representative had not been granted authority to administer the estate under this part.

Ca. Prob. Code § 10551
Enacted by Stats. 1990, Ch. 79.

Section 10552 - Powers as to claims

The personal representative has the power to do all of the following:
(a) Allow, pay, reject, or contest any claim by or against the estate.
(b) Compromise or settle a claim, action, or proceeding by or for the benefit of, or against, the decedent, the personal representative, or the estate.
(c) Release, in whole or in part, any claim belonging to the estate to the extent that the claim is uncollectible.
(d) Allow a claim to be filed after the expiration of the time for filing the claim.
Ca. Prob. Code § 10552
Amended by Stats. 1996, Ch. 862, Sec. 29. Effective January 1, 1997.

Section 10553 - Powers as to actions and proceedings

The personal representative has the power to do all of the following:
(a) Commence and maintain actions and proceedings for the benefit of the estate.
(b) Defend actions and proceedings against the decedent, the personal representative, or the estate.
Ca. Prob. Code § 10553
Enacted by Stats. 1990, Ch. 79.

Section 10554 - Powers as to obligations owing to estate

The personal representative has the power to extend, renew, or in any manner modify the terms of an obligation owing to or in favor of the decedent or the estate.
Ca. Prob. Code § 10554
Enacted by Stats. 1990, Ch. 79.

Section 10555 - Power to convey or transfer property

The personal representative has the power to convey or transfer property in order to carry out the exercise of a specific power granted by this part.

Ca. Prob. Code § 10555
Enacted by Stats. 1990, Ch. 79.

Section 10556 - Power to pay taxes and administration expenses

The personal representative has the power to pay all of the following:
(a) Taxes and assessments.
(b) Expenses incurred in the collection, care, and administration of the estate.

Ca. Prob. Code § 10556
Enacted by Stats. 1990, Ch. 79.

Section 10557 - Power to purchase annuity

The personal representative has the power to purchase an annuity from an insurer admitted to do business in this state to satisfy a devise of an annuity or other direction in the will for periodic payments to a devisee.

Ca. Prob. Code § 10557
Enacted by Stats. 1990, Ch. 79.

Section 10558 - Power to exercise option right

The personal representative has the power to exercise an option right that is property of the estate.

Ca. Prob. Code § 10558
Enacted by Stats. 1990, Ch. 79.

Section 10559 - Power to purchase securities or commodities

The personal representative has the power to purchase securities or commodities required to perform an incomplete contract of sale where the decedent died having sold but not delivered securities or commodities not owned by the decedent.

Ca. Prob. Code § 10559
Enacted by Stats. 1990, Ch. 79.

Section 10560 - Power to hold security in name of nominee

The personal representative has the power to hold a security in the name of a nominee or in any other form without disclosure of the estate, so that title to the security may pass by delivery.

Ca. Prob. Code § 10560
Enacted by Stats. 1990, Ch. 79.

Section 10561 - Power to exercise security subscription or conversion rights

The personal representative has the power to exercise security subscription or conversion rights.

Ca. Prob. Code § 10561
Enacted by Stats. 1990, Ch. 79.

Section 10562 - Power to make repairs and improvements

The personal representative has the power to make repairs and improvements to real and personal property of the estate.

Ca. Prob. Code § 10562
Enacted by Stats. 1990, Ch. 79.

Section 10563 - Power to accept deed subject to mortgage or deed of trust

The personal representative has the power to accept a deed to property which is subject to a mortgage or deed of trust in lieu of foreclosure of the mortgage or sale under the deed of trust.

Ca. Prob. Code § 10563
Enacted by Stats. 1990, Ch. 79.

Section 10564 - Power to give partial satisfaction of

mortgage

The personal representative has the power to give a partial satisfaction of a mortgage or to cause a partial reconveyance to be executed by a trustee under a deed of trust held by the estate.

Ca. Prob. Code § 10564
Enacted by Stats. 1990, Ch. 79.

Chapter 4 - NOTICE OF PROPOSED ACTION PROCEDURE

Section 10580 - Generally

(a) A personal representative who has been granted authority to administer the estate under this part shall give notice of proposed action as provided in this chapter prior to the taking of the proposed action without court supervision if the provision of Chapter 3 (commencing with Section 10500) giving the personal representative the power to take the action so requires. Nothing in this subdivision authorizes a personal representative to take an action under this part if the personal representative does not have the power to take the action under this part.

(b) A personal representative who has been granted authority to administer the estate under this part may give notice of proposed action as provided in this chapter even if the provision of Chapter 3 (commencing with Section 10500) giving the personal representative the power to take the action permits the personal representative to take the action without giving notice of proposed action. Nothing in this subdivision requires the personal representative to give notice of proposed action where not required under subdivision (a) or authorizes a personal representative to take any action that the personal representative is not otherwise authorized to take.

Ca. Prob. Code § 10580
Enacted by Stats. 1990, Ch. 79.

Section 10581 - Persons to whom notice given

Except as provided in Sections 10582 and 10583, notice of proposed action shall be given to all of the following:

(a) Each known devisee whose interest in the estate would be affected by the proposed action.

(b) Each known heir whose interest in the estate would be affected by the proposed action.

(c) Each person who has filed a request under Chapter 6 (commencing with Section 1250) of Part 2, of Division 3 for special notice of petitions filed in the administration proceeding.

(d) The Attorney General, at the office of the Attorney General in Sacramento, if any portion of the estate is to escheat to the state and its interest in the estate would be affected by the proposed action.

Ca. Prob. Code § 10581
Enacted by Stats. 1990, Ch. 79.

Section 10582 - Person consenting to proposed action

Notice of proposed action need not be given to any person who consents in writing to the proposed action. The consent may be executed at any time before or after the proposed action is taken.

Ca. Prob. Code § 10582
Enacted by Stats. 1990, Ch. 79.

Section 10583 - Person waiving right to notice

(a) Notice of proposed action need not be given to any person who, in writing, waives the right to notice of proposed action with respect to the particular proposed action. The waiver may be executed at any time before or after the proposed action is taken. The waiver shall describe the particular proposed action and may waive particular aspects of the notice, such as the delivery, mailing, or time requirements of Section 10586, or the giving of the notice in its entirety for the particular proposed action.

(b) Notice of proposed action need not be given to any person who has executed the Statutory Waiver of Notice of Proposed Action Form prescribed by the Judicial Council and in that form has made either of the following:

(1) A general waiver of the right to notice of proposed action.

(2) A waiver of the right to notice of proposed action for all transactions of a type which includes the particular proposed action.

Ca. Prob. Code § 10583
Enacted by Stats. 1990, Ch. 79.

Section 10584 - Revocation of waiver or consent

(a) A waiver or consent may be revoked only in writing and is effective only when the writing is received by the personal representative.

(b) A copy of the revocation may be filed with the court, but the effectiveness of the revocation is not dependent upon a copy being filed with the court.

Ca. Prob. Code § 10584
Enacted by Stats. 1990, Ch. 79.

Section 10585 - Contents; use of form

(a) The notice of proposed action shall state all of the following:

(1) The name, mailing address, and electronic address of the personal representative.

(2) The name, telephone number, and electronic address of a person who may be contacted for additional information.

(3) The action proposed to be taken, with a reasonably specific description of the action. If the proposed action involves the sale or exchange of real property, or the granting of an option to purchase real property, the notice of proposed action shall state the material terms of the transaction, including, if applicable, the sale price and the amount of, or method of calculating, any commission or compensation paid or to be paid to an agent or broker in connection with the transaction.

(4) The date on or after which the proposed action is to be taken.

(b) The notice of proposed action may be given using the most current Notice of Proposed Action form prescribed by the Judicial Council.

(c) If the most current form prescribed by the Judicial Council is not used to give notice of proposed action, the notice of proposed action shall satisfy all of the following requirements:

(1) The notice of proposed action shall be in substantially the same form as the form prescribed by the Judicial Council.

(2) The notice of proposed action shall contain the statements described in subdivision (a).

(3) The notice of proposed action shall contain a form for objecting to the proposed action in substantially the form set out in the Judicial Council form.

Ca. Prob. Code § 10585

Amended by Stats 2017 ch 319 (AB 976),s 80, eff. 1/1/2018.

Section 10586 - Mail or personal delivery

The notice of proposed action shall be delivered pursuant to Section 1215 to each person required to be given notice of proposed action not less than 15 days before the date specified in the notice of proposed action on or after which the proposed action is to be taken. If mailed, the notice of proposed action shall be addressed to the person at the person's last known address.

Ca. Prob. Code § 10586

Amended by Stats 2017 ch 319 (AB 976),s 81, eff. 1/1/2018.

Section 10587 - Objection to proposed action

(a) Any person entitled to notice of proposed action under Section 10581 may object to the proposed action as provided in this section.

(b) The objection to the proposed action is made by delivering pursuant to Section 1215 a written objection to the proposed action to the personal representative at the address stated in the notice of proposed action. The person objecting to the proposed action either may use the Judicial Council form or may make the objection in any other writing that identifies the proposed action with reasonable certainty and indicates that the person objects to the taking of the proposed action.

(c) The personal representative is deemed to have notice of the objection to the proposed action if it is delivered or received at the address stated in the notice of proposed action before whichever of the following times is the later:

(1) The date specified in the notice of proposed action on or after which the proposed action is to be taken.

(2) The date the proposed action is actually taken.

Ca. Prob. Code § 10587

Amended by Stats 2017 ch 319 (AB 976),s 82, eff. 1/1/2018.

Section 10588 - Application for order restraining proposed action

(a) Any person who is entitled to notice of proposed action for a proposed action described in subdivision (a) of Section 10580, or any person who is given notice of a proposed action described in subdivision (b) of Section 10580, may apply to the court having jurisdiction over the proceeding for an order restraining the personal representative from taking the proposed action without court supervision. The court shall grant the requested order without requiring notice to the personal representative and without cause being shown for the order.

(b) The personal representative is deemed to have notice of the restraining order if it is served upon the personal representative in the same manner as is provided for in Section 415.10 or 415.30 of the Code of Civil Procedure, or in the manner authorized by the court, before whichever of the following times is the later:

(1) The date specified in a notice of proposed action on or after which the proposed action is to be taken.

(2) The date the proposed action is actually taken.

Ca. Prob. Code § 10588

Enacted by Stats. 1990, Ch. 79.

Section 10589 - Taking proposed action under court supervision or requesting instructions from court

(a) If the proposed action is one that would require court supervision if the personal representative had not been granted authority to administer the estate under this part and the personal representative has notice of a written objection made under Section 10587 to the proposed action or a restraining order issued under Section 10588, the personal representative shall, if the personal representative desires to take the proposed action, take the proposed action under the provisions of this code dealing with court supervision of that kind of action.

(b) If the proposed action is one that would not require court supervision even if the personal representative had not been granted authority to administer the estate under this part but the personal representative has given notice of the proposed action and has notice of a written objection made under Section 10587 to the proposed action or a restraining order issued under Section 10588, the personal representative shall, if he or she desires to take the proposed action, request instructions from the court concerning the proposed action. The personal representative may take the proposed action only under such order as may be entered by the court.

(c) A person who objects to a proposed action as provided in Section 10587 or serves a restraining order issued under Section 10588 in the manner provided in that section shall be given notice of any hearing on a petition for court authorization or confirmation of the proposed action.

Ca. Prob. Code § 10589

Amended by Stats. 1991, Ch. 82, Sec. 26. Effective June 30, 1991. Operative July 1, 1991, by Sec. 31 of Ch. 82.

Section 10590 - Court review of proposed action

(a) Except as provided in subdivision (c), only a person described in Section 10581 has a right to have the court review the proposed action after it has been taken or otherwise to object to the proposed action after it has been taken. Except as provided in subdivisions (b) and (c), a person described in Section 10581 waives the right to have the court review the proposed action after it has been taken, or otherwise to object to the proposed action after it has been taken, if either of the following circumstances exists:

(1) The person has been given notice of a proposed action, as provided in Sections 10580 to 10586, inclusive, and fails to object as provided in subdivision (d).

(2) The person has waived notice of or consented to the proposed action as provided in Sections 10582 to 10584, inclusive. **(b)** Unless the person has waived notice of or consented to the proposed action as provided in Sections 10582 to 10584, inclusive, the court may review the action taken upon motion of a person described in Section 10581 who establishes that he or she did not actually receive the notice of proposed action before the time to object under subdivision (d) expires.
(c) The court may review the action of the personal representative upon motion of an heir or devisee who establishes all of the following:

(1) At the time the notice was given, the heir or devisee lacked capacity to object to the proposed action or was a minor.

(2) No notice of proposed action was actually received by the guardian, conservator, or other legal representative of the heir or devisee.

(3) The guardian, conservator, or other legal representative did not waive notice of proposed action.

(4) The guardian, conservator, or other legal representative did not consent to the proposed action.
(d) For the purposes of this section, an objection to a proposed

action is made only by one or both of the following methods:

(1) Delivering or mailing a written objection as provided in Section 10587 within the time specified in subdivision (c) of that section.

(2) Serving a restraining order obtained under Section 10588 in the manner prescribed and within the time specified in subdivision (b) of that section.

Ca. Prob. Code § 10590
Enacted by Stats. 1990, Ch. 79.

Section 10591 - Validity of action not affected by failure to comply with provisions

(a) The failure of the personal representative to comply with subdivision (a) of Section 10580 and with Sections 10581, 10585, 10586, and 10589, and the taking of the action by the personal representative without such compliance, does not affect the validity of the action so taken or the title to any property conveyed or transferred to bona fide purchasers or the rights of third persons who, dealing in good faith with the personal representative, changed their position in reliance upon the action, conveyance, or transfer without actual notice of the failure of the personal representative to comply with those provisions.
(b) No person dealing with the personal representative has any duty to inquire or investigate whether or not the personal representative has complied with the provisions listed in subdivision (a).

Ca. Prob. Code § 10591
Enacted by Stats. 1990, Ch. 79.

Section 10592 - Removal of personal representative

(a) In a case where notice of proposed action is required by this chapter, the court in its discretion may remove the personal representative from office unless the personal representative does one of the following:

(1) Gives notice of proposed action as provided in this chapter.

(2) Obtains a waiver of notice of proposed action as provided in this chapter.

(3) Obtains a consent to the proposed action as provided in this chapter.

(b) The court in its discretion may remove the personal representative from office if the personal representative takes a proposed action in violation of Section 10589.

Ca. Prob. Code § 10592

Enacted by Stats. 1990, Ch. 79.

Part 7 - COMPENSATION OF PERSONAL REPRESENTATIVE AND ATTORNEY FOR THE PERSONAL REPRESENTATIVE

Chapter 1 - AMOUNT OF COMPENSATION

Article 1 - COMPENSATION OF PERSONAL REPRESENTATIVE

Section 10800 - Compensation for ordinary services

(a) Subject to the provisions of this part, for ordinary services the personal representative shall receive compensation based on the value of the estate accounted for by the personal representative, as follows:

(1) Four percent on the first one hundred thousand dollars ($100,000).

(2) Three percent on the next one hundred thousand dollars ($100,000).

(3) Two percent on the next eight hundred thousand dollars ($800,000).

(4) One percent on the next nine million dollars ($9,000,000).

(5) One-half of one percent on the next fifteen million dollars ($15,000,000).

(6) For all amounts above twenty-five million dollars ($25,000,000), a reasonable amount to be determined by the court.
(b) For the purposes of this section, the value of the estate accounted for by the personal representative is the total amount of the appraisal value of property in the inventory, plus gains over the appraisal value on sales, plus receipts, less losses from the appraisal value on sales, without reference to encumbrances or other obligations on estate property.
Ca. Prob. Code § 10800
Amended by Stats 2001 ch 699 (AB 232), s 2, eff. 1/1/2002.

Section 10801 - Additional compensation for extraordinary services; employment of tax experts

(a) Subject to the provisions of this part, in addition to the compensation provided by Section 10800, the court may allow additional compensation for extraordinary services by the personal representative in an amount the court determines is just and reasonable.
(b) The personal representative may also employ or retain tax counsel, tax auditors, accountants, or other tax experts for the performance of any action which such persons, respectively, may lawfully perform in the computation, reporting, or making of tax returns, or in negotiations or litigation which may be necessary for the final determination and payment of taxes, and pay from the funds of the estate for such services.
Ca. Prob. Code § 10801
Amended by Stats. 1991, Ch. 82, Sec. 28. Effective June 30, 1991. Operative July 1, 1991, by Sec. 31 of Ch. 82.

Section 10802 - Compensation provided by will

(a) Except as otherwise provided in this section, if the decedent's will makes provision for the compensation of the personal representative, the compensation provided by the will shall be the full and only compensation for the services of the personal representative.

(b) The personal representative may petition the court to be relieved from a provision of the will that provides for the compensation of the personal representative.

(c) Notice of the hearing on the petition shall be given as provided in Section 1220 to all of the following persons:

(1) Each person listed in Section 1220.

(2) Each known heir whose interest in the estate would be affected by the petition.

(3) Each known devisee whose interest in the estate would be affected by the petition.

(4) The Attorney General, at the office of the Attorney General in Sacramento, if any portion of the estate is to escheat to the state and its interest in the estate would be affected by the petition.

(d) If the court determines that it is to the advantage of the estate and in the best interest of the persons interested in the estate, the court may make an order authorizing compensation for the personal representative in an amount greater than provided in the will.

Ca. Prob. Code § 10802
Enacted by Stats. 1990, Ch. 79.

Section 10803 - Agreement for higher compensation than provided by part

An agreement between the personal representative and an heir or devisee for higher compensation than that provided by this part is void.

Ca. Prob. Code § 10803
Enacted by Stats. 1990, Ch. 79.

Section 10804 - Personal representative who is attorney

Notwithstanding any provision in the decedent's will, a personal representative who is an attorney shall be entitled to receive the personal representative's compensation as provided in this part, but shall not receive compensation for services as the attorney for the personal representative unless the court specifically approves the right to the compensation in advance and finds that the arrangement is to the advantage, benefit, and best interests of the decedent's estate.

Ca. Prob. Code § 10804
Amended by Stats 2001 ch 699 (AB 232), s 3, eff. 1/1/2002.

Section 10805 - Apportionment of compensation

If there are two or more personal representatives, the personal representative's compensation shall be apportioned among the personal representatives by the court according to the services actually rendered by each personal representative or as agreed to by the personal representatives.

Ca. Prob. Code § 10805
Enacted by Stats. 1990, Ch. 79.

Article 2 - COMPENSATION OF ATTORNEY FOR THE PERSONAL REPRESENTATIVE

Section 10810 - Compensation for ordinary services

(a) Subject to the provisions of this part, for ordinary services the attorney for the personal representative shall receive compensation based on the value of the estate accounted for by the personal representative, as follows:

(1) Four percent on the first one hundred thousand dollars ($100,000).

(2) Three percent on the next one hundred thousand dollars ($100,000).

(3) Two percent on the next eight hundred thousand dollars ($800,000).

(4) One percent on the next nine million dollars ($9,000,000).

(5) One-half of 1 percent on the next fifteen million dollars ($15,000,000).

(6) For all amounts above twenty-five million dollars ($25,000,000), a reasonable amount to be determined by the court.
(b) For the purposes of this section, the value of the estate accounted for by the personal representative is the total amount of the appraisal of property in the inventory, plus gains over the appraisal value on sales, plus receipts, less losses from the appraisal value on sales, without reference to encumbrances or other obligations on estate property.

Ca. Prob. Code § 10810
Amended by Stats 2001 ch 699 (AB 232), s 4, eff. 1/1/2002.

Section 10811 - Additional compensation for extraordinary services

(a) Subject to the provisions of this part, in addition to the compensation provided by Section 10810, the court may allow additional compensation for extraordinary services by the attorney for the personal representative in an amount the court determines is just and reasonable.
(b) Extraordinary services by the attorney for which the court may allow compensation include services by a paralegal performing the extraordinary services under the direction and supervision of an attorney. The petition for compensation shall set forth the hours spent and services performed by the paralegal.
(c) An attorney for the personal representative may agree to perform extraordinary service on a contingent fee basis subject to the following conditions:

(1) The agreement is written and complies with all the

requirements of Section 6147 of the Business and Professions Code.

(2) The agreement is approved by the court following a hearing noticed as provided in Section 10812.

(3) The court determines that the compensation provided in the agreement is just and reasonable and the agreement is to the advantage of the estate and in the best interests of the persons who are interested in the estate.
Ca. Prob. Code § 10811
Amended by Stats. 1993, Ch. 527, Sec. 4. Effective January 1, 1994.

Section 10812 - Provision in will for compensation of attorney

(a) Except as otherwise provided in this section, if the decedent's will makes provision for the compensation of the attorney for the personal representative, the compensation provided by the will shall be the full and only compensation for the services of the attorney for the personal representative.
(b) The personal representative or the attorney for the personal representative may petition the court to be relieved from a provision of the will that provides for the compensation of the attorney for the personal representative.
(c) Notice of the hearing on the petition shall be given as provided in Section 1220 to all of the following persons:

(1) Each person listed in Section 1220.

(2) Each known heir whose interest in the estate would be affected by the petition.

(3) Each known devisee whose interest in the estate would be affected by the petition.

(4) The Attorney General, at the office of the Attorney General in Sacramento, if any portion of the estate is to escheat to the state and its interest in the estate would be affected by the petition.

(5) If the court determines that it is to the advantage of the estate and in the best interest of the persons interested in the estate, the court may make an order authorizing compensation of the attorney for the personal representative in an amount greater than provided in the will.

Ca. Prob. Code § 10812
Added by Stats. 1991, Ch. 82, Sec. 30. Effective June 30, 1991. Operative July 1, 1991, by Sec. 31 of Ch. 82.

Section 10813 - Agreement for higher compensation than provided by part

An agreement between the personal representative and the attorney for higher compensation for the attorney than that provided by this part is void.

Ca. Prob. Code § 10813
Added by Stats. 1991, Ch. 82, Sec. 30. Effective June 30, 1991. Operative July 1, 1991, by Sec. 31 of Ch. 82.

Section 10814 - Apportionment of compensation

If there are two or more attorneys for the personal representative, the attorney's compensation shall be apportioned among the attorneys by the court according to the services actually rendered by each attorney or as agreed to by the attorneys.

Ca. Prob. Code § 10814
Added by Stats. 1991, Ch. 82, Sec. 30. Effective June 30, 1991. Operative July 1, 1991, by Sec. 31 of Ch. 82.

Chapter 2 - ALLOWANCE OF COMPENSATION BY COURT

Section 10830 - Petition requesting allowance on compensation; notice of hearing; hearing

(a) At any time after four months from the issuance of letters:

(1) The personal representative may file a petition requesting an allowance on the compensation of the personal representative.

(2) The personal representative or the attorney for the personal representative may file a petition requesting an allowance on the compensation of the attorney for the personal representative.
(b) Notice of the hearing on the petition shall be given as provided in Section 1220 to all of the following:

(1) Each person listed in Section 1220.

(2) Each known heir whose interest in the estate would be affected by the payment of the compensation.

(3) Each known devisee whose interest in the estate would be affected by the payment of the compensation.

(4) The Attorney General, at the office of the Attorney General in Sacramento, if any portion of the estate is to escheat to the state and its interest in the estate would be affected by the petition.
(c) On the hearing, the court may make an order allowing the portion of the compensation of the personal representative or the attorney for the personal representative, as the case may be, on account of services rendered up to that time, that the court determines is proper. The order shall authorize the personal representative to charge against the estate the amount allowed.
Ca. Prob. Code § 10830
Amended by Stats. 1990, Ch. 710, Sec. 35. Operative July 1, 1991, by Sec. 48 of Ch. 710.

Section 10831 - Request for compensation when final accounting and petition for final distribution made

(a) At the time of the filing of the final account and petition for an order for final distribution:

(1) The personal representative may petition the court for an order fixing and allowing the personal representative's compensation for all services rendered in the estate proceeding.

(2) The personal representative or the attorney for the personal representative may petition the court for an order fixing and allowing the compensation, of the attorney for all services rendered in the estate proceeding.

(b) The request for compensation may be included in the final account or the petition for final distribution or may be made in a separate petition.

(c) Notice of the hearing on the petition shall be given as provided in Section 1220 to all of the following:

(1) Each person listed in Section 1220.

(2) Each known heir whose interest in the estate would be affected by the payment of the compensation.

(3) Each known devisee whose interest in the estate would be affected by the payment of the compensation.

(4) The Attorney General, at the office of the Attorney General in Sacramento, if any portion of the estate is to escheat to the state and its interest in the estate would be affected by the petition.

(d) On the hearing, the court shall make an order fixing and allowing the compensation for all services rendered in the estate proceeding. In the case of an allowance to the personal representative, the order shall authorize the personal representative to charge against the estate the amount allowed, less any amount previously charged against the estate pursuant to Section 10830. In the case of the attorney's compensation the order shall require the personal representative to pay the attorney out of the estate the amount allowed, less any amount paid to the attorney out of the estate pursuant to Section 10830.

Ca. Prob. Code § 10831

Amended by Stats. 1990, Ch. 710, Sec. 36. Operative July 1, 1991, by Sec. 48 of Ch. 710.

Section 10832 - Allowance of compensation for extraordinary services before final distribution

Notwithstanding Sections 10830 and 10831, the court may allow compensation to the personal representative or to the attorney for the personal representative for extraordinary services before final distribution when any of the following requirements is satisfied:

(a) It appears likely that administration of the estate will continue, whether due to litigation or otherwise, for an unusually long time.

(b) Present payment will benefit the estate or the beneficiaries of the estate.

(c) Other good cause is shown.

Ca. Prob. Code § 10832

Amended by Stats. 1994, Ch. 806, Sec. 33. Effective January 1, 1995.

Chapter 3 - APPLICATION OF PART

Section 10850 - Inapplicability to proceeding commenced before July 1, 1991

(a) This part does not apply in any proceeding for administration of a decedent's estate commenced before July 1, 1991.

(b) Notwithstanding its repeal, the applicable law in effect before July 1, 1991, governing the subject matter of this part continues to apply in any proceeding for administration of a decedent's estate commenced before July 1, 1991.

Ca. Prob. Code § 10850

Amended by Stats. 1990, Ch. 710, Sec. 37. Operative July 1, 1991, by Sec. 48 of Ch. 710.

Part 8 - ACCOUNTS

Chapter 1 - GENERAL PROVISIONS

Section 10900 - Financial statement and report of administration; statement of liabilities

(a) An account shall include both a financial statement and a report of administration as provided in Chapter 4 (commencing with Section 1060) of Part 1 of Division 3, and this section.

(b) The statement of liabilities in the report of administration shall include the following information:

(1) Whether notice to creditors was given under Section 9050.

(2) Creditor claims filed, including the date of filing the claim, the name of the claimant, the amount of the claim, and the action taken on the claim.

(3) Creditor claims not paid, satisfied, or adequately provided for. As to each such claim, the statement shall indicate whether the claim is due and the date due, the date any notice of rejection was given, and whether the creditor has brought an action on the claim. The statement shall identify any real or personal property that is security for the claim, whether by mortgage, deed of trust, lien, or other encumbrance.

(c) The amendments to this section made by Assembly Bill 2751 of the 1995-96 Regular Session shall become operative on July 1, 1997.

Ca. Prob. Code § 10900

Amended by Stats. 1996, Ch. 862, Sec. 30. Effective January 1, 1997. Amended version operative July 1, 1997, pursuant to earlier operation of new subdivision (c).

Section 10901 - Production of documents for inspection and audit

On court order, or on request by an interested person filed with the clerk and a copy served on the personal representative, the personal representative shall produce for inspection and audit by the court or interested person the documents specified in the order or request that support an account.

Ca. Prob. Code § 10901

Enacted by Stats. 1990, Ch. 79.

Section 10902 - Incorporation by reference of accounting provided by conservator or guardian

When a personal representative receives assets from the conservator of a deceased conservatee or the guardian of a deceased ward, the personal representative may incorporate by reference any accounting provided by the conservator or guardian for the decedent for the period subsequent to the date of death, and the personal representative is entitled to rely on the accounting by such other fiduciary, and shall not have a duty to independently investigate or verify the transactions reported in such an account.

Ca. Prob. Code § 10902
Repealed and added by Stats. 1996, Ch. 862, Sec. 32. Effective January 1, 1997. Operative July 1, 1997, by Sec. 49 of Ch. 862.

Chapter 2 - WHEN ACCOUNT REQUIRED

Section 10950 - Court ordered account

(a) On its own motion or on petition of an interested person, the court may order an account at any time.
(b) The court shall order an account on petition of an interested person made more than one year after the last account was filed or, if no previous account has been filed, made more than one year after issuance of letters to the personal representative.
(c) The court order shall specify the time within which the personal representative must file an account.

Ca. Prob. Code § 10950
Enacted by Stats. 1990, Ch. 79.

Section 10951 - When final account and petition for final distribution filed

The personal representative shall file a final account and petition for an order for final distribution of the estate when the estate is in a condition to be closed.

Ca. Prob. Code § 10951
Enacted by Stats. 1990, Ch. 79.

Section 10952 - Time for filing account when personal representative resigns or removed from office

A personal representative who resigns or is removed from office or whose authority is otherwise terminated shall, unless the court extends the time, file an account not later than 60 days after termination of authority. If the personal representative fails to so file the account, the court may compel the account pursuant to Chapter 4 (commencing with Section 11050).

Ca. Prob. Code § 10952
Enacted by Stats. 1990, Ch. 79.

Section 10953 - Accounting by legal representative appointed for deceased or incapacitated personal representative

(a) As used in this section:

(1) "Incapacitated" means lack of capacity to serve as personal representative.

(2) "Legal representative" means the personal representative of a deceased personal representative or the conservator of the estate of an incapacitated personal representative.
(b) If a personal representative dies or becomes incapacitated and a legal representative is appointed for the deceased or incapacitated personal representative, the legal representative shall not later than 60 days after appointment, unless the court extends the time, file an account of the administration of the deceased or incapacitated personal representative.
(c) If a personal representative dies or becomes incapacitated and no legal representative is appointed for the deceased or incapacitated personal representative, or if the personal representative absconds, the court may compel the attorney for the deceased, incapacitated, or absconding personal representative or attorney of record in the estate proceeding to file an account of the administration of the deceased, incapacitated, or absconding personal representative.
(d) The legal representative or attorney shall exercise reasonable diligence in preparing an account under this section. Verification of the account may be made on information and belief. The court shall settle the account as in other cases. The court shall allow reasonable compensation to the legal representative or the attorney for

preparing the account. The amount allowed is a charge against the estate that was being administered by the deceased, incapacitated, or absconding personal representative. Legal services for which compensation shall be allowed to the attorney under this subdivision include those services rendered by any paralegal performing the services under the direction and supervision of an attorney. The petition or application for compensation shall set forth the hours spent and services performed by the paralegal.

Ca. Prob. Code § 10953

Enacted by Stats. 1990, Ch. 79.

Section 10954 - Waiver or acknowledgment

(a) Notwithstanding any other provision of this part, the personal representative is not required to file an account if any of the following conditions is satisfied as to each person entitled to distribution from the estate:

(1) The person has executed and filed a written waiver of account or a written acknowledgment that the person's interest has been satisfied.

(2) Adequate provision has been made for satisfaction in full of the person's interest. This paragraph does not apply to a residuary devisee or a devisee whose interest in the estate is subject to abatement, payment of expenses, or accrual of interest or income. **(b)** A waiver or acknowledgment under subdivision (a) shall be executed as follows:

(1) If the person entitled to distribution is an adult and competent, by that person.

(2) If the person entitled to distribution is a minor, by a person authorized to receive money or property belonging to the minor. If the waiver or acknowledgment is executed by a guardian of the estate of the minor, the waiver or acknowledgment may be executed without the need to obtain approval of the court in which the guardianship proceeding is pending.

(3) If the person entitled to distribution is a conservatee, by the conservator of the estate of the conservatee. The waiver or acknowledgment may be executed without the need to obtain approval of the court in which the conservatorship proceeding is pending.

(4) If the person entitled to distribution is a trust, by the trustee, but only if the named trustee's written acceptance of the trust is filed with the court. In the case of a trust that is subject to the continuing jurisdiction of the court pursuant to Chapter 4 (commencing with Section 17300) of Part 5 of Division 9, the waiver or acknowledgment may be executed without the need to obtain approval of the court.

(5) If the person entitled to distribution is an estate, by the personal representative of the estate. The waiver or acknowledgment may be executed without the need to obtain approval of the court in which the estate is being administered.

(6) If the person entitled to distribution is incapacitated, unborn, unascertained, or is a person whose identity or address is unknown, or is a designated class of persons who are not ascertained or are not in being, and there is a guardian ad litem appointed to represent the person entitled to distribution, by the guardian ad litem.

(7) If the person entitled to distribution has designated an attorney in fact who has the power under the power of attorney to execute the waiver or acknowledgment, by either of the following:

(A) The person entitled to distribution if an adult and competent.

(B) The attorney in fact.

(c) Notwithstanding subdivision (a):

(1) The personal representative shall file a final report of administration at the time the final account would otherwise have been required. The final report shall include the amount of compensation paid or payable to the personal representative and to the attorney for the personal representative and shall set forth the basis for determining the amounts.

(2) A creditor whose interest has not been satisfied may petition under Section 10950 for an account.
Ca. Prob. Code § 10954
Amended by Stats. 1990, Ch. 710, Sec. 39. Operative July 1, 1991, by Sec. 48 of Ch. 710.

Chapter 3 - SETTLEMENT OF ACCOUNT

Section 11000 - Notice of hearing

(a) The personal representative shall give notice of the hearing as provided in Section 1220 to all of the following persons:

(1) Each person listed in Section 1220.

(2) Each known heir whose interest in the estate would be affected by the account.

(3) Each known devisee whose interest in the estate would be affected by the account.

(4) The Attorney General, at the office of the Attorney General in Sacramento, if any portion of the estate is to escheat to the state and its interest would be affected by the account.

(5) If the estate is insolvent, each creditor who has filed a claim that is allowed or approved but is unpaid in whole or in part.
(b) If the petition for approval of the account requests allowance of all or a portion of the compensation of the personal representative or the attorney for the personal representative, the notice of hearing shall so state.
(c) If the account is a final account and is filed together with a petition for an order for final distribution of the estate, the notice of

hearing shall so state.

Ca. Prob. Code § 11000

Amended by Stats. 1990, Ch. 710, Sec. 40. Operative July 1, 1991, by Sec. 48 of Ch. 710.

Section 11001 - Causes for contesting account

All matters relating to an account may be contested for cause shown, including, but not limited to:

(a) The validity of an allowed or approved claim not reported in a previous account and not established by judgment.

(b) The value of property for purposes of distribution.

(c) Actions taken by the personal representative not previously authorized or approved by the court, subject to Section 10590 (Independent Administration of Estates Act).

Ca. Prob. Code § 11001

Enacted by Stats. 1990, Ch. 79.

Section 11002 - Hearing; appointment of referees

(a) The court may conduct any hearing that may be necessary to settle the account, and may cite the personal representative to appear before the court for examination.

(b) The court may appoint one or more referees to examine the account and make a report on the account, subject to confirmation by the court. The court may allow a reasonable compensation to the referee to be paid out of the estate.

(c) The court may make any orders that the court deems necessary to effectuate the provisions of this section.

Ca. Prob. Code § 11002

Enacted by Stats. 1990, Ch. 79.

Section 11003 - Award of compensation and costs

(a) If the court determines that the contest was without reasonable cause and in bad faith, the court may award against the contestant the compensation and costs of the personal representative and other expenses and costs of litigation, including attorney's fees, incurred to defend the account. The amount awarded is a charge against any interest of the contestant in the estate and the contestant is personally liable for any amount that remains unsatisfied.

(b) If the court determines that the opposition to the contest was without reasonable cause and in bad faith, the court may award the contestant the costs of the contestant and other expenses and costs of litigation, including attorney's fees, incurred to contest the account. The amount awarded is a charge against the compensation or other interest of the personal representative in the estate and the personal representative is liable personally and on the bond, if any, for any amount that remains unsatisfied.

Ca. Prob. Code § 11003
Enacted by Stats. 1990, Ch. 79.

Section 11004 - Allowance of expenses in administration of estate

The personal representative shall be allowed all necessary expenses in the administration of the estate, including, but not limited to, necessary expenses in the care, management, preservation, and settlement of the estate.

Ca. Prob. Code § 11004
Enacted by Stats. 1990, Ch. 79.

Section 11005 - Debt paid but without claim filed

If a debt has been paid within the time prescribed in Section 9154 but without a claim having been filed and established in the manner prescribed by statute, in settling the account the court shall allow the amount paid if all of the following are proven:

(a) The debt was justly due.

(b) The debt was paid in good faith.

(c) The amount paid did not exceed the amount reasonably necessary to satisfy the indebtedness.

(d) The estate is solvent.

Ca. Prob. Code § 11005
Enacted by Stats. 1990, Ch. 79.

Chapter 4 - COMPELLING ACCOUNT

Section 11050 - Generally

Subject to the provisions of this chapter, if the personal representative does not file a required account, the court shall compel the account by punishment for contempt.

    Ca. Prob. Code § 11050
Enacted by Stats. 1990, Ch. 79.

Section 11051 - Issuance of citation

(a) A citation shall be issued, served, and returned, requiring a personal representative who does not file a required account to appear and show cause why the personal representative should not be punished for contempt.
(b) If the personal representative purposefully evades personal service of the citation, the personal representative shall be removed from office.

    Ca. Prob. Code § 11051
Enacted by Stats. 1990, Ch. 79.

Section 11052 - Failure to appear and file account

If the personal representative does not appear and file a required account, after having been duly cited, the personal representative may be punished for contempt or removed from office, or both, in the discretion of the court.

    Ca. Prob. Code § 11052
Enacted by Stats. 1990, Ch. 79.

Part 9 - PAYMENT OF DEBTS

Chapter 1 - DEFINITIONS AND PRELIMINARY PROVISIONS

Article 1 - DEFINITIONS

Section 11400 - Definitions govern construction

Unless the provision or context otherwise requires, the definitions in this article govern the construction of this part.

Ca. Prob. Code § 11400

Enacted by Stats. 1990, Ch. 79.

Section 11401 - Debt

"Debt" means:

(a) A claim that is established under Part 4 (commencing with Section 9000) or that is otherwise payable in the course of administration.

(b) An expense of administration.

(c) A charge against the estate including, but not limited to, taxes, expenses of last illness, and family allowance.

Ca. Prob. Code § 11401

Enacted by Stats. 1990, Ch. 79.

Section 11402 - Wage claim

"Wage claim" means a claim for wages, not exceeding two thousand dollars ($2,000), of each employee of the decedent for work done or personal services rendered within 90 days before the death of the decedent.

Ca. Prob. Code § 11402

Enacted by Stats. 1990, Ch. 79.

Article 2 - PROCEEDINGS COMMENCED BEFORE JULY 1, 1988

Section 11405 - Generally

(a) This part does not apply in any proceeding for the administration of a decedent's estate commenced before July 1, 1988.

(b) The applicable law in effect before July 1, 1988, governing the subject matter of this part continues to apply in any proceeding for administration of a decedent's estate commenced before July 1, 1988, notwithstanding its repeal by Chapter 923 of the Statutes of

1987.

Ca. Prob. Code § 11405
Enacted by Stats. 1990, Ch. 79.

Chapter 2 - GENERAL PROVISIONS

Section 11420 - Order of priority of payment

(a) Debts shall be paid in the following order of priority among classes of debts, except that debts owed to the United States or to this state that have preference under the laws of the United States or of this state shall be given the preference required by such laws:

(1) Expenses of administration. With respect to obligations secured by mortgage, deed of trust, or other lien, including, but not limited to, a judgment lien, only those expenses of administration incurred that are reasonably related to the administration of that property by which obligations are secured shall be given priority over these obligations.

(2) Obligations secured by a mortgage, deed of trust, or other lien, including, but not limited to, a judgment lien, in the order of their priority, so far as they may be paid out of the proceeds of the property subject to the lien. If the proceeds are insufficient, the part of the obligation remaining unsatisfied shall be classed with general debts.

(3) Funeral expenses.

(4) Expenses of last illness.

(5) Family allowance.

(6) Wage claims.

(7) General debts, including judgments not secured by a lien and all other debts not included in a prior class.
(b) Except as otherwise provided by statute, the debts of each class are without preference or priority one over another. No debt of any

class may be paid until all those of prior classes are paid in full. If property in the estate is insufficient to pay all debts of any class in full, each debt in that class shall be paid a proportionate share.

Ca. Prob. Code § 11420

Amended by Stats. 1996, Ch. 862, Sec. 33. Effective January 1, 1997.

Section 11421 - Expenses paid after payment of administration expenses

Subject to Section 11420, as soon as the personal representative has sufficient funds, after retaining sufficient funds to pay expenses of administration, the personal representative shall pay the following:

(a) Funeral expenses.

(b) Expenses of last illness.

(c) Family allowance.

(d) Wage claims.

Ca. Prob. Code § 11421

Enacted by Stats. 1990, Ch. 79.

Section 11422 - Court order to pay debts

(a) Except as provided in Section 11421, the personal representative is not required to pay a debt until payment has been ordered by the court.

(b) On the settlement of any account of the personal representative after the expiration of four months after the date letters are first issued to a general personal representative, the court shall order payment of debts, as the circumstances of the estate permit. If property in the estate is insufficient to pay all of the debts, the order shall specify the amount to be paid to each creditor.

(c) If the estate will be exhausted by the payment ordered, the account of the personal representative constitutes a final account, and notice of hearing shall be the notice given for the hearing of a final account. The personal representative is entitled to a discharge when the personal representative has complied with the terms of the order.

(d) Nothing in this section precludes settlement of an account of a personal representative for payment of a debt made without prior court authorization.

Ca. Prob. Code § 11422
Enacted by Stats. 1990, Ch. 79.

Section 11423 - Interest on debt

(a) Interest accrues on a debt from the date the court orders payment of the debt until the date the debt is paid. Interest accrues at the legal rate on judgments.

(b) Notwithstanding subdivision (a), in the case of a debt based on a written contract, interest accrues at the rate and in accordance with the terms of the contract. The personal representative may, by order of the court, pay all or part of the interest accumulated and unpaid at any time when there are sufficient funds, whether the debt is then due or not.

(c) Notwithstanding subdivision (a), in the case of a debt for unpaid taxes or any other debt for which interest is expressly provided by statute, interest accrues at the rate and in accordance with the terms of the statute.

Ca. Prob. Code § 11423
Enacted by Stats. 1990, Ch. 79.

Section 11424 - Liability for failure to make payment

The personal representative shall pay a debt to the extent of the order for payment of the debt, and is liable personally and on the bond, if any, for failure to make the payment.

Ca. Prob. Code § 11424
Enacted by Stats. 1990, Ch. 79.

Section 11428 - Debt not paid because creditor not found

(a) If an estate is in all other respects ready to be closed, and it appears to the satisfaction of the court, on affidavit or evidence taken in open court, that a debt has not been and cannot be paid because the creditor cannot be found, the court or judge shall make an order fixing the amount of the payment and directing the personal representative to deposit the payment with the county treasurer of the county in which the proceeding is pending.

(b) The county treasurer shall give a receipt for the deposit, for which the county treasurer is liable on the official bond. The receipt shall be treated by the court or judge in favor of the personal representative with the same force and effect as if executed by the creditor.

(c) A deposit with the county treasurer under the provisions of this section shall be received, accounted for, and disposed of as provided by Section 1444 of the Code of Civil Procedure. A deposit in the State Treasury under the provisions of this section shall be deemed to be made under the provisions of Article 1 (commencing with Section 1440) of Chapter 6 of Title 10 of Part 3 of the Code of Civil Procedure.

Ca. Prob. Code § 11428

Enacted by Stats. 1990, Ch. 79.

Section 11429 - Contribution from creditors who are paid

(a) Where the accounts of the personal representative have been settled and an order made for the payment of debts and distribution of the estate, a creditor who is not paid, whether or not included in the order for payment, has no right to require contribution from creditors who are paid or from distributees, except to the extent provided in Section 9392.

(b) Nothing in this section precludes recovery against the personal representative personally or on the bond, if any, by a creditor who is not paid, subject to Section 9053.

Ca. Prob. Code § 11429

Amended by Stats. 1990, Ch. 140, Sec. 14.1. Operative July 1, 1991, by Sec. 30 of Ch. 140.

Chapter 3 - ALLOCATION OF DEBTS BETWEEN ESTATE AND SURVIVING SPOUSE

Section 11440 - Petition for order to allocate debt

If it appears that a debt of the decedent has been paid or is payable in whole or in part by the surviving spouse, or that a debt of the surviving spouse has been paid or is payable in whole or in part from property in the decedent's estate, the personal representative, the surviving spouse, or a beneficiary may, at any time before an order for final distribution is made, petition for an order to allocate the debt.

Ca. Prob. Code § 11440
Enacted by Stats. 1990, Ch. 79.

Section 11441 - Contents of petition

The petition shall include a statement of all of the following:
(a) All debts of the decedent and surviving spouse known to the petitioner that are alleged to be subject to allocation and whether paid in whole or part or unpaid.
(b) The reason why the debts should be allocated.
(c) The proposed allocation and the basis for allocation alleged by the petitioner.

Ca. Prob. Code § 11441
Enacted by Stats. 1990, Ch. 79.

Section 11442 - Order to show cause why information should not be provided

If it appears from the petition that allocation would be affected by the value of the separate property of the surviving spouse and any community property and quasi-community property not administered in the estate and if an inventory and appraisal of the property has not been provided by the surviving spouse, the court shall make an order to show cause why the information should not be provided.

Ca. Prob. Code § 11442
Enacted by Stats. 1990, Ch. 79.

Section 11443 - Notice of hearing

The petitioner shall give notice of the hearing as provided in Section 1220, together with a copy of the petition and the order to show cause, if any.

Ca. Prob. Code § 11443
Enacted by Stats. 1990, Ch. 79.

Section 11444 - Allocation by agreement; allocation in absence of agreement

(a) The personal representative and the surviving spouse may provide for allocation by agreement and, on a determination by the court that the agreement substantially protects the rights of interested persons, the allocation provided in the agreement shall be ordered by the court.

(b) In the absence of an agreement, each debt subject to allocation shall first be characterized by the court as separate or community, in accordance with the laws of the state applicable to marital dissolution proceedings. Following that characterization, the debt or debts shall be allocated as follows:

(1) Separate debts of either spouse shall be allocated to that spouse's separate property assets, and community debts shall be allocated to the spouses' community property assets.

(2) If a separate property asset of either spouse is subject to a secured debt that is characterized as that spouse's separate debt, and the net equity in that asset available to satisfy that secured debt is less than that secured debt, the unsatisfied portion of that secured debt shall be treated as an unsecured separate debt of that spouse and allocated to the net value of that spouse's other separate property assets.

(3) If the net value of either spouse's separate property assets is less than that spouse's unsecured separate debt or debts, the unsatisfied portion of the debt or debts shall be allocated to the net value of that spouse's one-half share of the community property assets. If the net value of that spouse's one-half share of the community property assets is less than that spouse's unsatisfied unsecured separate debt or debts, the remaining unsatisfied portion of the debt or debts shall be allocated to the net value of the other spouse's one-half share of the community property assets.

(4) If a community property asset is subject to a secured debt that is characterized as a community debt, and the net equity in that asset available to satisfy that secured debt is less than that secured debt, the unsatisfied portion of that secured debt shall be treated as an unsecured community debt and allocated to the net value of the other community property assets.

(5) If the net value of the community property assets is less than the unsecured community debt or debts, the unsatisfied portion of the debt or debts shall be allocated equally between the separate property assets of the decedent and the surviving spouse. If the net value of either spouse's separate property assets is less than that spouse's share of the unsatisfied portion of the unsecured community debt or debts, the remaining unsatisfied portion of the debt or debts shall be allocated to the net value of the other spouse's separate property assets.

(c) For purposes of this section:

(1) The net value of either spouse's separate property asset shall refer to its fair market value as of the date of the decedent's death, minus the date-of-death balance of any liens and encumbrances on that asset that have been characterized as that spouse's separate debts.

(2) The net value of a community property asset shall refer to its fair market value as of the date of the decedent's death, minus the date-of-death balance of any liens and encumbrances on that asset that have been characterized as community debts.

(3) In the case of a nonrecourse debt, the amount of that debt shall be limited to the net equity in the collateral, based on the fair market value of the collateral as of the date of the decedent's death, that is available to satisfy that debt. For the purposes of this paragraph, "nonrecourse debt" means a debt for which the debtor's obligation to repay is limited to the collateral securing the debt, and for which a deficiency judgment against the debtor is not permitted by law.

(d) Notwithstanding the foregoing provisions of this section, the court may order a different allocation of debts between the decedent's estate and the surviving spouse if the court finds a different allocation to be equitable under the circumstances.
(e) Nothing contained in this section is intended to impair or affect the rights of third parties. If a personal representative or the surviving spouse incurs any damages or expense, including attorney's fees, on account of the nonpayment of a debt that was allocated to the other party pursuant to subdivision (b), or as the result of a debt being misallocated due to fraud or intentional misrepresentation by the other party, the party incurring damages shall be entitled to recover from the other party for damages or expense deemed reasonable by the court that made the allocation.

Ca. Prob. Code § 11444
Amended by Stats 2001 ch 72 (SB 668), s 1, eff. 1/1/2002.

Section 11445 - Order of court

On making a determination as provided in this chapter, the court shall make an order that:
(a) Directs the personal representative to make payment of the amounts allocated to the estate by payment to the surviving spouse or creditors.
(b) Directs the personal representative to charge amounts allocated to the surviving spouse against any property or interests of the surviving spouse that are in the possession or control of the personal representative. To the extent that property or interests of the surviving spouse in the possession or control of the personal representative are insufficient to satisfy the allocation, the court order shall summarily direct the surviving spouse to pay the allocation to the personal representative.

Ca. Prob. Code § 11445
Enacted by Stats. 1990, Ch. 79.

Section 11446 - Funeral expenses and expenses of last illness

Notwithstanding any other statute, funeral expenses and expenses of last illness shall be charged against the estate of the decedent and shall not be allocated to, or charged against the community share of, the surviving spouse, whether or not the surviving spouse is financially able to pay the expenses and whether or not the surviving spouse or any other person is also liable for the expenses.

Ca. Prob. Code § 11446
Enacted by Stats. 1990, Ch. 79.

Chapter 4 - DEBTS THAT ARE CONTINGENT, DISPUTED, OR NOT DUE

Section 11460 - Definitions

As used in this chapter:
(a) A debt is "contingent" if it is established under Part 4 (commencing with Section 9000) in either a fixed or an uncertain amount and will become absolute on occurrence of a stated event other than the passage of time. The term includes a secured obligation for which there may be recourse against property in the estate, other than the property that is the security, if the security is insufficient.
(b) A debt is "disputed" if it is a claim rejected in whole or in part under Part 4 (commencing with Section 9000) and is not barred under Section 9353 as to the part rejected.
(c) A debt is "not due" if it is established under Part 4 (commencing with Section 9000) and will become due on the passage of time. The term includes a debt payable in installments.

Ca. Prob. Code § 11460
Added by Stats. 1991, Ch. 1055, Sec. 31.

Section 11461 - Petition for order; notice of hearing

When all other debts have been paid and the estate is otherwise in a condition to be closed, on petition by an interested person, the court may make or modify an order or a combination of orders under this chapter that the court in its discretion determines is appropriate to provide adequately for a debt that is contingent, disputed, or not due, if the debt becomes absolute, established, or due. Notice of the hearing on the petition shall be given as provided in Section 1220 to the creditor whose debt is contingent, disputed, or not due, as well as to the persons provided in Section 11601.

Ca. Prob. Code § 11461
Added by Stats. 1991, Ch. 1055, Sec. 31.

Section 11462 - Agreement to manner of providing for debt

Notwithstanding any other provision of this chapter, if the court determines that all interested persons agree to the manner of providing for a debt that is contingent, disputed, or not due and that the agreement reasonably protects all interested persons and will not extend administration of the estate unreasonably, the court shall approve the agreement.

Ca. Prob. Code § 11462
Added by Stats. 1991, Ch. 1055, Sec. 31.

Section 11463 - Order of amount deposited in financial institution

The court may order an amount deposited in a financial institution, as provided in Chapter 3 (commencing with Section 9700) of Part 5, that would be payable if a debt that is contingent, disputed, or not due, were absolute, established, or due. The order shall provide that the amount deposited is subject to withdrawal only upon authorization of the court, to be paid to the creditor when the debt becomes absolute, established, or due, or to be distributed in the manner provided in Section 11642 if the debt does not become absolute or established.

Ca. Prob. Code § 11463
Added by Stats. 1991, Ch. 1055, Sec. 31.

Section 11464 - Assumption of liability for contingent or disputed debt

(a) The court may order property in the estate distributed to a person entitled to it under the final order for distribution, if the person files with the court an assumption of liability for a contingent or disputed debt as provided in subdivision (b). The court may impose any other conditions the court in its discretion determines are just, including that the distributee give a security interest in all or part of the property distributed or that the distributee give a bond in an amount determined by the court.

(b) As a condition for an order under subdivision (a), each distributee shall file with the court a signed and acknowledged agreement assuming personal liability for the contingent or disputed debt and consenting to jurisdiction within this state for the enforcement of the debt if it becomes absolute or established. The personal liability of each distributee shall not exceed the fair market value on the date of distribution of the property received by the distributee, less the amount of liens and encumbrances. If there is more than one distributee, the personal liability of the distributees is joint and several.

(c) If the debt becomes absolute or established, it may be enforced against each distributee in the same manner as it could have been enforced against the decedent if the decedent had not died. In an action based on the debt, the distributee may assert any defense, cross-complaint, or setoff that would have been available to the decedent if the decedent had not died.

(d) The statute of limitations applicable to a contingent debt is tolled from the time the creditor's claim is filed until 30 days after the order for distribution becomes final. The signing of an agreement under subdivision (b) neither extends nor revives any limitation period.

Ca. Prob. Code § 11464
Added by Stats. 1991, Ch. 1055, Sec. 31.

Section 11465 - Appointment of trustee to receive payment

(a) The court may order that a trustee be appointed to receive payment for a debt that is contingent, disputed, or not due. The court in determining the amount paid to the trustee shall compute the present value of the debt, giving consideration to a reasonable return on the amount to be invested. The trustee shall invest the payment in investments that would be proper for a personal representative or as authorized in the order.

(b) The trustee shall pay the debt as provided in the order. On completion of payment, any excess in possession of the trustee shall be distributed in the manner provided in Section 11642.

Ca. Prob. Code § 11465

Added by Stats. 1991, Ch. 1055, Sec. 31.

Section 11466 - Bond given conditioned on payment

The court may order property in the estate distributed to a person entitled to it under the final order for distribution, if the person gives a bond conditioned on payment by the person of the amount of a contingent or disputed debt that becomes absolute or established. The amount of the bond shall be determined by the court, not to exceed the fair market value on the date of distribution of the property received by the distributee, less the amount of liens and encumbrances. In the case of a disputed debt or in the case of a contingent debt where litigation is required to establish the contingency, the cost of the bond is recoverable from the unsuccessful party as a cost of litigation.

Ca. Prob. Code § 11466

Added by Stats. 1991, Ch. 1055, Sec. 31.

Section 11467 - Order continuing administration of estate

The court may order that the administration of the estate continue until the contingency, dispute, or passage of time of a debt that is contingent, disputed, or not due is resolved.

Ca. Prob. Code § 11467

Added by Stats. 1991, Ch. 1055, Sec. 31.

Part 10 - DISTRIBUTION OF ESTATE

Chapter 1 - ORDER FOR DISTRIBUTION

Article 1 - GENERAL PROVISIONS

Section 11600 - Petition for order of distribution

The personal representative or an interested person may petition the court under this chapter for an order for preliminary or final distribution of the decedent's estate to the persons entitled thereto.

Ca. Prob. Code § 11600

Enacted by Stats. 1990, Ch. 79.

Section 11601 - Notice of hearing

Notice of the hearing on the petition shall be given as provided in Section 1220 to all of the following persons:

(a) Each person listed in Section 1220.

(b) Each known heir whose interest in the estate would be affected by the petition.

(c) Each known devisee whose interest in the estate would be affected by the petition.

(d) The Attorney General, at the office of the Attorney General in Sacramento, if any portion of the estate is to escheat to the state and its interest in the estate would be affected by the petition.

(e) The Controller, if property is to be distributed to the state because there is no known beneficiary or if property is to be distributed to a beneficiary whose whereabouts is unknown. A copy of the latest account filed with the court shall be delivered to the Controller with the notice.

Ca. Prob. Code § 11601

Amended by Stats 2017 ch 319 (AB 976),s 83, eff. 1/1/2018.

Section 11602 - Opposition to petition

The personal representative or any interested person may oppose the petition.

Ca. Prob. Code § 11602

Enacted by Stats. 1990, Ch. 79.

Section 11603 - Court order; whereabouts of distributee named in order unknown

(a) If the court determines that the requirements for distribution are satisfied, the court shall order distribution of the decedent's estate, or such portion as the court directs, to the persons entitled thereto.

(b) The order shall:

(1) Name the distributees and the share to which each is entitled.

(2) Provide that property distributed subject to a limitation or condition, including, but not limited to, an option granted under Chapter 16 (commencing with Section 9960) of Part 5, is distributed to the distributees subject to the terms of the limitation or condition.

(c) If the whereabouts of a distributee named in the order is unknown, the order shall provide for alternate distributees and the share to which each is entitled. The alternate distributees shall be the persons, to the extent known or reasonably ascertainable, who would be entitled under the decedent's will or under the laws of intestate succession if the distributee named in the order had predeceased the decedent, or in the case of a devise for a charitable purpose, under the doctrine of cy pres. If the distributee named in the order does not claim the share to which the distributee is entitled within five years after the date of the order, the distributee is deemed to have predeceased the decedent for the purpose of this section and the alternate distributees are entitled to the share as provided in the order.

Ca. Prob. Code § 11603

Amended by Stats 2000 ch 17 (AB 1491), s 4.6, eff. 1/1/2001.

Section 11604 - Court inquiry into circumstances surrounding execution and consideration; refusal to order distribution or ordering on equitable terms

(a) This section applies where distribution is to be made to any of the following persons:

(1) The transferee of a beneficiary.

(2) Any person other than a beneficiary under an agreement, request, or instructions of a beneficiary or the attorney in fact of a beneficiary.

(b) The court on its own motion, or on motion of the personal representative or other interested person or of the public administrator, may inquire into the circumstances surrounding the execution of, and the consideration for, the transfer, agreement, request, or instructions, and the amount of any fees, charges, or consideration paid or agreed to be paid by the beneficiary.

(c) The court may refuse to order distribution, or may order distribution on any terms that the court deems just and equitable, if the court finds either of the following:

(1) The fees, charges, or consideration paid or agreed to be paid by a beneficiary are grossly unreasonable.

(2) The transfer, agreement, request, or instructions were obtained by duress, fraud, or undue influence.

(d) Notice of the hearing on the motion shall be served on the beneficiary and on the persons described in subdivision (a) at least 15 days before the hearing in the manner provided in Section 415.10 or 415.30 of the Code of Civil Procedure.

Ca. Prob. Code § 11604

Enacted by Stats. 1990, Ch. 79.

Section 11604.5 - Distribution to transferee for value

(a) This section applies when distribution from a decedent's estate is made to a transferee for value who acquires any interest of a beneficiary in exchange for cash or other consideration.

(b) For purposes of this section, a transferee for value is a person who satisfies both of the following criteria:

(1) The person purchases the interest from a beneficiary for consideration pursuant to a written agreement.

(2) The person, directly or indirectly, regularly engages in the purchase of beneficial interests in estates for consideration.

(c) This section does not apply to any of the following:

(1)A transferee who is a beneficiary of the estate or a person who has a claim to distribution from the estate under another instrument or by intestate succession.

(2)A transferee who is either the registered domestic partner of the beneficiary, or is related by blood, marriage, or adoption to the beneficiary or the decedent.

(3)A transaction made in conformity with the California Financing Law (Division 9 (commencing with Section 22000) of the Financial Code) and subject to regulation by the Department of Financial Protection and Innovation.

(4)A transferee who is engaged in the business of locating missing or unknown heirs and who acquires an interest from a beneficiary solely in exchange for providing information or services associated with locating the heir or beneficiary.

(d)A written agreement is effective only if all of the following conditions are met:

(1) The executed written agreement is filed with the court not later than 30 days following the date of its execution or, if administration of the decedent's estate has not commenced, then within 30 days of issuance of the letters of administration or letters testamentary, but in no event later than 15 days prior to the hearing on the petition for final distribution. Prior to filing or serving that written agreement, the transferee for value shall redact any personally identifying information about the beneficiary, other than the name and address of the beneficiary, and any financial information provided by the beneficiary to the transferee for value on the application for cash or other consideration, from the agreement.

(2) If the negotiation or discussion between the beneficiary and the transferee for value leading to the execution of the written agreement by the beneficiary was conducted in a language other than English, the beneficiary shall receive the written agreement in English, together with a copy of the agreement translated into the language in which it was negotiated or discussed. The written agreement and the translated copy, if any, shall be provided to the beneficiary.

(3)The documents signed by, or provided to, the beneficiary are printed in at least 10-point type.

(4)The transferee for value executes a declaration or affidavit attesting that the requirements of this section have been satisfied, and the declaration or affidavit is filed with the court within 30 days of execution of the written agreement or, if administration of the decedent's estate has not commenced, then within 30 days of issuance of the letters of administration or letters testamentary, but in no event later than 15 days prior to the hearing on the petition for final distribution.

(5)Notice of the assignment is served on the personal representative or the attorney of record for the personal representative within 30 days of execution of the written agreement or, if general or special letters of administration or letters testamentary have not been issued, then within 30 days of issuance of the letters of administration or letters testamentary, but in no event later than 15 days before the hearing on the petition for final distribution.

(e)The written agreement shall include the following terms, in addition to any other terms:

(1)The amount of consideration paid to the beneficiary.

(2)A description of the transferred interest.

(3)If the written agreement so provides, the amount by which the transferee for value would have its distribution reduced if the beneficial interest assigned is distributed prior to a specified date.

(4)A statement of the total of all costs or fees charged to the beneficiary resulting from the transfer for value, including, but not limited to, transaction or processing fees, credit report costs, title search costs, due diligence fees, filing fees, bank or electronic transfer costs, or any other fees or costs. If all the costs and fees are paid by the transferee for value and are included in the amount of the transferred interest, then the statement of costs need not itemize any costs or fees. This subdivision shall not apply to costs, fees, or damages arising out of a material breach of the agreement or fraud by or on the part of the beneficiary.

(f) A written agreement shall not contain any of the following provisions and, if any such provision is included, that provision shall be null and void:

(1) A provision holding harmless the transferee for value, other than for liability arising out of fraud by the beneficiary.

(2) A provision granting to the transferee for value agency powers to represent the beneficiary's interest in the decedent's estate beyond the interest transferred.

(3) A provision requiring payment by the beneficiary to the transferee for value for services not related to the written agreement or services other than the transfer of interest under the written agreement.

(4) A provision permitting the transferee for value to have recourse against the beneficiary if the distribution from the estate in satisfaction of the beneficial interest is less than the beneficial interest assigned to the transferee for value, other than recourse for any expense or damage arising out of the material breach of the agreement or fraud by the beneficiary.

(g) The court on its own motion, or on the motion of the personal representative or other interested person, may inquire into the circumstances surrounding the execution of, and the consideration for, the written agreement to determine that the requirements of this section have been satisfied.

(h) The court may refuse to order distribution under the written agreement, or may order distribution on any terms that the court considers equitable, if the court finds that the transferee for value did not substantially comply with the requirements of this section, or if the court finds that any of the following conditions existed at the time of transfer:

(1)The fees, charges, or consideration paid or agreed to be paid by the beneficiary were grossly unreasonable.

(2)The transfer of the beneficial interest was obtained by duress, fraud, or undue influence.

(i)In addition to any remedy specified in this section, for any willful violation of the requirements of this section found to be committed in bad faith, the court may require the transferee for value to pay to the beneficiary up to twice the value paid for the assignment.

(j)Notice of the hearing on any motion brought under this section shall be served on the beneficiary and on the transferee for value at least 15 days before the hearing in the manner provided in Section 415.10 or 415.30 of the Code of Civil Procedure.

(k)If the decedent's estate is not subject to a pending court proceeding under the Probate Code in California, but is the subject of a probate proceeding in another state, the transferee for value shall not be required to submit to the court a copy of the written agreement as required under paragraph (1) of subdivision (d). If the written agreement is entered into in California or if the beneficiary is domiciled in California, that written agreement shall otherwise conform to the provisions of subdivisions (d), (e), and (f) in order to be effective.

Ca. Prob. Code § 11604.5

Amended by Stats 2022 ch 452 (SB 1498),s 208, eff. 1/1/2023.
Amended by Stats 2019 ch 143 (SB 251),s 78, eff. 1/1/2020.
Amended by Stats 2015 ch 190 (AB 1517),s 71, eff. 1/1/2016.
Added by Stats 2005 ch 438 (SB 390),s 1, eff. 1/1/2006.

Section 11605 - Final order binding and conclusive

When a court order made under this chapter becomes final, the order binds and is conclusive as to the rights of all interested persons.

Ca. Prob. Code § 11605

Enacted by Stats. 1990, Ch. 79.

Article 2 - PRELIMINARY DISTRIBUTION

Section 11620 - Time for filing petition

A petition for an order for preliminary distribution of all, or a portion of, the share of a decedent's estate to which a beneficiary is entitled may not be filed unless at least two months have elapsed after letters are first issued to a general personal representative.

Ca. Prob. Code § 11620
Enacted by Stats. 1990, Ch. 79.

Section 11621 - When court will order distribution; order stayed until bond filed

(a) The court shall order distribution under this article if at the hearing it appears that the distribution may be made without loss to creditors or injury to the estate or any interested person.
(b) The order for distribution shall be stayed until any bond required by the court is filed.

Ca. Prob. Code § 11621
Enacted by Stats. 1990, Ch. 79.

Section 11622 - When bond required

(a) If the court orders distribution before four months have elapsed after letters are first issued to a general personal representative, the court shall require a bond. The bond shall be in the amount of the distribution.
(b) If the court orders distribution after four months have elapsed after letters are first issued to a general personal representative, the court may require a bond. The bond shall be in the amount the court orders.
(c) Any bond required by the court shall be given by the distributee and filed with the court. The bond shall be conditioned on payment of the distributee's proper share of the debts of the estate, not exceeding the amount distributed.

Ca. Prob. Code § 11622
Enacted by Stats. 1990, Ch. 79.

Section 11623 - Authority to administer estate without court supervision

(a) Notwithstanding Section 11601, if authority is granted to administer the estate without court supervision under the Independent Administration of Estates Act, Part 6 (commencing with Section 10400):

(1) The personal representative may petition the court for an order for preliminary distribution on notice as provided in Section 1220. Notwithstanding subdivision (c) of Section 1220, the court may not dispense with notice unless the time for filing creditor claims has expired.

(2) The aggregate of all property distributed under this section shall not exceed 50 percent of the net value of the estate. For the purpose of this subdivision, "net value of the estate" means the excess of the value of the property in the estate, as determined by all inventories and appraisals on file with the court, over the total amount of all creditor claims and of all liens and encumbrances recorded or known to the personal representative not included in a creditor claim, excluding any estate tax lien occasioned by the decedent's death.

(b) Nothing in this section limits the authority of the personal representative to make preliminary distribution under other provisions of this chapter, whether or not authority is granted to administer the estate under the Independent Administration of Estates Act, Part 6 (commencing with Section 10400).

Ca. Prob. Code § 11623

Amended (as amended by Stats. 1990, Ch. 710) by Stats. 1991, Ch. 82, Sec. 30.5. Effective June 30, 1991. Operative July 1, 1991, by Sec. 31 of Ch. 82.

Section 11624 - Payment of costs of proceeding

The costs of a proceeding under this article shall be paid by the distributee or the estate in proportions determined by the court.

Ca. Prob. Code § 11624
Enacted by Stats. 1990, Ch. 79.

Article 3 - FINAL DISTRIBUTION

Section 11640 - Petition for order; resolution of ademption by satisfaction or advancements; continuation of administration

(a) When all debts have been paid or adequately provided for, or if the estate is insolvent, and the estate is in a condition to be closed, the personal representative shall file a petition for, and the court shall make, an order for final distribution of the estate.
(b) The court shall hear and determine and resolve in the order all questions arising under Section 21135 (ademption by satisfaction) or Section 6409 (advancements).
(c) If debts remain unpaid or not adequately provided for or if, for other reasons, the estate is not in a condition to be closed, the administration may continue for a reasonable time, subject to Chapter 1 (commencing with Section 12200) of Part 11 (time for closing estate).
Ca. Prob. Code § 11640
Amended by Stats 2002 ch 138 (AB 1784), s 9, eff. 1/1/2003.

Section 11641 - Immediate distribution of property

When an order settling a final account and for final distribution is entered, the personal representative may immediately distribute the property in the estate to the persons entitled to distribution, without further notice or proceedings.
Ca. Prob. Code § 11641
Enacted by Stats. 1990, Ch. 79.

Section 11642 - Distribution of property acquired or discovered after distribution

Any property acquired or discovered after the court order for final distribution is made shall be distributed in the following manner:
(a) If the order disposes of the property, distribution shall be made

362

in the manner provided in the order. The court may, in an appropriate case, require a supplemental account and make further instructions relating to the property.

(b) If the order does not dispose of the property, distribution shall be made either (1) in the manner ordered by the court on a petition for instructions or (2) under Section 12252 (administration after discharge) if the personal representative has been discharged.

Ca. Prob. Code § 11642

Enacted by Stats. 1990, Ch. 79.

Chapter 2 - DETERMINATION OF PERSONS ENTITLED TO DISTRIBUTION

Section 11700 - Petition for determination

At any time after letters are first issued to a general personal representative and before an order for final distribution is made, the personal representative, or any person claiming to be a beneficiary or otherwise entitled to distribution of a share of the estate, may file a petition for a court determination of the persons entitled to distribution of the decedent's estate. The petition shall include a statement of the basis for the petitioner's claim.

Ca. Prob. Code § 11700

Enacted by Stats. 1990, Ch. 79.

Section 11701 - Notice of hearing

Notice of the hearing on the petition shall be given as provided in Section 1220 to all of the following persons:

(a) Each person listed in Section 1220.

(b) Each known heir whose interest in the estate would be affected by the petition.

(c) Each known devisee whose interest in the estate would be affected by the petition.

(d) The Attorney General, at the office of the Attorney General in Sacramento, if any portion of the estate is to escheat to the state and its interest in the estate would be affected by the petition.

Ca. Prob. Code § 11701

Enacted by Stats. 1990, Ch. 79.

Section 11702 - Written statement of person's interest in estate

(a) Any interested person may appear and, at or before the time of the hearing, file a written statement of the person's interest in the estate. The written statement may be in support of, or in opposition to, the petition. No other pleadings are necessary and the written statement of each claimant shall be deemed denied by each of the other claimants to the extent the written statements conflict.
(b) If a person fails timely to file a writen statement:

(1) The case is at issue notwithstanding the failure and the case may proceed on the petition and written statements filed by the time of the hearing, and no further pleadings by other persons are necessary.

(2) The person may not participate further in the proceeding for determination of persons entitled to distribution, but the person's interest in the estate is not otherwise affected.

(3) The person is bound by the decision in the proceeding.
Ca. Prob. Code § 11702
Enacted by Stats. 1990, Ch. 79.

Section 11703 - Attorney General deemed person entitled to distribution

The Attorney General shall be deemed to be a person entitled to distribution of the estate for purposes of this chapter if the estate involves or may involve any of the following:
(a) A charitable trust, other than a charitable trust with a designated trustee that may lawfully accept the trust.
(b) A devise for a charitable purpose without an identified beneficiary.
(c) An escheat to the State of California.
Ca. Prob. Code § 11703
Enacted by Stats. 1990, Ch. 79.

Section 11704 - Evidence in preceding; hearing on petition

(a) The court shall consider as evidence in the proceeding any statement made in a petition filed under Section 11700 and any statement of interest filed under Section 11702. The court shall not hear or consider a petition filed after the time prescribed in Section 11700.

(b)

(1) The personal representative may petition the court for authorization to participate, as necessary to assist the court, in the proceeding. Notice of the hearing on the petition shall be given to the persons identified in Section 11701 in the manner provided in Section 1220.

(2) The court may grant or deny this petition, in whole or in part, on the pleadings, without an evidentiary hearing or further discovery. A petition filed pursuant to this subdivision may be granted only upon a showing of good cause. The court shall determine the manner and capacity in which the personal representative may provide assistance in the proceeding. The court may direct the personal representative to file papers as a party to the proceeding, or to take other specified action, if deemed by the court to be necessary to assist the court.

Ca. Prob. Code § 11704
Amended by Stats 2013 ch 84 (AB 1160),s 1, eff. 1/1/2014.

Section 11705 - Order of court

(a) The court shall make an order that determines the persons entitled to distribution of the decedent's estate and specifies their shares.

(b) When the court order becomes final it binds and is conclusive as to the rights of all interested persons.

Ca. Prob. Code § 11705
Enacted by Stats. 1990, Ch. 79.

Chapter 3 - DISTRIBUTION OF PROPERTY IN ESTATE

Section 11750 - Generally

(a) The personal representative is responsible for distribution of the property in the estate in compliance with the terms of the court order for distribution.

(b) A distributee may demand, sue for, and recover from the personal representative or any person in possession, property to which the distributee is entitled.

(c) A distribution of property made in compliance with the terms of the court order for distribution is valid as to a person acting in good faith and for a valuable consideration.

Ca. Prob. Code § 11750
Enacted by Stats. 1990, Ch. 79.

Section 11751 - Receipt of distributee; recording court order for distribution of real property

The personal representative shall obtain the receipt of the distributee for property in the estate distributed by the personal representative. In the case of real property, the personal representative shall record the court order for distribution or the personal representative's deed or both in the county in which the real property is located. Recordation of the order or deed is deemed to be a receipt of the distributee for the property.

Ca. Prob. Code § 11751
Enacted by Stats. 1990, Ch. 79.

Section 11752 - Inventory from distributee if possession for life only

If personal property in the possession of a distributee is subject to possession by the distributee for life only, the personal representative shall demand an inventory of the property from the distributee. On receipt, the personal representative shall file the inventory with the court and deliver a copy to any distributee of the remainder.

Ca. Prob. Code § 11752
Enacted by Stats. 1990, Ch. 79.

Section 11753 - Discharge of personal representative

(a) Distribution in compliance with the court order entitles the personal representative to a full discharge with respect to property included in the order.

(b) The personal representative shall, before or at the time of the petition for discharge, file receipts for all property in the estate. In the case of real property, the personal representative shall file a statement that identifies the date and place of the recording and other appropriate recording information for the court order for distribution or the personal representative's deed.

(c) The court may excuse the filing of a receipt on a showing that the personal representative is unable, after reasonable effort, to obtain a receipt and that the property has been delivered to or is in the possession of the distributee.

Ca. Prob. Code § 11753
Enacted by Stats. 1990, Ch. 79.

Section 11754 - Reasonable storage, delivery and shipping costs

Expenses of administration of the estate shall include reasonable storage, delivery, and shipping costs for distribution of tangible personal property to a distributee.

Ca. Prob. Code § 11754
Added by Stats. 1994, Ch. 806, Sec. 34. Effective January 1, 1995.

Chapter 4 - DECEASED DISTRIBUTEE

Section 11801 - Distributed with same effect as if beneficiary living

(a) Except as provided in subdivision (b), the share in a decedent's estate of a beneficiary who survives the decedent but who dies before distribution shall be distributed under this chapter with the same effect as though the distribution were made to the beneficiary while living.

(b) Subject to Section 21525, distribution may not be made under this chapter if the decedent's will provides that the beneficiary is entitled to take under the will only if the beneficiary survives the date of distribution or other period stated in the will and the beneficiary fails to survive the date of distribution or other period.

Ca. Prob. Code § 11801

Enacted by Stats. 1990, Ch. 79.

Section 11802 - Distribution of beneficiary's share

If a beneficiary satisfies the requirement of Section 11801, the beneficiary's share in the decedent's estate shall be distributed as follows:

(a) Except as otherwise provided in this section, distribution shall be made to the personal representative of the estate of the beneficiary for the purpose of administration in the estate of the beneficiary.

(b) If the beneficiary was issue of the decedent and died intestate while under the age of majority and not having been emancipated, distribution shall be made directly to the heirs of the beneficiary without administration in the estate of the beneficiary.

(c) If a person entitled to the beneficiary's share proceeds under Division 8 (commencing with Section 13000) (disposition of estate without administration), distribution shall be made under Division 8.

Ca. Prob. Code § 11802

Enacted by Stats. 1990, Ch. 79.

Chapter 5 - DEPOSIT WITH COUNTY TREASURER

Section 11850 - Cases in which deposit in name of distributee allowed

Subject to Section 11851, the personal representative may deposit property to be distributed with the county treasurer of the county in which the proceedings are pending in the name of the distributee in any of the following cases:

(a) The property remains in the possession of the personal representative unclaimed or the whereabouts of the distributee is unknown.

(b) The distributee refuses to give a receipt for the property.

(c) The distributee is a minor or incompetent person who has no guardian, conservator, or other fiduciary to receive the property or person authorized to give a receipt for the property.

(d) For any other reason the property cannot be distributed, and the personal representative desires discharge. Notwithstanding Section 11851, deposit may not be made under this subdivision except on court order.

Ca. Prob. Code § 11850
Enacted by Stats. 1990, Ch. 79.

Section 11851 - Deposit of money; personal property other than money

(a) If property authorized by Section 11850 to be deposited with the county treasurer consists of money, the personal representative may deposit the money.

(b) If property authorized by Section 11850 to be deposited with the county treasurer consists of personal property other than money, the personal representative may not deposit the personal property except on court order. If it appears to the court that sale is for the benefit of interested persons, the court shall order the personal property sold, and the proceeds of sale, less expenses of sale allowed by the court, shall be deposited in the county treasury. If it appears to the court that sale is not for the benefit of interested persons, the court shall order the personal property deposited with the Controller, to be held subject to the provisions of Chapter 6 (commencing with Section 11900).

Ca. Prob. Code § 11851
Enacted by Stats. 1990, Ch. 79.

Section 11852 - Receipt for deposit

The county treasurer shall give a receipt for a deposit made under this chapter and is liable on the official bond of the county treasurer for the money deposited. The receipt has the same effect as if executed by the distributee.

Ca. Prob. Code § 11852
Enacted by Stats. 1990, Ch. 79.

Section 11853 - Delivery of certified copy of order for distribution

If money is deposited or is already on deposit with the county treasurer, the personal representative shall deliver to the county treasurer a certified copy of the order for distribution.

Ca. Prob. Code § 11853
Enacted by Stats. 1990, Ch. 79.

Section 11854 - Petition claiming money on deposit

(a) A person may claim money on deposit in the county treasury by filing a petition with the court that made the order for distribution. The petition shall show the person's claim or right to the property. Unless the petition is filed by the person named in the decree for distribution of a decedent's estate, or the legal representative of the person or the person's estate, the petition shall state the facts required to be stated in a petition for escheated property filed under Section 1355 of the Code of Civil Procedure. On the filing of the petition, the same proceedings shall be had as are required by that section, except that the hearing shall be ex parte unless the court orders otherwise.

(b) If so ordered by the court, a copy of the petition shall be served on the Attorney General. The Attorney General may answer the petition, at the Attorney General's discretion.

(c) If the court is satisfied that the claimant has a right to the property claimed, the court shall make an order establishing the right. On presentation of a certified copy of the order, the county auditor shall draw a warrant on the county treasurer for the amount of money covered by the order.

(d) A claim for money distributed in the estate of a deceased person made after the deposit of the property in the State Treasury is governed by the provisions of Chapter 3 (commencing with Section 1335) of Title 10 of Part 3 of the Code of Civil Procedure.

Ca. Prob. Code § 11854
Amended by Stats. 1994, Ch. 806, Sec. 35. Effective January 1, 1995.

Chapter 6 - DISTRIBUTION TO STATE

Section 11900 - Property not ordered distributed to known beneficiaries

(a) The court shall order property that is not ordered distributed to known beneficiaries to be distributed to the state.
(b) Insofar as practicable, any real property or tangible personal property shall be converted to money before distribution to the state.

Ca. Prob. Code § 11900
Enacted by Stats. 1990, Ch. 79.

Section 11901 - Order including words creating trust in favor of unknown or unidentified persons

If the court orders distribution of property in the decedent's estate to the state, and the order includes words that otherwise create a trust in favor of unknown or unidentified persons as a class, the distribution shall vest in the state both legal and equitable title to the property.

Ca. Prob. Code § 11901
Enacted by Stats. 1990, Ch. 79.

Section 11902 - Duty of personal representative to deliver property and record order

(a) If the court orders distribution to the state, the personal representative shall promptly:

(1) Deliver any money to the State Treasurer.

(2) Deliver any personal property other than money to the Controller for deposit in the State Treasury.

(3) Cause a certified copy of the order to be recorded in the office of the county recorder of each county in which any real property is located.

(b) At the time of making a delivery of property or recordation under this section, the personal representative shall deliver to the Controller a certified copy of the order for distribution together with a statement of the date and place of each recording and other appropriate recording information.

Ca. Prob. Code § 11902
Enacted by Stats. 1990, Ch. 79.

Section 11903 - Time property held; failure to timely claim property

(a) Property distributed to the state shall be held by the Treasurer for a period of five years from the date of the order for distribution, within which time any person may claim the property in the manner provided by Title 10 (commencing with Section 1300) of Part 3 of the Code of Civil Procedure.

(b) A person who does not claim the property within the time prescribed in this section is forever barred, and the property vests absolutely in the state, subject to the provisions of Title 10 (commencing with Section 1300) of Part 3 of the Code of Civil Procedure.

Ca. Prob. Code § 11903
Enacted by Stats. 1990, Ch. 79.

Section 11904 - Transmittal of property deposited in county treasury

No deposit of property in an estate shall be made in the county treasury by a personal representative if any other property in the estate is to be or has been distributed to the state under this chapter, but the property that would otherwise be deposited in the county treasury shall be transmitted promptly to the State Treasurer or Controller as provided in this chapter.

Ca. Prob. Code § 11904
Enacted by Stats. 1990, Ch. 79.

Chapter 7 - PARTITION OR ALLOTMENT OF PROPERTY

Section 11950 - Petition to make partition, allotment or other division

(a) If two or more beneficiaries are entitled to the distribution of undivided interests in property and have not agreed among themselves to a partition, allotment, or other division of the property, any of them, or the personal representative at the request of any of them, may petition the court to make a partition, allotment, or other division of the property that will be equitable and will avoid the distribution of undivided interests.
(b) A proceeding under this chapter is limited to interests in the property that are subject to administration and does not include other interests except to the extent the owners of other interests in the property consent to be bound by the partition, allotment, or other division.
Ca. Prob. Code § 11950
Enacted by Stats. 1990, Ch. 79.

Section 11951 - Filing petition; contents

(a) A petition under this chapter may be filed at any time before an order for distribution of the affected property becomes final.
(b) The petition shall:

(1) Describe the property.

(2) State the names of the persons having or claiming undivided interests.

(3) Describe the undivided interests, so far as known to the petitioner.
Ca. Prob. Code § 11951
Enacted by Stats. 1990, Ch. 79.

Section 11952 - Notice of hearing; parties; objection to jurisdiction

(a) Notice of the hearing on the petition shall be given as provided in Section 1220 to the personal representative and to the persons entitled to distribution of the undivided interests.

(b) At the hearing the persons entitled to distribution of the undivided interests shall be considered the parties to the proceeding whether or not they have appeared or filed a responsive pleading. No one shall be considered as a plaintiff or as a defendant.

(c) Any objection to the jurisdiction of the court shall be made and resolved in the manner prescribed in Part 19 (commencing with Section 850) of Division 2.

Ca. Prob. Code § 11952

Amended by Stats 2003 ch 32 (AB 167), s 12, eff. 1/1/2004.

Section 11953 - Value of property received; sale; agreement

(a) The court shall partition, allot, or otherwise divide the property so that each party receives property with a value proportionate to the value of the party's interest in the whole.

(b) The court may direct the personal representative to sell property where, under the circumstances, sale would be more equitable than partition and where the property cannot conveniently be allotted to any one party. The sale shall be conducted in the same manner as other sales made during administration of an estate.

(c) Any two or more parties may agree to accept undivided interests.

Ca. Prob. Code § 11953

Enacted by Stats. 1990, Ch. 79.

Section 11954 - Appointment of referees

(a) The court, in its discretion, may appoint one or three referees to partition property capable of being partitioned, if requested to do so by a party. The number of referees appointed must conform to the request of at least one of the parties.

(b) The referees shall have the powers and perform the duties of referees in, and the court shall have the same powers with respect to their report as in, partition actions under Title 10.5 (commencing with Section 872.010) of Part 2 of the Code of Civil Procedure.

Ca. Prob. Code § 11954
Enacted by Stats. 1990, Ch. 79.

Section 11955 - Expenses

The expenses of partition shall be equitably apportioned by the court among the parties, but each party must pay the party's own attorney's fees. The amount charged to each party shall be included and specified in the order and, to the extent unpaid, constitutes a lien on the property allotted to the party.

Ca. Prob. Code § 11955
Enacted by Stats. 1990, Ch. 79.

Section 11956 - Division made controls proceedings for distribution; appeal of proceedings leading to division

(a) The partition, allotment, or other division made by the court shall control in proceedings for distribution, unless modified for good cause on reasonable notice.
(b) The proceedings leading to the partition, allotment, or other division may be reviewed on appeal from the order for distribution.

Ca. Prob. Code § 11956
Enacted by Stats. 1990, Ch. 79.

Chapter 8 - INTEREST AND INCOME ACCRUING DURING ADMINISTRATION

Section 12000 - Testator's intention not otherwise indicated by will

The provisions of this chapter apply where the intention of the testator is not otherwise indicated by the will.

Ca. Prob. Code § 12000
Enacted by Stats. 1990, Ch. 79.

Section 12001 - Rate of interest

If interest is payable under this chapter, the rate of interest is three percentage points less than the legal rate on judgments in effect one year after the date of the testator's death and shall not be recomputed in the event of a change in the applicable rate thereafter.

Ca. Prob. Code § 12001

Amended by Stats. 1992, Ch. 871, Sec. 14. Effective January 1, 1993.

Section 12002 - Specific devise

(a) Except as provided in this section, a specific devise does not bear interest.

(b) A specific devise carries with it income on the devised property from the date of death, less expenses attributable to the devised property during administration of the estate. For purposes of this section, expenses attributable to property are expenses that result directly from the use or ownership of the property, including property tax and tax on the income from the property, but excluding estate and generation-skipping transfer taxes.

(c) If income of specifically devised property is not sufficient to pay expenses attributable to the property, the deficiency shall be paid out of the estate until the property is distributed to the devisee or the devisee takes possession of or occupies the property, whichever occurs first. To the extent a deficiency paid out of the estate is attributable to the period that commences one year after the testator's death, whether paid during or after expiration of the one year period following the date of death, the amount paid is a charge against the share of the devisee, and the personal representative has an equitable lien on the specifically devised property as against the devisee in the amount paid.

(d) If specifically devised property is sold during administration of the estate, the devisee is entitled to the net income from the property until the date of sale, and to interest on the net sale proceeds thereafter, but no interest accrues during the first year after the testator's death.

Ca. Prob. Code § 12002

Enacted by Stats. 1990, Ch. 79.

Section 12003 - General pecuniary devise

If a general pecuniary devise, including a general pecuniary devise in trust, is not distributed within one year after the testator's death, the devise bears interest thereafter.

Ca. Prob. Code § 12003
Enacted by Stats. 1990, Ch. 79.

Section 12004 - Annuity

(a) An annuity commences at the testator's death and shall be paid at the end of the annual, monthly, or other specified period.
(b) If an annuity is not paid at the end of the specified period, it bears interest thereafter, but no interest accrues during the first year after the testator's death.

Ca. Prob. Code § 12004
Enacted by Stats. 1990, Ch. 79.

Section 12005 - Devisee of devise of maintenance

A devisee of a devise for maintenance is entitled to interest on the amount of any unpaid accumulations of the payments held by the personal representative on each anniversary of the testator's death, computed from the date of the anniversary.

Ca. Prob. Code § 12005
Enacted by Stats. 1990, Ch. 79.

Section 12006 - Net income

Net income received during administration not paid under other provisions of this chapter and not otherwise devised shall be distributed pro rata as income among all distributees who receive either residuary or intestate property. If a distributee takes for life or for a term of years, the pro rata share of income belongs to the tenant for life or for the term of years.

Ca. Prob. Code § 12006
Enacted by Stats. 1990, Ch. 79.

Section 12007 - Law in effect when decedent died before July 1, 1969

This chapter does not apply in cases where the decedent died before July 1, 1989. In cases where the decedent died before July 1, 1989, the applicable law in effect before July 1, 1989, continues to apply.

Ca. Prob. Code § 12007
Enacted by Stats. 1990, Ch. 79.

Part 11 - CLOSING ESTATE ADMINISTRATION

Chapter 1 - TIME FOR CLOSING ESTATE

Section 12200 - Time for petition for order of final distribution or making report on administration status

The personal representative shall either petition for an order for final distribution of the estate or make a report of status of administration not later than the following times:

(a) In an estate for which a federal estate tax return is not required, within one year after the date of issuance of letters.

(b) In an estate for which a federal estate tax return is required, within 18 months after the date of issuance of letters.

Ca. Prob. Code § 12200
Enacted by Stats. 1990, Ch. 79.

Section 12201 - Contents of report on status of administration; filing; notice of hearing; hearing

If a report of status of administration is made under Section 12200:

(a) The report shall show the condition of the estate, the reasons why the estate cannot be distributed and closed, and an estimate of the time needed to close administration of the estate.

(b) The report shall be filed with the court. Notice of hearing of the report shall be given as provided in Section 1220 to persons then interested in the estate, and shall include a statement in not less than 10-point boldface type or a reasonable equivalent thereof if printed, or in all capital letters if not printed, in substantially the following words: "YOU HAVE THE RIGHT TO PETITION FOR AN ACCOUNT UNDER SECTION 10950 OF THE CALIFORNIA PROBATE CODE."

(c) On the hearing of the report, the court may order either of the following:

(1) That the administration of the estate continue for the time and on the terms and conditions that appear reasonable, including an account under Section 10950, if the court determines that continuation of administration is in the best interests of the estate or of interested persons.

(2) That the personal representative shall petition for final distribution.

Ca. Prob. Code § 12201
Enacted by Stats. 1990, Ch. 79.

Section 12202 - Personal representative cited to appear and show condition of estate

(a) The court may, on petition of any interested person or on its own motion, for good cause shown on the record, cite the personal representative to appear before the court and show the condition of the estate and the reasons why the estate cannot be distributed and closed.

(b) On the hearing of the citation, the court may either order the administration of the estate to continue or order the personal representative to petition for final distribution, as provided in Section 12201.

Ca. Prob. Code § 12202
Amended by Stats. 1996, Ch. 563, Sec. 28. Effective January 1, 1997.

Section 12203 - Continuation of administration in order to pay family allowance

(a) For purposes of this chapter, continuation of the administration of the estate in order to pay a family allowance is not in the best interests of the estate or interested persons unless the court determines both of the following:

(1) The family allowance is needed by the recipient to pay for necessaries of life, including education so long as pursued to advantage.

(2) The needs of the recipient for continued family allowance outweigh the needs of the decedent's beneficiaries whose interests would be adversely affected by continuing the administration of the estate for this purpose.

(b) Nothing in this section shall be construed to authorize continuation of a family allowance beyond the time prescribed in Section 6543.

(c) Nothing in this section limits the power of the court to order a preliminary distribution of the estate.

Ca. Prob. Code § 12203
Enacted by Stats. 1990, Ch. 79.

Section 12204 - Failure to comply with order

Failure of the personal representative to comply with an order made under this chapter is grounds for removal from office.

Ca. Prob. Code § 12204
Enacted by Stats. 1990, Ch. 79.

Section 12205 - Reduction of compensation of personal representative or attorney

(a) The court may reduce the compensation of the personal representative or the attorney for the personal representative by an amount the court determines to be appropriate if the court makes all of the following determinations:

(1) The time taken for administration of the estate exceeds the time required by this chapter or prescribed by the court.

(2) The time taken was within the control of the personal representative or attorney whose compensation is being reduced.

(3) The delay was not in the best interest of the estate or interested persons.

(b) An order under this section reducing compensation may be made regardless of whether the compensation otherwise allowable under Part 7 (commencing with Section 10800) would be reasonable compensation for the services rendered by the personal representative or attorney.

(c) An order under this section may be made at any of the following hearings:

(1) The hearing for final distribution.

(2) The hearing for an allowance on the compensation of the personal representative or attorney.

(d) In making a determination under this section, the court shall take into account any action taken under Section 12202 as a result of a previous delay.

Ca. Prob. Code § 12205
Amended by Stats. 1990, Ch. 710, Sec. 42. Operative July 1, 1991, by Sec. 48 of Ch. 710.

Section 12206 - Effect of limitation in will of time for administration

A limitation in a will of the time for administration of an estate is directory only and does not limit the power of the personal representative or the court to continue administration of the estate beyond the time limitation in the will if the continuation is necessary.

Ca. Prob. Code § 12206
Enacted by Stats. 1990, Ch. 79.

Chapter 2 - DISCHARGE OF PERSONAL REPRESENTATIVE

Section 12250 - Order discharging personal representative

(a) When the personal representative has complied with the terms of the order for final distribution and has filed the appropriate receipts or the court has excused the filing of a receipt as provided in Section 11753, the court shall, on ex parte petition, make an order discharging the personal representative from all liability incurred thereafter.

(b) Nothing in this section precludes discharge of the personal representative for distribution made without prior court order, so long as the terms of the order for final distribution are satisfied.

Ca. Prob. Code § 12250

Enacted by Stats. 1990, Ch. 79.

Section 12251 - Petition for termination of further proceedings and discharge

(a) At any time after appointment of a personal representative and whether or not letters have been issued, if it appears there is no property of any kind belonging to the estate and subject to administration, the personal representative may petition for the termination of further proceedings and for discharge of the personal representative. The petition shall state the facts required by this subdivision.

(b) Notice of the hearing on the petition shall be given as provided in Section 1220 to all interested persons.

(c) If it appears to the satisfaction of the court on the hearing that the facts stated in the petition are true, the court shall make an order terminating the proceeding and discharging the personal representative.

Ca. Prob. Code § 12251

Enacted by Stats. 1990, Ch. 79.

Section 12252 - Subsequent administration necessary after discharge

If subsequent administration of an estate is necessary after the personal representative has been discharged because other property is discovered or because it becomes necessary or proper for any other cause, both of the following shall apply:

(a) The court shall appoint as personal representative the person entitled to appointment in the same order as is directed in relation to an original appointment, except that the person who served as personal representative at the time of the order of discharge has priority.

(b) Notice of hearing of the appointment shall be given as provided in Section 1220 to the person who served as personal representative at the time of the order of discharge and to other interested persons. If property has been distributed to the State of California, a copy of any petition for subsequent appointment of a personal representative and the notice of hearing shall be given as provided in Section 1220 to the Controller.

Ca. Prob. Code § 12252
Amended by Stats 2009 ch 8 (AB 1163),s 3, eff. 1/1/2010.
Amended by Stats 2007 ch 388 (AB 403),s 1, eff. 1/1/2008.

Part 12 - ADMINISTRATION OF ESTATES OF MISSING PERSONS PRESUMED DEAD

Section 12400 - Missing person defined

Unless the provision or context otherwise requires, as used in this part, "missing person" means a person who is presumed to be dead under Section 12401.

Ca. Prob. Code § 12400
Enacted by Stats. 1990, Ch. 79.

Section 12401 - Death presumed

In proceedings under this part, a person who has not been seen or heard from for a continuous period of five years by those who are likely to have seen or heard from that person, and whose absence is not satisfactorily explained after diligent search or inquiry, is presumed to be dead. The person's death is presumed to have occurred at the end of the period unless there is sufficient evidence to establish that death occurred earlier.

Ca. Prob. Code § 12401
Enacted by Stats. 1990, Ch. 79.

Section 12402 - Manner of administering estate

Subject to the provisions of this part, the estate of a missing person may be administered in the manner provided generally for the administration of estates of deceased persons.

Ca. Prob. Code § 12402
Enacted by Stats. 1990, Ch. 79.

Section 12403 - Court having jurisdiction

(a) If the missing person was a resident of this state when last seen or heard from, the superior court of the county of the person's last known place of residence has jurisdiction for the purposes of this part.

(b) If the missing person was a nonresident of this state when last seen or heard from, the superior court of a county where real property of the missing person is located, or of a county where personal property is located if the missing person has no real property in this state, has jurisdiction for the purposes of this part.

Ca. Prob. Code § 12403
Enacted by Stats. 1990, Ch. 79.

Section 12404 - Petition for administration

(a) A petition may be filed in the court having jurisdiction under Section 12403 for the administration of the estate of a missing person.

(b) The petition may be filed by any person who may be appointed as a personal representative, other than a person described in subdivision (r) of Section 8461.

(c) In addition to the matters otherwise required in a petition for administration of the estate, the petition shall state all of the following:

(1) The last known place of residence and the last known address of the missing person.

(2) The time and circumstances when the missing person was last seen or heard from.

(3) That the missing person has not been seen or heard from for a continuous period of five years by the persons likely to have seen or heard from the missing person (naming them and their relationship to the missing person) and that the whereabouts of the missing person is unknown to those persons and to the petitioner.

(4) A description of the search or the inquiry made concerning the whereabouts of the missing person.

Ca. Prob. Code § 12404
Enacted by Stats. 1990, Ch. 79.

Section 12405 - Notice of hearing

Notice of hearing shall be served and published, and proof made, in the same manner as in proceedings for administration of the estate of a decedent, except that notice of hearing on the petition shall also be sent by registered mail to the missing person at his or her last known address.

Ca. Prob. Code § 12405
Enacted by Stats. 1990, Ch. 79.

Section 12406 - Hearing; petitioner ordered to conduct diligent search or inquiry

(a) At the hearing, the court shall determine whether the alleged missing person is a person who is presumed to be dead under Section 12401. The court may receive evidence and consider the affidavits and depositions of persons likely to have seen or heard from or know the whereabouts of the alleged missing person.
(b) If the court is not satisfied that a diligent search or inquiry has been made for the missing person, the court may order the petitioner to conduct a diligent search or inquiry and to report the results. The court may order the search or inquiry to be made in any manner that the court determines to be advisable, including any or all of the following methods:

(1) Inserting in one or more suitable newspapers or other

385

periodicals a notice requesting information from any person having knowledge of the whereabouts of the missing person.

(2) Notifying law enforcement officials and public welfare agencies in appropriate locations of the disappearance of the missing person.

(3) Engaging the services of an investigator.
(c) The costs of a search ordered by the court pursuant to subdivision (b) shall be paid by the estate of the missing person, but if there is no administration, the court in its discretion may order the petitioner to pay the costs.
Ca. Prob. Code § 12406
Enacted by Stats. 1990, Ch. 79.

Section 12407 - Court finding that person presumed dead

(a) If the court finds that the alleged missing person is a person presumed to be dead under Section 12401, the court shall do both of the following:

(1) Appoint a personal representative for the estate of the missing person in the manner provided for the estates of deceased persons.

(2) Determine the date of the missing person's death.
(b) The personal representative shall administer the estate of the missing person in the same general manner and method of procedure, and with the same force and effect, as provided for the administration of the estates of deceased persons, except as otherwise provided in this part.
Ca. Prob. Code § 12407
Enacted by Stats. 1990, Ch. 79.

Section 12408 - Missing person reappears

(a) If the missing person reappears:

(1) The missing person may recover property of the missing person's estate in the possession of the personal representative, less fees, costs, and expenses thus far incurred.

(2) The missing person may recover from distributees any property of the missing person's estate that is in their possession, or the value of distributions received by them, to the extent that recovery from distributees is equitable in view of all the circumstances, but an action under this paragraph is forever barred five years after the time the distribution was made.

(b) The remedies available to the missing person under subdivision (a) are exclusive, except for any remedy the missing person may have by reason of fraud or intentional wrongdoing.

(c) Except as provided in subdivisions (a) and (b), the order for final distribution, when it becomes final, is conclusive as to the rights of the missing person, the rights of the beneficiaries of the missing person, and the rights of all other persons interested in the estate.

(d) If a dispute arises as to the identity of a person claiming to be a reappearing missing person, the person making the claim or any other interested person may file a petition under Section 11700, notwithstanding the limitations of time prescribed in Section 11700, for the determination of the identity of the person claiming to be the reappearing missing person.

Ca. Prob. Code § 12408
Enacted by Stats. 1990, Ch. 79.

Part 13 - NONDOMICILIARY DECEDENTS

Chapter 1 - DEFINITIONS

Section 12500 - Definitions govern construction

Unless the provision or context otherwise requires, the definitions in this chapter govern the construction of this part.

Ca. Prob. Code § 12500
Enacted by Stats. 1990, Ch. 79.

Section 12501 - Ancillary administration

"Ancillary administration" means proceedings in this state for administration of the estate of a nondomiciliary decedent.

Ca. Prob. Code § 12501

Enacted by Stats. 1990, Ch. 79.

Section 12502 - Foreign nation

"Foreign nation" means a jurisdiction other than a state of the United States.

Ca. Prob. Code § 12502

Enacted by Stats. 1990, Ch. 79.

Section 12503 - Foreign nation personal representative

"Foreign nation personal representative" means a personal representative appointed in a jurisdiction other than a state of the United States.

Ca. Prob. Code § 12503

Enacted by Stats. 1990, Ch. 79.

Section 12504 - Local personal representative

"Local personal representative" means a nondomiciliary decedent's personal representative appointed in this state.

Ca. Prob. Code § 12504

Enacted by Stats. 1990, Ch. 79.

Section 12505 - Nondomiciliary decedent

"Nondomiciliary decedent" means a person who dies domiciled in a sister state or foreign nation.

Ca. Prob. Code § 12505

Enacted by Stats. 1990, Ch. 79.

Section 12506 - Sister state

"Sister state" means a state other than this state.

Ca. Prob. Code § 12506
Enacted by Stats. 1990, Ch. 79.

Section 12507 - Sister state personal representative

"Sister state personal representative" means a personal representative appointed in a sister state.
Ca. Prob. Code § 12507
Enacted by Stats. 1990, Ch. 79.

Chapter 2 - ANCILLARY ADMINISTRATION

Article 1 - OPENING ANCILLARY ADMINISTRATION

Section 12510 - Persons who may petition court for probate of will or appointment of local personal representative

Any interested person, or a sister state or foreign nation personal representative, may commence an ancillary administration proceeding by a petition to the court for either or both of the following:
(a) Probate of the nondomiciliary decedent's will.
(b) Appointment of a local personal representative.
Ca. Prob. Code § 12510
Enacted by Stats. 1990, Ch. 79.

Section 12511 - Venue for proceeding

The proper county for an ancillary administration proceeding under this chapter is the county determined pursuant to Section 7052.
Ca. Prob. Code § 12511
Enacted by Stats. 1990, Ch. 79.

Section 12512 - Notice of proceeding

Notice of an ancillary administration proceeding shall be given and, except as provided in Article 2 (commencing with Section 12520), the same proceedings had as in the case of a petition for probate of a will or appointment of a personal representative of a person who dies domiciled in this state.

Ca. Prob. Code § 12512
Enacted by Stats. 1990, Ch. 79.

Section 12513 - Priority of personal representative

If the decedent dies while domiciled in a sister state, a personal representative appointed by a court of the decedent's domicile has priority over all other persons except where the decedent's will nominates a different person to be the personal representative in this state. The sister state personal representative may nominate another person as personal representative and the nominee has the same priority as the sister state personal representative.

Ca. Prob. Code § 12513
Enacted by Stats. 1990, Ch. 79.

Article 2 - PROBATE OF NONDOMICILIARY DECEDENT'S WILL ADMITTED TO PROBATE IN SISTER STATE OR FOREIGN NATION

Section 12520 - Proceeding governed by article

(a) If a nondomiciliary decedent's will has been admitted to probate in a sister state or foreign nation and satisfies the requirements of this article, probate of the will in an ancillary administration proceeding is governed by this article.
(b) If a nondomiciliary decedent's will has been admitted to probate in a sister state or foreign nation, but does not satisfy the requirements of this article, the will may be probated in an ancillary administration proceeding pursuant to Part 2 (commencing with Section 8000).

Ca. Prob. Code § 12520
Enacted by Stats. 1990, Ch. 79.

Section 12521 - Contents of petition for probate

(a) A petition for probate of a nondomiciliary decedent's will under this article shall include both of the following:

(1) The will or an authenticated copy of the will.

(2) An authenticated copy of the order admitting the will to probate in the sister state or foreign nation or other evidence of the establishment or proof of the will in accordance with the law of the sister state or foreign nation.

(b) As used in this section, "authenticated copy" means a copy that satisfies the requirements of Article 2 (commencing with Section 1530) of Chapter 2 of Division 11 of the Evidence Code.

Ca. Prob. Code § 12521

Enacted by Stats. 1990, Ch. 79.

Section 12522 - Will admitted to probate in accordance of laws of sister state

If a will of a nondomiciliary decedent was admitted to probate, or established or proved, in accordance with the laws of a sister state, the court shall admit the will to probate in this state, and may not permit a contest or revocation of probate, unless one or more of the following are shown:

(a) The determination in the sister state is not based on a finding that at the time of death the decedent was domiciled in the sister state.

(b) One or more interested parties were not given notice and an opportunity for contest in the proceedings in the sister state.

(c) The determination in the sister state is not final.

Ca. Prob. Code § 12522

Enacted by Stats. 1990, Ch. 79.

Section 12523 - Will admitted to probate in accordance with laws of foreign nation

(a) Except as provided in subdivision (b), if a will of a nondomiciliary decedent was admitted to probate, or established or proved, in accordance with the laws of a foreign nation, the court shall admit the will to probate in this state, and may not permit a contest or revocation of probate, if it appears from the order admitting the will to probate in the foreign nation, or otherwise appears, that all of the following conditions are satisfied:

(1) The determination in the foreign nation is based on a finding that at the time of death the decedent was domiciled in the foreign nation.

(2) All interested parties were given notice and an opportunity for contest in the proceedings in the foreign nation.

(3) The determination in the foreign nation is final.
(b) The court may refuse to admit the will, even though it is shown to satisfy the conditions provided in subdivision (a), where the order admitting the will was made under a judicial system that does not provide impartial tribunals or procedures compatible with the requirements of due process of law.
Ca. Prob. Code § 12523
Enacted by Stats. 1990, Ch. 79.

Section 12524 - Force and effect of will admitted to probate

A nondomiciliary decedent's will admitted to probate under this article has the same force and effect as the will of a person who dies while domiciled in this state that is admitted to probate in this state.
Ca. Prob. Code § 12524
Enacted by Stats. 1990, Ch. 79.

Article 3 - APPLICATION OF GENERAL PROVISIONS

Section 12530 - Generally

Except to the extent otherwise provided in this chapter, ancillary administration of a decedent's estate is subject to all other provisions of this code concerning the administration of the decedent's estate, including, but not limited to, opening estate administration, inventory and appraisal, creditor claims, estate management, independent administration, compensation, accounts, payment of debts, distribution, and closing estate administration.

Ca. Prob. Code § 12530
Enacted by Stats. 1990, Ch. 79.

Article 4 - DISTRIBUTION OF PROPERTY TO SISTER STATE PERSONAL REPRESENTATIVE

Section 12540 - Order for distribution of decedent's personal property in California

(a) If a person dies while domiciled in a sister state, the court in an ancillary administration proceeding may make an order for preliminary or final distribution of all or part of the decedent's personal property in this state to the sister state personal representative if distribution is in the best interest of the estate or interested persons.

(b) The court order shall be made in the manner and pursuant to the procedure provided in, and is subject to the provisions of, Chapter 1 (commencing with Section 11600) of Part 10.

Ca. Prob. Code § 12540
Enacted by Stats. 1990, Ch. 79.

Section 12541 - Sale of real property and distribution of proceeds to sister state personal representative

If necessary to make distribution pursuant to this article, real property in the nondomiciliary decedent's estate may be sold and the court may order the proceeds to be distributed to the sister state personal representative. The sale shall be made in the same manner as other sales of real property of a decedent.

Ca. Prob. Code § 12541
Enacted by Stats. 1990, Ch. 79.

Section 12542 - Estate in sister state where decedent domiciled insolvent

If the nondomiciliary decedent's estate in the sister state where the decedent was domiciled is insolvent, distribution may be made only to the sister state personal representative and not to the beneficiaries.

Ca. Prob. Code § 12542
Enacted by Stats. 1990, Ch. 79.

Chapter 3 - COLLECTION OF PERSONAL PROPERTY OF SMALL ESTATE BY SISTER STATE PERSONAL REPRESENTATIVE WITHOUT ANCILLARY ADMINISTRATION

Section 12570 - Use of affidavit procedure to collect personal property

If a nondomiciliary decedent's property in this state satisfies the requirements of Section 13100, a sister state personal representative may, without petitioning for ancillary administration, use the affidavit procedure provided by Chapter 3 (commencing with Section 13100) of Part 1 of Division 8 to collect personal property of the decedent.

Ca. Prob. Code § 12570
Enacted by Stats. 1990, Ch. 79.

Section 12571 - Law governing payment, delivery or transfer property

The effect of payment, delivery, or transfer of personal property to the sister state personal representative pursuant to this chapter, and the effect of failure to do so, are governed by Chapter 3 (commencing with Section 13100) of Part 1 of Division 8.

Ca. Prob. Code § 12571
Enacted by Stats. 1990, Ch. 79.

Section 12572 - Action against holder of decedent's property

The sister state personal representative may bring an action against a holder of the decedent's property, and may be awarded attorney's fees, as provided in subdivision (b) of Section 13105.

Ca. Prob. Code § 12572
Enacted by Stats. 1990, Ch. 79.

Section 12573 - Liability of sister state personal representative

A sister state personal representative who takes property by affidavit under this chapter is not liable as a person to whom payment, delivery, or transfer of the decedent's property is made under Section 13109 or 13110 to the extent that the sister state personal representative restores the property to the nondomiciliary decedent's estate in the sister state in compliance with Section 13111.

Ca. Prob. Code § 12573
Enacted by Stats. 1990, Ch. 79.

Chapter 4 - JURISDICTION OVER FOREIGN PERSONAL REPRESENTATIVE

Section 12590 - Actions in which representative submits personally in representative capacity to jurisdiction of courts of state

A sister state personal representative or foreign nation personal representative submits personally in a representative capacity to the jurisdiction of the courts of this state in any proceeding relating to the estate by any of the following actions:

(a) Filing a petition for ancillary administration.

(b) Receiving money or other personal property pursuant to Chapter 3 (commencing with Section 12570). Jurisdiction under this subdivision is limited to the amount of money and the value of personal property received.

(c) Doing any act in this state as a personal representative that would have given this state jurisdiction over the personal representative as an individual.

Ca. Prob. Code § 12590
Enacted by Stats. 1990, Ch. 79.

Section 12591 - Subject to jurisdiction of courts of state to

same extent as nondomiciliary decedent

A sister state personal representative or foreign nation personal representative is subject to the jurisdiction of the courts of this state in a representative capacity to the same extent that the nondomiciliary decedent was subject to jurisdiction at the time of death.

Ca. Prob. Code § 12591
Enacted by Stats. 1990, Ch. 79.

Division 8 - DISPOSITION OF ESTATE WITHOUT ADMINISTRATION

Part 1 - COLLECTION OR TRANSFER OF SMALL ESTATE WITHOUT ADMINISTRATION

Chapter 1 - DEFINITIONS

Section 13000 - Definitions govern construction

Unless the provision or context otherwise requires, the definitions in this chapter govern the construction of this part.

Ca. Prob. Code § 13000
Enacted by Stats. 1990, Ch. 79.

Section 13002 - Holder of the decedent's property

"Holder of the decedent's property" or "holder" means, with respect to any particular item of property of the decedent, the person owing money to the decedent, having custody of tangible personal property of the decedent, or acting as registrar or transfer agent of the evidences of a debt, obligation, interest, right, security, or chose in action belonging to the decedent.

Ca. Prob. Code § 13002
Enacted by Stats. 1990, Ch. 79.

Section 13004 - Particular item of property

(a) "Particular item of property" means:

(1) Particular personal property of the decedent which is sought to be collected, received, or transferred by the successor of the decedent under Chapter 3 (commencing with Section 13100).

(2) Particular real property of the decedent, or particular real and personal property of the decedent, for which the successor of the decedent seeks a court order determining succession under Chapter 4 (commencing with Section 13150).

(3) Particular real property of the decedent with respect to which the successor of the decedent files an affidavit of succession under Chapter 5 (commencing with Section 13200).
(b) Subject to subdivision (a), "particular item of property" includes all interests specified in Section 62.
Ca. Prob. Code § 13004
Amended by Stats. 1991, Ch. 1055, Sec. 32.

Section 13005 - Property of decedent, decedent's property, money due decedent and similar phrases

"Property of the decedent," "decedent's property," "money due the decedent," and similar phrases, include property that becomes part of the decedent's estate on the decedent's death, whether by designation of the estate as beneficiary under an insurance policy on the decedent's life or under the decedent's retirement plan, or otherwise.
Ca. Prob. Code § 13005
Added by Stats. 1991, Ch. 1055, Sec. 33.

Section 13006 - Successor of the decedent

"Successor of the decedent" means:
(a) If the decedent died leaving a will, the sole beneficiary or all of the beneficiaries who succeeded to a particular item of property of the decedent under the decedent's will. For the purposes of this part, a trust is a beneficiary under the decedent's will if the trust

succeeds to the particular item of property under the decedent's will.

(b) If the decedent died without a will, the sole person or all of the persons who succeeded to the particular item of property of the decedent under Sections 6401 and 6402 or, if the law of a sister state or foreign nation governs succession to the particular item of property, under the law of the sister state or foreign nation.

    Ca. Prob. Code § 13006
Amended by Stats. 1991, Ch. 1055, Sec. 34.

Section 13007 - Proceeding

"Proceeding" means either that a petition is currently pending in this state for administration of a decedent's estate under Division 7 (commencing with Section 7000), a special administrator for the decedent's estate has been appointed in this state and is now serving, or a personal representative for the decedent's estate has been appointed in this state with general powers. "Proceeding" does not include a petition for administration which was dismissed without the appointment of a personal representative, any proceeding under Division 8 (commencing with Section 13000), or any action or proceeding in another state.

    Ca. Prob. Code § 13007
Added by Stats. 1992, Ch. 871, Sec. 15. Effective January 1, 1993.

Chapter 2 - GENERAL PROVISIONS

Section 13050 - Property excluded in determining property of estate of decedent

(a) For the purposes of this part:

(1) Any property or interest or lien thereon that, at the time of the decedent's death, was held by the decedent as a joint tenant, or in which the decedent had a life or other interest terminable upon the decedent's death, or that was held by the decedent and passed to the decedent's surviving spouse pursuant to Section 13500, shall be excluded in determining the property or estate of the decedent or its value. This excluded property shall include, but not be limited to, property in a trust revocable by the decedent during the decedent's lifetime.

(2) A multiple-party account to which the decedent was a party at the time of the decedent's death shall be excluded in determining the property or estate of the decedent or its value, whether or not all or a portion of the sums on deposit are community property, to the extent that the sums on deposit belong after the death of the decedent to a surviving party, P.O.D. payee, or beneficiary. For the purposes of this paragraph, the terms "multiple-party account," "party," "P.O.D. payee," and "beneficiary" are defined in Article 2 (commencing with Section 5120) of Chapter 1 of Part 2 of Division 5.

(b) For the purposes of this part, all of the following property shall be excluded in determining the property or estate of the decedent or its value:

(1) Any vehicle registered under Division 3 (commencing with Section 4000) of the Vehicle Code or titled under Division 16.5 (commencing with Section 38000) of the Vehicle Code.

(2) Any vessel numbered under Division 3.5 (commencing with Section 9840) of the Vehicle Code.

(3) Any manufactured home, mobilehome, commercial coach, truck camper, or floating home registered under Part 2 (commencing with Section 18000) of Division 13 of the Health and Safety Code.

(c) For the purposes of this part, the value of the following property shall be excluded in determining the value of the decedent's property in this state:

(1) Any amounts due to the decedent for services in the Armed Forces of the United States.

(2) The amount, not exceeding sixteen thousand six hundred twenty-five dollars ($16,625), as adjusted periodically in accordance with Section 890, of salary or other compensation, including compensation for unused vacation, owing to the decedent for personal services from any employment.

Ca. Prob. Code § 13050

Amended by Stats 2019 ch 122 (AB 473),s 4, eff. 1/1/2020.

Amended by Stats 2011 ch 117 (AB 1305),s 3, eff. 1/1/2012.

Section 13051 - Persons who may act without authorization or approval of court

For the purposes of this part:

(a) The guardian or conservator of the estate of a person entitled to any of the decedent's property may act on behalf of the person without authorization or approval of the court in which the guardianship or conservatorship proceeding is pending.

(b) The trustee of a trust may act on behalf of the trust. In the case of a trust that is subject to continuing jurisdiction of the court pursuant to Chapter 4 (commencing with Section 17300) of Part 5 of Division 9, the trustee may act on behalf of the trust without the need to obtain approval of the court.

(c) If the decedent's will authorizes a custodian under the Uniform Gifts to Minors Act or the Uniform Transfers to Minors Act of any state to receive a devise to a beneficiary, the custodian may act on behalf of the beneficiary until such time as the custodianship terminates.

(d) A sister state personal representative may act on behalf of the beneficiaries as provided in Chapter 3 (commencing with Section 12570) of Part 13 of Division 7.

(e) The attorney in fact authorized under a durable power of attorney may act on behalf of the beneficiary giving the power of attorney.

Ca. Prob. Code § 13051

Amended by Stats. 1991, Ch. 1055, Sec. 35.

Section 13052 - Date of valuation of property in making appraisal

In making an appraisal for the purposes of this part, the probate referee shall use the date of the decedent's death as the date of valuation of the property.

Ca. Prob. Code § 13052

Enacted by Stats. 1990, Ch. 79.

Section 13053 - Effective date of part

(a) Except as provided in subdivision (b), this part applies whether the decedent died before, on, or after July 1, 1987.

(b) This part does not apply and the law in effect at the time of payment, delivery, or transfer shall apply if the payment, delivery, or transfer was made prior to July 1, 1987, pursuant to former Probate Code Sections 630 to 632, inclusive, repealed by Chapter 783 of the Statutes of 1986.

Ca. Prob. Code § 13053

Enacted by Stats. 1990, Ch. 79.

Section 13054 - Reference to former sections 630 to 632 deemed reference to comparable provisions

A reference in any statute of this state or in a written instrument, including a will or trust, to a provision of former Sections 630 to 632, inclusive, repealed by Chapter 783, Statutes of 1986, shall be deemed to be a reference to the comparable provisions of Chapter 3 (commencing with Section 13100).

Ca. Prob. Code § 13054

Enacted by Stats. 1990, Ch. 79.

Chapter 3 - AFFIDAVIT PROCEDURE FOR COLLECTION OR TRANSFER OF PERSONAL PROPERTY

Section 13100 - Acts allowed successor of decedent without procuring letters or awaiting probate

Excluding the property described in Section 13050, if the gross value of the decedent's real and personal property in this state does not exceed one hundred sixty-six thousand two hundred fifty dollars ($166,250), as adjusted periodically in accordance with Section 890, and if 40 days have elapsed since the death of the decedent, the successor of the decedent may, without procuring letters of administration or awaiting probate of the will, do any of the following with respect to one or more particular items of property:

(a) Collect any particular item of property that is money due the decedent.

(b) Receive any particular item of property that is tangible personal property of the decedent.

(c) Have any particular item of property that is evidence of a debt, obligation, interest, right, security, or chose in action belonging to the decedent transferred, whether or not secured by a lien on real property.

Ca. Prob. Code § 13100

Amended by Stats 2019 ch 122 (AB 473),s 5, eff. 1/1/2020.
Amended by Stats 2011 ch 117 (AB 1305),s 4, eff. 1/1/2012.

Section 13100.5 - Transferee; Transferred property; Unsecured debts

The following definitions apply for the purposes of this chapter:

(a)"Transferee" means a person to whom payment, delivery, or transfer of property is made under this chapter.

(b)"Transferred property" means property that is paid, delivered, or transferred pursuant to an affidavit or declaration executed under Section 13101.

(c)"Unsecured debts" includes, but is not limited to, a decedent's funeral expenses, expenses of a decedent's last illness, and wage claims.

Ca. Prob. Code § 13100.5

Added by Stats 2022 ch 29 (AB 1716),s 2, eff. 1/1/2023.

Section 13101 - Affidavit or declaration furnished holder of decedent's property

(a) To collect money, receive tangible personal property, or have evidences of a debt, obligation, interest, right, security, or chose in action transferred under this chapter, an affidavit or a declaration under penalty of perjury under the laws of this state shall be furnished to the holder of the decedent's property stating all of the following:

(1) The decedent's name.

(2) The date and place of the decedent's death.

(3) "At least 40 days have elapsed since the death of the decedent, as shown in a certified copy of the decedent's death certificate attached to this affidavit or declaration."

(4) Either of the following, as appropriate:

    (A) "No proceeding is now being or has been conducted in California for administration of the decedent's estate."

    (B) "The decedent's personal representative has consented in writing to the payment, transfer, or delivery to the affiant or declarant of the property described in the affidavit or declaration."

(5) "The current gross fair market value of the decedent's real and personal property in California, excluding the property described in Section 13050 of the California Probate Code, does not exceed [Insert dollar amount specified in subdivision (g) of Section 13101 of the California Probate Code]."

(6) A description of the property of the decedent that is to be paid, transferred, or delivered to the affiant or declarant.

(7) The name of the successor of the decedent (as defined in Section 13006 of the California Probate Code) to the described property.

(8) Either of the following, as appropriate:

    (A) "The affiant or declarant is the successor of the decedent (as defined in Section 13006 of the California Probate Code) to the decedent's interest in the described property."

(B) "The affiant or declarant is authorized under Section 13051 of the California Probate Code to act on behalf of the successor of the decedent (as defined in Section 13006 of the California Probate Code) with respect to the decedent's interest in the described property."

(9) "No other person has a superior right to the interest of the decedent in the described property."

(10) "The affiant or declarant requests that the described property be paid, delivered, or transferred to the affiant or declarant."

(11) "The affiant or declarant affirms or declares under penalty of perjury under the laws of the State of California that the foregoing is true and correct."

(b) Where more than one person executes the affidavit or declaration under this section, the statements required by subdivision (a) shall be modified as appropriate to reflect that fact.

(c) If the particular item of property to be transferred under this chapter is a debt or other obligation secured by a lien on real property and the instrument creating the lien has been recorded in the office of the county recorder of the county where the real property is located, the affidavit or declaration shall satisfy the requirements both of this section and of Section 13106.5.

(d) A certified copy of the decedent's death certificate shall be attached to the affidavit or declaration.

(e) If the decedent's personal representative has consented to the payment, transfer, or delivery of the described property to the affiant or declarant, a copy of the consent and of the personal representative's letters shall be attached to the affidavit or declaration.

(f) If the decedent dies on or after April 1, 2022, the list of adjusted dollar amounts, published in accordance with subdivision (c) of Section 890, in effect on the date of the decedent's death, shall be attached to the affidavit or declaration.

(g)

(1) If the decedent dies prior to April 1, 2022, the dollar amount for paragraph (5) of subdivision (a) is one hundred sixty-six thousand two hundred fifty dollars ($166,250).

(2) If the decedent dies on or after April 1, 2022, the dollar amount for paragraph (5) of subdivision (a) is the adjusted dollar amount, published in accordance with subdivision (c) of Section 890, in effect on the date of the decedent's death.

Ca. Prob. Code § 13101
Amended by Stats 2019 ch 122 (AB 473),s 6, eff. 1/1/2020.
Amended by Stats 2011 ch 117 (AB 1305),s 5, eff. 1/1/2012.

Section 13102 - Presentation of evidence of ownership

(a) If the decedent had evidence of ownership of the property described in the affidavit or declaration and the holder of the property would have had the right to require presentation of the evidence of ownership before the duty of the holder to pay, deliver, or transfer the property to the decedent would have arisen, the evidence of ownership, if available, shall be presented with the affidavit or declaration to the holder of the decedent's property.

(b) If the evidence of ownership is not presented to the holder pursuant to subdivision (a), the holder may require, as a condition for the payment, delivery, or transfer of the property, that the person presenting the affidavit or declaration provide the holder with a bond or undertaking in a reasonable amount determined by the holder to be sufficient to indemnify the holder against all liability, claims, demands, loss, damages, costs, and expenses that the holder may incur or suffer by reason of the payment, delivery, or transfer of the property. Nothing in this subdivision precludes the holder and the person presenting the affidavit or declaration from dispensing with the requirement that a bond or undertaking be provided and instead entering into an agreement satisfactory to the holder concerning the duty of the person presenting the affidavit or declaration to indemnify the holder.

Ca. Prob. Code § 13102
Enacted by Stats. 1990, Ch. 79.

Section 13103 - Inventory and appraisal of real property

If the estate of the decedent includes any real property in this state, the affidavit or declaration shall be accompanied by an inventory and appraisal of the real property. The inventory and appraisal of the real property shall be made as provided in Part 3 (commencing with Section 8800) of Division 7. The appraisal shall be made by a probate referee selected by the affiant or declarant from those probate referees appointed by the Controller under Section 400 to appraise property in the county where the real property is located.

Ca. Prob. Code § 13103
Enacted by Stats. 1990, Ch. 79.

Section 13104 - Reasonable proof of identity of person executing affidavit or declaration

(a) Reasonable proof of the identity of each person executing the affidavit or declaration shall be provided to the holder of the decedent's property.
(b) Reasonable proof of identity is provided for the purposes of this section if both of the following requirements are satisfied:

(1) The person executing the affidavit or declaration is personally known to the holder.

(2) The person executes the affidavit or declaration in the presence of the holder.
(c) If the affidavit or declaration is executed in the presence of the holder, a written statement under penalty of perjury by a person personally known to the holder affirming the identity of the person executing the affidavit or declaration is reasonable proof of identity for the purposes of this section.
(d) If the affidavit or declaration is executed in the presence of the holder, the holder may reasonably rely on any of the following as reasonable proof of identity for the purposes of this section:

(1) An identification card or driver's license issued by the

Department of Motor Vehicles of this state that is current or was issued during the preceding five years.

(2) A passport issued by the Department of State of the United States that is current or was issued during the preceding five years.

(3) Any of the following documents if the document is current or was issued during the preceding five years and contains a photograph and description of the person named on it, is signed by the person, and bears a serial or other identifying number:

(A) A passport issued by a foreign government that has been stamped by the United States Immigration and Naturalization Service.

(B) A driver's license issued by a state other than California.

(C) An identification card issued by a state other than California.

(D) An identification card issued by any branch of the armed forces of the United States.

(e) For the purposes of this section, a notary public's certificate of acknowledgment identifying the person executing the affidavit or declaration is reasonable proof of identity of the person executing the affidavit or declaration.

(f) Unless the affidavit or declaration contains a notary public's certificate of acknowledgment of the identity of the person, the holder shall note on the affidavit or declaration either that the person executing the affidavit or declaration is personally known or a description of the identification provided by the person executing the affidavit or declaration.

Ca. Prob. Code § 13104
Enacted by Stats. 1990, Ch. 79.

Section 13105 - Payment, delivery or transfer of property

(a) If the requirements of Sections 13100 to 13104, inclusive, are satisfied:

(1) The person or persons executing the affidavit or declaration as successor of the decedent are entitled to have the property described in the affidavit or declaration paid, delivered, or transferred to them.

(2) A transfer agent of a security described in the affidavit or declaration shall change the registered ownership on the books of the corporation from the decedent to the person or persons executing the affidavit or declaration as successor of the decedent. **(b)** If the holder of the decedent's property refuses to pay, deliver, or transfer any personal property or evidence thereof to the successor of the decedent within a reasonable time, the successor may recover the property or compel its payment, delivery, or transfer in an action brought for that purpose against the holder of the property. If an action is brought against the holder under this section, the court shall award reasonable attorney's fees to the person or persons bringing the action if the court finds that the holder of the decedent's property acted unreasonably in refusing to pay, deliver, or transfer the property to them as required by subdivision (a).

Ca. Prob. Code § 13105
Enacted by Stats. 1990, Ch. 79.

Section 13106 - Sufficient acquittance for payment of money, delivery or property or changing registered ownership

(a) If the requirements of Sections 13100 to 13104, inclusive, are satisfied, receipt by the holder of the decedent's property of the affidavit or declaration constitutes sufficient acquittance for the payment of money, delivery of property, or changing registered ownership of property pursuant to this chapter and discharges the holder from any further liability with respect to the money or property. The holder may rely in good faith on the statements in the affidavit or declaration and has no duty to inquire into the truth of any statement in the affidavit or declaration.

(b) If the requirements of Sections 13100 to 13104, inclusive, are satisfied, the holder of the decedent's property is not liable for any taxes due to this state by reason of paying money, delivering property, or changing registered ownership of property pursuant to this chapter.

Ca. Prob. Code § 13106
Enacted by Stats. 1990, Ch. 79.

Section 13106.5 - Affidavit or declaration recorded in office of county recorder

(a) If the particular item of property transferred under this chapter is a debt or other obligation secured by a lien on real property and the instrument creating the lien has been recorded in the office of the county recorder of the county where the real property is located, the affidavit or declaration described in Section 13101 shall be recorded in the office of the county recorder of that county and, in addition to the contents required by Section 13101, shall include both of the following:

(1) The recording reference of the instrument creating the lien.

(2) A notary public's certificate of acknowledgment identifying each person executing the affidavit or declaration.

(b) The transfer under this chapter of the debt or obligation secured by a lien on real property has the same effect as would be given to an assignment of the right to collect the debt or enforce the obligation. The recording of the affidavit or declaration under subdivision (a) shall be given the same effect as is given under Sections 2934 and 2935 of the Civil Code to recording an assignment of a mortgage and an assignment of the beneficial interest under a deed of trust.

(c) If a deed of trust upon the real property was given to secure the debt and the requirements of subdivision (a) and of Sections 13100 to 13103, inclusive, are satisfied:

(1) The trustee under the deed of trust may rely in good faith on the statements made in the affidavit or declaration and has no duty to inquire into the truth of any statement in the affidavit or declaration.

(2) A person acting in good faith and for a valuable consideration may rely upon a recorded reconveyance of the trustee under the deed of trust.

(d) If a mortgage upon the real property was given to secure the debt and the requirements of subdivision (a) and of Sections 13100 to 13103, inclusive, are satisfied, a person acting in good faith and for a valuable consideration may rely upon a recorded discharge of the mortgage executed by the person or persons executing the affidavit or declaration as successor of the decedent or by their successors in interest.

Ca. Prob. Code § 13106.5
Enacted by Stats. 1990, Ch. 79.

Section 13107 - Presentation of affidavit or declaration to court in which estate administered

Where the money or property claimed in an affidavit or declaration presented under this chapter is that of a deceased heir or devisee of a deceased person whose estate is being administered in this state, the personal representative of the person whose estate is being administered shall present the affidavit or declaration to the court in which the estate is being administered. The court shall direct the personal representative to pay the money or deliver the property to the person or persons identified by the affidavit or declaration as the successor of the decedent to the extent that the order for distribution determines that the deceased heir or devisee was entitled to the money or property under the will or the laws of succession.

Ca. Prob. Code § 13107
Enacted by Stats. 1990, Ch. 79.

Section 13107.5 - Substitution of successor as party in place of decedent in pending action or proceeding

Where the money or property claimed in an affidavit or declaration executed under this chapter is the subject of a pending action or proceeding in which the decedent was a party, the successor of the decedent shall, without procuring letters of administration or awaiting probate of the will, be substituted as a party in place of the decedent by making a motion under Article 3 (commencing with Section 377.30) of Chapter 4 of Title 2 of Part 2 of the Code of Civil Procedure. The successor of the decedent shall file the affidavit or declaration with the court when the motion is made. For the purpose of Article 3 (commencing with Section 377.30) of Chapter 4 of Title 2 of Part 2 of the Code of Civil Procedure, a successor of the decedent who complies with this chapter shall be considered as a successor in interest of the decedent.

Ca. Prob. Code § 13107.5
Amended by Stats. 1992, Ch. 178, Sec. 39. Effective January 1, 1993.

Section 13108 - Requirements for using procedure provided for in chapter

(a) The procedure provided by this chapter may be used only if one of the following requirements is satisfied:

(1) No proceeding for the administration of the decedent's estate is pending or has been conducted in this state.

(2) The decedent's personal representative consents in writing to the payment, transfer, or delivery of the property described in the affidavit or declaration pursuant to this chapter.
(b) Payment, delivery, or transfer of a decedent's property pursuant to this chapter does not preclude later proceedings for administration of the decedent's estate.

Ca. Prob. Code § 13108
Amended by Stats. 1991, Ch. 1055, Sec. 38.

Section 13109 - Liability for unsecured debts of decedent

(a)A transferee is personally liable, to the extent provided in this section for the unsecured debts of the decedent. That debt may be enforced against the transferee in the same manner as it could have been enforced against the decedent if the decedent had not died. In any action based upon the debt, the transferee may assert any defense, cross-complaint, or setoff that would have been available to the decedent if the decedent had not died. Nothing in this section permits enforcement of a claim that is barred under Part 4 (commencing with Section 9000) of Division 7. Section 366.2 of the Code of Civil Procedure applies in an action under this section.

(b) The personal liability under subdivision (a) shall not exceed the fair market value of the transferred property at the time the affidavit or declaration is presented under this chapter, less the amount of any liens and encumbrances on the transferred property at that time, and less the amount of any payment made pursuant to subdivision (a) of Section 13110.

(c)A transferee is not liable under this section if the transferee has satisfied the requirements of Section 13109.5, 13110.5, or 13111.

Ca. Prob. Code § 13109

Amended by Stats 2022 ch 29 (AB 1716),s 3, eff. 1/1/2023.
Amended by Stats. 1992, Ch. 178, Sec. 40. Effective January 1, 1993.

Section 13109.5 - Transferee personally liable estate for share of decedent's unsecured debts

(a) If proceedings for the administration of the decedent's estate are commenced, a transferee is personally liable to the estate for a share of the decedent's unsecured debts.

(b) In calculating the transferee's share of liability under subdivision (a), the abatement rules provided in Part 4 (commencing with Section 21400) of Division 11 shall be applied, using all of the following assumptions:

(1) Transferred property shall be treated as if it had remained in the estate for administration.

(2) Any unsecured debts of the decedent that were paid by the transferee pursuant to Section 13109 shall be treated as if they were claims made against the decedent's estate.

(c) The personal representative shall provide a written statement of liability to the transferee, which specifies the amount that must be paid to the estate.

(d) The transferee is personally liable to the estate for the amount specified in the statement of liability. Any amount that the transferee paid pursuant to Section 13109 or 13110 shall be credited against the amount that the transferee owes the estate under this subdivision. If the amount that the transferee paid pursuant to Section 13109 or 13110 exceeds the amount specified in the written statement of liability, the estate shall reimburse the difference to the transferee. For the purposes of Section 11420, that reimbursement shall be deemed an expense of administration.

(e) The reasonable cost of proceeding under this section shall be reimbursed as an extraordinary service under Sections 10801 and 10811. The transferee is liable for the payment of that cost, which shall be separately identified in the statement of liability.

(f)A transferee is not liable under this section if the transferee has satisfied the requirements of Section 13110.5 or 13111.

Ca. Prob. Code § 13109.5

Added by Stats 2022 ch 29 (AB 1716),s 4, eff. 1/1/2023.

Section 13110 - Liability to person having superior right to testate or intestate succession

(a) Except as provided in subdivision (b), a transferee is personally liable to any person having a superior right to the transferred property by testate or intestate succession from the decedent. Except as provided in subdivision (b), the personal liability established by this subdivision shall not exceed the sum of the following, less the amount of any payment made pursuant to Section 13109 or 13109.5:

(1) The fair market value of the transferred property at the time the affidavit or declaration is presented under this chapter, less the amount of any liens and encumbrances on the transferred property at that time.

(2) Income received from the property, if that income would have accrued to the estate had the property not been transferred to the transferee.

413

(3) If the property has been disposed of, interest on the fair market value of the transferred property from the date of disposition at the rate of 7 percent per annum. For the purposes of this paragraph, "fair market value of the transferred property" means the fair market value of the transferred property, determined as of the time of the disposition of the property, less the amount of any liens and encumbrances on the property at the time the property was paid, delivered, or transferred to the transferee.

(b) In addition to any other liability the transferee has under this section and Sections 13109, 13109.5, 13111, and 13113.5 a person who fraudulently secures the payment, delivery, or transfer of the decedent's property under this chapter is liable to the person having a superior right to that property by testate or intestate succession from the decedent for three times the fair market value of the property. For the purposes of this subdivision, the "fair market value of the property" is the fair market value of the property paid, delivered, or transferred to the person liable under this subdivision, valued as of the time the person liable under this subdivision presents the affidavit or declaration under this chapter to the holder of the decedent's property, less any liens and encumbrances on that property at that time.

(c) An action to impose liability under this section is forever barred three years after the affidavit or declaration is presented under this chapter to the holder of the decedent's property, or three years after the discovery of the fraud, whichever is later. The three-year period specified in this subdivision is not tolled for any reason.

(d)A transferee is not liable under subdivision (a) if the transferee has satisfied the requirements of Section 13110.5 or 13111.

Ca. Prob. Code § 13110

Amended by Stats 2022 ch 29 (AB 1716),s 5, eff. 1/1/2023.
Amended by Stats. 1991, Ch. 1055, Sec. 39.

Section 13110.5 - Transferee may voluntarily return transferred property to decedent's estate for administration

(a) If proceedings for the administration of a decedent's estate are commenced, a transferee may voluntarily return transferred property to the decedent's estate for administration.

(b) The property to be restored to the estate under this section shall be reduced or increased as provided in Section 13113.5.

Ca. Prob. Code § 13110.5

Added by Stats 2022 ch 29 (AB 1716),s 6, eff. 1/1/2023.

Section 13111 - Liability upon request that property be restored to estate

(a) If property is paid, delivered, or transferred to a transferee under this chapter, and the decedent's personal representative determines that another person has a superior right to the property by testate or intestate succession from the decedent, the personal representative may request that the transferred property be restored to the estate. Subject to subdivisions (b), (c), (d), (e), and (g) if the personal representative makes that request, the transferee is liable for all of the following:

(1) If the transferee still has the transferred property, restitution of the transferred property to the decedent's estate.

(2) If the transferee no longer has the transferred property, restitution to the decedent's estate of the fair market value of the transferred property plus interest from the date of disposition at the rate of 7 percent per annum on the fair market value of the transferred property. For the purposes of this paragraph, the "fair market value of the transferred property" is the fair market value of the transferred property, determined as of the time of the disposition of the transferred property, less the amount of any liens and encumbrances on the transferred property at the time the property was paid, delivered, or transferred to the person under this chapter.

(b) Subject to subdivision (c) and subject to any additional liability the transferee has under Sections 13109 to 13113.5, inclusive, if the transferee fraudulently secured the payment, delivery, or transfer of the decedent's property under this chapter, the transferee is liable under this section for restitution of three times the fair market value of the transferred property. For the purposes of this subdivision, the "fair market value of the transferred property" is the fair market value of the transferred property, determined as of the time the person liable under this subdivision presents the affidavit or declaration under this chapter, less the amount of any liens and encumbrances on the property at that time. Restitution provided under this subdivision shall first be used to pay the estate's cost of proceeding under this section, with the remainder paid to the person who has a superior right to the property by testate or intestate succession.

(c)The property and amount required to be restored to the estate under this section shall be reduced or increased as provided in Section 13113.5.

(d)An action to enforce the liability under this section may be brought only by the personal representative of the estate of the decedent.

(e)An action to enforce the liability under this section is forever barred three years after presentation of the affidavit or declaration under this chapter to the holder of the decedent's property, or three years after the discovery of the fraud, whichever is later. The three-year period specified in this subdivision is not tolled for any reason.

(f)In the case of a nondomiciliary decedent, restitution under this section shall be made to the estate in an ancillary administration proceeding.

(g)A transferee is not liable under subdivision (a) if the transferred property was returned to the estate under Section 13110.5.

Ca. Prob. Code § 13111

Added by Stats 2022 ch 29 (AB 1716),s 8, eff. 1/1/2023.
Repealed by Stats 2022 ch 29 (AB 1716),s 7, eff. 1/1/2023.
Amended by Stats 2019 ch 122 (AB 473),s 7, eff. 1/1/2020.
Amended by Stats 2015 ch 293 (AB 139),s 18, eff. 1/1/2016.

Section 13112 - [Repealed]

Ca. Prob. Code § 13112

Repealed by Stats 2022 ch 29 (AB 1716),s 9, eff. 1/1/2023.
Amended by Stats 2019 ch 122 (AB 473),s 8, eff. 1/1/2020.

Section 13113 - Remedies in addition to remedies for fraud or intentional wrongdoing

The remedies available under Sections 13109 to 13111, inclusive, are in addition to any remedies available by reason of any fraud or intentional wrongdoing.
  Ca. Prob. Code § 13113
Amended by Stats 2022 ch 29 (AB 1716),s 10, eff. 1/1/2023.
Enacted by Stats. 1990, Ch. 79.

Section 13113.5 - Reimbursment to transferee

(a) If the transferee's action or inaction increased the value of property returned to the estate or decreased the estate's obligations, the personal representative shall reimburse the transferee by the same amount. Actions or inaction that increase the value of returned property or decrease the estate's obligations include, but are not necessarily limited to, the following actions:

   (1)A payment toward an unsecured debt of the decedent.

   (2)A payment toward a debt secured against the returned property.

   (3)A significant improvement of the returned property that increased the fair market value of the property.
(b) If the transferee's action or inaction decreased the value of property returned to the estate or increased the estate's obligations, the transferee is personally liable to the estate for that amount. Actions or inaction that decrease the value of the returned property or increase the estate's obligations include, but are not necessarily limited to, the following actions or inaction:

   (1) An action or inaction that resulted in a lien or encumbrance being recorded against the property.

   (2) The receipt of income from the property, if that income would have accrued to the estate had the property not been transferred to the transferee.

(c) The personal representative shall provide the transferee a written statement of any reimbursement or liability under this section, along with a statement of the reasons for the reimbursement or liability.

(d) For the purposes of Section 11420, reimbursement of the transferee under subdivision (a) shall be deemed an expense of administration.

(e) In the event that the transferee and the personal representative cannot agree on the reimbursement or liability due under this section, the transferee or personal representative may petition the court for an order determining the amount of the reimbursement or liability. In making a decision under this subdivision, the court should consider the surrounding circumstances, including whether the parties acted in good faith and whether a particular result would impose an unfair burden on the transferee or the estate.

Ca. Prob. Code § 13113.5
Added by Stats 2022 ch 29 (AB 1716),s 11, eff. 1/1/2023.

Section 13114 - Refusal by public administrator to pay money or deliver property; coroner

(a) A public administrator who has taken possession or control of property of a decedent under Article 1 (commencing with Section 7600) of Chapter 4 of Part 1 of Division 7 may refuse to pay money or deliver property pursuant to this chapter if payment of the costs and fees described in Section 7604 has not first been made or adequately assured to the satisfaction of the public administrator.

(b) A coroner who has property found upon the body of a decedent, or who has taken charge of property of the decedent pursuant to Section 27491.3 of the Government Code, may refuse to pay or deliver the property pursuant to this chapter if payment of the reasonable costs of holding or safeguarding the property has not first been made or adequately assured to the satisfaction of the coroner.

Ca. Prob. Code § 13114
Enacted by Stats. 1990, Ch. 79.

Section 13114.5 - Value of returned property included in total value of estate

If transferred property is returned to the estate under Sections 13110.5 or 13111, the value of that property shall be included in the total value of the estate, for all purposes.

Ca. Prob. Code § 13114.5
Added by Stats 2022 ch 29 (AB 1716),s 12, eff. 1/1/2023.

Section 13115 - Obtaining possession of real property

The procedure provided in this chapter may not be used to obtain possession or the transfer of real property.

Ca. Prob. Code § 13115
Enacted by Stats. 1990, Ch. 79.

Section 13116 - Procedure in addition to and supplemental to other procedures

The procedure provided in this chapter is in addition to and supplemental to any other procedure for (1) collecting money due to a decedent, (2) receiving tangible personal property of a decedent, or (3) having evidence of ownership of property of a decedent transferred. Nothing in this chapter restricts or limits the release of tangible personal property of a decedent pursuant to any other provision of law. This section is declaratory of existing law.

Ca. Prob. Code § 13116
Enacted by Stats. 1990, Ch. 79.

Section 13117 - Excuse from liability for acting reasonably and in good faith

If the court finds that a person to whom payment, delivery, or transfer of the decedent's property has been made under this chapter has acted reasonably and in good faith under the circumstances as known to the person, the court may, in its discretion, excuse the person from liability to pay interest, in whole or in part, under paragraph (2) of subdivision (a) of Section 13111, if it would be equitable to do so.

    Ca. Prob. Code § 13117

Amended by Stats 2022 ch 29 (AB 1716),s 13, eff. 1/1/2023.
Added by Stats 2019 ch 122 (AB 473),s 9, eff. 1/1/2020.

Chapter 4 - COURT ORDER DETERMINING SUCCESSION TO PROPERTY

Section 13150 - Requirements for using procedure

The procedure provided by this chapter may be used only if one of the following requirements is satisfied:

(a) No proceeding is being or has been conducted in this state for administration of the decedent's estate.

(b) The decedent's personal representative consents in writing to use of the procedure provided by this chapter to determine that real property of the decedent is property passing to the petitioners.

    Ca. Prob. Code § 13150

Amended by Stats. 1991, Ch. 1055, Sec. 42.

Section 13151 - Petition to determine that petitioner has succeeded to personal property

Exclusive of the property described in Section 13050, if a decedent dies leaving real property in this state and the gross value of the decedent's real and personal property in this state does not exceed one hundred sixty-six thousand two hundred fifty dollars ($166,250), as adjusted periodically in accordance with Section 890, and 40 days have elapsed since the death of the decedent, the successor of the decedent to an interest in a particular item of property that is real property, without procuring letters of administration or awaiting the probate of the will, may file a petition in the superior court of the county in which the estate of the decedent may be administered requesting a court order determining that the petitioner has succeeded to that real property. A petition under this chapter may include an additional request that the court make an order determining that the petitioner has succeeded to personal property described in the petition.

Ca. Prob. Code § 13151
Amended by Stats 2019 ch 122 (AB 473),s 10, eff. 1/1/2020.
Amended by Stats 2011 ch 117 (AB 1305),s 6, eff. 1/1/2012.

Section 13152 - Contents of petition

(a) The petition shall be verified by each petitioner, shall contain a request that the court make an order under this chapter determining that the property described in the petition is property passing to the petitioner, and shall state all of the following:

(1) The facts necessary to determine that the petition is filed in the proper county.

(2) The gross value of the decedent's real and personal property in this state, excluding the property described in Section 13050, as shown by the inventory and appraisal attached to the petition, does not exceed the dollar amount specified in subdivision (f).

(3) A description of the particular item of real property in this state that the petitioner alleges is property of the decedent passing to the petitioner, and a description of the personal property that the petitioner alleges is property of the decedent passing to the petitioner if the requested order also is to include a determination that the described personal property is property passing to the petitioner.

(4) The facts upon which the petitioner bases the allegation that the described property is property passing to the petitioner.

(5) Either of the following, as appropriate:

(A) A statement that no proceeding is being or has been conducted in this state for administration of the decedent's estate.

(B) A statement that the decedent's personal representative has consented in writing to use of the procedure provided by this chapter.

(6) Whether estate proceedings for the decedent have been commenced in any other jurisdiction and, if so, where those proceedings are pending or were conducted.

(7) The name, age, address, and relation to the decedent of each heir and devisee of the decedent, the names and addresses of all persons named as executors of the will of the decedent, and, if the petitioner is the trustee of a trust that is a devisee under the will of the decedent, the names and addresses of all persons interested in the trust, as determined in cases of future interests pursuant to paragraph (1), (2), or (3) of subdivision (a) of Section 15804, so far as known to any petitioner.

(8) The name and address of each person serving as guardian or conservator of the estate of the decedent at the time of the decedent's death, so far as known to any petitioner.

(b) An inventory and appraisal in the form set forth in Section 8802 of the decedent's real and personal property in this state, excluding the property described in Section 13050, shall be attached to the petition. The appraisal shall be made by a probate referee selected by the petitioner from those probate referees appointed by the Controller under Section 400 to appraise property in the county where the real property is located. The appraisal shall be made as provided in Part 3 (commencing with Section 8800) of Division 7. The petitioner may appraise the assets that a personal representative could appraise under Section 8901.

(c) If the petitioner bases the petitioner's claim to the described property upon the will of the decedent, a copy of the will shall be attached to the petition.

(d) If the decedent's personal representative has consented to use of the procedure provided by this chapter, a copy of the consent shall be attached to the petition.

(e) If the decedent dies on or after April 1, 2022, the list of adjusted dollar amounts, published in accordance with subdivision (c) of Section 890, in effect on the date of the decedent's death shall be attached to the petition.

(f)

(1) If the decedent dies prior to April 1, 2022, the dollar amount for paragraph (2) of subdivision (a) is one hundred sixty-six thousand two hundred fifty dollars ($166,250).

(2) If the decedent dies on or after April 1, 2022, the dollar amount for paragraph (2) of subdivision (a) is the adjusted dollar amount, published in accordance with subdivision (c) of Section 890, in effect on the date of the decedent's death.

Ca. Prob. Code § 13152
Amended by Stats 2019 ch 122 (AB 473),s 11, eff. 1/1/2020.
Amended by Stats 2011 ch 117 (AB 1305),s 7, eff. 1/1/2012.

Section 13153 - Notice of hearing

Notice of the hearing shall be given as provided in Section 1220 to each of the persons named in the petition pursuant to Section 13152.

Ca. Prob. Code § 13153
Enacted by Stats. 1990, Ch. 79.

Section 13154 - Court order

(a) If the court makes the determinations required under subdivision (b), the court shall issue an order determining (1) that real property, to be described in the order, of the decedent is property passing to the petitioners and the specific property interest of each petitioner in the described property and (2) if the petition so requests, that personal property, to be described in the order, of the decedent is property passing to the petitioners and the specific property interest of each petitioner in the described property.
(b) The court may make an order under this section only if the court makes all of the following determinations:

(1) The gross value of the decedent's real and personal property in this state, excluding the property described in Section 13050, does not exceed one hundred sixty-six thousand two hundred fifty dollars ($166,250), as adjusted periodically in accordance with

Section 890.

(2) Not less than 40 days have elapsed since the death of the decedent.

(3) Whichever of the following is appropriate:

(A) No proceeding is being or has been conducted in this state for administration of the decedent's estate.

(B) The decedent's personal representative has consented in writing to use of the procedure provided by this chapter.

(4) The property described in the order is property of the decedent passing to the petitioner.

(c) If the petition has attached an inventory and appraisal that satisfies the requirements of subdivision (b) of Section 13152, the determination required by paragraph (1) of subdivision (b) of this section shall be made on the basis of the verified petition and the attached inventory and appraisal, unless evidence is offered by a person opposing the petition that the gross value of the decedent's real and personal property in this state, excluding the property described in Section 13050, exceeds one hundred sixty-six thousand two hundred fifty dollars ($166,250), as adjusted periodically in accordance with Section 890.

Ca. Prob. Code § 13154
Amended by Stats 2019 ch 122 (AB 473),s 12, eff. 1/1/2020.
Amended by Stats 2011 ch 117 (AB 1305),s 8, eff. 1/1/2012.

Section 13155 - Final order conclusive on all persons

Upon becoming final, an order under this chapter determining that property is property passing to the petitioner is conclusive on all persons, whether or not they are in being.

Ca. Prob. Code § 13155
Amended by Stats. 1991, Ch. 1055, Sec. 46.

Section 13156 - Liability for unsecured debts of decedent

(a) Subject to subdivisions (b), (c), and (d), the petitioner who receives the decedent's property pursuant to an order under this chapter is personally liable for the unsecured debts of the decedent.
(b) The personal liability of any petitioner shall not exceed the fair market value at the date of the decedent's death of the property received by that petitioner pursuant to an order under this chapter, less the amount of any liens and encumbrances on the property.
(c) In any action or proceeding based upon an unsecured debt of the decedent, the petitioner may assert any defense, cross-complaint, or setoff which would have been available to the decedent if the decedent had not died.
(d) Nothing in this section permits enforcement of a claim that is barred under Part 4 (commencing with Section 9000) of Division 7.
(e) Section 366.2 of the Code of Civil Procedure applies in an action under this section.

    Ca. Prob. Code § 13156

Amended by Stats. 1992, Ch. 178, Sec. 41. Effective January 1, 1993.

Section 13157 - Attorney's fees

The attorney's fees for services performed in connection with the filing of a petition and obtaining a court order under this chapter shall be determined by private agreement between the attorney and the client and are not subject to approval by the court. If there is no agreement between the attorney and the client concerning the attorney's fees for services performed in connection with the filing of a petition and obtaining of a court order under this chapter and there is a dispute concerning the reasonableness of the attorney's fees for those services, a petition may be filed with the court in the same proceeding requesting that the court determine the reasonableness of the attorney's fees for those services. If there is an agreement between the attorney and the client concerning the attorney's fees for services performed in connection with the filing of a petition and obtaining a court order under this chapter and there is a dispute concerning the meaning of the agreement, a petition may be filed with the court in the same proceeding requesting that the court determine the dispute.

Ca. Prob. Code § 13157
Enacted by Stats. 1990, Ch. 79.

Section 13158 - Compliance with Chapter 3

Nothing in this chapter excuses compliance with Chapter 3 (commencing with Section 13100) by the holder of the decedent's personal property if an affidavit or declaration is furnished as provided in that chapter.

Ca. Prob. Code § 13158
Added by Stats. 1991, Ch. 1055, Sec. 47.

Chapter 5 - AFFIDAVIT PROCEDURE FOR REAL PROPERTY OF SMALL VALUE

Section 13200 - Filing affidavit; contents

(a) No sooner than six months from the death of a decedent, a person or persons claiming as successor of the decedent to a particular item of property that is real property may file in the superior court in the county in which the decedent was domiciled at the time of death, or if the decedent was not domiciled in this state at the time of death, then in any county in which real property of the decedent is located, an affidavit in the form prescribed by the Judicial Council pursuant to Section 1001 stating all of the following:

(1) The name of the decedent.

(2) The date and place of the decedent's death.

(3) A legal description of the real property and the interest of the decedent therein.

(4) The name and address of each person serving as guardian or conservator of the estate of the decedent at the time of the decedent's death, so far as known to the affiant.

(5) "The gross value of all real property in the decedent's estate located in California, as shown by the inventory and appraisal attached to this affidavit, excluding the real property described in Section 13050 of the California Probate Code, does not exceed [Insert dollar amount specified in subdivision (h)]."

(6) "At least six months have elapsed since the death of the decedent as shown in a certified copy of decedent's death certificate attached to this affidavit."

(7) Either of the following, as appropriate:

(A) "No proceeding is now being or has been conducted in California for administration of the decedent's estate."

(B) "The decedent's personal representative has consented in writing to use of the procedure provided by this chapter."

(8) "Funeral expenses, expenses of last illness, and all unsecured debts of the decedent have been paid."

(9) "The affiant is the successor of the decedent (as defined in Section 13006 of the Probate Code) and to the decedent's interest in the described property, and no other person has a superior right to the interest of the decedent in the described property."

(10) "The affiant declares under penalty of perjury under the laws of the State of California that the foregoing is true and correct." **(b)** For each person executing the affidavit, the affidavit shall contain a notary public's certificate of acknowledgment identifying the person.
(c) An inventory and appraisal of the decedent's real property in this state, excluding the real property described in Section 13050, shall be attached to the affidavit. The inventory and appraisal of the real property shall be made as provided in Part 3 (commencing with Section 8800) of Division 7. The appraisal shall be made by a probate referee selected by the affiant from those probate referees appointed by the Controller under Section 400 to appraise property in the county where the real property is located.

(d) If the affiant claims under the decedent's will and no estate proceeding is pending or has been conducted in California, a copy of the will shall be attached to the affidavit.

(e) A certified copy of the decedent's death certificate shall be attached to the affidavit. If the decedent's personal representative has consented to the use of the procedure provided by this chapter, a copy of the consent and of the personal representative's letters shall be attached to the affidavit.

(f) If the decedent dies on or after April 1, 2022, the list of adjusted dollar amounts, published in accordance with subdivision (c) of Section 890, in effect on the date of the decedent's death shall be attached to the affidavit.

(g) The affiant shall deliver pursuant to Section 1215 a copy of the affidavit and attachments to any person identified in paragraph (4) of subdivision (a).

(h)

(1) When the decedent dies prior to April 1, 2022, the dollar amount for paragraph (5) of subdivision (a) is fifty-five thousand four hundred twenty-five dollars ($55,425).

(2) When the decedent dies on or after April 1, 2022, the dollar amount for paragraph (5) of subdivision (a) is the adjusted dollar amount, published in accordance with subdivision (c) of Section 890, in effect on the date of the decedent's death.

Ca. Prob. Code § 13200
Amended by Stats 2019 ch 122 (AB 473),s 13, eff. 1/1/2020.
Amended by Stats 2017 ch 319 (AB 976),s 84, eff. 1/1/2018.
Amended by Stats 2011 ch 117 (AB 1305),s 9, eff. 1/1/2012.

Section 13201 - Fee for filing affidavit and issuance of copy

Notwithstanding any other provision of law, the total fee for the filing of an affidavit under Section 13200 and the issuance of one certified copy of the affidavit under Section 13202 is as provided in subdivision (b) of Section 70626 of the Government Code.

Ca. Prob. Code § 13201

Amended by Stats 2005 ch 75 (AB 145),s 150, eff. 7/19/2005, op. 1/1/2006

Section 13202 - Filing affidavit and copy and recording copy

Upon receipt of the affidavit and the required fee, the court clerk, upon determining that the affidavit is complete and has the required attachments, shall file the affidavit and attachments and shall issue a certified copy of the affidavit without the attachments. The certified copy shall be recorded in the office of the county recorder of the county where the real property is located. The county recorder shall index the certified copy in the index of grantors and grantees. The decedent shall be indexed as the grantor and each person designated as a successor to the property in the certified copy shall be indexed as a grantee.

Ca. Prob. Code § 13202
Enacted by Stats. 1990, Ch. 79.

Section 13202.5 - Transferee; Transferred property; Unsecured debts

For the purposes of this chapter, the following terms have the following meanings:
(a)"Transferee" means a person designated as a successor of the decedent in a certified copy of an affidavit issued under Section 13202.
(b)"Transferred property" means property transferred to a transferee pursuant to a certified copy of an affidavit issued under Section 13202.
(c)"Unsecured debts" includes, but is not limited to, a decedent's funeral expenses, expenses of a decedent's last illness, and wage claims.

Ca. Prob. Code § 13202.5
Added by Stats 2022 ch 29 (AB 1716),s 14, eff. 1/1/2023.

Section 13203 - Rights and protections of person acting in good faith and for valuable consideration

(a) A person acting in good faith and for a valuable consideration with a person designated as a successor of the decedent to a particular item of property in a certified copy of an affidavit issued under Section 13202 and recorded in the county in which the real property is located has the same rights and protections as the person would have if each person designated as a successor in the recorded certified copy of the affidavit had been named as a distributee of the real property in an order for distribution that had become final.

(b) The issuance and recording of a certified copy of an affidavit under this chapter does not preclude later proceedings for administration of the decedent's estate.

Ca. Prob. Code § 13203

Enacted by Stats. 1990, Ch. 79.

Section 13204 - Liability for unsecured debts of decedent

(a) A transferee is personally liable to the extent provided in this section for the unsecured debts of the decedent. That debt may be enforced against the transferee in the same manner as it could have been enforced against the decedent if the decedent had not died. In any action based upon the debt, the transferee may assert any defense, cross-complaint, or setoff that would have been available to the decedent if the decedent had not died. Nothing in this section permits enforcement of a claim that is barred under Part 4 (commencing with Section 9000) of Division 7. Section 366.2 of the Code of Civil Procedure applies in an action under this section.

(b) The personal liability under subdivision (a) shall not exceed the fair market value of the transferred property at the time of the issuance of the certified copy of the affidavit under Section 13202, less the amount of any liens and encumbrances on the transferred property at that time, and less the amount of any payment made pursuant to subdivision (a) of Section 13205.

(c) The transferee is not liable under this section if the transferee has satisfied the requirements of Section 13204.5, 13205.5, or 13206.

Ca. Prob. Code § 13204

Amended by Stats 2022 ch 29 (AB 1716),s 15, eff. 1/1/2023.
Amended by Stats. 1992, Ch. 178, Sec. 42. Effective January 1, 1993.

Section 13204.5 - Transferee personally liable estate for share of decedent's unsecured debts

(a) If proceedings for the administration of the decedent's estate are commenced, a transferee is personally liable to the estate for a share of the decedent's unsecured debts.

(b) In calculating the transferee's share of liability under subdivision (a), the abatement rules provided in Part 4 (commencing with Section 21400) of Division 11 shall be applied, using all of the following assumptions:

(1) Transferred property under this chapter shall be treated as if it had remained in the estate for administration.

(2) Any unsecured debts of the decedent that were paid by the transferee pursuant to Section 13204 shall be treated as if they were claims made against the decedent's estate.

(c) The personal representative shall provide a written statement of liability to the transferee, which specifies the amount that must be paid to the estate.

(d) The transferee is personally liable to the estate for the amount specified in the statement of liability. Any amount that the transferee paid pursuant to Section 13204 or 13205 shall be credited against the amount that the transferee owes the estate under this subdivision. If the amount that the transferee paid pursuant to Section 13204 or 13205 exceeds the amount specified in the written statement of liability, the estate shall reimburse the difference to the transferee. For the purposes of Section 11420, that reimbursement shall be deemed an expense of administration.

(e) The reasonable cost of proceeding under this section shall be reimbursed as an extraordinary service under Sections 10801 and 10811. The transferee is liable for the payment of that cost, which shall be separately identified in the statement of liability.

(f) The transferee is not liable under this section if the transferee has satisfied the requirements of Section 13205.5 or 13206.

Ca. Prob. Code § 13204.5
Added by Stats 2022 ch 29 (AB 1716),s 16, eff. 1/1/2023.

Section 13205 - Liability to person having superior rights by testate or intestate succession

(a)A transferee is personally liable to any person having a superior right to transferred property by testate or intestate succession from the decedent. Except as provided in subdivision (d), the personal liability established by this subdivision shall not exceed the sum of the following, less the amount of any payment made pursuant to Section 13204 or 13204.5:

(1) The fair market value at the time of the issuance of the certified copy of the affidavit under Section 13202 of the transferred property, less the amount of any liens and encumbrances on the transferred property at that time.

(2) Income received from the property, if that income would have accrued to the estate had the property not been transferred to the transferee.

(3) If the property has been disposed of, interest on the fair market value of the transferred property from the date of disposition at the rate of 7 percent per annum. For the purposes of this paragraph, "fair market value of the transferred property" means the fair market value of the transferred property, determined as of the time of the disposition of the property, less the amount of any liens and encumbrances on the property at the time the certified copy of the affidavit was issued.
(b) In addition to any other liability the transferee has under this section and Sections 13204, 13204.5, 13206, and 13208, if the transferee fraudulently executed or filed the affidavit under this chapter, the transferee is liable to the person having a superior right to that property by testate or intestate succession from the decedent for three times the fair market value of the transferred property. For the purposes of this subdivision, the "fair market value of the transferred property" is the fair market value of the transferred

432

property determined as of the time the certified copy of the affidavit was issued under Section 13202, less any liens and encumbrances on the transferred property at that time.

(c) An action to impose liability under this section is forever barred three years after the certified copy of the affidavit is issued under Section 13202, or three years after the discovery of the fraud, whichever is later. The three-year period specified in this subdivision is not tolled for any reason.

(d) The transferee is not liable under this section if the transferee has satisfied the requirements of Section 13205.5 or 13206.

Ca. Prob. Code § 13205

Amended by Stats 2022 ch 29 (AB 1716),s 17, eff. 1/1/2023.

Amended by Stats. 1991, Ch. 1055, Sec. 49.

Section 13205.5 - Transferee may voluntarily return transferred property to decedent's estate for administration

(a) If proceedings for the administration of the decedent's estate are commenced, a transferee may voluntarily return transferred property to the decedent's estate for administration.

(b) The property to be restored to the estate under this section shall be reduced or increased as provided in Section 13208.5.

Ca. Prob. Code § 13205.5

Added by Stats 2022 ch 29 (AB 1716),s 18, eff. 1/1/2023.

Section 13206 - Liability upon request that property be restored to estate

(a) If property is transferred to a transferee under this chapter, and the decedent's personal representative later determines that another person has a superior right to the property by testate or intestate succession from the decedent, the personal representative may request that the transferred property be restored to the estate. Subject to subdivisions (b), (c), (d), (e), and (g) if the personal representative makes that request, the transferee is liable for all of the following:

(1) If the transferee still has the transferred property, restitution of the transferred property to the decedent's estate.

(2) If the transferee no longer has the transferred property, restitution to the decedent's estate of the fair market value of the transferred property plus interest from the date of disposition at the rate of 7 percent per annum on the fair market value of the transferred property. For the purposes of this paragraph, the "fair market value of the transferred property" is the fair market value of the transferred property, determined as of the time of the disposition of the transferred property, less the amount of any liens and encumbrances on the transferred property at the time the certified copy of the affidavit was issued.

(b) Subject to subdivision (d), if the transferee fraudulently executed or filed the affidavit under this chapter, the transferee is liable under this section for restitution of three times the fair market value of the transferred property. For the purposes of this subdivision, the "fair market value of the transferred property" is the fair market value of the transferred property, determined as of the time the certified copy of the affidavit was issued, less the amount of any liens and encumbrances on the property at that time. Restitution provided under this subdivision shall first be used to pay the estate's cost of proceeding under this section, with the remainder paid to the person who has a superior right to the property by testate or intestate succession.

(c) Subject to subdivision (d), if the transferee made a significant improvement to the transferred property in the good faith belief that the transferee was the successor of the decedent to that property, the transferee is liable for whichever of the following the decedent's estate elects:

(1) The restitution of the transferred property to the estate of the decedent.

(2) The restoration to the decedent's estate of the fair market value of the transferred property, determined as of the time of the issuance of the certified copy of the affidavit under Section 13202, less the amount of any liens and encumbrances on the transferred

434

property at that time, together with interest on the net amount at the rate of 7 percent per annum running from the date of the issuance of the certified copy of the affidavit.

(d) The property and amount required to be restored to the estate under this section shall be reduced or increased as provided in Section 13208.5.

(e) An action to enforce the liability under this section may be brought only by the personal representative of the estate of the decedent.

(f) An action to enforce the liability under this section is forever barred three years after the certified copy of the affidavit is issued under Section 13202, or three years after the discovery of the fraud, whichever is later. The three-year period specified in this subdivision is not tolled for any reason.

(g) The transferee is not liable under subdivision (a) if the transferred property was returned to the estate under Section 13205.5.

Ca. Prob. Code § 13206
Added by Stats 2022 ch 29 (AB 1716),s 20, eff. 1/1/2023.
Repealed by Stats 2022 ch 29 (AB 1716),s 19, eff. 1/1/2023.
Amended by Stats 2019 ch 122 (AB 473),s 14, eff. 1/1/2020.
Amended by Stats 2015 ch 293 (AB 139),s 19, eff. 1/1/2016.

Section 13207 - [Repealed]

Ca. Prob. Code § 13207
Repealed by Stats 2022 ch 29 (AB 1716),s 21, eff. 1/1/2023.
Amended by Stats 2019 ch 122 (AB 473),s 15, eff. 1/1/2020.

Section 13208 - Remedies in addition to remedies for fraud or intentional wrongdoing

The remedies available under Sections 13204 to 13206, inclusive, are in addition to any remedies available by reason of any fraud or intentional wrongdoing.

Ca. Prob. Code § 13208
Amended by Stats 2022 ch 29 (AB 1716),s 22, eff. 1/1/2023.
Enacted by Stats. 1990, Ch. 79.

Section 13208.5 - Reimbursment to transferee

(a) If the transferee's action or inaction increased the value of property returned to the estate or decreased the estate's obligations, the personal representative shall reimburse the transferee by the same amount. Actions or inaction that increase the value of returned property or decrease the estate's obligations include, but are not necessarily limited to, the following actions:

(1)A payment toward an unsecured debt of the decedent.

(2)A payment toward a debt secured against the returned property.

(3)A significant improvement of the returned property that increased the fair market value of the property.
(b) If the transferee's action or inaction decreased the value of property returned to the estate or increased the estate's obligations, the transferee is personally liable to the estate for that amount. Actions or inaction that decrease the value of the returned property or increase the estate's obligations include, but are not necessarily limited to, the following actions or inaction:

(1) An action or inaction that resulted in a lien or encumbrance being recorded against the property.

(2) The receipt of income from the property, if that income would have accrued to the estate had the property not been transferred to the transferee.
(c) The personal representative shall provide the transferee a written statement of any reimbursement or liability under this section, along with a statement of the reasons for the reimbursement or liability.
(d) For the purposes of Section 11420, reimbursement of the transferee under subdivision (a) shall be deemed an expense of administration.
(e) In the event that the transferee and the personal representative

cannot agree on the reimbursement or liability due under this section, the transferee or personal representative may petition the court for an order determining the amount of the reimbursement or liability. In making a decision under this subdivision, the court should consider the surrounding circumstances, including whether the parties acted in good faith and whether a particular result would impose an unfair burden on the transferee or the estate.

Ca. Prob. Code § 13208.5

Added by Stats 2022 ch 29 (AB 1716),s 23, eff. 1/1/2023.

Section 13209 - Value of returned property included in total value of the estate

If transferred property is returned to the estate under Sections 13205.5 or 13206, the value of that property shall be included in the total value of the estate, for all purposes.

Ca. Prob. Code § 13209

Added by Stats 2022 ch 29 (AB 1716),s 24, eff. 1/1/2023.

Section 13210 - Requirements for using procedure provided

The procedure provided by this chapter may be used only if one of the following requirements is satisfied:

(a) No proceeding for the administration of the decedent's estate is pending or has been conducted in this state.

(b) The decedent's personal representative consents in writing to use of the procedure provided by this chapter.

Ca. Prob. Code § 13210

Added by Stats. 1991, Ch. 1055, Sec. 52.

Section 13211 - Excuse from liability for acting reasonably and in good faith

If the court finds that a person designated as a successor of the decedent in a certified copy of an affidavit issued under Section 13202 has acted reasonably and in good faith under the circumstances as known to the person, the court may, in its discretion, excuse the person from liability to pay interest, in whole or in part, under paragraph (2) of subdivision (a) of Section 13206 or paragraph (2) of subdivision (c) of Section 13206, if it would be equitable to do so.

Ca. Prob. Code § 13211
Amended by Stats 2022 ch 29 (AB 1716),s 25, eff. 1/1/2023.
Added by Stats 2019 ch 122 (AB 473),s 16, eff. 1/1/2020.

Part 2 - PASSAGE OF PROPERTY TO SURVIVING SPOUSE WITHOUT ADMINISTRATION

Chapter 1 - GENERAL PROVISIONS

Section 13500 - Generally

Except as provided in this chapter, when a spouse dies intestate leaving property that passes to the surviving spouse under Section 6401, or dies testate and by his or her will devises all or a part of his or her property to the surviving spouse, the property passes to the survivor subject to the provisions of Chapter 2 (commencing with Section 13540) and Chapter 3 (commencing with Section 13550), and no administration is necessary.

Ca. Prob. Code § 13500
Amended by Stats 2016 ch 50 (SB 1005),s 89, eff. 1/1/2017.

Section 13501 - Property subject to administration under article

Except as provided in Chapter 6 (commencing with Section 6600) of Division 6 and in Part 1 (commencing with Section 13000) of this division, the following property of the decedent is subject to administration under this code:
(a) Property passing to someone other than the surviving spouse under the decedent's will or by intestate succession.
(b) Property disposed of in trust under the decedent's will.
(c) Property in which the decedent's will limits the surviving spouse to a qualified ownership. For the purposes of this subdivision, a devise to the surviving spouse that is conditioned on the spouse surviving the decedent by a specified period of time is not a

"qualified ownership" interest if the specified period of time has expired.

Ca. Prob. Code § 13501

Enacted by Stats. 1990, Ch. 79.

Section 13502 - Property administered under code

(a) Upon the election of the surviving spouse or the personal representative, guardian of the estate, or conservator of the estate of the surviving spouse, all or a portion of the following property may be administered under this code:

(1) The one-half of the community property that belongs to the decedent under Section 100, the one-half of the quasi-community property that belongs to the decedent under Section 101, and the separate property of the decedent.

(2) The one-half of the community property that belongs to the surviving spouse under Section 100 and the one-half of the quasi-community property that belongs to the surviving spouse under Section 101.

(b) The election shall be made by a writing specifically evidencing the election filed in the proceedings for the administration of the estate of the deceased spouse within four months after the issuance of letters, or within any further time that the court may allow upon a showing of good cause, and before entry of an order under Section 13656.

Ca. Prob. Code § 13502

Enacted by Stats. 1990, Ch. 79.

Section 13502.5 - Order that pecuniary devise or fractional interest in any property be administered under code

(a) Upon a petition by the personal representative of a decedent and a showing of good cause, the court may order that a pecuniary devise to the surviving spouse, or a fractional interest passing to the surviving spouse in any property in which the remaining fraction is subject to the administration, may be administered under this code, except to the extent that it has passed by inheritance as determined by an order pursuant to Chapter 5 (commencing with Section 13650).

(b) Notice of this petition shall be given as provided in Section 1220 to the person designated in that section and to the surviving spouse.

Ca. Prob. Code § 13502.5

Added by Stats. 1992, Ch. 871, Sec. 16. Effective January 1, 1993.

Section 13503 - Election or agreement to have community property transferred to trustee under will of deceased spouse

(a) The surviving spouse or the personal representative, guardian of the estate, or conservator of the estate of the surviving spouse may file an election and agreement to have all or part of the one-half of the community property that belongs to the surviving spouse under Section 100 and the one-half of the quasi-community property that belongs to the surviving spouse under Section 101 transferred by the surviving spouse or the surviving spouse's personal representative, guardian, or conservator to the trustee under the will of the deceased spouse or the trustee of an existing trust identified by the will of the deceased spouse, to be administered and distributed by the trustee.

(b) The election and agreement shall be filed in the proceedings for the administration of the estate of the deceased spouse and before the entry of the order for final distribution in the proceedings.

Ca. Prob. Code § 13503

Enacted by Stats. 1990, Ch. 79.

Section 13504 - Community property held in revocable trust govern by trust provisions

Notwithstanding the provisions of this part, community property held in a revocable trust described in Section 761 of the Family Code is governed by the provisions, if any, in the trust for disposition in the event of death.

Ca. Prob. Code § 13504

Amended by Stats. 1994, Ch. 1269, Sec. 61.6. Effective January 1, 1995.

Section 13505 - Effect date

This part applies whether the deceased spouse died before, on, or after July 1, 1987.

Ca. Prob. Code § 13505

Enacted by Stats. 1990, Ch. 79.

Section 13506 - Construction of references to former sections 202 to 206 or 649 to 649.5

A reference in any statute of this state or in a written instrument, including a will or trust, to a provision of former Sections 202 to 206, inclusive, of the Probate Code (as repealed by Chapter 527 of the Statutes of 1984) or former Sections 649.1 to 649.5, inclusive, or Sections 650 to 658, inclusive, of the Probate Code (as repealed by Chapter 783 of the Statutes of 1986) shall be deemed to be a reference to the comparable provision of this part.

Ca. Prob. Code § 13506

Enacted by Stats. 1990, Ch. 79.

Chapter 2 - RIGHT OF SURVIVING SPOUSE TO DISPOSE OF PROPERTY

Section 13540 - Generally

(a) Except as provided in Section 13541, after 40 days from the death of a spouse, the surviving spouse or the personal representative, guardian of the estate, or conservator of the estate of the surviving spouse has full power to sell, convey, lease, mortgage, or otherwise deal with and dispose of the community or quasi-community real property, and the right, title, and interest of any grantee, purchaser, encumbrancer, or lessee shall be free of rights of the estate of the deceased spouse or of devisees or creditors of the deceased spouse to the same extent as if the property had been owned as the separate property of the surviving spouse.
(b) The surviving spouse or the personal representative, guardian

441

of the estate, or conservator of the estate of the surviving spouse
may record, prior to or together with the instrument that makes a
disposition of property under this section, an affidavit of the facts
that establish the right of the surviving spouse to make the
disposition.

(c) Nothing in this section affects or limits the liability of the
surviving spouse under Sections 13550 to 13553, inclusive, and
Chapter 3.5 (commencing with Section 13560).

Ca. Prob. Code § 13540

Amended by Stats. 1994, Ch. 806, Sec. 36. Effective January 1,
1995.

Section 13541 - Inapplicability of disposition after notice satisfying requirements of section recorded

(a) Section 13540 does not apply to a sale, conveyance, lease,
mortgage, or other disposition that takes place after a notice that
satisfies the requirements of this section is recorded in the office of
the county recorder of the county in which real property is located.

(b) The notice shall contain all of the following:

(1) A description of the real property in which an interest is
claimed.

(2) A statement that an interest in the property is claimed by a
named person under the will of the deceased spouse.

(3) The name or names of the owner or owners of the record
title to the property.

(c) There shall be endorsed on the notice instructions that it shall
be indexed by the recorder in the name or names of the owner or
owners of record title to the property, as grantor or grantors, and in
the name of the person claiming an interest in the property, as
grantee.

(d) A person shall not record a notice under this section for the
purpose of slandering title to the property. If the court in an action
or proceeding relating to the rights of the parties determines that a
person recorded a notice under this section for the purpose of

442

slandering title, the court shall award against the person the cost of the action or proceeding, including a reasonable attorney's fee, and the damages caused by the recording.

Ca. Prob. Code § 13541

Amended by Stats. 1991, Ch. 1055, Sec. 55.

Section 13542 - Disposition not affected by repeal of former section 649.2

The repeal of former Section 649.2 by Chapter 783 of the Statutes of 1986 does not affect any sale, lease, mortgage, or other transaction or disposition of real property made prior to July 1, 1987, to which that section applied, and such a sale, lease, mortgage, or other transaction or disposition shall continue to be governed by the provisions of former Section 649.2 notwithstanding the repeal of that section.

Ca. Prob. Code § 13542

Enacted by Stats. 1990, Ch. 79.

Section 13545 - Power to dispose of securities registered in name of surviving spouse

(a) After the death of a spouse, the surviving spouse, or the personal representative, guardian of the estate, or conservator of the estate of the surviving spouse has full power to sell, assign, pledge, or otherwise deal with and dispose of community or quasi-community property securities registered in the name of the surviving spouse alone, and the right, title, and interest of any purchaser, assignee, encumbrancer, or other transferee shall be free of the rights of the estate of the deceased spouse or of devisees or creditors of the deceased spouse to the same extent as if the deceased spouse had not died.

(b) Nothing in this section affects or limits the liability of a surviving spouse under Sections 13550 to 13553, inclusive, and Chapter 3.5 (commencing with Section 13560).

Ca. Prob. Code § 13545

Added by Stats. 1991, Ch. 1055, Sec. 56.

Chapter 3 - LIABILITY FOR DEBTS OF DECEASED SPOUSE

Section 13550 - Surviving spouse's liability

Except as provided in Sections 11446, 13552, 13553, and 13554, upon the death of a married person, the surviving spouse is personally liable for the debts of the deceased spouse chargeable against the property described in Section 13551 to the extent provided in Section 13551.

Ca. Prob. Code § 13550
Enacted by Stats. 1990, Ch. 79.

Section 13551 - Amount of surviving spouse's liability

The liability imposed by Section 13550 shall not exceed the fair market value at the date of the decedent's death, less the amount of any liens and encumbrances, of the total of the following:
(a) The portion of the one-half of the community and quasi-community property belonging to the surviving spouse under Sections 100 and 101 that is not exempt from enforcement of a money judgment and is not administered in the estate of the deceased spouse.
(b) The portion of the one-half of the community and quasi-community property belonging to the decedent under Sections 100 and 101 that passes to the surviving spouse without administration under this part.
(c) The separate property of the decedent that passes to the surviving spouse without administration under this part.

Ca. Prob. Code § 13551
Amended by Stats 2022 ch 29 (AB 1716),s 26, eff. 1/1/2023.
Enacted by Stats. 1990, Ch. 79.

Section 13552 - Action upon liability barred

If proceedings are commenced in this state for the administration of the estate of the deceased spouse and the time for filing claims has commenced, any action upon the liability of the surviving spouse pursuant to Section 13550 is barred to the same extent as provided for claims under Part 4 (commencing with Section 9000) of Division 7, except as to the following:

(a) Creditors who commence judicial proceedings for the enforcement of the debt and serve the surviving spouse with the complaint therein prior to the expiration of the time for filing claims.

(b) Creditors who have or who secure the surviving spouse's acknowledgment in writing of the liability of the surviving spouse for the debts.

(c) Creditors who file a timely claim in the proceedings for the administration of the estate of the deceased spouse.

Ca. Prob. Code § 13552
Enacted by Stats. 1990, Ch. 79.

Section 13553 - Liability if property administered under code

The surviving spouse is not liable under this chapter if all the property described in paragraphs (1) and (2) of subdivision (a) of Section 13502 is administered under this code.

Ca. Prob. Code § 13553
Enacted by Stats. 1990, Ch. 79.

Section 13554 - Enforcement of debt; defenses, cross-complaint or setoff asserted; applicability of section 366.2, Code of Civil Procedure

(a) Except as otherwise provided in this chapter, any debt described in Section 13550 may be enforced against the surviving spouse in the same manner as it could have been enforced against the deceased spouse if the deceased spouse had not died.

(b) In any action or proceeding based upon the debt, the surviving spouse may assert any defense, cross-complaint, or setoff which would have been available to the deceased spouse if the deceased spouse had not died.

(c) Section 366.2 of the Code of Civil Procedure applies in an action under this section.

Ca. Prob. Code § 13554
Amended by Stats. 1992, Ch. 178, Sec. 43. Effective January 1, 1993.

Chapter 3.5 - LIABILITY FOR DECEDENT'S PROPERTY

Section 13560 - Decedent's property defined

For the purposes of this chapter, "decedent's property" means the one-half of the community property that belongs to the decedent under Section 100 and the one-half of the quasi-community property that belongs to the decedent under Section 101.
Ca. Prob. Code § 13560
Added by Stats. 1991, Ch. 1055, Sec. 57.

Section 13561 - Decedent's property in possession or control of surviving spouse; limitation of action to impose liability

(a) If the decedent's property is in the possession or control of the surviving spouse at the time of the decedent's death, the surviving spouse is personally liable to the extent provided in Section 13563 to any person having a superior right by testate succession from the decedent.
(b) An action to impose liability under this section is forever barred three years after the death of the decedent. The three-year period specified in this subdivision is not tolled for any reason.
Ca. Prob. Code § 13561
Added by Stats. 1991, Ch. 1055, Sec. 57.

Section 13562 - Liability for restitution

(a) Subject to subdivisions (b), (c), and (d), if proceedings for the administration of the decedent's estate are commenced, the surviving spouse is liable for:

(1) The restitution to the decedent's estate of the decedent's property if the surviving spouse still has the decedent's property, together with (A) the net income the surviving spouse received from the decedent's property and (B) if the surviving spouse encumbered the decedent's property after the date of death, the amount necessary to satisfy the balance of the encumbrance as of the date the decedent's property is restored to the estate.

(2) The restitution to the decedent's estate of the fair market value of the decedent's property if the surviving spouse no longer has the decedent's property, together with (A) the net income the surviving spouse received from the decedent's property prior to disposing of it and (B) interest from the date of disposition at the rate of 7 percent per annum on the fair market value of the decedent's property. For the purposes of this paragraph, the "fair market value of the decedent's property" is the fair market value of the decedent's property, determined as of the time of the disposition of the decedent's property, less the amount of any liens and encumbrances on the decedent's property at the time of the decedent's death.

(b) Subject to subdivision (c), if proceedings for the administration of the decedent's estate are commenced and the surviving spouse made a significant improvement to the decedent's property in the good faith belief that the surviving spouse was the successor of the decedent to the decedent's property, the surviving spouse is liable for whichever of the following the decedent's estate elects:

(1) The restitution of the decedent's property, as improved, to the estate of the decedent upon the condition that the estate reimburse the surviving spouse for (A) the amount by which the improvement increases the fair market value of the decedent's property restored, valued as of the time of restitution, and (B) the amount paid by the surviving spouse for principal and interest on any liens or encumbrances that were on the decedent's property at the time of the decedent's death.

(2) The restoration to the decedent's estate of the fair market value of the decedent's property, valued as of the time of the decedent's death, excluding the amount of any liens and encumbrances on the decedent's property at that time, together with interest on the net amount at the rate of 7 percent per annum running from the date of the decedent's death.

(c) The property and amount required to be restored to the estate under this section shall be reduced by any property or amount paid by the surviving spouse to satisfy a liability under Chapter 3 (commencing with Section 13550).

(d) An action to enforce the liability under this section may be brought only by the personal representative of the estate of the decedent. Whether or not the personal representative brings an action under this section, the personal representative may enforce the liability only to the extent necessary to protect the interests of the heirs, devisees, and creditors of the decedent.

(e) An action to enforce the liability under this section is forever barred three years after the death of the decedent. The three-year period specified in this subdivision is not tolled for any reason.

   Ca. Prob. Code § 13562

Amended by Stats 2019 ch 122 (AB 473),s 17, eff. 1/1/2020.
Amended by Stats 2015 ch 293 (AB 139),s 20, eff. 1/1/2016.

Section 13563 - Liability if requirements of section 13582 satisfied; amount of liability

(a) The surviving spouse is not liable under Section 13561 if proceedings for the administration of the decedent's estate are commenced and the surviving spouse satisfies the requirements of Section 13562.

(b) The aggregate of the personal liability of the surviving spouse under Section 13561 shall not exceed the sum of the following:

   (1) The fair market value at the time of the decedent's death, less the amount of any liens and encumbrances on the decedent's property at that time, of the portion of the decedent's property that passes to any person having a superior right by testate succession from the decedent.

   (2) The net income the surviving spouse received from the portion of the decedent's property that passes to any person having a superior right by testate succession from the decedent.

   (3) If the decedent's property has been disposed of, interest on the fair market value of the portion of the decedent's property that passes to any person having a superior right by testate succession from the decedent from the date of disposition at the rate of 7 percent per annum. For the purposes of this paragraph, "fair market value" is fair market value, determined as of the time of disposition of the decedent's property, less the amount of any liens and encumbrances on the decedent's property at the time of the decedent's death.

Ca. Prob. Code § 13563
Amended by Stats 2019 ch 122 (AB 473),s 18, eff. 1/1/2020.

Section 13564 - Remedies in addition to other remedies

The remedies available under Sections 13561 to 13563, inclusive, are in addition to any remedies available by reason of any fraud or intentional wrongdoing.

Ca. Prob. Code § 13564
Added by Stats. 1991, Ch. 1055, Sec. 57.

Section 13565 - Excuse from liability for acting reasonably and in good faith

If the court finds that the surviving spouse has acted reasonably and in good faith under the circumstances as known to the surviving spouse, the court may, in its discretion, excuse the surviving spouse from liability to pay interest, in whole or in part, under paragraph (2) of subdivision (a) of Section 13562, paragraph (2) of subdivision (b) of Section 13562, or paragraph (3) of subdivision (b) of Section 13563, if it would be equitable to do so.

Ca. Prob. Code § 13565
Added by Stats 2019 ch 122 (AB 473),s 19, eff. 1/1/2020.

Chapter 4 - COLLECTION BY AFFIDAVIT OF COMPENSATION OWED TO DECEASED SPOUSE

Section 13600 - Generally

(a) At any time after a spouse dies, the surviving spouse or the guardian or conservator of the estate of the surviving spouse may, without procuring letters of administration or awaiting probate of the will, collect salary or other compensation owed by an employer for personal services of the deceased spouse, including compensation for unused vacation, not in excess of sixteen thousand six hundred twenty-five dollars ($16,625), as adjusted periodically in accordance with Section 890, net.

(b) Not more than sixteen thousand six hundred twenty-five dollars ($16,625), as adjusted periodically in accordance with Section 890, net in the aggregate may be collected by or for the surviving spouse under this chapter from all of the employers of the decedent.

(c) For the purposes of this chapter, a guardian or conservator of the estate of the surviving spouse may act on behalf of the surviving spouse without authorization or approval of the court in which the guardianship or conservatorship proceeding is pending.

(d) The dollar limit set forth in subdivisions (a) and (b) does not apply to the surviving spouse or the guardian or conservator of the estate of the surviving spouse of a firefighter or peace officer described in subdivision (a) of Section 22820 of the Government Code.

Ca. Prob. Code § 13600

Amended by Stats 2019 ch 122 (AB 473),s 20, eff. 1/1/2020.
Amended by Stats 2016 ch 50 (SB 1005),s 90, eff. 1/1/2017.
Amended by Stats 2012 ch 162 (SB 1171),s 140, eff. 1/1/2013.
Amended by Stats 2011 ch 117 (AB 1305),s 10, eff. 1/1/2012.
Amended by Stats 2004 ch 69 (SB 626), s 35, eff. 6/23/2004.
Amended by Stats 2002 ch 733 (AB 2059), s 2, eff. 9/20/2002.

Section 13601 - Affidavit or declaration furnished to employer to collect salary or other compensation

(a) To collect salary or other compensation under this chapter, an affidavit or a declaration under penalty of perjury under the laws of this state shall be furnished to the employer of the deceased spouse stating all of the following:

(1) The name of the decedent.

(2) The date and place of the decedent's death.

(3) Either of the following, as appropriate:

    (A) "The affiant or declarant is the surviving spouse of the decedent."

    (B) "The affiant or declarant is the guardian or conservator of the estate of the surviving spouse of the decedent."

(4) "The surviving spouse of the decedent is entitled to the earnings of the decedent under the decedent's will or by intestate succession and no one else has a superior right to the earnings."

(5) "No proceeding is now being or has been conducted in California for administration of the decedent's estate."

(6) "Sections 13600 to 13605, inclusive, of the California Probate Code require that the earnings of the decedent, including compensation for unused vacation, not in excess of [Insert dollar amount specified in subdivision (e) of Section 13601 of the California Probate Code] net, be paid promptly to the affiant or declarant."

(7) "Neither the surviving spouse, nor anyone acting on behalf of the surviving spouse, has a pending request to collect compensation owed by another employer for personal services of the decedent under Sections 13600 to 13605, inclusive, of the California Probate Code."

(8) "Neither the surviving spouse, nor anyone acting on behalf of the surviving spouse, has collected any compensation owed by an employer for personal services of the decedent under Sections 13600 to 13605, inclusive, of the California Probate Code except the sum of _____ dollars ($_____) that was collected from _____."

(9) "The affiant or declarant requests that the affiant or declarant be paid the salary or other compensation owed by you for personal services of the decedent, including compensation for unused vacation, not to exceed [Insert dollar amount specified in subdivision (e) of Section 13601 of the California Probate Code] net, less the amount of _____ dollars ($_____) that was previously collected."

(10) "The affiant or declarant affirms or declares under penalty of perjury under the laws of the State of California that the foregoing is true and correct."

(b) Where the decedent is a firefighter or peace officer described in subdivision (a) of Section 22820 of the Government Code, the affidavit or declaration need not include the content specified in paragraphs (6) to (9), inclusive, of subdivision (a). The affidavit shall instead include the following statements:

(1) "The decedent was a firefighter or peace officer described in subdivision (a) of Section 22820 of the Government Code. Sections 13600 to 13605, inclusive, of the California Probate Code require that the earnings of the decedent, including compensation for unused vacation, be paid promptly to the affiant or declarant."

(2) "The affiant or declarant requests to be paid the salary or other compensation owed by you for personal services of the decedent, including compensation for unused vacation."

(c) Reasonable proof of the identity of the surviving spouse shall be provided to the employer. If a guardian or conservator is acting for the surviving spouse, reasonable proof of the identity of the guardian or conservator shall also be provided to the employer. Proof of identity that is sufficient under Section 13104 is sufficient proof of identity for the purposes of this subdivision.

(d) If a person presenting the affidavit or declaration is a person claiming to be the guardian or conservator of the estate of the surviving spouse, the employer shall be provided with reasonable proof, satisfactory to the employer, of the appointment of the person to act as guardian or conservator of the estate of the surviving spouse.

(e)

(1) When the decedent dies prior to April 1, 2022, the dollar amount for paragraphs (6) and (9) of subdivision (a) is sixteen thousand six hundred twenty-five dollars ($16,625).

(2) When the decedent dies on or after April 1, 2022, the dollar amount for paragraphs (6) and (9) of subdivision (a) is the adjusted dollar amount, published in accordance with subdivision (c) of Section 890, in effect on the date of the decedent's death. The affiant or declarant shall attach the list of adjusted dollar amounts, published in accordance with subdivision (c) of Section 890, in effect on the date of the decedent's death to the affidavit or declaration.

Ca. Prob. Code § 13601
Amended by Stats 2019 ch 122 (AB 473),s 21, eff. 1/1/2020.
Amended by Stats 2011 ch 117 (AB 1305),s 11, eff. 1/1/2012.
Amended by Stats 2003 ch 32 (AB 167),s 13, eff. 1/1/2004.

Section 13602 - Amount of earnings promptly paid by employer

If the requirements of Section 13600 are satisfied, the employer to whom the affidavit or declaration is presented shall promptly pay the earnings of the decedent, including compensation for unused vacation, as provided in Section 13600, to the person presenting the affidavit or declaration.

Ca. Prob. Code § 13602
Amended by Stats 2019 ch 122 (AB 473),s 22, eff. 1/1/2020.
Amended by Stats 2011 ch 117 (AB 1305),s 12, eff. 1/1/2012.

Section 13603 - Receipt of affidavit or declaration constitutes sufficient acquittance for compensation

If the requirements of Section 13601 are satisfied, receipt by the employer of the affidavit or declaration constitutes sufficient acquittance for the compensation paid pursuant to this chapter and discharges the employer from any further liability with respect to the compensation paid. The employer may rely in good faith on the statements in the affidavit or declaration and has no duty to inquire into the truth of any statement in the affidavit or declaration.

Ca. Prob. Code § 13603
Enacted by Stats. 1990, Ch. 79.

Section 13604 - Action if employer refuses to pay; attorney's fees

(a) If the employer refuses to pay as required by this chapter, the surviving spouse may recover the amount the surviving spouse is entitled to receive under this chapter in an action brought for that purpose against the employer.

(b) If an action is brought against the employer under this section, the court shall award reasonable attorney's fees to the surviving spouse if the court finds that the employer acted unreasonably in refusing to pay as required by this chapter.

Ca. Prob. Code § 13604
Enacted by Stats. 1990, Ch. 79.

Section 13605 - Effect of payment

(a) Nothing in this chapter limits the rights of the heirs or devisees of the deceased spouse. Payment of a decedent's compensation pursuant to this chapter does not preclude later proceedings for administration of the decedent's estate.

(b) Any person to whom payment is made under this chapter is answerable and accountable therefor to the personal representative of the decedent's estate and is liable for the amount of the payment to any other person having a superior right to the payment received. In addition to any other liability the person has under this section, a person who fraudulently secures a payment under this chapter is liable to a person having a superior right to the payment for three times the amount of the payment.

Ca. Prob. Code § 13605
Enacted by Stats. 1990, Ch. 79.

Section 13606 - Procedure in addition to other methods

The procedure provided in this chapter is in addition to, and not in lieu of, any other method of collecting compensation owed to a decedent.

Ca. Prob. Code § 13606
Enacted by Stats. 1990, Ch. 79.

Chapter 5 - DETERMINATION OR CONFIRMATION OF PROPERTY PASSING OR BELONGING TO SURVIVING SPOUSE

Section 13650 - Petition that administration not necessary because estate passes to surviving spouse

(a) A surviving spouse or the personal representative, guardian of the estate, or conservator of the estate of the surviving spouse may file a petition in the superior court of the county in which the estate of the deceased spouse may be administered requesting an order that administration of all or part of the estate is not necessary for the reason that all or part of the estate is property passing to the surviving spouse. The petition may also request an order confirming the ownership of the surviving spouse of property belonging to the surviving spouse under Section 100 or 101.
(b) To the extent of the election, this section does not apply to property that the petitioner has elected, as provided in Section 13502, to have administered under this code.
(c) A guardian or conservator may file a petition under this section without authorization or approval of the court in which the guardianship or conservatorship proceeding is pending.

Ca. Prob. Code § 13650
Enacted by Stats. 1990, Ch. 79.

Section 13651 - Allegations and content of petition

(a) A petition filed pursuant to Section 13650 shall allege that administration of all or a part of the estate of the deceased spouse is not necessary for the reason that all or a part of the estate is property passing to the surviving spouse, and shall set forth all of the following information:

(1) If proceedings for the administration of the estate are not pending, the facts necessary to determine the county in which the estate of the deceased spouse may be administered.

(2) A description of the property of the deceased spouse which the petitioner alleges is property passing to the surviving spouse, including the trade or business name of any property passing to the surviving spouse that consists of an unincorporated business or an interest in an unincorporated business which the deceased spouse was operating or managing at the time of death, subject to any written agreement between the deceased spouse and the surviving spouse providing for a non pro rata division of the aggregate value of the community property assets or quasi-community assets, or both.

(3) The facts upon which the petitioner bases the allegation that all or a part of the estate of the deceased spouse is property passing to the surviving spouse.

(4) A description of any interest in the community property or quasi-community property, or both, which the petitioner requests the court to confirm to the surviving spouse as belonging to the surviving spouse pursuant to Section 100 or 101, subject to any written agreement between the deceased spouse and the surviving spouse providing for a non pro rata division of the aggregate value of the community property assets or quasi-community assets, or both.

(5) The name, age, address, and relation to the deceased spouse of each heir and devisee of the deceased spouse, the names and addresses of all persons named as executors of the will of the deceased spouse, and the names and addresses of all persons appointed as personal representatives of the deceased spouse, which are known to the petitioner. Disclosure of any written agreement between the deceased spouse and the surviving spouse providing for a non pro rata division of the aggregate value of the community property assets or quasi-community property assets, or both, or the affirmative statement that this agreement does not exist. If a dispute arises as to the division of the community property assets or quasi-community property assets, or both,

456

pursuant to this agreement, the court shall determine the division subject to terms and conditions or other remedies that appear equitable under the circumstances of the case, taking into account the rights of all interested persons.

(b) If the petitioner bases the allegation that all or part of the estate of the deceased spouse is property passing to the surviving spouse upon the will of the deceased spouse, a copy of the will shall be attached to the petition.

(c) If the petitioner bases the description of the property of the deceased spouse passing to the surviving spouse or the property to be confirmed to the surviving spouse, or both, upon a written agreement between the deceased spouse and the surviving spouse providing for a non pro rata division of the aggregate value of the community property assets or quasi-community assets, or both, a copy of the agreement shall be attached to the petition.

Ca. Prob. Code § 13651
Amended by Stats. 1998, Ch. 682, Sec. 6. Effective January 1, 1999.

Section 13652 - Petition filed in pending proceedings without payment of additional fee

If proceedings for the administration of the estate of the deceased spouse are pending, a petition under this chapter shall be filed in those proceedings without the payment of an additional fee.

Ca. Prob. Code § 13652
Enacted by Stats. 1990, Ch. 79.

Section 13653 - Petition filed with petition for probate or for administration

If proceedings for the administration of the estate of the deceased spouse are not pending, a petition under this chapter may, but need not, be filed with a petition for probate of the will of the deceased spouse or for administration of the estate of the deceased spouse.

Ca. Prob. Code § 13653
Enacted by Stats. 1990, Ch. 79.

Section 13654 - Admitting will to probate or appointing

personal representative not precluded by petition

The filing of a petition under this chapter does not preclude the court from admitting the will of the deceased spouse to probate or appointing a personal representative of the estate of the deceased spouse upon the petition of any person legally entitled, including any petition for probate of the will or for administration of the estate which is filed with a petition filed under this chapter.

Ca. Prob. Code § 13654
Enacted by Stats. 1990, Ch. 79.

Section 13655 - Notice of hearing

(a) If proceedings for the administration of the estate of the deceased spouse are pending at the time a petition is filed under this chapter, or if the proceedings are not pending and if the petition filed under this chapter is not filed with a petition for probate of the deceased spouse's will or for administration of the estate of the deceased spouse, notice of the hearing on the petition filed under this chapter shall be given as provided in Section 1220 to all of the following persons:

(1) Each person listed in Section 1220 and each person named as executor in any will of the deceased spouse.

(2) All devisees and known heirs of the deceased spouse and, if the petitioner is the trustee of a trust that is a devisee under the will of the decedent, all persons interested in the trust, as determined in cases of future interests pursuant to paragraph (1), (2), or (3) of subdivision (a) of Section 15804.

(b) The notice specified in subdivision (a) shall also be delivered as provided in subdivision (a) to the Attorney General, addressed to the office of the Attorney General at Sacramento, if the petitioner bases the allegation that all or part of the estate of the deceased spouse is property passing to the surviving spouse upon the will of the deceased spouse and the will involves or may involve either of the following:

(1) A testamentary trust of property for charitable purposes other than a charitable trust with a designated trustee, resident in this state.

(2) A devise for a charitable purpose without an identified devisee or beneficiary.

Ca. Prob. Code § 13655

Amended by Stats 2017 ch 319 (AB 976),s 85, eff. 1/1/2018.

Section 13656 - Issuance of order

(a) If the court finds that all of the estate of the deceased spouse is property passing to the surviving spouse, the court shall issue an order describing the property, determining that the property is property passing to the surviving spouse, and determining that no administration is necessary. The court may issue any further orders which may be necessary to cause delivery of the property or its proceeds to the surviving spouse.

(b) If the court finds that all or part of the estate of the deceased spouse is not property passing to the surviving spouse, the court shall issue an order (1) describing any property which is not property passing to the surviving spouse, determining that that property does not pass to the surviving spouse and determining that that property is subject to administration under this code and (2) describing the property, if any, which is property passing to the surviving spouse, determining that that property passes to the surviving spouse, and determining that no administration of that property is necessary. If the court determines that property passes to the surviving spouse, the court may issue any further orders which may be necessary to cause delivery of that property or its proceeds to the surviving spouse.

(c) If the petition filed under this chapter includes a description of the interest of the surviving spouse in the community or quasi-community property, or both, which belongs to the surviving spouse pursuant to Section 100 or 101 and the court finds that the interest belongs to the surviving spouse, the court shall issue an order describing the property and confirming the ownership of the surviving spouse and may issue any further orders which may be necessary to cause ownership of the property to be confirmed in the surviving spouse.

Ca. Prob. Code § 13656
Enacted by Stats. 1990, Ch. 79.

Section 13657 - Final order conclusive on all persons

Upon becoming final, an order under Section 13656 (1) determining that property is property passing to the surviving spouse or (2) confirming the ownership of the surviving spouse of property belonging to the surviving spouse under Section 100 or 101 shall be conclusive on all persons, whether or not they are in being.

Ca. Prob. Code § 13657
Enacted by Stats. 1990, Ch. 79.

Section 13658 - List of all known creditors of unincorporated business

If the court determines that all or a part of the property passing to the surviving spouse consists of an unincorporated business or an interest in an unincorporated business which the deceased spouse was operating or managing at the time of death, the court shall require the surviving spouse to file a list of all of the known creditors of the business and the amounts owing to each of them. The court may issue any order necessary to protect the interests of the creditors of the business, including, but not limited to, the filing of (1) an undertaking and (2) an inventory and appraisal in the form provided in Section 8802 and made as provided in Part 3 (commencing with Section 8800) of Division 7.

Ca. Prob. Code § 13658
Enacted by Stats. 1990, Ch. 79.

Section 13659 - Inventory and appraisal

Except as provided in Section 13658, no inventory and appraisal of the estate of the deceased spouse is required in a proceeding under this chapter. However, within three months after the filing of a petition under this chapter, or within such further time as the court or judge for reasonable cause may allow, the petitioner may file with the clerk of the court an inventory and appraisal made as provided in Part 3 (commencing with Section 8800) of Division 7. The petitioner may appraise the assets which a personal representative could appraise under Section 8901.

Ca. Prob. Code § 13659
Enacted by Stats. 1990, Ch. 79.

Section 13660 - Attorney's fees

The attorney's fees for services performed in connection with the filing of a petition and obtaining of a court order under this chapter shall be determined by private agreement between the attorney and the client and are not subject to approval by the court. If there is no agreement between the attorney and the client concerning the attorney's fees for services performed in connection with the filing of a petition and obtaining of a court order under this chapter and there is a dispute concerning the reasonableness of the attorney's fees for those services, a petition may be filed with the court in the same proceeding requesting that the court determine the reasonableness of the attorney's fees for those services. If there is an agreement between the attorney and the client concerning the attorney's fees for services performed in connection with the filing of a petition and obtaining a court order under this chapter and there is a dispute concerning the meaning of the agreement, a petition may be filed with the court in the same proceeding requesting that the court determine the dispute.

Ca. Prob. Code § 13660
Enacted by Stats. 1990, Ch. 79.

Division 9 - TRUST LAW

Part 1 - GENERAL PROVISIONS

Section 15000 - Title of division

This division shall be known and may be cited as the Trust Law.

Ca. Prob. Code § 15000
Enacted by Stats. 1990, Ch. 79.

Section 15001 - Applicability of division

Except as otherwise provided by statute:
(a) This division applies to all trusts regardless of whether they were created before, on, or after July 1, 1987.
(b) This division applies to all proceedings concerning trusts commenced on or after July 1, 1987.
(c) This division applies to all proceedings concerning trusts commenced before July 1, 1987, unless in the opinion of the court application of a particular provision of this division would substantially interfere with the effective conduct of the proceedings or the rights of the parties and other interested persons, in which case the particular provision of this division does not apply and prior law applies.
Ca. Prob. Code § 15001
Enacted by Stats. 1990, Ch. 79.

Section 15002 - Common law as to trusts

Except to the extent that the common law rules governing trusts are modified by statute, the common law as to trusts is the law of this state.
Ca. Prob. Code § 15002
Enacted by Stats. 1990, Ch. 79.

Section 15003 - Constructive and resulting trusts; fiduciary and confidential relationships; entities excluded from definition of trusts

(a) Nothing in this division affects the substantive law relating to constructive or resulting trusts.
(b) The repeal of Title 8 (commencing with Section 2215) of Part 4 of Division 3 of the Civil Code by Chapter 820 of the Statutes of 1986 was not intended to alter the rules applied by the courts to fiduciary and confidential relationships, except as to express trusts

governed by this division.

(c) Nothing in this division or in Section 82 is intended to prevent the application of all or part of the principles or procedures of this division to an entity or relationship that is excluded from the definition of "trust" provided by Section 82 where these principles or procedures are applied pursuant to statutory or common law principles, by court order or rule, or by contract.

Ca. Prob. Code § 15003

Amended by Stats. 1990, Ch. 710, Sec. 43. Operative July 1, 1991, by Sec. 48 of Ch. 710.

Section 15004 - Charitable trusts

Unless otherwise provided by statute, this division applies to charitable trusts that are subject to the jurisdiction of the Attorney General to the extent that the application of the provision is not in conflict with the Supervision of Trustees and Fundraisers for Charitable Purposes Act, Article 7 (commencing with Section 12580) of Chapter 6 of Part 2 of Division 3 of Title 2 of the Government Code.

Ca. Prob. Code § 15004

Amended by Stats 2020 ch 370 (SB 1371),s 232, eff. 1/1/2021.

Part 2 - CREATION, VALIDITY, MODIFICATION, AND TERMINATION OF TRUSTS

Chapter 1 - CREATION AND VALIDITY OF TRUSTS

Section 15200 - Methods of creating

Subject to other provisions of this chapter, a trust may be created by any of the following methods:

(a) A declaration by the owner of property that the owner holds the property as trustee.

(b) A transfer of property by the owner during the owner's lifetime to another person as trustee.

(c) A transfer of property by the owner, by will or by other instrument taking effect upon the death of the owner, to another person as trustee.

(d) An exercise of a power of appointment to another person as trustee.

(e) An enforceable promise to create a trust.

Ca. Prob. Code § 15200

Enacted by Stats. 1990, Ch. 79.

Section 15201 - Settlor's intention

A trust is created only if the settlor properly manifests an intention to create a trust.

Ca. Prob. Code § 15201

Enacted by Stats. 1990, Ch. 79.

Section 15202 - Trust property

A trust is created only if there is trust property.

Ca. Prob. Code § 15202

Enacted by Stats. 1990, Ch. 79.

Section 15203 - Purposes

A trust may be created for any purpose that is not illegal or against public policy.

Ca. Prob. Code § 15203

Enacted by Stats. 1990, Ch. 79.

Section 15204 - Indefinite or general purpose

A trust created for an indefinite or general purpose is not invalid for that reason if it can be determined with reasonable certainty that a particular use of the trust property comes within that purpose.

Ca. Prob. Code § 15204

Enacted by Stats. 1990, Ch. 79.

Section 15205 - Beneficiary required

(a) A trust, other than a charitable trust, is created only if there is a beneficiary.

(b) The requirement of subdivision (a) is satisfied if the trust instrument provides for either of the following:

(1) A beneficiary or class of beneficiaries that is ascertainable with reasonable certainty or that is sufficiently described so it can be determined that some person meets the description or is within the class.

(2) A grant of a power to the trustee or some other person to select the beneficiaries based on a standard or in the discretion of the trustee or other person.

Ca. Prob. Code § 15205
Enacted by Stats. 1990, Ch. 79.

Section 15206 - Methods of evidencing trust in relation to real property

A trust in relation to real property is not valid unless evidenced by one of the following methods:
(a) By a written instrument signed by the trustee, or by the trustee's agent if authorized in writing to do so.
(b) By a written instrument conveying the trust property signed by the settlor, or by the settlor's agent if authorized in writing to do so.
(c) By operation of law.

Ca. Prob. Code § 15206
Enacted by Stats. 1990, Ch. 79.

Section 15207 - Existence and terms of oral trust

(a) The existence and terms of an oral trust of personal property may be established only by clear and convincing evidence.
(b) The oral declaration of the settlor, standing alone, is not sufficient evidence of the creation of a trust of personal property.
(c) In the case of an oral trust, a reference in this division or elsewhere to a trust instrument or declaration means the terms of the trust as established pursuant to subdivision (a).

Ca. Prob. Code § 15207
Enacted by Stats. 1990, Ch. 79.

Section 15208 - Consideration not required; promise to create in future

Consideration is not required to create a trust, but a promise to create a trust in the future is enforceable only if the requirements for an enforceable contract are satisfied.
Ca. Prob. Code § 15208
Enacted by Stats. 1990, Ch. 79.

Section 15209 - Trust not invalid, merged or terminated

If a trust provides for one or more successor beneficiaries after the death of the settlor, the trust is not invalid, merged, or terminated in either of the following circumstances:
(a) Where there is one settlor who is the sole trustee and the sole beneficiary during the settlor's lifetime.
(b) Where there are two or more settlors, one or more of whom are trustees, and the beneficial interest in the trust is in one or more of the settlors during the lifetime of the settlors.
Ca. Prob. Code § 15209
Enacted by Stats. 1990, Ch. 79.

Section 15210 - Recording trust relating to real property

A trust created pursuant to this chapter which relates to real property may be recorded in the office of the county recorder in the county where all or a portion of the real property is located.
Ca. Prob. Code § 15210
Enacted by Stats. 1990, Ch. 79.

Section 15211 - Term of trust for noncharitable corporation or unincorporated society or for lawful noncharitable purpose

A trust for a noncharitable corporation or unincorporated society or for a lawful noncharitable purpose may be performed by the trustee for only 21 years, whether or not there is a beneficiary who can seek enforcement or termination of the trust and whether or not the terms of the trust contemplate a longer duration.

Ca. Prob. Code § 15211

Added by Stats. 1991, Ch. 156, Sec. 20.

Section 15212 - Trust for care of animal

(a) Subject to the requirements of this section, a trust for the care of an animal is a trust for a lawful noncharitable purpose. Unless expressly provided in the trust, the trust terminates when no animal living on the date of the settlor's death remains alive. The governing instrument of the animal trust shall be liberally construed to bring the trust within this section, to presume against the merely precatory or honorary nature of the disposition, and to carry out the general intent of the settlor. Extrinsic evidence is admissible in determining the settlor's intent.

(b) A trust for the care of an animal is subject to the following requirements:

(1) Except as expressly provided otherwise in the trust instrument, the principal or income shall not be converted to the use of the trustee or to any use other than for the benefit of the animal.

(2) Upon termination of the trust, the trustee shall distribute the unexpended trust property in the following order:

(A) As directed in the trust instrument.

(B) If the trust was created in a nonresiduary clause in the settlor's will or in a codicil to the settlor's will, under the residuary clause in the settlor's will.

(C) If the application of subparagraph (A) or (B) does not result in distribution of unexpended trust property, to the settlor's heirs under Section 21114.

(3) For the purposes of Section 21110, the residuary clause described in subparagraph (B) of paragraph (2) shall be treated as creating a future interest under the terms of a trust.

(c) The intended use of the principal or income may be enforced by a person designated for that purpose in the trust instrument or, if none is designated, by a person appointed by a court. In addition to a person identified in subdivision (a) of Section 17200, any person interested in the welfare of the animal or any nonprofit charitable organization that has as its principal activity the care of animals may petition the court regarding the trust as provided in Chapter 3 (commencing with Section 17200) of Part 5.

(d) If a trustee is not designated or no designated or successor trustee is willing or able to serve, a court shall name a trustee. A court may order the transfer of the trust property to a court-appointed trustee, if it is required to ensure that the intended use is carried out and if a successor trustee is not designated in the trust instrument or if no designated successor trustee agrees to serve or is able to serve. A court may also make all other orders and determinations as it shall deem advisable to carry out the intent of the settlor and the purpose of this section.

(e) The accountings required by Section 16062 shall be provided to the beneficiaries who would be entitled to distribution if the animal were then deceased and to any nonprofit charitable corporation that has as its principal activity the care of animals and that has requested these accountings in writing. However, if the value of the assets in the trust does not exceed forty thousand dollars ($40,000), no filing, report, registration, periodic accounting, separate maintenance of funds, appointment, or fee is required by reason of the existence of the fiduciary relationship of the trustee, unless ordered by the court or required by the trust instrument.

(f) Any beneficiary, any person designated by the trust instrument or the court to enforce the trust, or any nonprofit charitable corporation that has as its principal activity the care of animals may, upon reasonable request, inspect the animal, the premises where the animal is maintained, or the books and records of the trust.

(g) A trust governed by this section is not subject to termination pursuant to subdivision (b) of Section 15408.

(h) Section 15211 does not apply to a trust governed by this section.

(i) For purposes of this section, "animal" means a domestic or pet animal for the benefit of which a trust has been established.

Ca. Prob. Code § 15212
Added by Stats 2008 ch 168 (SB 685),s 2, eff. 1/1/2009.

Chapter 2 - RESTRICTIONS ON VOLUNTARY AND INVOLUNTARY TRANSFERS

Section 15300 - Beneficiary's interest in income not subject to transfer

Except as provided in Sections 15304 to 15307, inclusive, if the trust instrument provides that a beneficiary's interest in income is not subject to voluntary or involuntary transfer, the beneficiary's interest in income under the trust may not be transferred and is not subject to enforcement of a money judgment until paid to the beneficiary.

Ca. Prob. Code § 15300
Enacted by Stats. 1990, Ch. 79.

Section 15301 - Beneficiary's interest in principal not subject to transfer

(a) Except as provided in subdivision (b) and in Sections 15304 to 15307, inclusive, if the trust instrument provides that a beneficiary's interest in principal is not subject to voluntary or involuntary transfer, the beneficiary's interest in principal may not be transferred and is not subject to enforcement of a money judgment until paid to the beneficiary.

(b) After an amount of principal has become due and payable to the beneficiary under the trust instrument, upon petition to the court under Section 709.010 of the Code of Civil Procedure by a judgment creditor, the court may make an order directing the trustee to satisfy the money judgment out of that principal amount. The court in its discretion may issue an order directing the trustee to satisfy all or part of the judgment out of that principal amount.

Ca. Prob. Code § 15301
Enacted by Stats. 1990, Ch. 79.

Section 15302 - Trust to pay income or principal for education or support of beneficiary

Except as provided in Sections 15304 to 15307, inclusive, if the trust instrument provides that the trustee shall pay income or principal or both for the education or support of a beneficiary, the beneficiary's interest in income or principal or both under the trust, to the extent the income or principal or both is necessary for the education or support of the beneficiary, may not be transferred and is not subject to the enforcement of a money judgment until paid to the beneficiary.

Ca. Prob. Code § 15302
Enacted by Stats. 1990, Ch. 79.

Section 15303 - Trustee to pay beneficiary so much of income or principal as trustee in trustee's discretion sees fit

(a) If the trust instrument provides that the trustee shall pay to or for the benefit of a beneficiary so much of the income or principal or both as the trustee in the trustee's discretion sees fit to pay, a transferee or creditor of the beneficiary may not compel the trustee to pay any amount that may be paid only in the exercise of the trustee's discretion.
(b) If the trustee has knowledge of the transfer of the beneficiary's interest or has been served with process in a proceeding under Section 709.010 of the Code of Civil Procedure by a judgment creditor seeking to reach the beneficiary's interest, and the trustee pays to or for the benefit of the beneficiary any part of the income or principal that may be paid only in the exercise of the trustee's discretion, the trustee is liable to the transferee or creditor to the extent that the payment to or for the benefit of the beneficiary impairs the right of the transferee or creditor. This subdivision does not apply if the beneficiary's interest in the trust is subject to a restraint on transfer that is valid under Section 15300 or 15301.
(c) This section applies regardless of whether the trust instrument provides a standard for the exercise of the trustee's discretion.

(d) Nothing in this section limits any right the beneficiary may have to compel the trustee to pay to or for the benefit of the beneficiary all or part of the income or principal.

Ca. Prob. Code § 15303

Enacted by Stats. 1990, Ch. 79.

Section 15304 - Restraint on transfer of settlor's interest; principal and income paid for education or support settlor

(a) If the settlor is a beneficiary of a trust created by the settlor and the settlor's interest is subject to a provision restraining the voluntary or involuntary transfer of the settlor's interest, the restraint is invalid against transferees or creditors of the settlor. The invalidity of the restraint on transfer does not affect the validity of the trust.

(b) If the settlor is the beneficiary of a trust created by the settlor and the trust instrument provides that the trustee shall pay income or principal or both for the education or support of the beneficiary or gives the trustee discretion to determine the amount of income or principal or both to be paid to or for the benefit of the settlor, a transferee or creditor of the settlor may reach the maximum amount that the trustee could pay to or for the benefit of the settlor under the trust instrument, not exceeding the amount of the settlor's proportionate contribution to the trust.

(c) For purposes of this chapter, the settlor shall not be considered to be a beneficiary of an irrevocable trust created by the settlor solely by reason of a discretionary authority vested in the trustee to pay directly or reimburse the settlor for any federal or state income tax on trust income or principal that is payable by the settlor, and a transferee or creditor of the settlor shall not be entitled to reach any amount solely by a reason of that discretionary authority.

Ca. Prob. Code § 15304

Amended by Stats 2022 ch 32 (AB 1866),s 1, eff. 1/1/2023.

Enacted by Stats. 1990, Ch. 79.

Section 15305 - Order requiring trustee to satisfy support judgment

(a) As used in this section, "support judgment" means a money judgment for support of the trust beneficiary's spouse or former spouse or minor child.

(b) If the beneficiary has the right under the trust to compel the trustee to pay income or principal or both to or for the benefit of the beneficiary, the court may, to the extent that the court determines it is equitable and reasonable under the circumstances of the particular case, order the trustee to satisfy all or part of the support judgment out of all or part of those payments as they become due and payable, presently or in the future.

(c) Whether or not the beneficiary has the right under the trust to compel the trustee to pay income or principal or both to or for the benefit of the beneficiary, the court may, to the extent that the court determines it is equitable and reasonable under the circumstances of the particular case, order the trustee to satisfy all or part of the support judgment out of all or part of future payments that the trustee, pursuant to the exercise of the trustee's discretion, determines to make to or for the benefit of the beneficiary.

(d) This section applies to a support judgment notwithstanding any provision in the trust instrument.

Ca. Prob. Code § 15305
Enacted by Stats. 1990, Ch. 79.

Section 15305.5 - Order requiring trustee to satisfy restitution judgment

(a) As used in this section, "restitution judgment" means a judgment awarding restitution for the commission of a felony or a money judgment for damages incurred as a result of conduct for which the defendant was convicted of a felony.

(b) If the beneficiary has the right under the trust to compel the trustee to pay income or principal or both to or for the benefit of the beneficiary, the court may, to the extent that the court determines it is equitable and reasonable under the circumstances of the particular case, order the trustee to satisfy all or part of the restitution judgment out of all or part of those payments as they become due and payable, presently or in the future.

(c) Whether or not the beneficiary has the right under the trust to compel the trustee to pay income or principal or both to or for the benefit of the beneficiary, the court may, to the extent that the court determines it is equitable and reasonable under the circumstances of the particular case, order the trustee to satisfy all or part of the restitution judgment out of all or part of future payments that the trustee, pursuant to the exercise of the trustee's discretion, determines to make to or for the benefit of the beneficiary.

(d) This section applies to a restitution judgment notwithstanding any provision in the trust instrument.

Ca. Prob. Code § 15305.5
Added by Stats. 1991, Ch. 175, Sec. 1.

Section 15306 - Statute making beneficiary liable for reimbursement to state or local public entity for public support furnished beneficiary

(a) Notwithstanding any provision in the trust instrument, if a statute of this state makes the beneficiary liable for reimbursement of this state or a local public entity in this state for public support furnished to the beneficiary or to the beneficiary's spouse or minor child, upon petition to the court under Section 709.010 of the Code of Civil Procedure by the appropriate state or local public entity or public official, to the extent the court determines it is equitable and reasonable under the circumstances of the particular case, the court may do the following:

(1) If the beneficiary has the right under the trust to compel the trustee to pay income or principal or both to or for the benefit of the beneficiary, order the trustee to satisfy all or part of the liability out of all or part of the payments as they become due, presently or in the future.

(2) Whether or not the beneficiary has the right under the trust to compel the trustee to pay income or principal or both to or for the benefit of the beneficiary, order the trustee to satisfy all or part of the liability out of all or part of the future payments that the trustee, pursuant to the exercise of the trustee's discretion, determines to make to or for the benefit of the beneficiary.

(3) If the beneficiary is a settlor or the spouse or minor child of the settlor and the beneficiary does not have the right under the trust to compel the trustee to pay income or principal or both to or for the benefit of the beneficiary, to the extent that the trustee has the right to make payments of income or principal or both to or for the beneficiary pursuant to the exercise of the trustee's discretion, order the trustee to satisfy all or part of the liability without regard to whether the trustee has then exercised or may thereafter exercise the discretion in favor of the beneficiary.

(b) Subdivision (a) does not apply to any trust that is established for the benefit of an individual who has a disability that substantially impairs the individual's ability to provide for his or her own care or custody and constitutes a substantial handicap. If, however, the trust results in the individual being ineligible for needed public social services under Division 9 (commencing With Section 10000) of the Welfare and Institutions Code, this subdivision is not applicable and the provisions of subdivision (a) are to be applied.

Ca. Prob. Code § 15306
Enacted by Stats. 1990, Ch. 79.

Section 15306.5 - Order directing trustee to satisfy judgment out of payments to which beneficiary entitled

(a) Notwithstanding a restraint on transfer of the beneficiary's interest in the trust under Section 15300 or 15301, and subject to the limitations of this section, upon a judgment creditor's petition under Section 709.010 of the Code of Civil Procedure, the court may make an order directing the trustee to satisfy all or part of the judgment out of the payments to which the beneficiary is entitled under the trust instrument or that the trustee, in the exercise of the trustee's discretion, has determined or determines in the future to pay to the beneficiary.

(b) An order under this section may not require that the trustee pay in satisfaction of the judgment an amount exceeding 25 percent of the payment that otherwise would be made to, or for the benefit of, the beneficiary.

(c) An order under this section may not require that the trustee pay in satisfaction of the judgment any amount that the court determines is necessary for the support of the beneficiary and all the persons the beneficiary is required to support.

(d) An order for satisfaction of a support judgment, as defined in Section 15305, has priority over an order to satisfy a judgment under this section. Any amount ordered to be applied to the satisfaction of a judgment under this section shall be reduced by the amount of an order for satisfaction of a support judgment under Section 15305, regardless of whether the order for satisfaction of the support judgment was made before or after the order under this section.

(e) If the trust gives the trustee discretion over the payment of either principal or income of a trust, or both, nothing in this section affects or limits that discretion in any manner. The trustee has no duty to oppose a petition to satisfy a judgment under this section or to make any claim for exemption on behalf of the beneficiary. The trustee is not liable for any action taken, or omitted to be taken, in compliance with any court order made under this section.

(f) Subject to subdivision (d), the aggregate of all orders for satisfaction of money judgments against the beneficiary's interest in the trust may not exceed 25 percent of the payment that otherwise would be made to, or for the benefit of, the beneficiary.

Ca. Prob. Code § 15306.5
Enacted by Stats. 1990, Ch. 79.

Section 15307 - Application of amount to which beneficiary to receive to satisfaction of money judgment

Notwithstanding a restraint on transfer of a beneficiary's interest in the trust under Section 15300 or 15301, any amount to which the beneficiary is entitled under the trust instrument or that the trustee, in the exercise of the trustee's discretion, has determined to pay to the beneficiary in excess of the amount that is or will be necessary for the education and support of the beneficiary may be applied to the satisfaction of a money judgment against the beneficiary. Upon the judgment creditor's petition under Section

709.010 of the Code of Civil Procedure, the court may make an order directing the trustee to satisfy all or part of the judgment out of the beneficiary's interest in the trust.

Ca. Prob. Code § 15307
Enacted by Stats. 1990, Ch. 79.

Section 15308 - Modification of order

Any order entered by a court under Section 15305, 15306, 15306.5, or 15307 is subject to modification upon petition of an interested person filed in the court where the order was made.

Ca. Prob. Code § 15308
Enacted by Stats. 1990, Ch. 79.

Section 15309 - Disclaimer or renunciation by beneficiary not transfer

A disclaimer or renunciation by a beneficiary of all or part of his or her interest under a trust shall not be considered a transfer under Section 15300 or 15301.

Ca. Prob. Code § 15309
Enacted by Stats. 1990, Ch. 79.

Chapter 3 - MODIFICATION AND TERMINATION OF TRUSTS

Section 15400 - Trust revocable by settlor

Unless a trust is expressly made irrevocable by the trust instrument, the trust is revocable by the settlor. This section applies only where the settlor is domiciled in this state when the trust is created, where the trust instrument is executed in this state, or where the trust instrument provides that the law of this state governs the trust.

Ca. Prob. Code § 15400
Enacted by Stats. 1990, Ch. 79.

Section 15401 - Methods for revoking trust

(a) A trust that is revocable by the settlor or any other person may be revoked in whole or in part by any of the following methods:

(1) By compliance with any method of revocation provided in the trust instrument.

(2) By a writing, other than a will, signed by the settlor or any other person holding the power of revocation and delivered to the trustee during the lifetime of the settlor or the person holding the power of revocation. If the trust instrument explicitly makes the method of revocation provided in the trust instrument the exclusive method of revocation, the trust may not be revoked pursuant to this paragraph.

(b)

(1) Unless otherwise provided in the instrument, if a trust is created by more than one settlor, each settlor may revoke the trust as to the portion of the trust contributed by that settlor, except as provided in Section 761 of the Family Code.

(2) Notwithstanding paragraph (1), a settlor may grant to another person, including, but not limited to, his or her spouse, a power to revoke all or part of that portion of the trust contributed by that settlor, regardless of whether that portion was separate property or community property of that settlor, and regardless of whether that power to revoke is exercisable during the lifetime of that settlor or continues after the death of that settlor, or both.

(c) A trust may not be modified or revoked by an attorney in fact under a power of attorney unless it is expressly permitted by the trust instrument.

(d) This section shall not limit the authority to modify or terminate a trust pursuant to Section 15403 or 15404 in an appropriate case.

(e) The manner of revocation of a trust revocable by the settlor or any other person that was created by an instrument executed before July 1, 1987, is governed by prior law and not by this section.

Ca. Prob. Code § 15401
Amended by Stats 2012 ch 55 (AB 1683),s 1, eff. 1/1/2013.

Section 15402 - Modification of trust by procedure for

revocation

Unless the trust instrument provides otherwise, if a trust is revocable by the settlor, the settlor may modify the trust by the procedure for revocation.

Ca. Prob. Code § 15402
Enacted by Stats. 1990, Ch. 79.

Section 15403 - Consent of all beneficiaries; continuance necessary to carry out particular purpose; limitation of class

(a) Except as provided in subdivision (b), if all beneficiaries of an irrevocable trust consent, they may petition the court for modification or termination of the trust.

(b) If the continuance of the trust is necessary to carry out a material purpose of the trust, the trust cannot be modified or terminated unless the court, in its discretion, determines that the reason for doing so under the circumstances outweighs the interest in accomplishing a material purpose of the trust. If the trust is subject to a valid restraint on the transfer of a beneficiary's interest as provided in Chapter 2 (commencing with Section 15300), the trust may not be terminated unless the court determines there is good cause to do so.

(c) If the trust provides for the disposition of principal to a class of persons described only as "heirs" or "next of kin" of the settlor, or using other words that describe the class of all persons who would take under the rules of intestacy, the court may limit the class of beneficiaries whose consent is necessary to modify or terminate a trust to the beneficiaries who are reasonably likely to take under the circumstances.

Ca. Prob. Code § 15403
Amended by Stats 2017 ch 61 (SB 333),s 1, eff. 1/1/2018.

Section 15404 - Consent of settlor and beneficiaries

(a) A trust may be modified or terminated by the written consent of the settlor and all beneficiaries without court approval of the modification or termination.

(b) If any beneficiary does not consent to the modification or termination of the trust, the court may modify or partially terminate the trust upon petition to the court by the other beneficiaries, with the consent of the settlor, if the interests of the beneficiaries who do not consent are not substantially impaired.

(c) If the trust provides for the disposition of principal to a class of persons described only as "heirs" or "next of kin" of the settlor, or using other words that describe the class of all persons who would take under the rules of intestacy, the court may limit the class of beneficiaries whose consent is necessary to modify or terminate a trust to the beneficiaries who are reasonably likely to take under the circumstances.

Ca. Prob. Code § 15404
Amended by Stats 2017 ch 61 (SB 333),s 2, eff. 1/1/2018.

Section 15405 - Consent of beneficiary lacking legal capacity

For the purposes of Sections 15403 and 15404, the consent of a beneficiary who lacks legal capacity, including a minor, or who is an unascertained or unborn person may be given in proceedings before the court by a guardian ad litem, if it would be appropriate to do so. In determining whether to give consent, the guardian ad litem may rely on general family benefit accruing to living members of the beneficiary's family as a basis for approving a modification or termination of the trust.

Ca. Prob. Code § 15405
Enacted by Stats. 1990, Ch. 79.

Section 15406 - Presumption of fertility rebuttable

In determining the class of beneficiaries whose consent is necessary to modify or terminate a trust pursuant to Section 15403 or 15404, the presumption of fertility is rebuttable.

Ca. Prob. Code § 15406
Enacted by Stats. 1990, Ch. 79.

Section 15407 - Events causing termination

(a) A trust terminates when any of the following occurs:

  (1) The term of the trust expires.

  (2) The trust purpose is fulfilled.

  (3) The trust purpose becomes unlawful.

  (4) The trust purpose becomes impossible to fulfill.

  (5) The trust is revoked.
(b) On termination of the trust, the trustee continues to have the powers reasonably necessary under the circumstances to wind up the affairs of the trust.
  Ca. Prob. Code § 15407
Enacted by Stats. 1990, Ch. 79.

Section 15408 - Fair market value of principal so low in relation to cost of administration

(a) On petition by a trustee or beneficiary, if the court determines that the fair market value of the principal of a trust has become so low in relation to the cost of administration that continuation of the trust under its existing terms will defeat or substantially impair the accomplishment of its purposes, the court may, in its discretion and in a manner that conforms as nearly as possible to the intention of the settlor, order any of the following:

  (1) Termination of the trust.

  (2) Modification of the trust.

  (3) Appointment of a new trustee.
(b) Notwithstanding subdivision (a), if the trust principal does not exceed fifty thousand dollars ($50,000) in value, the trustee has the

power to terminate the trust.

(c) The existence of a trust provision restraining transfer of the beneficiary's interest does not prevent application of this section.

Ca. Prob. Code § 15408

Amended by Stats 2018 ch 78 (AB 2426),s 1, eff. 1/1/2019.

Amended by Stats 2010 ch 621 (SB 202),s 1, eff. 1/1/2011.

Section 15409 - Circumstances not known to or anticipated by settlor

(a) On petition by a trustee or beneficiary, the court may modify the administrative or dispositive provisions of the trust or terminate the trust if, owing to circumstances not known to the settlor and not anticipated by the settlor, the continuation of the trust under its terms would defeat or substantially impair the accomplishment of the purposes of the trust. In this case, if necessary to carry out the purposes of the trust, the court may order the trustee to do acts that are not authorized or are forbidden by the trust instrument.

(b) The court shall consider a trust provision restraining transfer of the beneficiary's interest as a factor in making its decision whether to modify or terminate the trust, but the court is not precluded from exercising its discretion to modify or terminate the trust solely because of a restraint on transfer.

Ca. Prob. Code § 15409

Enacted by Stats. 1990, Ch. 79.

Section 15410 - Disposition of property upon termination

At the termination of a trust, the trust property shall be disposed of as follows:

(a) In the case of a trust that is revoked by the settlor, the trust property shall be disposed of in the following order of priority:

(1) As directed by the settlor.

(2) As provided in the trust instrument.

(3) To the extent that there is no direction by the settlor or in

the trust instrument, to the settlor, or his or her estate, as the case may be.

(b) In the case of a trust that is revoked by any person holding a power of revocation other than the settlor, the trust property shall be disposed of in the following order of priority:

(1) As provided in the trust instrument.

(2) As directed by the person exercising the power of revocation.

(3) To the extent that there is no direction in the trust instrument or by the person exercising the power of revocation, to the person exercising the power of revocation, or his or her estate, as the case may be.

(c) In the case of a trust that is terminated by the consent of the settlor and all beneficiaries, as agreed by the settlor and all beneficiaries.

(d) In any other case, as provided in the trust instrument or in a manner directed by the court that conforms as nearly as possible to the intention of the settlor as expressed in the trust instrument.

(e) If a trust is terminated by the trustee pursuant to subdivision (b) of Section 15408, the trust property may be distributed as determined by the trustee pursuant to the standard provided in subdivision (d) without the need for a court order. If the trust instrument does not provide a manner of distribution at termination and the settlor's intent is not adequately expressed in the trust instrument, the trustee may distribute the trust property to the living beneficiaries on an actuarial basis.

Ca. Prob. Code § 15410

Amended by Stats 2012 ch 55 (AB 1683),s 2, eff. 1/1/2013.

Section 15411 - Combination of trusts into single trust

If the terms of two or more trusts are substantially similar, on petition by a trustee or beneficiary, the court, for good cause shown, may combine the trusts if the court determines that administration as a single trust will not defeat or substantially impair the accomplishment of the trust purposes or the interests of the beneficiaries.

Ca. Prob. Code § 15411
Enacted by Stats. 1990, Ch. 79.

Section 15412 - Division of trust into two or more trusts

On petition by a trustee or beneficiary, the court, for good cause shown, may divide a trust into two or more separate trusts, if the court determines that dividing the trust will not defeat or substantially impair the accomplishment of the trust purposes or the interests of the beneficiaries.

Ca. Prob. Code § 15412
Enacted by Stats. 1990, Ch. 79.

Section 15413 - Provision prohibiting termination purporting to be applicable after expiration of periods provided by statutory rule against perpetuities

A trust provision, express or implied, that the trust may not be terminated is ineffective insofar as it purports to be applicable after the expiration of the longer of the periods provided by the statutory rule against perpetuities, Article 2 (commencing with Section 21205) of Chapter 1 of Part 2 of Division 11.

Ca. Prob. Code § 15413
Added by Stats. 1991, Ch. 156, Sec. 22.

Section 15414 - Termination of trust continued after expiration of period provided by statutory rule against perpetuities

Notwithstanding any other provision in this chapter, if a trust continues in existence after the expiration of the longer of the periods provided by the statutory rule against perpetuities, Article 2 (commencing with Section 21205) of Chapter 1 of Part 2 of Division 11, the trust may be terminated in either of the following manners:

(a) On petition by a majority of the beneficiaries.

(b) On petition by the Attorney General or by any person who would be affected by the termination, if the court finds that the termination would be in the public interest or in the best interest of a majority of the persons who would be affected by the termination.

Ca. Prob. Code § 15414
Added by Stats. 1991, Ch. 156, Sec. 23.

Part 3 - TRUSTEES AND BENEFICIARIES

Chapter 1 - TRUSTEES

Article 1 - GENERAL PROVISIONS

Section 15600 - Acceptance of trust; preservation of trust without accepting trust

(a) The person named as trustee may accept the trust, or a modification of the trust, by one of the following methods:

(1) Signing the trust instrument or the trust instrument as modified, or signing a separate written acceptance.

(2) Knowingly exercising powers or performing duties under the trust instrument or the trust instrument as modified, except as provided in subdivision (b).
(b) In a case where there is an immediate risk of damage to the trust property, the person named as trustee may act to preserve the trust property without accepting the trust or a modification of the trust, if within a reasonable time after acting the person delivers a written rejection of the trust or the modification of the trust to the settlor or, if the settlor is dead or incompetent, to a beneficiary. This subdivision does not impose a duty on the person named as trustee to act.

Ca. Prob. Code § 15600
Enacted by Stats. 1990, Ch. 79.

Section 15601 - Rejection of trust

(a) A person named as trustee may in writing reject the trust or a modification of the trust.
(b) If the person named as trustee does not accept the trust or a

modification of the trust by a method provided in subdivision (a) of Section 15600 within a reasonable time after learning of being named as trustee or of the modification, the person has rejected the trust or the modification.

(c) A person named as trustee who rejects the trust or a modification of the trust is not liable with respect to the rejected trust or modification.

Ca. Prob. Code § 15601
Enacted by Stats. 1990, Ch. 79.

Section 15602 - Bond

(a) A trustee is not required to give a bond to secure performance of the trustee's duties, unless any of the following circumstances occurs:

(1) A bond is required by the trust instrument.

(2) Notwithstanding a waiver of a bond in the trust instrument, a bond is found by the court to be necessary to protect the interests of beneficiaries or other persons having an interest in the trust.

(3) An individual who is not named as a trustee in the trust instrument is appointed as a trustee by the court.

(b) Notwithstanding paragraphs (1) and (3) of subdivision (a), the court may excuse a requirement of a bond, reduce or increase the amount of a bond, release a surety, or permit the substitution of another bond with the same or different sureties. The court may not, however, excuse the requirement of a bond for an individual described in paragraph (3) of subdivision (a), except under compelling circumstances. For the purposes of this section, a request by all the adult beneficiaries of a trust that bond be waived for an individual described in paragraph (3) of subdivision (a) for their trust is deemed to constitute a compelling circumstance.

(c) If a bond is required, it shall be filed or served and shall be in the amount and with sureties and liabilities ordered by the court.

(d) Except as otherwise provided in the trust instrument or ordered by the court, the cost of the bond shall be charged against the trust.

(e) A trust company may not be required to give a bond, notwithstanding a contrary provision in the trust instrument.

Ca. Prob. Code § 15602

Amended by Stats 2004 ch 75 (AB 1883), s 1, eff. 1/1/2005.

Section 15603 - Certificate of appointment

On application by the trustee, the court clerk shall issue a certificate that the trustee is a duly appointed and acting trustee under the trust if the court file shows the incumbency of the trustee.

Ca. Prob. Code § 15603

Enacted by Stats. 1990, Ch. 79.

Section 15604 - Appointment of nonprofit charitable corporation as trustee

(a) Notwithstanding any other provision of law, a nonprofit charitable corporation may be appointed as trustee of a trust created pursuant to this division, if all of the following conditions are met:

(1) The corporation is incorporated in this state.

(2) The articles of incorporation specifically authorize the corporation to accept appointments as trustee.

(3) For the three years prior to the filing of a petition under this section, the nonprofit charitable corporation has been exempt from payment of income taxes pursuant to Section 501(c)(3)(c)(3) of the Internal Revenue Code and has served as a private professional conservator in the state.

(4) The settlor or an existing trustee consents to the appointment of the nonprofit corporation as trustee or successor trustee, either in the petition or in a writing signed either before or after the petition is filed.

(5) The court determines the trust to be in the best interest of the settlor.

(6) The court determines that the appointment of the nonprofit corporation as trustee is in the best interest of the settlor and the trust estate.

(b) A petition for appointment of a nonprofit corporation as trustee under this section may be filed by any of the following:

(1) The settlor or the spouse of the settlor.

(2) The nonprofit charitable corporation.

(3) An existing trustee.

(c) The petition shall include in the caption the name of a responsible corporate officer who shall act for the corporation for purposes of this section. If, for any reason, the officer so named ceases to act as the responsible corporate officer for purposes of this section, the corporation shall file with the court a notice containing (1) the name of the successor responsible corporate officer and (2) the date the successor becomes the responsible corporate officer.

(d) The petition shall request that a trustee be appointed for the estate, shall specify the name, address, and telephone number of the proposed trustee and the name, address, and telephone number of the settlor or proposed settlor, and state the reasons why the appointment of the trustee is necessary.

(e) The petition shall set forth, so far as the information is known to the petitioner, the names and addresses of all persons entitled to notice of a conservatorship petition, as specified in subdivision (b) of Section 1821.

(f) Notice of the hearing on the petition shall be given in the same manner as provided in Sections 1822 and 1824.

(g) The trustee appointed by the court pursuant to this section shall do all of the following:

(1) File the required bond for the benefit of the trust estate in the same manner provided for conservators of the estate as set forth in Section 2320. This bond may not be waived, but the court may, in its discretion, permit the filing of a bond in an amount less than would otherwise be required under Section 2320.

(2) Comply with the requirements for registration and filing of annual statements pursuant to Article 4 (commencing with Section 2340) of Chapter 4 of Part 4 of Division 4.

(3) File with the court inventories and appraisals of the trust estate and present its accounts of the trust estate in the manner provided for conservators of the estate set forth in Chapter 7 (commencing with Section 2600) of Part 4 of Division 4.

(4) Be reimbursed for expenses and compensated as trustee in the manner provided for conservators of the estate as described in Chapter 8 (commencing with Section 2640) of Part 4 of Division 4. However, compensation as trustee appointed under this section shall be allowed only for services actually rendered.

(5) Be represented by counsel in all proceedings before the court. Any fee allowed for an attorney for the nonprofit charitable corporation shall be for services actually rendered.
(h) The trustee appointed by the court under this section may be removed by the court, or may resign in accordance with Chapter 9 (commencing with Section 2650) of Part 4 of Division 4. If the nonprofit charitable corporation resigns or is removed by the court, the settlor may appoint another person as successor trustee, or another nonprofit charitable corporation as trustee under this section.
(i) The trustee appointed by the court under this section is bound by the trust instrument created by the settlor, and shall be subject to the duties and responsibilities of a trustee as provided in this code.
Ca. Prob. Code § 15604
Amended by Stats 2001 ch 351 (AB 479), s 2, eff. 1/1/2002.
Added September 16, 1999 (Bill Number SB 1090) (Chapter 424)

Article 2 - COTRUSTEES

Section 15620 - Exercise of power by unanimous action

Unless otherwise provided in the trust instrument, a power vested in two or more trustees may only be exercised by their unanimous action.

Ca. Prob. Code § 15620

Enacted by Stats. 1990, Ch. 79.

Section 15621 - Vacancy in office of cotrustee

Unless otherwise provided in the trust instrument, if a vacancy occurs in the office of a cotrustee, the remaining cotrustee or cotrustees may act for the trust as if they are the only trustees.

Ca. Prob. Code § 15621

Enacted by Stats. 1990, Ch. 79.

Section 15622 - Cotrustee unavailable to perform duties

Unless otherwise provided in the trust instrument, if a cotrustee is unavailable to perform the duties of the cotrustee because of absence, illness, or other temporary incapacity, the remaining cotrustee or cotrustees may act for the trust, as if they are the only trustees, where necessary to accomplish the purposes of the trust or to avoid irreparable injury to the trust property.

Ca. Prob. Code § 15622

Enacted by Stats. 1990, Ch. 79.

Article 3 - RESIGNATION AND REMOVAL OF TRUSTEES

Section 15640 - Methods of resignation

A trustee who has accepted the trust may resign only by one of the following methods:

(a) As provided in the trust instrument.

(b) In the case of a revocable trust, with the consent of the person holding the power to revoke the trust.

(c) In the case of a trust that is not revocable, with the consent of all adult beneficiaries who are receiving or are entitled to receive income under the trust or to receive a distribution of principal if the trust were terminated at the time consent is sought. If a beneficiary has a conservator, the conservator may consent to the trustee's resignation on behalf of the conservatee without obtaining court approval. Without limiting the power of the beneficiary to consent to the trustee's resignation, if the beneficiary has designated an attorney in fact who has the power under the power of attorney to consent to the trustee's resignation, the attorney in fact may consent to the resignation.

(d) Pursuant to a court order obtained on petition by the trustee under Section 17200. The court shall accept the trustee's resignation and may make any orders necessary for the preservation of the trust property, including the appointment of a receiver or a temporary trustee.

Ca. Prob. Code § 15640

Enacted by Stats. 1990, Ch. 79.

Section 15641 - Liability not released or affected

The liability for acts or omissions of a resigning trustee or of the sureties on the trustee's bond, if any, is not released or affected in any manner by the trustee's resignation.

Ca. Prob. Code § 15641

Enacted by Stats. 1990, Ch. 79.

Section 15642 - Removal

(a) A trustee may be removed in accordance with the trust instrument, by the court on its own motion, or on petition of a settlor, cotrustee, or beneficiary under Section 17200.

(b) The grounds for removal of a trustee by the court include the following:

(1) Where the trustee has committed a breach of the trust.

(2) Where the trustee is insolvent or otherwise unfit to administer the trust.

(3) Where hostility or lack of cooperation among cotrustees impairs the administration of the trust.

(4) Where the trustee fails or declines to act.

(5) Where the trustee's compensation is excessive under the circumstances.

(6) Where the sole trustee is a person described in subdivision (a) of Section 21380, whether or not the person is the transferee of a donative transfer by the transferor, unless, based upon any evidence of the intent of the settlor and all other facts and circumstances, which shall be made known to the court, the court finds that it is consistent with the settlor's intent that the trustee continue to serve and that this intent was not the product of fraud or undue influence. Any waiver by the settlor of this provision is against public policy and shall be void. This paragraph shall not apply to instruments that became irrevocable on or before January 1, 1994. This paragraph shall not apply if any of the following conditions are met:

(A) The settlor is related by blood or marriage to, or is a cohabitant with, any one or more of the trustees, the person who drafted or transcribed the instrument, or the person who caused the instrument to be transcribed.

(B) The instrument is reviewed by an independent attorney who (1) counsels the settlor about the nature of their intended trustee designation and (2) signs and delivers to the settlor and the designated trustee a certificate in substantially the following form:

"CERTIFICATE OF INDEPENDENT REVIEW
I, _____ (attorney's name) _____ , have reviewed
_____ (name of instrument) _____ and have counseled my client,
_____ (name of client) _____ , fully and privately on the nature and
legal effect of the designation as trustee of _____ (name of trustee) _____
contained in that instrument. I am so disassociated from the interest of the person named as trustee as to be in a position to

advise my client impartially and confidentially as to the consequences of the designation. On the basis of this counsel, I conclude that the designation of a person who would otherwise be subject to removal under paragraph (6) of subdivision (b) of Section 15642 of the Probate Code is clearly the settlor's intent and that intent is not the product of fraud, menace, duress, or undue influence.

_____ (Name of Attorney) _____ (Date) "

This independent review and certification may occur either before or after the instrument has been executed, and if it occurs after the date of execution, the named trustee shall not be subject to removal under this paragraph. Any attorney whose written engagement signed by the client is expressly limited to the preparation of a certificate under this subdivision, including the prior counseling, shall not be considered to otherwise represent the client.

(C) After full disclosure of the relationships of the persons involved, the instrument is approved pursuant to an order under Article 10 (commencing with Section 2580) of Chapter 6 of Part 4 of Division 4.

(7) If, as determined under Part 17 (commencing with Section 810) of Division 2, the trustee is substantially unable to manage the trust's financial resources or is otherwise substantially unable to execute properly the duties of the office. When the trustee holds the power to revoke the trust, substantial inability to manage the trust's financial resources or otherwise execute properly the duties of the office may not be proved solely by isolated incidents of negligence or improvidence.

(8) If the trustee is substantially unable to resist fraud or undue influence. When the trustee holds the power to revoke the trust, substantial inability to resist fraud or undue influence may not be proved solely by isolated incidents of negligence or improvidence.

(9) For other good cause.

(c) If, pursuant to paragraph (6) of subdivision (b), the court finds that the designation of the trustee was not consistent with the intent of the settlor or was the product of fraud or undue influence, the person being removed as trustee shall bear all costs of the proceeding, including reasonable attorney's fees.

(d) If the court finds that the petition for removal of the trustee was filed in bad faith and that removal would be contrary to the settlor's intent, the court may order that the person or persons seeking the removal of the trustee bear all or any part of the costs of the proceeding, including reasonable attorney's fees.

(e) If it appears to the court that trust property or the interests of a beneficiary may suffer loss or injury pending a decision on a petition for removal of a trustee and any appellate review, the court may, on its own motion or on petition of a cotrustee or beneficiary, compel the trustee whose removal is sought to surrender trust property to a cotrustee or to a receiver or temporary trustee. The court may also suspend the powers of the trustee to the extent the court deems necessary.

(f) For purposes of this section, the term "related by blood or marriage" shall include persons within the seventh degree.

Ca. Prob. Code § 15642

Amended by Stats 2020 ch 36 (AB 3364),s 43, eff. 1/1/2021.
Amended by Stats 2010 ch 620 (SB 105),s 3, eff. 1/1/2011.
Amended by Stats 2006 ch 84 (AB 2042),s 1, eff. 1/1/2007.

Section 15643 - Vacancy

There is a vacancy in the office of trustee in any of the following circumstances:

(a) The person named as trustee rejects the trust.

(b) The person named as trustee cannot be identified or does not exist.

(c) The trustee resigns or is removed.

(d) The trustee dies.

(e) A conservator or guardian of the person or estate of an individual trustee is appointed.

(f) The trustee is the subject of an order for relief in bankruptcy.

(g) A trust company's charter is revoked or powers are suspended, if the revocation or suspension is to be in effect for a period of 30 days or more.

(h) A receiver is appointed for a trust company if the appointment is not vacated within a period of 30 days.

Ca. Prob. Code § 15643

Amended by Stats 2009 ch 500 (AB 1059),s 57, eff. 1/1/2010.

Section 15644 - Delivery of trust property by former trustee to successor

When a vacancy has occurred in the office of trustee, the former trustee who holds property of the trust shall deliver the trust property to the successor trustee or a person appointed by the court to receive the property and remains responsible for the trust property until it is delivered. A trustee who has resigned or is removed has the powers reasonably necessary under the circumstances to preserve the trust property until it is delivered to the successor trustee and to perform actions necessary to complete the resigning or removed trustee's administration of the trust.

Ca. Prob. Code § 15644

Enacted by Stats. 1990, Ch. 79.

Section 15645 - Costs and attorney's fee in proceeding to remove trustee and appoint trust company as successor trustee

If the trustee of a trust that is not revocable has refused to transfer administration of the trust to a successor trust company on request of the beneficiaries described in subdivision (c) of Section 15640 and the court in subsequent proceedings under Section 17200 makes an order removing the existing trustee and appointing a trust company as successor trustee, the court may, in its discretion, award costs and reasonable attorney's fees incurred by the petitioner in the proceeding to be paid by the trustee or from the trust as ordered by the court.

Ca. Prob. Code § 15645

Enacted by Stats. 1990, Ch. 79.

Article 4 - APPOINTMENT OF TRUSTEES

Section 15660 - Appointing trustee to fill vacancy

(a) If the trust has no trustee or if the trust instrument requires a vacancy in the office of a cotrustee to be filled, the vacancy shall be filled as provided in this section.

(b) If the trust instrument provides a practical method of appointing a trustee or names the person to fill the vacancy, the vacancy shall be filled as provided in the trust instrument.

(c) If the vacancy in the office of trustee is not filled as provided in subdivision (b), the vacancy may be filled by a trust company that has agreed to accept the trust on agreement of all adult beneficiaries who are receiving or are entitled to receive income under the trust or to receive a distribution of principal if the trust were terminated at the time the agreement is made. If a beneficiary has a conservator, the conservator may agree to the successor trustee on behalf of the conservatee without obtaining court approval. Without limiting the power of the beneficiary to agree to the successor trustee, if the beneficiary has designated an attorney in fact who has the power under the power of attorney to agree to the successor trustee, the attorney in fact may agree to the successor trustee.

(d) If the vacancy in the office of trustee is not filled as provided in subdivision (b) or (c), on petition of any interested person or any person named as trustee in the trust instrument, the court may, in its discretion, appoint a trustee to fill the vacancy. If the trust provides for more than one trustee, the court may, in its discretion, appoint the original number or any lesser number of trustees. In selecting a trustee, the court shall give consideration to any nomination by the beneficiaries who are 14 years of age or older.

Ca. Prob. Code § 15660
Amended by Stats. 1992, Ch. 871, Sec. 17. Effective January 1, 1993.

Section 15660.5 - Appointment of public guardian or public administrator as trustee

(a) The court may appoint as trustee of a trust the public guardian or public administrator of the county in which the matter is pending subject to the following requirements:

(1) Neither the public guardian nor the public administrator shall be appointed as trustee unless the court finds, after reasonable inquiry, that no other qualified person is willing to act as trustee or the public guardian, public administrator, or his or her representative consents.

(2) The public administrator shall not be appointed as trustee unless either of the following is true:

(A) At the time of the appointment and pursuant to the terms of the trust, the entire trust is then to be distributed outright. For purposes of this paragraph, a trust that is "then to be distributed outright" does not include a trust pursuant to which payments to, or on behalf of, a beneficiary or beneficiaries are to be made from the trust on an ongoing basis for more than six months after the date of distribution.

(B) The public administrator consents.

(3) Neither the public guardian nor the public administrator shall be appointed as a cotrustee unless the public guardian, public administrator, or his or her representative consents.

(4) Neither the public guardian nor the public administrator shall be appointed as general trustee without a hearing and notice to the public guardian or public administrator, or his or her representative, and other interested persons as provided in Section 17203.

(5) Neither the public guardian nor the public administrator shall be appointed as temporary trustee without receiving notice of hearing as provided in Section 1220. The court shall not waive this notice of hearing, but may shorten the time for notice upon a finding of good cause.

(b)

(1) If the public guardian or the public administrator consents to the appointment as trustee under this section, he or she shall submit a written certification of the consent to the court no later than two court days after the noticed hearing date described in paragraph (4) or (5) of subdivision (a). The public administrator shall not be appointed as trustee under subparagraph (A) of paragraph (2) of subdivision (a) if, after receiving notice as required by this section, the public administrator files a written certification with the court that the public administrator is unable to provide the level of services needed to properly fulfill the obligations of a trustee of the trust.

(2) If the public administrator has been appointed as trustee without notice as required in paragraph (4) or (5) of subdivision (a), and the public administrator files a written certification with the court that he or she is unable to provide the level of services needed to properly fulfill the obligations of a trustee of the trust, this shall be good cause for the public administrator to be relieved as trustee.
(c) The order of appointment shall provide for an annual bond fee as described in Section 15688.

Ca. Prob. Code § 15660.5
Added by Stats 2008 ch 237 (AB 2343),s 5, eff. 1/1/2009.
Repealed by Stats 2008 ch 237 (AB 2343),s 4, eff. 1/1/2009.

Article 5 - COMPENSATION AND INDEMNIFICATION OF TRUSTEES

Section 15680 - Compensation in accordance to trust instrument; allowing greater or lesser compensation

(a) Subject to subdivision (b), and except as provided in Section 15688, if the trust instrument provides for the trustee's compensation, the trustee is entitled to be compensated in accordance with the trust instrument.
(b) Upon proper showing, the court may fix or allow greater or lesser compensation than could be allowed under the terms of the trust in any of the following circumstances:

(1) Where the duties of the trustee are substantially different from those contemplated when the trust was created.

(2) Where the compensation in accordance with the terms of the trust would be inequitable or unreasonably low or high.

(3) In extraordinary circumstances calling for equitable relief.
(c) An order fixing or allowing greater or lesser compensation under subdivision (b) applies only prospectively to actions taken in administration of the trust after the order is made.
   Ca. Prob. Code § 15680
Amended by Stats 2008 ch 237 (AB 2343),s 6, eff. 1/1/2009.

Section 15681 - Compensation not specified in trust instrument

If the trust instrument does not specify the trustee's compensation, the trustee is entitled to reasonable compensation under the circumstances.
   Ca. Prob. Code § 15681
Enacted by Stats. 1990, Ch. 79.

Section 15682 - Fixing amount of periodic compensation

The court may fix an amount of periodic compensation under Sections 15680 and 15681 to continue for as long as the court determines is proper.
   Ca. Prob. Code § 15682
Enacted by Stats. 1990, Ch. 79.

Section 15683 - Apportionment among cotrustees

Unless the trust instrument otherwise provides or the trustees otherwise agree, if the trust has two or more trustees, the compensation shall be apportioned among the cotrustees according to the services rendered by them.
   Ca. Prob. Code § 15683
Enacted by Stats. 1990, Ch. 79.

Section 15684 - Repayment out of trust property

A trustee is entitled to the repayment out of the trust property for the following:

(a) Expenditures that were properly incurred in the administration of the trust.

(b) To the extent that they benefited the trust, expenditures that were not properly incurred in the administration of the trust.

Ca. Prob. Code § 15684

Enacted by Stats. 1990, Ch. 79.

Section 15685 - Trustee's equitable lien

The trustee has an equitable lien on the trust property as against the beneficiary in the amount of advances, with any interest, made for the protection of the trust, and for expenses, losses, and liabilities sustained in the administration of the trust or because of ownership or control of any trust property.

Ca. Prob. Code § 15685

Enacted by Stats. 1990, Ch. 79.

Section 15686 - Increased trustee's fee

(a) As used in this section, "trustee's fee" includes, but is not limited to, the trustee's periodic base fee, rate of percentage compensation, minimum fee, hourly rate, and transaction charge, but does not include fees for extraordinary services.

(b) A trustee shall not charge an increased trustee's fee for administration of a particular trust unless the trustee first gives at least 60 days' written notice of that increased fee to all of the following persons:

(1) Each beneficiary who is entitled to an account under Section 16062.

(2) Each beneficiary who was given the last preceding account.

(3) Each beneficiary who has made a written request to the trustee for notice of an increased trustee's fee and has given an address for receiving notice.

(c) If a beneficiary files a petition under Section 17200 for review of the increased trustee's fee or for removal of the trustee and serves a copy of the petition on the trustee before the expiration of the 60-day period, the increased trustee's fee does not take effect as to that trust until otherwise ordered by the court or the petition is dismissed.

Ca. Prob. Code § 15686
Amended by Stats 2017 ch 319 (AB 976),s 86, eff. 1/1/2018.

Section 15687 - Compensation for legal services

(a) Notwithstanding any provision of a trust to the contrary, a trustee who is an attorney may receive only (1) the trustee's compensation provided in the trust or otherwise provided in this article or (2) compensation for legal services performed for the trustee, unless the trustee obtains approval for the right to dual compensation as provided in subdivision (d).

(b) No parent, child, sibling, or spouse of a person who is a trustee, and no law partnership or corporation whose partner, shareholder, or employee is serving as a trustee shall receive any compensation for legal services performed for the trustee unless the trustee waives trustee compensation or unless the trustee obtains approval for the right to dual compensation as provided in subdivision (d).

(c) This section shall not apply if the trustee is related by blood or marriage to, or is a cohabitant with, the settlor.

(d) After full disclosure of the nature of the compensation and relationship of the trustee to all persons receiving compensation under this section, the trustee may obtain approval for dual compensation by either of the following:

(1) An order pursuant to paragraph (21) of subdivision (b) of Section 17200.

(2) Giving 30 days' advance written notice to the persons entitled to notice under Section 17203. Within that 30-day period, any person entitled to notice may object to the proposed action by written notice to the trustee or by filing a petition pursuant to paragraph (21) of subdivision (b) of Section 17200. If the trustee receives this objection during that 30-day period and if the trustee wishes dual compensation, the trustee shall file a petition for approval pursuant to paragraph (21) of subdivision (b) of Section 17200.

(e) Any waiver of the requirements of this section is against public policy and shall be void.

(f) This section applies to services rendered on or after January 1, 1994.

Ca. Prob. Code § 15687

Amended by Stats. 1995, Ch. 730, Sec. 10. Effective January 1, 1996.

Section 15688 - Payment of public guardian or public administrator appointed as trustee

Notwithstanding any other provision of this article and the terms of the trust, a public guardian or public administrator who is appointed as a trustee of a trust pursuant to Section 15660.5 shall be paid from the trust property for all of the following:

(a) Reasonable expenses incurred in the administration of the trust.

(b) Compensation for services of the public guardian or public administrator and the attorney of the public guardian or public administrator, as follows:

(1) If the public guardian or public administrator is appointed as trustee of a trust that provides for the outright distribution of the entire trust estate, compensation for the public guardian or public administrator, and any attorney for the public guardian or public administrator, shall be calculated as that provided to a personal representative and attorney pursuant to Part 7 (commencing with Section 10800) of Division 7, based on the fair market value of the assets as of the date of the appointment, provided that the minimum amount of compensation for the public guardian or the public administrator shall be one thousand dollars ($1,000). Additionally, the minimum amount of compensation for the attorney for the public guardian or the public administrator, if any, shall be one thousand dollars ($1,000).

(2) For a trust other than that described in paragraph (1), the public guardian or public administrator shall be compensated as provided in Section 15680. Compensation shall be consistent with compensation allowed for professional fiduciaries or corporate fiduciaries providing comparable services.

(3) Except as provided in paragraph (1), reasonable compensation for the attorney for the public guardian or public administrator.

(c) An annual bond fee in the amount of twenty-five dollars ($25) plus one-fourth of 1 percent of the amount of the trust assets greater than ten thousand dollars ($10,000). The amount charged shall be deposited in the county treasury.

Ca. Prob. Code § 15688

Amended by Stats 2008 ch 237 (AB 2343),s 7, eff. 1/1/2009.
Amended by Stats 2002 ch 784 (SB 1316), s 581, eff. 1/1/2003.

Chapter 2 - BENEFICIARIES

Section 15800 - Rights afforded beneficiaries in person holding power to revoke

(a) Except to the extent that the trust instrument otherwise provides or where the joint action of the settlor and all beneficiaries is required, during the time that a trust is revocable and at least one person holding the power to revoke the trust, in whole or in part, is competent, the following shall apply:

(1) The person holding the power to revoke, and not the beneficiary, has the rights afforded beneficiaries under this division.

(2) The duties of the trustee are owed to the person holding the power to revoke.

(b) Except to the extent that the trust instrument otherwise provides or where the joint action of the settlor and all beneficiaries is required, if, during the time that a trust is revocable, no person holding the power to revoke the trust, in whole or in part, is competent, the following shall apply:

(1) Within 60 days of receiving information establishing the incompetency of the last person holding the power to revoke the trust, the trustee shall provide notice of the application of this subdivision and a true and complete copy of the trust instrument and any amendments to each beneficiary to whom the trustee would be required or authorized to distribute income or principal if the settlor had died as of the date of receipt of the information. If the trust has been completely restated, the trustee need not include the trust instrument or amendments superseded by the last restatement.

(2) The duties of the trustee to account at least annually or provide information requested under Section 16061 shall be owed to each beneficiary to whom the trustee would be required or authorized to distribute income or principal if the settlor had died during the account period or the period relating to the administration of the trust relevant to the report, as applicable.

(3)A beneficiary whose interest is conditional on some factor not yet in existence or not yet determinable shall not be considered a beneficiary for purposes of this section, unless the trustee, in the trustee's discretion, believes it is likely that the condition or conditions will be satisfied at the time of the settlor's death.

(4) If the interest of a beneficiary fails because a condition to receiving that interest has not been satisfied or the trustee does not believe that the condition will be satisfied at the time of the settlor's death, the duties in paragraphs (1) and (2) shall be owed to the beneficiary or beneficiaries who would next succeed to that interest at the relevant time or period as determined under the trust instrument, as amended and restated.
(c) Incompetency, for the purposes of subdivision (b), may be established by either of the following:

(1) The method for determining incompetency specified by the trust instrument, as amended or restated.

(2)A judicial determination of incompetency.
Ca. Prob. Code § 15800
Amended by Stats 2022 ch 420 (AB 2960),s 42, eff. 1/1/2023.
Amended by Stats 2021 ch 749 (AB 1079),s 1, eff. 1/1/2022.
Enacted by Stats. 1990, Ch. 79.
See Stats 2021 ch 749 (AB 1079), s 3.

Section 15801 - Power to consent in person holding power to revoke

(a) In any case where the consent of a beneficiary may be given or is required to be given before an action may be taken, during the time that a trust is revocable and the person holding the power to revoke the trust is competent, the person holding the power to revoke, and not the beneficiary, has the power to consent or withhold consent.
(b) This section does not apply where the joint consent of the settlor and all beneficiaries is required by statute.
Ca. Prob. Code § 15801
Enacted by Stats. 1990, Ch. 79.

Section 15802 - Notice given person holding power to revoke

Notwithstanding any other statute, during the time that a trust is revocable and the person holding the power to revoke the trust is competent, a notice that is to be given to a beneficiary shall be given to the person holding the power to revoke and not to the beneficiary.
Ca. Prob. Code § 15802
Enacted by Stats. 1990, Ch. 79.

Section 15803 - Rights of holder of presently exercisable power of appointment or power to withdraw property

The holder of a presently exercisable general power of appointment or power to withdraw property from the trust has the rights of a person holding the power to revoke the trust that are provided by Sections 15800 to 15802, inclusive, to the extent of the holder's power over the trust property.

Ca. Prob. Code § 15803
Enacted by Stats. 1990, Ch. 79.

Section 15804 - Notice to beneficiary or person interested in trust

(a) Subject to subdivisions (b) and (c), it is sufficient compliance with a requirement in this division that notice be given to a beneficiary, or to a person interested in the trust, if notice is given as follows:

(1) Where an interest has been limited on any future contingency to persons who will compose a certain class upon the happening of a certain event without further limitation, notice shall be given to the persons in being who would constitute the class if the event had happened immediately before the commencement of the proceeding or if there is no proceeding, if the event had happened immediately before notice is given.

(2) Where an interest has been limited to a living person and the same interest, or a share therein, has been further limited upon the happening of a future event to the surviving spouse or to persons who are or may be the distributees, heirs, issue, or other kindred of the living person, notice shall be given to the living person.

(3) Where an interest has been limited upon the happening of any future event to a person, or a class of persons, or both, and the interest, or a share of the interest, has been further limited upon the happening of an additional future event to another person, or a class of persons, or both, notice shall be given to the person or persons in being who would take the interest upon the happening of the first of these events.
(b) If a conflict of interest involving the subject matter of the trust

proceeding exists between a person to whom notice is required to be given and a person to whom notice is not otherwise required to be given under subdivision (a), notice shall also be given to persons not otherwise entitled to notice under subdivision (a) with respect to whom the conflict of interest exists.

(c) Nothing in this section affects any of the following:

(1) Requirements for notice to a person who has requested special notice, a person who has filed notice of appearance, or a particular person or entity required by statute to be given notice.

(2) Availability of a guardian ad litem pursuant to Section 1003.

(d) As used in this section, "notice" includes other papers.

Ca. Prob. Code § 15804

Amended by Stats. 1992, Ch. 178, Sec. 43.4. Effective January 1, 1993.

Section 15805 - Attorney General subject to limitations on beneficiaries' rights

Notwithstanding any other provision of law, the Attorney General is subject to the limitations on the rights of beneficiaries of revocable trusts provided by Sections 15800 to 15802, inclusive.

Ca. Prob. Code § 15805

Enacted by Stats. 1990, Ch. 79.

Part 4 - TRUST ADMINISTRATION

Chapter 1 - DUTIES OF TRUSTEES

Article 1 - TRUSTEE'S DUTIES IN GENERAL

Section 16000 - Duty to administer trust

On acceptance of the trust, the trustee has a duty to administer the trust according to the trust instrument and, except to the extent the trust instrument provides otherwise, according to this division.

Ca. Prob. Code § 16000

Enacted by Stats. 1990, Ch. 79.

Section 16001 - Duty to follow written direction

(a) Except as provided in subdivision (b), the trustee of a revocable trust shall follow any written direction acceptable to the trustee given from time to time (1) by the person then having the power to revoke the trust or the part thereof with respect to which the direction is given or (2) by the person to whom the settlor delegates the right to direct the trustee.

(b) If a written direction given under subdivision (a) would have the effect of modifying the trust, the trustee has no duty to follow the direction unless it complies with the requirements for modifying the trust.

Ca. Prob. Code § 16001
Enacted by Stats. 1990, Ch. 79.

Section 16002 - Duty to administer solely in interest of beneficiaries

(a) The trustee has a duty to administer the trust solely in the interest of the beneficiaries.

(b) It is not a violation of the duty provided in subdivision (a) for a trustee who administers two trusts to sell, exchange, or participate in the sale or exchange of trust property between the trusts, if both of the following requirements are met:

(1) The sale or exchange is fair and reasonable with respect to the beneficiaries of both trusts.

(2) The trustee gives to the beneficiaries of both trusts notice of all material facts related to the sale or exchange that the trustee knows or should know.

Ca. Prob. Code § 16002
Enacted by Stats. 1990, Ch. 79.

Section 16003 - Duty to deal impartially with beneficiaries

If a trust has two or more beneficiaries, the trustee has a duty to deal impartially with them and shall act impartially in investing and managing the trust property, taking into account any differing interests of the beneficiaries.

Ca. Prob. Code § 16003

Amended by Stats. 1995, Ch. 63, Sec. 1. Effective January 1, 1996.

Section 16004 - Duty to not use or deal with property for trustee's own interest or other purpose

(a) The trustee has a duty not to use or deal with trust property for the trustee's own profit or for any other purpose unconnected with the trust, nor to take part in any transaction in which the trustee has an interest adverse to the beneficiary.

(b) The trustee may not enforce any claim against the trust property that the trustee purchased after or in contemplation of appointment as trustee, but the court may allow the trustee to be reimbursed from trust property the amount that the trustee paid in good faith for the claim.

(c) A transaction between the trustee and a beneficiary which occurs during the existence of the trust or while the trustee's influence with the beneficiary remains and by which the trustee obtains an advantage from the beneficiary is presumed to be a violation of the trustee's fiduciary duties. This presumption is a presumption affecting the burden of proof. This subdivision does not apply to the provisions of an agreement between a trustee and a beneficiary relating to the hiring or compensation of the trustee.

Ca. Prob. Code § 16004

Enacted by Stats. 1990, Ch. 79.

Section 16004.5 - Requiring beneficiary to relieve trustee of liability as condition of making distribution or payment

(a) A trustee may not require a beneficiary to relieve the trustee of liability as a condition for making a distribution or payment to, or for the benefit of, the beneficiary, if the distribution or payment is required by the trust instrument.

(b) This section may not be construed as affecting the trustee's right to:

(1) Maintain a reserve for reasonably anticipated expenses, including, but not limited to, taxes, debts, trustee and accounting fees, and costs and expenses of administration.

(2) Seek a voluntary release or discharge of a trustee's liability from the beneficiary.

(3) Require indemnification against a claim by a person or entity, other than a beneficiary referred to in subdivision (a), which may reasonably arise as a result of the distribution.

(4) Withhold any portion of an otherwise required distribution that is reasonably in dispute.

(5) Seek court or beneficiary approval of an accounting of trust activities.

Ca. Prob. Code § 16004.5
Added by Stats 2003 ch 585 (AB 1705), s 1, eff. 1/1/2004.

Section 16005 - Duty to not to become trustee of trust adverse to beneficiary of first trust

The trustee of one trust has a duty not to knowingly become a trustee of another trust adverse in its nature to the interest of the beneficiary of the first trust, and a duty to eliminate the conflict or resign as trustee when the conflict is discovered.

Ca. Prob. Code § 16005
Enacted by Stats. 1990, Ch. 79.

Section 16006 - Duty to take steps to take and keep control of and to preserve trust

The trustee has a duty to take reasonable steps under the circumstances to take and keep control of and to preserve the trust property.

Ca. Prob. Code § 16006
Enacted by Stats. 1990, Ch. 79.

Section 16007 - Duty to make property productive

The trustee has a duty to make the trust property productive under the circumstances and in furtherance of the purposes of the trust.
Ca. Prob. Code § 16007
Enacted by Stats. 1990, Ch. 79.

Section 16009 - Duty to keep property separate and designated as trust property

The trustee has a duty to do the following:
(a) To keep the trust property separate from other property not subject to the trust.
(b) To see that the trust property is designated as property of the trust.
Ca. Prob. Code § 16009
Enacted by Stats. 1990, Ch. 79.

Section 16010 - Duty to enforce claims

The trustee has a duty to take reasonable steps to enforce claims that are part of the trust property.
Ca. Prob. Code § 16010
Enacted by Stats. 1990, Ch. 79.

Section 16011 - Duty to defend actions

The trustee has a duty to take reasonable steps to defend actions that may result in a loss to the trust.
Ca. Prob. Code § 16011
Enacted by Stats. 1990, Ch. 79.

Section 16012 - Delegation of duties

(a) The trustee has a duty not to delegate to others the performance of acts that the trustee can reasonably be required personally to perform and may not transfer the office of trustee to another person nor delegate the entire administration of the trust to a cotrustee or other person.

(b) In a case where a trustee has properly delegated a matter to an agent, cotrustee, or other person, the trustee has a duty to exercise general supervision over the person performing the delegated matter.

(c) This section does not apply to investment and management functions under Section 16052.

Ca. Prob. Code § 16012

Amended by Stats. 1995, Ch. 63, Sec. 3. Effective January 1, 1996.

Section 16013 - Cotrustee's duties

If a trust has more than one trustee, each trustee has a duty to do the following:

(a) To participate in the administration of the trust.

(b) To take reasonable steps to prevent a cotrustee from committing a breach of trust or to compel a cotrustee to redress a breach of trust.

Ca. Prob. Code § 16013

Enacted by Stats. 1990, Ch. 79.

Section 16014 - Duty to apply full extent of skills; special skills

(a) The trustee has a duty to apply the full extent of the trustee's skills.

(b) If the settlor, in selecting the trustee, has relied on the trustee's representation of having special skills, the trustee is held to the standard of the skills represented.

Ca. Prob. Code § 16014

Enacted by Stats. 1990, Ch. 79.

Section 16015 - Provision of services for compensation by regulated financial institution

The provision of services for compensation by a regulated financial institution or its affiliates in the ordinary course of business either to a trust of which it also acts as trustee or to a person dealing with the trust is not a violation of the duty provided in Section 16002 or 16004. For the purposes of this section, "affiliate" means a corporation that directly or indirectly through one or more intermediaries controls, is controlled by, or is under common control with another domestic or foreign corporation.

Ca. Prob. Code § 16015
Enacted by Stats. 1990, Ch. 79.

Article 2 - TRUSTEE'S STANDARD OF CARE

Section 16040 - Reasonable care, skill and caution; standard expanded or restricted by settlor

(a) The trustee shall administer the trust with reasonable care, skill, and caution under the circumstances then prevailing that a prudent person acting in a like capacity would use in the conduct of an enterprise of like character and with like aims to accomplish the purposes of the trust as determined from the trust instrument.
(b) The settlor may expand or restrict the standard provided in subdivision (a) by express provisions in the trust instrument. A trustee is not liable to a beneficiary for the trustee's good faith reliance on these express provisions.
(c) This section does not apply to investment and management functions governed by the Uniform Prudent Investor Act, Article 2.5 (commencing with Section 16045).

Ca. Prob. Code § 16040
Amended by Stats. 1995, Ch. 63, Sec. 4. Effective January 1, 1996.

Section 16041 - Standard of care not affected by receipt of compensation

A trustee's standard of care and performance in administering the trust is not affected by whether or not the trustee receives any compensation.

Ca. Prob. Code § 16041
Enacted by Stats. 1990, Ch. 79.

Section 16042 - Deposit or investment of trust funds

coming into custody of public guardian

(a) Notwithstanding the requirements of this article, Article 2.5 (commencing with Section 16045), and the terms of the trust, all trust funds that come within the custody of the public guardian who is appointed as trustee of the trust pursuant to Section 15660.5 may be deposited or invested in the same manner, and would be subject to the same terms and conditions, as a deposit or investment by the public administrator of funds in the estate of a decedent pursuant to Article 3 (commencing with Section 7640) of Chapter 4 of Part 1 of Division 7.

(b) Upon the deposit or investment of trust property pursuant to subdivision (a), the public guardian shall be deemed to have met the standard of care specified in this article and Article 2.5 (commencing with Section 16045) with respect to this trust property.

Ca. Prob. Code § 16042
Added by Stats. 1997, Ch. 93, Sec. 4. Effective January 1, 1998.

Article 2.5 - UNIFORM PRUDENT INVESTOR ACT

Section 16045 - Act constitutes prudent investment rule, citation

This article, together with subdivision (a) of Section 16002 and Section 16003, constitutes the prudent investor rule and may be cited as the Uniform Prudent Investor Act.

Ca. Prob. Code § 16045
Added by Stats. 1995, Ch. 63, Sec. 6. Effective January 1, 1996.

Section 16046 - Duty to comply with rule; expansion or restriction by settlor

(a) Except as provided in subdivision (b), a trustee who invests and manages trust assets owes a duty to the beneficiaries of the trust to comply with the prudent investor rule.

(b) The settlor may expand or restrict the prudent investor rule by express provisions in the trust instrument. A trustee is not liable to a beneficiary for the trustee's good faith reliance on these express provisions.

Ca. Prob. Code § 16046

Added by Stats. 1995, Ch. 63, Sec. 6. Effective January 1, 1996.

Section 16047 - Circumstances considered in investing and managing trust assets

(a) A trustee shall invest and manage trust assets as a prudent investor would, by considering the purposes, terms, distribution requirements, and other circumstances of the trust. In satisfying this standard, the trustee shall exercise reasonable care, skill, and caution.

(b) A trustee's investment and management decisions respecting individual assets and courses of action must be evaluated not in isolation, but in the context of the trust portfolio as a whole and as a part of an overall investment strategy having risk and return objectives reasonably suited to the trust.

(c) Among circumstances that are appropriate to consider in investing and managing trust assets are the following, to the extent relevant to the trust or its beneficiaries:

(1) General economic conditions.

(2) The possible effect of inflation or deflation.

(3) The expected tax consequences of investment decisions or strategies.

(4) The role that each investment or course of action plays within the overall trust portfolio.

(5) The expected total return from income and the appreciation of capital.

(6) Other resources of the beneficiaries known to the trustee as determined from information provided by the beneficiaries.

(7) Needs for liquidity, regularity of income, and preservation or appreciation of capital.

(8) An asset's special relationship or special value, if any, to the purposes of the trust or to one or more of the beneficiaries.
(d) A trustee shall make a reasonable effort to ascertain facts relevant to the investment and management of trust assets.
(e) A trustee may invest in any kind of property or type of investment or engage in any course of action or investment strategy consistent with the standards of this chapter.
  Ca. Prob. Code § 16047
Added by Stats. 1995, Ch. 63, Sec. 6. Effective January 1, 1996.

Section 16048 - Duty to diversity investments

In making and implementing investment decisions, the trustee has a duty to diversify the investments of the trust unless, under the circumstances, it is prudent not to do so.
  Ca. Prob. Code § 16048
Added by Stats. 1995, Ch. 63, Sec. 6. Effective January 1, 1996.

Section 16049 - Decisions concerning retention and disposition of trust assets

Within a reasonable time after accepting a trusteeship or receiving trust assets, a trustee shall review the trust assets and make and implement decisions concerning the retention and disposition of assets, in order to bring the trust portfolio into compliance with the purposes, terms, distribution requirements, and other circumstances of the trust, and with the requirements of this chapter.
  Ca. Prob. Code § 16049
Added by Stats. 1995, Ch. 63, Sec. 6. Effective January 1, 1996.

Section 16050 - Reasonable and appropriate costs

In investing and managing trust assets, a trustee may only incur costs that are appropriate and reasonable in relation to the assets, overall investment strategy, purposes, and other circumstances of the trust.

Ca. Prob. Code § 16050
Added by Stats. 1995, Ch. 63, Sec. 6. Effective January 1, 1996.

Section 16051 - Determination of compliance with rule

Compliance with the prudent investor rule is determined in light of the facts and circumstances existing at the time of a trustee's decision or action and not by hindsight.

Ca. Prob. Code § 16051
Added by Stats. 1995, Ch. 63, Sec. 6. Effective January 1, 1996.

Section 16052 - Delegation of functions

(a) A trustee may delegate investment and management functions as prudent under the circumstances. The trustee shall exercise prudence in the following:

(1) Selecting an agent.

(2) Establishing the scope and terms of the delegation, consistent with the purposes and terms of the trust.

(3) Periodically reviewing the agent's overall performance and compliance with the terms of the delegation.
(b) In performing a delegated function, an agent has a duty to exercise reasonable care to comply with the terms of the delegation.
(c) Except as otherwise provided in Section 16401, a trustee who complies with the requirements of subdivision (a) is not liable to the beneficiaries or to the trust for the decisions or actions of the agent to whom the function was delegated.
(d) By accepting the delegation of a trust function from the trustee of a trust that is subject to the law of this state, an agent submits to the jurisdiction of the courts of this state.

Ca. Prob. Code § 16052
Added by Stats. 1995, Ch. 63, Sec. 6. Effective January 1, 1996.

Section 16053 - Terms authorizing permitted investment

or strategy

The following terms or comparable language in the provisions of a trust, unless otherwise limited or modified, authorizes any investment or strategy permitted under this chapter: "investments permissible by law for investment of trust funds," "legal investments," "authorized investments," "using the judgment and care under the circumstances then prevailing that persons of prudence, discretion, and intelligence exercise in the management of their own affairs, not in regard to speculation but in regard to the permanent disposition of their funds, considering the probable income as well as the probable safety of their capital," "prudent man rule," "prudent trustee rule," "prudent person rule," and "prudent investor rule."

Ca. Prob. Code § 16053
Added by Stats. 1995, Ch. 63, Sec. 6. Effective January 1, 1996.

Section 16054 - Applicability to trusts existing on or after effective date

This article applies to trusts existing on and created after its effective date. As applied to trusts existing on its effective date, this article governs only decisions or actions occurring after that date.

Ca. Prob. Code § 16054
Added by Stats. 1995, Ch. 63, Sec. 6. Effective January 1, 1996.

Article 3 - TRUSTEE'S DUTY TO REPORT INFORMATION AND ACCOUNT TO BENEFICIARIES

Section 16060 - Duty to keep beneficiaries reasonably informed

The trustee has a duty to keep the beneficiaries of the trust reasonably informed of the trust and its administration.

Ca. Prob. Code § 16060
Enacted by Stats. 1990, Ch. 79.

Section 16060.5 - Terms of the trust defined

As used in this article, "terms of the trust" means the written trust instrument of an irrevocable trust or those provisions of a written trust instrument in effect at the settlor's death that describe or affect that portion of a trust that has become irrevocable at the death of the settlor. In addition, "terms of the trust" includes, but is not limited to, signatures, amendments, disclaimers, and any directions or instructions to the trustee that affect the disposition of the trust. "Terms of the trust" does not include documents which were intended to affect disposition only while the trust was revocable. If a trust has been completely restated, "terms of the trust" does not include trust instruments or amendments which are superseded by the last restatement before the settlor's death, but it does include amendments executed after the restatement. "Terms of the trust" also includes any document irrevocably exercising a power of appointment over the trust or over any portion of the trust which has become irrevocable.

Ca. Prob. Code § 16060.5

Amended by Stats 2000 ch 34 (AB 460), s 2, eff. 1/1/2001.

Section 16060.7 - Providing terms of trust to beneficiary

On the request of a beneficiary, the trustee shall provide the terms of the trust to the beneficiary unless the trustee is not required to provide the terms of the trust to the beneficiary in accordance with Section 16069.

Ca. Prob. Code § 16060.7

Added by Stats 2010 ch 621 (SB 202),s 2, eff. 1/1/2011.

Section 16061 - Providing requested information to beneficiary relating administration

Except as provided in Section 16069, on reasonable request by a beneficiary, the trustee shall report to the beneficiary by providing requested information to the beneficiary relating to the administration of the trust relevant to the beneficiary's interest.

Ca. Prob. Code § 16061

Amended by Stats 2010 ch 621 (SB 202),s 3, eff. 1/1/2011.

Section 16061.5 - Beneficiaries provided copy of terms of irrevocable trust

(a) A trustee shall provide a true and complete copy of the terms of the irrevocable trust, or irrevocable portion of the trust, to each of the following:

(1) Any beneficiary of the trust who requests it, and to any heir of a deceased settlor who requests it, when a revocable trust or any portion of a revocable trust becomes irrevocable because of the death of one or more of the settlors of the trust, when a power of appointment is effective or lapses upon the death of a settlor under the circumstances described in paragraph (3) of subdivision (a) of Section 16061.7, or because, by the express terms of the trust, the trust becomes irrevocable within one year of the death of a settlor because of a contingency related to the death of one or more of the settlors of the trust.

(2) Any beneficiary of the trust who requests it, whenever there is a change of trustee of an irrevocable trust.

(3) If the trust is a charitable trust subject to the supervision of the Attorney General, to the Attorney General, if requested, when a revocable trust or any portion of a revocable trust becomes irrevocable because of the death of one or more of the settlors of the trust, when a power of appointment is effective or lapses upon the death of a settlor under the circumstances described in paragraph (3) of subdivision (a) of Section 16061.7, or because, by the express terms of the trust, the trust becomes irrevocable within one year of the death of a settlor because of a contingency related to the death of one or more of the settlors of the trust, and whenever there is a change of trustee of an irrevocable trust.

(b) The trustee shall, for purposes of this section, rely upon any final judicial determination of heirship. However, the trustee shall have discretion to make a good faith determination by any reasonable means of the heirs of a deceased settlor in the absence of a final judicial determination of heirship known to the trustee.

Ca. Prob. Code § 16061.5
Amended by Stats 2010 ch 621 (SB 202),s 4, eff. 1/1/2011.
Amended by Stats 2000 ch 34 (AB 460), s 3, eff. 1/1/2001.

Section 16061.7 - Events requiring trustee to serve notice

(a) A trustee shall serve a notification by the trustee as described in this section in the following events:

(1) When a revocable trust or any portion thereof becomes irrevocable because of the death of one or more of the settlors of the trust, or because, by the express terms of the trust, the trust becomes irrevocable within one year of the death of a settlor because of a contingency related to the death of one or more of the settlors of the trust.

(2) Whenever there is a change of trustee of an irrevocable trust.

(3) Whenever a power of appointment retained by a settlor is effective or lapses upon death of the settlor with respect to an inter vivos trust which was, or was purported to be, irrevocable upon its creation. This paragraph shall not apply to a charitable remainder trust. For purposes of this paragraph, "charitable remainder trust" means a charitable remainder annuity trust or charitable remainder unitrust as defined in Section 664(d)(d) of the Internal Revenue Code.

(4) The duty to serve the notification by the trustee pursuant to this subdivision is the duty of the continuing or successor trustee, and any one cotrustee may serve the notification.
(b) The notification by the trustee required by subdivision (a) shall be served on each of the following:

(1) Each beneficiary of the irrevocable trust or irrevocable portion of the trust, subject to the limitations of Section 15804.

(2) Each heir of the deceased settlor, if the event that requires notification is the death of a settlor or irrevocability within one year of the death of the settlor of the trust by the express terms of the trust because of a contingency related to the death of a settlor.

(3) If the trust is a charitable trust subject to the supervision of the Attorney General, to the Attorney General.

(c) A trustee shall, for purposes of this section, rely upon any final judicial determination of heirship, known to the trustee, but the trustee shall have discretion to make a good faith determination by any reasonable means of the heirs of a deceased settlor in the absence of a final judicial determination of heirship known to the trustee.

(d) The trustee need not provide a copy of the notification by trustee to any beneficiary or heir (1) known to the trustee but who cannot be located by the trustee after reasonable diligence or (2) unknown to the trustee.

(e) The notification by trustee shall be served by any of the methods described in Section 1215 to the last known address.

(f) The notification by trustee shall be served not later than 60 days following the occurrence of the event requiring service of the notification by trustee, or 60 days after the trustee became aware of the existence of a person entitled to receive notification by trustee, if that person was not known to the trustee on the occurrence of the event requiring service of the notification. If there is a vacancy in the office of the trustee on the date of the occurrence of the event requiring service of the notification by trustee, or if that event causes a vacancy, then the 60-day period for service of the notification by trustee commences on the date the new trustee commences to serve as trustee.

(g) The notification by trustee shall contain the following information:

(1) The identity of the settlor or settlors of the trust and the date of execution of the trust instrument.

(2) The name, address, and telephone number of each trustee of the trust.

(3) The address of the physical location where the principal place of administration of the trust is located, pursuant to Section 17002.

(4) Any additional information that may be expressly required by the terms of the trust instrument.

(5) A notification that the recipient is entitled, upon reasonable request to the trustee, to receive from the trustee a true and complete copy of the terms of the trust.

(h) If the notification by the trustee is served because a revocable trust or any portion of it has become irrevocable because of the death of one or more settlors of the trust, or because, by the express terms of the trust, the trust becomes irrevocable within one year of the death of a settlor because of a contingency related to the death of one or more of the settlors of the trust, the notification by the trustee shall also include a warning, set out in a separate paragraph in not less than 10-point boldface type, or a reasonable equivalent thereof, that states as follows: "You may not bring an action to contest the trust more than 120 days from the date this notification by the trustee is served upon you or 60 days from the date on which a copy of the terms of the trust is delivered to you during that 120-day period, whichever is later."

(i) Any waiver by a settlor of the requirement of serving the notification by trustee required by this section is against public policy and shall be void.

(j) A trustee may serve a notification by trustee in the form required by this section on any person in addition to those on whom the notification by trustee is required to be served. A trustee is not liable to any person for serving or for not serving the notice on any person in addition to those on whom the notice is required to be served. A trustee is not required to serve a notification by trustee if the event that otherwise requires service of the notification by trustee occurs before January 1, 1998.

Ca. Prob. Code § 16061.7

Amended by Stats 2017 ch 319 (AB 976),s 87, eff. 1/1/2018.
Amended by Stats 2010 ch 621 (SB 202),s 5, eff. 1/1/2011.
Amended by Stats 2000 ch 592 (AB 1628), s 1, eff. 1/1/2001.

This section was also amended by Stats 2000 ch 34 (AB 460), s 4, but was superseded. See Ca. Gov. Code § 9605.

Section 16061.8 - Limitation of action to contest trust after notice serve

A person upon whom the notification by the trustee is served pursuant to paragraph (1) of subdivision (a) of Section 16061.7, whether the notice is served on the person within or after the time period set forth in subdivision (f) of Section 16061.7, shall not bring an action to contest the trust more than 120 days from the date the notification by the trustee is served upon the person, or 60 days from the date on which a copy of the terms of the trust is delivered pursuant to Section 1215 to the person during that 120-day period, whichever is later.

Ca. Prob. Code § 16061.8
Amended by Stats 2022 ch 30 (AB 1745),s 1, eff. 1/1/2023.
Amended by Stats 2017 ch 319 (AB 976),s 88, eff. 1/1/2018.
Amended by Stats 2010 ch 621 (SB 202),s 6, eff. 1/1/2011.
Amended by Stats 2000 ch 592 (AB 1628), s 2, eff. 1/1/2001.
This section was also amended by Stats 2000 ch 34 (AB 460), s 5, but was superseded. See Ca. Gov. Code § 9605.

Section 16061.9 - Liability of trustee for failure to serve notice

(a) A trustee who fails to serve the notification by trustee as required by Section 16061.7 on a beneficiary shall be responsible for all damages, attorney's fees, and costs caused by the failure unless the trustee makes a reasonably diligent effort to comply with that section.

(b) A trustee who fails to serve the notification by trustee as required by Section 16061.7 on an heir who is not a beneficiary and whose identity is known to the trustee shall be responsible for all damages caused to the heir by the failure unless the trustee shows that the trustee made a reasonably diligent effort to comply with that section. For purposes of this subdivision, "reasonably diligent effort" means that the trustee has delivered notice pursuant to

Section 1215 to the heir at the heir's last address actually known to the trustee.

(c) A trustee, in exercising discretion with respect to the timing and nature of distributions of trust assets, may consider the fact that the period in which a beneficiary or heir could bring an action to contest the trust has not expired.

Ca. Prob. Code § 16061.9

Amended by Stats 2017 ch 319 (AB 976),s 89, eff. 1/1/2018.
Added by Stats 2000 ch 34 (AB 460), s 6, eff. 1/1/2001.

Section 16062 - Duty to account at termination of trust and upon change of trustee

(a) Except as otherwise provided in this section and in Section 16064, the trustee shall account at least annually, at the termination of the trust, and upon a change of trustee, to each beneficiary to whom income or principal is required or authorized in the trustee's discretion to be currently distributed.

(b) A trustee of a living trust created by an instrument executed before July 1, 1987, is not subject to the duty to account provided by subdivision (a).

(c) A trustee of a trust created by a will executed before July 1, 1987, is not subject to the duty to account provided by subdivision (a), except that if the trust is removed from continuing court jurisdiction pursuant to Article 2 (commencing with Section 17350) of Chapter 4 of Part 5, the duty to account provided by subdivision (a) applies to the trustee.

(d) Except as provided in Section 16064, the duty of a trustee to account pursuant to former Section 1120.1a of the Probate Code (as repealed by Chapter 820 of the Statutes of 1986), under a trust created by a will executed before July 1, 1977, which has been removed from continuing court jurisdiction pursuant to former Section 1120.1a, continues to apply after July 1, 1987. The duty to account under former Section 1120.1a may be satisfied by furnishing an account that satisfies the requirements of Section 16063.

(e) Any limitation or waiver in a trust instrument of the obligation to account is against public policy and shall be void as to any sole trustee who is either of the following:

(1) A disqualified person as defined in former Section 21350.5 (as repealed by Chapter 620 of the Statutes of 2010).

(2) Described in subdivision (a) of Section 21380, but not described in Section 21382.

Ca. Prob. Code § 16062

Amended by Stats 2016 ch 86 (SB 1171),s 250, eff. 1/1/2017.
Amended by Stats 2011 ch 296 (AB 1023),s 244, eff. 1/1/2012.
Amended by Stats 2010 ch 620 (SB 105),s 4, eff. 1/1/2011.
Amended by Stats 2001 ch 159 (SB 662), s 165.5, eff. 1/1/2002.

Section 16063 - Contents of account furnished pursuant to section 16062

(a) An account furnished pursuant to Section 16062 shall contain the following information:

(1) A statement of receipts and disbursements of principal and income that have occurred during the last complete fiscal year of the trust or since the last account.

(2) A statement of the assets and liabilities of the trust as of the end of the last complete fiscal year of the trust or as of the end of the period covered by the account.

(3) The trustee's compensation for the last complete fiscal year of the trust or since the last account.

(4) The agents hired by the trustee, their relationship to the trustee, if any, and their compensation, for the last complete fiscal year of the trust or since the last account.

(5) A statement that the recipient of the account may petition the court pursuant to Section 17200 to obtain a court review of the account and of the acts of the trustee.

(6) A statement that claims against the trustee for breach of trust may not be made after the expiration of three years from the date the beneficiary receives an account or report disclosing facts giving rise to the claim.

(b) All accounts filed to be approved by a court shall be presented in the manner provided in Chapter 4 (commencing with Section 1060) of Part 1 of Division 3.

Ca. Prob. Code § 16063

Repealed and added by Stats. 1997, Ch. 724, Sec. 26. Effective January 1, 1998.

Section 16064 - Circumstances not requiring trustee to account

The trustee is not required to account to a beneficiary as described in subdivision (a) of Section 16062, in any of the following circumstances:

(a) To the extent the trust instrument waives the account, except that no waiver described in subdivision (e) of Section 16062 shall be valid or enforceable. Regardless of a waiver of accounting in the trust instrument, upon a showing that it is reasonably likely that a material breach of the trust has occurred, the court may compel the trustee to account.

(b) As to a beneficiary who has waived in writing the right to an account. A waiver of rights under this subdivision may be withdrawn in writing at any time as to accounts for transactions occurring after the date of the written withdrawal. Regardless of a waiver of accounting by a beneficiary, upon a showing that is reasonably likely that a material breach of the trust has occurred, the court may compel the trustee to account.

(c) In any of the circumstances set forth in Section 16069.

Ca. Prob. Code § 16064

Amended by Stats 2010 ch 621 (SB 202),s 7, eff. 1/1/2011.

Section 16068 - Waiver against public policy

Any waiver by a settlor of the obligation of the trustee of either of the following is against public policy and shall be void:

(a) To provide the terms of the trust to the beneficiary as required by Sections 16060.7 and 16061.5.

(b) To provide requested information to the beneficiary as required by Section 16061.

Ca. Prob. Code § 16068

Added by Stats 2010 ch 621 (SB 202),s 8, eff. 1/1/2011.

Section 16069 - Circumstances not requiring trustee to perform duties of article

(a) The trustee is not required to account to the beneficiary, provide the terms of the trust to a beneficiary, or provide requested information to the beneficiary pursuant to Section 16061, in any of the following circumstances:

(1) In the case of a beneficiary of a revocable trust, as provided in subdivision (a) of Section 15800, for the period when the trust may be revoked.

(2) If the beneficiary and the trustee are the same person.

(b) Notwithstanding subdivision (a), in the case of a revocable trust, if no person holding the power to revoke the trust, in whole or in part, is competent, the trustee's duties to account shall be owed to those beneficiaries specified in paragraph (2) of subdivision (b) of Section 15800.

Ca. Prob. Code § 16069

Amended by Stats 2021 ch 749 (AB 1079),s 2, eff. 1/1/2022.
Added by Stats 2010 ch 621 (SB 202),s 9, eff. 1/1/2011.
See Stats 2021 ch 749 (AB 1079), s 3.

Article 4 - DUTIES WITH REGARD TO DISCRETIONARY POWERS

Section 16080 - Power exercised reasonably and not arbitrarily

Except as provided in Section 16081, a discretionary power conferred upon a trustee is not left to the trustee's arbitrary discretion, but shall be exercised reasonably.

Ca. Prob. Code § 16080
Enacted by Stats. 1990, Ch. 79.

Section 16081 - Duty when trust confers absolute, sole or uncontrolled discretion on trustee

(a) Subject to the additional requirements of subdivisions (b), (c), and (d), if a trust instrument confers "absolute," "sole," or "uncontrolled" discretion on a trustee, the trustee shall act in accordance with fiduciary principles and shall not act in bad faith or in disregard of the purposes of the trust.

(b) Notwithstanding the use of terms like "absolute," "sole," or "uncontrolled" by a settlor or a testator, a person who is a beneficiary of a trust that permits the person, either individually or as trustee or cotrustee, to make discretionary distributions of income or principal to or for the benefit of himself or herself pursuant to a standard, shall exercise that power reasonably and in accordance with the standard.

(c) Unless a settlor or a testator clearly indicates that a broader power is intended by express reference to this subdivision, a person who is a beneficiary of a trust that permits the person, as trustee or cotrustee, to make discretionary distributions of income or principal to or for the benefit of himself or herself may exercise that power in his or her favor only for his or her health, education, support, or maintenance within the meaning of Sections 2041 and 2514 of the Internal Revenue Code. Notwithstanding the foregoing and the provisions of Section 15620, if a power to make discretionary distributions of income or principal is conferred upon two or more trustees, the power may be exercised by any trustee who is not a current permissible beneficiary of that power ; and provided further that if there is no trustee who is not a current permissible beneficiary of that power, any party in interest may apply to a court of competent jurisdiction to appoint a trustee who is not a current permissible beneficiary of that power, and the power may be exercised by the trustee appointed by the court.

(d) Subdivision (c) does not apply to either of the following:

(1) Any power held by the settlor of a revocable or amendable trust.

(2) Any power held by a settlor's spouse or a testator's spouse who is the trustee of a trust for which a marital deduction, as defined in Section 21520, has been allowed.
(e) Subdivision (c) applies to any of the following:

(1) Any trust executed on or after January 1, 1997.

(2) Any testamentary trust created under a will executed on or after January 1, 1997.

(3) Any irrevocable trust created under a document executed before January 1, 1997, or any revocable trust executed before that date if the settlor was incapacitated as of that date, unless all parties in interest elect affirmatively not to be subject to the application of subdivision (c) through a written instrument delivered to the trustee. That election shall be made on or before the latest of January 1, 1998, three years after the date on which the trust became irrevocable, or, in the case of a revocable trust where the settlor was incapacitated, three years after the date on which the settlor became incapacitated.
(f) Notwithstanding the foregoing, the provisions of subdivision (c) neither create a new cause of action nor impair an existing cause of action that, in either case, relates to any power limited by subdivision (c) that was exercised before January 1, 1997.
(g) For purposes of this section, the term "party in interest" means any of the following persons:

(1) If the trust is revocable and the settlor is incapacitated, the settlor's legal representative under applicable law, or the settlor's attorney-in-fact under a durable power of attorney that is sufficient to grant the authority required under subdivision (c) or (e), as applicable.

(2) If the trust is irrevocable, each trustee, each beneficiary then entitled or authorized to receive income distributions from the trust, or each remainder beneficiary who would be entitled to receive notice of a trust proceeding under Section 15804. Any beneficiary who lacks legal capacity may be represented by the beneficiary's legal representative, attorney-in-fact under a durable power of attorney that is sufficient to grant the authority required under subdivision (c) or (e), as applicable, or in the absence of a legal representative or attorney-in-fact, a guardian ad litem appointed for that purpose.

Ca. Prob. Code § 16081
Amended by Stats. 1996, Ch. 410, Sec. 1. Effective January 1, 1997.

Section 16082 - Power to distribute not used to discharge legal obligation

Except as otherwise specifically provided in the trust instrument, a person who holds a power to appoint or distribute income or principal to or for the benefit of others, either as an individual or as trustee, may not use the power to discharge the legal obligations of the person holding the power.

Ca. Prob. Code § 16082
Enacted by Stats. 1990, Ch. 79.

Article 5 - DUTIES OF TRUSTEES OF PRIVATE FOUNDATIONS, CHARITABLE TRUSTS, AND SPLIT-INTEREST TRUSTS

Section 16100 - Definitions

As used in this article, the following definitions shall control:
(a) "Charitable trust" means a charitable trust as described in Section 4947(a)(1)(a)(1) of the Internal Revenue Code.
(b) "Private foundation" means a private foundation as defined in Section 509 of the Internal Revenue Code.
(c) "Split-interest trust" means a split-interest trust as described in Section 4947(a)(2)(a)(2) of the Internal Revenue Code.

Ca. Prob. Code § 16100
Enacted by Stats. 1990, Ch. 79.

Section 16101 - Distribution of income so as not to subject trust property to tax

During any period when a trust is deemed to be a charitable trust or a private foundation, the trustee shall distribute its income for each taxable year (and principal if necessary) at a time and in a manner that will not subject the property of the trust to tax under Section 4942 of the Internal Revenue Code.

Ca. Prob. Code § 16101
Enacted by Stats. 1990, Ch. 79.

Section 16102 - Prohibited acts by trustee

During any period when a trust is deemed to be a charitable trust, a private foundation, or a split-interest trust, the trustee shall not do any of the following:

(a) Engage in any act of self-dealing as defined in Section 4941(d)(d) of the Internal Revenue Code.

(b) Retain any excess business holdings as defined in Section 4943(c)(c) of the Internal Revenue Code.

(c) Make any investments in such manner as to subject the property of the trust to tax under Section 4944 of the Internal Revenue Code.

(d) Make any taxable expenditure as defined in Section 4945(d)(d) of the Internal Revenue Code.

Ca. Prob. Code § 16102
Enacted by Stats. 1990, Ch. 79.

Section 16103 - Provisions applicable to split-interest trusts

With respect to split-interest trusts:

(a) Subdivisions (b) and (c) of Section 16102 do not apply to any trust described in Section 4947(b)(3)(b)(3) of the Internal Revenue Code.

(b) Section 16102 does not apply with respect to any of the following:

(1) Any amounts payable under the terms of such trust to income beneficiaries, unless a deduction was allowed under Section

170(f)(2)(B)(f)(2)(B), 2055(e)(2)(B)(e)(2)(B), or 2522(c)(2)(B)(c)(2)(B) of the Internal Revenue Code.

(2) Any amounts in trust other than amounts for which a deduction was allowed under Section 170, 545(b)(2)(b)(2), 556(b)(2)(b)(2), 642(c)(c), 2055, 2106(a)(2)(a)(2), or 2522 of the Internal Revenue Code, if the amounts are segregated, as that term is defined in Section 4947(a)(3)(a)(3) of the Internal Revenue Code, from amounts for which no deduction was allowable.

(3) Any amounts irrevocably transferred in trust before May 27, 1969.

Ca. Prob. Code § 16103
Enacted by Stats. 1990, Ch. 79.

Section 16104 - Provisions deemed contained in trust instrument

The provisions of Sections 16101, 16102, and 16103 shall be deemed to be contained in the instrument creating every trust to which this article applies. Any provision of the instrument inconsistent with or contrary to this article is without effect.

Ca. Prob. Code § 16104
Enacted by Stats. 1990, Ch. 79.

Section 16105 - Commencement of proceeding contemplated by section 101(l)(3), federal Tax Reform Act of 1969

(a) A proceeding contemplated by Section 101(l)(3)(l)(3) of the federal Tax Reform Act of 1969 (Public Law 91-172) may be commenced pursuant to Section 17200 by the organization involved. All specifically named beneficiaries of the organization and the Attorney General shall be parties to the proceedings. Notwithstanding Section 17000, this provision is not exclusive and does not limit any jurisdiction that otherwise exists.

(b) If an instrument creating a trust affected by this section has been recorded, a notice of pendency of judicial proceedings under this section shall be recorded in a similar manner within 10 days from the commencement of the proceedings. A duly certified copy of any final judgment or decree in the proceedings shall be similarly recorded.

Ca. Prob. Code § 16105
Enacted by Stats. 1990, Ch. 79.

Section 16106 - Notice from trustee required prior to disposal of assets

(a) On and after July 1, 2022, a trustee holding assets subject to a charitable trust shall give written notice to the Attorney General at least 20 days before the trustee sells, leases, conveys, exchanges, transfers, or otherwise disposes of all or substantially all of the charitable assets.

(b) On or after January 1, 2022, the Attorney General shall establish rules and regulations necessary to administer this section.

Ca. Prob. Code § 16106
Amended by Stats 2022 ch 28 (SB 1380),s 128, eff. 1/1/2023.
Added by Stats 2021 ch 708 (AB 900),s 1, eff. 1/1/2022.

Chapter 2 - POWERS OF TRUSTEES

Article 1 - GENERAL PROVISIONS

Section 16200 - Powers without need to obtain court authorization

A trustee has the following powers without the need to obtain court authorization:

(a) The powers conferred by the trust instrument.

(b) Except as limited in the trust instrument, the powers conferred by statute.

(c) Except as limited in the trust instrument, the power to perform any act that a trustee would perform for the purposes of the trust under the standard of care provided in Section 16040 or 16047.

Ca. Prob. Code § 16200
Amended by Stats. 1995, Ch. 63, Sec. 7. Effective January 1, 1996.

Section 16201 - Power of court to relieve trustee from restrictions

This chapter does not affect the power of a court to relieve a trustee from restrictions on the exercise of powers under the trust instrument.

Ca. Prob. Code § 16201
Enacted by Stats. 1990, Ch. 79.

Section 16202 - Exercise of power subject to fiduciary duties

The grant of a power to a trustee, whether by the trust instrument, by statute, or by the court, does not in itself require or permit the exercise of the power. The exercise of a power by a trustee is subject to the trustee's fiduciary duties.

Ca. Prob. Code § 16202
Enacted by Stats. 1990, Ch. 79.

Section 16203 - Instrument incorporating powers provided in repealed section 1120.2

An instrument that incorporates the powers provided in former Section 1120.2 (repealed by Chapter 820 of the Statutes of 1986) shall be deemed to refer to the powers provided in Article 2 (commencing with Section 16220). For this purpose, the trustee's powers under former Section 1120.2 are not diminished and the trustee is not required to obtain court approval for exercise of a power for which court approval was not required by former law.

Ca. Prob. Code § 16203
Enacted by Stats. 1990, Ch. 79.

Article 2 - SPECIFIC POWERS OF TRUSTEES

Section 16220 - Power to collect, hold and retain trust property

The trustee has the power to collect, hold, and retain trust property received from a settlor or any other person until, in the judgment of the trustee, disposition of the property should be made. The property may be retained even though it includes property in which the trustee is personally interested.

Ca. Prob. Code § 16220
Enacted by Stats. 1990, Ch. 79.

Section 16221 - Power to accept additions to property

The trustee has the power to accept additions to the property of the trust from a settlor or any other person.

Ca. Prob. Code § 16221
Enacted by Stats. 1990, Ch. 79.

Section 16222 - Power to continue or participate in operation of business

(a) Subject to subdivision (b), the trustee has the power to continue or participate in the operation of any business or other enterprise that is part of the trust property and may effect incorporation, dissolution, or other change in the form of the organization of the business or enterprise.

(b) Except as provided in subdivision (c), the trustee may continue the operation of a business or other enterprise only as authorized by the trust instrument or by the court. For the purpose of this subdivision, the lease of four or fewer residential units is not considered to be the operation of a business or other enterprise.

(c) The trustee may continue the operation of a business or other enterprise for a reasonable time pending a court hearing on the matter or pending a sale of the business or other enterprise.

(d) The limitation provided in subdivision (b) does not affect any power to continue or participate in the operation of a business or other enterprise that the trustee has under a trust created by an instrument executed before July 1, 1987.

Ca. Prob. Code § 16222
Enacted by Stats. 1990, Ch. 79.

Section 16224 - Power to invest in obligations of United

States government

(a) In the absence of an express provision to the contrary in a trust instrument, where the instrument directs or permits investment in obligations of the United States government, the trustee has the power to invest in those obligations directly or in the form of an interest in a money market mutual fund registered under the Investment Company Act of 1940 (15 U.S.C. Sec. 80a-1 et seq.) or an investment vehicle authorized for the collective investment of trust funds pursuant to Section 9.18 of Part 9 of Title 12 of the Code of Federal Regulations, the portfolios of which are limited to United States government obligations maturing not later than five years from the date of investment or reinvestment and to repurchase agreements fully collateralized by United States government obligations.

(b) This section applies only to trusts created on or after January 1, 1985.

Ca. Prob. Code § 16224
Enacted by Stats. 1990, Ch. 79.

Section 16225 - Power to deposit trust funds

(a) The trustee has the power to deposit trust funds at reasonable interest in any of the following accounts:

(1) An insured account in a financial institution.

(2) To the extent that the account is collateralized, an account in a bank, an account in an insured savings and loan association, or an account in an insured credit union.

(b) A trustee may deposit trust funds pursuant to subdivision (a) in a financial institution operated by, or that is an affiliate of, the trustee. For the purpose of this subdivision, "affiliate" means a corporation that directly or indirectly through one or more intermediaries controls, is controlled by, or is under common control with another domestic or foreign corporation.

(c) This section does not limit the power of a trustee in a proper case to deposit trust funds in an account described in subdivision

(a) that is subject to notice or other conditions respecting withdrawal prescribed by law or governmental regulation.

(d) The court may authorize the deposit of trust funds in an account described in subdivision (a) in an amount greater than the maximum insured or collateralized amount.

(e) Nothing in this section prevents the trustee from holding an amount of trust property reasonably necessary for the orderly administration of the trust in the form of cash or in a checking account without interest.

Ca. Prob. Code § 16225
Enacted by Stats. 1990, Ch. 79.

Section 16226 - Power to acquire or dispose of property

The trustee has the power to acquire or dispose of property, for cash or on credit, at public or private sale, or by exchange.

Ca. Prob. Code § 16226
Enacted by Stats. 1990, Ch. 79.

Section 16227 - Powers to manage, control, divide, etc. trust property

The trustee has the power to manage, control, divide, develop, improve, exchange, partition, change the character of, or abandon trust property or any interest therein.

Ca. Prob. Code § 16227
Enacted by Stats. 1990, Ch. 79.

Section 16228 - Power to encumber, mortgage or pledge trust property

The trustee has the power to encumber, mortgage, or pledge trust property for a term within or extending beyond the term of the trust in connection with the exercise of any power vested in the trustee.

Ca. Prob. Code § 16228
Enacted by Stats. 1990, Ch. 79.

Section 16229 - Power to repair, alter or improve trust

property

The trustee has the power to do any of the following:
(a) Make ordinary or extraordinary repairs, alterations, or improvements in buildings or other trust property.
(b) Demolish any improvements.
(c) Raze existing or erect new party walls or buildings.
   Ca. Prob. Code § 16229
Enacted by Stats. 1990, Ch. 79.

Section 16230 - Power to subdivide, develop, dedicate, vacate, etc. land

The trustee has the power to do any of the following:
(a) Subdivide or develop land.
(b) Dedicate land to public use.
(c) Make or obtain the vacation of plats and adjust boundaries.
(d) Adjust differences in valuation on exchange or partition by giving or receiving consideration.
(e) Dedicate easements to public use without consideration.
   Ca. Prob. Code § 16230
Enacted by Stats. 1990, Ch. 79.

Section 16231 - Power to enter into lease

The trustee has the power to enter into a lease for any purpose as lessor or lessee with or without the option to purchase or renew and for a term within or extending beyond the term of the trust.
   Ca. Prob. Code § 16231
Enacted by Stats. 1990, Ch. 79.

Section 16232 - Power to lease or arrange for exploration and removal of gas, oil, other minerals

The trustee has the power to enter into a lease or arrangement for exploration and removal of gas, oil, or other minerals or geothermal energy, and to enter into a community oil lease or a pooling or unitization agreement, and for a term within or extending beyond

the term of the trust.
Ca. Prob. Code § 16232
Enacted by Stats. 1990, Ch. 79.

Section 16233 - Power to grant option involving disposition

The trustee has the power to grant an option involving disposition of trust property or to take an option for the acquisition of any property, and an option may be granted or taken that is exercisable beyond the term of the trust.
Ca. Prob. Code § 16233
Enacted by Stats. 1990, Ch. 79.

Section 16234 - Power as to stock or membership in nonprofit corporation

With respect to any shares of stock of a domestic or foreign corporation, any membership in a nonprofit corporation, or any other property, a trustee has the power to do any of the following:
(a) Vote in person, and give proxies to exercise, any voting rights with respect to the shares, memberships, or property.
(b) Waive notice of a meeting or give consent to the holding of a meeting.
(c) Authorize, ratify, approve, or confirm any action that could be taken by shareholders, members, or property owners.
Ca. Prob. Code § 16234
Enacted by Stats. 1990, Ch. 79.

Section 16235 - Power to pay calls, assessments, other charges on account of securities

The trustee has the power to pay calls, assessments, and any other sums chargeable or accruing against or on account of securities.
Ca. Prob. Code § 16235
Enacted by Stats. 1990, Ch. 79.

Section 16236 - Power as to stock subscription or

conversion rights

The trustee has the power to sell or exercise stock subscription or conversion rights.

    Ca. Prob. Code § 16236
Enacted by Stats. 1990, Ch. 79.

Section 16237 - Power to consent to reorganization, consolidation, merger, etc. of corporation or other business

The trustee has the power to consent, directly or through a committee or other agent, to the reorganization, consolidation, merger, dissolution, or liquidation of a corporation or other business enterprise, and to participate in voting trusts, pooling arrangements, and foreclosures, and in connection therewith, to deposit securities with and transfer title and delegate discretion to any protective or other committee as the trustee may deem advisable.

    Ca. Prob. Code § 16237
Enacted by Stats. 1990, Ch. 79.

Section 16238 - Power to hold security in name of nominee

The trustee has the power to hold a security in the name of a nominee or in other form without disclosure of the trust so that title to the security may pass by delivery.

    Ca. Prob. Code § 16238
Enacted by Stats. 1990, Ch. 79.

Section 16239 - Power to deposit securities in securities depository

The trustee has the power to deposit securities in a securities depository, as defined in Section 30004 of the Financial Code, which is licensed under Section 30200 of the Financial Code or is exempt from licensing by Section 30005 or 30006 of the Financial

Code. The securities may be held by the securities depository in the manner authorized by Section 775 of the Financial Code.

Ca. Prob. Code § 16239

Enacted by Stats. 1990, Ch. 79.

Section 16240 - Power to insure trust property

The trustee has the power to insure the property of the trust against damage or loss and to insure the trustee against liability with respect to third persons.

Ca. Prob. Code § 16240

Enacted by Stats. 1990, Ch. 79.

Section 16241 - Power to borrow

The trustee has the power to borrow money for any trust purpose to be repaid from trust property. The lender may include, but is not limited to, a bank holding company, affiliate, or subsidiary of the trustee.

Ca. Prob. Code § 16241

Enacted by Stats. 1990, Ch. 79.

Section 16242 - Power to pay or contest, settle or release claims

The trustee has the power to do any of the following:

(a) Pay or contest any claim.

(b) Settle a claim by or against the trust by compromise, arbitration, or otherwise.

(c) Release, in whole or in part, any claim belonging to the trust.

Ca. Prob. Code § 16242

Enacted by Stats. 1990, Ch. 79.

Section 16243 - Power to pay taxes, assessments, compensation and other expenses

The trustee has the power to pay taxes, assessments, reasonable compensation of the trustee and of employees and agents of the trust, and other expenses incurred in the collection, care, administration, and protection of the trust.

Ca. Prob. Code § 16243

Enacted by Stats. 1990, Ch. 79.

Section 16244 - Power as to loans out of trust property

The trustee has the following powers:

(a) To make loans out of trust property to the beneficiary on terms and conditions that the trustee determines are fair and reasonable under the circumstances.

(b) To guarantee loans to the beneficiary by encumbrances on trust property.

Ca. Prob. Code § 16244

Enacted by Stats. 1990, Ch. 79.

Section 16245 - Power to pay principal or income distributable to beneficiary

The trustee has the power to pay any sum of principal or income distributable to a beneficiary, without regard to whether the beneficiary is under a legal disability, by paying the sum to the beneficiary or by paying the sum to another person for the use or benefit of the beneficiary. Any sum distributable under this section to a custodian under the California Uniform Transfers to Minors Act (Part 9 (commencing with Section 3900)) shall be subject to Section 3906.

Ca. Prob. Code § 16245

Amended by Stats. 1996, Ch. 862, Sec. 39. Effective January 1, 1997.

Section 16246 - Power to distribute property and money and adjust differences of valuation

The trustee has the power to effect distribution of property and money in divided or undivided interests and to adjust resulting differences in valuation. A distribution in kind may be made pro rata or non pro rata, and may be made pursuant to any written agreement providing for a non pro rata division of the aggregate value of the community property assets or quasi-community property assets, or both.

Ca. Prob. Code § 16246
Amended by Stats. 1998, Ch. 682, Sec. 12. Effective January 1, 1999.

Section 16247 - Power to hire

The trustee has the power to hire persons, including accountants, attorneys, auditors, investment advisers, appraisers (including probate referees appointed pursuant to Section 400), or other agents, even if they are associated or affiliated with the trustee, to advise or assist the trustee in the performance of administrative duties.

Ca. Prob. Code § 16247
Amended by Stats. 1994, Ch. 806, Sec. 38. Effective January 1, 1995.

Section 16248 - Power to execute and deliver instruments

The trustee has the power to execute and deliver all instruments which are needed to accomplish or facilitate the exercise of the powers vested in the trustee.

Ca. Prob. Code § 16248
Enacted by Stats. 1990, Ch. 79.

Section 16249 - Power to prosecute or defend actions, claims, other proceedings

The trustee has the power to prosecute or defend actions, claims, or proceedings for the protection of trust property and of the trustee in the performance of the trustee's duties.

Ca. Prob. Code § 16249
Amended by Stats 2001 ch 49 (SB 669), s 5, eff. 1/1/2002.

Chapter 3 - UNIFORM PRINCIPAL AND INCOME ACT

Article 1 - SHORT TITLE AND DEFINITIONS

Section 16320 - Title of chapter

This chapter may be cited as the Uniform Principal and Income Act.

Ca. Prob. Code § 16320

EFFECTIVE 1/1/2000. Added7/22/1999 (Bill Number: AB 846) (Chapter 145).

Section 16321 - Definitions govern construction

The definitions in this article govern the construction of this chapter.

Ca. Prob. Code § 16321

EFFECTIVE 1/1/2000. Added7/22/1999 (Bill Number: AB 846) (Chapter 145).

Section 16322 - Accounting period

"Accounting period" means a calendar year unless another 12-month period is selected by a fiduciary. The term includes a portion of a calendar year or other 12-month period that begins when an income interest begins or ends when an income interest ends.

Ca. Prob. Code § 16322

EFFECTIVE 1/1/2000. Added7/22/1999 (Bill Number: AB 846) (Chapter 145).

Section 16323 - Fiduciary

"Fiduciary" means a personal representative or a trustee.

Ca. Prob. Code § 16323

EFFECTIVE 1/1/2000. Added7/22/1999 (Bill Number: AB 846) (Chapter 145).

Section 16324 - Income

"Income" means money or property that a fiduciary receives as current return from a principal asset. The term includes a portion of receipts from a sale, exchange, or liquidation of a principal asset, to the extent provided in Article 5.1 (commencing with Section 16350), 5.2 (commencing with Section 16355), or 5.3 (commencing with

Section 16360).

Ca. Prob. Code § 16324
EFFECTIVE 1/1/2000. Added7/22/1999 (Bill Number: AB 846)
(Chapter 145).

Section 16325 - Income beneficiary

"Income beneficiary" means a person to whom net income of a trust
is or may be payable.
Ca. Prob. Code § 16325
EFFECTIVE 1/1/2000. Added7/22/1999 (Bill Number: AB 846)
(Chapter 145).

Section 16326 - Income interest

"Income interest" means the right of an income beneficiary to
receive all or part of net income, whether the trust requires it to be
distributed or authorizes it to be distributed in the trustee's
discretion.
Ca. Prob. Code § 16326
EFFECTIVE 1/1/2000. Added7/22/1999 (Bill Number: AB 846)
(Chapter 145).
EFFECTIVE 1/1/2000. Added July 22, 1999 (Bill Number: AB 846)
(Chapter 145).

Section 16327 - Mandatory income interest

"Mandatory income interest" means the right of an income
beneficiary to receive net income that the trust requires the
fiduciary to distribute.
Ca. Prob. Code § 16327
EFFECTIVE 1/1/2000. Added7/22/1999 (Bill Number: AB 846)
(Chapter 145).
EFFECTIVE 1/1/2000. Added July 22, 1999 (Bill Number: AB 846)
(Chapter 145).

Section 16328 - Net income

"Net income" means the total receipts allocated to income during an accounting period minus the disbursements made from income during the accounting period, plus or minus transfers under this chapter to or from income during the accounting period. During any period in which the trust is being administered as a unitrust, either pursuant to the powers conferred by Sections 16336.4 to 16336.6, inclusive, or pursuant to the terms of the governing instrument, "net income" means the unitrust amount, if the unitrust amount is no less than 3 percent and no more than 5 percent of the fair market value of the trust assets, whether determined annually or averaged on a multiple year basis.

Ca. Prob. Code § 16328

Amended by Stats 2005 ch 100 (SB 754),s 1, eff. 1/1/2006
EFFECTIVE 1/1/2000. Added July 22, 1999 (Bill Number: AB 846) (Chapter 145).

Article 2 - GENERAL PROVISIONS AND FIDUCIARY DUTIES

Section 16335 - Fiduciary's duties in allocating receipts and disbursements; exercising discretionary power

(a) In allocating receipts and disbursements to or between principal and income, and with respect to any other matter within the scope of this chapter, a fiduciary:

(1) Shall administer a trust or decedent's estate in accordance with the trust or the will, even if there is a different provision in this chapter.

(2) May administer a trust or decedent's estate by the exercise of a discretionary power of administration given to the fiduciary by the trust or the will, even if the exercise of the power produces a result different from a result required or permitted by this chapter, and no inference that the fiduciary has improperly exercised the discretion arises from the fact that the fiduciary has made an allocation contrary to a provision of this chapter.

(3) Shall administer a trust or decedent's estate in accordance with this chapter if the trust or the will does not contain a different provision or does not give the fiduciary a discretionary power of administration.

(4) Shall add a receipt or charge a disbursement to principal to the extent that the trust or the will and this chapter do not provide a rule for allocating the receipt or disbursement to or between principal and income.

(b) In exercising a discretionary power of administration regarding a matter within the scope of this chapter, whether granted by a trust, a will, or this chapter, including the trustee's power to adjust under subdivision (a) of Section 16336, and the trustee's power to convert into a unitrust or reconvert or change the unitrust payout percentage pursuant to Sections 16336.4 to 16336.6, inclusive, the fiduciary shall administer the trust or decedent's estate impartially, except to the extent that the trust or the will expresses an intention that the fiduciary shall or may favor one or more of the beneficiaries. The exercise of discretion in accordance with this chapter is presumed to be fair and reasonable to all beneficiaries.

Ca. Prob. Code § 16335

Amended by Stats 2005 ch 100 (SB 754),s 2, eff. 1/1/2006
EFFECTIVE 1/1/2000. Added July 22, 1999 (Bill Number: AB 846) (Chapter 145).

Section 16336 - Adjustment between principal and income

(a) Subject to subdivision (b), a trustee may make an adjustment between principal and income to the extent the trustee considers necessary if all of the following conditions are satisfied:

(1) The trustee invests and manages trust assets under the prudent investor rule.

(2) The trust describes the amount that shall or may be distributed to a beneficiary by referring to the trust's income.

(3) The trustee determines, after applying the rules in subdivision (a) of Section 16335, and considering any power the trustee may have under the trust to invade principal or accumulate income, that the trustee is unable to comply with subdivision (b) of Section 16335.

(b) A trustee may not make an adjustment between principal and income in any of the following circumstances:

(1) Where it would diminish the income interest in a trust (A) that requires all of the income to be paid at least annually to a spouse and (B) for which, if the trustee did not have the power to make the adjustment, an estate tax or gift tax marital deduction would be allowed, in whole or in part.

(2) Where it would reduce the actuarial value of the income interest in a trust to which a person transfers property with the intent to qualify for a gift tax exclusion.

(3) Where it would change the amount payable to a beneficiary as a fixed annuity or a fixed fraction of the value of the trust assets.

(4) Where it would be made from any amount that is permanently set aside for charitable purposes under a will or trust, unless both income and principal are so set aside.

(5) Where possessing or exercising the power to make an adjustment would cause an individual to be treated as the owner of all or part of the trust for income tax purposes, and the individual would not be treated as the owner if the trustee did not possess the power to make an adjustment.

(6) Where possessing or exercising the power to make an adjustment would cause all or part of the trust assets to be included for estate tax purposes in the estate of an individual who has the power to remove a trustee or appoint a trustee, or both, and the assets would not be included in the estate of the individual if the trustee did not possess the power to make an adjustment.

(7) Where the trustee is a beneficiary of the trust.

548

(8) During any period in which the trust is being administered as a unitrust pursuant to the trustee's exercise of the power to convert provided in Section 16336.4 or 16336.5, or pursuant to the terms of the governing instrument.

(c) Notwithstanding Section 15620, if paragraph (5), (6), or (7) of subdivision (b) applies to a trustee and there is more than one trustee, a cotrustee to whom the provision does not apply may make the adjustment unless the exercise of the power by the remaining trustee or trustees is not permitted by the trust.

(d) A trustee may release the entire power conferred by subdivision (a) or may release only the power to adjust from income to principal or the power to adjust from principal to income in either of the following circumstances:

(1) If the trustee is uncertain about whether possessing or exercising the power will cause a result described in paragraphs (1) to (6), inclusive, of subdivision (b).

(2) If the trustee determines that possessing or exercising the power will or may deprive the trust of a tax benefit or impose a tax burden not described in subdivision (b).

(e) A release under subdivision (d) may be permanent or for a specified period, including a period measured by the life of an individual.

(f) A trust that limits the power of a trustee to make an adjustment between principal and income does not affect the application of this section unless it is clear from the trust that it is intended to deny the trustee the power of adjustment provided by subdivision (a).

(g) In deciding whether and to what extent to exercise the power to make adjustments under this section, the trustee may consider, but is not limited to, any of the following:

(1) The nature, purpose, and expected duration of the trust.

(2) The intent of the settlor.

(3) The identity and circumstances of the beneficiaries.

(4) The needs for liquidity, regularity of income, and preservation and appreciation of capital.

(5) The assets held in the trust; the extent to which they consist of financial assets, interests in closely held enterprises, tangible and intangible personal property, or real property; the extent to which an asset is used by a beneficiary; and whether an asset was purchased by the trustee or received from the settlor.

(6) The net amount allocated to income under other statutes and the increase or decrease in the value of the principal assets, which the trustee may estimate as to assets for which market values are not readily available.

(7) Whether and to what extent the trust gives the trustee the power to invade principal or accumulate income or prohibit the trustee from invading principal or accumulating income, and the extent to which the trustee has exercised a power from time to time to invade principal or accumulate income.

(8) The actual and anticipated effect of economic conditions on principal and income and effects of inflation and deflation.

(9) The anticipated tax consequences of an adjustment.
(h) Nothing in this section or in this chapter is intended to create or imply a duty to make an adjustment, and a trustee is not liable for not considering whether to make an adjustment or for choosing not to make an adjustment.

Ca. Prob. Code § 16336
Amended by Stats 2005 ch 100 (SB 754),s 3, eff. 1/1/2006
EFFECTIVE 1/1/2000. Added July 22, 1999 (Bill Number: AB 846) (Chapter 145).

Section 16336.4 - Conversion of trust into unitrust without court order

(a) Unless expressly prohibited by the governing instrument, a trustee may convert a trust into a unitrust, as described in this section. A trust that limits the power of the trustee to make an adjustment between principal and income or modify the trust does not affect the application of this section unless it is clear from the governing instrument that it is intended to deny the trustee the power to convert into a unitrust.

(b) The trustee may convert a trust into a unitrust without a court order if all of the following apply:

(1) The conditions set forth in subdivision (a) of Section 16336 are satisfied.

(2) The unitrust proposed by the trustee conforms to the provisions of paragraphs (1) to (8), inclusive, of subdivision (e).

(3) The trustee gives written notice of the trustee's intention to convert the trust into a unitrust and furnishes the information required by subdivision (c). The notice shall comply with the requirements of Chapter 5 (commencing with Section 16500), including notice to a beneficiary who is a minor and to the minor's guardian, if any.

(4) No beneficiary objects to the proposed action in a writing delivered to the trustee within the period prescribed by subdivision (d) of Section 16502 or a longer period as is specified in the notice described in subdivision (c).

(c) The notice described in paragraph (3) of subdivision (b) shall include a copy of Sections 16336.4 to 16336.7, inclusive, and all of the following additional information:

(1) A statement that the trust shall be administered in accordance with the provisions of subdivision (e) and the effective date of the conversion.

(2) A description of the method to be used for determining the fair market value of trust assets.

(3) The amount actually distributed to the income beneficiary during the previous accounting year of the trust.

(4) The amount that would have been distributed to the income beneficiary during the previous accounting year of the trust had the trustee's proposed changes been in effect during that entire year.

(5) The discretionary decisions the trustee proposes to make as of the conversion date pursuant to subdivision (f).
(d) In deciding whether to exercise the power conferred by this section, a trustee may consider, among other things, the factors set forth in subdivision (g) of Section 16336.
(e) Except to the extent that the court orders otherwise or the parties agree otherwise pursuant to Section 16336.5 after a trust is converted to a unitrust, all of the following shall apply:

(1) The trustee shall make regular distributions in accordance with the governing instrument construed in accordance with the provisions of this section.

(2) The term "income" in the governing instrument shall mean an annual distribution, the unitrust amount, equal to 4 percent, which is the payout percentage, of the net fair market value of the trust's assets, whether those assets would be considered income or principal under other provisions of this chapter, averaged over the lesser of the following:

(A) The three preceding years.

(B) The period during which the trust has been in existence.

(3) During each accounting year of the trust following its conversion into a unitrust, the trustee shall, as early in the year as is practicable, furnish each income beneficiary with a statement describing the computation of the unitrust amount for that accounting year.

(4) The trustee shall determine the net fair market value of each asset held in the trust no less often than annually. However, the following property shall not be included in determining the unitrust amount:

(A) Any residential property or any tangible personal property that, as of the first business day of the current accounting year, one or more current beneficiaries of the trust have or have had the right to occupy, or have or have had the right to possess or control, other than in his or her capacity as trustee of the trust, which property shall be administered according to other provisions of this chapter as though no conversion to a unitrust had occurred.

(B) Any asset specifically devised to a beneficiary to the extent necessary, in the trustee's reasonable judgment, to avoid a material risk of exhausting other trust assets prior to termination of the trust. All net income generated by a specifically devised asset excluded from the unitrust computation pursuant to this subdivision shall be accumulated or distributed by the trustee according to the rules otherwise applicable to that net income pursuant to other provisions of this chapter.

(C) Any asset while held in a testator's estate or a terminating trust.

(5) The unitrust amount, as otherwise computed pursuant to this subdivision, shall be reduced proportionately for any material distribution made to accomplish a partial termination of the trust required by the governing instrument or made as a result of the exercise of a power of appointment or withdrawal, other than distributions of the unitrust amount, and shall be increased proportionately for the receipt of any material addition to the trust, other than a receipt that represents a return on investment, during the period considered in paragraph (2) in computing the unitrust amount. For the purpose of this paragraph, a distribution or an addition shall be "material" if the net value of the distribution or addition, when combined with all prior distributions made or additions received during the same accounting year, exceeds 10 percent of the value of the assets used to compute the unitrust amount as of the most recent prior valuation date. The trustee may, in the reasonable exercise of his or her discretion, adjust the unitrust amount pursuant to this subdivision even if the distributions or additions are not sufficient to meet the definition of materiality set forth in the preceding sentence.

(6) In the case of a short year in which a beneficiary's right to payments commences or ceases, the trustee shall prorate the unitrust amount on a daily basis.

(7) Unless otherwise provided by the governing instrument or determined by the trustee, the unitrust amount shall be considered paid in the following order from the following sources:

(A) From the net taxable income, other than capital gains, determined as if the trust were other than a unitrust.

(B) From net realized short-term capital gains.

(C) From net realized long-term capital gains.

(D) From tax-exempt and other income.

(E) From principal of the trust.

(8) Expenses that would be deducted from income if the trust were not a unitrust may not be deducted from the unitrust amount. **(f)** The trustee shall determine, in the trustee's discretion, all of the following matters relating to administration of a unitrust created pursuant to this section:

(1) The effective date of a conversion to a unitrust.

(2) The frequency of payments in satisfaction of the unitrust amount.

(3) Whether to value the trust's assets annually or more frequently.

(4) What valuation dates to use.

(5) How to value nonliquid assets.

(6) The characterization of the unitrust payout for income tax reporting purposes. However, the trustee's characterization shall be consistent.

(7) Any other matters that the trustee deems appropriate for the proper functioning of the unitrust.

(g) A conversion into a unitrust does not affect a provision in the governing instrument directing or authorizing the trustee to distribute principal or authorizing the exercise of a power of appointment over or withdrawal of all or a portion of the principal.

(h) A trustee may not convert a trust into a unitrust in any of the following circumstances:

(1) If payment of the unitrust amount would change the amount payable to a beneficiary as a fixed annuity or a fixed fraction of the value of the trust assets.

(2) If the unitrust distribution would be made from any amount that is permanently set aside for charitable purposes under the governing instrument and for which a federal estate or gift tax deduction has been taken, unless both income and principal are set aside.

(3) If possessing or exercising the power to convert would cause an individual to be treated as the owner of all or part of the trust for federal income tax purposes, and the individual would not be treated as the owner if the trustee did not possess the power to convert.

(4) If possessing or exercising the power to convert would cause all or part of the trust assets to be subject to federal estate or gift tax with respect to an individual, and the assets would not be subject to federal estate or gift tax with respect to the individual if the trustee did not possess the power to convert.

(5) If the conversion would result in the disallowance of a federal estate tax or gift tax marital deduction that would be allowed if the trustee did not have the power to convert.

(i) If paragraph (3) or (4) of subdivision (h) applies to a trustee and there is more than one trustee, a cotrustee to whom the provision does not apply may convert the trust unless the exercise of the power by the remaining trustee or trustees is prohibited by the governing instrument. If paragraph (3) or (4) of subdivision (h) applies to all of the trustees, the court may order the conversion as provided in subdivision (b) of Section 16336.5.

(j)

(1) A trustee may release the power conferred by this section to convert to a unitrust if either of the following circumstances exist:

(A) The trustee is uncertain about whether possessing or experiencing the power will cause a result described in paragraph (3), (4), or (5) of subdivision (h).

(B) The trustee determines that possessing or exercising the power will or may deprive the trust of a tax benefit or impose a tax burden not described in subdivision (h).

(2) A release pursuant to paragraph (1) may be permanent or for a specified period, including a period measured by the life of an individual.

Ca. Prob. Code § 16336.4

Amended by Stats 2010 ch 621 (SB 202),s 10, eff. 1/1/2011.
Added by Stats 2005 ch 100 (SB 754),s 4, eff. 1/1/2006.

Section 16336.5 - Conversion of trust into unitrust upon terms other those set forth in section 16336.4(e) without court order

(a) The trustee may convert a trust into a unitrust upon terms other than those set forth in subdivision (e) of Section 16336.4, without court order, if all of the following apply:

(1) The conditions set forth in subdivision (a) of Section 16336 are satisfied.

(2) The trustee gives written notice of the trustee's intention to convert the trust into a unitrust and furnishes the information required by subdivision (c) of Section 16336.4. The notice shall comply with the requirements of Chapter 5 (commencing with Section 16500), including notice to a beneficiary who is a minor and to the minor's guardian, if any.

(3) The payout percentage to be adopted is at least 3 percent and no greater than 5 percent.

(4) All beneficiaries entitled to notice under Section 16501 consent in writing to the proposed action after having been furnished with the notice described in subdivision (c) of Section 16336.4.
(b) The court may order the conversion of a trust into a unitrust as provided in this subdivision.

(1)

(A) The trustee may petition the court to approve the conversion to a unitrust for any one of the following reasons:

(i) A beneficiary timely objects to a proposed conversion to a unitrust.

(ii) The trustee proposes to make the conversion upon terms other than those described in subdivision (e) of Section 16336.4.

(iii) Paragraph (3) or (4) of subdivision (h) of Section 16336.4 applies to all currently acting trustees.

(iv) If the trustee determines, in its discretion, that a petition is advisable.

(B) In no event, however, may the court authorize conversion to a unitrust with a payout percentage of less than 3 percent or greater than 5 percent of the fair market value of the trust assets.

(2) A beneficiary may petition the court to order the conversion.

(3) The court shall approve the conversion proposed by the trustee or direct the conversion requested by the beneficiary if the conditions set forth in subdivision (a) of Section 16336 are satisfied and the court concludes that conversion of the trust on the terms proposed will enable the trustee to better comply with the provisions of subdivision (b) of Section 16335.

(4) In deciding whether to approve a proposed conversion or direct a requested conversion, the court may consider, among other factors, those described in subdivision (g) of Section 16336.

Ca. Prob. Code § 16336.5
Added by Stats 2005 ch 100 (SB 754),s 5, eff. 1/1/2006.

Section 16336.6 - Reconversion from unitrust or change payout percentage of unitrust

Unless expressly prohibited by the governing instrument, a trustee may reconvert the trust from a unitrust or change the payout percentage of a unitrust.

(a) The trustee may make the reconversion or change in payout percentage without a court order if all of the following conditions are satisfied:

(1) At least three years have elapsed since the most recent conversion to a unitrust.

(2) The trustee determines that reconversion or change in payout percentage would enable the trustee to better comply with the provisions of subdivision (b) of Section 16335.

(3) One of the following notice requirements is satisfied:

(A) In the case of a proposed reconversion, the trustee gives written notice of the trustee's intention to convert that complies with the requirements of Chapter 5 (commencing with Section 16500) and no beneficiary objects to the proposed action in a writing delivered pursuant to Section 1215 to the trustee within the period prescribed by subdivision (d) of Section 16502. The trustee's notice shall include the information described in paragraphs (3) and (4) of subdivision (c) of Section 16336.4.

(B) In the case of a proposed change in payout percentage, the trustee gives written notice stating the new payout percentage that the trustee proposes to adopt, which notice shall comply with the requirements of Chapter 5 (commencing with Section 16500), and no beneficiary objects to the proposed action in a writing delivered pursuant to Section 1215 to the trustee within the period prescribed by subdivision (d) of Section 16502.

(b) The trustee may make the reconversion or change in payout percentage at any time pursuant to court order provided that:

(1) the court determines that reconversion or change in payout percentage will enable the trustee to better comply with the provisions of subdivision (b) of Section 16335, and

(2) in the case of a change in payout percentage, the new payout percentage is at least 3 percent and no greater than 5 percent. The court may enter an order pursuant to this subdivision upon the petition of the trustee or any beneficiary.

Ca. Prob. Code § 16336.6
Amended by Stats 2017 ch 319 (AB 976),s 90, eff. 1/1/2018.
Added by Stats 2005 ch 100 (SB 754),s 6, eff. 1/1/2006.

Section 16336.7 - Duty not imposed on trustee to convert or reconvert

(a) Sections 16336.4 to 16336.6, inclusive, shall not impose any duty on the trustee to convert or reconvert a trust or to consider a conversion or reconversion.

(b) Subdivision (b) of Section 16503 applies to all actions pursuant to Sections 16336.4 to 16336.6, inclusive, for which notice of proposed action is given in compliance with Chapter 5 (commencing with Section 16500), including notice to a beneficiary who is a minor and to the minor's guardian, if any.

Ca. Prob. Code § 16336.7
Added by Stats 2005 ch 100 (SB 754),s 7, eff. 1/1/2006.

Section 16337 - Notice of proposed action

A trustee may give a notice of proposed action regarding a matter governed by this chapter as provided in Chapter 5 (commencing with Section 16500). For the purpose of this section, a proposed action includes a course of action and a decision not to take action.

Ca. Prob. Code § 16337
Amended by Stats 2004 ch 54 (SB 1021), s 1, eff. 1/1/2005.
EFFECTIVE 1/1/2000. Added July 22, 1999 (Bill Number: AB 846) (Chapter 145).

Section 16338 - Remedies in proceedings with respect to trustee exercise or nonexercise of powers

In a proceeding with respect to a trustee's exercise or nonexercise of the power to make an adjustment under Section 16336, the sole remedy is to direct, deny, or revise an adjustment between principal and income. In a proceeding with respect to a trustee's exercise or nonexercise of a power conferred by Sections 16336.4 to 16336.6, inclusive, the sole remedy is to obtain an order directing the trustee to convert the trust to a unitrust, to reconvert from a unitrust, to change the distribution percentage, or to order any administrative procedures the court determines to be necessary or helpful for the proper functioning of the trust.

Ca. Prob. Code § 16338
Amended by Stats 2005 ch 100 (SB 754),s 8, eff. 1/1/2006
EFFECTIVE 1/1/2000. Added July 22, 1999 (Bill Number: AB 846) (Chapter 145).

Section 16339 - Effective date

This chapter applies to every trust or decedent's estate existing on or after January 1, 2000, except as otherwise expressly provided in the trust or will or in this chapter.

Ca. Prob. Code § 16339

EFFECTIVE 1/1/2000. Added7/22/1999 (Bill Number: AB 846) (Chapter 145).

Article 3 - DECEDENT'S ESTATE OR TERMINATING INCOME INTEREST

Section 16340 - Rules applicable

After the decedent's death, in the case of a decedent's estate, or after an income interest in a trust ends, the following rules apply:

(a) If property is specifically given to a beneficiary, by will or trust, the fiduciary of the estate or of the terminating income interest shall distribute the net income and principal receipts to the beneficiary who is to receive the property, subject to the following rules:

(1) The net income and principal receipts from the specifically given property are determined by including all of the amounts the fiduciary receives or pays with respect to the property, whether the amounts accrued or became due before, on, or after the decedent's death or an income interest in a trust ends, and by making a reasonable provision for amounts the fiduciary believes the estate or terminating income interest may become obligated to pay after the property is distributed.

(2) The fiduciary may not reduce income and principal receipts from the specifically given property on account of a payment described in Section 16370 or 16371, to the extent that the will, the trust, or Section 12002 requires payment from other property or to the extent that the fiduciary recovers the payment from a third person.

(3) A specific gift distributable under a trust shall carry with it the same benefits and burdens as a specific devise under a will, as set forth in Chapter 8 (commencing with Section 12000) of Part 10 of Division 7.

(b) A general pecuniary gift, an annuity, or a gift of maintenance distributable under a trust carries with it income and bears interest in the same manner as a general pecuniary devise, an annuity, or a gift of maintenance under a will, as set forth in Chapter 8 (commencing with Section 12000) of Part 10 of Division 7. The fiduciary shall distribute to a beneficiary who receives a pecuniary amount, whether outright or in trust, the interest or any other amount provided by the will, the trust, this subdivision, or Chapter 8 (commencing with Section 12000) of Part 10 of Division 7, from the remaining net income determined under subdivision (c) or from principal to the extent that net income is insufficient.

(c) The fiduciary shall determine the remaining net income of the decedent's estate or terminating income interest as provided in this chapter and by doing the following:

(1) Including in net income all income from property used to discharge liabilities.

(2) Paying from income or principal, in the fiduciary's discretion, fees of attorneys, accountants, and fiduciaries, court costs and other expenses of administration, and interest on death taxes, except that the fiduciary may pay these expenses from income of property passing to a trust for which the fiduciary claims an estate tax marital or charitable deduction only to the extent that the payment of these expenses from income will not cause the reduction or loss of the deduction.

(3) Paying from principal all other disbursements made or incurred in connection with the settlement of a decedent's estate or the winding up of a terminating income interest, including debts, funeral expenses, disposition of remains, family allowances, and death taxes and related penalties that are apportioned to the estate or terminating income interest by the will, the trust, or Division 10 (commencing with Section 20100).

(d) After distributions required by subdivision (b), the fiduciary shall distribute the remaining net income determined under subdivision (c) in the manner provided in Section 16341 to all other beneficiaries.

(e) For purposes of this section, a reference in Chapter 8 (commencing with Section 12000) of Part 10 of Division 7 to the date of the testator's death means the date of the settlor's death or of the occurrence of some other event on which the distributee's right to receive the gift depends.

(f) If a trustee has distributed a specific gift or a general pecuniary gift before January 1, 2007, the trustee may allocate income and principal as set forth in this chapter or in any other manner permissible under the law in effect at the time of the distribution. If the trustee distributes a specific gift or a general pecuniary gift after December 31, 2006, then the trustee shall allocate income and principal as provided in this chapter.

Ca. Prob. Code § 16340

Amended by Stats 2006 ch 569 (AB 2347),s 1, eff. 1/1/2007.
EFFECTIVE 1/1/2000. Added July 22, 1999 (Bill Number: AB 846) (Chapter 145).

Section 16341 - Net income beneficiary entitled to receive

(a) Each beneficiary described in subdivision (d) of Section 16340 is entitled to receive a portion of the net income equal to the beneficiary's fractional interest in undistributed principal assets, using values as of the distribution dates and without reducing the values by any unpaid principal obligations.

(b) If a fiduciary does not distribute all of the collected but undistributed net income to each beneficiary as of a distribution date, the fiduciary shall maintain appropriate records showing the interest of each beneficiary in that net income.

(c) The distribution date for purposes of this section may be the date as of which the fiduciary calculates the value of the assets if that date is reasonably near the date on which assets are actually distributed.

Ca. Prob. Code § 16341

EFFECTIVE 1/1/2000. Added7/22/1999 (Bill Number: AB 846) (Chapter 145).

Article 4 - APPORTIONMENT AT BEGINNING AND END OF INCOME INTEREST

Section 16345 - When income beneficiary entitled to net income; when income interest begins; when assets become subject to trust

(a) An income beneficiary is entitled to net income from the date on which the income interest begins. An income interest begins on the date specified in the trust or, if no date is specified, on the date an asset becomes subject to a trust or successive income interest. **(b)** An asset becomes subject to a trust at the following times:

(1) In the case of an asset that is transferred to a trust during the transferor's life, on the date it is transferred to the trust.

(2) In the case of an asset that becomes subject to a trust by reason of a will, even if there is an intervening period of administration of the testator's estate, on the date of the testator's death.

(3) In the case of an asset that is transferred to a fiduciary by a third party because of the individual's death, on the date of the individual's death.
(c) An asset becomes subject to a successive income interest on the day after the preceding income interest ends, as determined under subdivision (d), even if there is an intervening period of administration to wind up the preceding income interest.
(d) An income interest ends on the day before an income beneficiary dies, or another terminating event occurs, or on the last day of a period during which there is no beneficiary to whom a trustee may distribute income.

be comeCa. Prob. Code § 16345
EFFECTIVE 1/1/2000. Added7/22/1999 (Bill Number: AB 846) (Chapter 145).

Section 16346 - Allocation of income receipt or disbursement

(a) A trustee shall allocate an income receipt or disbursement other than one to which subdivision (a) of Section 16340 applies to principal if its due date occurs before a decedent dies in the case of an estate or before an income interest begins in the case of a trust or successive income interest.

(b) A trustee shall allocate an income receipt or disbursement to income if its due date occurs on or after the date on which a decedent dies or an income interest begins and it is a periodic due date. An income receipt or disbursement shall be treated as accruing from day to day if its due date is not periodic or it has no due date. The portion of the receipt or disbursement accruing before the date on which a decedent dies or an income interest begins shall be allocated to principal and the balance shall be allocated to income.

(c) An item of income or an obligation is due on the date the payer is required to make a payment. If a payment date is not stated, there is no due date for the purposes of this chapter. Distributions to shareholders or other owners from an entity to which Section 16350 applies are deemed to be due on the date fixed by the entity for determining who is entitled to receive the distribution or, if no date is fixed, on the declaration date for the distribution. A due date is periodic for receipts or disbursements that must be paid at regular intervals under a lease or an obligation to pay interest or if an entity customarily makes distributions at regular intervals.

Ca. Prob. Code § 16346
EFFECTIVE 1/1/2000. Added7/22/1999 (Bill Number: AB 846) (Chapter 145).

Section 16347 - Payment of beneficiary's share of undistributed income

(a) For the purposes of this section, "undistributed income" means net income received before the date on which an income interest ends. The term does not include an item of income or expense that is due or accrued or net income that has been added or is required to be added to principal by the trust.

(b) Except as provided in subdivision (c), on the date when a mandatory income interest ends, the trustee shall pay to a mandatory income beneficiary who survives that date, or to the estate of a deceased mandatory income beneficiary whose death causes the interest to end, the beneficiary's share of the undistributed income that is not disposed of under the trust.

(c) If immediately before the income interest ends, the beneficiary under subdivision (b) has an unqualified power to revoke more than 5 percent of the trust, the undistributed income from the portion of the trust that may be revoked shall be added to principal.

(d) When a trustee's obligation to pay a fixed annuity or a fixed fraction of the value of the trust's assets ends, the trustee shall prorate the final payment.

Ca. Prob. Code § 16347

EFFECTIVE 1/1/2000. Added7/22/1999 (Bill Number: AB 846) (Chapter 145).

Article 5.1 - ALLOCATION OF RECEIPTS DURING ADMINISTRATION OF TRUST: RECEIPTS FROM ENTITIES

Section 16350 - Allocation of money received from entity

(a) As used in this section, "entity" shall mean a corporation, partnership, limited-liability company, regulated investment company, real estate investment trust, common trust fund, or any other organization in which a trustee has an interest other than a trust or estate to which Section 16351 applies, a business or activities to which Section 16352 applies, or an asset-backed security to which Section 16367 applies.

(b) Except as otherwise provided in this section, a trustee shall allocate to income money received from an entity.

(c) A trustee shall allocate to principal the following receipts from an entity:

(1) Property other than money.

(2) Money received in one distribution or a series of related distributions in exchange for part or all of a trust's interest in the entity.

(3) Money received in a distribution if and to the extent that the trustee determines that the distribution is a return of capital under subdivision (d), (e), (f), or (g).

(4) Money received from an entity that is a regulated investment company or a real estate investment trust if the money distributed is a capital gain dividend for federal income tax purposes.

(d) A trustee may determine that money is received as a return of capital if and to the extent that the money received exceeds the total amount of income tax that the beneficiaries must pay on their respective shares of the taxable income of the entity and the trust must pay from income under Article 4 (commencing with Section 16345), Article 5.1 (commencing with Section 16350), Article 5.2 (commencing with Section 16355), and Article 5.3 (commencing with Section 16360), inclusive, on its share of the taxable income of the entity. A trustee may determine that money which represents gain upon the sale or other disposition of property described in subdivision (e) is a return of capital.

(e) In determining if and to what extent a distribution is a return of capital, a trustee may rely upon and determine the weight to be given to any information concerning the source of the money from which the distribution is made which is reasonably available to the trustee, including, but not limited to, information concerning any of the following:

(1) The amount of the distribution in question compared to the amount of the entity's regular, periodic distributions, if any, during the year in which the distribution is made and in prior years.

(2) If the primary activity of the entity is not an investment activity described in paragraph (3), the amount of money the entity has received from the conduct of its normal business activities compared to the amount of money the entity has received from all other sources, including, but not limited to, any of the following:

(A) The sale of all or part of a business conducted by the entity or by another entity in which it owns an interest, directly or indirectly, including, but not limited to, money representing any gain realized on such a sale.

(B) The sale of one or more business assets that are not sold to customers in the normal course of the entity's business, including, but not limited to, money representing any gain realized on such a sale.

(C) The sale of one or more investment assets, including, but not limited to, money representing any gain realized on such a sale.

(3) If the primary activity of the entity is to invest funds in another entity or in investment property that the entity owns directly for the purpose of realizing gain on the disposition of all or a part of an investment, the amount of money that the entity has received from the sale of all or part of one or more of those investments, including, but not limited to, money representing any gain realized on a disposition.

(4) The amount of money the entity has accumulated, to the extent that the governing body of the entity has decided the money is no longer needed for the business or investment needs of the entity.

(5) The amount of income tax, if any, that each beneficiary has paid on the undistributed income of the entity before the year of the distribution and the amount of income tax on the undistributed income of the entity that the trust has paid from the income or principal of the trust.

(6) The amount of money the entity has borrowed, whether or not repayment of the loan is secured to any extent by one or more of the entity's assets.

(7) The amount of money the entity has received from the sources described in Sections 16358, 16362, 16363, and 16364.

(8) The amount of money the entity has received from a source not described in this subdivision.

(f) If a trustee determines that only a portion of a distribution is a return of capital and is in doubt about the amount of the distribution that is a return of capital, the trustee shall resolve the doubt by allocating to income the amount, if any, the trustee determines is not a return of capital and by allocating the balance of the distribution to principal.

(g) A trustee shall consider and may rely upon, without independent investigation, the financial statements of an entity and any other information provided by an entity about the character of a distribution or the source of funds from which the distribution is made if the information is provided at or near the time of distribution by the entity's board of directors or other person or group of persons authorized to exercise powers to pay money or transfer property comparable to those of a corporation's board of directors. The trustee is not bound by any statement made or implied by the entity about the extent to which a distribution is or is not a return of capital. If the trustee receives additional information about the distribution and the trustee has not yet made a distribution to a trust beneficiary of any portion of that distribution from the entity for which the trustee has made the determination of whether the amount is a return of capital, the trustee shall consider the additional information received and may make an adjustment to that decision. If the trustee receives additional information about the distribution after the trustee has made a distribution to a trust beneficiary of any portion of that distribution from the entity for which the trustee has made the determination of whether the amount is a return of capital, the trustee is not required to change that decision.

(h) In exercising the discretion provided to the trustee pursuant to subdivisions (d), (e), (f), and (g), the trustee shall comply with the duties provided for under Article 1 (commencing with Section 16000) of Chapter 1, including, but not limited to, Sections 16000, 16003, and 16004.

Ca. Prob. Code § 16350

Added by Stats 2017 ch 577 (AB 307),s 2, eff. 1/1/2018.

Section 16351 - Allocation to income amount received as distribution of income

A trustee shall allocate to income an amount received as a distribution of income from a trust or a decedent's estate (other than an interest in an investment entity) in which the trust has an interest other than a purchased interest, and shall allocate to principal an amount received as a distribution of principal from the trust or estate.

Ca. Prob. Code § 16351
EFFECTIVE 1/1/2000. Added7/22/1999 (Bill Number: AB 846) (Chapter 145).

Section 16352 - Accounting separately for business or other activity

(a) If a trustee who conducts a business or other activity determines that it is in the best interest of all the beneficiaries to account separately for the business or other activity instead of accounting for it as part of the trust's general accounting records, the trustee may maintain separate accounting records for its transactions, whether or not its assets are segregated from other trust assets.

(b) A trustee who accounts separately for a business or other activity may determine the extent to which its net cash receipts must be retained for working capital, the acquisition or replacement of fixed assets, and its other reasonably foreseeable needs, and the extent to which the remaining net cash receipts are accounted for as principal or income in the trust's general accounting records. If a trustee sells assets of the business or other activity, other than in the ordinary course of the business or other activity, the trustee shall account for the net amount received as principal in the trust's general accounting records to the extent the trustee determines that the amount received is no longer required in the conduct of the business or other activity.

(c) Businesses and other activities for which a trustee may maintain separate accounting records include the following:

(1) Retail, manufacturing, service, and other traditional business activities.

(2) Farming.

(3) Raising and selling livestock and other animals.

(4) Managing rental properties.

(5) Extracting minerals and other natural resources.

(6) Timber operations.

(7) Activities to which Section 16366 applies.

Ca. Prob. Code § 16352

EFFECTIVE 1/1/2000. Added7/22/1999 (Bill Number: AB 846) (Chapter 145).

Article 5.2 - ALLOCATION OF RECEIPTS DURING ADMINISTRATION OF TRUST: RECEIPTS NOT NORMALLY APPORTIONED

Section 16355 - Allocations to principal

A trustee shall allocate to principal:

(a) To the extent not allocated to income under this chapter, assets received from a transferor during the transferor's lifetime, a decedent's estate, a trust with a terminating income interest, or a payer under a contract naming the trust or its trustee as beneficiary.

(b) Subject to any contrary rules in this article and in Articles 5.1 (commencing with Section 16350) and 5.3 (commencing with Section 16360), money or other property received from the sale, exchange, liquidation, or change in form of a principal asset, including realized profit.

(c) Amounts recovered from third parties to reimburse the trust because of disbursements described in paragraph (7) of subdivision (a) of Section 16371 or for other reasons to the extent not based on the loss of income.

(d) Proceeds of property taken by eminent domain, but a separate award made for the loss of income with respect to an accounting period during which a current income beneficiary had a mandatory income interest is income.

(e) Net income received in an accounting period during which there is no beneficiary to whom a trustee may or must distribute income.

(f) Other receipts allocated to principal as provided in Article 5.3 (commencing with Section 16360).

    Ca. Prob. Code § 16355

EFFECTIVE 1/1/2000. Added7/22/1999 (Bill Number: AB 846) (Chapter 145).

Section 16356 - Amount received as rent

Unless the trustee accounts for receipts from rental property pursuant to Section 16352, the trustee shall allocate to income an amount received as rent of real or personal property, including an amount received for cancellation or renewal of a lease. An amount received as a refundable deposit, including a security deposit or a deposit that is to be applied as rent for future periods, shall be added to principal and held subject to the terms of the lease, and is not available for distribution to a beneficiary until the trustee's contractual obligations have been satisfied with respect to that amount.

    Ca. Prob. Code § 16356

EFFECTIVE 1/1/2000. Added7/22/1999 (Bill Number: AB 846) (Chapter 145).

Section 16357 - Amount received as interest; amount received from sale, redemption or other obligation to pay money

(a) An amount received as interest, whether determined at a fixed, variable, or floating rate, on an obligation to pay money to the trustee, including an amount received as consideration for prepaying principal, shall be allocated to income without any provision for amortization of premium.

(b) An amount received from the sale, redemption, or other disposition of an obligation to pay money to the trustee more than one year after it is purchased or acquired by the trustee, including an obligation whose purchase price, or its value when it is otherwise acquired, is less than its value at maturity, shall be allocated to principal. If the obligation matures within one year after it is purchased or acquired by the trustee, an amount received in excess of its purchase price, or its value when it is otherwise acquired, shall be allocated to income.

(c) This section does not apply to an obligation to which Section 16361, 16362, 16363, 16364, 16366, or 16367 applies.

Ca. Prob. Code § 16357

EFFECTIVE 1/1/2000. Added7/22/1999 (Bill Number: AB 846) (Chapter 145).

Section 16358 - Proceeds of life insurance or other contract in which trust or trustee named as beneficiary; proceeds from contract insuring against loss

(a) Except as otherwise provided in subdivision (b), a trustee shall allocate to principal the proceeds of a life insurance policy or other contract in which the trust or its trustee is named as beneficiary, including a contract that insures the trust or its trustee against loss for damage to, destruction of, or loss of title to a trust asset. The trustee shall allocate dividends on an insurance policy to income if the premiums on the policy are paid from income, and to principal if the premiums are paid from principal.

(b) A trustee shall allocate to income proceeds of a contract that insures the trustee against loss of occupancy or other use by an income beneficiary, loss of income, or, subject to Section 16352, loss of profits from a business.

(c) This section does not apply to a contract to which Section 16361 applies.

Ca. Prob. Code § 16358

EFFECTIVE 1/1/2000. Added7/22/1999 (Bill Number: AB 846) (Chapter 145).

Article 5.3 - ALLOCATION OF RECEIPTS DURING ADMINISTRATION OF TRUST: RECEIPTS NORMALLY APPORTIONED

Section 16360 - Allocation of entire insubstantial amount to principal; allocation presumed insubstantial

(a) If a trustee determines that an allocation between principal and income required by Section 16361, 16362, 16363, 16364, or 16367 is insubstantial, the trustee may allocate the entire amount to principal unless one of the circumstances described in subdivision (b) of Section 16336 applies to the allocation. This power may be exercised by a cotrustee in the circumstances described in subdivision (c) of Section 16336 and may be released for the reasons and in the manner provided in subdivisions (d) and (e) of Section 16336.

(b) An allocation is presumed to be insubstantial in either of the following cases:

(1) Where the amount of the allocation would increase or decrease net income in an accounting period, as determined before the allocation, by less than 10 percent.

(2) Where the value of the asset producing the receipt for which the allocation would be made is less than 10 percent of the total value of the trust's assets at the beginning of the accounting period.

(c) Nothing in this section imposes a duty on the trustee to make an allocation under this section, and the trustee is not liable for failure to make an allocation under this section.

Ca. Prob. Code § 16360
EFFECTIVE 1/1/2000. Added7/22/1999 (Bill Number: AB 846) (Chapter 145).

Section 16361 - Payment characterized as interest dividend or payment in lieu of interest or dividend

(a) For purposes of this section, the following terms have the following meanings:

(1) "Payment" means a payment that a trustee may receive over a fixed number of years or during the life of an individual because of services rendered or property transferred to the payer in exchange for future payments. The term also includes a payment made in money or property from the payer's general assets or from a separate fund created by the payer. For purposes of subdivisions (d), (e), (f), and (g), "payment" also includes any payment from a separate fund, regardless of the reason for the payment.

(2) "Separate fund" includes a private or commercial annuity, an individual retirement account, and a pension, profit-sharing, stock bonus, or stock ownership plan.

(b) To the extent that any portion of the payment is characterized by the payer as interest, a dividend, or a payment made in lieu of interest or a dividend, a trustee shall allocate that portion of the payment to income. The trustee shall allocate to principal the balance of the payment.

(c) If no part of a payment is characterized as interest, a dividend, or an equivalent payment, and all or part of the payment is required to be made, a trustee shall allocate to income 10 percent of the part that is required to be made during the accounting period and the balance to principal. If no part of a payment is required to be made or the payment received is the entire amount to which the trustee is entitled, the trustee shall allocate the entire payment to principal. For purposes of this subdivision, a payment is not "required to be made" to the extent that it is made because the trustee exercises a right of withdrawal.

(d) Subdivisions (f) and (g) shall apply, except as provided in subdivision (e), and subdivisions (b) and (c) shall not apply, in determining the allocation of a payment made from a separate fund to either of the following:

(1) A trust to which an election to qualify for a marital deduction is made under Section 2056(b)(7)(b)(7) of the Internal Revenue Code.

(2) A trust that qualifies for the marital deduction under Section

2056(b)(5)(b)(5) of the Internal Revenue Code.

(e) Subdivisions (d), (f), and (g) shall not apply if the series of payments would, without the application of subdivision (d), qualify for the marital deduction under Section 2056(b)(7)(C)(b)(7)(C) of the Internal Revenue Code.

(f) If the separate fund payer provides documentation reflecting the internal income of the separate fund to the trustee, the trustee shall allocate the internal income of each separate fund for the accounting period as if the separate fund were a trust subject to this act. Upon request of the surviving spouse, the trustee shall require that the person administering the separate fund distribute this internal income to the trust. The trustee shall allocate a payment from the separate fund to income to the extent of the internal income of the separate fund and distribute that amount to the surviving spouse. The trustee shall allocate the balance to principal. Upon request of the surviving spouse, the trustee shall allocate principal to income to the extent the internal income of the separate fund exceeds payments made from the separate fund to the trust during the accounting period.

(g) If the separate fund payer does not provide documentation reflecting the internal income of the separate fund to the trustee, but the trustee can determine the value of the separate fund, the internal income of the separate fund is deemed to equal 4 percent of the fund's value, according to the most recent statement of value preceding the beginning of the accounting period. If the separate fund payer does not provide documentation reflecting the internal income of the separate fund to the trustee and the trustee cannot determine the value of the separate fund, the internal income of the fund is deemed to equal the product of the interest rate and the present value of the expected future payments, as determined under Section 7520 of the Internal Revenue Code for the month preceding the accounting period for which the computation is made.

(h) This section does not apply to a payment to which Section 16362 applies.

Ca. Prob. Code § 16361

Amended by Stats 2010 ch 71 (AB 229),s 1, eff. 1/1/2011.
Amended by Stats 2009 ch 152 (AB 1545),s 1, eff. 1/1/2010.
Added by Stats 2006 ch 569 (AB 2347),s 3, eff. 1/1/2007.

EFFECTIVE 1/1/2000. Added July 22, 1999 (Bill Number: AB 846) (Chapter 145).

Section 16361.1 - Trust described in section 16361(d)

Section 16361, as amended by the act adding this section, applies to a trust described in subdivision (d) of Section 16361, on and after the following dates:

(a) If the trust is not funded as of January 1, 2010, the date of the decedent's death.

(b) If the trust is initially funded in the calendar year beginning January 1, 2010, the date of the decedent's death.

(c) If the trust is not described in subdivision (a) or (b), on January 1, 2010.

   Ca. Prob. Code § 16361.1
Added by Stats 2009 ch 152 (AB 1545),s 2, eff. 1/1/2010.

Section 16362 - Liquidating asset defined

(a) In this section, "liquidating asset" means an asset whose value will diminish or terminate because the asset is expected to produce receipts for a period of limited duration. The term includes a leasehold, patent, copyright, royalty right, and right to receive payments under an arrangement that does not provide for the payment of interest on the unpaid balance. The term does not include a payment subject to Section 16361, resources subject to Section 16363, timber subject to Section 16364, an activity subject to Section 16366, an asset subject to Section 16367, or any asset for which the trustee establishes a reserve for depreciation under Section 16372.

(b) A trustee shall allocate to income 10 percent of the receipts from a liquidating asset and the balance to principal.

   Ca. Prob. Code § 16362
EFFECTIVE 1/1/2000. Added7/22/1999 (Bill Number: AB 846) (Chapter 145).

Section 16363 - Receipts from interest in minerals, water or other natural resources

(a) To the extent that a trustee accounts for receipts from an interest in minerals, water, or other natural resources pursuant to this section, the trustee shall allocate them as follows:

(1) If received as a nominal bonus, nominal delay rental, or nominal annual rent on a lease, a receipt shall be allocated to income.

(2) If received from a production payment, a receipt shall be allocated to income if and to the extent that the agreement creating the production payment provides a factor for interest or its equivalent. The balance shall be allocated to principal.

(3) If an amount received as a royalty, shut-in-well payment, take-or-pay payment, bonus, or delay rental is more than nominal, 90 percent shall be allocated to principal and the balance to income.

(4) If an amount is received from a working interest or any other interest in mineral or other natural resources not described in paragraph (1), (2), or (3), 90 percent of the net amount received shall be allocated to principal and the balance to income.
(b) An amount received on account of an interest in water that is renewable shall be allocated to income. If the water is not renewable, 90 percent of the amount shall be allocated to principal and the balance to income.
(c) This chapter applies whether or not a decedent or donor was extracting minerals, water, or other natural resources before the interest became subject to the trust.
(d) If a trust owned an interest in minerals, water, or other natural resources on January 1, 2000, the trustee may at all times allocate receipts from the interest as provided in this chapter or in the manner reasonably used by the trustee prior to that date. Receipts from an interest in minerals, water, or other natural resources acquired after January 1, 2000, shall be allocated by the trustee as provided in this chapter. If the interest was owned by the trust on January 1, 2000, a trustee that allocated receipts from the interest between January 1, 2000, and December 31, 2006, as provided in

this chapter shall not have a duty to review that allocation and shall not have liability arising from the allocation. Nothing in this section is intended to create or imply a duty to allocate in a manner used by the trustee prior to January 1, 2000, and a trustee is not liable for not considering whether to make such an allocation or for choosing not to make such an allocation.

Ca. Prob. Code § 16363

Amended by Stats 2006 ch 569 (AB 2347),s 4, eff. 1/1/2007. EFFECTIVE 1/1/2000. Added July 22, 1999 (Bill Number: AB 846) (Chapter 145).

Section 16364 - Receipts from sale of timber and related products

(a) To the extent that a trustee accounts for receipts from the sale of timber and related products pursuant to this section, the trustee shall allocate the net receipts as follows:

(1) To income to the extent that the amount of timber removed from the land does not exceed the rate of growth of the timber during the accounting periods in which a beneficiary has a mandatory income interest.

(2) To principal to the extent that the amount of timber removed from the land exceeds the rate of growth of the timber or the net receipts are from the sale of standing timber.

(3) To or between income and principal if the net receipts are from the lease of timberland or from a contract to cut timber from land owned by a trust, by determining the amount of timber removed from the land under the lease or contract and applying the rules in paragraphs (1) and (2).

(4) To principal to the extent that advance payments, bonuses, and other payments are not allocated pursuant to paragraph (1), (2), or (3).

(b) In determining net receipts to be allocated under subdivision (a), a trustee shall deduct and transfer to principal a reasonable amount for depletion.

(c) This chapter applies whether or not a decedent or transferor was harvesting timber from the property before it became subject to the trust.

(d) If a trust owned an interest in timberland on January 1, 2000, the trustee may at all times allocate net receipts from the sale of timber and related products as provided in this chapter or in the manner reasonably used by the trustee prior to that date. Net receipts from an interest in timberland acquired after January 1, 2000, shall be allocated by the trustee as provided in this chapter. If the interest was owned by the trust on January 1, 2000, a trustee that allocated net receipts from the interest between January 1, 2000, and December 31, 2006, as provided in this chapter shall not have a duty to review that allocation and shall not have liability arising from the allocation. Nothing in this section is intended to create or imply a duty to allocate in a manner used by the trustee prior to January 1, 2000, and a trustee is not liable for not considering whether to make such an allocation or for choosing not to make such an allocation.

Ca. Prob. Code § 16364

Amended by Stats 2006 ch 569 (AB 2347),s 5, eff. 1/1/2007.
EFFECTIVE 1/1/2000. Added July 22, 1999 (Bill Number: AB 846) (Chapter 145).

Section 16365 - Insufficient distribution to provide spouse with beneficial enjoyment of marital deduction

(a) If a marital deduction is allowed for all or part of a trust whose assets consist substantially of property that does not provide the spouse with sufficient income from or use of the trust assets, and if the amounts that the trustee transfers from principal to income under Section 16336 and distributes to the spouse from principal pursuant to the terms of the trust are insufficient to provide the spouse with the beneficial enjoyment required to obtain the marital deduction, the spouse may require the trustee to make property productive of income or convert it into productive property or exercise the power under subdivision (a) of Section 16336 within a reasonable time. The trustee may decide which action or

580

combination of actions to take.

(b) In cases not governed by subdivision (a), proceeds from the sale or other disposition of a trust asset are principal without regard to the amount of income the asset produces during any accounting period.

Ca. Prob. Code § 16365

EFFECTIVE 1/1/2000. Added7/22/1999 (Bill Number: AB 846) (Chapter 145).

Section 16366 - Receipts from and disbursement made in connection with derivatives

(a) In this section, "derivative" means a contract or financial instrument or a combination of contracts and financial instruments that gives a trust the right or obligation to participate in some or all changes in the price of a tangible or intangible asset or group of assets, or changes in a rate, an index of prices or rates, or other market indicator for an asset or a group of assets.

(b) To the extent that a trustee does not account under Section 16352 for transactions in derivatives, the trustee shall allocate to principal receipts from and disbursements made in connection with those transactions.

(c) If a trustee grants an option to buy property from the trust, whether or not the trust owns the property when the option is granted, grants an option that permits another person to sell property to the trust, or acquires an option to buy property for the trust or an option to sell an asset owned by the trust, and the trustee or other owner of the asset is required to deliver the asset if the option is exercised, an amount received for granting the option shall be allocated to principal. An amount paid to acquire the option shall be paid from principal. A gain or loss realized upon the exercise of an option, including an option granted to a settlor of the trust for services rendered, shall be allocated to principal.

Ca. Prob. Code § 16366

EFFECTIVE 1/1/2000. Added7/22/1999 (Bill Number: AB 846) (Chapter 145).

Section 16367 - Proceeds of collateral financial assets;

asset-backed security

(a) In this section, "asset-backed security" means an asset whose value is based upon the right it gives the owner to receive distributions from the proceeds of financial assets that provide collateral for the security. The term includes an asset that gives the owner the right to receive from the collateral financial assets only the interest or other current return or only the proceeds other than interest or current return. The term does not include an asset to which Section 16350 or 16361 applies.

(b) If a trust receives a payment from interest or other current return and from other proceeds of the collateral financial assets, the trustee shall allocate to income the portion of the payment which the payer identifies as being from interest or other current return and shall allocate the balance of the payment to principal.

(c) If a trust receives one or more payments in exchange for the trust's entire interest in an asset-backed security in one accounting period, the trustee shall allocate the payments to principal. If a payment is one of a series of payments that will result in the liquidation of the trust's interest in the security over more than one accounting period, the trustee shall allocate 10 percent of the payment to income and the balance to principal.

Ca. Prob. Code § 16367
EFFECTIVE 1/1/2000. Added7/22/1999 (Bill Number: AB 846) (Chapter 145).

Article 6 - ALLOCATION OF DISBURSEMENTS DURING ADMINISTRATION OF TRUST

Section 16370 - Disbursements from income

A trustee shall make the following disbursements from income to the extent that they are not disbursements to which paragraph (2) or (3) of subdivision (c) of Section 16340 applies:

(a) Except as otherwise ordered by the court, one-half of the regular compensation of the trustee and of any person providing investment advisory or custodial services to the trustee.

(b) Except as otherwise ordered by the court, one-half of all expenses for accountings, judicial proceedings, or other matters that involve both the income and remainder interests.

(c) All of the other ordinary expenses incurred in connection with the administration, management, or preservation of trust property and the distribution of income, including interest, ordinary repairs, regularly recurring taxes assessed against principal, and expenses of a proceeding or other matter that concerns primarily the income interest.

(d) All recurring premiums on insurance covering the loss of a principal asset or the loss of income from or use of the asset.

Ca. Prob. Code § 16370

EFFECTIVE 1/1/2000. Added7/22/1999 (Bill Number: AB 846) (Chapter 145).

Section 16371 - Disbursements from principal

(a) A trustee shall make the following disbursements from principal:

(1) Except as otherwise ordered by the court, the remaining one-half of the disbursements described in subdivisions (a) and (b) of Section 16370.

(2) Except as otherwise ordered by the court, all of the trustee's compensation calculated on principal as a fee for acceptance, distribution, or termination, and disbursements made to prepare property for sale.

(3) Payments on the principal of a trust debt.

(4) Expenses of a proceeding that concerns primarily principal, including a proceeding to construe the trust or to protect the trust or its property.

(5) Premiums paid on a policy of insurance not described in subdivision (d) of Section 16370 of which the trust is the owner and beneficiary.

(6) Estate, inheritance, and other transfer taxes, including penalties, apportioned to the trust.

(7) Disbursements related to environmental matters, including reclamation, assessing environmental conditions, remedying and removing environmental contamination, monitoring remedial activities and the release of substances, preventing future releases of substances, collecting amounts from persons liable or potentially liable for the costs of those activities, penalties imposed under environmental laws or regulations and other payments made to comply with those laws or regulations, statutory or common law claims by third parties, and defending claims based on environmental matters.

(b) If a principal asset is encumbered with an obligation that requires income from that asset to be paid directly to the creditor, the trustee shall transfer from principal to income an amount equal to the income paid to the creditor in reduction of the principal balance of the obligation.

Ca. Prob. Code § 16371
EFFECTIVE 1/1/2000. Added7/22/1999 (Bill Number: AB 846) (Chapter 145).

Section 16372 - Principal asset subject to depreciation

(a) For purposes of this section, "depreciation" means a reduction in value due to wear, tear, decay, corrosion, or gradual obsolescence of a fixed asset having a useful life of more than one year.

(b) A trustee may transfer from income to principal a reasonable amount of the net cash receipts from a principal asset that is subject to depreciation, under generally accepted accounting principles, but may not transfer any amount for depreciation under this section in any of the following circumstances:

(1) As to the portion of real property used or available for use by a beneficiary as a residence or of tangible personal property held or made available for the personal use or enjoyment of a beneficiary.

(2) During the administration of a decedent's estate.

(3) If the trustee is accounting under Section 16352 for the business or activity in which the asset is used.

(c) An amount transferred from income to principal need not be held as a separate fund.

Ca. Prob. Code § 16372

EFFECTIVE 1/1/2000. Added7/22/1999 (Bill Number: AB 846) (Chapter 145).

Section 16373 - Principal disbursement transferred in one or more accounting periods

(a) If a trustee makes or expects to make a principal disbursement described in this section, the trustee may transfer an appropriate amount from income to principal in one or more accounting periods to reimburse principal or to provide a reserve for future principal disbursements.

(b) Principal disbursements to which subdivision (a) applies include the following, but only to the extent that the trustee has not been and does not expect to be reimbursed by a third party:

(1) An amount chargeable to income but paid from principal because it is unusually large, including extraordinary repairs.

(2) A capital improvement to a principal asset, whether in the form of changes to an existing asset or the construction of a new asset, including special assessments.

(3) Disbursements made to prepare property for rental, including tenant allowances, leasehold improvements, and broker's commissions.

(4) Periodic payments on an obligation secured by a principal asset to the extent that the amount transferred from income to principal for depreciation is less than the periodic payments.

(5) Disbursements described in paragraph (7) of subdivision (a) of Section 16371.

(c) If the asset whose ownership gives rise to the disbursements becomes subject to a successive income interest after an income interest ends, a trustee may continue to transfer amounts from income to principal as provided in subdivision (a).

Ca. Prob. Code § 16373

EFFECTIVE 1/1/2000. Added7/22/1999 (Bill Number: AB 846) (Chapter 145).

Section 16374 - Payment of tax

(a) A tax required to be paid by a trustee based on receipts allocated to income shall be paid from income.

(b) A tax required to be paid by a trustee based on receipts allocated to principal shall be paid from principal, even if the tax is called an income tax by the taxing authority.

(c) A tax required to be paid by a trustee on the trust's share of an entity's taxable income shall be paid as follows:

(1) From income to the extent that receipts from the entity are allocated only to income.

(2) From principal to the extent that receipts from the entity are allocated only to principal.

(3) Proportionately from principal and income to the extent that receipts from the entity are allocated to both income and principal.

(4) From principal to the extent that the tax exceeds the total receipts from the entity.

(d) After applying subdivisions (a), (b), and (c), the trustee shall adjust income or principal receipts to the extent that the trust's taxes are reduced because the trust receives a deduction for payments made to a beneficiary.

Ca. Prob. Code § 16374

Amended by Stats 2009 ch 152 (AB 1545),s 3, eff. 1/1/2010. EFFECTIVE 1/1/2000. Added July 22, 1999 (Bill Number: AB 846) (Chapter 145).

Section 16374.5 - Order and sources distributions

considered paid

Unless otherwise provided by the governing instrument, determined by the trustee, or ordered by the court, distributions to beneficiaries shall be considered paid in the following order from the following sources:
(a) From net taxable income other than capital gains.
(b) From net realized short-term capital gains.
(c) From net realized long-term capitalized gains.
(d) From tax-exempt and other income.
(e) From principal of the trust.
  Ca. Prob. Code § 16374.5
Added by Stats 2006 ch 569 (AB 2347),s 6, eff. 1/1/2007.

Section 16375 - Adjustments to offset shifting of economic interests or tax benefits

(a) A fiduciary may make adjustments between principal and income to offset the shifting of economic interests or tax benefits between income beneficiaries and remainder beneficiaries that arise from any of the following:

   (1) Elections and decisions, other than those described in subdivision (b), that the fiduciary makes from time to time regarding tax matters.

   (2) An income tax or any other tax that is imposed upon the fiduciary or a beneficiary as a result of a transaction involving or a distribution from the estate or trust.

   (3) The ownership by a decedent's estate or trust of an interest in an entity whose taxable income, whether or not distributed, is includable in the taxable income of the estate, trust, or a beneficiary.
(b) If the amount of an estate tax marital deduction or charitable contribution deduction is reduced because a fiduciary deducts an amount paid from principal for income tax purposes instead of deducting it for estate tax purposes, and as a result estate taxes paid

from principal are increased and income taxes paid by a decedent's estate, trust, or beneficiary are decreased, each estate, trust, or beneficiary that benefits from the decrease in income tax shall reimburse the principal from which the increase in estate tax is paid. The total reimbursement must equal the increase in the estate tax to the extent that the principal used to pay the increase would have qualified for a marital deduction or charitable contribution deduction but for the payment. The proportionate share of the reimbursement for each estate, trust, or beneficiary whose income taxes are reduced must be the same as its proportionate share of the total decrease in income tax. An estate or trust shall reimburse principal from income.

 Ca. Prob. Code § 16375
EFFECTIVE 1/1/2000. Added7/22/1999 (Bill Number: AB 846) (Chapter 145).

Chapter 4 - LIABILITY OF TRUSTEES TO BENEFICIARIES

Article 1 - LIABILITY FOR BREACH OF TRUST

Section 16400 - Breach of trust defined

A violation by the trustee of any duty that the trustee owes the beneficiary is a breach of trust.

 Ca. Prob. Code § 16400
Enacted by Stats. 1990, Ch. 79.

Section 16401 - Liability for acts or omissions of agent;

(a) Except as provided in subdivision (b), the trustee is not liable to the beneficiary for the acts or omissions of an agent.
(b) Under any of the circumstances described in this subdivision, the trustee is liable to the beneficiary for an act or omission of an agent employed by the trustee in the administration of the trust that would be a breach of the trust if committed by the trustee:

 (1) Where the trustee directs the act of the agent.

(2) Where the trustee delegates to the agent the authority to perform an act that the trustee is under a duty not to delegate.

(3) Where the trustee does not use reasonable prudence in the selection of the agent or the retention of the agent selected by the trustee.

(4) Where the trustee does not periodically review the agent's overall performance and compliance with the terms of the delegation.

(5) Where the trustee conceals the act of the agent.

(6) Where the trustee neglects to take reasonable steps to compel the agent to redress the wrong in a case where the trustee knows of the agent's acts or omissions.

(c) The liability of a trustee for acts or omissions of agents that occurred before July 1, 1987, is governed by prior law and not by this section.

Ca. Prob. Code § 16401

Amended by Stats. 1995, Ch. 63, Sec. 9. Effective January 1, 1996.

Section 16402 - Liability for breach of trust committed by cotrustee

(a) Except as provided in subdivision (b), a trustee is not liable to the beneficiary for a breach of trust committed by a cotrustee.

(b) A trustee is liable to the beneficiary for a breach committed by a cotrustee under any of the following circumstances:

(1) Where the trustee participates in a breach of trust committed by the cotrustee.

(2) Where the trustee improperly delegates the administration of the trust to the cotrustee.

(3) Where the trustee approves, knowingly acquiesces in, or conceals a breach of trust committed by the cotrustee.

(4) Where the trustee negligently enables the cotrustee to commit a breach of trust.

(5) Where the trustee neglects to take reasonable steps to compel the cotrustee to redress a breach of trust in a case where the trustee knows or has information from which the trustee reasonably should have known of the breach.

(c) The liability of a trustee for acts or omissions of a cotrustee that occurred before July 1, 1987, is governed by prior law and not by this section.

Ca. Prob. Code § 16402

Enacted by Stats. 1990, Ch. 79.

Section 16403 - Liability of successor trustee for breach committee by predecessor

(a) Except as provided in subdivision (b), a successor trustee is not liable to the beneficiary for a breach of trust committed by a predecessor trustee.

(b) A successor trustee is liable to the beneficiary for breach of trust involving acts or omissions of a predecessor trustee in any of the following circumstances:

(1) Where the successor trustee knows or has information from which the successor trustee reasonably should have known of a situation constituting a breach of trust committed by the predecessor trustee and the successor trustee improperly permits it to continue.

(2) Where the successor trustee neglects to take reasonable steps to compel the predecessor trustee to deliver the trust property to the successor trustee.

(3) Where the successor trustee neglects to take reasonable steps to redress a breach of trust committed by the predecessor trustee in a case where the successor trustee knows or has information from which the successor trustee reasonably should have known of the predecessor trustee's breach.

(c) The liability of a trustee for acts or omissions of a predecessor trustee that occurred before July 1, 1987, is governed by prior law and not by this section.

Ca. Prob. Code § 16403
Enacted by Stats. 1990, Ch. 79.

Article 2 - REMEDIES FOR BREACH OF TRUST

Section 16420 - Generally

(a) If a trustee commits a breach of trust, or threatens to commit a breach of trust, a beneficiary or cotrustee of the trust may commence a proceeding for any of the following purposes that is appropriate:

(1) To compel the trustee to perform the trustee's duties.

(2) To enjoin the trustee from committing a breach of trust.

(3) To compel the trustee to redress a breach of trust by payment of money or otherwise.

(4) To appoint a receiver or temporary trustee to take possession of the trust property and administer the trust.

(5) To remove the trustee.

(6) Subject to Section 18100, to set aside acts of the trustee.

(7) To reduce or deny compensation of the trustee.

(8) Subject to Section 18100, to impose an equitable lien or a constructive trust on trust property.

(9) Subject to Section 18100, to trace trust property that has been wrongfully disposed of and recover the property or its proceeds.

(b) The provision of remedies for breach of trust in subdivision (a) does not prevent resort to any other appropriate remedy provided by statute or the common law.

Ca. Prob. Code § 16420
Enacted by Stats. 1990, Ch. 79.

Section 16421 - Exclusively in equity

The remedies of a beneficiary against the trustee are exclusively in equity.

Ca. Prob. Code § 16421
Enacted by Stats. 1990, Ch. 79.

Article 3 - MEASURE OF LIABILITY FOR BREACH OF TRUST

Section 16440 - Generally

(a) If the trustee commits a breach of trust, the trustee is chargeable with any of the following that is appropriate under the circumstances:

(1) Any loss or depreciation in value of the trust estate resulting from the breach of trust, with interest.

(2) Any profit made by the trustee through the breach of trust, with interest.

(3) Any profit that would have accrued to the trust estate if the loss of profit is the result of the breach of trust.
(b) If the trustee has acted reasonably and in good faith under the circumstances as known to the trustee, the court, in its discretion, may excuse the trustee in whole or in part from liability under subdivision (a) if it would be equitable to do so.

Ca. Prob. Code § 16440
Enacted by Stats. 1990, Ch. 79.

Section 16441 - Liability for interest

(a) If the trustee is liable for interest pursuant to Section 16440, the trustee is liable for the greater of the following amounts:

(1) The amount of interest that accrues at the legal rate on judgments in effect during the period when the interest accrued.

(2) The amount of interest actually received.
(b) If the trustee has acted reasonably and in good faith under the circumstances as known to the trustee, the court, in its discretion, may excuse the trustee in whole or in part from liability under subdivision (a) if it would be equitable to do so.
   Ca. Prob. Code § 16441
Amended by Stats. 1998, Ch. 77, Sec. 5. Effective January 1, 1999.

Section 16442 - Resort to other remedies

The provisions in this article for liability of a trustee for breach of trust do not prevent resort to any other remedy available under the statutory or common law.
   Ca. Prob. Code § 16442
Enacted by Stats. 1990, Ch. 79.

Article 4 - LIMITATIONS AND EXCULPATION

Section 16460 - Limitation of action for claim

(a) Unless a claim is previously barred by adjudication, consent, limitation, or otherwise:

(1) If a beneficiary has received an interim or final account in writing, or other written report, that adequately discloses the existence of a claim against the trustee for breach of trust, the claim is barred as to that beneficiary unless a proceeding to assert the claim is commenced within three years after receipt of the account or report. An account or report adequately discloses existence of a claim if it provides sufficient information so that the beneficiary knows of the claim or reasonably should have inquired into the existence of the claim.

(2) If an interim or final account in writing or other written report does not adequately disclose the existence of a claim against the trustee for breach of trust or if a beneficiary does not receive any written account or report, the claim is barred as to that beneficiary unless a proceeding to assert the claim is commenced within three years after the beneficiary discovered, or reasonably should have discovered, the subject of the claim.

(b) For the purpose of subdivision (a), a beneficiary is deemed to have received an account or report, as follows:

(1) In the case of an adult who is reasonably capable of understanding the account or report, if it is received by the adult personally.

(2) In the case of an adult who is not reasonably capable of understanding the account or report, if it is received by the person's legal representative, including a guardian ad litem or other person appointed for this purpose.

(3) In the case of a minor, if it is received by the minor's guardian or, if the minor does not have a guardian, if it is received by the minor's parent so long as the parent does not have a conflict of interest.

(c) A written account or report under this section may, but need not, satisfy the requirements of Section 16061 or 16063 or any other provision.

Ca. Prob. Code § 16460

Amended by Stats. 1996, Ch. 862, Sec. 40. Effective January 1, 1997.

Section 16461 - Relief of trustee from liability; release from liability if beneficiary fails to object to item in report within specified period

(a) Except as provided in subdivision (b), (c), or (d), the trustee can be relieved of liability for breach of trust by provisions in the trust instrument.

(b) A provision in the trust instrument is not effective to relieve the trustee of liability (1) for breach of trust committed intentionally, with gross negligence, in bad faith, or with reckless indifference to the interest of the beneficiary, or (2) for any profit that the trustee derives from a breach of trust.

(c) Subject to subdivision (b), a provision in a trust instrument that releases the trustee from liability if a beneficiary fails to object to an item in an interim or final account or other written report within a specified time period is effective only if all of the following conditions are met:

(1) The account or report sets forth the item.

(2) The period specified in the trust instrument for the beneficiary to object is not less than 180 days, or the trustee elects to follow the procedure provided in subdivision (d).

(3) Written notice in 12-point boldface type is provided to a beneficiary with the account or report in the following form: NOTICE TO BENEFICIARIES YOU HAVE [insert "180 days" or the period specified in the trust instrument, whichever is longer] FROM YOUR RECEIPT OF THIS ACCOUNT OR REPORT TO MAKE AN OBJECTION TO ANY ITEM SET FORTH IN THIS ACCOUNT OR REPORT. ANY OBJECTION YOU MAKE MUST BE IN WRITING; IT MUST BE DELIVERED TO THE TRUSTEE WITHIN THE PERIOD STATED ABOVE; AND IT MUST STATE YOUR OBJECTION. YOUR FAILURE TO DELIVER A WRITTEN OBJECTION TO THE TRUSTEE WITHIN THE PERIOD STATED ABOVE WILL PERMANENTLY PREVENT YOU FROM LATER ASSERTING THIS OBJECTION AGAINST THE TRUSTEE. IF YOU DO MAKE AN OBJECTION TO THE TRUSTEE, THE THREE-YEAR PERIOD PROVIDED IN SECTION 16460 OF THE PROBATE CODE FOR COMMENCEMENT OF LITIGATION WILL APPLY TO CLAIMS BASED ON YOUR OBJECTION AND WILL BEGIN TO RUN ON THE DATE THAT YOU RECEIVE THIS ACCOUNT OR REPORT.

(d) A provision in a trust instrument that provides for a period less than 180 days to object to an item in an account or report shall be ineffective to release the trustee from liability. A trustee of a trust created by an instrument with an ineffective period may elect to be governed by the provisions of subdivision (c) by complying with the requirements of subdivision (c), except that "180 days" shall be substituted in the notice form for the ineffective period.

(e) Subject to subdivision (b), a beneficiary who fails to object in writing to an account or report that complies with the requirements of subdivision (c) within the specified, valid period shall be barred from asserting any claim against the trustee regarding an item that is adequately disclosed in the account or report. An item is adequately disclosed if the disclosure regarding the item meets the requirements of paragraph (1) of subdivision (a) of Section 16460.

(f) Except as provided in subdivision (a) of Section 16460, the trustee may not be released from liability as to any claim based on a written objection made by a beneficiary if the objection is delivered to the trustee within the specified, effective period. If a beneficiary has filed a written objection to an account or report that complies with the requirements of subdivision (c) within the specified, valid period that concerns an item that affects any other beneficiary of the trust, any affected beneficiary may join in the objection anytime within the specified, valid period or while the resolution of the objection is pending, whichever is later. This section is not intended to establish a class of beneficiaries for actions on an account and report or provide that the action of one beneficiary is for the benefit of all beneficiaries. This section does not create a duty for any trustee to notify beneficiaries of objections or resolution of objections.

(g) Provided that a beneficiary has filed a written objection to an account or report that complies with the requirements of subdivision (c) within the specified, valid period, a supplemental written objection may be delivered in the same manner as the objection not later than 180 days after the receipt of the account or report or no later than the period specified in the trust instrument, whichever is longer.

(h) Compliance with subdivision (c) excuses compliance with paragraph (6) of subdivision (a) of Section 16063 for the account or report to which that notice relates.

(i) Subject to subdivision (b), if proper notice has been given and a beneficiary has not made a timely objection, the trustee is not liable for any other claims adequately disclosed by any item in the account or report.

(j) Subdivisions (c) to (i), inclusive, apply to all accounts and reports submitted after the effective date of the act adding these subdivisions.

Ca. Prob. Code § 16461

Amended by Stats 2004 ch 538 (AB 1990), s 1, eff. 1/1/2005.

Section 16462 - Act performed or omitted pursuant to written instruction of person holding power to revoke

(a) Notwithstanding Section 16461, a trustee of a revocable trust is not liable to a beneficiary for any act performed or omitted pursuant to written directions from the person holding the power to revoke, including a person to whom the power to direct the trustee is delegated.

(b) Subdivision (a) applies to a trust that is revocable in part with respect to the interest of the beneficiary in that part of the trust property.

Ca. Prob. Code § 16462

Enacted by Stats. 1990, Ch. 79.

Section 16463 - Consent of beneficiary to act or omission

(a) Except as provided in subdivisions (b) and (c), a beneficiary may not hold the trustee liable for an act or omission of the trustee as a breach of trust if the beneficiary consented to the act or omission before or at the time of the act or omission.

(b) The consent of the beneficiary does not preclude the beneficiary from holding the trustee liable for a breach of trust in any of the following circumstances:

(1) Where the beneficiary was under an incapacity at the time of the consent or of the act or omission.

(2) Where the beneficiary at the time consent was given did not know of his or her rights and of the material facts (A) that the trustee knew or should have known and (B) that the trustee did not reasonably believe that the beneficiary knew.

(3) Where the consent of the beneficiary was induced by improper conduct of the trustee.

(c) Where the trustee has an interest in the transaction adverse to the interest of the beneficiary, the consent of the beneficiary does not preclude the beneficiary from holding the trustee liable for a breach of trust under any of the circumstances described in subdivision (b) or where the transaction to which the beneficiary consented was not fair and reasonable to the beneficiary.

Ca. Prob. Code § 16463
Enacted by Stats. 1990, Ch. 79.

Section 16464 - Release or contract effective to discharge trustee's liability

(a) Except as provided in subdivision (b), a beneficiary may be precluded from holding the trustee liable for a breach of trust by the beneficiary's release or contract effective to discharge the trustee's liability to the beneficiary for that breach.

(b) A release or contract is not effective to discharge the trustee's liability for a breach of trust in any of the following circumstances:

(1) Where the beneficiary was under an incapacity at the time of making the release or contract.

(2) Where the beneficiary did not know of his or her rights and of the material facts (A) that the trustee knew or reasonably should have known and (B) that the trustee did not reasonably believe that the beneficiary knew.

(3) Where the release or contract of the beneficiary was induced by improper conduct of the trustee.

(4) Where the transaction involved a bargain with the trustee that was not fair and reasonable.

Ca. Prob. Code § 16464
Enacted by Stats. 1990, Ch. 79.

Section 16465 - Affirmation of transaction that beneficiary had option to affirm or reject

(a) Except as provided in subdivision (b), if the trustee, in breach of trust, enters into a transaction that the beneficiary may at his or her option reject or affirm, and the beneficiary affirms the transaction, the beneficiary shall not thereafter reject it and hold the trustee liable for any loss occurring after the trustee entered into the transaction.
(b) The affirmance of a transaction by the beneficiary does not preclude the beneficiary from holding a trustee liable for a breach of trust if, at the time of the affirmance, any of the following circumstances existed:

(1) The beneficiary was under an incapacity.

(2) The beneficiary did not know of his or her rights and of the material facts (A) that the trustee knew or reasonably should have known and (B) that the trustee did not reasonably believe that the beneficiary knew.

(3) The affirmance was induced by improper conduct of the trustee.

(4) The transaction involved a bargain with the trustee that was not fair and reasonable.

Ca. Prob. Code § 16465
Enacted by Stats. 1990, Ch. 79.

Chapter 5 - NOTICE OF PROPOSED ACTION BY TRUSTEE

Section 16500 - Generally

Subject to subdivision (d) of Section 16501, a trustee may give a notice of proposed action regarding a matter governed by Chapter 2 (commencing with Section 16200) or Chapter 3 (commencing with Section 16320) as provided in this chapter. For the purpose of this chapter, a proposed action includes a course of action or a decision not to take action. This chapter does not preclude an application or assertion of any other rights or remedies available to an interested party as otherwise provided in this part regarding an action to be taken or not to be taken by the trustee.

Ca. Prob. Code § 16500

Added by Stats 2004 ch 54 (SB 1021), s 2, eff. 1/1/2005.

Section 16501 - Persons notice mailed to; actions for which notice not used

(a) The trustee who elects to provide notice pursuant to this chapter shall deliver notice pursuant to Section 1215 of the proposed action to each of the following:

(1) A beneficiary who is receiving, or is entitled to receive, income under the trust, including a beneficiary who is entitled to receive income at the discretion of the trustee.

(2) A beneficiary who would receive a distribution of principal if the trust were terminated at the time the notice is given.

(b) Notice of proposed action is not required to be given to a person who consents in writing to the proposed action. The consent may be executed at any time before or after the proposed action is taken.

(c) A trustee is not required to provide a copy of the notice of proposed action to a beneficiary who is known to the trustee but who cannot be located by the trustee after reasonable diligence or who is unknown to the trustee.

(d) Notwithstanding any other provision of this chapter, the trustee may not use a notice of proposed action in any of the following actions:

(1) Allowance of the trustee's compensation.

(2) Allowance of compensation of the attorney for the trustee.

(3) Settlement of accounts.

(4) Discharge of the trustee.

(5) Sale of property of the trust to the trustee or to the attorney for the trustee.

(6) Exchange of property of the trust for property of the trustee or for property of the attorney for the trustee.

(7) Grant of an option to purchase property of the trust to the trustee or to the attorney for the trustee.

(8) Allowance, payment, or compromise of a claim of the trustee, or the attorney for the trustee, against the trust.

(9) Compromise or settlement of a claim, action, or proceeding by the trust against the trustee or against the attorney for the trust.

(10) Extension, renewal, or modification of the terms of a debt or other obligation of the trustee, or the attorney for the trustee, owing to or in favor of the trust.

Ca. Prob. Code § 16501
Amended by Stats 2017 ch 319 (AB 976),s 91, eff. 1/1/2018.
Amended by Stats 2016 ch 64 (AB 1700),s 1, eff. 1/1/2017.
Added by Stats 2004 ch 54 (SB 1021), s 2, eff. 1/1/2005.

Section 16502 - Contents

The notice of proposed action shall state that it is given pursuant to this section and shall include all of the following:
(a) The name, mailing address, and electronic address of the trustee.
(b) The name, telephone number, and electronic address of a person who may be contacted for additional information.
(c) A description of the action proposed to be taken and an explanation of the reasons for the action.
(d) The time within which objections to the proposed action can be made, which shall be at least 45 days from the delivery or receipt of the notice of proposed action.
(e) The date on or after which the proposed action may be taken or

is effective.

Ca. Prob. Code § 16502

Amended by Stats 2017 ch 319 (AB 976),s 92, eff. 1/1/2018.
Added by Stats 2004 ch 54 (SB 1021), s 2, eff. 1/1/2005.

Section 16503 - Objection to proposed action

(a) A beneficiary may object to the proposed action by delivering a written objection pursuant to Section 1215 to the trustee at the address stated in the notice of proposed action within the time period specified in the notice of proposed action.

(b) A trustee is not liable to a beneficiary for an action regarding a matter governed by this part if the trustee does not receive a written objection to the proposed action from a beneficiary within the applicable period and the other requirements of this section are satisfied. If no beneficiary entitled to notice objects under this section, the trustee is not liable to any current or future beneficiary with respect to the proposed action. This subdivision does not apply to a person who is a minor or an incompetent adult at the time of receiving the notice of proposed action unless the notice is served on a guardian or conservator of the estate of the person.

(c) If the trustee receives a written objection within the applicable period, either the trustee or a beneficiary may petition the court to have the proposed action taken as proposed, taken with modifications, or denied. In the proceeding, a beneficiary objecting to the proposed action has the burden of proving that the trustee's proposed action should not be taken. A beneficiary who has not objected is not estopped from opposing the proposed action in the proceeding.

(d) If the trustee decides not to implement the proposed action, the trustee shall notify the beneficiaries of the decision not to take the action and the reasons for the decision, and the trustee's decision not to implement the proposed action does not itself give rise to liability to any current or future beneficiary. A beneficiary may petition the court to have the action taken, and has the burden of proving that it should be taken.

Ca. Prob. Code § 16503

Amended by Stats 2017 ch 319 (AB 976),s 93, eff. 1/1/2018.
Added by Stats 2004 ch 54 (SB 1021), s 2, eff. 1/1/2005.

Section 16504 - Procedures prior to taking action

This chapter does not require a trustee to use these procedures prior to taking any action.

    Ca. Prob. Code § 16504

Added by Stats 2004 ch 54 (SB 1021), s 2, eff. 1/1/2005.

Part 5 - JUDICIAL PROCEEDINGS CONCERNING TRUSTS

Chapter 1 - JURISDICTION AND VENUE

Section 17000 - Exclusive jurisdiction; concurrent jurisdiction

(a) The superior court having jurisdiction over the trust pursuant to this part has exclusive jurisdiction of proceedings concerning the internal affairs of trusts.

(b) The superior court having jurisdiction over the trust pursuant to this part has concurrent jurisdiction of the following:

    (1) Actions and proceedings to determine the existence of trusts.

    (2) Actions and proceedings by or against creditors or debtors of trusts.

    (3) Other actions and proceedings involving trustees and third persons.

    Ca. Prob. Code § 17000

Enacted by Stats. 1990, Ch. 79.

Section 17001 - Court of general jurisdiction

In proceedings commenced pursuant to this division, the court is a court of general jurisdiction and has all the powers of the superior court.

    Ca. Prob. Code § 17001

Amended by Stats. 1990, Ch. 710, Sec. 44. Operative July 1, 1991, by Sec. 48 of Ch. 710.

Section 17002 - Principal place of administration

(a) The principal place of administration of the trust is the usual place where the day-to-day activity of the trust is carried on by the trustee or its representative who is primarily responsible for the administration of the trust.
(b) If the principal place of administration of the trust cannot be determined under subdivision (a), it shall be determined as follows:

  (1) If the trust has a single trustee, the principal place of administration of the trust is the trustee's residence or usual place of business.

  (2) If the trust has more than one trustee, the principal place of administration of the trust is the residence or usual place of business of any of the cotrustees as agreed upon by them or, if not, the residence or usual place of business of any of the cotrustees.
  Ca. Prob. Code § 17002
Enacted by Stats. 1990, Ch. 79.

Section 17003 - Personal jurisdiction

Subject to Section 17004:
(a) By accepting the trusteeship of a trust having its principal place of administration in this state the trustee submits personally to the jurisdiction of the court under this division.
(b) To the extent of their interests in the trust, all beneficiaries of a trust having its principal place of administration in this state are subject to the jurisdiction of the court under this division.
  Ca. Prob. Code § 17003
Enacted by Stats. 1990, Ch. 79.

Section 17004 - Exercise of jurisdiction pursuant to section 410.10, Code of Civil Procedure

The court may exercise jurisdiction in proceedings under this division on any basis permitted by Section 410.10 of the Code of Civil Procedure.

Ca. Prob. Code § 17004
Enacted by Stats. 1990, Ch. 79.

Section 17005 - Venue for commencement of proceedings

(a) The proper county for commencement of a proceeding pursuant to this division is either of the following:

(1) In the case of a living trust, the county where the principal place of administration of the trust is located.

(2) In the case of a testamentary trust, either the county where the decedent's estate is administered or where the principal place of administration of the trust is located.

(b) If a living trust has no trustee, the proper county for commencement of a proceeding for appointing a trustee is the county where the trust property, or some portion of the trust property, is located.

(c) Except as otherwise provided in subdivisions (a) and (b), the proper county for commencement of a proceeding pursuant to this division is determined by the rules applicable to civil actions generally.

Ca. Prob. Code § 17005
Enacted by Stats. 1990, Ch. 79.

Section 17006 - No right to jury trial

There is no right to a jury trial in proceedings under this division concerning the internal affairs of trusts.

Ca. Prob. Code § 17006
Enacted by Stats. 1990, Ch. 79.

Chapter 2 - NOTICE

Section 17100 - Generally

Except as otherwise provided in this division, notice in proceedings commenced pursuant to this division, or notice otherwise required by this division, is governed by Part 2 (commencing with Section 1200) of Division 3.

Ca. Prob. Code § 17100
Added by Stats. 1990, Ch. 79, Sec. 14.

Section 17105 - Notice given without court order

A petitioner or other person required to give notice may cause notice to be given to any person interested in the trust without the need for a court order.

Ca. Prob. Code § 17105
Added by Stats. 1990, Ch. 79, Sec. 14.

Chapter 3 - PROCEEDINGS CONCERNING TRUSTS

Section 17200 - Petition concerning internal affairs or determine existence; internal affairs of trust

(a) Except as provided in Section 15800, a trustee or beneficiary of a trust may petition the court under this chapter concerning the internal affairs of the trust or to determine the existence of the trust.

(b) Proceedings concerning the internal affairs of a trust include, but are not limited to, proceedings for any of the following purposes:

(1) Determining questions of construction of a trust instrument.

(2) Determining the existence or nonexistence of any immunity, power, privilege, duty, or right.

(3) Determining the validity of a trust provision.

(4) Ascertaining beneficiaries and determining to whom property shall pass or be delivered upon final or partial termination of the trust, to the extent the determination is not made by the trust instrument.

(5) Settling the accounts and passing upon the acts of the trustee, including the exercise of discretionary powers.

(6) Instructing the trustee.

(7) Compelling the trustee to do any of the following:

    (A) Provide a copy of the terms of the trust.

    (B) Provide information about the trust under Section 16061 if the trustee has failed to provide the requested information within 60 days after the beneficiary's reasonable written request, and the beneficiary has not received the requested information from the trustee within the six months preceding the request.

    (C) Account to the beneficiary, subject to the provisions of Section 16064, if the trustee has failed to submit a requested account within 60 days after written request of the beneficiary and no account has been made within six months preceding the request.

(8) Granting powers to the trustee.

(9) Fixing or allowing payment of the trustee's compensation or reviewing the reasonableness of the trustee's compensation.

(10) Appointing or removing a trustee.

(11) Accepting the resignation of a trustee.

(12) Compelling redress of a breach of the trust by any available remedy.

(13) Approving or directing the modification or termination of the trust.

(14) Approving or directing the combination or division of trusts.

(15) Amending or conforming the trust instrument in the manner required to qualify a decedent's estate for the charitable estate tax deduction under federal law, including the addition of mandatory governing instrument requirements for a charitable remainder trust as required by final regulations and rulings of the United States Internal Revenue Service.

(16) Authorizing or directing transfer of a trust or trust property to or from another jurisdiction.

(17) Directing transfer of a testamentary trust subject to continuing court jurisdiction from one county to another.

(18) Approving removal of a testamentary trust from continuing court jurisdiction.

(19) Reforming or excusing compliance with the governing instrument of an organization pursuant to Section 16105.

(20) Determining the liability of the trust for any debts of a deceased settlor. However, nothing in this paragraph shall provide standing to bring an action concerning the internal affairs of the trust to a person whose only claim to the assets of the decedent is as a creditor.

(21) Determining petitions filed pursuant to Section 15687 and reviewing the reasonableness of compensation for legal services authorized under that section. In determining the reasonableness of compensation under this paragraph, the court may consider, together with all other relevant circumstances, whether prior approval was obtained pursuant to Section 15687.

(22) If a member of the State Bar of California has transferred the economic interest of his or her practice to a trustee and if the member is a deceased member under Section 9764, a petition may be brought to appoint a practice administrator. The procedures, including, but not limited to, notice requirements, that apply to the appointment of a practice administrator for a deceased member shall apply to the petition brought under this section.

(23) If a member of the State Bar of California has transferred the economic interest of his or her practice to a trustee and if the member is a disabled member under Section 2468, a petition may be brought to appoint a practice administrator. The procedures, including, but not limited to, notice requirements, that apply to the appointment of a practice administrator for a disabled member shall apply to the petition brought under this section.

(c) The court may, on its own motion, set and give notice of an order to show cause why a trustee who is a professional fiduciary, and who is required to be licensed under Chapter 6 (commencing with Section 6500) of Division 3 of the Business and Professions Code, should not be removed for failing to hold a valid, unexpired, unsuspended license.

Ca. Prob. Code § 17200

Amended by Stats 2010 ch 621 (SB 202),s 11, eff. 1/1/2011.
Amended by Stats 2003 ch 629 (SB 294), s 8, eff. 1/1/2004.
EFFECTIVE 1/1/2000. Amended July 26, 1999 (Bill Number: AB 239) (Chapter 175).

Section 17200.1 - Proceedings concerning transfer of property

All proceedings concerning the transfer of property of the trust shall be conducted pursuant to the provisions of Part 19 (commencing with Section 850) of Division 2.

Ca. Prob. Code § 17200.1

Added by Stats 2001 ch 49 (SB 669), s 7, eff. 1/1/2002.
Former § 17200.1 was repealed by Stats 2001 ch 49 (SB 669), s 6.

Section 17200.2 - [Repealed]

Ca. Prob. Code § 17200.2

Repealed by Stats 2001 ch 49 (SB 669), s 8, eff. 1/1/2002.

Section 17201 - Petition commencing proceedings

A proceeding under this chapter is commenced by filing a petition stating facts showing that the petition is authorized under this chapter. The petition shall also state the grounds of the petition and the names and addresses of each person entitled to notice of the petition.

Ca. Prob. Code § 17201
Amended by Stats. 1996, Ch. 862, Sec. 44. Effective January 1, 1997.

Section 17201.1 - Discovery upon trustee

A petitioner in a proceeding under Section 17200 may commence discovery upon a trustee in accordance with the same time periods set forth in the Civil Discovery Act (Title 4 (commencing with Section 2016.010) of Part 4 of the Code of Civil Procedure) except that the time periods shall commence to run upon service of the petition and notice of hearing upon the trustee or the trustee's appearance in the proceeding, whichever first occurs. Nothing in this section shall alter when a respondent in such a proceeding may commence discovery.

Ca. Prob. Code § 17201.1
Added by Stats 2017 ch 32 (AB 308),s 4, eff. 1/1/2018.

Section 17202 - Proceeding not reasonably necessary for protection of interests

The court may dismiss a petition if it appears that the proceeding is not reasonably necessary for the protection of the interests of the trustee or beneficiary.

Ca. Prob. Code § 17202
Enacted by Stats. 1990, Ch. 79.

Section 17203 - Notice of hearing

(a) At least 30 days before the time set for the hearing on the petition, the petitioner shall cause notice of hearing to be delivered pursuant to Section 1215 to all of the following persons:

(1) All trustees.

(2) All beneficiaries, subject to Chapter 2 (commencing with Section 15800) of Part 3.

(3) The Attorney General, if the petition relates to a charitable trust subject to the jurisdiction of the Attorney General.
(b) At least 30 days before the time set for hearing on the petition, the petitioner shall cause notice of the hearing and a copy of the petition to be served in the manner provided in Chapter 4 (commencing with Section 413.10) of Title 5 of Part 2 of the Code of Civil Procedure on any person, other than a trustee or beneficiary, whose right, title, or interest would be affected by the petition and who does not receive notice pursuant to subdivision (a). The court may not shorten the time for giving notice under this subdivision.
(c) If a person to whom notice otherwise would be given has been deceased for at least 40 days, and no personal representative has been appointed for the estate of that person, and the deceased person's right, title, or interest has not passed to any other person pursuant to Division 8 (commencing with Section 13000) or otherwise, notice may instead be given to the following persons:

(1) Each heir and devisee of the decedent, and all persons named as executors of the will of the decedent, so far as known to the petitioner.

(2) Each person serving as guardian or conservator of the decedent at the time of the decedent's death, so far as known to the petitioner.
Ca. Prob. Code § 17203
Amended by Stats 2017 ch 319 (AB 976),s 94, eff. 1/1/2018.

Section 17204 - Request of special notice by beneficiary

(a) If proceedings involving a trust are pending, a beneficiary of the trust may, in person or by attorney, file with the court clerk where the proceedings are pending a written request stating that the beneficiary desires special notice of the filing of petitions in the proceeding relating to any or all of the purposes described in Section 17200 and giving an address for receiving notice by mail. A copy of the request shall be delivered pursuant to Section 1215 to the trustee or the trustee's attorney. If personally delivered, the request shall be effective when it is delivered. If mailed or electronically delivered, the request shall be effective when it is received. When the original of the request is filed with the court clerk, it shall be accompanied by a written admission or proof of service. A request for special notice may be modified or withdrawn in the same manner as provided for the making of the initial request.

(b)

(1) An interested person may request special notice in the same manner as a beneficiary under subdivision (a), for the purpose set forth in paragraph (9) of subdivision (b) of Section 17200. The request for special notice shall be accompanied by a verified statement of the person's interest.

(2) For purposes set forth in paragraphs (2), (4) to (6), inclusive, (8), (12), (16), (20), and (21) of subdivision (b) of Section 17200, an interested person may petition the court for an order for special notice of proceedings involving a trust. The petition shall include a verified statement of the creditor's interest and may be served on the trustee or the trustee's attorney in a manner described in Section 1215. The petition may be made by ex parte application.

(3) For purposes of this subdivision, an "interested person" means only a creditor of a trust or, if the trust has become irrevocable upon the death of a trustor, a creditor of the trustor.

(4) This section does not confer standing on an interested person if standing does not otherwise exist.

(c) Except as provided in subdivision (d), after serving and filing a request and proof of service pursuant to subdivision (a) or paragraph (1) of subdivision (b), the beneficiary or the interested person is entitled to notice pursuant to Section 17203. If the petition of an interested person filed pursuant to paragraph (2) of subdivision (b) is granted by the court, the interested person is entitled to notice pursuant to Section 17203.

(d) A request for special notice made by a beneficiary whose right to notice is restricted by Section 15802 is not effective.

Ca. Prob. Code § 17204

Amended by Stats 2017 ch 319 (AB 976),s 95, eff. 1/1/2018.

Amended by Stats 2004 ch 334 (AB 2872), s 1, eff. 1/1/2005.

Section 17205 - Copy of petition mailed to person

If a trustee or beneficiary has served and filed either a notice of appearance, in person or by counsel, directed to the petitioner or the petitioner's counsel in connection with a particular petition and proceeding or a written request for a copy of the petition, and has given an address to which notice or a copy of the petition may be delivered pursuant to Section 1215, the petitioner shall cause a copy of the petition to be delivered to that person within five days after service of the notice of appearance or receipt of the request.

Ca. Prob. Code § 17205

Amended by Stats 2017 ch 319 (AB 976),s 96, eff. 1/1/2018.

Section 17206 - Discretion of court

The court in its discretion may make any orders and take any other action necessary or proper to dispose of the matters presented by the petition, including appointment of a temporary trustee to administer the trust in whole or in part.

Ca. Prob. Code § 17206

Enacted by Stats. 1990, Ch. 79.

Section 17209 - Administration intended to proceed expeditiously

The administration of trusts is intended to proceed expeditiously and free of judicial intervention, subject to the jurisdiction of the court.

Ca. Prob. Code § 17209
Enacted by Stats. 1990, Ch. 79.

Section 17210 - Petition in case involving charitable trust

In a case involving a charitable trust subject to the jurisdiction of the Attorney General, the Attorney General may petition under this chapter.

Ca. Prob. Code § 17210
Enacted by Stats. 1990, Ch. 79.

Section 17211 - Costs of litigation in proceeding contesting trustee's account

(a) If a beneficiary contests the trustee's account and the court determines that the contest was without reasonable cause and in bad faith, the court may award against the contestant the compensation and costs of the trustee and other expenses and costs of litigation, including attorney's fees, incurred to defend the account. The amount awarded shall be a charge against any interest of the beneficiary in the trust. The contestant shall be personally liable for any amount that remains unsatisfied.

(b) If a beneficiary contests the trustee's account and the court determines that the trustee's opposition to the contest was without reasonable cause and in bad faith, the court may award the contestant the costs of the contestant and other expenses and costs of litigation, including attorney's fees, incurred to contest the account. The amount awarded shall be a charge against the compensation or other interest of the trustee in the trust. The trustee shall be personally liable and on the bond, if any, for any amount that remains unsatisfied.

Ca. Prob. Code § 17211
Added by Stats. 1996, Ch. 563, Sec. 31. Effective January 1, 1997.

Chapter 4 - TESTAMENTARY TRUSTS SUBJECT TO CONTINUING COURT JURISDICTION

Article 1 - ADMINISTRATION OF TESTAMENTARY TRUSTS SUBJECT TO CONTINUING COURT JURISDICTION

Section 17300 - Applicability

This article applies only to the following:

(a) A trust created by a will executed before July 1, 1977, and not incorporated by reference in a will on or after July 1, 1977.

(b) A trust created by a will which provides that the trust is subject to the continuing jurisdiction of the superior court.

Ca. Prob. Code § 17300
Enacted by Stats. 1990, Ch. 79.

Section 17301 - Retention of jurisdiction

If a trust described in Section 17300 continues after distribution of the decedent's estate, the court in which the decedent's estate was administered retains jurisdiction over the trust for any of the purposes specified in Section 17200.

Ca. Prob. Code § 17301
Enacted by Stats. 1990, Ch. 79.

Section 17302 - Part governs proceedings

Except as otherwise provided in this article, proceedings relating to trusts under continuing court jurisdiction are governed by this part.

Ca. Prob. Code § 17302
Enacted by Stats. 1990, Ch. 79.

Section 17303 - Inapplicable to trust described in section 17300

This article does not apply to a trust described in Section 17300 that has been removed from continuing court jurisdiction.

Ca. Prob. Code § 17303
Enacted by Stats. 1990, Ch. 79.

Section 17304 - Transfer of trust to different county; petition; hearing

(a) At any time after final distribution of the decedent's estate, a trust described in Section 17300 may be transferred to a different county in this state as provided in this section.
(b) The petition for transfer shall set forth all of the following:

(1) The name of the county to which jurisdiction over the trust is sought to be transferred.

(2) The names, ages, and places of residence of the trustees and all beneficiaries of the trust, so far as known to the petitioner.

(3) A brief description of the character, condition, value, and location of property of the trust.

(4) A brief statement of the reasons for transfer.
(c) If, after hearing, it appears to the court that the transfer of jurisdiction to the county designated in the petition or to any other county in this state will be in the best interests of the estate, or that economical and convenient administration of the trust will be facilitated by the transfer, the court shall make an order transferring jurisdiction over the trust. Upon such order, the court clerk shall certify a copy of the order of transfer to the clerk of the court to which jurisdiction is transferred, together with copies of the instrument creating the trust, the decree of distribution, and any other documents or matters of record the court determines by order to be necessary to define the powers and duties of the trustee, or otherwise to be necessary in connection with further administration of the trust.
(d) The court to which jurisdiction is transferred may from time to time require by order the filing of certified copies of additional papers or matters of record from the court in which the decedent's estate was administered as are required.

(e) Upon the filing of a certified copy of the order of transfer, together with supporting documents, the court to which jurisdiction is transferred has the same jurisdiction over the trust as the court in which the decedent's estate was administered but for the transfer.

Ca. Prob. Code § 17304
Enacted by Stats. 1990, Ch. 79.

Article 2 - REMOVAL OF TRUSTS FROM CONTINUING COURT JURISDICTION

Section 17350 - Applicability

This article applies only to trusts created by will executed before July 1, 1977, and not incorporated by reference in a will on or after July 1, 1977.

Ca. Prob. Code § 17350
Enacted by Stats. 1990, Ch. 79.

Section 17351 - Removal if trustee is trust company; notice of removal

(a) If any of the trustees of a trust described in Section 17350 is a trust company, the trust shall be removed from continuing court jurisdiction as provided in this section. Within six months after the initial funding of the trust, the trustee shall give a notice of removal of the trust from continuing court jurisdiction to each beneficiary. Notice of removal shall be sent by registered or certified mail or by first-class mail, but notice sent by first-class mail is effective only if an acknowledgment of receipt of notice is signed by the beneficiary and returned to the trustee.

(b) The notice of removal of the trust from continuing court jurisdiction shall contain the following:

(1) A statement that as of January 1, 1983, the law was changed to remove the necessity for continuing court jurisdiction over the trust.

(2) A statement that Section 17200 of the Probate Code gives any beneficiary the right to petition a court to determine important matters relating to the administration of the trust.

(3) A copy of the text of Sections 17200 and 17201.

(4) A statement that each income beneficiary, as defined in Section 16325, is entitled to an annual statement of the principal and income receipts and disbursements of the trust and that any other beneficiary is entitled to such information upon written request to the trustee.

(5) The name and location of the court in the county in which it is appropriate to file a petition pursuant to Section 17200, the name and location of the court that had jurisdiction over the administration of the decedent's estate, and a statement that it is appropriate to file a petition pursuant to Section 17200 with either court.

(c) The trustee shall file with the court that had jurisdiction over the administration of the decedent's estate proof of giving notice under this section within seven months after the initial funding of the trust.

Ca. Prob. Code § 17351

EFFECTIVE 1/1/2000. Amended July 22, 1999 (Bill Number: AB 846) (Chapter 145).

Section 17352 - Removal if none of trustees is trust company

(a) If none of the trustees of a trust described in Section 17350 is a trust company, the trust may be removed from continuing court jurisdiction only with approval of the court. The trustee may petition for court approval at any time, and from time to time, in the trustee's discretion.

(b) The petition for removal shall set forth the trust accounts in detail, report the trustee's acts, and show the condition of the trust estate. A copy of the trust instrument shall be attached to the petition.

(c) At the hearing the court may receive testimony from any interested person and may grant or deny the petition, or may grant the petition on such conditions as the court in its discretion deems proper.

(d) If the petition is granted, the trustee shall send the notice of removal of the trust provided in subdivision (b) of Section 17351 and file proof of service as required by subdivision (c) of Section 17351 within six months and seven months, respectively, from the date the petition is granted. A copy of the court order granting the petition shall be attached to the notice.

(e) If the petition is not granted, the trust shall continue to be administered under Article 1 (commencing with Section 17300) as if the settlor had provided in the will that the court does not lose jurisdiction of the estate by final distribution.

Ca. Prob. Code § 17352
Enacted by Stats. 1990, Ch. 79.

Section 17353 - Trust company appointed as successor trustee

If a trust company is appointed as a successor trustee of a trust which, at the time of the appointment, is subject to continuing court jurisdiction because it was not removed pursuant to Section 17352, the successor trustee shall comply with Section 17351. For the purpose of complying with Section 17351, the date of appointment of the successor trustee shall be treated as the date of initial funding of the trust.

Ca. Prob. Code § 17353
Enacted by Stats. 1990, Ch. 79.

Section 17354 - Events not causing trust to be subject to continuing jurisdiction

After a trust is removed from continuing court jurisdiction pursuant to this article, neither a change in trustees nor any other event causes the trust to be subject to continuing court jurisdiction under Article 1 (commencing with Section 17300).

Ca. Prob. Code § 17354
Enacted by Stats. 1990, Ch. 79.

Chapter 5 - TRANSFER OF TRUST TO ANOTHER JURISDICTION

Section 17400 - Applicability

(a) This chapter applies to all of the following:

(1) A trust that is subject to this division.

(2) A trust subject to Chapter 8 (commencing with Section 6320) of Part 1 of Division 6.

(3) Any other trust to which the provisions of this chapter are made applicable by statute or trust instrument.
(b) This chapter does not prevent the transfer of the place of administration of a trust or of trust property to another jurisdiction by any other available means.
Ca. Prob. Code § 17400
Enacted by Stats. 1990, Ch. 79.

Section 17401 - Generally

(a) The court may make an order for the transfer of the place of administration of a trust or the transfer of some or all of the trust property to a jurisdiction outside this state as provided in this chapter.
(b) Except as otherwise provided in this chapter, proceedings under this chapter are governed by this part.
Ca. Prob. Code § 17401
Enacted by Stats. 1990, Ch. 79.

Section 17402 - Petition for transfer

The petition for transfer shall set forth all of the following:
(a) The names and places of residence of the following:

(1) The trustee administering the trust in this state.

(2) The trustee, including any domiciliary trustee, who will administer the trust or trust property in the other jurisdiction.

(b) The names, ages, and places of residence of the living beneficiaries, as far as known to the petitioner.

(c) Whether the trustee who will administer the trust in the other jurisdiction has agreed to accept the trust. If so, the acceptance or a copy shall be attached as an exhibit to the petition or otherwise filed with the court.

(d) A general statement of the qualifications of the trustee who will administer the trust in the other jurisdiction and the amount of fiduciary bond, if any. If the trustee is an individual, the statement shall include the trustee's age.

(e) A general statement of the nature and value of the property of any trust of the same settlor being administered in the other jurisdiction by the trustee who will administer the trust in the other jurisdiction.

(f) The name of the court, if any, having jurisdiction of the trustee in the other jurisdiction or of its accounts or in which a proceeding may be had with respect to administration of the trust or the trustee's accounts.

(g) A statement of the character, condition, location, and value of the trust property sought to be transferred.

(h) Whether there is any pending civil action in this state against the trustee arising out of the administration of the trust sought to be transferred.

(i) A statement of the reasons for the transfer.

Ca. Prob. Code § 17402

Enacted by Stats. 1990, Ch. 79.

Section 17403 - Notice of hearing

(a) At least 30 days before the time set for the hearing on the petition, the petitioner shall cause notice of the time and place of the hearing to be delivered pursuant to Section 1215 to each of the persons named in the petition at their respective addresses as stated in the petition.

(b) Any person interested in the trust, as trustee, beneficiary, or otherwise, may appear and file written grounds in opposition to the petition.

Ca. Prob. Code § 17403
Amended by Stats 2017 ch 319 (AB 976),s 97, eff. 1/1/2018.

Section 17404 - Findings required for order

The court may, in its discretion, grant the petition and order the trustee to transfer the trust property or to transfer the place of administration of the trust to the other jurisdiction if, after hearing, all of the following appear to the court:

(a) The transfer of the trust property to a trustee in another jurisdiction, or the transfer of the place of administration of the trust to another jurisdiction, will promote the best interests of the trust and those interested in it, taking into account the interest in the economical and convenient administration of the trust.

(b) The transfer will not violate the trust instrument.

(c) Any new trustee to whom the trust property is to be transferred is qualified, willing, and able to administer the trust or trust property under the trust instrument.

Ca. Prob. Code § 17404
Enacted by Stats. 1990, Ch. 79.

Section 17405 - Transfer order

If a transfer is ordered under this chapter, the court may direct the manner of transfer and impose terms and conditions as may be just, including, but not limited to, a requirement for the substitution of a successor trustee in any pending litigation in this state. The delivery of property in accordance with the order of the court is a full discharge of the trustee in relation to all property embraced in the order.

Ca. Prob. Code § 17405
Enacted by Stats. 1990, Ch. 79.

Chapter 6 - TRANSFER OF TRUST FROM ANOTHER JURISDICTION

Section 17450 - Applicability

(a) This chapter applies to a trust, or portion thereof, administered in a jurisdiction outside this state.

(b) This chapter does not prevent the transfer of the place of administration of a trust or of trust property to this state by any other available means.

Ca. Prob. Code § 17450
Enacted by Stats. 1990, Ch. 79.

Section 17451 - Generally

(a) The court may make an order accepting the transfer of the place of administration of a trust from another jurisdiction to this state or the transfer of some or all of the trust property in another jurisdiction to a trustee in this state as provided in this chapter.

(b) Except as otherwise provided in this chapter, proceedings under this chapter are governed by this part.

Ca. Prob. Code § 17451
Enacted by Stats. 1990, Ch. 79.

Section 17452 - Venue for filing petition

(a) If the petition requests that a resident of this state be appointed trustee, the petition shall be filed in the court of the county where the proposed principal place of administration of the trust pursuant to Section 17002 is located.

(b) If the petition requests that only a nonresident of this state be appointed trustee, the petition shall be filed in the court of the county where either (1) any beneficiary resides or (2) a substantial portion of the trust property to be transferred is located or will be located.

Ca. Prob. Code § 17452
Enacted by Stats. 1990, Ch. 79.

Section 17453 - Contents of petition for transfer

The petition for transfer shall set forth all of the following:

(a) The names and places of residence of the following:

(1) The trustee administering the trust in the other jurisdiction.

(2) The proposed trustee to whom administration of the trust or trust property will be transferred.

(b) The names, ages, and places of residence of all living beneficiaries, as far as known to the petitioner.

(c) Whether administration of the trust has been subject to supervision in a jurisdiction outside this state. If so, the petition shall state whether a petition or appropriate request for transfer of place of administration of the trust or trust property to this state has been filed, if necessary, with the court in the other jurisdiction, and the status of the petition or request.

(d) Whether the trustee proposed to administer the trust in this state has agreed to accept the trust in this state. If the trustee has agreed, the acceptance shall be attached as an exhibit to the petition or otherwise filed with the court.

(e) A general statement of the qualifications of the trustee proposed to administer the trust in this state and the amount of any bond to be requested. If the trustee is an individual, the statement shall include the trustee's age.

(f) A copy of the trust instrument or a statement of the terms of the trust instrument in effect at the time the petition is filed, including all amendments thereto.

(g) A statement of the character, condition, location, and value of the trust property sought to be transferred.

(h) A statement of the reasons for the transfer.

Ca. Prob. Code § 17453
Enacted by Stats. 1990, Ch. 79.

Section 17454 - Notice of hearing

(a) At least 30 days before the time set for the hearing on the petition, the petitioner shall cause notice of the time and place of the hearing to be delivered pursuant to Section 1215 to each of the persons named in the petition at their respective addresses as stated in the petition.

(b) Any person interested in the trust, as trustee, beneficiary, or otherwise, may appear and file written grounds in opposition to the petition.

Ca. Prob. Code § 17454
Amended by Stats 2017 ch 319 (AB 976),s 98, eff. 1/1/2018.

Section 17455 - Findings required for order

(a) The court may, in its discretion, grant the petition and issue an order accepting transfer of trust property or the place of administration of the trust to this state and appoint a trustee to administer the trust in this state, if, after hearing, all of the following appear to the court:

   (1) The transfer of the trust property to a trustee in this state, or the transfer of the place of administration of the trust to this state, will promote the best interests of the trust and those interested in it, taking into account the interest in the economical and convenient administration of the trust.

   (2) The transfer will not violate the trust instrument.

   (3) The trustee appointed by the court to administer the trust in this state, and to whom the trust property is to be transferred, is qualified, willing, and able to administer the trust or trust property under the trust instrument.

   (4) The proper court in the other jurisdiction has approved the transfer if approval is necessary under the law of the other jurisdiction.

(b) If the court grants the petition under subdivision (a), the court shall require the trustee to give a bond, if necessary under the law of the other jurisdiction or of this state, and may require bond as provided in Section 15602.

Ca. Prob. Code § 17455
Enacted by Stats. 1990, Ch. 79.

Section 17456 - Conditional order

If appropriate to facilitate transfer of the trust property or the place of administration of a trust to this state, the court may issue a conditional order appointing a trustee to administer the trust in this state and indicating that transfer to this state will be accepted if transfer is approved by the proper court of the other jurisdiction.

Ca. Prob. Code § 17456
Enacted by Stats. 1990, Ch. 79.

Section 17457 - Administration of trust

A trust transferred to this state pursuant to this chapter shall be administered in the same manner as a trust of that type created in this state. The validity of a trust and the construction of the beneficial provisions of a trust transferred to this state are not affected by this section.

Ca. Prob. Code § 17457
Enacted by Stats. 1990, Ch. 79.

Part 6 - RIGHTS OF THIRD PERSONS

Chapter 1 - LIABILITY OF TRUSTEE TO THIRD PERSONS

Section 18000 - Contract properly entered into in trustee's fiduciary capacity

(a) Unless otherwise provided in the contract or in this chapter, a trustee is not personally liable on a contract properly entered into in the trustee's fiduciary capacity in the course of administration of the trust unless the trustee fails to reveal the trustee's representative capacity or identify the trust in the contract.
(b) The personal liability of a trustee on a contract entered into before July 1, 1987, is governed by prior law and not by this section.

Ca. Prob. Code § 18000
Enacted by Stats. 1990, Ch. 79.

Section 18001 - Obligations arising from ownership or control of trust property

A trustee is personally liable for obligations arising from ownership or control of trust property only if the trustee is personally at fault.

Ca. Prob. Code § 18001
Enacted by Stats. 1990, Ch. 79.

Section 18002 - Torts committed in course of administration

A trustee is personally liable for torts committed in the course of administration of the trust only if the trustee is personally at fault.
Ca. Prob. Code § 18002
Enacted by Stats. 1990, Ch. 79.

Section 18003 - Cotrustee not joining in exercise of power; dissenting cotrustee joining in action at direction of majority

(a) A cotrustee who does not join in exercising a power held by three or more cotrustees is not liable to third persons for the consequences of the exercise of the power.
(b) A dissenting cotrustee who joins in an action at the direction of the majority cotrustees is not liable to third persons for the action if the dissenting cotrustee expresses the dissent in writing to any other cotrustee at or before the time the action is taken.
(c) This section does not excuse a cotrustee from liability for failure to discharge the cotrustee's duties as a trustee.
Ca. Prob. Code § 18003
Enacted by Stats. 1990, Ch. 79.

Section 18004 - Claim asserted by proceeding against trustee in trustee's representative capacity

A claim based on a contract entered into by a trustee in the trustee's representative capacity, on an obligation arising from ownership or control of trust property, or on a tort committed in the course of administration of the trust may be asserted against the trust by proceeding against the trustee in the trustee's representative capacity, whether or not the trustee is personally liable on the claim.

Ca. Prob. Code § 18004
Enacted by Stats. 1990, Ch. 79.

Section 18005 - Determining liability between estate and trustee personally

The question of liability as between the trust estate and the trustee personally may be determined in a proceeding under Section 17200.
Ca. Prob. Code § 18005
Enacted by Stats. 1990, Ch. 79.

Chapter 2 - PROTECTION OF THIRD PERSONS

Section 18100 - Third person acting in good faith and for valuable consideration without actual knowledge

With respect to a third person dealing with a trustee or assisting a trustee in the conduct of a transaction, if the third person acts in good faith and for a valuable consideration and without actual knowledge that the trustee is exceeding the trustee's powers or improperly exercising them:

(a) The third person is not bound to inquire whether the trustee has power to act or is properly exercising a power and may assume without inquiry the existence of a trust power and its proper exercise.

(b) The third person is fully protected in dealing with or assisting the trustee just as if the trustee has and is properly exercising the power the trustee purports to exercise.
Ca. Prob. Code § 18100
Enacted by Stats. 1990, Ch. 79.

Section 18100.5 - Certificate of trust in lieu of providing copy of trust instrument

(a) The trustee may present a certification of trust to any person in lieu of providing a copy of the trust instrument to establish the existence or terms of the trust. A certification of trust may be executed by the trustee voluntarily or at the request of the person with whom the trustee is dealing.

(b) The certification of trust may confirm the following facts or contain the following information:

(1) The existence of the trust and date of execution of the trust instrument.

(2) The identity of the settlor or settlors and the currently acting trustee or trustees of the trust.

(3) The powers of the trustee.

(4) The revocability or irrevocability of the trust and the identity of any person holding any power to revoke the trust.

(5) When there are multiple trustees, the signature authority of the trustees, indicating whether all, or less than all, of the currently acting trustees are required to sign in order to exercise various powers of the trustee.

(6) The trust identification number, whether a social security number or an employer identification number.

(7) The manner in which title to trust assets should be taken.

(8) The legal description of any interest in real property held in the trust.

(c) The certification shall contain a statement that the trust has not been revoked, modified, or amended in any manner which would cause the representations contained in the certification of trust to be incorrect and shall contain a statement that it is being signed by all of the currently acting trustees of the trust. The certification shall be in the form of an acknowledged declaration signed by all currently acting trustees of the trust. The certification signed by the currently acting trustee may be recorded in the office of the county recorder in the county where all or a portion of the real property is located.

(d) The certification of trust may, but is not required to, include excerpts from the original trust documents, any amendments thereto, and any other documents evidencing or pertaining to the succession of successor trustees. The certification of trust shall not be required to contain the dispositive provisions of the trust which set forth the distribution of the trust estate.

(e) A person whose interest is, or may be, affected by the certification of trust may require that the trustee offering or recording the certification of trust provide copies of those excerpts from the original trust documents, any amendments thereto, and any other documents which designate, evidence, or pertain to the succession of the trustee or confer upon the trustee the power to act in the pending transaction, or both. Nothing in this section is intended to require or imply an obligation to provide the dispositive provisions of the trust or the entire trust and amendments thereto.

(f) A person who acts in reliance upon a certification of trust without actual knowledge that the representations contained therein are incorrect is not liable to any person for so acting. A person who does not have actual knowledge that the facts contained in the certification of trust are incorrect may assume without inquiry the existence of the facts contained in the certification of trust. Actual knowledge shall not be inferred solely from the fact that a copy of all or part of the trust instrument is held by the person relying upon the trust certification. Any transaction, and any lien created thereby, entered into by the trustee and a person acting in reliance upon a certification of trust shall be enforceable against the trust assets. However, if the person has actual knowledge that the trustee is acting outside the scope of the trust, then the transaction is not enforceable against the trust assets. Nothing contained herein shall limit the rights of the beneficiaries of the trust against the trustee.

(g) A person's failure to demand a certification of trust does not affect the protection provided that person by Section 18100, and no inference as to whether that person has acted in good faith may be drawn from the failure to demand a certification of trust. Nothing in this section is intended to create an implication that a person is liable for acting in reliance upon a certification of trust under circumstances where the requirements of this section are not satisfied.

(h) Except when requested by a beneficiary or in the context of litigation concerning a trust and subject to the provisions of subdivision (e), any person making a demand for the trust documents in addition to a certification of trust to prove facts set forth in the certification of trust acceptable to the third party shall be liable for damages, including attorney's fees, incurred as a result of the refusal to accept the certification of trust in lieu of the requested documents if the court determines that the person acted in bad faith in requesting the trust documents.

(i) Any person may record a certification of trust that relates to an interest in real property in the office of the county recorder in any county in which all or a portion of the real property is located. The county recorder shall impose any fee prescribed by law for recording that document sufficient to cover all costs incurred by the county in recording the document. The recorded certification of trust shall be a public record of the real property involved. This subdivision does not create a requirement to record a certification of trust in conjunction with the recordation of a transfer of title of real property involving a trust.

Ca. Prob. Code § 18100.5
Amended by Stats 2004 ch 136 (AB 1848), s 1, eff. 1/1/2005.

Section 18101 - Not bound to ensure proper application of trust property

A third person who acts in good faith is not bound to ensure the proper application of trust property paid or delivered to the trustee.

Ca. Prob. Code § 18101
Enacted by Stats. 1990, Ch. 79.

Section 18102 - Transaction with former trustee without knowledge person no longer trustee

If a third person acting in good faith and for a valuable consideration enters into a transaction with a former trustee without knowledge that the person is no longer a trustee, the third person is fully protected just as if the former trustee were still a trustee.

Ca. Prob. Code § 18102
Enacted by Stats. 1990, Ch. 79.

Section 18103 - Express trust relating to real property not contained or declared in grant to trustee

If an express trust relating to real property is not contained or declared in the grant to the trustee, or in an instrument signed by the trustee and recorded in the same office with the grant to the trustee, the grant shall be deemed absolute in favor of a person dealing with the trustee in good faith and for a valuable consideration.

Ca. Prob. Code § 18103
Enacted by Stats. 1990, Ch. 79.

Section 18104 - Presumption person holds interest, lien or encumbrance absolutely and free of trust

(a) If an interest in or lien or encumbrance on real property is conveyed, created, or affected by an instrument in favor of a person in trust but no beneficiary is indicated in the instrument, it is presumed that the person holds the interest, lien, or encumbrance absolutely and free of the trust. This is a presumption affecting the burden of proof. In an action or proceeding involving the interest, lien, or encumbrance instituted against the person, the person shall be deemed the only necessary representative of the undisclosed beneficiary and of the original grantor or settlor and anyone claiming under them. A judgment is binding upon and conclusive against these persons as to all matters finally adjudicated in the judgment.

(b) An instrument executed by the person holding an interest, lien, or encumbrance described in subdivision (a), whether purporting to be the act of that person in his or her own right or in the capacity of a trustee, is presumed to affect the interest, lien, or encumbrance according to the tenor of the instrument. This is a presumption affecting the burden of proof. Upon the recording of the instrument in the county where the land affected by the instrument is located, the presumption is conclusive in favor of a person acting in good faith and for valuable consideration.

Ca. Prob. Code § 18104

Enacted by Stats. 1990, Ch. 79.

Section 18105 - Affidavit of change of trustee

If title to an interest in real property is affected by a change of trustee, the successor trustee may execute and record in the county in which the property is located an affidavit of change of trustee. The county recorder shall impose any fee prescribed by law for recording that document in an amount sufficient to cover all costs incurred by the county in recording the document. The affidavit shall include the legal description of the real property, the name of the former trustee or trustees and the name of the successor trustee or trustees. The affidavit may also, but is not required to, include excerpts from the original trust documents, any amendments thereto, and any other documents evidencing or pertaining to the succession of the successor trustee or trustees.

Ca. Prob. Code § 18105

Added by Stats 2004 ch 136 (AB 1848), s 2, eff. 1/1/2005.

Section 18106 - Requirements for recording document establishing change of trustee

(a) A document establishing the fact of change of trustee recorded pursuant to this chapter is subject to all statutory requirements for recorded documents.

(b) The county recorder shall index a document establishing the fact of change of a trustee recorded pursuant to this section in the index of grantors and grantees. The index entry shall be for the grantor, and for the purpose of this index, the person who has been succeeded as trustee shall be deemed to be the grantor. The county recorder shall impose any fee prescribed by law for indexing that document in an amount sufficient to cover all costs incurred by the county in indexing the document.

Ca. Prob. Code § 18106

Added by Stats 2004 ch 136 (AB 1848), s 3, eff. 1/1/2005.

Section 18107 - Prima facie evidence of change of trustee

A document establishing the change of a trustee recorded pursuant to this chapter is prima facie evidence of the change of trustee insofar as the document identifies an interest in real property located in the county, title to which is affected by the change of trustee. The presumption established by this section is a presumption affecting the burden of producing evidence.

Ca. Prob. Code § 18107
Added by Stats 2004 ch 136 (AB 1848), s 4, eff. 1/1/2005.

Section 18108 - Copies of documents pertaining to succession

Any person whose interest is, or may be, affected by the recordation of an affidavit of change of trustee pursuant to this chapter may require that the successor trustee provide copies of those excerpts from the original trust documents, any amendments thereto, and any other documents which evidence or pertain to the succession of the successor trustee or trustees. Nothing in this section is intended to require or imply an obligation to provide the dispositive provisions of the trust or the entire trust and any amendments thereto.

Ca. Prob. Code § 18108
Added by Stats 2004 ch 136 (AB 1848), s 5, eff. 1/1/2005.

Chapter 3 - RIGHTS OF CREDITORS OF SETTLOR

Section 18200 - Property subject to claims of creditors of settlor

If the settlor retains the power to revoke the trust in whole or in part, the trust property is subject to the claims of creditors of the settlor to the extent of the power of revocation during the lifetime of the settlor.

Ca. Prob. Code § 18200
Enacted by Stats. 1990, Ch. 79.

Section 18201 - Settlor entitled to exemptions

Any settlor whose trust property is subject to the claims of creditors pursuant to Section 18200 shall be entitled to all exemptions as provided in Chapter 4 (commencing with Section 703.010) of Division 2 of Title 9 of Part 2 of the Code of Civil Procedure.

Ca. Prob. Code § 18201
Added by Stats. 1998, Ch. 682, Sec. 14. Effective January 1, 1999.

Part 7 - UNIFORM PRUDENT MANAGEMENT OF INSTITUTIONAL FUNDS ACT

Section 18500 - [Repealed]

Ca. Prob. Code § 18500
Repealed by Stats 2008 ch 715 (SB 1329),s 3, eff. 1/1/2009.

Section 18501 - Title of part

This part may be cited as the Uniform Prudent Management of Institutional Funds Act.

Ca. Prob. Code § 18501
Added by Stats 2008 ch 715 (SB 1329),s 4, eff. 1/1/2009.

Section 18502 - Definitions

As used in this part, the following terms shall have the following meanings:

(a) "Charitable purpose" means the relief of poverty, the advancement of education or religion, the promotion of health, the promotion of a governmental purpose, or any other purpose the achievement of which is beneficial to the community.

(b) "Endowment fund" means an institutional fund or part thereof that, under the terms of a gift instrument, is not wholly expendable by the institution on a current basis. The term does not include assets that an institution designates as an endowment fund for its own use.

(c) "Gift instrument" means a record or records, including an institutional solicitation, under which property is granted to, transferred to, or held by an institution as an institutional fund.

(d) "Institution" means any of the following:

(1) A person, other than an individual, organized and operated exclusively for charitable purposes.

(2) A government or governmental subdivision, agency, or instrumentality, to the extent that it holds funds exclusively for a charitable purpose.

(3) A trust that had both charitable and noncharitable interests, after all noncharitable interests have terminated.

(e) "Institutional fund" means a fund held by an institution exclusively for charitable purposes. The term does not include any of the following:

(1) Program-related assets.

(2) A fund held for an institution by a trustee that is not an institution.

(3) A fund in which a beneficiary that is not an institution has an interest, other than an interest that could arise upon violation or failure of the purposes of the fund.

(f) "Person" means an individual, corporation, business trust, estate, trust, partnership, limited liability company, association, joint venture, public corporation, government or governmental subdivision, agency, or instrumentality, or any other legal or commercial entity.

(g) "Program-related asset" means an asset held by an institution primarily to accomplish a charitable purpose of the institution and not primarily for investment.

(h) "Record" means information that is inscribed on a tangible medium or that is stored in an electronic or other medium and is retrievable in perceivable form.

Ca. Prob. Code § 18502

Added by Stats 2008 ch 715 (SB 1329),s 4, eff. 1/1/2009.

Section 18503 - Duties in managing and investing institutional funds; pooling funds; factors considered

(a) Subject to the intent of a donor expressed in a gift instrument, an institution, in managing and investing an institutional fund, shall consider the charitable purposes of the institution and the purposes of the institutional fund.

(b) In addition to complying with the duty of loyalty imposed by law other than this part, each person responsible for managing and investing an institutional fund shall manage and invest the fund in good faith and with the care an ordinarily prudent person in a like position would exercise under similar circumstances.

(c) In managing and investing an institutional fund, an institution is subject to both of the following:

(1) It may incur only costs that are appropriate and reasonable in relation to the assets, the purposes of the institution, and the skills available to the institution.

(2) It shall make a reasonable effort to verify facts relevant to the management and investment of the fund.

(d) An institution may pool two or more institutional funds for purposes of management and investment.

(e) Except as otherwise provided by a gift instrument, the following rules apply:

(1) In managing and investing an institutional fund, all of the following factors, if relevant, must be considered:

(A) General economic conditions.

(B) The possible effect of inflation or deflation.

(C) The expected tax consequences, if any, of investment decisions or strategies.

(D) The role that each investment or course of action plays

within the overall investment portfolio of the fund.

    (E) The expected total return from income and the appreciation of investments.

    (F) Other resources of the institution.

    (G) The needs of the institution and the fund to make distributions and to preserve capital.

    (H) An asset's special relationship or special value, if any, to the charitable purposes of the institution.

    (2) Management and investment decisions about an individual asset must be made not in isolation but rather in the context of the institutional fund's portfolio of investments as a whole and as a part of an overall investment strategy having risk and return objectives reasonably suited to the fund and to the institution.

    (3) Except as otherwise provided by law other than this part, an institution may invest in any kind of property or type of investment consistent with this section.

    (4) An institution shall diversify the investments of an institutional fund unless the institution reasonably determines that, because of special circumstances, the purposes of the fund are better served without diversification.

    (5) Within a reasonable time after receiving property, an institution shall make and carry out decisions concerning the retention or disposition of the property or to rebalance a portfolio, in order to bring the institutional fund into compliance with the purposes, terms, and distribution requirements of the institution as necessary to meet other circumstances of the institution and the requirements of this part.

    (6) A person that has special skills or expertise, or is selected in reliance upon the person's representation that the person has special skills or expertise, has a duty to use those skills or that expertise in managing and investing institutional funds.

(f) Nothing in this section alters the duties and liabilities of a director of a nonprofit public benefit corporation under Section 5240 of the Corporations Code.

Ca. Prob. Code § 18503

Added by Stats 2008 ch 715 (SB 1329),s 4, eff. 1/1/2009.

Section 18504 - Decision to appropriate for expenditure or accumulate so much of endowment fund as determined prudent

(a) Subject to the intent of a donor expressed in the gift instrument, an institution may appropriate for expenditure or accumulate so much of an endowment fund as the institution determines is prudent for the uses, benefits, purposes, and duration for which the endowment fund is established. Unless stated otherwise in the gift instrument, the assets in an endowment fund are donor-restricted assets until appropriated for expenditure by the institution. In making a determination to appropriate or accumulate, the institution shall act in good faith, with the care that an ordinarily prudent person in a like position would exercise under similar circumstances, and shall consider, if relevant, all of the following factors:

(1) The duration and preservation of the endowment fund.

(2) The purposes of the institution and the endowment fund.

(3) General economic conditions.

(4) The possible effect of inflation or deflation.

(5) The expected total return from income and the appreciation of investments.

(6) Other resources of the institution.

(7) The investment policy of the institution.

(b) To limit the authority to appropriate for expenditure or accumulate under subdivision (a), a gift instrument must specifically state the limitation.

(c) Terms in a gift instrument designating a gift as an endowment, or a direction or authorization in the gift instrument to use only "income," "interest," "dividends," or "rents, issues, or profits," or "to preserve the principal intact," or words of similar import have both of the following effects:

(1) To create an endowment fund of permanent duration unless other language in the gift instrument limits the duration or purpose of the fund.

(2) To not otherwise limit the authority to appropriate for expenditure or accumulate under subdivision (a).

(d) The appropriation for expenditure in any year of an amount greater than 7 percent of the fair market value of an endowment fund, calculated on the basis of market values determined at least quarterly and averaged over a period of not less than three years immediately preceding the year in which the appropriation for expenditure is made, creates a rebuttable presumption of imprudence. For an endowment fund in existence for fewer than three years, the fair market value of the endowment fund shall be calculated for the period the endowment fund has been in existence. This subdivision does not do any of the following:

(1) Apply to an appropriation for expenditure permitted under law other than this part or by the gift instrument.

(2) Apply to a private or public postsecondary educational institution, or to a campus foundation established by and operated under the auspices of such an educational institution.

(3) Create a presumption of prudence for an appropriation for expenditure of an amount less than or equal to 7 percent of the fair market value of the endowment fund.

Ca. Prob. Code § 18504
Added by Stats 2008 ch 715 (SB 1329),s 4, eff. 1/1/2009.

Section 18505 - Delegation to external agent management and investment of fund

(a) Subject to any specific limitation set forth in a gift instrument or in law other than this part, an institution may delegate to an external agent the management and investment of an institutional fund to the extent that an institution could prudently delegate under the circumstances. An institution shall act in good faith, with the care that an ordinarily prudent person in a like position would exercise under similar circumstances, in all of the following:

(1) Selecting an agent.

(2) Establishing the scope and terms of the delegation, consistent with the purposes of the institution and the institutional fund.

(3) Periodically reviewing the agent's actions in order to monitor the agent's performance and compliance with the scope and terms of the delegation.
(b) In performing a delegated function, an agent owes a duty to the institution to exercise reasonable care to comply with the scope and terms of the delegation.
(c) An institution that complies with subdivision (a) is not liable for the decisions or actions of an agent to which the function was delegated except to the extent a trustee would be liable for those actions or decisions under Sections 16052 and 16401.
(d) By accepting delegation of a management or investment function from an institution that is subject to the laws of this state, an agent submits to the jurisdiction of the courts of this state in all proceedings arising from or related to the delegation or the performance of the delegated function.
(e) An institution may delegate management and investment functions to its committees, officers, or employees as authorized by law of this state other than this part.

Ca. Prob. Code § 18505
Added by Stats 2008 ch 715 (SB 1329),s 4, eff. 1/1/2009.

Section 18506 - Release or modification of restriction contained in gift instrument

(a) If the donor consents in a record, an institution may release or modify, in whole or in part, a restriction contained in a gift instrument on the management, investment, or purpose of an institutional fund. A release or modification may not allow a fund to be used for a purpose other than a charitable purpose of the institution.

(b) The court, upon application of an institution, may modify a restriction contained in a gift instrument regarding the management or investment of an institutional fund if the restriction has become impracticable or wasteful, if it impairs the management or investment of the fund, or if, because of circumstances not anticipated by the donor, a modification of a restriction will further the purposes of the fund. The institution shall notify the Attorney General of the application, and the Attorney General must be given an opportunity to be heard. To the extent practicable, any modification must be made in accordance with the donor's probable intention.

(c) If a particular charitable purpose or a restriction contained in a gift instrument on the use of an institutional fund becomes unlawful, impracticable, impossible to achieve, or wasteful, the court, upon application of an institution, may modify the purpose of the fund or the restriction on the use of the fund in a manner consistent with the charitable purposes expressed in the gift instrument. The institution shall notify the Attorney General of the application, and the Attorney General must be given an opportunity to be heard.

(d) If an institution determines that a restriction contained in a gift instrument on the management, investment, or purpose of an institutional fund is unlawful, impracticable, impossible to achieve, or wasteful, the institution, 60 days after notification to the Attorney General and to the donor at the donor's last known address in the records of the institution, may release or modify the restriction, in whole or part, if all of the following apply:

(1) The institutional fund subject to the restriction has a total value of less than one hundred thousand dollars ($100,000).

(2) More than 20 years have elapsed since the fund was established.

(3) The institution uses the property in a manner consistent with the charitable purposes expressed in the gift instrument. An institution that releases or modifies a restriction under this subdivision may, if appropriate circumstances arise thereafter, use the property in accordance with the restriction notwithstanding its release or modification, and that use is deemed to satisfy the consistency requirement of this paragraph.

Ca. Prob. Code § 18506
Added by Stats 2008 ch 715 (SB 1329),s 4, eff. 1/1/2009.

Section 18507 - Determination of compliance with part

Compliance with this part is determined in light of the facts and circumstances existing at the time a decision is made or action is taken, and not by hindsight.

Ca. Prob. Code § 18507
Added by Stats 2008 ch 715 (SB 1329),s 4, eff. 1/1/2009.

Section 18508 - Effective date

This part applies to institutional funds existing on or established after January 1, 2009. As applied to institutional funds existing on January 1, 2009, this part governs only decisions made or actions taken on or after that date.

Ca. Prob. Code § 18508
Added by Stats 2008 ch 715 (SB 1329),s 4, eff. 1/1/2009.

Section 18509 - Effect on Electronic Signatures in Global and National Commerce Act

This part modifies, limits, and supersedes the Electronic Signatures in Global and National Commerce Act (15 U.S.C. Sec. 7001 et seq.), but does not modify, limit, or supersede Section 101 of that act (15 U.S.C. Sec. 7001(a)) , or authorize electronic delivery of any of the notices described in Section 103 of that act (15 U.S.C. Sec. 7003(b))
.

Ca. Prob. Code § 18509
Added by Stats 2008 ch 715 (SB 1329),s 4, eff. 1/1/2009.

Section 18510 - Construction of part

In applying and construing this uniform act, consideration must be given to the need to promote uniformity of the law with respect to its subject matter among states that enact it.
Ca. Prob. Code § 18510
Added by Stats 2008 ch 715 (SB 1329),s 4, eff. 1/1/2009.

Part 8 - PAYMENT OF CLAIMS, DEBTS, AND EXPENSES FROM REVOCABLE TRUST OF DECEASED SETTLOR

Chapter 1 - GENERAL PROVISIONS

Section 19000 - Definitions

As used in this part:
(a) "Claim" means a demand for payment for any of the following, whether due, not due, accrued or not accrued, or contingent, and whether liquidated or unliquidated:

(1) Liability of the deceased settlor, whether arising in contract, tort, or otherwise.

(2) Liability for taxes incurred before the deceased settlor's death, whether assessed before or after the deceased settlor's death, other than property taxes and assessments secured by real property liens.

(3) Liability for the funeral expenses of the deceased settlor.
(b) "Claim" does not include a dispute regarding title to specific

property alleged to be included in the trust estate.

(c) "Creditor" means a person who may have a claim against the trust property.

(d) "Trust" means a trust described in Section 18200, or, if a portion of a trust, that portion that remained subject to the power of revocation at the deceased settlor's death.

(e) "Deceased settlor" means a deceased person who, at the time of his or her death, held the power to revoke the trust in whole or in part.

(f) "Debts" means all claims, as defined in subdivision (a), all expenses of administration, and all other proper charges against the trust estate, including taxes.

(g) "Probate estate" means a decedent's estate subject to administration pursuant to Division 7 (commencing with Section 7000).

(h) "Trust estate" means a decedent's property, real and personal, that is titled in the name of the trustee of the deceased settlor's trust or confirmed by order of the court to the trustee of the deceased settlor's trust.

Ca. Prob. Code § 19000

Amended by Stats 2015 ch 48 (SB 785),s 1, eff. 1/1/2016.
Amended by Stats 2007 ch 159 (AB 341),s 8, eff. 1/1/2008.

Section 19001 - Property subject to creditors' claims and administration expenses; instruction directing priority of sources of payment

(a) Upon the death of a settlor, the property of the deceased settlor that was subject to the power of revocation at the time of the settlor's death is subject to the claims of creditors of the deceased settlor's probate estate and to the expenses of administration of the probate estate to the extent that the deceased settlor's probate estate is inadequate to satisfy those claims and expenses.

(b) The deceased settlor, by appropriate direction in the trust instrument, may direct the priority of sources of payment of debts among subtrusts or other gifts established by the trust at the deceased settlor's death. Notwithstanding this subdivision, no direction by the settlor shall alter the priority of payment, from whatever source, of the matters set forth in Section 11420 which shall be applied to the trust as it applies to a probate estate.

Ca. Prob. Code § 19001

Amended by Stats 2015 ch 48 (SB 785),s 2, eff. 1/1/2016.

Section 19002 - Right of creditor to recover not affected

(a) Except as expressly provided, this part shall not be construed to affect the right of any creditor to recover from any revocable trust established by the deceased settlor.

(b) Nothing in this part shall be construed as a construction or alteration of any claims procedure set forth under Part 4 (commencing with Section 9000) of Division 7.

Ca. Prob. Code § 19002

Added by Stats. 1991, Ch. 992, Sec. 3.

Section 19003 - Proposed notice to creditors

(a) At any time following the death of the settlor, and during the time that there has been no filing of a petition to administer the probate estate of the deceased settlor in this state of which the trustee has actual knowledge, the trustee may file with the court a proposed notice to creditors. Upon the court's assignment of a proceeding number to the proposed notice, the trustee shall publish and serve notice to creditors of the deceased settlor in the form and within the time prescribed in Chapters 3 (commencing with Section 19040) and 4 (commencing with Section 19050). That action shall constitute notice to creditors of the requirements of this part.

(b) The filing shall be made with the superior court for the county in this state where the deceased settlor resided at the time of death, or if none, in any county in this state in which trust property was located at the time of the settlor's death, or if none, in the county in this state that was the principal place of administration of the trust at the time of the settlor's death.

(c) Nothing in subdivision (a) affects a notice or request to a public entity required by Chapter 7 (commencing with Section 19200).

Ca. Prob. Code § 19003

Amended by Stats 2015 ch 48 (SB 785),s 3, eff. 1/1/2016.

Section 19004 - Rules applicable to filing claims

If the trustee files, publishes, and serves notice as set forth in Section 19003, then:

(a) All claims against the trust shall be filed in the manner and within the time provided in this part.

(b) A claim that is not filed as provided in this part is barred from collection from trust assets.

(c) The holder of a claim may not maintain an action on the claim against the trust unless the claim is first filed as provided in this part.

Ca. Prob. Code § 19004
Added by Stats. 1991, Ch. 992, Sec. 3.

Section 19005 - Powers of trustee

The trustee may at any time pay, reject, or contest any claim against the deceased settlor or settle any claim by compromise, arbitration, or otherwise. The trustee may also file a petition in the manner set forth in Chapter 2 (commencing with Section 19020) to settle any claim.

Ca. Prob. Code § 19005
Added by Stats. 1991, Ch. 992, Sec. 3.

Section 19006 - Extent of protection from creditors afforded by filing notice

(a) If a trustee of a trust established by the deceased settlor files, publishes, and serves notice as provided in Section 19003 the protection from creditors afforded that trustee and trust shall also be afforded to any other trusts established by the deceased settlor and the trustees and beneficiaries of those trusts.

(b) If the personal representative of the deceased settlor's probate estate has published notice under Section 8120 and given notice of administration of the probate estate of the deceased settlor under Chapter 2 (commencing with Section 9050) of Part 4 of Division 7, the protection from creditors afforded the personal representative of the deceased settlor's probate estate shall be afforded to the trustee and to the beneficiaries of the trust.

(c) In the event that, following the filing and publication of the notice set forth in Section 19003, there shall be commenced any proceeding under which a notice pursuant to Section 8120 is required to be published, then the trustee shall have a right of collection against that probate estate to recover the amount of any debts paid from trust assets that would otherwise have been satisfied (whether by law or by direction in the deceased settlor's will or trust) by the property subject to probate proceedings.

Ca. Prob. Code § 19006
Amended by Stats 2015 ch 48 (SB 785),s 4, eff. 1/1/2016.

Section 19007 - Determination of liability of trust

Nothing in this part shall determine the liability of any trust established by the deceased settlor as against any other trust established by that settlor, except to the extent that the trustee of the other trust shall file, publish, and serve the notice specified in Section 19003 and thereafter seek a determination of relative liability pursuant to Chapter 2 (commencing with Section 19020).

Ca. Prob. Code § 19007
Added by Stats. 1991, Ch. 992, Sec. 3.

Section 19008 - Liability of trust if notice not filed

If there is no proceeding to administer the probate estate of the deceased settlor, and if the trustee does not file a proposed notice to creditors pursuant to Section 19003 and does not publish notice to creditors pursuant to Chapter 3 (commencing with Section 19040), then the liability of the trust to any creditor of the deceased settlor shall be as otherwise provided by law.

Ca. Prob. Code § 19008
Amended by Stats 2015 ch 48 (SB 785),s 5, eff. 1/1/2016.

Section 19009 - Disclosure of existence or contents of trust

Nothing in this part shall be construed to permit or require disclosure of the existence of the trust or the contents of any of its provisions to any creditor or beneficiary except as that creditor or beneficiary may otherwise be entitled to that information.

Ca. Prob. Code § 19009
Added by Stats. 1991, Ch. 992, Sec. 3.

Section 19010 - No duty on trustee to initiate notice proceeding

Nothing in this part imposes any duty on the trustee to initiate the notice proceeding set forth in Section 19003, and the trustee is not liable for failure to initiate the proceeding under this part.

Ca. Prob. Code § 19010
Added by Stats. 1991, Ch. 992, Sec. 3.

Section 19011 - Adoption of form and contents of petition, notice, etc.

(a) The Judicial Council may prescribe the form and contents of the petition, notice, claim form, and allowance or rejection form to be used pursuant to this part. The allowance or rejection form may be part of the claim form.
(b) Any claim form adopted by the Judicial Council shall inform the creditor that the claim must be filed with the court and a copy delivered pursuant to Section 1215 to the trustee. The claim form shall include a proof of delivery of a copy of the claim to the trustee, which may be completed by the claimant.

Ca. Prob. Code § 19011
Amended by Stats 2017 ch 319 (AB 976),s 99, eff. 1/1/2018.
Amended by Stats 2007 ch 159 (AB 341),s 9, eff. 1/1/2008.

Section 19012 - Effective date

(a) This part applies to claims against any deceased settlor who dies on or after January 1, 1992.
(b) The applicable law in effect before January 1, 1992, continues to apply to claims against any deceased settlor who dies before

January 1, 1992.

Ca. Prob. Code § 19012

Added by Stats. 1991, Ch. 992, Sec. 3.

Chapter 2 - PETITION FOR APPROVAL AND SETTLEMENT OF CLAIMS AGAINST DECEASED SETTLOR

Section 19020 - Generally

At any time after the filing and first publication of notice pursuant to Chapter 3 (commencing with Section 19040), and after expiration of the time to file claims provided in that chapter, a trustee or beneficiary may petition the court under this chapter to approve either of the following:

(a) Allowance, compromise, or settlement of any claims that have not been rejected by the trustee under the procedure provided in this part and for which trust property may be liable.

(b) An allocation of any amounts due by reason of an action described in subdivision (a) to two or more trusts which may be liable for the claims.

Ca. Prob. Code § 19020

Added by Stats. 1991, Ch. 992, Sec. 3.

Section 19021 - Venue for filing petition

The petition shall be filed in that county as may be determined pursuant to Section 19003. In the event this action seeks approval of allocation to two or more trusts for which the notice proceeding in Section 19003 would prescribe superior courts for more than one county, the court located in the county so prescribed for the trustee initiating the proceeding under this chapter shall have jurisdiction.

Ca. Prob. Code § 19021

Added by Stats. 1991, Ch. 992, Sec. 3.

Section 19022 - Commencement of proceeding; contents of petition

(a) A proceeding under this chapter is commenced by filing a verified petition stating facts showing that the petition is authorized under this chapter and the grounds of the petition.

(b) The petition shall set forth a description of the trust and the names of creditors with respect to which action is requested and a description of each claim, together with the requested determination by the court with respect to the claims, provided, however, that this section does not require the filing of a copy of the trust or disclosure of the beneficial interests of the trust. That petition shall also set forth the beneficiaries of the trust, those claimants whose interest in the trust may be affected by the petition, and the trustees of any other trust to which an allocation of liability may be approved by the court pursuant to the petition.

(c) The clerk shall set the matter for hearing.

Ca. Prob. Code § 19022
Amended by Stats 2007 ch 159 (AB 341),s 10, eff. 1/1/2008.

Section 19023 - Service of notice of hearing and petition

At least 30 days before the time set for the hearing on the petition, the petitioner shall cause notice of the time and place of the hearing and a copy of the petition to be served on each of the creditors whose interests in the estate may be affected by the petition in the manner provided in Chapter 4 (commencing with Section 413.10) of Title 5 of Part 2 of the Code of Civil Procedure.

Ca. Prob. Code § 19023
Amended by Stats 2007 ch 159 (AB 341),s 11, eff. 1/1/2008.

Section 19024 - Service of notice of hearing and petition by mail

At least 30 days before the time set for the hearing on the petition, the petitioner shall cause notice of the time and place of the hearing, together with a copy of the petition, to be delivered pursuant to Section 1215 to each of the following persons who is not a petitioner:

(a) All trustees of the trust and of any other trusts to which an allocation of liability may be approved by the court pursuant to the petition.

(b) All beneficiaries affected.

(c) The personal representative of the deceased settlor's probate estate, if any is known to the trustee.

(d) The Attorney General, if the petition relates to a charitable trust subject to the jurisdiction of the Attorney General, unless the Attorney General waives notice.

Ca. Prob. Code § 19024

Amended by Stats 2017 ch 319 (AB 976),s 100, eff. 1/1/2018.
Amended by Stats 2015 ch 48 (SB 785),s 6, eff. 1/1/2016.

Section 19025 - Failure to timely file written pleading upon notice; final order binding

(a) If any creditor, beneficiary, or trustee fails timely to file a written pleading upon notice, then the case is at issue, notwithstanding the failure. The case may proceed on the petition and written statements filed by the time of the hearing, and no further pleadings by other persons are necessary. The creditor, beneficiary, or trustee who failed timely to file a written pleading upon notice may not participate further in the proceeding for the determination requested, and that creditor, beneficiary, or trustee shall be bound by the decision in the proceeding.

(b) The court's order, when final, shall be conclusive as to the liability of the trust property with respect to the claims at issue in the petition. In the event of a subsequent administration of the probate estate of the deceased settlor, that order shall be binding on the personal representative of the probate estate of the deceased settlor as well as all creditors and beneficiaries who had notice of the petition.

Ca. Prob. Code § 19025

Amended by Stats 2015 ch 48 (SB 785),s 7, eff. 1/1/2016.
Amended by Stats 2007 ch 159 (AB 341),s 12, eff. 1/1/2008.

Section 19026 - Proceeding not reasonably necessary

The court may dismiss a petition if it appears that the proceeding is not reasonably necessary for the protection of the interests of the trustee or any beneficiary of the trust.

Ca. Prob. Code § 19026
Added by Stats. 1991, Ch. 992, Sec. 3.

Section 19027 - Court order

(a) The court in its discretion may make any orders and take any other action necessary or proper to dispose of the matters presented by the petition.
(b) If the court determines that the assets of the trust estate are insufficient to pay all debts, then the court shall order payment in the manner specified by Section 11420.
Ca. Prob. Code § 19027
Added by Stats. 1991, Ch. 992, Sec. 3.

Section 19029 - Appointment of guardian ad litem

The court may, on its own motion or on request of a trustee or other person interested in the trust, appoint a guardian ad litem in accordance with Section 1003.
Ca. Prob. Code § 19029
Added by Stats. 1991, Ch. 992, Sec. 3.

Section 19030 - Cases involving charitable trusts

In a case involving a charitable trust subject to the jurisdiction of the Attorney General, the Attorney General may petition under this chapter.
Ca. Prob. Code § 19030
Added by Stats. 1991, Ch. 992, Sec. 3.

Chapter 3 - PUBLICATION OF NOTICE

Section 19040 - Generally

(a) Publication of notice pursuant to this section shall be for at least 15 days. Three publications in a newspaper published once a week or more often, with at least five days intervening between the first and last publication dates, not counting the first and last publication dates as part of the five-day period, are sufficient.

Notice shall be published in a newspaper of general circulation in the city, county, or city and county in this state where the deceased settlor resided at the time of death, or if none, in the city, county, or city and county in this state wherein trust property was located at the time of the settlor's death, or if none, in the city, county, or city and county in this state wherein the principal place of administration of the trust was located at the time of the settlor's death. If there is no newspaper of general circulation published in the applicable city, county, or city and county, notice shall be published in a newspaper of general circulation published in this state nearest to the applicable city, county, or city and county seat, and which is circulated within the applicable city, county, or city and county. If there is no such newspaper, notice shall be given in written or printed form, posted at three of the most public places within the community. For purposes of this section, "city" means a charter city as defined in Section 34101 of the Government Code or a general law city as defined in Section 34102 of the Government Code.

(b) The caption of the notice, the deceased settlor's name, and the name of the trustee shall be in at least 8-point type, the text of the notice shall be in at least 7-point type, and the notice shall state substantially as follows:

NOTICE TO CREDITORSOF _____

\# _____SUPERIOR COURT OF CALIFORNIACOUNTY OF _____Notice is hereby given to the creditors and contingent creditors of the above-named decedent, that all persons having claims against the decedent are required to file them with the Superior Court, at _____, and deliver pursuant to Section 1215 of the California Probate Code a copy to _____, as trustee of the trust dated _____ wherein the decedent was the settlor, at _____, within the later of four months after _____ (the date of the first publication of notice to creditors) or, if notice is mailed or personally delivered to you, 60 days after the date this notice is mailed or personally delivered to you. A claim form may be obtained from the court clerk. For your protection, you are encouraged to file your claim by certified mail, with return receipt requested.

(name and address of trustee or attorney)

(c) An affidavit showing due publication of notice shall be filed with the clerk upon completion of the publication. The affidavit shall contain a copy of the notice, and state the date of its first publication.

Ca. Prob. Code § 19040
Amended by Stats 2017 ch 319 (AB 976),s 101, eff. 1/1/2018.
Amended by Stats 2007 ch 159 (AB 341),s 13, eff. 1/1/2008.

Section 19041 - Notice published in good faith attempt to comply with section 19040

The Legislature finds and declares that to be most effective, notice to creditors should be published in compliance with the procedures specified in Section 19040. However, the Legislature recognizes the possibility that in unusual cases due to confusion over jurisdictional boundaries or oversights the notice may inadvertently be published in a newspaper which does not meet these requirements. Therefore, to prevent a minor error in publication from invalidating what would otherwise be a proper proceeding, the Legislature further finds and declares that notice published in a good faith attempt to comply with Section 19040 shall be sufficient to provide notice to creditors and establish jurisdiction if the court expressly finds that the notice was published in a newspaper of general circulation published within the city, county, or city and county and widely circulated within a true cross section of the community in which the deceased settlor resided or wherein the principal place of administration of the trust was located or the property was located in substantial compliance with Section 19040.

Ca. Prob. Code § 19041
Added by Stats. 1991, Ch. 992, Sec. 3.

Chapter 4 - ACTUAL NOTICE TO CREDITORS

Section 19050 - When trustee has knowledge of creditor

Except as provided in Section 19054, if the trustee has knowledge of a creditor of the deceased settlor, the trustee shall give notice to the creditor. The notice shall be given as provided in Section 1215. For the purpose of this section, a trustee has knowledge of a creditor of the deceased settlor if the trustee is aware that the creditor has demanded payment from the deceased settlor or the trust estate.

Ca. Prob. Code § 19050

Amended by Stats 2007 ch 159 (AB 341),s 14, eff. 1/1/2008.

Section 19051 - Time for giving notice

The notice shall be given before expiration of the later of the following times:

(a) Four months after the first publication of notice under Section 19040.

(b) Thirty days after the trustee first has knowledge of the creditor.

Ca. Prob. Code § 19051

Amended by Stats 2007 ch 159 (AB 341),s 15, eff. 1/1/2008.

Section 19052 - Form

The notice shall be in substantially the following form:

NOTICE TO CREDITORS

OF _____

_____ SUPERIOR COURT OF CALIFORNIA

COUNTY OF _____

Notice is hereby given to the creditors and contingent creditors of the above-named decedent, that all persons having claims against the decedent are required to file them with the Superior Court, at _____, and deliver pursuant to Section 1215 of the California Probate Code a copy to _____, as trustee of the trust dated _____ wherein the decedent was the settlor, at _____, within the later of four months after _____ (the date of the first publication of notice to creditors) or, if notice is mailed or personally delivered to you, 60 days after the date this notice is mailed or personally delivered to you, or you must petition to file a late claim as provided in Section 19103 of the Probate Code. A claim form may be obtained from the court clerk. For your protection, you are encouraged to file your claim by certified mail, with return receipt requested.

_____

(Date of mailing this notice if applicable)

_____

(name and address of trustee or attorney)

Ca. Prob. Code § 19052

Amended by Stats 2017 ch 319 (AB 976),s 102, eff. 1/1/2018.

Amended by Stats 2007 ch 159 (AB 341),s 16, eff. 1/1/2008.

Section 19053 - Liability of trustee for giving notice; not giving notice

(a) If the trustee believes that notice to a particular creditor is or may be required by this chapter and gives notice based on that belief, the trustee is not liable to any person for giving the notice, whether or not required by this chapter.

(b) If the trustee fails to give notice required by this chapter, the trustee is not liable to any person for that failure, unless a creditor establishes all of the following:

(1) The failure was in bad faith.

(2) The creditor did not have actual knowledge of the proceedings under Chapter 1 (commencing with Section 19000) sooner than one year after publication of notice to creditors under Section 19040, and payment would have been made on the creditor's claim if the claim had been properly filed.

(3) Within 16 months after the first publication of notice under Section 19040, the creditor did both of the following:

(A) Filed a petition requesting that the court in which the proceedings under Chapter 1 (commencing with Section 19000) were initiated make an order determining the liability of the trustee under this subdivision.

(B) At least 30 days before the hearing on the petition, caused notice of the hearing and a copy of the petition to be served on the trustee in the manner provided in Chapter 4 (commencing with Section 413.10) of Title 5 of Part 2 of the Code of Civil Procedure.

(c) Nothing in this section affects the liability of the trust estate, if any, for the claim of a creditor, and the trustee is not liable to the extent the claim is paid out of the trust estate.

(d) Nothing in this chapter imposes a duty on the trustee to make a search for creditors of the deceased settlor.

Ca. Prob. Code § 19053

Amended by Stats 2007 ch 159 (AB 341),s 17, eff. 1/1/2008.

Section 19054 - When trustee need not give notice

Notwithstanding Section 19050, the trustee need not give notice to a creditor even though the trustee has knowledge of the creditor if either of the following conditions is satisfied:

(a) The creditor has filed a claim as provided in this part.

(b) The creditor has demanded payment and the trustee elects to treat the demand as a claim under Section 19154.

Ca. Prob. Code § 19054

Amended by Stats 2003 ch 32 (AB 167), s 14, eff. 1/1/2004.

Chapter 5 - TIME FOR FILING CLAIMS

Section 19100 - Generally

(a) A creditor shall file a claim before expiration of the later of the following times:

(1) Four months after the first publication of notice to creditors under Section 19040.

(2) Sixty days after the date actual notice is mailed or personally delivered to the creditor. This paragraph does not extend the time provided in Section 366.2 of the Code of Civil Procedure.

(b) A reference in another statute to the time for filing a claim means the time provided in paragraph (1) of subdivision (a).

(c) This section shall not be interpreted to extend or toll any other statute of limitations, including that provided by Section 366.2 of the Code of Civil Procedure.

Ca. Prob. Code § 19100

Amended by Stats 2007 ch 159 (AB 341),s 18, eff. 1/1/2008.

Section 19101 - Vacancy in office of trustee

A vacancy in the office of the trustee that occurs before expiration of the time for filing a claim does not extend the time.

Ca. Prob. Code § 19101

Added by Stats. 1991, Ch. 992, Sec. 3.

Section 19102 - Claim not acted on until after expiration of time

A claim that is filed before expiration of the time for filing the claim is timely even if acted on by the trustee or the court after expiration of the time for filing claims.

Ca. Prob. Code § 19102

Added by Stats. 1991, Ch. 992, Sec. 3.

Section 19103 - Allowance of filing of claim after expiration of time

(a) Except as provided in subdivision (b), upon petition by a creditor or a trustee, the court may allow a claim to be filed after expiration of the time for filing a claim provided in Section 19100 if either of the following conditions are satisfied:

(1) The trustee failed to send proper and timely notice to the creditor and the petition is filed within 60 days after the creditor has actual knowledge of the administration of the trust.

(2) The creditor did not have knowledge of the facts giving rise to the existence of the claim more than 30 days prior to the time for filing a claim as provided in Section 19100, and the petition is filed within 60 days after the creditor has actual knowledge of both of the following:

(A) The existence of the facts reasonably giving rise to the existence of the claim.

(B) The administration of the trust.

(b) Notwithstanding subdivision (a), the court shall not allow a claim to be filed under this section more than one year after the date of first publication of notice to creditors under Section 19040. Nothing in this subdivision authorizes allowance or approval of a claim barred by, or extends the time provided in, Section 366.2 of the Code of Civil Procedure.

(c) The court may condition the claim on terms that are just and equitable. The court may deny the claimant's petition if a distribution to trust beneficiaries or payment to general creditors has been made and it appears the filing or establishment of the claim would cause or tend to cause unequal treatment among beneficiaries or creditors.

(d) Regardless of whether the claim is later established in whole or in part, property distributed under the terms of the trust subsequent to an order settling claims under Chapter 2 (commencing with Section 19020) and payments otherwise properly made before a claim is filed under this section are not subject to the claim. Except to the extent provided in Chapter 12 (commencing with Section 19400) and subject to Section 19053, the trustee, distributee, or payee is not liable on account of the prior distribution or payment. This subdivision does not limit the liability of a person who receives a preliminary distribution of property to restore to the trust an amount sufficient for payment of the beneficiary's proper share of the claim, not exceeding the amount distributed.

Ca. Prob. Code § 19103
Amended by Stats 2007 ch 159 (AB 341),s 19, eff. 1/1/2008.

Section 19104 - Amendment or revision of timely filed claim

(a) Subject to subdivision (b), if a claim is filed within the time provided in this chapter, the creditor may later amend or revise the claim. The amendment or revision shall be filed in the same manner as the claim.

(b) An amendment or revision may not be made to increase the amount of the claim after the time for filing a claim has expired. An amendment or revision to specify the amount of a claim that, at the time of filing, was not due, was contingent, or was not yet ascertainable, is not an increase in the amount of the claim within the meaning of this subdivision. An amendment or revision of a claim may not be made for any purpose after the earlier of the following times:

(1) The time the court makes an order approving settlement of the claim against the deceased settlor under Chapter 2 (commencing with Section 19020).

(2) One year after the date of the first publication of notice to creditors under Section 19040. Nothing in this paragraph authorizes allowance or approval of a claim barred by, or extends the time provided in, Section 366.2 of the Code of Civil Procedure.

Ca. Prob. Code § 19104

Amended by Stats 2007 ch 159 (AB 341),s 20, eff. 1/1/2008.

Chapter 6 - FILING OF CLAIMS

Section 19150 - Generally

(a) A claim may be filed by the creditor or a person acting on behalf of the claimant.

(b) A claim shall be filed with the court and a copy shall be delivered to the trustee pursuant to Section 1215. Failure to deliver a copy to the trustee does not invalidate a properly filed claim, but any loss that results from the failure shall be borne by the creditor.

Ca. Prob. Code § 19150

Amended by Stats 2017 ch 319 (AB 976),s 103, eff. 1/1/2018.

Amended by Stats 2007 ch 159 (AB 341),s 21, eff. 1/1/2008.

Section 19151 - Affidavit supporting claim

(a) A claim shall be supported by the affidavit of the creditor or the person on behalf of the claimant stating:

(1) The claim is a just claim.

(2) If the claim is due, the facts supporting the claim, the amount of the claim, and that all payments on and offsets to the claim have been credited.

(3) If the claim is not due or contingent, or the amount is not yet ascertainable, the facts supporting the claim.

(4) If the affidavit is made by a person other than the creditor, the reason it is not made by the creditor.

(b) The trustee may require satisfactory vouchers or proof to be produced to support the claim. An original voucher may be withdrawn after a copy is provided. If a copy is provided, the copy shall be attached to the claim.

Ca. Prob. Code § 19151

Amended by Stats 2007 ch 159 (AB 341),s 22, eff. 1/1/2008.

Section 19152 - Claim based on written instrument

(a) If a claim is based on a written instrument, either the original or a copy of the original with all endorsements shall be attached to the claim. If a copy is attached, the original instrument shall be exhibited to the trustee on demand unless it is lost or destroyed, in which case the fact that it is lost or destroyed shall be stated in the claim.

(b) If the claim or a part of the claim is secured by a mortgage, deed of trust, or other lien that is recorded in the office of the recorder of the county in which the property subject to the lien is located, it is sufficient to describe the mortgage, deed of trust, or lien and the recording reference for the instrument that created the mortgage, deed of trust, or other lien.

Ca. Prob. Code § 19152

Added by Stats. 1991, Ch. 992, Sec. 3.

Section 19153 - Adoption of claim form

The Judicial Council may adopt a claim form which shall inform the creditor that the claim must be filed with the court and a copy delivered to the trustee pursuant to Section 1215. Any such claim form shall include a proof of delivery of a copy of the claim to the trustee which may be completed by the creditor.

Ca. Prob. Code § 19153
Amended by Stats 2017 ch 319 (AB 976),s 104, eff. 1/1/2018.

Section 19154 - Waiver of formal defects and election to treat demand as claim

(a) Notwithstanding any other provision of this part, if a creditor makes a written demand for payment within the time specified in Section 19100, the trustee may waive formal defects and elect to treat the demand as a claim that is filed and established under this part by paying the amount demanded.

(b) Nothing in this section limits application of the doctrines of waiver, estoppel, laches, or detrimental reliance or any other equitable principle.

Ca. Prob. Code § 19154
Amended by Stats 2007 ch 159 (AB 341),s 23, eff. 1/1/2008.

Chapter 7 - CLAIMS BY PUBLIC ENTITIES

Section 19200 - Time for filing; public entity defined

(a) Except as provided in this chapter, a claim by a public entity shall be filed within the time otherwise provided in this part. A claim not so filed is barred, including any lien imposed for the claim.

(b) As used in this chapter, "public entity" has the meaning provided in Section 811.2 of the Government Code, and includes an officer authorized to act on behalf of the public entity.

Ca. Prob. Code § 19200
Added by Stats. 1991, Ch. 992, Sec. 3.

Section 19201 - Claim arising under listed law, act or code

(a) Notwithstanding any other statute, if a claim of a public entity arises under a law, act, or code listed in subdivision (b):

(1) The public entity may provide a form to be used for the written notice or request to the public entity required by this chapter. Where appropriate, the form may require the decedent's social security number, if known.

(2) The claim is barred only after written notice or request to the public entity and expiration of the period provided in the applicable section. If no written notice or request is made, the claim is enforceable by the remedies, and is barred at the time, otherwise provided in the law, act, or code.

(b)

Law, Act, or Code	Applicable Section
Sales and Use Tax Law (commencing with Section 6001 of the Revenue and Taxation Code)	Section 6487.1 of the Revenue and Taxation Code
Bradley-Burns Uniform Local Sales and Use Tax Law (commencing with Section 7200 of the Revenue and Taxation Code)	Section 6487.1 of the Revenue and Taxation Code
Transactions and Use Tax Law (commencing with Section 7251 of the Revenue and Taxation Code)	Section 6487.1 of the Revenue and Taxation Code

Motor Vehicle Fuel License Tax Law (commencing with Section 7301 of the Revenue and Taxation Code)	Section 7675.1 of the Revenue and Taxation Code
Use Fuel Tax Law (commencing with Section 8601 of the Revenue and Taxation Code)	Section 8782.1 of the Revenue and Taxation Code
Administration of Franchise and Income Tax Law (commencing with Section 18401 of the Revenue and Taxation Code)	Section 19517 of the Revenue and Taxation Code
Cigarette Tax Law (commencing with Section 30001 of the Revenue and Taxation Code)	Section 30207.1 of the Revenue and Taxation Code
Alcoholic Beverage Tax Law (commencing with Section 32001 of the Revenue and Taxation Code)	Section 32272.1 of the Revenue and Taxation Code
Unemployment Insurance Code	Section 1090 of the Unemployment Insurance Code

State Hospitals (commencing with Section 7200 of the Welfare andInstitutions Code)	Section 7277.1 of the Welfare and Institutions Code
Medi-Cal Act (commencing with Section 14000 of the Welfare and Institutions Code)	Section 9202 of the Probate Code
Waxman-Duffy Prepaid Health Plan Act (commencing with Section 14200 of the Welfare and Institutions Code)	Section 9202 of the Probate Code

Ca. Prob. Code § 19201
Amended by Stats 2014 ch 144 (AB 1847),s 50, eff. 1/1/2015.
Amended by Stats 2007 ch 159 (AB 341),s 24, eff. 1/1/2008.

Section 19202 - Notice to State Director of Health Services of death

(a) If the trustee knows or has reason to believe that the deceased settlor received health care under Chapter 7 (commencing with Section 14000) or Chapter 8 (commencing with Section 14200) of Part 3 of Division 9 of the Welfare and Institutions Code, or was the surviving spouse of a person who received that health care, the trustee shall give the State Director of Health Services notice of the death of the deceased settlor or surviving spouse in the manner provided in Section 215.

(b) The director has four months after notice is given in which to file a claim.

Ca. Prob. Code § 19202
Amended by Stats 2007 ch 159 (AB 341),s 25, eff. 1/1/2008.

Section 19203 - Claim against distributees

If property in the trust is distributed before expiration of the time allowed a public entity to file a claim, the public entity has a claim against the distributees to the full extent of the public entity's claim or each distributee's share of the distributed property, as set forth in Section 19402, whichever is less. The public entity's claim against distributees includes interest at a rate equal to that specified in Section 19521 of the Revenue and Taxation Code, from the date of distribution or the date of filing the claim by the public entity, whichever is later, plus other accruing costs as in the case of enforcement of a money judgment.

Ca. Prob. Code § 19203
Amended by Stats 2007 ch 159 (AB 341),s 26, eff. 1/1/2008.

Section 19204 - Order of priority of debts not affected

Nothing in this chapter shall be construed to affect the order of priority of debts provided for under other provisions of law.

Ca. Prob. Code § 19204
Added by Stats. 1991, Ch. 992, Sec. 3.

Section 19205 - Inapplicability to amounts illegally acquired

This chapter does not apply to liability for the restitution of amounts illegally acquired through the means of a fraudulent, false, or incorrect representation, or a forged or unauthorized endorsement.

Ca. Prob. Code § 19205
Added by Stats. 1991, Ch. 992, Sec. 3.

Chapter 8 - ALLOWANCE AND REJECTION OF CLAIMS

Section 19250 - Generally

When a claim is filed, the trustee shall allow or reject the claim in whole or in part.

Ca. Prob. Code § 19250

Added by Stats. 1991, Ch. 992, Sec. 3.

Section 19251 - Allowance or rejection in writing; filing and notice; contents; form

(a) Any allowance or rejection shall be in writing. The trustee shall file the allowance or rejection with the court clerk and give notice to the claimant, together with a copy of the allowance or rejection, as provided in Section 1215.

(b) The allowance or rejection shall contain the following information:

(1) The name of the claimant.

(2) The date of the settlor's death.

(3) The total amount of the claim.

(4) The amount allowed or rejected by the trustee.

(5) A statement that the claimant has 90 days from the time the notice of rejection is given, or 90 days after the claim becomes due, whichever is later, in which to bring an action on a claim rejected in whole or in part.

(c) The Judicial Council shall prescribe an allowance or rejection form, which may be part of the claim form. Use of a form prescribed by the Judicial Council is deemed to satisfy the requirements.

(d) This section does not apply to a demand the trustee elects to treat as a claim under Section 19154.

Ca. Prob. Code § 19251

Added by Stats. 1991, Ch. 992, Sec. 3.

Section 19252 - Payment constitutes allowance; power to compromise; trustee creditor of deceased settlor

The trustee shall have the power to pay any claim or portion of a claim and payment shall constitute allowance of the claim to the extent of the payment. The trustee shall have the power to compromise any claim or portion of a claim. If the trustee or the attorney for the trustee is a creditor of the deceased settlor, the trustee shall have the same powers regarding allowance, rejection, payment, or compromise set forth in this chapter.

Ca. Prob. Code § 19252
Amended by Stats 2007 ch 159 (AB 341),s 27, eff. 1/1/2008.

Section 19253 - Statute of limitations

(a) A claim barred by the statute of limitations may not be allowed by the trustee.
(b) The filing of a claim tolls the statute of limitations otherwise applicable to the claim until the trustee gives notice of allowance or rejection.
(c) The allowance of a claim further tolls the statute of limitations as to the part of the claim allowed until the allowed portion of the claim is paid.
(d) Notwithstanding the statute of limitations otherwise applicable to a claim, if an action on a rejected claim is not commenced or if the matter is not referred to a referee or to arbitration within the time prescribed in Section 19255, it is forever barred.

Ca. Prob. Code § 19253
Added by Stats. 1991, Ch. 992, Sec. 3.

Section 19254 - Refusal or neglect to act deemed equivalent to notice of rejection

If within 30 days after a claim is filed the trustee has refused or neglected to act on the claim, the refusal or neglect may, at the option of the claimant, be deemed equivalent to the giving of a notice of rejection on the 30th day.

Ca. Prob. Code § 19254
Added by Stats. 1991, Ch. 992, Sec. 3.

Section 19255 - Action on rejected claim

(a) A rejected claim is barred as to the part rejected unless the creditor brings an action on the claim or the matter is referred to a referee or to arbitration within the following times, excluding any time during which there is a vacancy in the office of the trustee:

(1) If the claim is due at the time of giving the notice of rejection, 90 days after the notice is given.

(2) If the claim is not due at the time of giving the notice of rejection, 90 days after the claim becomes due.

(b) In addition to any other county in which an action on a rejected claim may be commenced, the action may be commenced in the county or city and county wherein the principal place of administration of the trust is located.

(c) The creditor shall file a notice of the pendency of the action or the referral to a referee or to arbitration with the court clerk in the trust proceeding, together with proof of giving a copy of the notice to the trustee as provided in Section 1215. Personal service of a copy of the summons and complaint on the trustee is equivalent to the filing and giving of the notice.

(d) Any property distributed by the trustee under the terms of the trust after 120 days from the later of the time the notice of rejection is given or the claim is due and before the notice of pendency of action or referral or arbitration is filed and given, excluding therefrom any time during which there is a vacancy in the office of the trustee, is not subject to the claim. Neither the trustee nor the distributee is liable on account of the distribution.

(e) The prevailing party in the action shall be awarded court costs and, if the court determines that the prosecution or defense of the action against the prevailing party was unreasonable, the prevailing party shall be awarded reasonable litigation expenses, including attorney's fees. For the purpose of this subdivision, the prevailing party shall be the trustee if the creditor recovers an amount equal to or less than the amount of the claim allowed by the trustee, and shall be the creditor if the creditor recovers an amount greater than the amount of the claim allowed by the trustee.

Ca. Prob. Code § 19255
Amended by Stats 2007 ch 159 (AB 341),s 28, eff. 1/1/2008.

Chapter 9 - CLAIMS ESTABLISHED BY JUDGMENT

Section 19300 - Money judgment payable in course of administration; filing judgments

(a) Except as provided in Section 19303, after the death of the settlor all money judgments against the deceased settlor on a claim against the deceased settlor or against the trustee on a claim against the decedent or the trust estate are payable in the course of administration and are not enforceable against property in the trust estate of the deceased settlor under the Enforcement of Judgments Law (Title 9 (commencing with Section 680.010) of Part 2 of the Code of Civil Procedure).
(b) Subject to Section 19301, a judgment referred to in subdivision (a) shall be filed in the same manner as other claims.
Ca. Prob. Code § 19300
Added by Stats. 1991, Ch. 992, Sec. 3.

Section 19301 - Final judgment against trustee in representative capacity

When a money judgment against a trustee in a representative capacity becomes final, it conclusively establishes the validity of the claim for the amount of the judgment. The judgment shall provide that it is payable out of property in the deceased settlor's trust estate in the course of administration. An abstract of the judgment shall be filed in the trust administration proceedings.
Ca. Prob. Code § 19301
Added by Stats. 1991, Ch. 992, Sec. 3.

Section 19302 - Enforcement of judgment for possession or sale of trust property

(a) Notwithstanding the death of the settlor, a judgment for possession of trust property or a judgment for sale of trust property may be enforced under the Enforcement of Judgments Law (Title 9 (commencing with Section 680.010) of Part 2 of the Code of Civil Procedure). Nothing in this subdivision authorizes enforcement under the Enforcement of Judgments Law against any property in the trust estate of the deceased settlor other than the property described in the judgment for possession or sale.

(b) After the death of the settlor, a demand for money that is not satisfied from the trust property described in a judgment for sale of property shall be filed as a claim in the same manner as other claims and is payable in the course of administration.

Ca. Prob. Code § 19302
Added by Stats. 1991, Ch. 992, Sec. 3.

Section 19303 - Trust property subject to execution lien

If trust property of the deceased settlor is subject to an execution lien at the time of the settlor's death, enforcement against the property may proceed under the Enforcement of Judgments Law (Title 9 (commencing with Section 680.010) of Part 2 of the Code of Civil Procedure) to satisfy the judgment. The levying officer, as defined in Section 680.260 of the Code of Civil Procedure, shall account to the trustee for any surplus. If the judgment is not satisfied, the balance of the judgment remaining unsatisfied is payable in the course of administration.

Ca. Prob. Code § 19303
Added by Stats. 1991, Ch. 992, Sec. 3.

Section 19304 - Conversion of attachment lien to judgment lien on property

(a) An attachment lien may be converted into a judgment lien on property in the trust estate subject to the attachment lien, with the same priority as the attachment lien, in either of the following cases:

(1) Where the judgment debtor dies after entry of judgment in an action in which the property was attached.

(2) Where a judgment is entered after the death of the

defendant in an action in which the property was attached.

(b) To convert the attachment lien into a judgment lien, the levying officer shall, after entry of judgment in the action in which the property was attached and before the expiration of the attachment lien, do one of the following:

(1) Serve an abstract of the judgment, and a notice that the attachment lien has become a judgment lien, on the trustee or other person holding property subject to the attachment lien.

(2) Record or file in any office where the writ of attachment and notice of attachment are recorded or filed an abstract of the judgment and a notice that the attachment lien has become a judgment lien. If the attached property is real property, the plaintiff or the plaintiff's attorney may record the required abstract and notice with the same effect as if recorded by the levying officer.

(c) After the death of the settlor, any members of the deceased settlor's family who were supported in whole or in part by the deceased settlor may claim an exemption provided in Section 487.020 of the Code of Civil Procedure for property levied on under the writ of attachment if the right to the exemption exists at the time the exemption is claimed. The trustee may claim the exemption on behalf of members of the deceased settlor's family. The claim of exemption may be made at any time before the time the abstract and notice are served, recorded, or filed under subdivision (b) with respect to the property claimed to be exempt. The claim of exemption shall be made in the same manner as an exemption is claimed under Section 482.100 of the Code of Civil Procedure.

Ca. Prob. Code § 19304
Amended by Stats 2007 ch 159 (AB 341),s 29, eff. 1/1/2008.

Chapter 10 - ALLOCATION OF DEBTS BETWEEN TRUST AND SURVIVING SPOUSE

Section 19320 - Petition for order to allocate debt

If it appears that a debt of the deceased settlor has been paid or is payable in whole or in part from property in the deceased settlor's trust, then the trustee, the surviving spouse, the personal representative, if any, of a deceased settlor's probate estate, or a beneficiary may petition for an order to allocate the debt.

Ca. Prob. Code § 19320

Amended by Stats 2015 ch 48 (SB 785),s 8, eff. 1/1/2016.

Section 19321 - Contents of petition

A petition under Section 19320 shall include a statement of all of the following:

(a) All debts of the deceased settlor and surviving spouse known to the petitioner that are alleged to be subject to allocation and whether paid in whole or in part or unpaid.

(b) The reason why the debts should be allocated.

(c) The proposed allocation and the basis for allocation alleged by the petitioner.

Ca. Prob. Code § 19321

Added by Stats. 1991, Ch. 992, Sec. 3.

Section 19322 - Order to show cause why information should not be provided

If it appears from the petition under Section 19320 that allocation would be affected by the value of the separate property of the surviving spouse and any community property and quasi-community property not administered in the trust, and if an inventory and appraisal of the property has not been provided by the surviving spouse, the court shall make an order to show cause why the information should not be provided.

Ca. Prob. Code § 19322

Added by Stats. 1991, Ch. 992, Sec. 3.

Section 19323 - Notice of hearing

(a) At least 30 days before the time set for the hearing on the petition, the petitioner shall cause notice of the time and place of the hearing and a copy of the petition to be served on the surviving spouse in the manner provided in Chapter 4 (commencing with

Section 413.10) of Title 5 of Part 2 of the Code of Civil Procedure.
(b) At least 30 days before the time set for the hearing on the petition, the petitioner shall cause notice of the time and place of hearing, together with a copy of the petition, to be delivered pursuant to Section 1215 to each of the following persons who are not petitioners:

(1) All trustees of the trust and of any trusts to which an allocation of liability may be approved by the court pursuant to the petition.

(2) All beneficiaries affected.

(3) The personal representative of the deceased settlor's probate estate, if any is known to the trustee.

(4) The Attorney General, if the petition relates to a charitable trust subject to the jurisdiction of the Attorney General, unless the Attorney General waives notice.
Ca. Prob. Code § 19323
Amended by Stats 2017 ch 319 (AB 976),s 105, eff. 1/1/2018.
Amended by Stats 2015 ch 48 (SB 785),s 9, eff. 1/1/2016.

Section 19324 - Allocation of debts by agreement; allocation after characterization of debts as separate or community property

(a) The trustee, the personal representative, if any, of a deceased settlor's probate estate, and the surviving spouse may provide for allocation of debts by agreement so long as the agreement substantially protects the rights of other interested persons. The trustee, the personal representative, or the spouse may request and obtain court approval of the allocation provided in the agreement.
(b) In the absence of an agreement, each debt subject to allocation shall first be characterized by the court as separate or community, in accordance with the laws of the state applicable to marital dissolution proceedings. Following that characterization, the debt or debts shall be allocated as follows:

(1) Separate debts of either spouse shall be allocated to that spouse's separate property assets, and community debts shall be allocated to the spouses' community property assets.

(2) If a separate property asset of either spouse is subject to a secured debt that is characterized as that spouse's separate debt, and the net equity in that asset available to satisfy that secured debt is less than that secured debt, the unsatisfied portion of that secured debt shall be treated as an unsecured separate debt of that spouse and allocated to the net value of that spouse's other separate property assets.

(3) If the net value of either spouse's separate property assets is less than that spouse's unsecured separate debt or debts, the unsatisfied portion of the debt or debts shall be allocated to the net value of that spouse's one-half share of the community property assets. If the net value of that spouse's one-half share of the community property assets is less than that spouse's unsatisfied unsecured separate debt or debts, the remaining unsatisfied portion of the debt or debts shall be allocated to the net value of the other spouse's one-half share of the community property assets.

(4) If a community property asset is subject to a secured debt that is characterized as a community debt, and the net equity in that asset available to satisfy that secured debt is less than that secured debt, the unsatisfied portion of that secured debt shall be treated as an unsecured community debt and allocated to the net value of the other community property assets.

(5) If the net value of the community property assets is less than the unsecured community debt or debts, the unsatisfied portion of the debt or debts shall be allocated equally between the separate property assets of the deceased settlor and the surviving spouse. If the net value of either spouse's separate property assets is less than that spouse's share of the unsatisfied portion of the unsecured community debt or debts, the remaining unsatisfied portion of the debt or debts shall be allocated to the net value of the other spouse's separate property assets.

(c) For purposes of this section:

(1) The net value of either spouse's separate property asset shall refer to its fair market value as of the date of the deceased settlor's death, minus the date-of-death balance of any liens and encumbrances on that asset that have been characterized as that spouse's separate debts.

(2) The net value of a community property asset shall refer to its fair market value as of the date of the deceased settlor's death, minus the date-of-death balance of any liens and encumbrances on that asset that have been characterized as community debts.

(3) In the case of a nonrecourse debt, the amount of that debt shall be limited to the net equity in the collateral, based on the fair market value of the collateral as of the date of the decedent's death, that is available to satisfy that debt. For the purposes of this paragraph, "nonrecourse debt" means a debt for which the debtor's obligation to repay is limited to the collateral securing the debt, and for which a deficiency judgment against the debtor is not permitted by law.

(d) Notwithstanding the foregoing provisions of this section, the court may order a different allocation of debts between the deceased settlor's probate estate, trust, and the surviving spouse if the court finds a different allocation to be equitable under the circumstances.

(e) Nothing contained in this section is intended to impair or affect the rights of third parties. If a trustee, a personal representative, if any, of a deceased settlor's probate estate, or the surviving spouse incurs any damages or expense, including attorney's fees, on account of the nonpayment of a debt that was allocated to the other party pursuant to subdivision (b), or as the result of a debt being misallocated due to fraud or intentional misrepresentation by the other party, the party incurring damages shall be entitled to recover from the other party for damages or expense deemed reasonable by the court that made the allocation.

Ca. Prob. Code § 19324
Amended by Stats 2001 ch 72 (SB 668), s 2, eff. 1/1/2002.

Section 19325 - Court order

On making a determination as provided in this chapter, the court shall make an order that:

(a) Directs the trustee to make payment of the amounts allocated to the trust by payment to the surviving spouse or creditors.

(b) Directs the trustee to charge amounts allocated to the surviving spouse against any property or interests of the surviving spouse that are in the possession or control of the trustee. To the extent that property or interests of the surviving spouse in the possession or control of the trustee are insufficient to satisfy the allocation, the court order shall summarily direct the surviving spouse to pay the allocation to the trustee.

Ca. Prob. Code § 19325
Added by Stats. 1991, Ch. 992, Sec. 3.

Section 19326 - Funeral expenses and expenses of last illness

Notwithstanding any other statute, funeral expenses and expenses of last illness, in the absence of specific provisions in a will or trust to the contrary, shall be charged against the deceased settlor's probate estate and thereafter, against the deceased settlor's share of the trust and shall not be allocated to or charged against, the community share of the surviving spouse, whether or not the surviving spouse is financially able to pay the expenses and whether or not the surviving spouse or any other person is also liable for the expenses.

Ca. Prob. Code § 19326
Added by Stats. 1991, Ch. 992, Sec. 3.

Chapter 11 - LIABILITY OF SETTLOR'S SURVIVING SPOUSE

Section 19330 - Action barred, exceptions

If proceedings are commenced under this part for the settlement of claims against the trust, and the time for filing claims has commenced, any action upon the liability of the surviving spouse under Chapter 3 (commencing with Section 13550) is barred to the same extent as provided for claims under this part, except as to the following:

(a) Any creditor who commences judicial proceedings to enforce a claim and serves the surviving spouse with the complaint prior to the expiration of the time for filing claims.

(b) Any creditor who has or who secures the surviving spouse's acknowledgment in writing of the liability of the surviving spouse for the claim.

(c) Any creditor who files a timely claim in the proceedings for the administration of the estate of the deceased spouse.

Ca. Prob. Code § 19330
Added by Stats. 1991, Ch. 992, Sec. 3.

Chapter 12 - DISTRIBUTEE LIABILITY

Section 19400 - Beneficiary personally liable

Subject to Section 366.2 of the Code of Civil Procedure, if there is no proceeding to administer the probate estate of the deceased settlor, and if the trustee does not file a proposed notice to creditors pursuant to Section 19003 and does not publish notice to creditors pursuant to Chapter 3 (commencing with Section 19040), then a beneficiary of the trust to whom payment, delivery, or transfer of the deceased settlor's property is made pursuant to the terms of the trust is personally liable, to the extent provided in Section 19402, for the unsecured claims of the creditors of the deceased settlor's probate estate.

Ca. Prob. Code § 19400
Amended by Stats 2015 ch 48 (SB 785),s 10, eff. 1/1/2016.

Section 19401 - Person to property distributed personally liable

Subject to Section 19402, if the trustee filed a proposed notice to creditors pursuant to Section 19003 and published notice to creditors pursuant to Section 19040, and if the identity of the creditor was known to, or reasonably ascertainable by, the trustee within four months of the first publication of notice pursuant to Section 19040, then a person to whom property is distributed is personally liable for the claim of the creditor, without a claim first having been filed, if all of the following conditions are satisfied:

(a) The claim of the creditor was not merely conjectural.

(b) Notice to the creditor was not given to the creditor under Chapter 4 (commencing with Section 19050) and neither the creditor nor the attorney representing the creditor in the matter had actual knowledge of the administration of the trust estate sooner than one year after the date of first publication of notice pursuant to Section 19040.

(c) The statute of limitations applicable to the claim under Section 366.2 of the Code of Civil Procedure has not expired at the time of commencement of an action under this section.

Ca. Prob. Code § 19401

Amended by Stats. 1992, Ch. 178, Sec. 47. Effective January 1, 1993.

Section 19402 - Distributee's rights in action

(a) In any action under this chapter, subject to Section 366.2 of the Code of Civil Procedure, the distributee may assert any defenses, cross-complaints, or setoffs that would have been available to the deceased settlor if the settlor had not died.

(b) Personal liability under this chapter is applicable only to the extent the claim of the creditor cannot be satisfied out of the trust estate of the deceased settlor and is limited to a pro rata portion of the claim of the creditor, based on the proportion that the value of the property distributed to the person out of the trust estate bears to the total value of all property distributed to all persons out of the trust estate. Personal liability under this chapter for all claims of all creditors shall not exceed the value of the property distributed to the person out of the trust estate. As used in this chapter, the value of the property is the fair market value of the property on the date of its distribution, less the amount of any liens and encumbrances on the property at that time.

Ca. Prob. Code § 19402
Amended by Stats. 1992, Ch. 178, Sec. 48. Effective January 1, 1993.

Section 19403 - Purchasers for value from person personally liable under chapter

Nothing in this chapter affects the rights of a purchaser or encumbrancer of property in good faith and for value from a person who is personally liable under this section.

Ca. Prob. Code § 19403
Amended by Stats 2004 ch 183 (AB 3082), s 280, eff. 1/1/2005.

Part 9 - UNIFORM TRUST DECANTING ACT

Section 19501 - Short title

This part may be cited as the Uniform Trust Decanting Act.

Ca. Prob. Code § 19501
Added by Stats 2018 ch 407 (SB 909),s 1, eff. 1/1/2019.

Section 19502 - Definitions

For purposes of this part:

(a) "Appointive property" means the property or property interest subject to a power of appointment.

(b) "Ascertainable standard" means a standard relating to an individual's health, education, support, or maintenance within the meaning of Section 2041(b)(1)(A)(b)(1)(A) or Section 2514(c)(1)(c)(1) of the Internal Revenue Code (26 U.S.C. Secs. 2041(b)(1)(A), 2514(c)(1)) and any applicable regulations.

(c) "Authorized fiduciary" means any of the following:

(1) A trustee or other fiduciary, other than a settlor, that has discretion to distribute or direct a trustee to distribute part or all of the principal of the first trust to one or more current beneficiaries.

(2) A special fiduciary appointed under Section 19509.

(3) A special-needs fiduciary under Section 19513.

(d) "Beneficiary" means a person that meets one of the following conditions:

(1) Has a present or future, vested or contingent, beneficial interest in a trust.

(2) Holds a power of appointment over trust property.

(3) Is an identified charitable organization that will or may receive distributions under the terms of the trust.
(e) "Charitable interest" means an interest in a trust that meets one of the following conditions:

(1) Is held by an identified charitable organization and makes the organization a qualified beneficiary.

(2) Benefits only charitable organizations and, if the interest were held by an identified charitable organization, would make the organization a qualified beneficiary.

(3) Is held solely for charitable purposes and, if the interest were held by an identified charitable organization, would make the organization a qualified beneficiary.
(f) "Charitable organization" means either of the following:

(1) A person, other than an individual, organized and operated exclusively for charitable purposes.

(2) A government or governmental subdivision, agency, or instrumentality, to the extent it holds funds exclusively for a charitable purpose.
(g) "Charitable purpose" means the relief of poverty, the advancement of education or religion, the promotion of health, a municipal or other governmental purpose, or another purpose the achievement of which is beneficial to the community.
(h) "Court" means the court in this state having jurisdiction in matters relating to trusts.
(i) "Current beneficiary" means a beneficiary that on the date the

beneficiary's qualification is determined is a distributee or permissible distributee of trust income or principal. The term includes the holder of a presently exercisable general power of appointment but does not include a person that is a beneficiary only because the person holds any other power of appointment.

(j) "Decanting power" or "the decanting power" means the power of an authorized fiduciary under this part to distribute property of a first trust to one or more second trusts or to modify the terms of the first trust.

(k) "Expanded distributive discretion" means a discretionary power of distribution that is not limited to an ascertainable standard or a reasonably definite standard.

(l) "First trust" means a trust over which an authorized fiduciary may exercise the decanting power.

(m) "First trust instrument" means the trust instrument for a first trust.

(n) "General power of appointment" means a power of appointment exercisable in favor of a powerholder, the powerholder's estate, a creditor of the powerholder, or a creditor of the powerholder's estate.

(o) "Jurisdiction," with respect to a geographic area, includes a state or country.

(p) "Person" means an individual, estate, business or nonprofit entity, public corporation, government or governmental subdivision, agency, or instrumentality, or other legal entity.

(q) "Power of appointment" means a power that enables a powerholder acting in a nonfiduciary capacity to designate a recipient of an ownership interest in, or another power of appointment over, the appointive property. The term does not include a power of attorney.

(r) "Powerholder" means a person in which a donor creates a power of appointment.

(s) "Presently exercisable power of appointment" means a power of appointment exercisable by the powerholder at the relevant time.

(1) The term includes a power of appointment exercisable only after the occurrence of a specified event, the satisfaction of an ascertainable standard, or the passage of a specified time only after one of the following, respectively:

    (A) The occurrence of the specified event.

    (B) The satisfaction of the ascertainable standard.

    (C) The passage of the specified time.

    (2) The term does not include a power exercisable only at the powerholder's death.
(t) "Qualified beneficiary" means a beneficiary that, on the date the beneficiary's qualification is determined, satisfies one of the following conditions:

    (1) Is a distributee or permissible distributee of trust income or principal.

    (2) Would be a distributee or permissible distributee of trust income or principal if the interests of the distributees described in paragraph (1) terminated on that date without causing the trust to terminate.

    (3) Would be a distributee or permissible distributee of trust income or principal if the trust terminated on that date.
(u) "Reasonably definite standard" means a clearly measurable standard under which a holder of a power of distribution is legally accountable within the meaning of Section 674(b)(5)(A)(b)(5)(A) of the Internal Revenue Code (26 U.S.C. Sec. 674(b)(5)(A)) and any applicable regulations.
(v) "Second trust" means either of the following:

    (1) A first trust after modification under this part.

    (2) A trust to which a distribution of property from a first trust is or may be made under this part.
(w) "Second trust instrument" means the trust instrument for a second trust.
(x) "Settlor," except as otherwise provided in Section 19525, means

a person, including a testator, that creates or contributes property to a trust. If more than one person creates or contributes property to a trust, each person is a settlor of the portion of the trust property attributable to the person's contribution except to the extent another person has power to revoke or withdraw that portion.

(y) "State" means a state of the United States, the District of Columbia, Puerto Rico, the United States Virgin Islands, or any territory or insular possession subject to the jurisdiction of the United States.

(z) "Terms of the trust" means the manifestation of the settlor's intent regarding a trust's provisions as expressed in the trust instrument, as may be established by other evidence that would be admissible in a judicial proceeding, or as may be established by court order or nonjudicial settlement agreement.

(aa) "Trust instrument" means a trust executed by the settlor to create a trust or by any person to create a second trust that contains some or all of the terms of the trust, including any amendments.

Ca. Prob. Code § 19502

Added by Stats 2018 ch 407 (SB 909),s 1, eff. 1/1/2019.

Section 19503 - Scope

(a) Except as otherwise provided in subdivisions (b) and (c), this part applies to an express trust that is irrevocable or revocable by the settlor only with the consent of the trustee or a person holding an adverse interest.

(b) This part does not apply to a trust held solely for charitable purposes.

(c) Subject to Section 19515, a trust instrument may restrict or prohibit exercise of the decanting power.

(d) This part does not limit the power of a trustee, powerholder, or other person to distribute or appoint property in further trust or to modify a trust under the trust instrument, law of this state other than this part, common law, a court order, or a nonjudicial settlement agreement.

(e) This part does not affect the ability of a settlor to provide in a trust instrument for the distribution of the trust property or appointment in further trust of the trust property or for modification of the trust instrument.

Ca. Prob. Code § 19503

Added by Stats 2018 ch 407 (SB 909),s 1, eff. 1/1/2019.

Section 19504 - Fiduciary duty

(a) In exercising the decanting power, an authorized fiduciary shall act in accordance with its fiduciary duties, including the duty to act in accordance with the purposes of the first trust.

(b) This part does not create or imply a duty to exercise the decanting power or to inform beneficiaries about the applicability of this part.

(c) Except as otherwise provided in a first trust instrument, for purposes of this part, the terms of the first trust are deemed to include the decanting power.

Ca. Prob. Code § 19504

Added by Stats 2018 ch 407 (SB 909),s 1, eff. 1/1/2019.

Section 19505 - Application; governing law

This part applies to a trust created before, on, or after January 1, 2019, that satisfies either of the following conditions:

(a) Has its principal place of administration in this state, including a trust whose principal place of administration has been changed to this state.

(b) Provides by its trust instrument that it is governed by the law of this state or is governed by the law of this state for the purpose of any of the following:

(1) Administration, including administration of a trust whose governing law for purposes of administration has been changed to the law of this state.

(2) Construction of terms of the trust.

(3) Determining the meaning or effect of terms of the trust.

Ca. Prob. Code § 19505
Added by Stats 2018 ch 407 (SB 909),s 1, eff. 1/1/2019.

Section 19507 - Notice; exercise of decanting power

(a) In this section, a notice period begins on the day notice is given under subdivision (c) and ends 59 days after the day notice is given.
(b) An authorized fiduciary may exercise the decanting power without the consent of any person and without court approval in compliance with this part.
(c) Except as otherwise provided in subdivision (h), an authorized fiduciary shall give notice of the intended exercise of the decanting power not later than 60 days before the exercise to all of the following:

(1) Each settlor of the first trust, if living or then in existence.

(2) Each qualified beneficiary of the first trust.

(3) Each holder of a presently exercisable power of appointment over any part or all of the first trust.

(4) Each person that currently has the right to remove or replace the authorized fiduciary.

(5) Each other fiduciary of the first trust.

(6) Each fiduciary of the second trust.

(7) The Attorney General, if subdivision (b) of Section 19514 applies.
(d) Unless the trust instrument provides otherwise, an authorized fiduciary shall give notice under subdivision (c) to the guardian ad litem for a qualified beneficiary who is a minor and has no representative or who is an unascertained or unborn person. If a guardian ad litem has not been appointed at the time of the notice, the authorized fiduciary shall seek the appointment of one. The court may appoint a guardian ad litem, for purposes of this section,

in instances where the only matter before the court is that appointment.

(e) If an authorized fiduciary knows, or has reason to know, that a person entitled to notice under subdivision (c) is substantially unable to manage that person's own financial resources or resist fraud or undue influence, the authorized fiduciary shall give notice under subdivision (c) to that person and to the individual appointed to act on that person's behalf, including, but not limited to, an attorney-in-fact under a power of attorney. If no such individual has been appointed at the time of the notice, the authorized fiduciary shall seek the appointment of such an individual. The court may appoint a guardian ad litem, for purposes of this section, in instances where the only matter before the court is that appointment.

(f) An authorized fiduciary is not required to give notice under subdivision (c) to a person who is known to the fiduciary but cannot be located by the fiduciary after reasonable diligence.

(g) A notice under subdivision (c) shall include all of the following:

(1) A description of the manner in which the authorized fiduciary intends to exercise the decanting power, which shall include a statement as to the authorized fiduciary's reason for the proposed decanting and an explanation as to the differences between the first trust and the second trust or trusts.

(2) The proposed effective date for exercise of the power.

(3) A copy of the first trust instrument.

(4) A copy of all second trust instruments.

(5) A warning, set out in a separate paragraph in not less than 10-point bold type, or a reasonable equivalent thereof, that states the following: "If you do not bring a court action to contest the proposed trust decanting (the proposed changes to the trust) within 59 days of this notice, you will lose your right to contest the decanting."

(h) The decanting power may be exercised before expiration of the notice period under subdivision (a) if all persons entitled to receive notice waive the period in a signed waiver.

(i) The receipt of notice, waiver of the notice period, or expiration of the notice period does not affect the right of a person to file an application under Section 19509 that asserts either of the following:

(1) An attempted exercise of the decanting power is ineffective because it did not comply with this part or was an abuse of discretion or breach of fiduciary duty.

(2) Section 19522 applies to the exercise of the decanting power. **(j)** The notice required by this section shall be served by mail to the last known address, pursuant to Section 1215, or by personal delivery.

Ca. Prob. Code § 19507
Added by Stats 2018 ch 407 (SB 909),s 1, eff. 1/1/2019.

Section 19508 - Representation

(a) Notice to a person with authority to represent and bind another person under this code or a first trust instrument has the same effect as notice given directly to the person represented.
(b) Consent of or waiver by a person with authority to represent and bind another person under this code or a first trust instrument is binding on the person represented unless the person represented objects to the representation before the consent or waiver otherwise would become effective.
(c) A person with authority to represent and bind another person under this code or a first trust instrument may file an application under Section 19509 on behalf of the person represented.
(d) A settlor may not represent or bind a beneficiary under this part.

Ca. Prob. Code § 19508
Added by Stats 2018 ch 407 (SB 909),s 1, eff. 1/1/2019.

Section 19509 - Court involvement

(a) On application of an authorized fiduciary, a person entitled to notice under subdivision (c) of Section 19507, a beneficiary, or, with respect to a charitable interest, the Attorney General or other person that has standing to enforce the charitable interest, the court may do any of the following:

(1) Provide instructions to the authorized fiduciary regarding whether a proposed exercise of the decanting power is permitted under this part and is consistent with the fiduciary duties of the authorized fiduciary.

(2) Appoint a special fiduciary and authorize the special fiduciary to determine whether the decanting power should be exercised under this part and to exercise the decanting power.

(3) Approve an exercise of the decanting power.

(4) Determine that a proposed or attempted exercise of the decanting power is ineffective because of either of the following:

(A) After applying Section 19522, the proposed or attempted exercise does not or did not comply with this part.

(B) The proposed or attempted exercise would be or was an abuse of the fiduciary's discretion or a breach of fiduciary duty.

(5) Determine the extent to which Section 19522 applies to a prior exercise of the decanting power.

(6) Provide instructions to the trustee regarding the application of Section 19522 to a prior exercise of the decanting power.

(7) Order other relief to carry out the purposes of this part.
(b) If an application is made under subdivision (a), the burden is on the authorized fiduciary to establish that notice was given as required by Section 19507 and that the authorized fiduciary may exercise the decanting power.
(c) On application of an authorized fiduciary, the court may approve either or both of the following:

(1) An increase in the fiduciary's compensation under Section 19516.

(2) A modification under Section 19518 of a provision granting a person the right to remove or replace the fiduciary.
Ca. Prob. Code § 19509
Added by Stats 2018 ch 407 (SB 909),s 1, eff. 1/1/2019.

Section 19510 - Formalities

An exercise of the decanting power shall be made in a writing signed by an authorized fiduciary. The signed writing shall, directly or by reference to the notice required by Section 19507, identify the first trust and the second trust or trusts and state the property of the first trust being distributed to each second trust and the property, if any, that remains in the first trust.
Ca. Prob. Code § 19510
Added by Stats 2018 ch 407 (SB 909),s 1, eff. 1/1/2019.

Section 19511 - Decanting power under expanded distributive discretion

(a) For purposes of this section:

(1) "Noncontingent right" means a right that is not subject to the exercise of discretion or the occurrence of a specified event that is not certain to occur. The term does not include a right held by a beneficiary if any person has discretion to distribute property subject to the right to any person other than the beneficiary or the beneficiary's estate.

(2) "Presumptive remainder beneficiary" means a qualified beneficiary other than a current beneficiary.

(3) "Successor beneficiary" means a beneficiary that is not a qualified beneficiary on the date the beneficiary's qualification is determined. The term does not include a person that is a beneficiary only because the person holds a nongeneral power of appointment.

(4) "Vested interest" means any of the following:

(A) A right to a mandatory distribution that is a noncontingent right as of the date of the exercise of the decanting power.

(B) A current and noncontingent right, annually or more frequently, to a mandatory distribution of income, a specified dollar amount, or a percentage of value of some or all of the trust property.

(C) A current and noncontingent right, annually or more frequently, to withdraw income, a specified dollar amount, or a percentage of value of some or all of the trust property.

(D) A presently exercisable general power of appointment.

(E) A right to receive an ascertainable part of the trust property on the trust's termination that is not subject to the exercise of discretion or to the occurrence of a specified event that is not certain to occur.

(b) Subject to subdivision (c) and Section 19514, an authorized fiduciary that has expanded distributive discretion over the principal of a first trust for the benefit of one or more current beneficiaries may exercise the decanting power over the principal of the first trust.

(c) Subject to Section 19513, in an exercise of the decanting power under this section, a second trust may not do any of the following:

(1) Include as a current beneficiary a person that is not a current beneficiary of the first trust, except as otherwise provided in subdivision (d).

(2) Include as a presumptive remainder beneficiary or successor beneficiary a person that is not a current beneficiary, presumptive

remainder beneficiary, or successor beneficiary of the first trust, except as otherwise provided in subdivision (d).

(3) Reduce or eliminate a vested interest.

(d) Subject to paragraph (3) of subdivision (c) and Section 19514, in an exercise of the decanting power under this section, a second trust may be a trust created or administered under the law of any jurisdiction and may do each of the following:

(1) Retain a power of appointment granted in the first trust.

(2) Omit a power of appointment granted in the first trust, other than a presently exercisable general power of appointment.

(3) Create or modify a power of appointment if the powerholder is a current beneficiary of the first trust and the authorized fiduciary has expanded distributive discretion to distribute principal to the beneficiary.

(4) Create or modify a power of appointment if the powerholder is a presumptive remainder beneficiary or successor beneficiary of the first trust, but the exercise of the power may take effect only after the powerholder becomes, or would have become if then living, a current beneficiary.

(e) A power of appointment described in paragraphs (1) to (4), inclusive, of subdivision (d) may be general or nongeneral. The class of permissible appointees in favor of which the power may be exercised may be broader than, or different from, the beneficiaries of the first trust.

(f) If an authorized fiduciary has expanded distributive discretion over part but not all of the principal of a first trust, the fiduciary may exercise the decanting power under this section over that part of the principal over which the authorized fiduciary has expanded distributive discretion.

Ca. Prob. Code § 19511

Added by Stats 2018 ch 407 (SB 909),s 1, eff. 1/1/2019.

Section 19512 - Decanting power under limited

distributive discretion

(a) For purposes of this section, "limited distributive discretion" means a discretionary power of distribution that is limited to an ascertainable standard or a reasonably definite standard.

(b) An authorized fiduciary that has limited distributive discretion over the principal of the first trust for benefit of one or more current beneficiaries may exercise the decanting power over the principal of the first trust.

(c) Under this section and subject to Section 19514, a second trust may be created or administered under the law of any jurisdiction. Under this section, the second trusts, in the aggregate, shall grant each beneficiary of the first trust beneficial interests which are substantially similar to the beneficial interests of the beneficiary in the first trust. For purposes of this subdivision, "substantially similar" means that there is no material change in a beneficiary's beneficial interests, except as provided in subdivision (d).

(d) A power to make a distribution under a second trust for the benefit of a beneficiary who is an individual is substantially similar to a power under the first trust to make a distribution directly to the beneficiary. A distribution is for the benefit of a beneficiary if it satisfies any of the following conditions:

(1) The distribution is applied for the benefit of the beneficiary.

(2) The beneficiary is under a legal disability or the trustee reasonably believes the beneficiary is incapacitated, and the distribution is made as permitted under this code.

(3) The distribution is made as permitted under the terms of the first trust instrument and the second trust instrument for the benefit of the beneficiary.

(e) If an authorized fiduciary has limited distributive discretion over part but not all of the principal of a first trust, the fiduciary may exercise the decanting power under this section over that part of the principal over which the authorized fiduciary has limited distributive discretion.

Ca. Prob. Code § 19512
Added by Stats 2018 ch 407 (SB 909),s 1, eff. 1/1/2019.

Section 19513 - Trust for beneficiary with disability

(a) For purposes of this section:

(1) "Beneficiary with a disability" means a beneficiary of a first trust who the special needs fiduciary believes may qualify for governmental benefits based on disability, whether or not the beneficiary currently receives those benefits or is an individual who has been adjudicated legally incompetent.

(2) "Governmental benefits" means financial aid or services from a state, federal, or other public agency.

(3) "Special needs fiduciary" means, with respect to a trust that has a beneficiary with a disability, any of the following:

(A) A trustee or other fiduciary, other than a settlor, that has discretion to distribute part or all of the principal of a first trust to one or more current beneficiaries.

(B) If no trustee or fiduciary has discretion under subparagraph (A), a trustee or other fiduciary, other than a settlor, that has discretion to distribute part or all of the income of the first trust to one or more current beneficiaries.

(C) If no trustee or fiduciary has discretion under subparagraphs (A) and (B), a trustee or other fiduciary, other than a settlor, that is required to distribute part or all of the income or principal of the first trust to one or more current beneficiaries.

(4) "Special needs trust" means a trust the trustee believes would not be considered a resource for purposes of determining whether a beneficiary with a disability is eligible for governmental benefits.
(b) A special needs fiduciary may exercise the decanting power

under Section 19511 over the principal of a first trust as if the fiduciary had authority to distribute principal to a beneficiary with a disability subject to expanded distributive discretion if both of the following conditions are satisfied:

(1) A second trust is a special needs trust that benefits the beneficiary with a disability.

(2) The special needs fiduciary determines that exercise of the decanting power will further the purposes of the first trust.
(c) In an exercise of the decanting power under this section, all of the following rules apply:

(1) Notwithstanding paragraph (2) of subdivision (c) of Section 19511, the interest in the second trust of a beneficiary with a disability may fulfill either of the following:

(A) Be a pooled trust as defined by Medicaid law for the benefit of the beneficiary with a disability under Section 1396p(d)(4)(C)(d)(4)(C) of the Public Health and Welfare Code (42 U.S.C. Sec. 1396p(d)(4)(C)) .

(B) Contain payback provisions complying with reimbursement requirements of Medicaid law under Section 1396p(d)(4)(A)(d)(4)(A) of the Public Health and Welfare Code (42 U.S.C. Sec. 1396p(d)(4)(A)) .

(2) Paragraph (3) of subdivision (c) of Section 19511 does not apply to the interests of the beneficiary with a disability.

(3) Except as affected by any change to the interests of the beneficiary with a disability, the second trust, or if there are two or more second trusts, the second trusts in the aggregate, shall grant each other beneficiary of the first trust beneficial interests in the second trusts which are substantially similar to the beneficiary's beneficial interests in the first trust.
Ca. Prob. Code § 19513
Added by Stats 2018 ch 407 (SB 909),s 1, eff. 1/1/2019.

Section 19514 - Protection of charitable interest

(a) For purposes of this section:

(1) "Determinable charitable interest" means a charitable interest that is a right to a mandatory distribution currently, periodically, on the occurrence of a specified event, or after the passage of a specified time and that is unconditional or will be held solely for charitable purposes.

(2) "Unconditional" means not subject to the occurrence of a specified event that is not certain to occur, other than a requirement in a trust instrument that a charitable organization be in existence or qualify under a particular provision of the United States Internal Revenue Code of 1986 on the date of the distribution, if the charitable organization meets the requirement on the date of determination.

(b) If a first trust contains a determinable charitable interest, the Attorney General has the rights of a qualified beneficiary and may represent and bind the charitable interest.

(c) If a first trust contains a charitable interest, the second trust or trusts may not do any of the following:

(1) Diminish the charitable interest.

(2) Diminish the interest of an identified charitable organization that holds the charitable interest.

(3) Alter any charitable purpose stated in the first trust instrument.

(4) Alter any condition or restriction related to the charitable interest.

(d) If there are two or more second trusts, the second trusts shall be treated as one trust for purposes of determining whether the exercise of the decanting power diminishes the charitable interest or diminishes the interest of an identified charitable organization for purposes of subdivision (c).

(e) If a first trust contains a determinable charitable interest, the second trust or trusts that include a charitable interest pursuant to subdivision (c) shall be administered under the law of this state unless any of the following occur:

(1) The Attorney General, after receiving notice under Section 19507, fails to object in a signed writing delivered to the authorized fiduciary within the notice period.

(2) The Attorney General consents in a signed writing to the second trust or trusts being administered under the law of another jurisdiction.

(3) The court approves the exercise of the decanting power.
(f) This part does not limit the powers and duties of the Attorney General under law of this state other than this part.

Ca. Prob. Code § 19514
Added by Stats 2018 ch 407 (SB 909),s 1, eff. 1/1/2019.

Section 19515 - Trust limitation on decanting

(a) An authorized fiduciary may not exercise the decanting power to the extent the first trust instrument expressly prohibits exercise of either of the following:

(1) The decanting power.

(2) A power granted by state law to the fiduciary to distribute part or all of the principal of the trust to another trust or to modify the trust.
(b) Exercise of the decanting power is subject to any restriction in the first trust instrument that expressly applies to exercise of either of the following:

(1) The decanting power.

(2) A power granted by state law to a fiduciary to distribute part or all of the principal of the trust to another trust or to modify the trust.

(c) A general prohibition of the amendment or revocation of a first trust, a spendthrift clause, or a clause restraining the voluntary or involuntary transfer of a beneficiary's interest does not preclude exercise of the decanting power.

(d) Subject to subdivisions (a) and (b), an authorized fiduciary may exercise the decanting power under this part even if the first trust instrument permits the authorized fiduciary or another person to modify the first trust instrument or to distribute part or all of the principal of the first trust to another trust.

(e) If a first trust instrument contains an express prohibition described in subdivision (a) or an express restriction described in subdivision (b), the authorized fiduciary shall include that provision or restriction in the second trust instrument.

Ca. Prob. Code § 19515
Added by Stats 2018 ch 407 (SB 909),s 1, eff. 1/1/2019.

Section 19516 - Change in compensation

(a) If a first trust instrument specifies an authorized fiduciary's compensation, the fiduciary may not exercise the decanting power to increase the fiduciary's compensation above the specified compensation unless either of the following occurs:

(1) All qualified beneficiaries of the second trust consent to the increase in a signed writing.

(2) The increase is approved by the court.

(b) If a first trust instrument does not specify an authorized fiduciary's compensation, the fiduciary may not exercise the decanting power to increase the fiduciary's compensation above the compensation permitted by this code unless either of the following occurs:

(1) All qualified beneficiaries of the second trust consent to the increase in a signed writing.

(2) The increase is approved by the court.

(c)

(1) A change in an authorized fiduciary's compensation which is incidental to other changes made by the exercise of the decanting power is not an increase in the fiduciary's compensation for purposes of subdivisions (a) and (b).

(2) For purposes of this subdivision, an incidental change to an authorized fiduciary's compensation includes, but is not limited to, an increase in the compensation of the authorized fiduciary for either of the following reasons:

(A) The second trust lasts longer than the first trust.

(B) The second trust has a greater value than the first trust.
Ca. Prob. Code § 19516
Added by Stats 2018 ch 407 (SB 909),s 1, eff. 1/1/2019.

Section 19517 - Relief from liability and indemnification

(a) Except as otherwise provided in this section, a second trust instrument may not relieve an authorized fiduciary from liability for breach of trust to a greater extent than the first trust instrument.
(b) A second trust instrument may provide for indemnification of an authorized fiduciary of the first trust or another person acting in a fiduciary capacity under the first trust for any liability or claim that would have been payable from the first trust if the decanting power had not been exercised.
(c) A second trust instrument may not reduce fiduciary liability in the aggregate.
(d) Subject to subdivision (c), a second trust instrument may reallocate fiduciary powers among fiduciaries as permitted by the law of this state other than this part.
Ca. Prob. Code § 19517
Added by Stats 2018 ch 407 (SB 909),s 1, eff. 1/1/2019.

Section 19518 - Removal or replacement of authorized

fiduciary

An authorized fiduciary may not exercise the decanting power to modify a provision in a first trust instrument granting another person power to remove or replace the fiduciary unless any of the following occurs:

(a) The person holding the power consents to the modification in a signed writing and the modification applies only to the person.

(b) The person holding the power and the qualified beneficiaries of the second trust consent to the modification in a signed writing and the modification grants a substantially similar power to another person.

(c) The court approves the modification and the modification grants a substantially similar power to another person.

Ca. Prob. Code § 19518

Added by Stats 2018 ch 407 (SB 909),s 1, eff. 1/1/2019.

Section 19519 - Tax-related limitations

(a) For purposes of this section:

(1) "Grantor trust" means a trust as to which a settlor of a first trust is considered the owner under Sections 671 to 677, inclusive, or Section 679 of the Internal Revenue Code (26 U.S.C. Secs. 671 to 677, 679) .

(2) "Nongrantor trust" means a trust that is not a grantor trust.

(3) "Qualified benefits property" means property subject to the minimum distribution requirements of Section 401(a)(9)(a)(9) of the Internal Revenue Code (26 U.S.C. Sec. 401(a)(9)) , and any applicable regulations, or to any similar requirements that refer to Section 401(a)(9)(a)(9) of the Internal Revenue Code (26 U.S.C. Sec. 401(a)(9)) or the regulations.

(b) An exercise of the decanting power is subject to all of the following limitations:

(1) If a first trust contains property that qualified, or would have qualified but for provisions of this part other than this section, for a marital deduction for purposes of the gift or estate tax under the Internal Revenue Code or a state gift, estate, or inheritance tax, the second trust instrument shall not include or omit any term that, if included in or omitted from the trust instrument for the trust to which the property was transferred, would have prevented the transfer from qualifying for the deduction, or would have reduced the amount of the deduction, under the same provisions of the Internal Revenue Code or state law under which the transfer qualified.

(2) If the first trust contains property that qualified, or would have qualified but for provisions of this part other than this section, for a charitable deduction for purposes of the income, gift, or estate tax under the Internal Revenue Code or a state income, gift, estate, or inheritance tax, the second trust instrument shall not include or omit any term that, if included in or omitted from the trust instrument for the trust to which the property was transferred, would have prevented the transfer from qualifying for the deduction, or would have reduced the amount of the deduction, under the same provisions of the Internal Revenue Code or state law under which the transfer qualified.

(3) If the first trust contains property that qualified, or would have qualified but for provisions of this part other than this section, for the exclusion from the gift tax described in Section 2503(b)(b) of the Internal Revenue Code (26 U.S.C. Sec. 2503(b)), the second trust instrument shall not include or omit a term that, if included in or omitted from the trust instrument for the trust to which the property was transferred, would have prevented the transfer from qualifying under Section 2503(b)(b) of the Internal Revenue Code (26 U.S.C. Sec. 2503(b)). If the first trust contains property that qualified, or would have qualified but for provisions of this part other than this section, for the exclusion from the gift tax described in Section 2503(b)(b) of the Internal Revenue Code (26 U.S.C. Sec. 2503(b)) by application of Section 2503(c)(c) of the Internal Revenue Code (26 U.S.C. Sec. 2503(c)), the second trust instrument shall not include or omit a term that, if included or omitted from the trust instrument for the trust to which the property was transferred, would have prevented the transfer from qualifying under Section 2503(c)(c) of the Internal Revenue Code (26 U.S.C. Sec. 2503(c)).

(4) If the property of the first trust includes shares of stock in an S-corporation, as defined in Section 1361 of the Internal Revenue Code (26 U.S.C. Sec. 1361) and the first trust is, or but for provisions of this part other than this section would be, a permitted shareholder under any provision of Section 1361 of the Internal Revenue Code (26 U.S.C. Sec. 1361), an authorized fiduciary may exercise the power with respect to part or all of the S-corporation stock only if any second trust receiving the stock is a permitted shareholder under Section 1361(c)(2)(c)(2) of the Internal Revenue Code (26 U.S.C. Sec. 1361(c)(2)). If the property of the first trust includes shares of stock in an S-corporation and the first trust is, or but for provisions of this part other than this section would be, a qualified subchapter-S trust within the meaning of Section 1361(d)(d) of the Internal Revenue Code (26 U.S.C. Sec. 1361(d)), the second trust instrument shall not include or omit a term that prevents the second trust from qualifying as a qualified subchapter-S trust.

(5) If the first trust contains property that qualified, or would have qualified but for provisions of this part other than this section, for a zero inclusion ratio for purposes of the generation-skipping transfer tax under Section 2642(c)(c) of the Internal Revenue Code (26 U.S.C. Sec. 2642(c)), the second trust instrument shall not include or omit a term that, if included in or omitted from the first trust instrument, would have prevented the transfer to the first trust from qualifying for a zero inclusion ratio under Section 2642(c)(c) of the Internal Revenue Code (26 U.S.C. Sec. 2642(c)).

(6) If the first trust is directly or indirectly the beneficiary of qualified benefits property, the second trust instrument may not include or omit any term that, if included in or omitted from the first trust instrument, would have increased the minimum distributions required with respect to the qualified benefits property under Section 401(a)(9)(a)(9) of the Internal Revenue Code (26 U.S.C. Sec. 401(a)(9)) and any applicable regulations, or any similar requirements that refer to Section 401(a)(9)(a)(9) of the Internal Revenue Code (26 U.S.C. Sec. 401(a)(9)) or the regulations. If an attempted exercise of the decanting power violates the preceding sentence, the trustee is deemed to have held the qualified benefits property and any reinvested distributions of the property as a separate share from the date of the exercise of the power and Section 19522 applies to the separate share.

(7) If the first trust qualifies as a grantor trust because of the application of Section 672(f)(2)(A)(f)(2)(A) of the Internal Revenue Code (26 U.S.C. Sec. 672(f)(2)(A)) , the second trust may not include or omit a term that, if included in or omitted from the first trust instrument, would have prevented the first trust from qualifying under Section 672(f)(2)(A)(f)(2)(A) of the Internal Revenue Code (26 U.S.C. Sec. 672(f)(2)(A)) .

(8) In this paragraph, "tax benefit" means a federal or state tax deduction, exemption, exclusion, or other benefit not otherwise listed in this section, except for a benefit arising from being a grantor trust. Subject to paragraph (9), a second trust instrument may not include or omit a term that, if included in or omitted from the first trust instrument, would have prevented qualification for a tax benefit if both of the following apply:

(A) The first trust instrument expressly indicates an intent to qualify for the benefit or the first trust instrument clearly is designed to enable the first trust to qualify for the benefit.

(B) The transfer of property held by the first trust or the first trust qualified, or, but for provisions of this part other than this section, would have qualified for the tax benefit.

(9)

(A) Subject to paragraph (4), and except as otherwise provided in paragraph (7), the second trust may be a nongrantor trust, even if the first trust is a grantor trust.

(B) Subject to paragraph (4), and except as otherwise provided in paragraph (10), the second trust may be a grantor trust, even if the first trust is a nongrantor trust.

(10) An authorized fiduciary may not exercise the decanting power if a settlor objects in a signed writing delivered to the fiduciary within the notice period and either of the following conditions is satisfied:

(A) The first trust and a second trust are both grantor trusts, in whole or in part, the first trust grants the settlor or another person the power to cause the first trust to cease to be a grantor trust, and the second trust does not grant an equivalent power to the settlor or other person.

(B) The first trust is a nongrantor trust and a second trust is a grantor trust, in whole or in part, with respect to the settlor, unless either of the following apply:

(i) The settlor has the power at all times to cause the second trust to cease to be a grantor trust.

(ii) The first trust instrument contains a provision granting the settlor or another person a power that would cause the first trust to cease to be a grantor trust and the second trust instrument contains the same provision.
Ca. Prob. Code § 19519
Added by Stats 2018 ch 407 (SB 909),s 1, eff. 1/1/2019.

Section 19520 - Duration of second trust

(a) Subject to subdivision (b), a second trust may have a duration that is the same as, or different from, the duration of the first trust.
(b) To the extent that property of a second trust is attributable to property of the first trust, the property of the second trust is subject to any rules governing maximum perpetuity, accumulation, or

suspension of the power of alienation that apply to property of the first trust.

Ca. Prob. Code § 19520
Added by Stats 2018 ch 407 (SB 909),s 1, eff. 1/1/2019.

Section 19521 - Need to distribute not required

An authorized fiduciary may exercise the decanting power whether or not under the first trust's discretionary distribution standard the fiduciary would have made or could have been compelled to make a discretionary distribution of principal at the time of the exercise.

Ca. Prob. Code § 19521
Added by Stats 2018 ch 407 (SB 909),s 1, eff. 1/1/2019.

Section 19522 - Saving provision

(a) If exercise of the decanting power would be effective under this part, except that the second trust instrument in part does not comply with this part, the exercise of the power is effective and the following rules apply with respect to the principal of the second trust attributable to the exercise of the power:

(1) A provision in the second trust instrument that is not permitted under this part is void to the extent necessary to comply with this part.

(2) A provision required by this part to be in the second trust instrument, which is not contained in the instrument, is deemed to be included in the instrument to the extent necessary to comply with this part.

(b) If a trustee or other fiduciary of a second trust determines that subdivision (a) applies to a prior exercise of the decanting power, the fiduciary shall take corrective action consistent with the fiduciary's duties.

Ca. Prob. Code § 19522
Added by Stats 2018 ch 407 (SB 909),s 1, eff. 1/1/2019.

Section 19523 - Trust for care of animal

(a) For purposes of this section:

(1) "Animal trust" means a trust or an interest in a trust described in Section 15212.

(2) "Protector" means either of the following:

(A) A person appointed in an animal trust to enforce the trust on behalf of the animal as described in subdivision (c) of Section 15212 or, if no person is appointed in the trust for that purpose, a person appointed by the court for that purpose.

(B) A nonprofit charitable corporation described in subdivision (e) of Section 15212 that has requested an accounting in writing.

(b) The decanting power may be exercised over an animal trust that has a protector to the extent the trust could be decanted under this part if each animal that benefits from the trust were an individual, if the protector consents in a signed writing to the exercise of the power.

(c) A protector for an animal has the rights under this part of a qualified beneficiary.

(d) Notwithstanding any other provision of this part, if a first trust is an animal trust, in an exercise of the decanting power, the second trust shall provide that trust property may be applied only to its intended purpose for the period the first trust benefited the animal.

Ca. Prob. Code § 19523
Added by Stats 2018 ch 407 (SB 909),s 1, eff. 1/1/2019.

Section 19524 - Terms of second trust

A reference in this code to a trust instrument or terms of the trust includes a second trust instrument and the terms of the second trust.

Ca. Prob. Code § 19524
Added by Stats 2018 ch 407 (SB 909),s 1, eff. 1/1/2019.

Section 19525 - Settlor

(a) For purposes of the law of this state other than this part and subject to subdivision (b), a settlor of a first trust is deemed to be the settlor of the second trust with respect to the portion of the principal of the first trust subject to the exercise of the decanting power.

(b) In determining settlor intent with respect to a second trust, the intent of a settlor of the first trust, a settlor of the second trust, and the authorized fiduciary may be considered.

Ca. Prob. Code § 19525
Added by Stats 2018 ch 407 (SB 909),s 1, eff. 1/1/2019.

Section 19526 - Later-discovered property

(a) Except as otherwise provided in subdivision (c), if exercise of the decanting power was intended to distribute all the principal of the first trust to one or more second trusts, later-discovered property belonging to the first trust and property paid to or acquired by the first trust after the exercise of the power is part of the trust estate of the second trust or trusts.

(b) Except as otherwise provided in subdivision (c), if exercise of the decanting power was intended to distribute less than all the principal of the first trust to one or more second trusts, later-discovered property belonging to the first trust or property paid to or acquired by the first trust after exercise of the power remains part of the trust estate of the first trust.

(c) An authorized fiduciary may provide in an exercise of the decanting power or by the terms of a second trust for disposition of later-discovered property belonging to the first trust or property paid to or acquired by the first trust after exercise of the power.

Ca. Prob. Code § 19526
Added by Stats 2018 ch 407 (SB 909),s 1, eff. 1/1/2019.

Section 19527 - Obligations

A debt, liability, or other obligation enforceable against property of a first trust is enforceable to the same extent against the property when held by the second trust after exercise of the decanting power.

Ca. Prob. Code § 19527

Added by Stats 2018 ch 407 (SB 909),s 1, eff. 1/1/2019.

Section 19529 - Petition for instructions or modification

This part does not limit a trustee's ability to petition for instructions or other approval under a trust pursuant to Chapter 3 (commencing with Section 17200) of Part 5 or to petition for modification of a trust pursuant to Chapter 3 (commencing with Section 15400) of Part 2.

Ca. Prob. Code § 19529

Amended by Stats 2019 ch 497 (AB 991),s 212, eff. 1/1/2020.

Added by Stats 2018 ch 407 (SB 909),s 1, eff. 1/1/2019.

Section 19530 - Severability

The provisions of this part are severable. If any provision of this part or its application is held invalid, that invalidity shall not affect other provisions or applications that can be given effect without the invalid provision or application.

Ca. Prob. Code § 19530

Added by Stats 2018 ch 407 (SB 909),s 1, eff. 1/1/2019.

Division 10 - PRORATION OF TAXES

Chapter 1 - PRORATION OF ESTATE TAXES

Article 1 - GENERAL PROVISIONS

Section 20100 - Definitions

Except where the context otherwise requires, the following definitions shall govern the construction of this chapter:

(a) "Estate tax" means a tax imposed by any federal or California estate tax law, now existing or hereafter enacted, and includes interest and penalties on any deficiency.

(b) "Person interested in the estate" means any person, including a personal representative, entitled to receive, or who has received, from a decedent while alive or by reason of the death of the decedent any property or interest therein.

(c) "Personal representative" includes a guardian, conservator, trustee, or other person charged with the responsibility of paying the estate tax.

(d) "Property" means property included in the gross estate for federal estate tax purposes.

(e) "Value" means fair market value as determined for federal estate tax purposes.

Ca. Prob. Code § 20100

Enacted by Stats. 1990, Ch. 79.

Section 20101 - Effective date

(a) This chapter does not apply to persons interested in the estate of a decedent who died before January 1, 1987.

(b) Notwithstanding the repeal of former Article 4a (commencing with Section 970) of Chapter 15 of Division 3 of the Probate Code by Chapter 783 of the Statutes of 1986, the provisions of that former article remain applicable where the decedent died before January 1, 1987. No inference as to the applicable law in effect before January 1, 1987, shall be drawn from the enactment of this chapter.

Ca. Prob. Code § 20101

Enacted by Stats. 1990, Ch. 79.

Article 2 - PRORATION

Section 20110 - Generally

(a) Except as provided in subdivision (b), any estate tax shall be equitably prorated among the persons interested in the estate in the manner prescribed in this article.

(b) This section does not apply:

    (1) To the extent the decedent in a written inter vivos or testamentary instrument disposing of property specifically directs that the property be applied to the satisfaction of an estate tax or that an estate tax be prorated to the property in the manner provided in the instrument. As used in this paragraph, an "instrument disposing of property" includes an instrument that creates an interest in property or an amendment to an instrument that disposes of property or creates an interest in property.

(2) Where federal law directs otherwise. If federal law directs the manner of proration of the federal estate tax, the California estate tax shall be prorated in the same manner.

Ca. Prob. Code § 20110
Enacted by Stats. 1990, Ch. 79.

Section 20111 - Proration made in proportion to value received by interested person to total value of property received by all persons

The proration required by this article shall be made in the proportion that the value of the property received by each person interested in the estate bears to the total value of all property received by all persons interested in the estate, subject to the provisions of this article.

Ca. Prob. Code § 20111
Enacted by Stats. 1990, Ch. 79.

Section 20112 - Allowances made for credits

(a) In making a proration of the federal estate tax, allowances shall be made for credits allowed for state or foreign death taxes in determining the federal tax payable and for exemptions and deductions allowed for the purpose of determining the taxable estate.

(b) In making a proration of the California estate tax, allowances shall be made for (1) credits (other than the credit for state death taxes paid) allowed by the federal estate tax law and attributable to property located in this state, and (2) exemptions and deductions allowed by the federal estate tax law for the purpose of determining the taxable estate attributable to property located in this state.

(c) In making a proration of an estate tax, interest on extension of

taxes and interest and penalties on any deficiency shall be charged
to equitably reflect the benefits and burdens of the extension or
deficiency and of any tax deductions associated with the interest
and penalties.

Ca. Prob. Code § 20112

Enacted by Stats. 1990, Ch. 79.

Section 20113 - Estate tax on temporary interest and remainder

If a trust is created, or other provision made whereby a person is
given an interest in the income of, an estate for years or for life in,
or other temporary interest in, any property, the estate tax on both
the temporary interest and on the remainder thereafter shall be
charged against and paid out of the corpus of the property without
apportionment between remainders and temporary estates.

Ca. Prob. Code § 20113

Enacted by Stats. 1990, Ch. 79.

Section 20114 - Election made pursuant to section 2032A, Internal Revenue Code

(a) As used in this section, "qualified real property" means
qualified real property as defined in Section 2032A of the Internal
Revenue Code (26 U.S.C. Sec. 2032A) .

(b) If an election is made pursuant to Section 2032A of the Internal
Revenue Code (26 U.S.C. Sec. 2032A) , the proration shall be based
upon the amount of federal estate tax that would be payable but for
the election. The amount of the reduction in federal estate tax
resulting from an election pursuant to Section 2032A of the
Internal Revenue Code (26 U.S.C. Sec. 2032A) shall reduce the tax
that is otherwise attributable to the qualified real property that is
the subject of the election. If the tax that is otherwise attributable to
the qualified real property is reduced to zero pursuant to this
subdivision, any excess amount of reduction shall reduce the tax
otherwise payable with respect to the other property, this amount to
be equitably prorated in accordance with Section 20111.

(c) If additional federal estate tax is imposed under subsection (c) of Section 2032A of the Internal Revenue Code (26 U.S.C. Sec. 2032A) by reason of early disposition or cessation of qualified use, the additional tax shall be a charge against the portion of the qualified real property to which the additional tax is attributable, and shall be equitably prorated among the persons interested in that portion of the qualified real property in proportion to their interests.

Ca. Prob. Code § 20114
Enacted by Stats. 1990, Ch. 79.

Section 20114.5 - Federal estate tax increase under section 4980A(d), Internal Revenue Code

(a) As used in this section:

(1) A reference to Section 4980A of the Internal Revenue Code means Section 4980A of the federal Internal Revenue Code of 1986 as amended (26 U.S.C. Sec. 4980A) and also means former Section 4981A of the federal Internal Revenue Code of 1986.

(2) "Excess retirement accumulation" has the meaning given it in paragraph (3) of subsection (d) of Section 4980A.
(b) If the federal estate tax is increased under subsection (d) of Section 4980A of the Internal Revenue Code, the amount of the increase shall be a charge against the persons who receive the excess retirement accumulation that gives rise to the increase, and shall be equitably prorated among all persons who receive interests in qualified employer plans and individual retirement plans to which the excess retirement accumulation is attributable.

Ca. Prob. Code § 20114.5
Amended by Stats 2004 ch 183 (AB 3082),s 281, eff. 1/1/2005

Section 20115 - Amount of extended tax

Where the payment of any portion of the federal estate tax is extended under the provisions of the federal estate tax law, the amount of extended tax shall be a charge against the persons who receive the specific property that gives rise to the extension.

Ca. Prob. Code § 20115
Enacted by Stats. 1990, Ch. 79.

Section 20116 - All property not in possession of personal representative; proration of amount not recoverable

(a) If all property does not come into the possession of the personal representative, the personal representative is entitled, and has the duty, to recover from the persons interested in the estate the proportionate amount of the estate tax with which the persons are chargeable under this chapter.
(b) If the personal representative cannot collect from any person interested in the estate the amount of an estate tax apportioned to the person, the amount not recoverable shall be equitably prorated among the other persons interested in the estate who are subject to proration.

Ca. Prob. Code § 20116
Enacted by Stats. 1990, Ch. 79.

Section 20117 - Right of reimbursement

(a) If a person is charged with or required to pay an estate tax greater than the amount prorated to that person because another person does not pay the amount of estate tax prorated to the other person, the person charged with or required to pay the greater amount has a right of reimbursement against the other person.
(b) The right of reimbursement may be enforced through the personal representative in the discretion of the personal representative, or may be enforced directly by the person charged with or required to pay the greater amount, and for the purpose of direct enforcement the person is subrogated to the position of the personal representative.
(c) The personal representative or person who has a right of reimbursement may commence a proceeding to have a court determine the right of reimbursement. The provisions of Article 3 (commencing with Section 20120) shall govern the proceeding, with changes necessary to make the provisions appropriate for application to the proceeding, and the court order determining the

right of reimbursement is an enforceable judgment.

Ca. Prob. Code § 20117
Enacted by Stats. 1990, Ch. 79.

Article 3 - JUDICIAL PROCEEDINGS

Section 20120 - Commencement of proceedings; venue; combining with administration proceedings

(a) The personal representative or any person interested in the estate may commence a proceeding to have a court determine the proration pursuant to this chapter.

(b) A proceeding under this article shall be commenced in the court in which the estate of the decedent was administered or, if no administration proceedings have been commmenced, in the superior court of any county in which the estate of the decedent may be administered.

(c) If proceedings for the administration of the decedent's estate are pending, a proceeding under this article shall be combined with the administration proceedings. If a proceeding is commenced at any time before final distribution, there shall be no additional filing fee.

Ca. Prob. Code § 20120
Enacted by Stats. 1990, Ch. 79.

Section 20121 - Filing petition

A proceeding under this article shall be commenced by filing a petition that sets forth all of the following information:

(a) The jurisdictional facts.

(b) Other facts necessary for the court to determine the proration of estate taxes.

Ca. Prob. Code § 20121
Enacted by Stats. 1990, Ch. 79.

Section 20122 - Notice of hearing

Not less than 30 days before the hearing, the petitioner shall do both of the following:

(a) Cause notice of the hearing and a copy of the petition to be delivered pursuant to Section 1215 to the personal representative and to each person interested in the estate against whom prorated amounts may be charged pursuant to paragraph (1) of subdivision (a) of Section 20123.

(b) Cause a summons and a copy of the petition to be served on each person interested in the estate who may be directed to make payment of prorated amounts pursuant to paragraph (2) of subdivision (a) of Section 20123. The summons shall be in the form and shall be served in the manner prescribed in Title 5 (commencing with Section 410.10) of Part 2 of the Code of Civil Procedure.

Ca. Prob. Code § 20122

Amended by Stats 2017 ch 319 (AB 976),s 106, eff. 1/1/2018.

Section 20123 - Court order upon making determination

(a) The court, upon making a determination as provided in this article, shall make an order:

(1) Directing the personal representative to charge the prorated amounts against the persons against whom an estate tax has been prorated insofar as the personal representative is in possession of any property or interests of the persons against whom the charge may be made.

(2) Summarily directing all other persons against whom an estate tax has been prorated to make payment of the prorated amounts to the personal representative.

(b) A court order made under this section is a judgment that may be enforced against the persons against whom an estate tax has been prorated.

Ca. Prob. Code § 20123

Amended by Stats. 1997, Ch. 724, Sec. 31. Effective January 1, 1998.

Section 20124 - Petition to modify order

Upon petition by the personal representative or any person

interested in the estate, the court shall modify an order made pursuant to this article whenever it appears that the amount of estate tax as actually determined is different from the amount of estate tax on which the court based the order.

Ca. Prob. Code § 20124
Enacted by Stats. 1990, Ch. 79.

Section 20125 - Action to recover amount of taxes payable to another state

(a) A personal representative acting or resident in another state may commence an action in this state to recover from a person interested in the estate, who either is resident in this state or owns property in this state, the amount of the federal estate tax, or an estate tax or death duty payable to another state, apportioned to the person.

(b) The action shall be commenced in the superior court of any county in which administration of the estate of the decedent would be proper or, if none, in which any defendant resides.

(c) For purposes of the action the apportionment by the court having jurisdiction of the administration of the decedent's estate in the other state is prima facie correct.

Ca. Prob. Code § 20125
Enacted by Stats. 1990, Ch. 79.

Chapter 2 - PRORATION OF TAXES ON GENERATION-SKIPPING TRANSFER

Article 1 - GENERAL PROVISIONS

Section 20200 - Definitions

Except where the context otherwise requires, the following definitions shall govern the construction of this chapter:

(a) "Generation-skipping transfer tax" means a tax imposed by any federal or California generation-skipping transfer tax law, now existing or hereafter enacted, and includes interest and penalties on any deficiency.

(b) "Property" means property on which a generation-skipping transfer tax is imposed.

(c) "Transferee" means any person who receives, who is deemed to receive, or who is the beneficiary of, any property.

(d) "Trustee" means any person who is a trustee within the meaning of the federal generation-skipping transfer tax law, or who is otherwise required to pay a generation-skipping transfer tax.

(e) "Value" means fair market value as determined for generation-skippi ng transfer tax purposes.

Ca. Prob. Code § 20200

Enacted by Stats. 1990, Ch. 79.

Section 20201 - Effective date

(a) This chapter does not apply to transferees of property of a decedent who died before January 1, 1987.

(b) No inference as to the applicable law in effect before January 1, 1987, shall be drawn from the enactment of this chapter.

Ca. Prob. Code § 20201

Enacted by Stats. 1990, Ch. 79.

Article 2 - PRORATION

Section 20210 - Equitable proration among transferees

(a) Except as provided in subdivision (b), any generation-skipping transfer tax shall be equitably prorated among the transferees in the manner prescribed in this article.

(b) This section does not apply:

(1) To the extent the transferor in a written instrument transferring property specifically directs that the property be applied to the satisfaction of a generation-skipping transfer tax or that a generation-skipping transfer tax be prorated to the property in the manner provided in the instrument.

(2) Where federal law directs otherwise. If federal law directs the manner of proration of the federal generation-skipping transfer tax, the California generation-skipping transfer tax shall be prorated in the same manner.

Ca. Prob. Code § 20210
Enacted by Stats. 1990, Ch. 79.

Section 20211 - Proration made in proportion to value of property received by each transferee to total value of property received by all transferees

The proration required by this article shall be made in the proportion that the value of the property received by each transferee bears to the total value of all property received by all transferees, subject to the provisions of this article.
Ca. Prob. Code § 20211
Enacted by Stats. 1990, Ch. 79.

Section 20212 - Allowances made; interest and penalties on deficiency

In making a proration required by this article:
(a) Allowances shall be made for credits, exemptions, and deductions allowed for the purpose of determining the tax payable.
(b) Interest and penalties on any deficiency shall be charged to equitably reflect the benefits and burdens of the deficiency and of any tax deductions associated with the interest and penalties.
Ca. Prob. Code § 20212
Enacted by Stats. 1990, Ch. 79.

Section 20213 - Tax on both temporary interest and other interests charged

If a trust is created or other provision made whereby a transferee is given an interest in income, or an estate for years or for life, or another temporary interest in property, the tax on both the temporary interest and other interests in the property shall be charged against, and paid out of, the corpus of the property without apportionment between the temporary and other interests.
Ca. Prob. Code § 20213
Enacted by Stats. 1990, Ch. 79.

Section 20214 - All property not in trustee's possession; amount not recoverable

(a) If all property does not come into the possession of the trustee, the trustee is entitled, and has the duty, to recover from the transferees, the proportionate amount of the tax with which the transferees are chargeable under this chapter.

(b) If the trustee cannot collect from any transferee the amount of tax apportioned to the transferee, the amount not recoverable shall be equitably prorated among the other transferees who are subject to proration.

Ca. Prob. Code § 20214
Enacted by Stats. 1990, Ch. 79.

Section 20215 - Right of reimbursement

(a) If a person is charged with, or required to pay, a generation-skipping transfer tax greater than the amount prorated to that person because another person does not pay the amount of generation-skipping transfer tax prorated to the other person, the person charged with or required to pay the greater amount has a right of reimbursement against the other person.

(b) The right of reimbursement may be enforced through the trustee in the discretion of the trustee, or may be enforced directly by the person charged with, or required to pay, the greater amount and, for the purpose of direct enforcement, the person is subrogated to the position of the trustee.

(c) The trustee or person who has a right of reimbursement may commence a proceeding to have a court determine the right of reimbursement. The provisions of Article 3 (commencing with Section 20220) shall govern the proceeding, with changes necessary to make the provisions appropriate for application to the proceeding, and the court order determining the right of reimbursement is an enforceable judgment.

Ca. Prob. Code § 20215
Enacted by Stats. 1990, Ch. 79.

Article 3 - JUDICIAL PROCEEDINGS

Section 20220 - Commencement; venue; combining proceeding with administration proceeding

(a) The trustee or any transferee may commence a proceeding to have a court determine the proration pursuant to this chapter.

(b) A proceeding under this article shall be commenced in the court in which the estate of the decedent was administered or, if no administration proceedings have been commenced, in the superior court of any county in which the estate of the decedent may be administered.

(c) If proceedings for the administration of the decedent's estate are pending, a proceeding under this article shall be combined with the administration proceedings. If a proceeding is commenced at any time before final distribution, there shall be no additional filing fee.

Ca. Prob. Code § 20220
Enacted by Stats. 1990, Ch. 79.

Section 20221 - Filing petition

A proceeding under this article shall be commenced by filing a petition that sets forth all of the following information:

(a) The jurisdictional facts.

(b) Other facts necessary for the court to determine the proration of the generation-skipping transfer tax.

Ca. Prob. Code § 20221
Enacted by Stats. 1990, Ch. 79.

Section 20222 - Notice of hearing

Not less than 30 days before the hearing the petitioner shall do both of the following:

(a) Cause notice of the hearing and a copy of the petition to be delivered pursuant to Section 1215 to the trustee and each transferee against whom prorated amounts may be charged pursuant to paragraph (1) of subdivision (a) of Section 20223.

(b) Cause a summons and a copy of the petition to be served on each transferee who may be directed to make payment of prorated amounts pursuant to paragraph (2) of subdivision (a) of Section 20223. The summons shall be in the form and shall be served in the manner prescribed in Title 5 (commencing with Section 410.10) of Part 2 of the Code of Civil Procedure.

Ca. Prob. Code § 20222
Amended by Stats 2017 ch 319 (AB 976),s 107, eff. 1/1/2018.

Section 20223 - Court order upon making determination

(a) The court, upon making a determination as provided in this article, shall make an order:

(1) Directing the trustee to charge the prorated amounts against the transferees against whom the generation-skipping transfer tax has been prorated insofar as the trustee is in possession of any property or interests of the transferees against whom the charge may be made.

(2) Summarily directing all other transferees against whom the generation-skipping transfer tax has been prorated to make payment of the prorated amounts to the trustee.
(b) A court order made under this section is a judgment that may be enforced against the persons against whom a generation-skipping transfer tax has been prorated.

Ca. Prob. Code § 20223
Amended by Stats. 1997, Ch. 724, Sec. 32. Effective January 1, 1998.

Section 20224 - Petition to modify order

Upon petition by the trustee or any transferee, the court shall modify an order made pursuant to this article whenever it appears that the amount of generation-skipping transfer tax as actually determined is different from the amount of tax on which the court based the order.

Ca. Prob. Code § 20224
Enacted by Stats. 1990, Ch. 79.

Section 20225 - Recovery of tax payable to another state

(a) A trustee acting or resident in another state may commence an action in this state to recover from a transferee, who either is resident in this state or owns property in this state, the amount of the federal generation-skipping transfer tax, or a generation-skipping transfer tax payable to another state, apportioned to the person.

(b) The action shall be commenced in the superior court of any county in which administration of the estate of the decedent would be proper or, if none, in which any defendant resides.

(c) For purposes of the action an apportionment by the court having jurisdiction of the administration of the decedent's estate in the other state is prima facie correct.

Ca. Prob. Code § 20225

Enacted by Stats. 1990, Ch. 79.

Division 11 - CONSTRUCTION OF WILLS, TRUSTS, AND OTHER INSTRUMENTS

Part 1 - RULES FOR INTERPRETATION OF INSTRUMENTS

Chapter 1 - GENERAL PROVISIONS

Section 21101 - Applicability

Unless the provision or context otherwise requires, this part applies to a will, trust, deed, and any other instrument.

Ca. Prob. Code § 21101

Amended by Stats 2002 ch 138 (AB 1784),s 10, eff. 1/1/2003.

Section 21102 - Intention of transferor

(a) The intention of the transferor as expressed in the instrument controls the legal effect of the dispositions made in the instrument.

(b) The rules of construction in this part apply where the intention of the transferor is not indicated by the instrument.

(c) Nothing in this section limits the use of extrinsic evidence, to the extent otherwise authorized by law, to determine the intention of the transferor.

Ca. Prob. Code § 21102

Amended by Stats 2002 ch 138 (AB 1784),s 11, eff. 1/1/2003.

Section 21103 - Meaning and legal effect of disposition in instrument

The meaning and legal effect of a disposition in an instrument is determined by the local law of a particular state selected by the transferor in the instrument unless the application of that law is contrary to the rights of the surviving spouse to community and quasi-community property, to any other public policy of this state applicable to the disposition, or, in the case of a will, to Part 3 (commencing with Section 6500) of Division 6.

Ca. Prob. Code § 21103

Amended by Stats 2002 ch 138 (AB 1784),s 12, eff. 1/1/2003.

Section 21104 - At death transfer defined

As used in this part, "at-death transfer" means a transfer that is revocable during the lifetime of the transferor, but does not include a joint tenancy or joint account with right of survivorship.

Ca. Prob. Code § 21104

Amended by Stats 2002 ch 138 (AB 1784),s 13, eff. 1/1/2003.

Section 21105 - Property passed by will

Except as otherwise provided in Sections 641 and 642, a will passes all property the testator owns at death, including property acquired after execution of the will.

Ca. Prob. Code § 21105

Amended by Stats 2002 ch 138 (AB 1784),s 14, eff. 1/1/2003.

Section 21106 - [Repealed]

Ca. Prob. Code § 21106
Repealed by Stats 2002 ch 138 (AB 1784),s 15, eff. 1/1/2003.

Section 21107 - Conversion of real property to money at transferor's death

If an instrument directs the conversion of real property into money at the transferor's death, the real property and its proceeds shall be deemed personal property from the time of the transferor's death.
Ca. Prob. Code § 21107
Amended by Stats 2002 ch 138 (AB 1784),s 16, eff. 1/1/2003.

Section 21108 - Determination of meaning of transfer of legal or equitable interest

The law of this state does not include (a) the common law rule of worthier title that a transferor cannot devise an interest to his or her own heirs or (b) a presumption or rule of interpretation that a transferor does not intend, by a transfer to his or her own heirs or next of kin, to transfer an interest to them. The meaning of a transfer of a legal or equitable interest to a transferor's own heirs or next of kin, however designated, shall be determined by the general rules applicable to the interpretation of instruments.
Ca. Prob. Code § 21108
Amended by Stats 2002 ch 138 (AB 1784),s 17, eff. 1/1/2003.

Section 21109 - Failure of transferee to survive transferor

(a) A transferee who fails to survive the transferor of an at-death transfer or until any future time required by the instrument does not take under the instrument.
(b) If it cannot be determined by clear and convincing evidence that the transferee survived until a future time required by the instrument, it is deemed that the transferee did not survive until the required future time.
Ca. Prob. Code § 21109
Amended by Stats 2002 ch 138 (AB 1784),s 18, eff. 1/1/2003.

Section 21110 - Issue of deceased transferee take in transferee's place

(a) Subject to subdivision (b), if a transferee is dead when the instrument is executed, or fails or is treated as failing to survive the transferor or until a future time required by the instrument, the issue of the deceased transferee take in the transferee's place in the manner provided in Section 240. A transferee under a class gift shall be a transferee for the purpose of this subdivision unless the transferee's death occurred before the execution of the instrument and that fact was known to the transferor when the instrument was executed.

(b) The issue of a deceased transferee do not take in the transferee's place if the instrument expresses a contrary intention or a substitute disposition. A requirement that the initial transferee survive the transferor or survive for a specified period of time after the death of the transferor constitutes a contrary intention. A requirement that the initial transferee survive until a future time that is related to the probate of the transferor's will or administration of the estate of the transferor constitutes a contrary intention.

(c) As used in this section, "transferee" means a person who is kindred of the transferor or kindred of a surviving, deceased, or former spouse of the transferor, but does not mean a spouse of the transferor.

Ca. Prob. Code § 21110
Amended by Stats 2018 ch 71 (AB 1960),s 1, eff. 1/1/2019.
Amended by Stats 2002 ch 138 (AB 1784),s 19, eff. 1/1/2003.

Section 21111 - Property transferred if transfer fails

(a) Except as provided in subdivision (b) and subject to Section 21110, if a transfer fails for any reason, the property is transferred as follows:

(1) If the transferring instrument provides for an alternative disposition in the event the transfer fails, the property is transferred according to the terms of the instrument.

(2) If the transferring instrument does not provide for an alternative disposition but does provide for the transfer of a residue, the property becomes a part of the residue transferred under the instrument.

(3) If the transferring instrument does not provide for an alternative disposition and does not provide for the transfer of a residue, or if the transfer is itself a residuary gift, the property is transferred to the decedent's estate.
(b) Subject to Section 21110, if a residuary gift or a future interest is transferred to two or more persons and the share of a transferee fails for any reason, and no alternative disposition is provided, the share passes to the other transferees in proportion to their other interest in the residuary gift or the future interest.
(c) A transfer of "all my estate" or words of similar import is a residuary gift for purposes of this section.
(d) If failure of a future interest results in an intestacy, the property passes to the heirs of the transferor determined pursuant to Section 21114.

Ca. Prob. Code § 21111
Amended by Stats 2002 ch 138 (AB 1784),s 20, eff. 1/1/2003.
Amended by Stats 2001 ch 417 (AB 873), s 11, eff. 1/1/2002.

Section 21112 - Condition referring to person's death with or without issue or to person having or leaving issue

A condition in a transfer of a present or future interest that refers to a person's death "with" or "without" issue, or to a person's "having" or "leaving" issue or no issue, or a condition based on words of similar import, is construed to refer to that person's being dead at the time the transfer takes effect in enjoyment and to that person either having or not having, as the case may be, issue who are alive at the time of enjoyment.

Ca. Prob. Code § 21112
Amended by Stats 2002 ch 138 (AB 1784),s 21, eff. 1/1/2003.

Section 21113 - [Repealed]

Ca. Prob. Code § 21113
Repealed by Stats 2002 ch 138 (AB 1784),s 22, eff. 1/1/2003.

Section 21114 - Present or future interest created in heirs, heirs at law, next of kin, etc.

(a) If a statute or an instrument provides for transfer of a present or future interest to, or creates a present or future interest in, a designated person's "heirs," "heirs at law," "next of kin," "relatives," or "family," or words of similar import, the transfer is to the persons, including the state under Section 6800, and in the shares that would succeed to the designated person's intestate estate under the intestate succession law of the transferor's domicile, if the designated person died when the transfer is to take effect in enjoyment. If the designated person's surviving spouse is living but is remarried at the time the transfer is to take effect in enjoyment, the surviving spouse is not an heir of the designated person for purposes of this section.
(b) As used in this section, "designated person" includes the transferor.

Ca. Prob. Code § 21114
Amended by Stats 2002 ch 138 (AB 1784),s 23, eff. 1/1/2003.

Section 21115 - Persons included in terms of class gift or relationship; transferor not natural parent

(a) Except as provided in subdivision (b), halfbloods, adopted persons, persons born out of wedlock, stepchildren, foster children, and the issue of these persons when appropriate to the class, are included in terms of class gift or relationship in accordance with the rules for determining relationship and inheritance rights for purposes of intestate succession.
(b) In construing a transfer by a transferor who is not the natural parent, a person born to the natural parent shall not be considered the child of that parent unless the person lived while a minor as a

regular member of the household of the natural parent or of that parent's parent, brother, sister, spouse, or surviving spouse. In construing a transfer by a transferor who is not the adoptive parent, a person adopted by the adoptive parent shall not be considered the child of that parent unless the person lived while a minor (either before or after the adoption) as a regular member of the household of the adopting parent or of that parent's parent, brother, sister, or surviving spouse.

(c) Subdivisions (a) and (b) shall also apply in determining:

(1) Persons who would be kindred of the transferor or kindred of a surviving, deceased, or former spouse of the transferor under Section 21110.

(2) Persons to be included as issue of a deceased transferee under Section 21110.

(3) Persons who would be the transferor's or other designated person's heirs under Section 21114.

(d) The rules for determining intestate succession under this section are those in effect at the time the transfer is to take effect in enjoyment.

Ca. Prob. Code § 21115
Amended by Stats 2002 ch 138 (AB 1784),s 24, eff. 1/1/2003.

Section 21116 - [Repealed]

Ca. Prob. Code § 21116
Repealed by Stats 2002 ch 138 (AB 1784),s 25, eff. 1/1/2003.

Section 21117 - Classification of death transfers

At-death transfers are classified as follows:
(a) A specific gift is a transfer of specifically identifiable property.
(b) A general gift is a transfer from the general assets of the transferor that does not give specific property.
(c) A demonstrative gift is a general gift that specifies the fund or property from which the transfer is primarily to be made.

(d) A general pecuniary gift is a pecuniary gift within the meaning of Section 21118.

(e) An annuity is a general pecuniary gift that is payable periodically.

(f) A residuary gift is a transfer of property that remains after all specific and general gifts have been satisfied.

Ca. Prob. Code § 21117

Amended by Stats 2002 ch 138 (AB 1784),s 26, eff. 1/1/2003.

Section 21118 - Value of property selected to satisfy pecuniary gift by distribution of property other than money

(a) If an instrument authorizes a fiduciary to satisfy a pecuniary gift wholly or partly by distribution of property other than money, property selected for that purpose shall be valued at its fair market value on the date of distribution, unless the instrument expressly provides otherwise. If the instrument permits the fiduciary to value the property selected for distribution as of a date other than the date of distribution, then, unless the instrument expressly provides otherwise, the property selected by the fiduciary for that purpose shall fairly reflect net appreciation and depreciation (occurring between the valuation date and the date of distribution) in all of the assets from which the distribution could have been made.

(b) As used in this section, "pecuniary gift" means a transfer of property made in an instrument that either is expressly stated as a fixed dollar amount or is a dollar amount determinable by the provisions of the instrument.

Ca. Prob. Code § 21118

Amended by Stats 2002 ch 138 (AB 1784),s 27, eff. 1/1/2003.

Chapter 2 - ASCERTAINING MEANING OF LANGUAGE USED IN THE INSTRUMENT

Section 21120 - Every expression given effect

The words of an instrument are to receive an interpretation that will give every expression some effect, rather than one that will render any of the expressions inoperative. Preference is to be given to an interpretation of an instrument that will prevent intestacy or failure of a transfer, rather than one that will result in an intestacy or failure of a transfer.

Ca. Prob. Code § 21120

Amended by Stats 2002 ch 138 (AB 1784),s 28, eff. 1/1/2003.

Section 21121 - All parts of instrument construed in relation to each other

All parts of an instrument are to be construed in relation to each other and so as, if possible, to form a consistent whole. If the meaning of any part of an instrument is ambiguous or doubtful, it may be explained by any reference to or recital of that part in another part of the instrument.

Ca. Prob. Code § 21121

Amended by Stats 2002 ch 138 (AB 1784),s 29, eff. 1/1/2003.

Section 21122 - Words given ordinary and grammatical meaning

The words of an instrument are to be given their ordinary and grammatical meaning unless the intention to use them in another sense is clear and their intended meaning can be ascertained. Technical words are not necessary to give effect to a disposition in an instrument. Technical words are to be considered as having been used in their technical sense unless (a) the context clearly indicates a contrary intention or (b) it satisfactorily appears that the instrument was drawn solely by the transferor and that the transferor was unacquainted with the technical sense.

Ca. Prob. Code § 21122

Amended by Stats 2002 ch 138 (AB 1784),s 30, eff. 1/1/2003.

Chapter 3 - EXONERATION; ADEMPTION

Section 21131 - Specific gift passes property without right of exoneration

A specific gift passes the property transferred subject to any mortgage, deed of trust, or other lien existing at the date of death, without right of exoneration, regardless of a general directive to pay debts contained in the instrument.

Ca. Prob. Code § 21131

Amended by Stats 2002 ch 138 (AB 1784),s 31, eff. 1/1/2003.

Section 21132 - At-death transfer of securities

(a) If a transferor executes an instrument that makes an at-death transfer of securities and the transferor then owned securities that meet the description in the instrument, the transfer includes additional securities owned by the transferor at death to the extent the additional securities were acquired by the transferor after the instrument was executed as a result of the transferor's ownership of the described securities and are securities of any of the following types:

(1) Securities of the same organization acquired by reason of action initiated by the organization or any successor, related, or acquiring organization, excluding any acquired by exercise of purchase options.

(2) Securities of another organization acquired as a result of a merger, consolidation, reorganization, or other distribution by the organization or any successor, related, or acquiring organization.

(3) Securities of the same organization acquired as a result of a plan of reinvestment.

(b) Distributions in cash before death with respect to a described security are not part of the transfer.

Ca. Prob. Code § 21132

Added by Stats 2002 ch 138 (AB 1784),s 33, eff. 1/1/2003.

Section 21133 - Right to property specifically given

A recipient of an at-death transfer of a specific gift has a right to the property specifically given, to the extent the property is owned by the transferor at the time the gift takes effect in possession or enjoyment, and all of the following:

(a) Any balance of the purchase price (together with any security agreement) owing from a purchaser to the transferor at the time the gift takes effect in possession or enjoyment by reason of sale of the property.

(b) Any amount of an eminent domain award for the taking of the property unpaid at the time the gift takes effect in possession or enjoyment.

(c) Any proceeds unpaid at the time the gift takes effect in possession or enjoyment on fire or casualty insurance on or other recovery for injury to the property.

(d) Property owned by the transferor at the time the gift takes effect in possession or enjoyment and acquired as a result of foreclosure, or obtained in lieu of foreclosure, of the security interest for a specifically given obligation.

Ca. Prob. Code § 21133

Amended by Stats 2002 ch 138 (AB 1784),s 34, eff. 1/1/2003.

Section 21134 - Right of transferee of specific gift to general pecuniary gift equal to net sale price

(a) Except as otherwise provided in this section, if, after the execution of the instrument of gift, specifically given property is sold, or encumbered by a deed of trust, mortgage, or other instrument, by a conservator, by an agent acting within the authority of a durable power of attorney for an incapacitated principal, or by a trustee acting for an incapacitated settlor of a trust established by the settlor as a revocable trust, the transferee of the specific gift has the right to a general pecuniary gift equal to the net sale price of the property unreduced by the payoff of any such encumbrance, or the amount of the unpaid encumbrance on the property as well as the property itself.

(b) Except as otherwise provided in this section, if an eminent domain award for the taking of specifically given property is paid to a conservator, to an agent acting within the authority of a durable power of attorney for an incapacitated principal, or to a trustee acting for an incapacitated settlor of a trust established by the settlor as a revocable trust, or if the proceeds on fire or casualty insurance on, or recovery for injury to, specifically gifted property are paid to a conservator, to an agent acting within the authority of a durable power of attorney for an incapacitated principal, or to a trustee acting for an incapacitated settlor of a trust established by the settlor as a revocable trust, the recipient of the specific gift has the right to a general pecuniary gift equal to the eminent domain award or the insurance proceeds or recovery unreduced by the payoff of any encumbrance placed on the property by the conservator, agent, or trustee, after the execution of the instrument of gift.

(c) For the purpose of the references in this section to a conservator, this section does not apply if, after the sale, mortgage, condemnation, fire, or casualty, or recovery, the conservatorship is terminated and the transferor survives the termination by one year.

(d) For the purpose of the references in this section to an agent acting with the authority of a durable power of attorney for an incapacitated principal, or to a trustee acting for an incapacitated settlor of a trust established by the settlor as a revocable trust, (1) "incapacitated principal" or "incapacitated settlor" means a principal or settlor who is an incapacitated person, (2) no adjudication of incapacity before death is necessary, and (3) the acts of an agent within the authority of a durable power of attorney are presumed to be for an incapacitated principal. However, there shall be no presumption of a settlor's incapacity concerning the acts of a trustee.

(e) The right of the transferee of the specific gift under this section shall be reduced by any right the transferee has under Section 21133.

Ca. Prob. Code § 21134

Amended by Stats 2012 ch 195 (AB 1985),s 1, eff. 1/1/2013.
Amended by Stats 2002 ch 138 (AB 1784),s 35, eff. 1/1/2003.

Section 21135 - Property given by transferor during lifetime treated as satisfaction of at-death transfer

(a) Property given by a transferor during his or her lifetime to a person is treated as a satisfaction of an at-death transfer to that person in whole or in part only if one of the following conditions is satisfied:

(1) The instrument provides for deduction of the lifetime gift from the at-death transfer.

(2) The transferor declares in a contemporaneous writing that the gift is in satisfaction of the at-death transfer or that its value is to be deducted from the value of the at-death transfer.

(3) The transferee acknowledges in writing that the gift is in satisfaction of the at-death transfer or that its value is to be deducted from the value of the at-death transfer.

(4) The property given is the same property that is the subject of a specific gift to that person.

(b) Subject to subdivision (c), for the purpose of partial satisfaction, property given during lifetime is valued as of the time the transferee came into possession or enjoyment of the property or as of the time of death of the transferor, whichever occurs first.

(c) If the value of the gift is expressed in the contemporaneous writing of the transferor, or in an acknowledgment of the transferee made contemporaneously with the gift, that value is conclusive in the division and distribution of the estate.

(d) If the transferee fails to survive the transferor, the gift is treated as a full or partial satisfaction of the gift, as the case may be, in applying Sections 21110 and 21111 unless the transferor's contemporaneous writing provides otherwise.

Ca. Prob. Code § 21135
Amended by Stats 2002 ch 138 (AB 1784),s 36, eff. 1/1/2003.

Section 21136 - [Repealed]

Ca. Prob. Code § 21136
Repealed by Stats 2002 ch 138 (AB 1784),s 37, eff. 1/1/2003.

Section 21137 - [Repealed]

Ca. Prob. Code § 21137
Repealed by Stats 2002 ch 138 (AB 1784),s 38, eff. 1/1/2003.

Section 21138 - [Repealed]

Ca. Prob. Code § 21138
Repealed by Stats 2002 ch 138 (AB 1784),s 39, eff. 1/1/2003.

Section 21139 - Rules not exhaustive

The rules stated in Sections 21133 to 21135, inclusive, are not
exhaustive, and nothing in those sections is intended to increase the
incidence of ademption under the law of this state.
Ca. Prob. Code § 21139
Amended by Stats 2002 ch 138 (AB 1784),s 40, eff. 1/1/2003.

Chapter 4 - EFFECTIVE DATES

Section 21140 - Generally

This part applies to all instruments, regardless of when they were
executed.
Ca. Prob. Code § 21140
Amended by Stats 2002 ch 138 (AB 1784),s 41, eff. 1/1/2003.

Part 2 - PERPETUITIES

Chapter 1 - UNIFORM STATUTORY RULE AGAINST PERPETUITIES

Article 1 - GENERAL PROVISIONS

Section 21200 - Title of chapter

This chapter shall be known and may be cited as the Uniform
Statutory Rule Against Perpetuities.
Ca. Prob. Code § 21200
Added by Stats. 1991, Ch. 156, Sec. 24.

Section 21201 - Common law rule superseded

This chapter supersedes the common law rule against perpetuities.

Ca. Prob. Code § 21201

Added by Stats. 1991, Ch. 156, Sec. 24.

Section 21202 - Effective date

(a) Except as provided in subdivision (b), this part applies to nonvested property interests and unexercised powers of appointment regardless of whether they were created before, on, or after January 1, 1992.

(b) This part does not apply to any property interest or power of appointment the validity of which has been determined in a judicial proceeding or by a settlement among interested persons.

Ca. Prob. Code § 21202

Added by Stats. 1991, Ch. 156, Sec. 24.

Article 2 - STATUTORY RULE AGAINST PERPETUITIES

Section 21205 - Nonvested property interest

A nonvested property interest is invalid unless one of the following conditions is satisfied:

(a) When the interest is created, it is certain to vest or terminate no later than 21 years after the death of an individual then alive.

(b) The interest either vests or terminates within 90 years after its creation.

Ca. Prob. Code § 21205

Added by Stats. 1991, Ch. 156, Sec. 24.

Section 21206 - General power of appointment not presently exercisable

A general power of appointment not presently exercisable because of a condition precedent is invalid unless one of the following conditions is satisfied:

(a) When the power is created, the condition precedent is certain to be satisfied or become impossible to satisfy no later than 21 years after the death of an individual then alive.

(b) The condition precedent either is satisfied or becomes impossible to satisfy within 90 years after its creation.

Ca. Prob. Code § 21206
Added by Stats. 1991, Ch. 156, Sec. 24.

Section 21207 - Nongeneral power of appointment or general testamentary power of appointment

A nongeneral power of appointment or a general testamentary power of appointment is invalid unless one of the following conditions is satisfied:

(a) When the power is created, it is certain to be irrevocably exercised or otherwise to terminate no later than 21 years after the death of an individual then alive.

(b) The power is irrevocably exercised or otherwise terminates within 90 years after its creation.

Ca. Prob. Code § 21207
Added by Stats. 1991, Ch. 156, Sec. 24.

Section 21208 - Possibility that child will be born after individual's death

In determining whether a nonvested property interest or a power of appointment is valid under this article, the possibility that a child will be born to an individual after the individual's death is disregarded.

Ca. Prob. Code § 21208
Added by Stats. 1991, Ch. 156, Sec. 24.

Section 21209 - Language inoperative to extent it produces period exceeding 21 year period

(a) If, in measuring a period from the creation of a trust or other property arrangement, language in a governing instrument (1) seeks to disallow the vesting or termination of any interest or trust beyond, (2) seeks to postpone the vesting or termination of any interest or trust until, or (3) seeks to operate in effect in any similar fashion upon, the later of (A) the expiration of a period of time not exceeding 21 years after the death of the survivor of specified lives in being at the creation of the trust or other property arrangement or (B) the expiration of a period of time that exceeds or might exceed 21 years after the death of the survivor of lives in being at the creation of the trust or other property arrangement, that language is inoperative to the extent it produces a period that exceeds 21 years after the death of the survivor of the specified lives.

(b) Notwithstanding Section 21202, this section applies only to governing instruments, including instruments exercising powers of appointment, executed on or after January 1, 1992.

Ca. Prob. Code § 21209

Added by Stats. 1991, Ch. 156, Sec. 24.

Article 3 - TIME OF CREATION OF INTEREST

Section 21210 - Generally

Except as provided in Sections 21211 and 21212, the time of creation of a nonvested property interest or a power of appointment is determined by other applicable statutes or, if none, under general principles of property law.

Ca. Prob. Code § 21210

Added by Stats. 1991, Ch. 156, Sec. 24.

Section 21211 - Interest created when power to become unqualified beneficial owner terminates

For purposes of this chapter:

(a) If there is a person who alone can exercise a power created by a governing instrument to become the unqualified beneficial owner of (1) a nonvested property interest or (2) a property interest subject to a power of appointment described in Section 21206 or 21207, the nonvested property interest or power of appointment is created when the power to become the unqualified beneficial owner terminates.

(b) A joint power with respect to community property held by individuals married to each other is a power exercisable by one person alone.

Ca. Prob. Code § 21211

Added by Stats. 1991, Ch. 156, Sec. 24.

Section 21212 - Interest arising from transfer of property to previously funded trust or other existing property arrangement

For purposes of this chapter, a nonvested property interest or a power of appointment arising from a transfer of property to a previously funded trust or other existing property arrangement is created when the nonvested property interest or power of appointment in the original contribution was created.

Ca. Prob. Code § 21212
Added by Stats. 1991, Ch. 156, Sec. 24.

Article 4 - REFORMATION

Section 21220 - Generally

On petition of an interested person, a court shall reform a disposition in the manner that most closely approximates the transferor's manifested plan of distribution and is within the 90 years allowed by the applicable provision in Article 2 (commencing with Section 21205), if any of the following conditions is satisfied:
(a) A nonvested property interest or a power of appointment becomes invalid under the statutory rule against perpetuities provided in Article 2 (commencing with Section 21205).
(b) A class gift is not but might become invalid under the statutory rule against perpetuities provided in Article 2 (commencing with Section 21205), and the time has arrived when the share of any class member is to take effect in possession or enjoyment.
(c) A nonvested property interest that is not validated by subdivision (a) of Section 21205 can vest but not within 90 years after its creation.

Ca. Prob. Code § 21220
Added by Stats. 1991, Ch. 156, Sec. 24.

Article 5 - EXCLUSIONS FROM STATUTORY RULE AGAINST PERPETUITIES

Section 21225 - Inapplicability of Article 2

Article 2 (commencing with Section 21205) does not apply to any of the following:

(a) A nonvested property interest or a power of appointment arising out of a nondonative transfer, except a nonvested property interest or a power of appointment arising out of (1) a premarital or postmarital agreement, (2) a separation or divorce settlement, (3) a spouse's election, (4) or a similar arrangement arising out of a prospective, existing, or previous marital relationship between the parties, (5) a contract to make or not to revoke a will or trust, (6) a contract to exercise or not to exercise a power of appointment, (7) a transfer in satisfaction of a duty of support, or (8) a reciprocal transfer.

(b) A fiduciary's power relating to the administration or management of assets, including the power of a fiduciary to sell, lease, or mortgage property, and the power of a fiduciary to determine principal and income.

(c) A power to appoint a fiduciary.

(d) A discretionary power of a trustee to distribute principal before termination of a trust to a beneficiary having an indefeasibly vested interest in the income and principal.

(e) A nonvested property interest held by a charity, government, or governmental agency or subdivision, if the nonvested property interest is preceded by an interest held by another charity, government, or governmental agency or subdivision.

(f) A nonvested property interest in or a power of appointment with respect to a trust or other property arrangement forming part of a pension, profit-sharing, stock bonus, health, disability, death benefit, income deferral, or other current or deferred benefit plan for one or more employees, independent contractors, or their beneficiaries or spouses, to which contributions are made for the purpose of distributing to or for the benefit of the participants or their beneficiaries or spouses the property, income, or principal in the trust or other property arrangement, except a nonvested property interest or a power of appointment that is created by an election of a participant or a beneficiary or spouse.

(g) A property interest, power of appointment, or arrangement that was not subject to the common law rule against perpetuities or is excluded by another statute of this state.

(h) A trust created for the purpose of providing for its beneficiaries under hospital service contracts, group life insurance, group disability insurance, group annuities, or any combination of such insurance, as defined in the Insurance Code.

Ca. Prob. Code § 21225
Amended by Stats. 1996, Ch. 563, Sec. 33. Effective January 1, 1997.

Chapter 2 - RELATED PROVISIONS

Section 21230 - Evidence of deaths unreasonably difficult to obtain

The lives of individuals selected to govern the time of vesting pursuant to Article 2 (commencing with Section 21205) of Chapter 1 may not be so numerous or so situated that evidence of their deaths is likely to be unreasonably difficult to obtain.

Ca. Prob. Code § 21230
Added by Stats. 1991, Ch. 156, Sec. 24.

Section 21231 - Person deemed to be individual alive when interest created

In determining the validity of a nonvested property interest pursuant to Article 2 (commencing with Section 21205) of Chapter 1, an individual described as the spouse of an individual alive at the commencement of the perpetuities period shall be deemed to be an individual alive when the interest is created, whether or not the individual so described was then alive.

Ca. Prob. Code § 21231
Added by Stats. 1991, Ch. 156, Sec. 24.

Part 3 - [Repealed] NO CONTEST CLAUSE

Chapter 1 - [Repealed] GENERAL PROVISIONS

Section 21300 - [Repealed]

Ca. Prob. Code § 21300

Repealed by Stats 2008 ch 174 (SB 1264),s 1, eff. 1/1/2010.
Amended by Stats 2002 ch 150 (SB 1878),s 1, eff. 1/1/2003.

Section 21301 - [Repealed]

Ca. Prob. Code § 21301

Section 21302 - [Repealed]

Ca. Prob. Code § 21302

Section 21303 - [Repealed]

Ca. Prob. Code § 21303

Section 21304 - [Repealed]

Ca. Prob. Code § 21304

Section 21305 - [Repealed]

Ca. Prob. Code § 21305
Amended by Stats 2002 ch 150 (SB 1878),s 2, eff. 1/1/2003.
Added by Stats 2000 ch 17 (AB 1491), s 5, eff. 1/1/2001.

Section 21306 - [Repealed]

Ca. Prob. Code § 21306
Amended by Stats 2000 ch 17 (AB 1491), s 6, eff. 1/1/2001.

Section 21307 - [Repealed]

Ca. Prob. Code § 21307

Section 21308 - [Repealed]

Ca. Prob. Code § 21308

Chapter 2 - [Repealed] DECLARATORY RELIEF

Section 21320 - [Repealed]

Ca. Prob. Code § 21320
Amended by Stats 2004 ch 183 (AB 3082),s 282, eff. 1/1/2005
Amended by Stats 2002 ch 150 (SB 1878),s 3, eff. 1/1/2003.
Amended by Stats 2000 ch 17 (AB 1491), s 7, eff. 1/1/2001.

Section 21321 - [Repealed]

Ca. Prob. Code § 21321

Section 21322 - [Repealed]

Ca. Prob. Code § 21322

Part 3 - NO CONTEST CLAUSE

Section 21310 - Definitions

As used in this part:
(a) "Contest" means a pleading filed with the court by a beneficiary that would result in a penalty under a no contest clause, if the no contest clause is enforced.
(b) "Direct contest" means a contest that alleges the invalidity of a protected instrument or one or more of its terms, based on one or more of the following grounds:

(1) Forgery.

(2) Lack of due execution.

(3) Lack of capacity.

(4) Menace, duress, fraud, or undue influence.

(5) Revocation of a will pursuant to Section 6120, revocation of a trust pursuant to Section 15401, or revocation of an instrument other than a will or trust pursuant to the procedure for revocation that is provided by statute or by the instrument.

(6) Disqualification of a beneficiary under Section 6112, 21350, or 21380.

(c) "No contest clause" means a provision in an otherwise valid instrument that, if enforced, would penalize a beneficiary for filing a pleading in any court.

(d) "Pleading" means a petition, complaint, cross-complaint, objection, answer, response, or claim.

(e) "Protected instrument" means all of the following instruments:

(1) The instrument that contains the no contest clause.

(2) An instrument that is in existence on the date that the instrument containing the no contest clause is executed and is expressly identified in the no contest clause, either individually or as part of an identifiable class of instruments, as being governed by the no contest clause.

Ca. Prob. Code § 21310

Amended by Stats 2010 ch 620 (SB 105),s 5, eff. 1/1/2011.
Added by Stats 2008 ch 174 (SB 1264),s 2, eff. 1/1/2010.

Section 21311 - Types of contests

(a) A no contest clause shall only be enforced against the following types of contests:

(1) A direct contest that is brought without probable cause.

(2) A pleading to challenge a transfer of property on the grounds that it was not the transferor's property at the time of the transfer. A no contest clause shall only be enforced under this paragraph if the no contest clause expressly provides for that application.

(3) The filing of a creditor's claim or prosecution of an action based on it. A no contest clause shall only be enforced under this paragraph if the no contest clause expressly provides for that application.

(b) For the purposes of this section, probable cause exists if, at the time of filing a contest, the facts known to the contestant would cause a reasonable person to believe that there is a reasonable likelihood that the requested relief will be granted after an opportunity for further investigation or discovery.

Ca. Prob. Code § 21311

Added by Stats 2008 ch 174 (SB 1264),s 2, eff. 1/1/2010.

Section 21312 - Determining intent of transferor

In determining the intent of the transferor, a no contest clause shall be strictly construed.

Ca. Prob. Code § 21312

Added by Stats 2008 ch 174 (SB 1264),s 2, eff. 1/1/2010.

Section 21313 - Common law

This part is not intended as a complete codification of the law governing enforcement of a no contest clause. The common law governs enforcement of a no contest clause to the extent this part does not apply.

Ca. Prob. Code § 21313

Added by Stats 2008 ch 174 (SB 1264),s 2, eff. 1/1/2010.

Section 21314 - Contrary provision in instrument

This part applies notwithstanding a contrary provision in the instrument.

Ca. Prob. Code § 21314

Added by Stats 2008 ch 174 (SB 1264),s 2, eff. 1/1/2010.

Section 21315 - Effective date

(a) This part applies to any instrument, whenever executed, that became irrevocable on or after January 1, 2001.

(b) This part does not apply to an instrument that became irrevocable before January 1, 2001.

Ca. Prob. Code § 21315

Added by Stats 2008 ch 174 (SB 1264),s 2, eff. 1/1/2010.

Part 3.5 - LIMITATIONS ON TRANSFERS TO DRAFTERS AND OTHERS

Section 21350 et seq - [Repealed]

Ca. Prob. Code § 21350 et seq

Repealed pursuant to Stats 2011 ch 296 (AB 1023),s 245, eff. 1/1/2012.

Amended by Stats 2003 ch 444 (AB 1349),s 1, eff. 1/1/2004.

Part 3.7 - PRESUMPTION OF FRAUD OR UNDUE INFLUENCE

Chapter 1 - DEFINITIONS

Section 21360 - Definitions govern construction

The definitions in this chapter govern the construction of this part.

Ca. Prob. Code § 21360

Added by Stats 2010 ch 620 (SB 105),s 7, eff. 1/1/2011.

Section 21362 - Care custodian; health and social services

(a) "Care custodian" means a person who provides health or social services to a dependent adult, except that "care custodian" does not include a person who provided services without remuneration if the person had a personal relationship with the dependent adult (1) at least 90 days before providing those services, (2) at least six months before the dependent adult's death, and (3) before the dependant adult was admitted to hospice care, if the dependent adult was admitted to hospice care. As used in this subdivision, "remuneration" does not include the donative transfer at issue under this chapter or the reimbursement of expenses.

(b) For the purposes of this section, "health and social services" means services provided to a dependent adult because of the person's dependent condition, including, but not limited to, the administration of medicine, medical testing, wound care, assistance with hygiene, companionship, housekeeping, shopping, cooking, and assistance with finances.

Ca. Prob. Code § 21362
Added by Stats 2010 ch 620 (SB 105),s 7, eff. 1/1/2011.

Section 21364 - Cohabitant

"Cohabitant" has the meaning provided in Section 13700 of the Penal Code.

Ca. Prob. Code § 21364
Added by Stats 2010 ch 620 (SB 105),s 7, eff. 1/1/2011.

Section 21366 - Dependent adult

"Dependent adult" means a person who, at the time of executing the instrument at issue under this part, was a person described in either of the following:

(a) The person was 65 years of age or older and satisfied one or both of the following criteria:

(1) The person was unable to provide properly for his or her personal needs for physical health, food, clothing, or shelter.

(2) Due to one or more deficits in the mental functions listed in paragraphs (1) to (4), inclusive, of subdivision (a) of Section 811, the person had difficulty managing his or her own financial resources or resisting fraud or undue influence.

(b) The person was 18 years of age or older and satisfied one or both of the following criteria:

(1) The person was unable to provide properly for his or her personal needs for physical health, food, clothing, or shelter.

(2) Due to one or more deficits in the mental functions listed in paragraphs (1) to (4), inclusive, of subdivision (a) of Section 811, the person had substantial difficulty managing his or her own financial

resources or resisting fraud or undue influence.
   Ca. Prob. Code § 21366
Added by Stats 2010 ch 620 (SB 105),s 7, eff. 1/1/2011.

Section 21368 - Domestic partner

"Domestic partner" has the meaning provided in Section 297 of the
Family Code.
   Ca. Prob. Code § 21368
Added by Stats 2010 ch 620 (SB 105),s 7, eff. 1/1/2011.

Section 21370 - Independent attorney

"Independent attorney" means an attorney who has no legal,
business, financial, professional, or personal relationship with the
beneficiary of a donative transfer at issue under this part, and who
would not be appointed as a fiduciary or receive any pecuniary
benefit as a result of the operation of the instrument containing the
donative transfer at issue under this part.
   Ca. Prob. Code § 21370
Added by Stats 2010 ch 620 (SB 105),s 7, eff. 1/1/2011.

Section 21374 - Related by blood or affinity

(a) A person who is "related by blood or affinity" to a specified
person means any of the following persons:

   (1) A spouse or domestic partner of the specified person.

   (2) A relative within a specified degree of kinship to the
specified person or within a specified degree of kinship to the
spouse or domestic partner of the specified person.

   (3) The spouse or domestic partner of a person described in
paragraph (2).
(b) For the purposes of this section, "spouse or domestic partner"
includes a predeceased spouse or predeceased domestic partner.
(c) In determining a relationship under this section, Sections 6406

and 6407, and Chapter 2 (commencing with Section 6450) of Part 2 of Division 6, are applicable.

Ca. Prob. Code § 21374

Added by Stats 2010 ch 620 (SB 105),s 7, eff. 1/1/2011.

Chapter 2 - OPERATION AND EFFECT OF PRESUMPTION

Section 21380 - Donative transfers presumed product of fraud or undue influence

(a) A provision of an instrument making a donative transfer to any of the following persons is presumed to be the product of fraud or undue influence:

(1) The person who drafted the instrument.

(2) A person who transcribed the instrument or caused it to be transcribed and who was in a fiduciary relationship with the transferor when the instrument was transcribed.

(3) A care custodian of a transferor who is a dependent adult, but only if the instrument was executed during the period in which the care custodian provided services to the transferor, or within 90 days before or after that period.

(4) A care custodian who commenced a marriage, cohabitation, or domestic partnership with a transferor who is a dependent adult while providing services to that dependent adult, or within 90 days after those services were last provided to the dependent adult, if the donative transfer occurred, or the instrument was executed, less than six months after the marriage, cohabitation, or domestic partnership commenced.

(5) A person who is related by blood or affinity, within the third degree, to any person described in paragraphs (1) to (3), inclusive.

(6) A cohabitant or employee of any person described in paragraphs (1) to (3), inclusive.

(7) A partner, shareholder, or employee of a law firm in which a person described in paragraph (1) or (2) has an ownership interest.
(b) The presumption created by this section is a presumption affecting the burden of proof. The presumption may be rebutted by proving, by clear and convincing evidence, that the donative transfer was not the product of fraud or undue influence.
(c) Notwithstanding subdivision (b), with respect to a donative transfer to the person who drafted the donative instrument, or to a person who is related to, or associated with, the drafter as described in paragraph (5), (6), or (7) of subdivision (a), the presumption created by this section is conclusive.
(d) If a beneficiary is unsuccessful in rebutting the presumption, the beneficiary shall bear all costs of the proceeding, including reasonable attorney's fees.

Ca. Prob. Code § 21380

Amended by Stats 2019 ch 10 (AB 328),s 1, eff. 1/1/2020.
Amended by Stats 2017 ch 56 (SB 153),s 1, eff. 1/1/2018.
Added by Stats 2010 ch 620 (SB 105),s 7, eff. 1/1/2011.

Section 21382 - Inapplicable instruments or transfers

Section 21380 does not apply to any of the following instruments or transfers:
(a) Except as provided in paragraph (4) of subdivision (a) of Section 21380, a donative transfer to a person who is related by blood or affinity, within the fourth degree, to the transferor or is the cohabitant of the transferor.
(b) An instrument that is drafted or transcribed by a person who is related by blood or affinity, within the fourth degree, to the transferor or is the cohabitant of the transferor.
(c) An instrument that is approved pursuant to an order under Article 10 (commencing with Section 2580) of Chapter 6 of Part 4 of Division 4, after full disclosure of the relationships of the persons involved.
(d) A donative transfer to a federal, state, or local public entity, an entity that qualifies for an exemption from taxation under Section 501(c)(3)(c)(3) or 501(c)(19)(c)(19) of the Internal Revenue Code, or a trust holding the transferred property for the entity.

(e) A donative transfer of property valued at five thousand dollars ($5,000) or less, if the total value of the transferor's estate equals or exceeds the amount stated in Section 13100.

(f) An instrument executed outside of California by a transferor who was not a resident of California when the instrument was executed.

Ca. Prob. Code § 21382

Amended by Stats 2019 ch 10 (AB 328),s 2, eff. 1/1/2020.
Added by Stats 2010 ch 620 (SB 105),s 7, eff. 1/1/2011.

Section 21384 - Review by independent attorney; certificate of independent review

(a) A donative transfer is not subject to Section 21380 if the instrument is reviewed by an independent attorney who counsels the transferor, out of the presence of any heir or proposed beneficiary, about the nature and consequences of the intended transfer, including the effect of the intended transfer on the transferor's heirs and on any beneficiary of a prior donative instrument, attempts to determine if the intended transfer is the result of fraud or undue influence, and signs and delivers to the transferor an original certificate in substantially the following form:

"CERTIFICATE OF INDEPENDENT REVIEW
I, , have reviewed
(attorney's name)
and have counseled the transferor,
(name of instrument)
, on the nature and consequences of any
(name of transferor)
transfers of property to
(name of person described in
Section 21380 of the Probate
Code)
that would be made by the instrument.
I am an "independent attorney" as defined in Section 21370 of the Probate Code and am in a position to advise the transferor

independently, impartially, and confidentially as to the consequences of the transfer.
On the basis of this counsel, I conclude that the transfers to that would
(name of person described in
Section 21380 of the Probate
Code)
be made by the instrument are not the product of fraud or undue influence.

"

(Name of Attorney)   (Date)

(b) An attorney whose written engagement, signed by the transferor, is expressly limited solely to compliance with the requirements of this section, shall not be considered to otherwise represent the transferor as a client.
(c) An attorney who drafts an instrument can review and certify the same instrument pursuant to this section, but only as to a donative transfer to a care custodian. In all other circumstances, an attorney who drafts an instrument may not review and certify the instrument.
(d) If the certificate is prepared by an attorney other than the attorney who drafted the instrument that is under review, a copy of the signed certification shall be provided to the drafting attorney.
   Ca. Prob. Code § 21384
Amended by Stats 2017 ch 56 (SB 153),s 2, eff. 1/1/2018.
Added by Stats 2010 ch 620 (SB 105),s 7, eff. 1/1/2011.

Section 21385 - Presumptions for at-death transfer between spouses

(a) An at-death transfer, as defined in Section 21104, between spouses by will, revocable trust, beneficiary form, or other instrument is not subject to Section 721 of the Family Code or any presumptions of undue influence created by that section.
(b) This section does not limit the application of any other statutory or common law presumptions of undue influence that may apply to an at-death transfer between spouses.

Ca. Prob. Code § 21385
Added by Stats 2019 ch 43 (AB 327),s 2, eff. 1/1/2020.

Section 21386 - Operation of donative gift failing under part

If a donative transfer fails under this part, the instrument making the donative transfer shall operate as if the beneficiary had predeceased the transferor without spouse, domestic partner, or issue.

Ca. Prob. Code § 21386
Amended by Stats 2017 ch 56 (SB 153),s 3, eff. 1/1/2018.
Added by Stats 2010 ch 620 (SB 105),s 7, eff. 1/1/2011.

Section 21388 - Liability

(a) A person is not liable for transferring property pursuant to an instrument that is subject to the presumption created under this part, unless the person is served with notice, prior to transferring the property, that the instrument has been contested under this part.
(b) A person who is served with notice that an instrument has been contested under this part is not liable for failing to transfer property pursuant to the instrument, unless the person is served with notice that the validity of the transfer has been conclusively determined by a court.

Ca. Prob. Code § 21388
Added by Stats 2010 ch 620 (SB 105),s 7, eff. 1/1/2011.

Section 21390 - Contrary provision in instrument

This part applies notwithstanding a contrary provision in an instrument.

Ca. Prob. Code § 21390
Added by Stats 2010 ch 620 (SB 105),s 7, eff. 1/1/2011.

Section 21392 - Effective date

(a) This part shall apply to instruments that become irrevocable on or after January 1, 2011. For the purposes of this section, an instrument that is otherwise revocable or amendable shall be deemed to be irrevocable if, on or after January 1, 2011, the transferor by reason of incapacity was unable to change the disposition of the transferor's property and did not regain capacity before the date of the transferor's death.

(b) It is the intent of the Legislature that this part supplement the common law on fraud and undue influence, without superseding or interfering in the operation of that law. Nothing in this part precludes an action to contest a donative transfer under the common law or under any other applicable law. This subdivision is declarative of existing law.

Ca. Prob. Code § 21392

Amended by Stats 2017 ch 56 (SB 153),s 4, eff. 1/1/2018.
Added by Stats 2010 ch 620 (SB 105),s 7, eff. 1/1/2011.

Part 4 - ABATEMENT

Section 21400 - Shares abate when necessary to effectuate instrument, plan or purpose

Notwithstanding any other provision of this part, if the instrument provides for abatement, or if the transferor's plan or if the purpose of the transfer would be defeated by abatement as provided in this part, the shares of beneficiaries abate as is necessary to effectuate the instrument, plan, or purpose.

Ca. Prob. Code § 21400

Enacted by Stats. 1990, Ch. 79.

Section 21401 - Shares abate for all purposes

Except as provided in Sections 21612 (omitted spouse) and 21623 (omitted children) and in Division 10 (commencing with Section 20100) (proration of taxes), shares of beneficiaries abate as provided in this part for all purposes, including payment of the debts, expenses, and charges specified in Section 11420, satisfaction of gifts, and payment of expenses on specifically devised property pursuant to Section 12002, and without any priority as between real and personal property.

Ca. Prob. Code § 21401

Amended by Stats 2003 ch 32 (AB 167),s 15, eff. 1/1/2004.

Section 21402 - Order of abatement of shares

(a) Shares of beneficiaries abate in the following order:

(1) Property not disposed of by the instrument.

(2) Residuary gifts.

(3) General gifts to persons other than the transferor's relatives.

(4) General gifts to the transferor's relatives.

(5) Specific gifts to persons other than the transferor's relatives.

(6) Specific gifts to the transferor's relatives.

(b) For purposes of this section, a "relative" of the transferor is a person to whom property would pass from the transferor under Section 6401 or 6402 (intestate succession) if the transferor died intestate and there were no other person having priority.

Ca. Prob. Code § 21402

Enacted by Stats. 1990, Ch. 79.

Section 21403 - Pro rata abatement; treatment of gifts of annuities and demonstrative gifts

(a) Subject to subdivision (b), shares of beneficiaries abate pro rata within each class specified in Section 21402.

(b) Gifts of annuities and demonstrative gifts are treated as specific gifts to the extent they are satisfied out of the fund or property specified in the gift and as general gifts to the extent they are satisfied out of property other than the fund or property specified in the gift.

Ca. Prob. Code § 21403

Enacted by Stats. 1990, Ch. 79.

Section 21404 - Specific gift required to be exonerated from mortgage, deed of trust or other lien

If an instrument requires property that is the subject of a specific gift to be exonerated from a mortgage, deed of trust, or other lien, a specific gift of other property does not abate for the purpose of exonerating the encumbered property.

Ca. Prob. Code § 21404
Enacted by Stats. 1990, Ch. 79.

Section 21405 - Contribution for abatement

(a) In any case in which there is abatement when a distribution is made during estate administration, the court shall fix the amount each distributee must contribute for abatement. The personal representative shall reduce the distributee's share by that amount.
(b) If a specific gift must be abated, the beneficiary of the specific gift may satisfy the contribution for abatement out of the beneficiary's property other than the property that is the subject of the specific gift.

Ca. Prob. Code § 21405
Enacted by Stats. 1990, Ch. 79.

Section 21406 - Effective date

(a) This part does not apply to a gift made before July 1, 1989. In the case of a gift made before July 1, 1989, the law that would have applied had this part not been enacted shall apply.
(b) For purposes of this section a gift by will is made on the date of the decedent's death.

Ca. Prob. Code § 21406
Enacted by Stats. 1990, Ch. 79.

Part 5 - COMPLIANCE WITH INTERNAL REVENUE CODE

Chapter 1 - GENERAL PROVISIONS

Section 21500 - Internal Revenue Code defined

As used in this part, "Internal Revenue Code" means the Internal Revenue Code of 1986, as amended from time to time. A reference to a provision of the Internal Revenue Code includes any subsequent provision of law enacted in its place.

Ca. Prob. Code § 21500

Enacted by Stats. 1990, Ch. 79.

Section 21501 - Effective date

(a) This part applies to a distribution made on or after January 1, 1988, whether the transferor died before, on, or after that date.

(b) A distribution made on or after January 1, 1983, and before January 1, 1988, is governed by the applicable law in effect before January 1, 1988.

Ca. Prob. Code § 21501

Enacted by Stats. 1990, Ch. 79.

Section 21502 - Instrument making part inapplicable; incorporation of part by reference

(a) This part does not apply to an instrument the terms of which expressly or by necessary implication make this part inapplicable.

(b) By an appropriate statement made in an instrument, the transferor may incorporate by reference any or all of the provisions of this part. The effect of incorporating a provision of this part in an instrument is to make the incorporated provision a part of the instrument as though the language of the incorporated provision were set forth verbatim in the instrument. Unless an instrument incorporating a provision of this part provides otherwise, the instrument automatically incorporates the provision's amendments.

Ca. Prob. Code § 21502

Enacted by Stats. 1990, Ch. 79.

Section 21503 - Formula included in instrument

(a) If an instrument includes a formula intended to eliminate the federal estate tax, the formula shall be applied to eliminate or to reduce to the maximum extent possible the federal estate tax.

(b) If an instrument includes a formula that refers to a maximum fraction or amount that will not result in a federal estate tax, the formula shall be construed to refer to the maximum fraction or amount that will not result in or increase the federal estate tax.

Ca. Prob. Code § 21503

Enacted by Stats. 1990, Ch. 79.

Chapter 2 - MARITAL DEDUCTION GIFTS

Section 21520 - Definitions

As used in this chapter:

(a) "Marital deduction" means the federal estate tax deduction allowed for transfers under Section 2056 of the Internal Revenue Code or the federal gift tax deduction allowed for transfers under Section 2523 of the Internal Revenue Code.

(b) "Marital deduction gift" means a transfer of property that is intended to qualify for the marital deduction.

Ca. Prob. Code § 21520

Enacted by Stats. 1990, Ch. 79.

Section 21521 - Inapplicability

Sections 21524 and 21526 do not apply to a trust that qualifies for the marital deduction under Section 20.2056(e)-2(b)(e)-2(b) of the Code of Federal Regulations (commonly referred to as the "estate trust").

Ca. Prob. Code § 21521

Enacted by Stats. 1990, Ch. 79.

Section 21522 - Effect if instrument contains gift

If an instrument contains a marital deduction gift:

(a) The provisions of the instrument, including any power, duty, or discretionary authority given to a fiduciary, shall be construed to comply with the marital deduction provisions of the Internal Revenue Code.

(b) The fiduciary shall not take any action or have any power that impairs the deduction as applied to the marital deduction gift.

(c) The marital deduction gift may be satisfied only with property that qualifies for the marital deduction.

Ca. Prob. Code § 21522
Enacted by Stats. 1990, Ch. 79.

Section 21523 - Economic Recovery Tax Act of 1981

(a) The Economic Recovery Tax Act of 1981 was enacted August 13, 1981. This section applies to an instrument executed before September 12, 1981 (before 30 days after enactment of the Economic Recovery Tax Act of 1981).

(b) If an instrument described in subdivision (a) indicates the transferor's intention to make a gift that will provide the maximum allowable marital deduction, the instrument passes to the recipient an amount equal to the maximum amount of the marital deduction that would have been allowed as of the date of the gift under federal law as it existed before enactment of the Economic Recovery Tax Act of 1981, with adjustments for the following, if applicable:

(1) The provisions of Section 2056(c)(1)(B)(c)(1)(B) and (C) of the Internal Revenue Code in effect immediately before enactment of the Economic Recovery Tax Act of 1981.

(2) To reduce the amount passing under the gift by the final federal estate tax values of any other property that passes under or outside of the instrument and qualifies for the marital deduction. This subdivision does not apply to qualified terminable interest property under Section 2056(b)(7)(b)(7) of the Internal Revenue Code.

Ca. Prob. Code § 21523
Enacted by Stats. 1990, Ch. 79.

Section 21524 - Provisions applicable to marital deduction trust

If a marital deduction gift is made in trust, in addition to the other provisions of this chapter, each of the following provisions also applies to the marital deduction trust:

(a) The transferor's spouse is the only beneficiary of income or principal of the marital deduction property as long as the spouse is alive. Nothing in this subdivision precludes exercise by the transferor's spouse of a power of appointment included in a trust that qualifies as a general power of appointment marital deduction trust.

(b) The transferor's spouse is entitled to all of the income of the marital deduction property not less frequently than annually, as long as the spouse is alive. For purposes of this subdivision, income shall be construed in a manner consistent with subdivision (b) of Section 2056 and subdivision (f) of Section 2523 of the Internal Revenue Code and shall include a unitrust payment or other allocation of income determined pursuant to a reasonable apportionment of total investment return that meets the requirements of Section 643 of the Internal Revenue Code and the regulations adopted pursuant to that statute.

(c) The transferor's spouse has the right to require that the trustee of the trust make unproductive marital deduction property productive or to convert it into productive property within a reasonable time.

Ca. Prob. Code § 21524

Amended by Stats 2016 ch 140 (SB 1265),s 1, eff. 1/1/2017. EFFECTIVE 1/1/2000. Amended July 22, 1999 (Bill Number: AB 846) (Chapter 145).

Section 21525 - Condition that transferor's spouse survive transferor

(a) If an instrument that makes a marital deduction gift includes a condition that the transferor's spouse survive the transferor by a period that exceeds or may exceed six months, other than a condition described in subdivision (b), the condition shall be limited to six months as applied to the marital deduction gift.

(b) If an instrument that makes a marital deduction gift includes a condition that the transferor's spouse survive a common disaster that results in the death of the transferor, the condition shall be limited to the time of the final audit of the federal estate tax return for the transferor's estate, if any, as applied to the marital deduction gift.

(c) The amendment of subdivision (a) made by Chapter 113 of the Statutes of 1988 is declaratory of, and not a change in, either existing law or former Section 1036 (repealed by Chapter 923 of the Statutes of 1987).

Ca. Prob. Code § 21525
Enacted by Stats. 1990, Ch. 79.

Section 21526 - Good faith election to make or not make election

A fiduciary is not liable for a good faith decision to make any election, or not to make any election, referred to in Section 2056(b)(7)(b)(7) or Section 2523(f)(f) of the Internal Revenue Code.

Ca. Prob. Code § 21526
Enacted by Stats. 1990, Ch. 79.

Chapter 3 - CHARITABLE GIFTS

Section 21540 - Charitable remainder unitrust or charitable remainder annuity trust

If an instrument indicates the transferor's intention to comply with the Internal Revenue Code requirements for a charitable remainder unitrust or a charitable remainder annuity trust as each is defined in Section 664 of the Internal Revenue Code, the provisions of the instrument, including any power, duty, or discretionary authority given to a fiduciary, shall be construed to comply with the charitable deduction provisions of Section 2055 or Section 2522 of the Internal Revenue Code and the charitable remainder trust provisions of Section 664 of the Internal Revenue Code in order to conform to that intent. In no event shall the fiduciary take an action or have a power that impairs the charitable deduction. The provisions of the instrument may be augmented in any manner consistent with Section 2055(e)(e) or Section 2522(c)(c) of the Internal Revenue Code on a petition provided for in Section 17200.

Ca. Prob. Code § 21540
Enacted by Stats. 1990, Ch. 79.

Section 21541 - Charitable lead trust

If an instrument indicates the transferor's intention to comply with the requirements for a charitable lead trust as described in Section 170(f)(2)(B)(f)(2)(B) and Section 2055(e)(2)(e)(2) or Section 2522(c)(2)(c)(2) of the Internal Revenue Code, the provisions of the instrument, including any power, duty, or discretionary authority given to a fiduciary, shall be construed to comply with the provisions of that section in order to conform to that intent. In no event shall the fiduciary take any action or have any power that impairs the charitable deduction. The provisions of the instrument may be augmented in any manner consistent with that intent upon a petition provided for in Section 17200.

Ca. Prob. Code § 21541
Enacted by Stats. 1990, Ch. 79.

Part 6 - FAMILY PROTECTION: OMITTED SPOUSES AND CHILDREN

Chapter 1 - GENERAL PROVISIONS

Section 21600 - Applicability

This part shall apply to property passing by will through a decedent's estate or by a trust, as defined in Section 82, that becomes irrevocable only on the death of the settlor.

Ca. Prob. Code § 21600
Added by Stats. 1997, Ch. 724, Sec. 34. Effective January 1, 1998.

Section 21601 - Definitions

(a) For purposes of this part, "decedent's testamentary instruments" means the decedent's will or revocable trust.
(b) "Estate" as used in this part shall include a decedent's probate estate and all property held in any revocable trust that becomes irrevocable on the death of the decedent.

Ca. Prob. Code § 21601
Added by Stats. 1997, Ch. 724, Sec. 34. Effective January 1, 1998.

Chapter 2 - OMITTED SPOUSES

Section 21610 - Share of omitted spouse

Except as provided in Section 21611, if a decedent fails to provide in a testamentary instrument for the decedent's surviving spouse who married the decedent after the execution of all of the decedent's testamentary instruments, the omitted spouse shall receive a share in the decedent's estate, consisting of the following property in said estate:

(a) The one-half of the community property that belongs to the decedent under Section 100.

(b) The one-half of the quasi-community property that belongs to the decedent under Section 101.

(c) A share of the separate property of the decedent equal in value to that which the spouse would have received if the decedent had died without having executed a testamentary instrument, but in no event is the share to be more than one-half the value of the separate property in the estate.

Ca. Prob. Code § 21610
Added by Stats. 1997, Ch. 724, Sec. 34. Effective January 1, 1998.

Section 21611 - Spouse not to receive share

The spouse shall not receive a share of the estate under Section 21610 if any of the following is established:

(a) The decedent's failure to provide for the spouse in the decedent's testamentary instruments was intentional and that intention appears from the testamentary instruments.

(b) The decedent provided for the spouse by transfer outside of the estate passing by the decedent's testamentary instruments and the intention that the transfer be in lieu of a provision in said instruments is shown by statements of the decedent or from the amount of the transfer or by other evidence.

(c) The spouse made a valid agreement waiving the right to share in the decedent's estate.

(d)

(1) If both of the following apply:

(A) The spouse was a care custodian, as that term is defined in Section 21362, of the decedent who was a dependent adult, as that term is defined in Section 21366, and the marriage commenced while the care custodian provided services to the decedent, or within 90 days after those services were last provided to the decedent.

(B) The decedent died less than six months after the marriage commenced.

(2) Notwithstanding paragraph (1), a spouse described by this subdivision shall be entitled to receive a share of the estate pursuant to Section 21610 if the spouse proves by clear and convincing evidence that the marriage between the spouse and the decedent was not the product of fraud or undue influence.

Ca. Prob. Code § 21611

Amended by Stats 2019 ch 10 (AB 328),s 3, eff. 1/1/2020.

Section 21612 - Satisfying share

(a) Except as provided in subdivision (b), in satisfying a share provided by this chapter:

(1) The share will first be taken from the decedent's estate not disposed of by will or trust, if any.

(2) If that is not sufficient, so much as may be necessary to satisfy the share shall be taken from all beneficiaries of decedent's testamentary instruments in proportion to the value they may respectively receive. The proportion of each beneficiary's share that may be taken pursuant to this subdivision shall be determined based on values as of the date of the decedent's death.

(b) If the obvious intention of the decedent in relation to some specific gift or devise or other provision of a testamentary instrument would be defeated by the application of subdivision (a), the specific devise or gift or provision may be exempted from the apportionment under subdivision (a), and a different apportionment, consistent with the intention of the decedent, may be adopted.

Ca. Prob. Code § 21612

Renumbered from Ca. Prob. Code §26112 and amended by Stats 2003 ch 32 (AB 167),s 17, eff. 1/1/2004.

Chapter 3 - OMITTED CHILDREN

Section 21620 - Share received by omitted child

Except as provided in Section 21621, if a decedent fails to provide in a testamentary instrument for a child of decedent born or adopted after the execution of all of the decedent's testamentary instruments, the omitted child shall receive a share in the decedent's estate equal in value to that which the child would have received if the decedent had died without having executed any testamentary instrument.

Ca. Prob. Code § 21620

Added by Stats. 1997, Ch. 724, Sec. 34. Effective January 1, 1998.

Section 21621 - Child not to receive share

A child shall not receive a share of the estate under Section 21620 if any of the following is established:

(a) The decedent's failure to provide for the child in the decedent's testamentary instruments was intentional and that intention appears from the testamentary instruments.

(b) The decedent had one or more children and devised or otherwise directed the disposition of substantially all the estate to the other parent of the omitted child.

(c) The decedent provided for the child by transfer outside of the estate passing by the decedent's testamentary instruments and the intention that the transfer be in lieu of a provision in said instruments is show by statements of the decedent or from the amount of the transfer or by other evidence.

Ca. Prob. Code § 21621
Added by Stats. 1997, Ch. 724, Sec. 34. Effective January 1, 1998.

Section 21622 - Decedent believed child dead or unaware of child's birth

If, at the time of the execution of all of decedent's testamentary instruments effective at the time of decedent's death, the decedent failed to provide for a living child solely because the decedent believed the child to be dead or was unaware of the birth of the child, the child shall receive a share in the estate equal in value to that which the child would have received if the decedent had died without having executed any testamentary instruments.

Ca. Prob. Code § 21622
Added by Stats. 1997, Ch. 724, Sec. 34. Effective January 1, 1998.

Section 21623 - Satisfying share

(a) Except as provided in subdivision (b), in satisfying a share provided by this chapter:

(1) The share will first be taken from the decedent's estate not disposed of by will or trust, if any.

(2) If that is not sufficient, so much as may be necessary to satisfy the share shall be taken from all beneficiaries of decedent's testamentary instruments in proportion to the value they may respectively receive. The proportion of each beneficiary's share that may be taken pursuant to this subdivision shall be determined based on values as of the date of the decedent's death.

(b) If the obvious intention of the decedent in relation to some specific gift or devise or other provision of a testamentary instrument would be defeated by the application of subdivision (a), the specific devise or gift or provision of a testamentary instrument may be exempted from the apportionment under subdivision (a), and a different apportionment, consistent with the intention of the decedent, may be adopted.

Ca. Prob. Code § 21623
Amended by Stats 2003 ch 32 (AB 167),s 16, eff. 1/1/2004.

Chapter 4 - APPLICABILITY

Section 21630 - Effective date

This part does not apply if the decedent died before January 1, 1998. The law applicable prior to January 1, 1998, applies if the decedent died before January 1, 1998.

Ca. Prob. Code § 21630
Added by Stats. 1997, Ch. 724, Sec. 34. Effective January 1, 1998.

Part 7 - CONTRACTS REGARDING TESTAMENTARY OR INTESTATE SUCCESSION

Section 21700 - Establishing contract

(a) A contract to make a will or devise or other instrument, or not to revoke a will or devise or other instrument, or to die intestate, if made after the effective date of this statute, can be established only by one of the following:

(1) Provisions of a will or other instrument stating the material provisions of the contract.

(2) An expressed reference in a will or other instrument to a contract and extrinsic evidence proving the terms of the contract.

(3) A writing signed by the decedent evidencing the contract.

(4) Clear and convincing evidence of an agreement between the decedent and the claimant or a promise by the decedent to the claimant that is enforceable in equity.

(5) Clear and convincing evidence of an agreement between the decedent and another person for the benefit of the claimant or a promise by the decedent to another person for the benefit of the claimant that is enforceable in equity.

(b) The execution of a joint will or mutual wills does not create a presumption of a contract not to revoke the will or wills.

(c) A contract to make a will or devise or other instrument, or not to revoke a will or devise or other instrument, or to die intestate, if made prior to the effective date of this section, shall be construed under the law applicable to the contract prior to the effective date of this section.

Ca. Prob. Code § 21700

Added by Stats 2000 ch 17 (AB 1491), s 8, eff. 1/1/2001.